Lecture Notes in Computer Science 7657

Commenced Publication in 1973
Founding and Former Series Editors:
Gerhard Goos, Juris Hartmanis, and Jan van Leeuwen

T0223890

José Bravo   Ramón Hervás
Marcela Rodríguez (Eds.)

Ambient Assisted Living and Home Care

4th International Workshop, IWAAL 2012
Vitoria-Gasteiz, Spain, December 3-5, 2012
Proceedings

 Springer

Volume Editors

José Bravo
Castilla-La Mancha University
Ciudad Real, Spain
E-mail: jose.bravo@uclm.es

Ramón Hervás
Castilla-La Mancha University
Ciudad Real, Spain
E-mail: ramon.hlucas@uclm.es

Marcela Rodríguez
University of Baja California
Mexicali, Mexico
E-mail: marcerod@uabc.mx

ISSN 0302-9743   e-ISSN 1611-3349
ISBN 978-3-642-35394-9   e-ISBN 978-3-642-35395-6
DOI 10.1007/978-3-642-35395-6
Springer Heidelberg Dordrecht London New York

Library of Congress Control Number: 2012953007

CR Subject Classification (1998): H.5.2-3, J.3-4, C.2, H.4, H.3, K.4.2, D.2

LNCS Sublibrary: SL 3 – Information Systems and Application, incl. Internet/Web and HCI

Typesetting: Camera-ready by author, data conversion by Scientific Publishing Services, Chennai, India

Printed on acid-free paper

Springer is part of Springer Science+Business Media (www.springer.com)

Preface

This volume contains the papers presented at IWAAL 2012: the 4th International Workshop on Ambient Assisted Living held during December 3–5, 2012, in Vitoria-Gasteiz (Spain). The IWAAL conference is an expanding event that emerged in 2009. This event responds to the European Union initiative "Ambient Assisted Living Joint Program (AALJP)," an ICT funding framework for "ageing well" that started in 2008. The AALJP aims to develop solutions that increase independence for dependent and older people, and also for their formal or informal carers. It is very important to address these solutions providing ways for older people to remain active and connected to society.

Home-care is a specific challenge involved in ambient assisted living. Particularly, the European Union focused their last call for proposals (AAL 5) on an important dimension of the topic of "ICT-Based Solutions for (Self-) Management of Daily Life Activities of Older Adults at Home." Home-care was the main topic of the IWAAL 2012 edition. Consequently, we received a significant number of contributions that aim at enhancing older adults' quality of life. The proposed products, systems, and services enable and sustain older people to continue managing their daily activities in their home.

Beyond home-care, the IWAAL proceedings also include research works describing progress on other research topics for AAL such as human–computer interaction at assistive environments, semantic modelling for realizing reactive and proactive assistive environments, sensing, monitoring, and key applications for AAL. Altogether, this fourth edition includes 58 research articles.

Finally, we would like to thank all the organizers (MAmI Research group, University of Deusto, CIC Tourgune and Technological University of Panama) and collaborators of this event (Vitoria-Gasteiz Council), together with the hard work of the Program Committee members cross-reviewing all the submitted papers.

December 2012

José Bravo
Ramón Hervás
Marcela Rodríguez

Organization

General Co-chairs

José Bravo   University of Castilla-La Mancha, Spain
Diego López-de-Ipiña   University of Deusto, Spain

IWAAL Program Committee Co-chairs

Ramon Herves   University of Castilla-La Mancha, Spain
Marcela Rodriguez   Autonomous University of Baja California,
    Mexico

Program Committee

Julio Abascal   University of the Basque Country, Spain
Hamid Aghajan   Standford University, USA
Xavier Alaman   UAM, Spain
Rosa Alarcon   Pontificia Universidad Católica de Chile, Chile
Mariano Alcañiz   UPV - i3bh/LabHuman, Spain
Roberto Aldunate   Applied Research Associates, USA
Jan Alexandersson   DFKI GmbH, Germany
Cecilio Angulo   Universitat Politécnica de Catalunya, Spain
Rosa Arriaga   Georgia Institute of Technology, USA
Mohamed Bakhouya   University of Technology of Belfort
    Montbeliard, France

Mert Bal   Miami University, USA
Javier Baliosian   University of the Republic, Uruguay
Francisco Ballesteros   Rey Juan Carlos University, Spain
Nelson Baloian   University of Chile, Chile
Francisco Bellido   University of Cordoba, Spain
Juan Botia   Universidad de Murcia, Spain
Jose Bravo   Universidad de Castilla La Mancha, Spain
Davide Brunelli   University of Trento, Italy
Yang Cai   Carnegie Mellon University, USA
Luis Carriço   University of Lisbon, Portugal
Sophie Chabridon   Telecom SudParis, France
Ignacio Chang   Technological University of Panama, Panama
Liming Luke Chen   University of Ulster, UK
Wei Chen   Eindhoven University of Technology,
    The Netherlands

Carlos Juiz	University of the Balearic Islands, Spain
Marting Kampel	Vienna University of Technology, Austria
Wolfgang Kastner	TU Vienna, Austria
Henry Kautz	University of Rochester, USA
Abdelmajid Khelil	TU Darmstadt, Germany
Ryszard Klempous	Wroclaw University of Technology, Poland
Vaclav Kremen	Czech Technical University of Prague, Czech Republic
Latif Ladid	University of Luxembourg - IPv6 Forum, Luxembourg
Carlos Lamsfus	CICtourGUNE, Spain
Ernst Leiss	University of Houston, USA
Lenka Lhotska	Czech Technical University of Prague, Czech Republic
Wenfeng Li	Wuhan University of Technology, P.R. China
Vincenzo Loia	Università degli Studi di Salerno, Italy
Diego Lopez-De-Ipiña	Deusto Institute of Technology, University of Deusto, Spain
Vesselin Lossifov	HTW-Berlin, Germany
Tun Lu	Fudan University, P.R. China
Wolfram Luther	University of Duisburg-Essen, Germany
Juan Carlos López	University of Castilla-La Mancha, Spain
Miren Karmele López de Ipiña	University of the Basque Country, Spain
Ricardo J. Machado	University of Minho, Portugal
Stephen Makonin	Simon Fraser University, Canada
Pedro Jose Marron	University of Duisburg-Essen and Fraunhofer IAIS, Germany
Oscar Mayora	Create-Net, Trento, Italy
Rene Mayrhofer	Upper Austrian University, Austria
Rene Meier	Trinity College Dublin, Ireland
Peter Mikulecky	University of Hradec Kralove, Czech Republic
Roberto Moreno-Díaz	University of Las Palmas de Gran Canaria, Spain
Francisco Moya	University of Castilla-La Mancha, Spain
Angelica Munoz-Melendez	INAOE, Mexico
Lilia Muñoz Arracera	Technological University of Panama, Panama
Andres Neyem	Pontificia Universidad Católica de Chile, Chile
David H. Nguyen	University of California, Irvine, USA
Chris Nugent	University of Ulster, UK
Nicolae Objelean	Moldova State University, Moldova
Sergio Ochoa	University of Chile, Chile
Juan Antonio Ortega	University of Seville, Spain
Emerson Paraiso	Pontificia Universidade Catolica do Parana, Brazil
Vicente Pelechano	Universidad Politécnica de Valencia, Spain

Dennis Pfisterer	University of Lübeck, Germany
Franz Pichler	Johannes Kepler University, Austria
Jose A. Pino	Universidad de Chile, Chile
Till Plumbaum	Technische Universität Berlin, Germany
Davy Preuveneers	K.U. Leuven, Belgium
Milton Ramos	TECPAR - Paraná Institute of Technology, Brazil
Anand Ranganathan	IBM T.J. Watson Research Center, USA
Patrick Reignier	I.P. Grenoble, France
Bernhard Rinner	University of Klagenfurt, Austria
Marcela Rodriguez	UABC, Mexico
Mario Romero	Georgia Institute of Technology, USA
Jerzy W. Rozenblit	University of Arizona, USA
Jonathan Ruiz-De-Garibay	University of Deusto, Spain
Rodrigo Santos	Universidad Nacional del Sur - Bahía Blanca, Argentina
Klaus Schmidt	Illinois State University, USA
Horst Schwetlick	HTW-Berlin, Germany
Boon-Chong Seet	Auckland University of Technology, New Zealand
Ripdudam Sohan	University of Cambridge, UK
Chantal Taconet	TELECOM & Management SudParis, France
Monica Tentori	CICESE, Mexico
Gabriel Urzaiz Lares	Anahuac Mayab University, Mexico
Vladimir Villarreal	Technological University of Panama, Panama
Andreas Voss	University of Applied Sciences from Jena, Germany
Nadir Weibel	University of California San Diego, USA
Benjamin Weyers	University of Duisburg-Essen, Germany
Erik Wilde	UC Berkeley, USA
Jacak Witold	Upper Austrian University of Applied Sciences, Austria
Hen-I Yang	Iowa State University, USA
Rui Zhang	Palo Alto Research Center, USA

Additional Reviewers

Aguilera, Unai
Almeida, Aitor
Alvarez-Lozano, Jorge
Amor Pinilla, Mercedes
Ayala, Inmaculada
Bountris, Panagiotis
Caloca, Carlos
Castanedo, Federico

Castillejo, Eduardo
Duarte, Lus
Fernández, Alejandro
Fuentes, Carolina
Gamez, Nadia
García, Carmelo R.
Gerla, Václav
Guerrero, Carlos

Gómez-Goiri, Aitor
Huptych, Michal
Jablonski, Bartosz
Ježek, Filip
Khan, Umair
Klempous, Joanna
Krammer, Lukas
Lera, Isaac
Lhotska, Lenka
López de Ipiña, Karmele
Marquez Vazquez, Jose Manuel
Melia-Segui, Joan
Orduña, Pablo
Ostkamp, Morin
Parak, Jakub

Pascual, Gustavo G.
Pokorny, Matous
Reinisch, Christian
Rusiecki, Andrzej
Santofimia Romero, Maria Jose
Schranz, Melanie
Tagaris, Anastassios
Testa, Alessandro
Tsirmpas, Haris
Ubeda, Benito
Vaccaro, Alfredo
Villa, David
Villanueva Molina, Félix Jesús
Winkler, Thomas

Table of Contents

Session 2: AAL Environments

Session 3: Sensing and Monitoring

Session 4: Human-Computer Interaction at Assistive Environments

Session 5: Semantic Modeling for Realizing AAL

Session 6: Key Application Domains

Adaptive Collaborative Environment for Vascular Problems Telediagnosis

María Aydeé Sánchez Santana[1], Jean-Baptiste Aupet[1],
Marie-Laure Betbeder[1], Jean-Christophe Lapayre[1],
and José Antonito Camarena Ibarrola[2]

[1] Institut Femto-ST/DISC - UMR CNRS 6174 -UFC
16 Rte de Gray, F-25030 Besançon Cedex - France
(ma.sanchez,jb.aupet,ml.betbeder,jc.lapayre)@femto-st.fr
[2] UMSNH, Gral. Francisco J. Mugica, Felicitas del Río, 58030 Morelia, Mexico
camarena@umich.mx

Abstract. The goal of this paper is to present a distributed tool for the medical community. This tool is called *VACODIS* (**VA***scular* **CO***llaborative tele***DI***agnosi***S**) enables to identification and quantification of the potential cardiovascular complications of a patient in a semi-automatic way. The first step consists of producing an automatic detection of cardiovascular abnormalities from Echo-Doppler images. The second step shares in a collaborative and adaptive way images and results from the first step. This sharing eases a collaborative diagnosis. Thus, this method enables multiple distant hospital workers (nurses, practitioners ...) to contribute to a collaborative diagnosis in the cardiovascular domain.

1 Introduction

This work is the result of the combined effort of UMSNH University (Morelia, Mexico) and the University of Franche-Comté (France). The team from Morelia is specialized in algorithms for image processing and segmentation, particularly in ultrasonography images (echo-doppler). The team from Franche-Comté is specialized in distributed algorithms for collaborative telediagnosis. The objective of this work is to provide the medical community with a distributed tool for semi-automatic diagnosis to identify and quantify potential cardiovascular complications of a patient. This diagnosis is done in two steps: Aautomatic detection of cardiovascular anomalies from echo-doppler images, and sharing results and images to help medics achieve to a collaborative diagnosis. This way, multiple practitioners will use this tool to collaborate in a consensed diagnosis independently of their locations.

The second section of this article presents the medical aspect and the pathology. Then, in the third section, algorithms of automatic image processing are presented. These algorithms enable detection of three kinds of anomalies: atherosclerosis, endothelial dysfunction, and atherosclerosis plaque. In the fourth

J. Bravo, R. Hervás, and M. Rodríguez (Eds.): IWAAL 2012, LNCS 7657, pp. 1–8, 2012.

section, we introduce a platform for automatic adaptation: WAVA. This platform enables sharing of information (ultrasonography images) and results of automatic detections of cardiovascular anomalies, adapting shared data in function of available hardware capacity of each. Finally, we end with a summary and some perspectives.

2   Medical Context

Cardiovascular diseases (CVD) are still the most important cause of death worldwide. In CVD domain, practitioners normally use echography to obtain a reliable diagnosis. Echography provides images in real-time in a non-intrusive and inexpensive approach. On the other hand, echography remains one of the most complicated challenges in the field of image processing [1,2].

Atherosclerosis is a condition in which artery's walls thicken as a result of the accumulation of fat residuals. It is a syndrome affecting arterial blood vessels, a chronic inflammatory response in the walls of arteries [3,4]. It is caused by the formation of multiple plaques within the arteries. In addition, endothelial dysfunction is a systemic pathological state of the endothelium (the inner lining of blood vessels) and can be broadly defined as an imbalance between vasodilating and vasoconstricting substances [4]. Endothelial dysfunction may result from and/or contribute to several disease processes. Endothelial function testing may have great potential prognostic value for the detection of CVD, but currently the available tests are too difficult, expensive, and/or variable for routine clinical use [5].

3   Methodology

Existing methods for assessing endothelial dysfunction and atherosclerosis are based on functional tests in the brachial and carotid artery. Endothelial dysfunction precedes over vascular disease and may itself be a potentially modifiable CVD risk factor.

3.1   Use of Ultrasonography Image with DICOM Format

Ultrasound is the most widely used technique for in vivo measurement Intima-Media Thickness (IMT) of carotid and brachial artery [6]. The major drawback of ultrasound is that it is highly operator-dependent [2]. This means that a number of technical and methodological requirements need to be fulfilled in order to perform a correct and effective computer-based endothelium measurement. To fully exploit the potential of ultrasound imaging in atherosclerosis research, image acquisition and image analysis should meet DICOM standards [7,8].

3.2   Segmentation: Automatic Recognition of Artery

The automatic segmentation of anatomical structures in ultrasound imagery is a real challenge due to acoustic interferences (*speckle noise*), which are inherent to these images. For our study of CVDs, speckle noise has not been a problem in automated recognition. The first issue in automatic image analysis is the segmentation of the distal wall of the carotid and brachial artery in order to extract the characteristic pattern of the artery. The basic idea consists of assuming the artery as the dark region (lumen: space where blood circulates), comprised by two bright stripes (the near and far wall artery layers). Therefore, the artery is recognized when the boundaries of the near and far wall endothelium are traced. The image is processed by column to locate the maximum intensity of each generated column by a linear discriminant to detect the artery wall (Fig. 1). These points are called *seed points*. Then, *seed points* are used to link all sequences of segmentation lines. An intelligent procedure removes false positives inside the segmentation lines and join nearest aligned segments. This step avoids over-segmentation. Speckle noise is removed with a Gaussian filter through a sliding kernel.

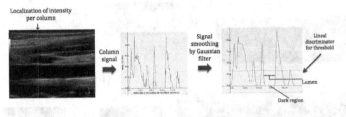

Fig. 1. Artery recognition

3.3   Automatic Detection of Vascular Anomalies

Segmentation of IMT and lumen in artery is perhaps the most challenging problem for our purpose. Three concentric layers constitute the arterial wall and are denominated from inside to outside: tunica intima, tunica media and adventitia. Only the tunica intima and the tunica media are controlled.

In our work, we propose three new tools for assisting physicians to detect vascular anomalies. These three methods will provide to hospital GP (or general practitioner) three images and an automatic diagnosis report:

- *Measure of light in brachial artery*: measures of light diameter in brachial artery must be done between the two artery walls in intima-light. The pressure of light must be detected to treat edges. We use cellular automaton introduced by Ullman and von Neumann [9]. A triplet (i, j, k) (cells) characterizes each pixel ((i, j) represents the position, and k-level intensity). The ultrasound can be considered as a particular cellular space. In our process, we consider two kinds of cells: alive cells (light) and death cells (muscle) (Fig. 2(a)).
- *Measure of endothelium in the carotid artery*: The determinant diagnosis of atherosclerosis is the measure of the carotid IMT that is defined on a side of the artery wall. Method ARC-Potential [10] can rapidly determine the IMT and preserve edge. The IMT measure is based on the edge and an approximation of seed points on gradient approach. The adventitia generally

bright enables to indicate precisely the end of IMT. This measure is possible for the transition between the light and the artery wall (Lumen-Intima or LI) and the transition between the media and the adventitia (MA) (Fig. 2(b)). The gradient satisfies the problem of LI/MA detection. Generally, an image gradient is calculated to find LI/MA points for all the image columns (Fig. 2(c)).

- *Measure of atherosclerosis plaque*: For automatic edge detection, we used quad-trees by combining a nonparametric classifier [11] based on a clustering algorithm, with a quad-tree representation of the image, the scheme is performs well and is simple to implement, giving satisfactory results at signal-to-noise speckle (Fig. 2(d)).
- *Diagnosis automatic generation*: after the three previous measures, our protocol provides a diagnosis automatically.

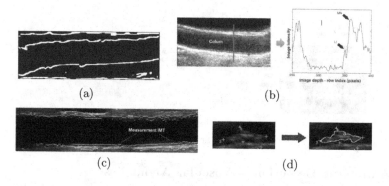

Fig. 2. Cellular automaton for outline recognition, (b) Carotid artery wall segmentation based on intensity criterion and on gradient approach, (c) Measure of IMT carotid by segmentationm (d) Plaque segmentation by using the quad-tree technic

In the following section, it is important to know how to adapt these four medias (three images and a text) in function of devices and networks. The goal is to enable practitioners to work together and elaborate a final diagnosis in the best conditions. In the next section, we define what is real-time collaborative environment for telemedicine and our new adaptive platform.

4   Collaborative Environments for Telemedicine

The CNOM (French National Council of Health Practitioners) defines Telemedicine as the practice that allows a patient to receive medical attention remotely by one or more practitioners through the use of technologies of information and communication for delivering the required medical data [12].

A few years ago, Telemedicine was used for patient control or eLearning [13] and was recently introduced for emergency care. These new technologies are now used to help practitioners from distant sites to perform diagnosis procedures and clinical examination by transferring medical images [14].

Collaborative software for Telemedicine enables practitioners to use collaborative tools for on-line telediagnosis, for this software, user interfaces and complementary tools help users to overcome large distances by creating a virtual examination room. Our goal is to obtain a reliable and secured environment to exchange medical data and optimized interaction to perform diagnosis.

5   A New Service of Data Flow Adaptation

We propose a new web service to adapt data and provide information. This web service is called WAVA and adapts the properties of exchanged data taking into account the constraints of the environment capacity manager and the exchanged data type.

5.1   WAVA: Web Service for Automatic Adaptation

WAVA adaptation works by establishing marks as a function of the properties used by specific devices. The adaptation server determines and reports the best quality/capacity so data would meet the requirements of the devices in turn. The quality is determined by adaptation of the specific encoding used by a any device as well as the resolution and compression rate. According to device performances (number of kind of processors, graphic card, resolution, etc.) and network used, the system provides for each property a corresponding mark. This information on devices and their properties are stored in a database. We distinguish two kinds of capacities evaluation: static mark that does not change during a session (Mark global (Mg)). This mark refers to CPU (Mcpu), resolution (Mres) and graphic card (Mgrph) that do not change during a session. If the devices are near each other then Mg is determined as the average of Mcpu, Mre, and Mgrph, otherwise the lowest one of them is used. The second kind of notation is a dynamic one. It is

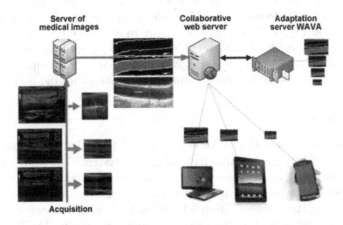

Fig. 3. WAVA Principle

calculated with bandwidth (MBW) and the CPU load (MC) that change during a session. To obtain the final mark (M), we re-evaluate the global mark with the dynamic one by taking the lower mark between the two marks to validate that the chosen adaptation is in concordance with the system. The use of WAVA is depicted in Fig. 3. WAVA receives periodically information of bandwidth and CPU load of users computers/devices thanks to information retrieved by the coordinator. The new mark is determined as a function of the newest available information.

5.2 WAVA Implementation

This prototype is based on provided services that enable to give a data skeleton to applications that want to use this service. The algorithm to calculate associated marks is shown in Fig. 4. This algorithm marks the terminal that needs access to a resource according to the configuration manager. The mark ranges from 0 to 5 being 5 the highest performance. This phase is totally transparent to the user.

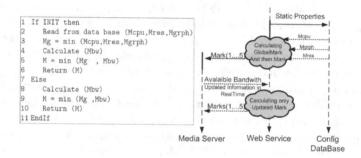

Fig. 4. WAVA Algorithm

5.3 WAVA Service Architecture

This prototype is based on provided services that enable to give a data skeleton to applications that want to use this service. The algorithm to calculate associated mark is shown in Fig. 4. This algorithm allows to mark the terminal that need to access to a resource from data provided by the configuration manager. The mark ranges from 0 to 5 being 5 the highest performance. This phase is totally transparent for the user. This phase is totally transparent for the user.

5.4 Performance

Research medical laboratories in Mexico provided 1 062 DICOM images from real patients for assessing our automatic diagnosis system. The ROC curve obtained after the sensitivity analysis performed to asses the diagnostic accuracy of Atherosclerosis in carotid artery ultrasound is shown in Fig. 5(a), this ROC curve was build varying the threshold from 0.1 mm to 1.3 mm with a step size of 0.01 mm, such threshold is used by the system to emit a diagnosis. The ROC curve obtained after our tests to evaluate the diagnostic accuracy in determination of

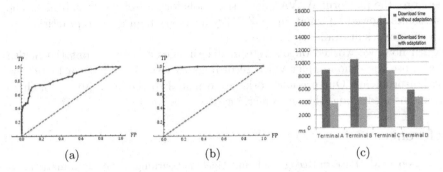

Fig. 5. Roc curve (a) atherosclerosis diagnosis, (b) endothelium dysfuction diagnosis, (c) WAVA Performances

endothelial dysfunction in humeral artery ultrasound pre and post stimulation is shown in Fig. 5(b), this ROC curve was build comparing the percentage of arterial dilation with a threshold that was varied from 5% to 40% with a step size of 0.1%.

In the context of our telediagnosis application called VACODIS, the system provides three images to physicians (lumen, endothelium, and plaque measurements) and a generated synthetic text report with an automatically generated diagnosis. The WAVA platform is used for the three images but is not required for the text report. In the following tests, we have used gray images produced by our segmentation algorithms in 1200 by 1200 pixels with an initial size of approximately 1,5 Mo. The web service converts images to the required format depending on the previously determined mark automatically. The lowest quality corresponds to a usable format on a Smartphone without lost of quality.

To test the performance of this platform, we have used different kinds of terminals to connect the practitioner to the platform for him to diagnose. Terminal (A) android tablet connected by WiFi, (B) iPad connected by HSDPA, (C) smart-phone connected in 3G, and (D) laptop connected on WiFi. Results are shown in Fig. 5(c). The adapted images are faster to display in the terminals (less CPU usage) and use less space (less memory usage). These points are really important for mobile terminals.

6   Conclusion

This work comes from collaboration between the University UMSNH of Morelia (Mexico) and the University of Franche-Comté (France). We proposed a new tool for detection of cardiovascular abnormalities in a patient. This automatic tool (but with a professional validation) is in use among hospital practitioners in Mexico, but it remains a local and individual tool. As part of small hospitals (for example as a Regional Hospital which is attached to a remote University Hospital Center), it is important to guarantee the same offer of healthcare regardless of the location of the patient. It is important that the hospital's experts are able to send their opinions and participate remotely and collaboratively to the telediagnosis.

Therefore, the platform WAVA allows this tools for an innovative solution. The first results showed information availability at a very high level to practitioners: performance results validate this use.

Until now, we worked on discrete media (images and text), but the health experts use the echo-doppler video recordings to visualize a part of blood circulation problems. Our present works are oriented to the adaptability of these continuous media, and the new emerging problems induced.

References

1. Bishop, C.M.: Pattern Recognition and Machine Learning. Series: Information Science and Statistics. Springer (2000) ISBN 978-0-387-31073-2
2. Theodoridis, S., Koutroumbas, K.: Pattern Recognition. Elsevier Academic Press (2005) ISBN: 9780080949123
3. Brusseau, E., de Korte, L., Mastik, F., Schaar, J., van der Steen, A.: Fully automatic luminal contour segmentation in intercoronary ultrasound imaging - a statistical approach. IEEE Trans. Med. Imag. 23(1), 555–566 (2004)
4. Campbell, N.W., Thomas, B.T., Troscianko, T.: A two-stage process for accurate image segmentation. In: Proc. Sixth International Conference on Image Processing and its Applications, pp. 655–659. IEEE (July 1997)
5. Rubin D.N., Yazbek N., Garcia M.J., Stewart W.J., Thomas J.D.: Qualitative and quantitative effects of harmonic echocardiographic imaging on endo-cardial edge definition and side-lobe artifacts. Journal of the American Society of Echocardiography, 32–45 (2000)
6. Pianykh, O.S.: Digital imaging and communications in medicine (dicom): A practical introduction and survival guide. Springer (2011) ISBN 3642108490
7. Loizou, C., Pattichis, C., Christodoulou, C., Istepanian, R., Pantziaris, M., Nicolaides, A.: comparative evaluation of despeckle filtering in ultrasound imaging of the carotid artery. IEEE Trans. on Ultrasonics, Ferroelectrics, and Frecuency Control 52, 885–3010 (2005)
8. Pham, M., Susomboon, R., Disney, T., Raicu, D., Furst, J.: A comparison of texture models for automatic liver segmentation. In: SPIE In Medical Imaging, vol. 6512 (2007)
9. Chun-Ling, C., Yun-Jie, Z., Gdong, Y.Y.: Cellular automata for edge detection of images. In: IEEE Proceedings of the Third International Conference on Machine Learning and Cybernetics, pp. 26–29 (2004)
10. Rivera, M., Marroquin, J.L.: Adaptive rest condition potentials: First and second order edge-preserving regularization, vol. 88, pp. 76–93 (2002)
11. Hunter, M., Steiglitz, K.: Operations on images using quadtrees. IEEE Transactions on Pattern Analysis and Machine Intelligence 1(2), 145–153 (1979)
12. Aupet, J.B., Garcia, E., Guyennet, H., Lapayre, J.C., Martins, D.: Security in medical telediagnosis. In: Book Multimedia Services in Intelligent Environments - Integrated Systems, ch. 9. Springer (2009)
13. Watkins, R.: e-learning - tool for training and professional development services, e-learning, development of knowledge and/or skills for building competence. In: Handbook of Improving Performance in the Workplace: Selecting and Implementing Performance Interventions, pp. 577–597. John Wiley and Sons, Inc. (2010)
14. Fuin, D., Garcia, E., Guyennet, H., Lapayre, J.C.: Collaborative interactions for medical e-Diagnosis. Int. Journal on High-Performance Computing and Networking, HPCN 5, 189–197 (2008)

Towards Secure e-Health Interoperable Personal Networks

Alexandru Egner[1], Alexandru Soceanu[2], Florica Moldoveanu[3],
Carlo Ferrari[1], and Michele Moro[1]

[1] Dept. of Information Engineering, University of Padova, Italy
`{egner,carlo,mike}@dei.unipd.it`
[2] Dept. of Computer Science and Mathematics,
Munich University of Applied Sciences, Germany
`soceanu@cs.hm.edu`
[3] Dept. of Computer Science, University Politehnica of Bucharest, Romania
`florica.moldoveanu@cs.pub.ro`

Abstract. The ISO/IEEE 11073 family of standards recently announced was
established to ensure plug-and-play interoperability between medical devices
within personal area networks. The new standards transfer the responsibility for
implementing security solutions for the mobile health systems to the manufac-
turer. The paper proposes an enhancement of the current specification of
ISO/IEEE 11073-20601 standard with a patient authentication and identity
management procedure which functions on the basis of biometric technology.
The proposed identification procedure works with biometric keys derived from
fingerprint measurements. The use of biometrics gives patients greater confidence in the identity management system, and fosters the trust in using mobile
medical devices on a larger scale. The test system, implemented using the
Continua Health Alliance framework, proved that the proposed identity
management solution is easily embeddable into the ISO/IEEE 11073 family of
standards.

Keywords: biometric key, ISO/IEEE 11073, authentication and identity
management.

1 Introduction

In response to the urgent request of "eHealth European Commission Information Society" [12] for focusing on technical, syntactical and semantic interoperability,
ISO/IEEE recently announced the family of 11073(X73) open standards. It ensures
the possibility to plug-and-play the various vendor's mobile medical devices manu-
factured according to these standards. These specifications do not, [1] however, feature any security procedures for patient authentication, identity management and data
encryption. Instead, they simply contain a recommendation addressed to the imple-
menters who are made responsible for designing and implementing the security
procedures. To promote the large-scale usage of mobile healthcare systems, a secure

J. Bravo, R. Hervás, and M. Rodríguez (Eds.): IWAAL 2012, LNCS 7657, pp. 9–16, 2012.

and user-friendly patient authentication concept needs to be urgently developed and implemented as an extension to the X73 family of standards already announced.

This paper presents a proposal for enhancing the ISO/IEEE 11073 family of specifications with a secure, easy-to-use and easy-to-implement mutual authentication procedure, supplemented by an identity management based on biometric measurements. We propose the use of fingerprints. This type of strong authentication gives patients greater confidence in a secure and unique identification procedure, thereby reinforcing the trust in using the mobile medical system on a larger scale. The method is based on a low cost technology which is easily embeddable into mobile medical devices. Moreover, fingerprint-based authentication may prove more comfortable than the traditional password-based one which requires the use of a keyboard. A test system was implemented in order to validate the easy embeddability of the proposed identity management solution into the existing ISO/IEEE 11073-20601 standard and to ensure backward compatibility with versions already implemented.

2   Secure Identity Management for IEEE 11073-20601 Using Biometric Keys

ISO/IEEE 11073 is a family of standards that regulates information exchange between mobile medical devices and external information systems. The paper refers to the ISO/IEEE 11073-20601 member of the X73 family of standards. To facilitate reading, we refer to the standard "ISO/IEEE 11073-20601: Application Profile – Optimized Exchange Protocol" as "OEP" [1]. OEP defines a point-to-point communication protocol between two entities which are called Agent and Manager. The Agent represents the device that directly collects information on a patient's vital signs. This can be, for instance, a thermometer or blood pressure monitor. In order to specify the behaviour of these heterogeneous devices, several medical device specializations were defined: the ISO/IEEE 11073-104zz specializations [2]. The Manager represents the device that collects personal health data from the Agents. It is represented by a local hosting device, i.e. a smart phone, a notebook, a PC, or similar devices.

OEP specifications recognized the importance of the issue of security in the context of this protocol and included the following important note [1] in the final version of the standard: *"This standard is not intended to ensure safety, security, health, or environmental protection in all circumstances"*. We recommend that the OEP protocol should not be used in practice if the extension of this standard with an appropriate security mechanism is not specified and implemented.

There are two important issues concerning OEP security: 1) the lack of any authentication mechanism certifying that the data collected correspond to the rightful patient and 2) the vulnerability of the wireless networks on which the communication protocol is based.

On the one hand, OEP does not in any way specify how the source of the medical data collected from the mobile medical devices (Agents) can be detected. This may lead to different types of attacks or mistakes which can affect the diagnosis of a person or the medical prescription. On the other, wireless networks are not very safe communication channels. Bluetooth, for example, has been proven to have significant security flaws as well as vulnerabilities to different types of attacks, such as sniffing, denial of service, or man-in-the-middle. Common Bluetooth security issues and the way vulnerabilites can be exploited have been discussed very extensively by Dunning [4] and Bialoglowy [5][6].

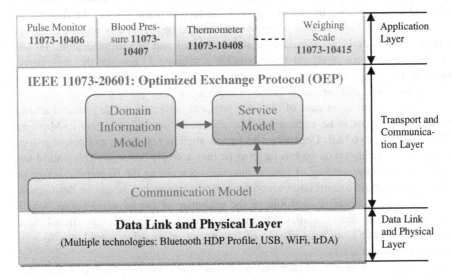

Fig. 1. Optimized Exchange Protocol architecture [1]

Identity management is an important requirement, especially for medical environments where Agents are shared among hospital patients or when Agents are provided for homecare monitoring. The authors believe that OEP should be extended to include mechanisms that offer solutions to the aforementioned problems: identity management and security of the vital signs data transfer. This paper only addresses the identity management aspect, and proposes a solution for enhancing the device authentication specified by the OEP standard by incorporating the patient identity.

There are many solutions that would be suitable for implementing an authentication procedure between the Agent and the Manager. In a system that employs a mutual authentication procedure, unauthorized Agents are unable to send medical data to the Manager, and an unauthorized Manager cannot collect Agents' clinical data. Thus, an authentication procedure would prevent: 1) storing erroneous data and 2) medical data leakage. This would be the first step in ensuring the security of transmitted medical data between mobile medical devices and the Manager. Moreover, the identity recognition of the patient is especially important as the medical data transferred must be reliably assigned to the corresponding patients.

A mechanism based on biometrics would meet the two objectives of the authentication, namely ensuring the verification of the identity of the patient using a specific medical device and identity management. The approach presented in this paper is the usage of fingerprints to uniquely and reliably identify the patients prior to using the mobile medical devices (Agents or Managers), so that the data transferred can be correctly and securely mapped to the person using the device. This procedure ensures patient authentication and identity management, which are two of the security features the protocol lacks. This approach raises several problems. The first stage would consist of fingerprint matching by the Manager since the Manager is responsible for identity management. Sending the fingerprint through an insecure communication channel could lead to exploitation by eavesdroppers. The second feature is that the fingerprint cannot be revoked. Unlike cards or passwords that can be revoked or replaced, fingerprints are permanently associated with the individual and are irreplaceable. To address these issues, we analyzed three possible solutions: 1) encrypt the message(s) containing the fingerprint image, 2) use cancellable biometrics and 3) use a mutual challenge-response authentication based on biometrics.

The first solution is, in case of the OEP protocol, unfeasible. The protocol allows only small messages to be exchanged. The maximum size of an Agent-to-Manager APDU is limited to 63KB. Depending on factors such as resolution and compression, the fingerprint image could be too large to fit into a single message. This would necessitate either a) the sending of several messages containing the fingerprint image or b) the application of compression algorithms. Both approaches would be detrimental to performance. Alternative c) would be the exchange of the minutiae points, which would convey the same essential information as the fingerprint image. In all three cases, however, the plain transmission of fingerprint information would lead to serious security breaches.

The second solution is the better one as communication is not affected by the large number or size of the messages. Instead, the Agent is required to have enough processing power to convert the fingerprint image into a cancellable biometric template [10]. Given the rapid development of embedded systems, we can safely assume that the processing power needed for this conversion will not pose an issue.

The third solution is the most advantageous, also in comparison with the proposition of cancellable fingerprints (solution 2). This approach relies on implementing a mutual challenge-response authentication, based on fingerprints. The difference between the two approaches lies in the way the systems authenticate themselves. Challenge-response is a form of authentication through which entities prove knowledge of a secret, which can be a password or a pre-shared key, without actually sending it to the other party [8]. This type of authentication offers little information to an attacker since the challenge [9] is changed for each authentication. We propose that this solution should be implemented in a session-based manner which will prohibit attackers from running brute-force or dictionary attacks.

In order to describe the challenge-response authentication protocol, we define the following terms:

Let Σ be an alphabet, defined as $\Sigma = \{0, 1\}$.

Let Σ^l be the set of all strings of length l over Σ.

Let ch_{gen} be a challenge generator function, defined as $ch_{gen} : \mathbb{N} \to \Sigma^l$, with $ch_{gen}(n) = RN_n$, where RN_n is a random value from Σ^n.

The mutual challenge-response authentication consists of the following steps:

Step 1: The Manager generates its challenge, i.e. a 64-bits random string.

Step 2: The Manager sends its challenge **KM** to the Agent.

Step 3: The Agent generates its own challenge, another 64-bits random string.

Step 4: The Agent calculates its response to the Manager's challenge:
$$RA = KA \oplus KM \oplus BIO_{KEY}.$$

Step 5: The Agent sends the Manager a message containing its response, **RA**, and its own challenge, **KA.**

Step 6: The Manager verifies the response **RA**. If the response is correct, it authenticates the Agent.

Step 7: The Manager calculates its response to the Agent's challenge:
$$RM = KM \oplus KA \oplus BIO_{KEY}.$$

Step 8: The Manager sends the Agent a message containing its own response **RM**.

Step 9: The Agent verifies the response **RM**. If the response is correct, it connects to the Manager.

The *BIO_KEY*, which is used in the procedure described above, is generated based on fingerprint measurements. This key is neither pre-shared, nor exchanged between the Agent and the Manager. The *BIO_KEY* is generated and stored by the Manager during the enrolment phase and it is generated also at the Agent site each time the authentication process starts. The authentication procedure begins when patients are connected to the vital signs monitoring devices (i.e. Agents). The Agent generates a new *BIO_KEY* which is used in the authentication process. The *BIO_KEY* is generated identically by the Agent and the Manager. The generation process consists of extracting the minutiae points from the fingerprint template, normalizing and converting them into a fixed length string, i.e. the *BIO_KEY*.

The protocol proposed above ensures both authentication and identity recognition. It does not significantly affect the number and size of the messages communicated, and it does not require a great deal of processing power. Recently developed wireless controllers, such as the ones from Bluegiga [7], have already implemented the OEP protocol and the Health Data Profile (HDP) in small embeddable chips. Consequently, we expect that the processing power available within medical devices will be able to satisfy the requirements needed for capturing fingerprint images and processing the algorithms necessary for generating the biometric key.

3   Implementation and Results

Validating the proposed solutions in the context of different mobile medical Agents and proving the suitability of the proposed identity management procedure in practice were also part of this research. The case study consists of extending the source code of the Agent and Manager to include authentication and identity management, as described in Section 2. The source code used in the validation process is part of an open source implementation of OEP, namely the OpenHealth Project [11]. The extended OEP protocol flow enabling biometric authentication is shown in Fig. 2.

1. <u>AarqApdu</u> – Agent's request for association with the Manager. This message is identical to the one in the IEEE version of the protocol.

2. <u>AareApdu</u> – Manager's response to the Agent's association request. The parameter that holds the actual response contains a new type of response called *rejected-authentication-required* which denotes that the Manager requests authentication in the association phase. The challenge for the authentication procedure is stored as an attribute in the OptionList parameter.

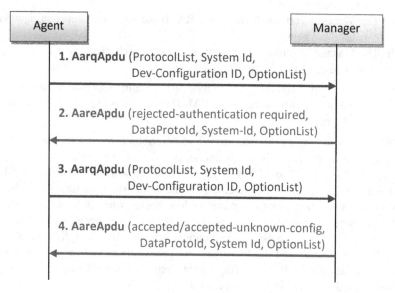

Fig. 2. Association procedure enabling secure authentication

3. <u>AarqApdu</u> – Agent's response to the Manager's challenge. The message contains the response to the Manager's challenge, as well as its own challenge for the Manager. Both pieces of information are stored in the OptionList parameter (Step 4 of the algorithm presented in Section 2).

4. <u>AareApdu</u> – the authentication result. If the authentication fails the first parameter will be set to *rejected-authentication-required*, and a new challenge is sent to the Agent. In the case of a successful authentication, the response is implicit. The message is similar to the response in the current version of the protocol except that it also contains the response to the Agent's challenge, stored in the OptionList parameter. After the fourth message is sent, the communication can follow the course defined in the current version of the protocol. The extension we propose is optional and does not change any specification of the current protocol, thus making it backward compatible.

In order to analyze the results of the authentication implementation using the biometric key, a Wireshark plug-in for dissecting OEP messages was developed. Figures 3 and 4 show the Manager requesting authentication prior to establishing the association and the Agent's response to the Manager's challenge, respectively.

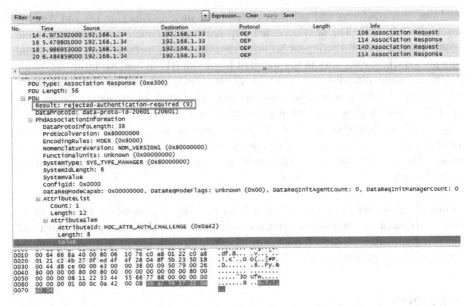

Fig. 3. Manager requesting authentication: result type is *rejected-authentication-required* (purple highlight); challenge is *value* (blue highlight)

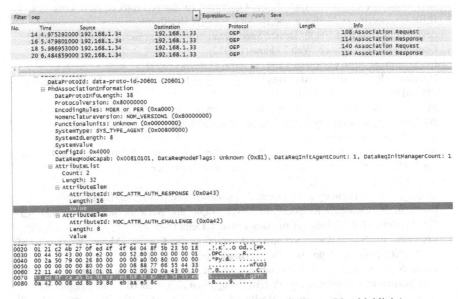

Fig. 4. The Agent's response to the Manager's challenge (blue highlight)

4   Conclusions

The publication of the final versions of various specifications of the ISO/IEEE 11073 family of standards between 2008 and 2010 elicited a huge response from the hardware manufacturers and software developers, such as Bluegiga [7] and Andago Ingenieria S.L. [11]. The next expected step requires that such mobile interoperable health systems prove a stringent security capability in respect of both patients and care personnel. The security in the standard Bluetooth (BT 2.1+EDR) layer, are insufficient and even vulnerable. The existing X73 standards at the application layer do not address any security aspects. The paper presents a proposal for enhancing the security of OEP by introducing a patient authentication with an identity management procedure based on biometric technology. The biometric key for the Agent-Manager authentication is derived from fingerprint measurements and it ensures a high degree of security for the patient authentication and for the Manager systems archiving patient's data.

Acknowledgements. This research has been partially supported by the project ex 60% "Advanced Application of Computer Science" of the University of Padova and by "Competitiveness and performance in research through quality doctoral programs (ProDOC) POSDRU/88/1.5/S61178" by the University Politehnica of Bucharest.

References

1. IEEE Engineering in Medicine and Biology Society, Health informatics—Personal health device comm. Part 20601: Appl. Profile-Optimized Exchange Protocol, New York (2008)
2. IEEE Engineering in Medicine and Biology Society, Health informatics — Personal health device comm. — Part 10408: Device Specialization — Thermometer, New York (2010)
3. Continua Health Alliance, Web 7 (January 2012), http://www.continuaalliance.org/index.html
4. Dunning, J.P.: Taming the Blue Beast - A Survey of Bluetooth-Based Threats. IEEE Security and Privacy, 20–27 (2010)
5. M. Bialoglowy, Bluetooth Security Review part 1, October 2, 2010, Web 2 (December 2011), http://www.symantec.com/connect/articles/bluetooth-security-review-part-1
6. Bialoglowy, M.: Bluetooth Security Review, Part 2, November 2, 2010, Web 2 (December 2011), http://www.symantec.com/connect/articles/bluetooth-security-review-part-2
7. Bluegiga, Web 2 (January 2012), http://www.bluegiga.com/home
8. Forouzan, B.: Challenge Response. In: Cryptography and Network Security, pp. 421–426. Tata McGraw-Hill Publishing Company Limited, Delhi (2007)
9. Rogaway, P.: Nonce-Based Symmetric Encryption. In: Roy, B., Meier, W. (eds.) FSE 2004. LNCS, vol. 3017, pp. 348–359. Springer, Heidelberg (2004)
10. Ratha, N., Connell, J., et al.: Cancelable Biometrics: A Case Study in Fingerprints. In: The 18th International Conference on Pattern Recognition (ICPR 2006), Hong Kong (2006)
11. Andago Ingineria S.L.: Open Health Assistant Project, Web 9 (January 2012), http://openhealthassistant.andago.com
12. Connected Health: Quality and Safety for European Citizens, Report of the Unit ICT for Health and of eHealth European Commission Information Society, Web 20 (August 2012), http://ec.europa.eu/information_society/activities/ict_psp/documents/connected-health.pdf

A New Approach to Prevent Cardiovascular Diseases Based on SCORE Charts through Reasoning Methods and Mobile Monitoring

Jesús Fontecha[1], David Ausín[2], Federico Castanedo[2], Diego López-de-Ipiña[2], Ramón Hervás[1], and José Bravo[1]

[1] MAmI Research Lab, University of Castilla-La Mancha, Ciudad Real, Spain
{jesus.fontecha,ramon.hlucas,jose.bravo}@uclm.es
[2] Deusto Institute of Technology, DeustoTech. University of Deusto, Bilbao, Spain
{david.ausin,fcastanedo,dipina}@deusto.es

Abstract. Nowadays, vital signs monitoring with mobile devices such as smartphones and tablets is possible through Bluetooth-enabled biometric devices. In this paper, we propose a system to monitor the risk of cardiovascular diseases in Ambient Assisted Living environments through blood pressure monitoring and other clinical factors, using mobile devices and reasoning techniques based on the Systematic Coronary Risk Evaluation Project (SCORE) charts. Mobile applications for patients and doctors, and a reasoning engine based on SWRL rules have been developed.

Keywords: Mobile Monitoring, Ambient Assisted Living, CVD Risk, Blood Pressure, Reasoning.

1 Introduction

Increasingly, the concept of Ubiquitous Computing in Healthcare environments is becoming a reality. This is explained by the advent of new embedded technologies, the wide use of universally deployed devices such as smartphones and tablets, and advances in wireless communications.

The Ambient Assisted Living (AAL) initiative[1] promotes the adoption of ICT technologies for helping elderly people, who live alone at home, to perform their daily activities, increasing their quality of life, but bearing in mind that it is crucial serving users in terms of usability. In this sense, the continuous monitoring of vital signs is essential to determine the health condition of the person at any moment, especially when the person suffers from a chronic disease or pathology which must be checked continuously. Many times, a continuous monitoring implies the use of biometric devices to obtain measures related to clinical parameters such as glucose or blood pressure among others. Also, other factors from the patient profile and/or personal medical record must be taken into account, for example: age, sex, healthy habits, measures from analytical tests

---

[1] http://www.aal-europe.eu/

J. Bravo, R. Hervás, and M. Rodríguez (Eds.): IWAAL 2012, LNCS 7657, pp. 17–24, 2012.

(e.g. cholesterol level) and even social factors (e.g. the country where the person lives). All of them have a specific importance, depending on the monitoring goal.

In this paper, we will focus on blood pressure monitoring and several related factors to determine the total risk of suffering a CardioVascular Disease (CVD) for a patient. For that, we will combine a reasoning engine based on Systematic Coronary Risk Evaluation Project (SCORE) chart [1] hosted in a server with Bluetooth-mediated mobile monitoring software.

2   Related Work

In recent years, mobile technologies have been integrated in many AAL systems to improve and monitor several tasks of people who live alone at home. Nowadays, there are approaches based on mobile devices and sensors to know the health condition of the person.

In our particular domain, Villareal et al. [2] propose an architecture for diabetes monitoring by using next-generation mobile devices. Meanwhile, other projects such as the Health Buddy System project [3], connect patients in their homes with doctors to avoid hospitalization situations. In these cases, monitoring tasks are based on questionnaires, and the final results are made available to the doctor via Internet. However, these systems need a direct interaction between devices and the monitored users. On the other hand, Bluetooth specifications[2] are being integrated in standard biometric devices, facilitating many kinds of monitoring. In fact, the Continua Health Alliance[3] promotes the use of a standard datasheet or protocol to receive and manage information from Bluetooth biometric devices.

The MoMo project [4] presents a framework based on several ontological models to facilitate the development of mobile monitoring systems which integrate biometric and mobile devices. In this work, we collect monitoring data from Bluetooth biometric devices, in our case blood pressure, by means of the MoMo framework. These data are saved into the patient record.

Description logics have been employed in medical informatics for several tasks [5], such as terminology modeling (e.g. OpenGALEN [6] and SNOMED CT [7]) or decision support (e.g PRODIGY project [8]). Description logics are the base of the OWL Web Ontology Language (OWL) [9]. The OWL application areas are not only reduced to the medical field and have been applied successfully in many fields associated to Ambient Intelligence where there is a need to model data and reason upon them. In OWL, there is a trade-off between the expressivity and the reasoning time: the more expressive an ontology is, the slower the reasoning task is. Another feature of the OWL ontology is that it can be combined with SWRL rules [10], thus new knowledge about a given semantic model cannot only be generated though the built-in ontological reasoning but also through expert-defined rules. Thus, we propose the use of reasoning mechanisms taking into account OWL and SWRL features for the final CVD risk estimation.

---

[2] http://bluetooth.com
[3] http://www.continuaalliance.org

Nowadays, SCORE is the main method used by the European Societies of Cardiology to determine CVD risk percentage in European and Mediterranean countries. However, our proposal can be extrapolated to non-European regions turning their CVD standardized charts into SWRL rules to be used by our system depending on the specific region. For example, the Framingham Risk Score [11] is the most common method for CVD risk estimation in USA, but this is also used elsewhere in the world. All existing methods are based on clinical evidences and their results are often very similar because these have been created from a base chart score proposed for the World Health Organization (WHO) and the International Society of Hypertension (ISH) [12], but adjusted to different regions. We have chose SCORE because the system is being developed and evaluated in Spain.

3   CVD Risk Estimation Approach

The aim of our proposal is to support clinical decisions facilitating the estimation of CVD risk and related recommendations from a continuous monitoring of blood pressure at home, using the MoMo framework principles and its combination with several clinical factors from the patient record. All collected data are the inputs to the reasoning module which uses an adaptation of the MoMo ontology and a reasoning engine based on OWL and SWRL as mentioned above.

3.1   Principles and Adaptation of MoMo Framework

MoMo framework [4] allows the development of mobile applications in an adaptive, generic and remote. *Generic*, allowing the development of apps for any kind of disease. *Adaptive*, providing services adjusted to each disease depending on a patient profile. *Remote*, Medical staff is able to know all data gathered by the patient biometric devices in a non-intrusive. *Mobile*, the development of applications is based on the integration of small wireless devices.

This framework proposes the use of different patterns to design user interfaces, to specify features and to develop standardized modules, allowing the reuse of these. Also, it describes an ontological classification called *MoMOntology* providing a framework data formalization (this includes data of patient profile, diseases and recommendations among other).

In our proposal, we have used the previous principles and an adaptation of the MoMo patient profile ontology with a set of SWRL rules for CVD risk estimation.

3.2   Blood Pressure Monitoring

The European guidelines on cardiovascular disease prevention in clinical practice [1] suggest to check the blood pressure levels frequently to prevent and monitor many coronary diseases. In this sense, the number of times in one day blood pressure should be measured depends on the health condition of the person and his patient record [13].

First, we have developed an Android mobile application to get measures from a Bluetooth-powered pressure monitor, namely Stabil O GRAPH SBPM-Control[4]. These measures are stored in a remote database by means of web services. Besides, this mobile application promotes the autonomy of the monitored user because direct intervention of the physician to take new measures is not needed. In Fig. 1 is shown the sequence diagram for blood pressure monitoring.

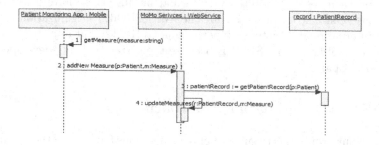

Fig. 1. Sequence diagram: A new measure of blood pressure has been taken

Most of the time, single measures do not provide sufficient information, therefore, more complex analysis are carried out. Thus, we must take into account other factors in order to make a proper assessment of risks. In the case of hypertensive people, there are 10 top high blood pressure risk factors [14]. These are: Age, Ethnicity, Gender, Family history, Smoking, Activity level, Diet, Medication and street drugs, Kidney problems, and Other medical problems. A continuous blood pressure monitoring is needed to find out hypertension problems.

3.3   CVD and SCORE Risk Charts

The analysis of blood pressure levels and other risk factors can be used to determine CVDs. In this sense, the SCORE method (see section 2), is able to estimate the 10-year risk of a first fatal atherosclerotic event, whether heart attack, stroke, aneurysm of the aorta, or other kind of CVD. Besides, SCORE charts provide a set of variables which identify the inputs to the reasoning engine. These ones are shown in Table 1 and below.

On the other hand, the outputs of the reasoning module from the previous variables have been grouped as follows.

- **Very High.** If a user presents a risk of 15% and over.
- **High.** If the risk is in the range 10% - 14%.
- **Mid High.** User presents a risk from 5% to 9%.
- **Mid.** User presents a risk from 3% - 4%.

---

[4] http://www.iem.de/stabil_o_graph_mobil2

Table 1. Input Variables

Variable	Description	Type	Range
Sex	Gender of the person	Binary	Male or Female
Age	Age of the person	Discrete	[40,50,55,60,65]
Smoker	Indicates if the person smokes	Binary	True or False
Cholesterol	Cholesterol level (mmol/L)	Double	[4,5,6,7,8]
Blood Pressure	Average of Systolic Blood Pressure(mmHg)	Discrete	[120,140,160,180)
High Risk Country	Indicates if the person lives in a high risk country (view the list of the countries below)	Binary	True or False

List of High Risk Countries: Countries not listed below.
List of Low Risk Countries: Andorra (AN), Austria (AU), Belgium (BE), Cyprus (CY), Denmark (DE), Finland (FI), France (FR), Germany (DE), Greece (GR), Iceland (IC), Ireland (IR), Israel (IS), Italy (IT), Luxembourg (LU), Malta (MA), Monaco (MO), The Netherlands (NL), Norway (NO), Portugal (PO), San Marino (SM), Slovenia (SL), Spain (SP), Sweden ILAR(SW), Switzerland (CH), United Kingdom (UK).

- *Mid Low.* If the risk is 2%.
- *Low.* If the risk presented corresponds to 1%.
- *None.* No risk is presented.

In addition, recommendations can be offered to the physician through a specific mobile application. These recommendations can be formed from the reasoning outputs and other clinical factors (including chronic diseases such as diabetes, and other pathologies). However, our initial prototype determines the risk of CVD from the patient profile and an average of latest blood pressure measures.

3.4 Reasoning Module

The reasoning module calculates the CVD risk associated to a patient and has the ability to create patient recommendations to decrease his CVD risk. The reasoning engine uses the OWL API [15] to load the patient ontology and the SWRL rules and Pellet [16] reasoner to perform the reasoning task. SWRL rules are divided in two parts: the antecedent and the consequent. In our case, more than 250 rules have been described according to SCORE charts.

The antecedent describes the conditions which must be fulfilled to infer the consequent assumptions. In this case, the antecedents are the patient's health condition and the consequences are his CVD risk and a set of recommendation adapted to him. Final results are sent to a medical mobile application through the corresponding web services. Fig 2 shows the sequence diagram from this process, and table 2 shows an example of a complete SWRL rule according to the specific output provided by SCORE.

4   System Deployment

Our proposal consists of two Android mobile applications with which the users (patients and doctors) interact.

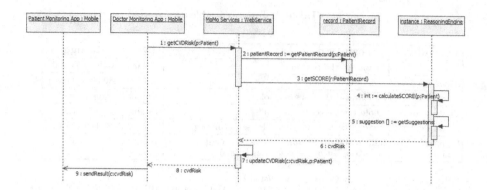

Fig. 2. Sequence diagram: CVD Risk calculation

Table 2. Example of SWRL Rule based on SCORE for a fourty-years-old non smoker woman who lives in a low CVD risk country, whose systolic blood pressure is between 120 and 160 mmHg and whose cholesterol is between 4 and 6 mmol/L

Antecedents	
Conditions	*SWRL Translation*
Pick up an individual which is a Patient	talismanPlus:Patient(?patient) ∧
Where does she live?	talismanPlus:livesIn(?patient,?country)∧ talismanPlus:LowCVDRiskCountry(?country)∧
Is she a female?	talismanPlus:isMale(?patient,?isMale)∧ sqwrl:equal(?isMale,false)∧
How old is she?	talismanPlus:isYearsOld(?patient,?years)∧ swrlb:greaterThanOrEqual(?years,40)∧ swrlb:lessThan(?years,50)∧
Does she smoke?	talismanPlus:isSmoker(?patient,?smoke)∧ sqwrl:equal(?smoke,false)∧
Obtain her record	talismanPlus:hasRecord(?patient,?history)∧
Check her systolic blood pressure	talismanPlus:hasTest(?history,?systolic)∧ talismanPlus:SystolicBloodPressureAvgTest(?systolic)∧ talismanPlus:hasSystolicBloodPressure(?systolic,?systolicMeasure)∧ swrlb:greaterThanOrEqual(?systolicMeasure,120)∧ swrlb:lessThan(?systolicMeasure,160)∧
Check cholesterol	talismanPlus:hasTest(?history,?cholesterol)∧ talismanPlus:CholesterolTest(?cholesterol)∧ talismanPlus:hasCholesterol(?cholesterol,?cholesterolMeasure)∧ swrlb:greaterThanOrEqual(?cholesterolMeasure,4)∧ swrlb:lessThan(?cholesterolMeasure,6)
Consequent	
Action	*SWRL translation*
Set her CVD risk	→ talismanPlus:hasCVDRisk(?patient,"none")

The first mobile app allows patients to monitor their vital signs such as blood pressure as explained in this paper (see Fig. 3, step 1). Data storage and retrieval processes are carried out by transactions with web services (2). This mobile app

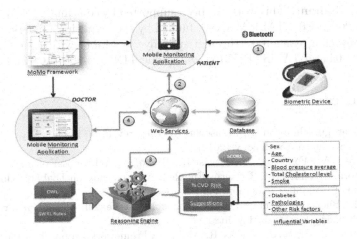

Fig. 3. System Overview

also provides a support to receive recommendations from the doctor and create charts related to the monitored tasks. Moreover, the second mobile app allows doctors to know the health condition of patients in real time (4) by means of retrieved data from the database (including patient record) using web services. Thus, the system sends recommendations and suggestions to patients thanks to the continuous monitoring without having a direct contact with the patient and also, these suggestions may be completed and enriched by doctors.

Finally, the reasoning module developed is responsible for calculating the CVD risk and create the related recommendations taking into account the set of influential variables from the patient record. Several web services provide access to the data and the results (3).

5 Discussions and Future Work

In this work, we have presented a system to monitor the blood pressure of a patient and calculate his CVD risk applying the SCORE method.

Ongoing work is to create a set of recommendation to reduce the patient's CVD risk and deploy the system in a real AAL environment to evaluate these recommendations inferred by the reasoner. Besides, the feedback gathered will be employed to enhance the mobile user interface and to ease the human-computer interaction.

In the future, we would like to extend the application to also monitor user's dietary habits and his daily physical activity by using the accelerometer integrated into the mobile phone to check if he follows the previously issued system recommendations, thus not only monitoring his health variables but also tracking the fulfilment of the recommendations issued to prevent any coronary incident.

Acknowledgment. This work has been supported by coordinated project grant TIN2010-20510-C04 (TALISMAN+), funded by the Spanish Ministerio de Ciencia e Innovación, concretely through subproyects MoMo with code TIN2010-20510-C04-04 and TALIS+ENGINE with code TIN2010-20510-C04-03.

References

1. European guidelines on cardiovascular disease prevention in clinical practice. European Society of Cardiology (2012)
2. Villarreal, V., Fontecha, J., Hervás, R., Bravo, J.: A Proposal of an Ubiquitous Monitoring Architecture Patterns-Enabled: A case study on Diabetes. Journal of Science of Computer Programming (in press, 2012)
3. Health Buddy System, http://www.bosch-telehealth.com/en/us/products/health_buddy/health_buddy.html
4. Villarreal, V., Bravo, J., Hervás, R.: MoMo: A Framework Proposal for Patient Mobile Monitoring. In: Proceedings of the 5th Conference of the Euro-American Association on Telematics and Information Systems, EATIS 2010, Panama, September 22-24. ACM Publication (2010)
5. Rector, A.: Medical Informatics, The description logic handbook, pp. 406–426. Cambridge University Press (2003)
6. Rector, A.L., Rogers, J.E., Zanstra, P.E., Van Der Haring, E.: OpenGALEN: open source medical terminology and tools. In: AMIA Annual Symposium Proceedings, American Medical Informatics Association, p. 982 (2003)
7. SNOMEDCT, http://www.nlm.nih.gov/research/umls/Snomed/snomed_main.html
8. Purves, I.N.: PRODIGY: implementing clinical guidance using computers. The British Journal of General Practice 48(434), 1552 (1998)
9. W3C, Web Ontology Language, OWL (2007), http://www.w3.org/2004/OWL/
10. W3C, SWRL: A Semantic Web Rule Language Combining OWL and RuleML (2004), http://www.w3.org/Submission/SWRL/
11. D'Agostino, R.B., Vasan, R.S., Pencina, M.J., Wolf, P.A., Cobain, M., Massaro, J.M., Kannel, W.B.: General cardiovascular risk profile for use in primary care: the Framingham Heart Study. Circulation 117(6), 743–753 (2008)
12. World Health Organization, World Health Report 2002: reducing risks, promoting healthy life, Geneva: WHO (2002a)
13. Victor, R.G.: Systemic hypertension: Mechanisms and diagnosis, 9th edn. Braunwald's Heart Disease: A Textbook of Cardiovascular Medicine, ch. 45. Saunders Elsevier, Philadelphia (2011)
14. Weber, C.: Top 10 High Blood Pressure Risk Factors (2007), http://highbloodpressure.about.com/od/understandyourrisk/tp/risk_tp.htm
15. Horridge, M., Bechhofer, S.: The OWL API: a Java API for working with OWL 2 ontologies. In: Proc. of OWL Experiences and Directions (2009)
16. Sirin, E., Parsia, B., Grau, B.C., Kalyanpur, A., Katz, Y.: Pellet: A practical owl-dl reasoner. Web Semantics: Science, Services and Agents on the World Wide Web 5(2), 51–53 (2007)

PeerAssist: A P2P Platform Supporting Virtual Communities to Assist Independent Living of Senior Citizens

Nikos Passas[1], Michael Fried[2], and Elias S. Manolakos[1]

[1] Dept. of Informatics & Telecommunications, University of Athens, Greece
{passas,eliasm}@di.uoa.gr
[2] Semantic Technology Institute, Innsbruck, Austria
michael.fried@sti2.at

Abstract. This paper describes the system architecture and status of PeerAssist, an Ambient Assisted Living (AAL) project that aims at designing, implementing, and demonstrating a flexible Peer-to Peer (P2P) platform, which will allow elderly people (not necessarily familiar with information technology) to build virtual communities dynamically based on interests and needs they share. The PeerAssist technology platform will facilitate establishing on demand ad-hoc communities with friends, family, neighbors, caregivers, etc. The community building and P2P interaction is achieved using information extracted from peer roles and profiles, context that describes the overall user environment, and the specific request initiated or service provided by a peer, all of which are represented semantically in a machine understandable form. An end-user request (query) is first represented semantically and then routed through the network in order to find semantically matching peers. The selected peer-to-peer platform exploits the system's intelligence to provide connectivity at the network level optimized to efficiently serve the objectives of the system.

Keywords: elderly, social networking, peer-to-peer.

1 Introduction

The shift in the distribution of earth's population towards older ages makes research for improving the quality of life for elderly people an urgent priority. Support mechanisms need to be put in place to allow elderly people to continue living normal lives and make it easier for them to remain fully integrated in their local societies. It is well known that retirement from a profession and age-related health problems or disabilities force the elderly to spend longer periods at home, away from social activities. As their involvement with social activities diminishes, they start feeling lonely and disconnected despite their interests and desires. Properly designed information and communication technologies can help them overcome this isolation and prolong the period of their active engagement with the rest of society. As a result, the whole society can reap the social and financial benefits associated with improving

J. Bravo, R. Hervás, and M. Rodríguez (Eds.): IWAAL 2012, LNCS 7657, pp. 25–32, 2012.

the quality of life for the elderly, as well as alleviating the financial burden of prolonged elderly people care which may severely stress family budgets.

Towards this direction, this paper presents PeerAssist, a flexible Peer-to-Peer (P2P) platform, which allows elderly people to build virtual communities dynamically based on interests and needs they share. PeerAssist can form the basis for developing a wide number of applications including (but not limited to): (i) peer-driven organization of social activities (such as going out, going to the movies, exchanging books, organizing a social gathering, etc.); (ii) soliciting peer help with housekeeping and other daily activities; (iii) allowing support organizations to "push" relevant content to interested elderly users; (iii) allowing caregivers, facilitators and family members to receive alerts if certain expected home activities of the elderly people are interrupted; (iv) responding to emergency situations that may ask for immediate action.

The paper is organized as follows: Section 2 presents the related state-of-the-art to set up the framework for the system description. Section 3 includes the main part of our contribution, i.e., the system architecture. It starts with the conceptual basis, and moves to the description of the PeerAssist node. Section 4 and 5 describe two of the most critical parts of the platform, the community networks, and the query processing system, respectively. Section 6 contains details on the platform implementation, while Section 7 contains information about the system evaluation and user trials. Section 8 concludes the paper.

2   State-of-the-Art

One of the PeerAssist project's main goals, to connect elderly people via virtual ad-hoc communities, can be viewed as an extension to general purpose social networks which helps users to feel socially connected and active. A multitude of publications and research projects for building AAL centric online communities have emerged in recent history.

One notable example is the interLiving project [1] which dealt with exploring and developing technologies for inter-generational communication between remotely located family members. Within this project the PeerCare initiative studied habits and social behavior of elderly people. Current AAL projects researching in similar directions include GO-myLife [2] a mobile social networking platform and Co-Living [3] a virtual collaborative community for elderly people. Also in recent history semantically enabled context aware platforms for (mobile) communications services, including multi-modal interaction [8] have been a topic within ICT research.

However, the roots of research in the direction of supporting elderly people through online networks can be found earlier in literature. Already in 2001, Camarinha-Matos et al. [4] wrote about the concept of "Virtual Communities and Elderly Support". As part of the European IST project TeleCARE, aimed at developing a configurable framework for virtual communities supporting elderly people, the authors already took into account many emerging topics like mobile agents as well as rising privacy issues.

In contrast to existing approaches PeerAssist's emphasis on P2P services will have high impact within the field because they: (1) constitute social communication that goes beyond a regular service provider/client interaction, (2) foster exchange between more than two parties additionally stimulating the processes of community building; (3) can be integrated into a network of added-value components of caregiver and technical service providers. This functionality is further extended by context aware, preference based suggestions and user interface adaptations.

3   The PeerAssist System Architecture

3.1   Conceptual Basis of PeerAssist

Before presenting the PeerAssist architecture let us establish a clear view of the Peer-Assist concepts summarized by the UML diagram shown in Figure 1.

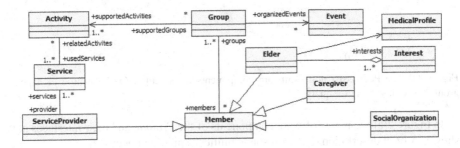

Fig. 1. PeerAssist concepts and their relation (UML diagram)

According to this conceptual model, a *Group* is a community of people driven by common interests which has a unique identifier, and is characterized by a name, a description, a type (i.e. either private or public), a purpose (i.e. general, event, caregiving, or healthcare related), and a time-to-live. A group may participate or organize *Events* (e.g. a social gathering) or support an *Activity* (e.g. an online discussion activity).

A Group is populated by at least one *Member* and, reversely, a *Member* may participate in one or more groups. There are many specializations of the core *Member* concept, namely the *Caregiver*, the *Social Organization*, the *Service Provider*, and the *Elder*. The latter specifies one or more Interests and has a specific *Medical Profile*.

Each *Group* supports one or more *Activities* (e.g. a discussion about a specific topic, playing an online game, etc.), which are realized through a set of *Services*. It should be noted that, a particular *Activity* may be supported by more than one *Group*. Also, a particular *Service* may be used in the context of more than one *Activity*. For example, the chat service can be used both in the discussion and online game activities. Finally, *Services* are provided by *Service Providers*, which are seen as a specialization of the *Member* concept. Each *Group* may organize one or more *Events* with a date associated.

3.2   The PeerAssist Node

The PeerAssist node (*PAnode*) is the main software entity of the PeerAssist platform. A *PAnode* is a software components architecture running in each user's PC and interacting with the rest of the entities of the PeerAssist platform (i.e. the portable user interface device, available sensors etc.) in order to orchestrate the execution of use cases that provide the PeerAssist functionality.

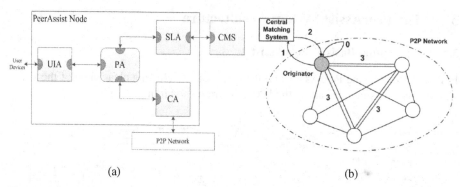

(a)   (b)

Fig. 2. (a) The PeerAssist node software components architecture. (b) Formation of a peer group in response to a user query.

In Figure 2(a) the main software components of the *PAnode* and their interfaces are shown. A brief description of their responsibilities is provided below:

User Interface Agent (UIA). It is responsible for: (i) Capturing user intent by interacting with the portable end-user device, (ii) gathering and communicating data that are used to form user queries.

Semantic Layer Agent (SLA). It is responsible for: (i) Maintaining the user profile and local context information in the Local Semantic Information (LSI) knowledge base, and (ii) interacting with the Central Matching System (CMS) (that is in a central server) whenever needed to process user queries.

Personal Assistant (PA). It is used to: (i) Dispatch information between the rest of the agents acting as an intelligent intermediary, (ii) mediate whenever needed on behalf of the user to facilitate interaction and support limited autonomy in certain use cases, (ii) maintain relevant information to improve interaction with the user through machine learning.

Communication Agent (CA).It is responsible to handle P2P communication with the other *PAnodes* in the PeerAssist community network, thus abstracting the communication aspect of the design for the rest of the agents. It also handles security and distributed trust related issues.

Home Automation Controller (HAC). It handles the control of and communication with local user devices and sensors.

4   The PeerAssist Community Networks

A typical use case in PeerAssist consists of a workflow with the following sequence of steps (not all steps are necessarily present in every use case):

1. Capturing end-user intent: This is accomplished using the UIA and is facilitated by taking into account the elderly user's profile and context. Potentially it may also involve the PA in an assistive/suggestive role.
2. Building a user community (group) to participate in an event/activity: The Semantic layer of PeerAssist (SLA-CMS) suggests which users may join the group based on intent, constraints, user context, profile, etc. Existing groups are presented to the user (through the UIA) and allowed to join the associated peer group (an ad-hoc user community maintained by the SLA). Users can join and leave a group dynamically on demand.
3. Execution and progress monitoring of the use case (application task): A task may involve calling several services. Some services may be offered by local devices interacting with the PAnode, and some others may be global services with implementations obtained from a remote service repository.

Following this generic use case paradigm, a PeerAssist task execution may necessitate the creation and maintenance of a logically fully connected graph of PAnodes. As shown in Figure 2(b) a specific end-user (called the "originator") uses its PAnode (shaded node) to create a group (peer community). Through interaction with the user interface a query is formed (step 0). The query may need to be sent all the way to the remote Central Matching System (CMS) in order to find matching users (step 1). The CMS returns a list of matching users rank ordered based on relevance (step 2). The originator's PAnode filters the matches and sends invitations to a selected subset. Once these users accept the invitation a logical communication channel (pipe) is opened among pairs of peers participating in the formed peer community (step 3). These pipes (shown as red edges) are maintained by the CA for as long as they are needed to support the interaction of members of the formed group.

5   The PeerAssist Query Processing System

With the exception of actually communicating with a peer, every other action that the user wants to perform using the PeerAssist platform is interpreted as a query that either retrieves information (for example Search Item scenario), or triggers changes of the stored information (for example Join Group or Leave Group scenarios).

The Matching and Query System's functionalities are as follows:

1. Formulate queries based on user inputs and query templates: The users provide inputs through the user interface, which is forwarded to the Semantic Layer Agent. A sub-component of the SLA translates the captured user intent into a machine interpretable formalism, namely SPARQL queries.
2. Execute a query against internal (local) semantic data: Every PAnode stores information about the end-user locally. A local matching system is available in

every node for executing queries referring to locally stored data. It is optimal for minimizing processing time and reducing network traffic, to execute queries locally, whenever possible.

3. Execute the query on the central data repository: There are two scenarios under which queries need to be executed against the central matching system (CMS). Firstly, if the user performs some updates on its own node, these updates need to be propagated to the global repository (e.g. updating a user's list of friends is performed both locally and on the global repository). Secondly, if the user searches for data not available locally (e.g. searching for a group with certain interests).

4. Filter data based on additional criteria: It refers to filtering query results based on user preferences expressed via the User Interface (e.g. according to location, gender etc.).

6   The PeerAssist Platform Implementation

The central element of the home network is the PeerAssist end user device, running the PAnode software components, providing home services, interacting with the user and managing the home infrastructure. This local server is a simple PC (desktop or laptop). The Portable User Interface Device is used to interact with the user and can be either a tablet, or a laptop, and it will connect to the PeerAssist end user device (in case they are two separate devices) through a graphical user interface, or a voice user interface using a headset or a microphone and a set of speakers. This device may also be part of the PeerAssist end user device.

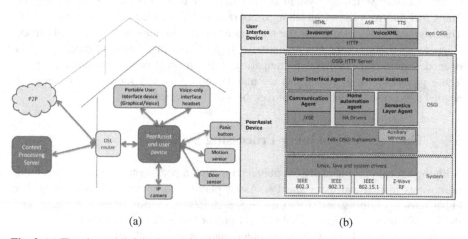

(a)   (b)

Fig. 3. (a) The elements of the PeerAssist home network. (b) The PeerAssist platform software implementation.

Added value services are enabled by supporting several home peripherals: panic button, motion/door sensor, camera, microphone etc. The panic button is connected to the local server and when pushed it triggers an alarm to notify the elderly user's caregivers. The camera is connected to the local server and it is employed in monitoring activities. Sensors, e.g. motion and door sensors are used to provide context monitoring during specific activities. The home devices (camera, speakers, microphone, panic button etc.) may be connected to the local server directly via cable, or through Bluetooth or some other wireless networking protocol.

The PeerAssist end user device acts as an edge peer to the P2P network. It runs an instance of the Apache Felix OSGi framework [6] (see Figure 3(b)) and it hosts all the main components that need to be accessed as OSGi bundles. It also runs a Web server (as an OSGi bundle or as a standalone server), that hosts the Web applications that must run locally in order to use the equipment (microphone, speakers) that connect locally to the end user device. The Web server sits behind a firewall and can be accessed only from within the home network, for security reasons and because there is no application that needs to be accessed from outside. The applications that run on the Web server, can access the Internet and the P2P network only through the OSGi interface and the JXTA [7] network, by communicating with the rendezvous and relay peers that have the ability to communicate through firewalls.

The end user device also runs a VoiceXML browser, which hosts the VoiceXML scenarios for the voice user interface. The end user device finally hosts the automatic speech recognition (ASR) and Text to Speech (TTS) modules that are used by the voice user interface, for the voice recognition of the user voice commands and response to the user. The VoiceXML browser is hosted on the same machine as the application server, but they communicate through HTTP calls so they could be hosted on different machines, or even different platforms. The ASR and TTS modules are not part of the VoiceXML browser, but third party components serving the need for supporting different languages, other than the default English language that is integrated in the browser. The scenarios supported by the VoiceXML browser, include the same actions that the user can perform with the graphical user interface, so that the user can either learn one of the two different options and use the other the same way, or switch back and forth from one option (graphical, voice) to the other during an action.

7   Evaluation and User Trials

As integral part of the project, the partners agreed on testing the software in two different countries, namely Greece and Spain. In a first step we conducted a user survey regarding the usability of the interface with existing mockups. Targeted were elderly people with mild computer experience e.g. using the PC multiple times a week, ability to check emails. The following findings were discovered as part of the assessment: So far the user interface was accepted well and participants were able to perform the given tasks (search users, join groups, etc.)mostly without problems. However in some points regarding for example the font size and spacing the user interface still needs improvement. These outcomes will influence the final version of the system used for the trials which we decided to split into two parts: A first test run will take place with users from Spain by the end of this year with 10-20 elderly participants and 1-2 doctors. After the system has been changed and extended according to the collected feedback the Greek trials will take place in2013.

8   Conclusions

With the use of peer-to-peer technology and advanced semantic representation and matching techniques, PeerAssist aims at providing an efficient yet simplified way for communication and social networking for the elderly. Entering its last project year, preliminary system evaluation results have been extracted from focus groups that show increased user interest for the kind of applications the platform targets. With the introduction of sophisticated user interfaces, such as graphical touch screens, television and voice input, average user impairments can be handled, reducing the need for prior computer knowledge. What remains critical is the construction of a convincing and realistic business plan, to make the service work in large scales after the end of the project.

Acknowledgements. The work in this paper has been partially funded by the AAL Joint Programme and partially by the funding agencies of Greece (General Secretariat for Research and Technology) and Austria (FFG). The authors are grateful for the support they received from their colleagues in the project from the University of Athens, InAccess Networks, Athens Development Agency, Warp, Ingema, STIInnsbruck and seekda.

References

[1] PeerAssist project, http://cnl.di.uoa.gr/peerassist
[2] interLiving project, http://interliving.kth.se/
[3] GO-myLife project, http://www.gomylife-project.eu/
[4] Co-Living project, http://www.project-coliving.eu/
[5] Camarinha-Matos, L.M., Afsarmanesh, H.: Virtual communities and elderly support. In: Kluev, V.V., D'Attellis, C.E., Mastorakis, N.E. (eds.) Advances in Automation, Multimedia and Video Systems, and Modern Computer Science, pp. 279–284. WSES (September 2001) ISBN 960-8052-44-0
[6] OSGi Alliance, http://www.osgi.org
[7] JXTA Language and Protocol for P2P Networking, http://jxta.kenai.com/
[8] Kernchen, R., Boussard, M., Hesselman, C., Villalonga, C., Clavier, E., Zhdanova, A.V., Cesar, P.: Managing Personal Communication Environments in Next Generation Service Platforms. In: Proceedings of the 16th Ist Mobileand Wireless Communications Summit, July 1-5. IEEE, Budapest (2007)

Validation Tool for Smart Screening of Language Disorders in Pediatrics Care

María Luisa Martín Ruiz[*], Miguel Angel Valero, and Iván Pau De Cruz

DIATEL, EUIT de Telecomunicación, Universidad Politécnica de Madrid, Spain
{marisam,mavalero,ipau}@diatel.upm.es

Abstract. Primary-care pediatricians could play a key role in early detection of development disorders as quick as they might have enough time and knowledge for suitable screenings at clinical routine. This research paper focuses on the development and validation of a knowledge-based web tool whose aim is to support a smart detection of developmental disorders in early childhood. Thus, the use of the system can trigger the necessary preventive and therapeutic actions from birth until the age of six. The platform was designed on the basis of an analysis of significant 21 cases of children with language disorders that supported the creation of a specific knowledge base, its ontology and a set of description logic relations. The resulting system is being validated in a scalable approach with a team of seven experts from the fields of neonathology, pediatrics, neurology and language therapy.

Keywords: Intelligent healthcare system, Decision Support Systems, Knowledge Management, Early attention, e-Health.

1 Introduction

Primary health care in Spain is currently close to collapse due to the high number of patients seen by a doctor through traditional consultations. In order to attend all the patients, they have seen reduced the time shared with the doctor in a consultation. This situation makes the quality of that care being eroded from the clinical point of view and a sense of lack of follow-up care received by the patients. Children, when are patients, are in the same situation.

This research focuses on promoting the welfare of children and their families. The early and appropriate diagnosis for the child's health status can lead to better treatment and effect on their development. The problems that could be detected in a routine visit to the pediatrician should be referred without delay to the appropriate specialist. This way the specialist can identify the disorder in the first stages and provide a proper medical treatment. This work aims to facilitate the task of pediatricians in the diagnosis and monitoring of children with language disorders. We propose a Decision Support System (DSS) that complements the actions of the pediatricians in the state of saturation in which they find themselves, helping them to find out early signs of language disorders. Thus, it is intended to catalyze processes of early intervention, early

---

[*] Corresponding author.

J. Bravo, R. Hervás, and M. Rodríguez (Eds.): IWAAL 2012, LNCS 7657, pp. 33–40, 2012.
© Springer-Verlag Berlin Heidelberg 2012

diagnosis and therapy, to improve the care of children with possible developmental disorders.

Primary-care pediatricians use information systems that fulfill the WONCA standards. Spanish healthcare system uses OMI, which does not gather aspects of the children's neuro-evolutive development and only it is thought to register information. Primary-care pediatricians play a key role in early detection of development alterations as they can undertake the preventive and therapeutic actions necessary in the interest of a child's optimal development. Present rates of detection of development disorders are lower than their real incidence [1], which means that early identification of children with such disorders remains a pending task. For these reasons, it is considered to be particularly valuable for a pediatrician to have access to an intelligent healthcare system in primary care to enable efficient screening of such disorders. This research paper describes the process of building of a tool for smart screening of language disorders in pediatrics care.

2   Background

Medicine is one of the fields to have benefited most from the use of computers, as a pioneer in the use of Decision Support Systems (DSS). HEPAXPERT (1991, Austrian) embedded knowledge-based diagnostic intelligence to interpret hepatitis serology test results. VIE-PNN was an expert system used for parenteral nutrition of neonates, (1993, Austrian). ERA project (2001, UK) is a DDS for interactive decision-making for identifying patients suspected of having cancer. ATENÍA project (2002, US) was used to control of hypertension in primary care. LISA project (2004, UK) assists in decision-making for children with lymphoblastic leukemia and the SimulConsult tool (2008, US) can detect health problems in children. In our study of DDS in medicine, no tool was found for the early detection of language disorders in children. Early detection of development disorders is very important, however, in clinical practice, pediatricians do not have enough time to perform proper screening of the children's neuro-evolutionary development, and their background in disabilities is not always as complete as would be desirable [2].

The use of smart systems in primary care becomes of greater interest as it can allow for detection of neurological disorders in children and prevention of added pathologies, achievement of functional improvements and allow for a more adaptive adjustment between a child and his or her surroundings. Paul and Fejerman studies stressed that a complete neurological and pediatric evaluation can reveal related developmental disorders, starting with detection of a language disorder [3,4]. Narbona highlights the fact that a neurological disorder does not manifest itself solely in a delay in the correct acquisition of speech and language, although a delay in the correct acquisition of language is the first alarm sign of a future neurological disorder [5]. Although medical procedures are available to detect a number of neurological disorders in children [1], these procedures are difficult to apply in primary pediatric care, as many require significant time and specialized knowledge. The review in this research found no solutions that exploit the potential of DSS in combination with artificial intelligence to efficiently and effectively assist pediatricians in the early detection of these disorders.

3   Methodology

The following team of experts from the field of healthcare participated in the construction of the Knowledge Base (KB) needed to enable knowledge inference in the DSS to perform early screening of language disorders in primary care: a neonatologist with high expertise in development disorders and child disability, former director of the neonatology department of San Carlos Hospital in Madrid, two primary care pediatricians, a neuropediatrician presently working in the Quirón Hospital of Madrid and two experts in specific language impairment who are therapists at the Language Intervention Center (LIC) at La Salle Campus (UAM) of Madrid.

The acquisition and systematization of needed knowledge required for the early referral of a DSS of a smart system proposed in this paper is a critical aspect that determines its effective use in primary care. The process of Knowledge Acquisition (KA) is the first step for creating a DSS and it strongly influences the conditions for correct operation. This process covers up to the final stage of DSS development. The methodology for KA requires consideration of both the definition of the knowledge to be systematized and the conceptualization and formal design of the information compiled from human and materials sources in order to model the functioning of the DSS [6]. The main methodologies available for extracting knowledge were studied (GROVER, CommonKADS (CK) [6], Methontology [7] and IDEAL). The conclusion of this study was to use a combination of CK and Methontology. The application of CK for the system design provided a set of early detection items to be considered by the pediatrician. This structured knowledge reflects all important aspects of the DSS to be implemented and verified through a user tool. CK was used in KA meetings as it is most suitable for modeling the knowledge extracted from language specialists in the form of ontology. Methontology defines a set of tasks that enabled moving from an informal specification of the domain of application, collected with the language specialists, to a semi-formal specification of the domain. This facility makes easier the understanding of the ontology for smart screening of language disorders by consulted neuropediatricians and language therapists as well as the system developer. Figure 1 summarizes the empirical design methodology for the construction of the DSS.

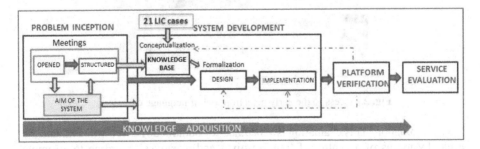

Fig. 1. Development methodology

DSS development has been carried out in four steps:

Problem inception: aims to fully define the problem to be solved for early intervention. In this phased, the group of experts involved in the KA process were – a pediatrician, a neuropediatrician and a neonatologist– held five open meetings between September 2009 and May 2011 in order to fully define the problem to be solved, work on early screening of language disorders, with the construction of a smart detection system.

System development: includes the implementation phase of the DSS. The main result is the KB. In this phased, the group of experts were – a neuropediatrician and two experts in specific language impairment who are therapists at the Language Intervention Center (LIC) at La Salle Campus (UAM) of Madrid specialized in neurological disorders in children – created the KB through ten structured meetings. The process of building and purging the KB was developed through a retrospective analysis of information on levels of language acquisition of 21 children who received therapy in the LIC [8]. The KB has been developed using Protégé (ontology creation platform) [9] and Pellet (reasoning engine) [10]. The verification of the KB required a usable tool so that specialists might interact with the KBS in an efficient way.

Platform verification: experts should be able to evaluate whether the system proposal to refer to a specialist arising from a detection of language development disorders was correct or not. Thus, a web tool (Figure 2) was built to facilitate the work of experts and primary care pediatricians. Five specialists have been involved in the verification stages both for usability and system performance tests along six months (two pediatricians, two language therapists and one neuropediatrician). This process contributed in a satisfactory way to improve the graphical user interface and the reasoning rules of the KB. End users pointed out that they could use the tool by themselves in clinical routine.

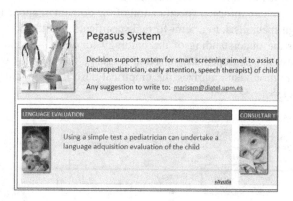

Fig. 2. Access to the early detection tool of language disorders

Service evaluation: This evaluation is scheduled for autumn 2012. We will evaluate the results by means of a control of false positives and negatives according to a sample give 100 children chosen at random by the pediatricians who will take part in the evaluation phase.

4   Results

This section contains the main results of this research. First, it describes the general System Architecture. Secondly, it describes the construction of the KB and then the process of formalization of the KB. Lastly, an example is shown of an ad-hoc web interface for verification of the resulting KB.

4.1   General System Architecture

The functional architecture of the resulting system must facilitate dynamic interaction between the actors involved, distributed platforms for the management of information, models of reasoning and processes in line with the health care model in which it is located (Figure 3).

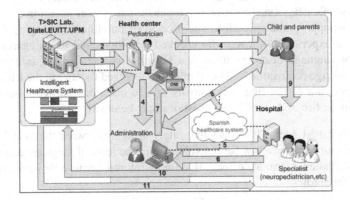

Fig. 3. General System Architecture

1. The child goes to the family pediatrician accompanied by a family member.
2. Primary health-care doctor decides to use the DSS to assess whether there is a language disorder in the child. The doctor will introduce the required information.
3. The DSS returns the result to the pediatrician.
4. Three possibilities:

(A) The result is that everything is normal.

(B) The result changes the visitation schedule the child's pediatrician, or the DSS proposed to be derived from the relevant specialist hospital. In this case the doctor decides whether to accept the decision of DSS and pursue the request for appointment at the hospital, or decide it is not necessary. As always the decision of DSS support to the pediatrician, never an imposition on the decisions that the doctor makes.

5. An appointment with the specialist is requested to the hospital
6. Response is received to the request for appointment with the hospital,
7. The details of the appointment with the specialist will be received by the pediatrician.
8. The appointment details reach the child and his family.

9. The child goes to the specialist.

10. The specialist checks the response of the DSS for the corresponding case.

11. The DSS returns the result of the evaluation process for that case.

12. The DSS notifies the pediatrician that the specialist has accessed to the system. The specialist will validate the outcome of DSS in order to improve the KB.

4.2   Knowledge Base for Language Disorders

The KB has been built through an iterative process of structured meetings between September 2011 and May 2012. Only the two language therapists and the neuropediatrician participated in the meetings, using CK techniques to extract information such as structured interviews to complete the KB with questions to be asked by the primary care pediatrician children's tutor upon arriving at the care facility. The questions were sharpened to focus on language, with a view to enabling the primary care pediatrician to detect possible delays in children's development that   closer attention or immediate referral to an appropriate specialist. The process of building and purging the KB is based on the experience of LIC, who checked developmental items against the appearance of language disorders through a retrospective analysis of information on levels of language acquisition of 21 children who received therapy in the LIC [8].

The structuring of the final KB consists of 136 questions between month 1 and month 72 in the life of the child, and questions may be of two types:

- Questions called Alert Milestones that imply bringing forward the visit. The child makes a return visit to allow for re-evaluation of the level of language acquisition.
- Questions called Alarm Milestones that imply referral because they are considered reasons for alarm.

Table 1 details the KB questions for a child between the ages of 1 and 4 months. The first column indicates the child's age in months at the time of evaluation and the question type (alert or alarm). The second column shows the question the pediatrician asks the child's tutor to evaluate the child's state of language acquisition and the "System decision" column contains the system's answer in the event of a negative answer to the question (referral to specialist or bring forward visit).

Table 1. Shows KB questions for 1, 2 and 3months

Age – Milestone	Question to be answered by pediatrician	System decision
1 month Alarm	Reacts to a bell	Send to specialist to check hearing
1 month Alarm	Vocalizes without crying	Send to specialist to check hearing
2 months Alert	Emits "OOO/AAH"	Bring forward visit (three months)
2 months Alert	Screams to interact	Bring forward visit (three months)
3 months Alert	Turns around or reacts (closing eyes) to a clap	Bring forward visit (three months)
3 months Alert	Turns at the sound of mother's voice	Bring forward visit (three months)
3 months Alarm	Emits "OOO/AAH"	Check if hearing problem ruled out Refer to neuropediatrician
3 months Alarm	Laughs in response to stimulus	Refer to neuropediatrician

Protégé [9] was used in formalization of the knowledge model to create the KB and the inference engine needed to support decision making. The ontology of Protégé was built with a class hierarchy for the first 6 years, including a sub-hierarchy of classes for each month corresponding to the questions to be asked by the pediatrician.

4.3   Web Tool for Accessing the DSS

Objective verification of the proposal to refer to a specialist arising from possible detection of language development disorders, suggested by the KB, required development of a useful web tool to facilitate the work of experts and users of pediatrics in primary care. For this reason, the DSS was implemented, offering the final user a simple verification interface based on an internal connection of the KB. The definition of the binary relationships established between ontology classes will sustain the system's reasoning process through axioms such as: If the child is 2 months old and we get a negative answer to the question "Emits OOO/AAH" or "Cries to interact", then "To anticipate the next visit in three months". Figure 4 shows in greater detail the questions the DSS proposes to the pediatrician for the language evaluation process in a two month-old child (Pegasus):

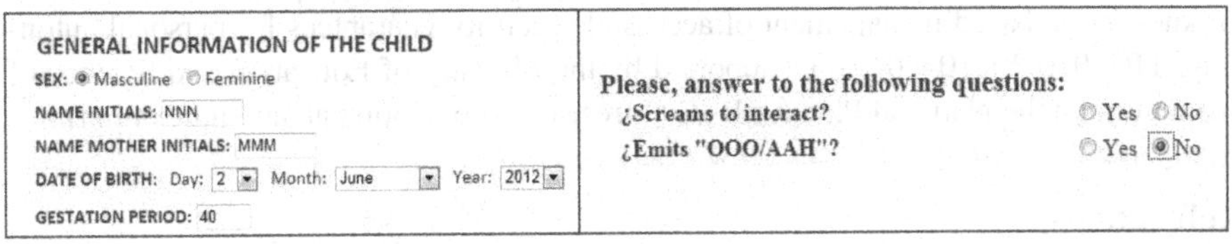

Fig. 4. Process of language evaluation

Figure 5 shows the result provided by the early detection tool based on a negative answer to the question "Emits OOO/AAH". At this point, the system proposes bringing forward the next visit and also suggests that the pediatrician enter an opinion on the system's decision or an alternative to the proposal of the system.

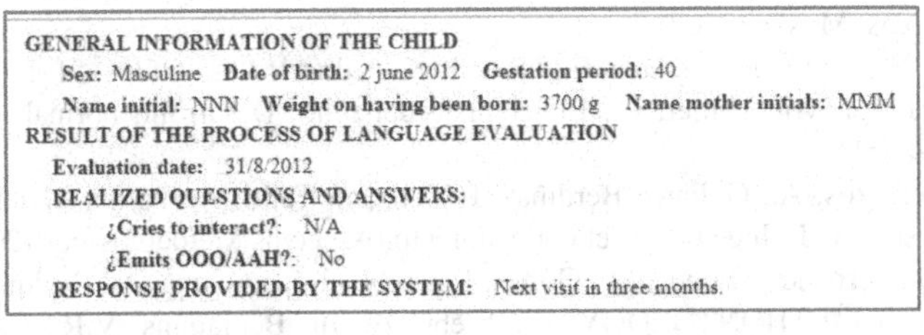

Fig. 5. Result of language evaluation process

5   Conclusions

The system proposes an innovative solution for the difficult task of detecting language disorders among children aged 0 to 6 in routine visits to pediatricians in primary care. Open web applications allow the easy utilization of the KB by pediatricians and specialist. The developed system does usable a DSS for early attention in primary care. The involvement of 4 experts in neuropediatrics, neonatology and language disorders was crucial for both defining the problem and for selecting 21 real, proven cases to refine the knowledge base with existing experience in primary care.

The opinion of the experts involved allows for a forthcoming start of the stage of validation, with a view to deployment and evaluation in routine clinical practice. The service evaluation is scheduled for autumn 2012 in cases considered of interest by the two pediatricians already involved in the final stage. The intelligent system is ripe for turn the withdrawal of information of the language acquisition state of the child by means of question - response, into an environmental intelligence based solutions.

Acknowledgements. Dr. José Arizcun, expert neonatologist in developmental disorders. Dra. Mª Teresa Ferrando, neuropediatrician in the Quiron Hospital (Madrid). Dra. Beatriz Chiclana and Dr. Erwin Kirchschlager, pediatricians in the Jazmin Health Center. Dra. Teresa Díaz, pediatrician in the Quiron Hospital (Madrid). Mª Peñafiel and Paloma Tejeda of the Language Intervention Center (CIL) La Salle Campus Madrid, Universidad Autónoma de Madrid.

This article is part of research we're conducting in the Talisec+ project (a framework for knowledge-based management of accessible security guarantees for personal autonomy; TIN2010-20510-C04-01), supported by the Ministry of Education and Science of Spain through the National Plan for R+D+I (research, development, and innovation).

References

1. Council on Children With Disabilities, Section on Developmental Behavioral Pediatrics, Bright Futures Steering Committee and Medical Home Initiatives for Children With Special Needs Project Advisory Committee. Identifying infants and young children with developmental disorders in the medical home. Pediatrics (2006)
2. Arrabal Terán, M.C., Arizcun Pineda, J.: Alteraciones del desarrollo y discapacidad. Grado de pediatría en España. Genysi (2007)
3. Paul, R.: Language disorders from infancy through adolescence: Assessment and intervention. St. Louis. Mosby (2007)
4. Fejerman, N., Fernández Álvarez, E.: Neurología pediátrica. Capitulos, 51–54 (2007)
5. Narbona, J., Chevrie-Muller, C.: El lenguaje del niño. Desarrollo normal, evaluación y trastornos (2003)
6. Alonso Betanzos, A., Guijarro Berdiñas, B., Lozano Tello, A., Palma Méndez, J.T., Taboada Iglesias, M.J.: Ingeniería del conocimiento. Aspectos Metodológicos (2004)
7. Corcho, O., Fernández-López, M., Gómez-Pérez, A., López-Cima, A.: Building Legal Ontologies with METHONTOLOGY and WebODE. In: Benjamins, V.R., Casanovas, P., Breuker, J., Gangemi, A. (eds.) Law and the Semantic Web. LNCS (LNAI), vol. 3369, pp. 142–157. Springer, Heidelberg (2005)
8. Peñafiel Puerto, M.: Mejorando las habilidades en indicadores tempranos de los trastornos del lenguaje. FAPap, vol. 5 (2012)
9. Protégé (2000), Planning a Project http://protege.stanford.edu/doc/users_guide/planning_a_project.html
10. Pellet OWL Reasoner for Java (2012), http://clarkparsia.com/pellet/docs/

A Novel Visualizer of Medical Images by Integrating an Extensible Plugin Framework

Alberto Rey, Alfonso Castro, Jose Carlos Dafonte, and Bernardino Arcay

Faculty of Computer Science, Campus Elviña, University of A Coruña, Spain
{alberto.rey,alfonso.castro,dafonte,bernardino.arcay}@udc.es

Abstract. The use of medical imaging for the diagnosis and, to a lesser extent, the prognosis and treatment of disease, is a common practice in modern medicine. Consequently, the need has arisen to develop applications that combine the ability to visualize digital medical images with the features required by clinical personnel in order to manage them. A number of medical image viewers are currently available, but nearly all of them are oriented towards visualizing and managing a single study of a patient, which limits the analysis of the expert. This paper introduces a novel application that contains the basic functionality required for common medical image analysis and which may be extended by a plug-in system with new features that could be demanded in the future. The application also makes it possible to visualize and analyze several studies at the same time, completely independently, increasing the accuracy of the analysis and facilitating the work of experts.

Keywords: DICOM, GUI, ITK, MITK.

1 Introduction

From the 1990s onwards, the use of digital devices for medical image acquisition has become widespread partly due to cheaper manufacturing costs and mainly due to the popularization of the DICOM standard [1] as a protocol for acquisition and communications between medical devices. This defines the protocols that medical image devices must support in order to communicate with each other and exchange and store images, regardless of their origin.

In addition, the emergence of new types of image acquisition techniques such as computed tomography (CT), magnetic resonance imaging (MRI) and PET (Positron Emission Tomography) have revolutionized the field of medical imaging and medical treatment, accelerating the transition from analogue to digital information [1]. These techniques have contributed to the appearance of new types of digital medical images that contain large amounts of information: a CT scan may contain more than 600 slices, meaning that its analysis is a time-consuming task for clinicians.

These advances in the digitalization of medical imaging have led to the need to create applications that would handle and display these images in a simple and comfortable way for the physician. Currently, a wide range of DICOM image

J. Bravo, R. Hervás, and M. Rodríguez (Eds.): IWAAL 2012, LNCS 7657, pp. 41–48, 2012.

viewers are available, both as Open Source and paid applications, for displaying medical images with a wide range of different features. Several publications [2,3,4] present a number of applications that are used to manage medical images, although they frequently lack the features for experts to be able to manage and visualize more than one study at a time, which limits the analysis and diagnosis of the images. Moreover, some applications such as 3D slicer [3] contain a large number of features that clinicians are unlikely to ever use due to their complexity.

These shortcomings frequently result in experts not using these tools, as many of their functions are not required for their daily routine, and their interfaces are often difficult to learn and manage.

This main aim of this work is to develop an application that offers physicians the basic functionality required for medical image analysis and which provides a versatile environment that can be modified according to their needs, allowing them to manage and visualize several studies at the same time. On this basis, the application can be extended to include new features encapsulated as plug-ins, which may be necessary according to the type of the tasks undertaken by the clinicians, such as integration with CAD systems. The application has been developed using Open Source libraries and can be executed on Linux, Windows and Mac.

2   Related Work and Materials

Currently, a wide range of applications focusing on medical image analysis and visualization are available under both paid and Open Source licenses. These include 3DSlicer [3], MITK 3M3 [4] and Volview [5]. All of them support DICOM image visualization, have different ways of extending their functions using plug-ins and are distributed under Open source licenses.

Slicer 3D is the most complete application in terms of functionality out of all of these systems. It offers functions that focus on segmentation and registration, as well as several algorithms for image processing and image-guided radiation therapy. It supports the visualization of both 2D and 3D views of data.

MITK 3M3 is the application developed using the MITK SDK, and it should be noted that our viewer has several of the same visualization components, such as renderers and mappers. It provides functions such as the visualization of 2D, 3D and 3D+t images, measurement tools, data fusion and several algorithms.

Volview focuses on the volume visualization of both 2D and 3D views, providing tools for visualization, complex rendering and annotation management.

In the process of carrying out this work, we have selected several toolkits to design and implement the different layers that comprise the architecture of the application.

In this case, we used The Medical Imaging Interaction Toolkit (MITK) [6,7,8] as the base library to design the interaction with images and visualization. This library combines the Insight Toolkit (ITK) [9] and the Visualization Toolkit (VTK) [10]. Some of the features not covered by this toolkit have been developed in this work using ITK and VTK. These toolkits are Open Source.

The user interface has been designed and developed using the Qt Development Framework [11]. This toolkit provides the necessary classes to develop widgets to support visualization, interaction and rendering images, and also provides tools to support internationalization, testing and a plug-in system.

3   Architecture

The system architecture provides a high level view of the collaboration between components and the flow of information to be carried out in order to accomplish tasks. Figure 1 shows the system architecture based on the relationship between the different toolkits used and the application components that are implemented.

The application is primarily based on Qt and MITK libraries (Figure 1a). However, it may be necessary to create or extend several classes to provide features not provided by MITK, so ITK and VTK are used for this purpose.

The viewer is divided in three general components (Figure 1b) that are grouped as libraries. The *Core* component groups classes that are independent of the interface and are used to represent the model and adapt libraries. The *guiWid* component includes the visual objects that comprise the user interface and perform the interaction with images. Finally, the *guiMod* component contains a set of independent modules grouping an application functionality, such as image and video management, and in general any function that can be incorporated as a plug-in representing a module.

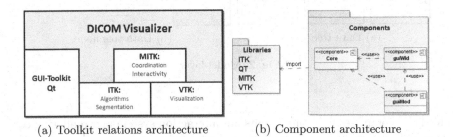

(a) Toolkit relations architecture   (b) Component architecture

Fig. 1. System architecture

This project follows the Model-View architectural pattern introduced by Qt. In this case, the model is based on MITK trees, which are responsible for encapsulating images or surfaces that will be rendered and displayed. The View provides the functionality needed by the viewer and for interaction with users, and is developed using several components of all selected toolkits.

3.1   Model

The central elements that represent the model are objects derived from ITK, and data trees derived from MITK. These objects are abstract representations of physical elements that can be present in a visualization scene, such as images, surfaces and data points. In contrast, data trees (Figure 2a) make it possible to manage multiple objects of different types in a hierarchical way, representing logical dependencies and physical interrelations between objects.

Each node (Figure 2b) that comprises each tree encapsulates the following elements: a data object with its geometry, the visualization support for the object (2D or 3D), an interactor to manage the object and a series of specific properties of the object. As a result, each scene is represented by a data tree that can contain several data objects representing different nodes.

Using this schema, the viewer can manage different elements (studies, images, surfaces, etc.) as each data tree is independent from the others and can be rendered at the same time, although the user can only interact with one.

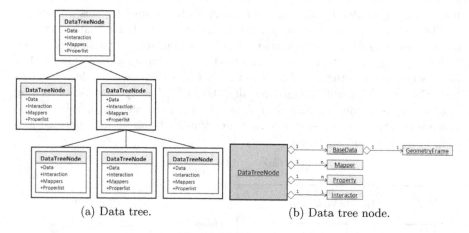

(a) Data tree.   (b) Data tree node.

Fig. 2. Model layer

3.2   View

This layer comprises two components: an interaction system and rendering controllers. The first component controls the interactive creation and modification of data objects, while the second block is responsible for rendering images and controlling cameras in the scene.

The interaction system is organized through state machines that describe and configure the events produced in response to the user interaction. These transitions and states for a particular interaction are detailed in a XML file that is loaded in execution time.

Figure 3 shows the general interaction process. The *EventMapper* translates the events from input devices (keyboard, mouse, etc.) into events that can be managed by MITK. In this way, the *GlobalInteraction* decides which specific *Interactor* must manage the event and control its future transitions. Finally, the operations that must be carried out in each state on the data objects are encapsulated using the Command Pattern in *Operation* objects.

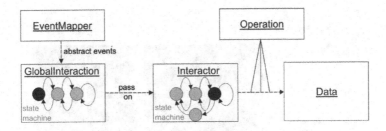

Fig. 3. Interaction System

The rendering controllers can be associated with data trees. One data tree can be associated with several controllers that perform the rendering of several objects or several views over one object. This behaviour means it is possible, for example, for the application to display and combine the Coronal, Transversal, Sagittal and 3D view of a CT study simultaneously.

The rendering process is finally carried out by Mappers that transform the data objects in primitive graphics rendered in VTK scenes by *OpenGL* processes.

The basic component in the application to display objects is the MITK rendering window. This element can display a set of data objects using the combination of classes provided by the Qt Toolkit and the rendering controllers referred to above.

The main widget of the application is a combination of rendering windows that can be combined in several distributions, meaning the application can display a scene from different view planes. By default, the distribution of the central widget consists of four views of a scene: Sagittal, Coronal, Transversal and 3D. The user can change that distribution by selecting a new one from a list included in the application menu.

4   User Interface

The user interface of the application is presented as a main window consisting of several blocks using the Qt toolkit.

The central widget makes it possible to manage and visualize several scenes grouped as tabs. Users can only control one tab at a time, but can view all of them by splitting or regrouping tabs (dragging and dropping) in vertical and horizontal configurations. Figure 4 shows the application with three studies open in the central widget, with the tabs arranged vertically and horizontally. In addition, each scene presents different layout combining rendering windows that display the scene objects from different viewpoints.

The user can choose to open a new file in a new scene, which will create a new tab grouped in the central widget, or to open this file in the active scene showing all the objects grouped in the same render window. In Figure 4, the bottom scene of the viewer shows a render of a set of two objects: a CT thorax study and a surface that overlaps a region of the image.

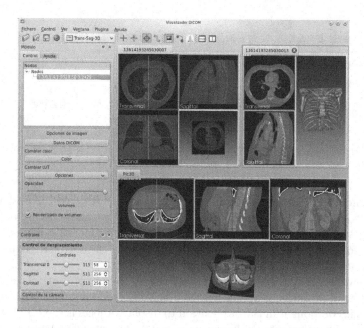

Fig. 4. Example of the application layout with three scenes

User interaction is modelled by obtaining events from input devices such as a keyboard or a mouse. These signals are collected using Qt observers that will invoke an interaction on data objects. Only observers associated with the active scene will provoke a reaction, while the rest of the observers associated with deactivated tabs will ignore the events. Users can activate or deactivate scenes just by clicking on a specific zone of each tab.

5 Plugin Framework

The application is designed in modules that implement similar functions. In this paper, the application consists of the following modules: Visualization, Intensity, Measurement and Video.

Each module must implement an Interface that models the interaction inside the application with the model and the view. In this sense, each module is in essence a plug-in that encapsulates similar functionalities performing several operations on a model, and incorporating a user interface to control this behaviour in the view layer. Figure 5a shows the result after the user has made several measurements using the features of the *Measurement module*. Figure 5b shows the interface block of the *Intensity module* in which the user can modify the image contrast with a level threshold.

The plug-in integration is performed transparently to the user; in this sense, we have developed a module manager that controls the loading and the states of the module interface and its classes in the application. The new module will

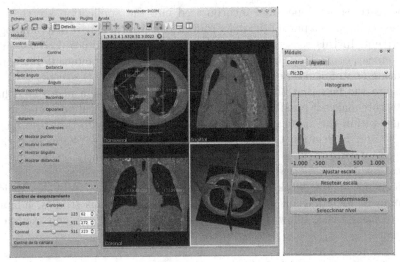

(a) Application interface showing the measurement module.

(b) User interface for the intensity module.

Fig. 5. User interface

appear as an icon in the viewer toolbar. Moreover, users can switch between modules using this bar, and at the same time their interface control will be shown, keeping their state separate for each scene.

6   Conclusion

In this paper we present an application that allows to visualize several types of medical images in a versatile way. The solution has been developed using Open Source toolkits and can be executed on multiple platforms. The main aim is to develop a versatile application that supports DICOM images combining the main characteristics of common image viewers and features of clinical applications.

In this case, the application makes it possible to visualize the most common medical image formats, such as DICOM, MetaImage or Analize. In general, it can be extended to support new formats by designing new classes that extend the IO Factory provided by ITK.

The application is highly versatile, as users can modify the user interface in numerous ways and adapt it to their needs within their clinical work. In this case, the major challenge has been to permit the simultaneous visualization and management of several studies, as the selected toolkits do not focus on this specific feature and several classes and design a manager had to be modified in order to maintain the independency between scenes.

We introduce a novel solution to manage scenes, at the same time as applying a method based on splitting and grouping tabs by drag and drop actions. In the same context, users can decide to render objects by grouping them into the same scene, or to visualize them in different split scenes.

The features developed and incorporated into the application are the basic features required as a part of the daily routine of a clinical expert in a radiological department. In this sense, we have developed several modules used for image management, controlling the contrast of the image using its intensity histogram, measuring anatomical objects, and finally video editing for the scene.

Despite the fact that these modules are basic, the design of a new Plugin architecture makes it possible to develop new features that will be loaded as new modules within the application, extending its functionality to the requirements of each user. In relation to this, we have developed a new plugin to perform the segmentation of lungs from CT thorax studies previously opened into the application. The segmentation result is displayed as a new scene.

In conclusion, this work presents a versatile solution that provides an ideal environment for clinicians to manage and visualize various studies, adapting them to their tasks, allowing them to improve their analysis and facilitating their work.

References

1. Fitzpatrick, J.M., Sonka, M.: Handbook of Medical Imaging. Medical Image Processing and Analysis, vol. PM80. SPIE Press Monograph (2000)
2. Bitter, I., Van Uitert Jr., R.L., Wolf, I., Ibáñez, L., Kuhnigk, J.: Comparison of Four Freely Available Frameworks for Image Processing and Visualization That Use ITK. IEEE Trans. Vis. Comput. Graph. 13(3), 483–493 (2007)
3. Pieper, S., Halle, M., Kikinis, R.: 3D SLICER. In: Proceedings of the 1st IEEE International Symposium on Biomedical Imaging: From Nano to Macro, pp. 632–635 (2004)
4. MITK 3M3 Image Analysis (November 2010),
   http://www.mint-medical.de/productssolutions/mitk3m3/mitk3m3/
5. Martin, K., Ibáñez, L., Avila, L., Barré, S., Kaspersen, J.H.: Integrating segmentation methods from the Insight Toolkit into a visualization application. Med. Image Anal. 9(6), 579–593 (2005)
6. Wolf, I., Vetter, M., Wegner, I., Böttger, T., Nolden, M., Schöbinger, M., et al.: The Medical Imaging Interaction Toolkit. Med. Image Analysis 9(6), 594–604 (2005)
7. Wolf I., Nolden M., Böttger T., Wegner I., Schöbinger M., Hastenteufel M., et al.: The MITK Approach. In: Insight Journal - 2005 MICCAI Open-Source Workshop (2005)
8. Wolf, I., Vetter, M., Wegner, I., Nolden, M., et al.: The Medical Imaging Interaction Toolkit (MITK) a toolkit facilitating the creation of interactive software by extending VTK and ITK. In: Med. Imag. 2004: Visualization, Image-Guided Procedures, and Display. Proc. of the SPIE, vol. 5367, pp. 16–27 (2004)
9. Ibáñez, L., Schroeder, W., Ng, L., Cates, J., Consortium, T.I.S., Hamming, R.: The ITK Software Guide. Kitware, Inc. (January 2003)
10. Schroeder, W.V., Martin, K., Lorensen, B.: The Visualization Toolkit An Object-Oriented Approach To 3D Graphics, 4th edn. Kitware, Inc. (December2006)
11. Blanchette, J.: Summerfield M.: C++ GUI Programming with Qt 4, 2nd edn. The official C++/Qt book. Prentice Hall (February 14, 2008)

Mobile System for Medical Control of Chronic Diseases through Intelligent Devices

Vladimir Villarreal[1], Jesus Manzano[2], Ramón Hervás[2], and José Bravo[2]

[1] Technological University of Panama, David, Chiriquí, Panamá
vladimir.villarreal@utp.ac.pa
[2] MamI Research Lab - Castilla-La Mancha University, Ciudad Real, Spain
manzanocaminojesus@gmail.com,
{ramon.hlucas,jose.bravo}@uclm.es

Abstract. The ageing of the population is a factor that in the future will increase the percentage of dependent people, given that there is a close relationship between dependence and age. When patients are in a health care environment, it is often isolated from their social environment; a situation which greatly complicates the medical follow-up, either complicated patient privacy. In this paper, we present a solution, through an application, which allows the patients monitoring, integrating the use of mobile phones in their activities. Through this device the patient keep updated all your medical information, from the reading of their vital signs, diet control, administration of medications, physical analyses, recommendations and others monitoring modules. We have evaluated the application in a group of patients. This application is evaluated in design, functionality and utility like efficiency.

Keywords: software architecture development, web services, communication technologies, users interfaces design, ambient assisted living.

1 Introduction

"Liz, is a girl diagnosed with diabetes. She uses a glucose meter to control the level of sugar in blood. Daily, she keeps the adequate level of glucose through several measurements of the diseases. In the same way, she has to do all the annotations in her notebook, whenever a measurement is realized, annotating the irregularities and changes presented in the day. If it has some problem it has to call the doctor to consult the happened him. To Liz it would like to have a constant follow-up of her measures, obtaining recommendations and messages whenever it changes her levels of glucose in blood. In the other way, she would like to have to hand, without need to register in her notebook, all the incidents that she has presented in the last days. She wanted also that her doctor was informed without she should be calling him. This would give him better quality of life and a more constant follow-up of her disease".

This is a situation that would like to take a patient who suffers from a chronic illness and need constant monitoring. We are developed and implemented an application to

J. Bravo, R. Hervás, and M. Rodríguez (Eds.): IWAAL 2012, LNCS 7657, pp. 49–57, 2012.

facilitate this every day, allowing patients to lead normal lives, without worry of how to control this follow-up medical. This is a not intrusive application with low level of interaction that once obtained the measurement of vital sign; the application can perform all activities of processing and visualization of the results.

In this article we present some related works that we have studied the structure of the application developed and finally the outcome of the assessment to a number of patients suffering from diabetes problems. Some aspects of quality have been assessed like the design of interfaces, the content of the modules and functionality of responses generated by the application.

2   Related Works

The use of such technologies is contemplated due to the low cost and energy consumption. Some research have brought with it the creation of different technological platforms that have offered a timely solution to problems of health care, some of them are mentioned in this section.

Health Buddy System [1] is a system that provides health monitoring of patients by reducing the scope of hospitalization. This system connects to patients in their homes to their healthcare providers. What distinguishes it from others is its ability not only to communicate the historical information of the patients with chronic diseases, but also to facilitate the education of the patient and encourage compliance with medication and lifestyle. AirStrip Patient Monitoring [2] is a platform for software development with a vision of safe critical patient information delivery directly from the monitoring systems of the hospital, devices of header, and health mobile clinical records. AirStrip was also designed to solve major challenges in the development of mobile software, such as the development of native applications that provide a rich user experience requirements, while at the same time, be able to scale and adapt to an ever-changing world of operating systems and mobile devices. WellDoc [3] is an application designed to be a service of monitoring for diabetics, integrated with Ford Sync, designed for iOS, which allows to monitor the current status of a patient using manual registry of food and glucose. Thanks to its integration with Sync, it will synchronize with this service via Bluetooth, which will detect if not we have not introduced a record recently, and through a system of questions (Yes or No), will make sure see if our blood levels are correct. It is not be so, it will suggest the next recommended action to take, or in extreme cases, will send an *SMS* to the contact that we have previously selected in emergencies, with the option to send another message to arrive home, confirming that we are safe.

Ambulation [4] is an important tool to assess the health of patients suffering from chronic diseases that affect mobility such as multiple sclerosis (MS), that of Parkinson's and muscular dystrophy through the assessment when they walk. Ambulation is a monitoring system of mobility that uses Android and Nokia N95 mobile phones to automatically detect the mobility of the user mode. The interaction that the user needs with the phone is turn it on and keep it with him throughout the day, with the intention that could be used as your everyday mobile phone for voice, data and applications, while Ambulation is running in the background. SenSAVE [5] with his project senSave developed a system for mobile monitoring of vital signs parameters. It defined the user interface and interaction adapted specifically for patients. Take measures of blood pressure and the pulse of people related to cardiovascular problems in real time. In summary this system, studied the way that presents information, Windows of dialogue and the role of alarms, proving the usability of mobile devices. Bravo [6] propose a solution to enabling NFC technology for supporting chronic diseases, specially in Alzheimer caregivers.

Our solution [7] [8] search to reduced the interaction with the mobile device, that all processing is done from the initial capture of vital signs. This information is used to offer messages to patient automatically. Avoid relying on a platform in particular, and provides additional patient information such as results of analyses and tests in general. It is implemented for different kinds of diseases. We have developed to interact with large number of diseases that can be monitored through vital signs. It proposes a communication between multiple biometric and mobile phone devices based on a profile of specific patient and disease afflicting. Control information is generated from these vital signs for patients.

3   Development a Patient Application to Control Diseases

We have developed an adaptable and parametric mobile application for multiple contexts like technological solution. The developed architecture is distributed in two specific areas. The first one is an application to be installed on the patient and the doctor mobile phone and the other one corresponding to the elements distributed on the main server, which contains the stored data. Mobile architecture has been developed in Android 2.2 [9], as an operating system for mobile devices. In addition the connectivity has been implemented through a database in MySQL, which is accessed by defined web services. These web services have been developed based on ksoap2. The application to monitor patients allows the adaptation in different medical settings and using different technologies. To facilitate its implementation, has defined three elements in the development of the application, these are: a container area, the schema definition and the interface and the origin and data flow relationship.

- **Container area:** It is the area that will contain the graphical user interface to design. Each user interface has a container area, which differs from other user interfaces, for the way in which they are implemented. This area for most of the interfaces has been defined thus facilitating the subsequent design and the scalability of the application.
- **Scheme and relationship of the interface:** Here is defined the scheme make up the user interface, based on the functionality of each one of them. Each functionality of the module is added to the parent zone to generate specific to each module interfaces.
- **Origin and flow of data:** Data flows involved in each of the modules or developed interfaces are defined here. The database defines this structure; this allows us to identify the relationship container-area and interface - data.

3.1   Patient Profile

One of the main features of the propose is associate the application to a patient that allow the data obtain, addition of activities, making recommendations and other control modules go according to the profile of the patient. In the application the patient can insert, view and edit the information about your disease. Many of the fields are just information (address, phone, e-mail address, etc.) except the contact number, which will be used to send a SMS to the contact person that the patient has been defined. This option allows the application to inform that person about high-risk situations, keeping him informed of the situation of the patient before variations of their vital signs monitored (Figure 1).

Fig. 1. Screenshot of patient profile: (a) container area specification, (b) patient registration and (c) patient information stored

If the application loses connectivity with the central server then all the application data are stored the device has the automatic option to keep the data in a local database, in such a way that don't miss relevant information of the patient. When the application has again connectivity, synchronize the local database with the remote database in such a way that updates the data for a particular patient.

3.2   Doctor Application

The doctor application is focuses on the management and monitoring of their patients. As shown in Figure 2, the doctor application can monitor their patient data, as well as the latest shots of action, notifications of risk showing in format graphic/list. But still, the application allows you to send messages to their associated patients, looking for a communication more direct between doctors and patients. The doctor, however, cannot only monitor patients who already have assigned, but may delete, search and add new patients to the list. The application has a system of recommendations with which to add a new measure, the user may see one set of recommendations of a diverse nature related both with the disease that monitors at that time, as with the last added measure. Such a system is to provide the patient important information about possible recommendations based on your last introduced measure in such a way that this information will help the patient concerning his illness. The recommendations are generated based on the analysis of the complete history of measurements.

(a)   (b)   (c)

Fig. 2. Screenshot of doctor application: (a) patient information, (c) measures patient records (c) additional information

3.3   Control Modules Doctor - Patient

The change of interface depending on the type of recommendation has been made for the convenience of the patient, as there are recommendations that can be viewed without loading a different interface and others that must be viewed on a different interface. For this reason, we can distinguish two types of interfaces; an interface in which we will show recommendations that are more complex (Figure 3(a)), and an interface type pop-up window (Figure 3(b)) that will show the recommendations that are simpler.

To be an interface that shows lots of information, requires that the information be accessed quickly to improve the performance of the application, this should not delay long in showing the services requested. Therefore, the data source must be local, not preventing that in another moment in the course of implementation, this load local from remote databases to the database content.

Therefore, the flow of data in the schema will be directed towards the local database that will provide us the information faster than if accessing to a network database. In Figure 3(c), shows the schema that represents the flow of data that uses the defined interface.

4   Evaluating the Functionality of the Application

We present an evaluation of the functionality of the developed software architecture. Patients with diabetes and blood pressure, needing to give follow-up to his illness, have evaluated these domains. We will assess aspects of content, design and usefulness of architecture. To evaluate the criteria of content, they responded to questions related to the organization of the content, the presence of aid during the use of the application, ease of interpretation, ease of identification of the elements and degree of value of the submitted content. For the design criteria, they responded to questions about the distribution of visual elements, displays, interpretation and identification of menu specifications. For the usefulness criteria they responded to questions about the usefulness degree of the generated recommendations, prevention and education messages and satisfaction degree of the information shown.

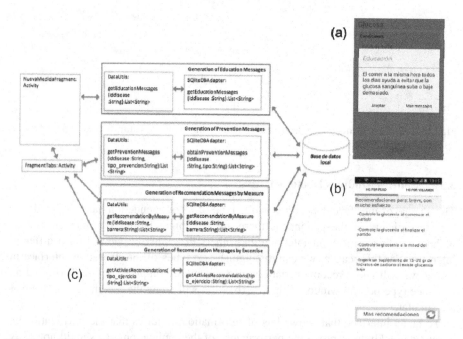

Fig. 3. Activities control interfaces developed: (a) pop-up window format, (b) list format, (c) data flow diagram

The initial aspects of the evaluation are:

- **Evaluation technique:** A questionnaire was applied where the participants complete the specific questions about the use of the application.
- **Aspects of quality to assess:** We assessed the aspects of content, design and usefulness of the application for end users.
- **Context to assess:** The patient used the application to monitor for a twenty minutes, the vital signs was associate with your disease, reviewed the activities of medical control that offers (recommendations, messages and prevention, education and self-control) and added physical activities to do.
- **Population to assess:** The assessment has been applied to ten people (6 men and 4 women). The population has been formed by two candidates to doctor, one doctor, one undergraduate university and six persons unrelated to the university between ages of 25 to 60. Users associated with the university are related to technology while non-university users have little knowledge with technology.
- **Time to assess:** The time that the patient will take using the application in the defined context will be 45 minutes. Then take 15 minutes to respond to the evaluation questionnaire.
- **Scale to use:** A Likert Scale from 1 to 5 has been established to evaluate each answer, 1 being the lowest evaluation for a question (very much in disagreement) and 5 the highest evaluation (very of agreement).

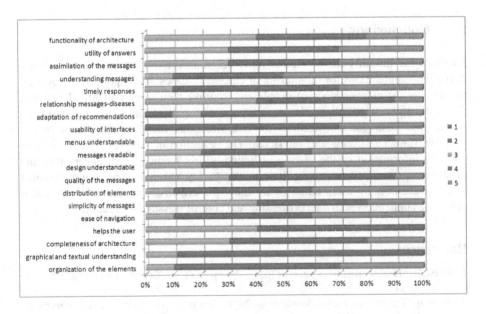

Fig. 4. Quality aspects by the end-user assessment

Criteria 1. Content: The majority of participants considered a good content of the application, facility of navigation has been evaluated between 4 and 5, understanding of the elements that make up the application, clarity in the information shown (figure 4). The content is one of the aspects over time in such a way that offered to the patient information better and more detailed according to the disease that has.

Criteria 2. Design: The design criteria have been the feature more highly valued by the participants. Weights between 4 and 5 according to the total number of participants have been obtained. The majority of patients, on the other hand feel that the application offers an interface or screens very understanding in each screen. This is because it has much careful design to familiarize patients with the application. The everyday use of the application will make the patient feel better and more secure in the follow-up of the disease.

Criteria 3. Utility: In general, the results of the evaluation carried out in this first approach, have been quite satisfactory. The aspects that have a lower valuation have been those of utility, this may be due to patients are used to make annotations in a diabetes book, and on other occasions do not make annotations, so do not perceive the difference when using the application evaluated. Another reason may be that difficulty that some patients have for using this type of technology, where either by age or inexperienced in the use of mobile devices, they feel some rejection for new technologies that consider takes them time to learn. These results help us to detect possible corrections in such a way that the user should be offered a more robust and friendly architecture.

5   Conclusions

Facilitate the mobility of the patient must be an aspect to take into account when developing applications for monitoring of chronic diseases. This application has tried to facilitate the independence of people and improve their quality of life. Therefore, the application must allow the mobility of the patient allowing a continuous monitoring. Data and notifications on risk situations must, to the extent of the possible, further reaching staff physician. The definition of the profile of the patient with the information of the disease afflicting allows medical practitioners take the most appropriate decisions to facilitate its day-to-day activities. The results obtained in the evaluation by users allow us to know the effectiveness and robustness that offers the application both data processing and control message generation.

References

1. BOSCH. Health Buddy System (2011), http://www.bosch-telehealth.com (cited 2012)
2. AirStrip, T.: AirStrip Patient Monitoring (2011), http://www.airstriptech.com/ (cited 2011)
3. WellDoc. WellDoc Health Platform (2011), http://www.welldoc.com/Products-and-Services/Our-Products.aspx (cited 2012)

4. Ryder, J., et al.: Ambulation: A Tool for Monitoring Mobility Patterns over Time Using Mobile Phones. In: International Conference on Computational Science and Engineering, CSE 2009 (2009)
5. Lorenz, A., et al.: Personalized mobile health monitoring for elderly. In: 9th International Conference on Human Computer Interaction with Mobile Devices and Services. ACM, Singapore (2007)
6. Bravo, J., López-de-Ipiña, D., Fuentes, C., Hervás, R., Peña, R., Vergara, M., Casero, G.: Enabling NFC Technology for Supporting Chronic Diseases: A Proposal for Alzheimer Caregivers. In: Aarts, E., Crowley, J.L., de Ruyter, B., Gerhäuser, H., Pflaum, A., Schmidt, J., Wichert, R. (eds.) AmI 2008. LNCS, vol. 5355, pp. 109–125. Springer, Heidelberg (2008)
7. Villarreal, V., et al.: Diabetes Patients' Care based on Mobile Monitoring. In: IADIS International Conference, Applied Computing 2009, Rome, Italy (2009)
8. Villarreal, V., Laguna, J., López, S., Fontecha, J., Fuentes, C., Hervás, R., de Ipiña, D.L., Bravo, J.: A Proposal for Mobile Diabetes Self-control: Towards a Patient Monitoring Framework. In: Omatu, S., Rocha, M.P., Bravo, J., Fernández, F., Corchado, E., Bustillo, A., Corchado, J.M. (eds.) IWANN 2009, Part II. LNCS, vol. 5518, pp. 870–877. Springer, Heidelberg (2009)
9. Android Developer. The Developer's Guide (2011), http://developer.android.com/index.html (cited 2012)

A Multi-sensor Mobile System Based on Agents for People Monitoring

Pilar Castro Garrido, Irene Luque Ruiz, and Miguel Ángel Gómez-Nieto

University of Córdoba, Department of Computing and Numerical Analysis
Albert Einstein Building, E-14071 Córdoba, Spain
{pcgarrido,iluque,mangel}@uco.es

Abstract. A multi-sensor mobile system for people monitoring is described in this paper. The system uses mobile phones to monitor a set of restrictions defined for the users. The effectiveness of the monitoring process is its continuing ability to detect changes on user activities and movements. Monitoring control is possible thanks to a set of agents installed on the mobile phone and server. Agents are responsible of collect the data from phone sensors activating the appropriate alarms by a set of defined rules. The applicability of the system will be illustrated with an example for Alzheimer patient monitoring.

Keywords: Mobile Phone, Sensors, Monitoring, Agent, JADE.

1 Introduction

In 1969, the Study of Critical Environmental Problems (SCEP) defined the monitoring term as: "systematic observation of parameters related to a specific problem, designed to provide information on the characteristic of the problem and their changes with the time" [1]. SCEP is the first study that analyzes the monitoring concept.

Through monitoring can be assessed the state of the object under supervision. The monitoring is made up through an automated process that collects the information about control parameters; this process uses electronic devices to monitor.

Currently, there are a large variety of devices for monitoring. It is possible to find a Sociometer [2] to sensing and modeling human networks; Caalyx [3] a patient monitoring device that can measure vital signs, detect falls and alert the signs about emergences to the nearest healthcare; Keruve [4] a watch pager that sends signals to a receiver with the position of the person wearing the watch and it is used primarily for people with Alzheimer.

Most of the monitoring devices are often specifically designed for monitoring one or more parameters, but do not allow the incorporation of new sensors or to be used to monitor a different set of parameters, being necessary to find other devices for monitoring. It is also desirable to enable the incorporation into these devices of new sensors in a simple and dynamic way.

Nowadays, mobile phones have more processing power, memory and a large number of sensors that provide a fairly comprehensive environmental status. They also

J. Bravo, R. Hervás, and M. Rodríguez (Eds.): IWAAL 2012, LNCS 7657, pp. 58–65, 2012.
© Springer-Verlag Berlin Heidelberg 2012

provide information about the activity made by the person who brings the mobile phone. For these reasons, they are the appropriate instrument to remain continuously connected and reachable allowing a process of monitoring. These features allow that mobile phones can be both the instrument of monitoring and control.

The use of mobile devices for monitoring is an important area of development. For instance, Cornelius et al. [5], presents Anonysense a framework that collect data from anonymous users, but they do not considers that exists many situation where the most important it is the source of the data. Kukkonen et al. [6], propose BeTelGeuse, an extensible data collection platform for mobile devices that automatically infers higher-level context from sensor data available for J2ME, but today smart phones need new programming languages because there is new platforms. Froehlich et al. [7] describe MyExperience, a System for in situ tracing and capturing of user Feedback on mobile phones but it is only applicable to Windows Phone devices.

None of the aforementioned monitoring systems allows alarm management or process control monitoring via the mobile device. In addition, those systems have as aim to provide context information but do not process it.

This paper describes the AGATHA System, a multi-sensor system using mobile phones focused on people monitoring the compliance of a set of defined constraints. The mechanisms for collecting data and triggering alarms are based on the definition of agents. In this system, mobile devices are not only used as elements to monitor people, but are also used to control the monitoring process. Depending on the user role (supervised or supervisor), the system component installed on the mobile device performs different types of actions showing different kind of information. The system sends alarm notifications to users when the supervised makes inappropriate activities related with their constraints.

The paper is structured as follows: section 2 and 3 describe an overview of the monitoring process and architecture of AGATHA, section 4 describe an application of the systems for Alzheimer patient monitoring. Finally, discussion and remark are presented in section 5.

2   Monitoring Process for AGATHA System

AGATHA is an innovative monitoring system and alarm management using the mobile phone capabilities and sensors to collect information about the environment and about the user carrying the mobile phone. Mobile phone is used to detect small changes in the position and activity of the use, at time to activate the necessary alarms that will allow correcting an inappropriate user action.

As all monitoring system, AGATHA should have the appropriate media to obtain specific and continuous information of the parameters involved in a monitoring process. The first step is the choice of the object or process to monitor as well as the parameters to be measured. These parameters must be valid, reliable and appropriate to detect user changes and violation of restrictions in order to act accordingly.

Once the parameters have been selected, the next step is to plan the monitoring process, including: a) the frequency of measurements, b) mechanisms for the gathering of parameter values, c) methods for processing and interpreting these values, and d) alarm mechanisms responsible for notifying the incidences or violation of restrictions.

2.1   Supervision Parameters

AGATHA monitors the compliance of a set of restrictions associated to users. Each restriction has a set of parameters to be measured. Restrictions are: geographical, communications (calls, messages, etc.) or movements.

Geographical restrictions are constraints related to physical spaces establishing where the users can move. In this type of restrictions are primarily used the values provide by the GPS and compass, but also are used other as the accelerometer or gyroscope. The system considers three types of geographical restrictions:

- *Prohibited zones*: fixed areas in which the user cannot enter.
- *Required zones*: fixed areas in which the subject must necessarily remain.
- *Relative zones*: dynamic areas in which the user cannot enter. These areas are constructed from the GPS positions two or more users, representing the prohibited areas common to two or more users.

The communication restrictions limit the use of the phone line, that is, the number of calls, SMS or MMS. Such restrictions can be of two types, depending on whether it limits the number of target line:

- *Phone restrictions*: limit the use that a user makes of his/her phone line, in terms of calls, SMS and MMS.
- *Contact restrictions*: restrict the communications that a user can have with another one.

Movement restrictions set a specific time that a user can remain in a specific point or area. Positions are determined through GPS and by means of the accelerometer and gyroscope is determined if the user stand still in one position making another kind of movement different to walk. Finally, light and proximity sensors determine if the device is being manipulated.

The system considers two basic user roles: supervisor and supervised. The supervised is the person to be monitored and the supervisor is who bears the monitoring control and who sets the monitoring parameters, as well as restrictions. In addition, supervisors are whom the system should report the activity monitored from supervised user. The system also informs to the supervised user about any incorrect action or movement in order to be known and corrected.

The frequency of the measurements is defined by the supervisor and it is specific to every monitoring process. During the monitoring process, the frequency may vary, and the system will inform to mobile devices.

2.2   Alarm Definition

Alarms inform to users (supervisor and supervised) the activation of any of the defined restrictions. Alarms notifications are performed as a *Toast* and *Push* notification. Table 1 shows the different alarms defined on the system. It can be distinguished two types of alarms, related to user restrictions and related with the configuration of the system. These last allow the correct performance of the system.

Table 1. Types of Alarm defined on AGATHA

Alarm	Sensors
User Restrictions	
Prohibited zones	GPS/Network, Compass
Required zones	GPS/Network, Compass
Relative zones	GPS/Network, Compass
Phone restrictions	Call, SMS and MMS Log
Contact restrictions	Call, SMS and MMS Log
Movement restrictions	GPS/Network, Accelerometer, Gyroscope, Light
Configuration	
Low battery	Battery level
Switch off mobile	Battery level, Network
No network coverage	Network
No sensor readings	Sensor reading

Each alarm has associated different severity levels. These levels are established considering defined limits for the different values of each sensor reading. In addition, for each level are defined a set of degrees of persistence. Persistence levels are based on the time during the supervised persist in the violation of some of the restrictions that he/she has associated.

For the different alarms defined in the system, it has been established a set of rules based on a set of preconditions. These preconditions are composed of a set of parameters corresponding to different values gathered from the sensors. Rules are implemented inside subagents' behaviour in charge of alarms management.

2.3   Mechanisms for the Collection, Processing and Interpreting Data

Mechanisms for the gathering process and analysis data are based on the definition of agents. The mobile phone has a set of agents ready to react to different events produced by the device sensors that capture information from the environment. This information is sent to a central agent, which is responsible for verifying that the information is valid and the user to be informed if any constraint has been violated. If the information received by the central agent is not correct, the data are forwarded to the agent in charge of receiving this information on the server, which will report to agents responsible for triggering the alarms (see Fig. 1). The server agents receive different information from monitored devices and it send two types of information:

- Information about the status of monitoring. This information is displayed in the mobile phone using maps and in textual form. The information displayed depends on the role played by the user of the mobile device.
- The different alarms that are sent to a type or to other of user.

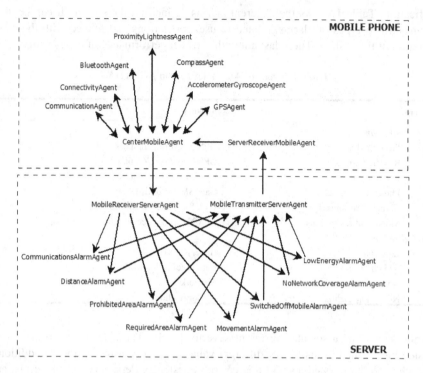

Fig. 1. System architecture based on agents

As shown in Fig. 1, AGATHA is client-server architecture. Clients are the mobile devices, composed by a set of agents collecting data from sensors and sending them to the server. The server is compound by another set of agents, responsible for collecting, storing and processing information from mobile devices as well as the activation of different alarms.

Software agents are developed on the JADE platform [8] (Java Agents Development Environment). JADE is a platform implemented in Java and the agents can communicate each other using a pattern specified by FIPA, called protocols. Each of these protocols provides the basic exchange of messages between two agents for a given type of conversation. The content of messages is JSON objects.

3   Agatha System Components

AGATHA is composed of three main components: a) a web application in charge of user registration, management of user roles and constraints and rules definition, b) a server in charge of alert service provider, and c) a mobile application installed on the mobile device of supervisor and supervised. Mobile and server applications interact via wireless communication.

3.1   AGATHA Web

AGATHA Web is a web site that provides the mechanisms needed to establish the parameters of the alert system. That is, it allows the management of information about users, relationship between the users, geographical areas, alert types, frequency of the gathering of information from mobile devices, etc.

Definition of users, user relationships, roles and alerts is managed by a powerful database also storing real-time information about users' activity. This database is used for the rule component in order to analyze the user status and to trigger the necessary agents in charge of sending back information to users.

3.2   AGATHA Mobile

This subsystem consists of a set of software agents and a graphical interface. The agents collect measures from the environment according to the phone sensors: GPS, accelerometer, gyroscope, compass, proximity sensor, lighting sensor, Bluetooth, Wi-Fi, and activity in the mobile: phone calls, SMS and MMS.

Fig. 2. Some screenshots of AGATHA mobile component

The mobile interface provides graphical information in form of maps about user location, as well as zones and routes (see Fig. 2). In addition, it provides textual information such as security level, distance between users (only with supervisor role), list of alarms activated, and much more.

3.3   AGATHA Alarm Provider

This component is responsible for receiving the information from the mobile device. This information must be processed to obtain the actions to be executed. Depending on the source of information, user under surveillance or supervisor, activity of related users, and so on, the system evaluates a set of rules defined for the involved users, and it returns to the users the results depending on the current context.

4   Use Case: Care of People with Alzheimer

The Alzheimer is a progressive, irreversible neurological disorder that affects the brain causing the death of neurons [9]. It produces a deterioration of all cognitive functions. This disease has different stages, during which the patient usually loses memory, ability to follow directions, can be lost in the street and, in advanced stages may lose the ability to walk and move, reaching a vegetative state.

Bravo et al. [10] propose a solution which aims to improve and complement Alzheimer's care in two ways: to manage the information easily, and as a complement for Alzheimer care visualization activities at home. This solution does not monitor parameters.

For these patients, the system AGATHA is like a nurse, who monitors their behavior, being able to activate the alarms defined for patients and to notify valuable information to the supervisor as well as the own patient. In this use case, we have defined initially the following main alarms:

- Alarms related to when a patient leaves a defined security zone (required zone).
- Alarms related to when a patient stands still for too long.
- Alarms related to when a patient is not capable of handling the device when he/she receives a phone call.

Notifications of the triggered alarms will be sent to the supervisor and depending of the alarm type, level and persistence, also will be sent to the patient (supervised).

As shown in Fig. 2, the system allows defining all type of constraints coloring different type of areas in the map screen.

The supervisor uses the mobile device for monitoring and he/she can display on the screen all Alzheimer patients under their care. Supervisor may at any time checks the status of alarms and even, directly from the interface of AGATHA, he/she may make a call to some patient simply touching on the user's avatar displayed on the map.

5   Discussion and Remarks

The aim of this work is to propose a novelty system to monitor the movements and activities of different kinds of users. The system collects data from mobile device sensors through agents. They send the data to the server responsible of its processing. When the server receives the data, it checks the activation ranges of alarms in order to return notifications to the involved users, if it is necessary.

An important characteristic of AGATHA it this system allows defining new alarms, agents and functionalities, including new sensors by Bluetooth or another network technology in an easy way, allowing the scalability of the system. New alarms can be included through web interface, an application form with different field related with the parameters that the new alarm must control. AGATHA also allows including new java agents only copying them inside the appropriate packet and compiling the project again. The advantage it is that the general behaviour it is not affected because each agent is independent and they can interact with the interface and with other agents without change anything. To include a new sensor, only it is necessary to include an agent that collects the data, other that controls the parameters and a new tuple in the sensors table of the database.

The system could be used for any monitoring process where a user with supervisor role monitors another user with supervised role, for instance, children surveillance. Thus, we show how AGATHA could be used for the surveillance of patients with not severe Alzheimer. The main advantages are not only that it is possible collect a large number of parameters used on the alarm definition; else it is possible to know the patient Alzheimer stage thank to history of sensors reading.

Acknowledgments. The Ministry of Science and Innovation of Spain (MICINN) supported this work (Project: TIN2011-24312).

References

1. SCEP: Man's Impact on the Global Environment. Assessment and Recommendations for Action. The MIT Press, Cambridge, MA and London, England (1970)
2. Choudhury, T., Pentland, A.: Sensing and Modeling Human Networks using the Sociometer. In: Fensel, D., Sycara, K.P., Mylopoulus, J. (eds.) ISWC 2003. LNCS, vol. 2870. Springer, Heidelberg (2003).
3. Al Shamsi, H., Ahmed, S., Redha, F.: Monitoring device for elders in UAE. In: International Conference and Workshop on Current Trends in Information Technology, pp. 32–36 (2011)
4. Keruve, http://www.keruve.com/
5. Cornelius, C., Kapadia, A., Kotz, D., Peebles, D., Shin, M., Triandopoulos, N.: Anonysense: privacy-aware people-centric sensing. In: ACM Conf. on Mobile Systems, Applications and Services (2008)
6. Kukkonen, J., Lagerspetz, E., Nurmi, P., Andersson, M.: BeTelGeuse: A Platform for Gathering and Processing Situational Data. IEEE Perv. Comp. 8, 49–56 (2009)
7. Froehlich, J., Chen, M.Y., Consolvo, S., Harrison, B., Landay, J.A.: MyExperience: a system for in situ tracing and capturing of user feedback on mobile phones. In: ACM Conf. on MobiSys (2007)
8. JADE, http://jade.tilab.com/index.html
9. Aguera-Ortiz, L., Frank-Garcia, A., Gil, P., Moreno, A.: Clinical progression of moderate-to-severe Alzheimer's disease and caregiver burden: a 12-month multicenter prospective observational study. International Psychogeriatrics 22(8), 1265–1279 (2010)
10. Bravo, J., López-de-Ipiña, D., Fuentes, C., Hervás, R., Peña, R., Vergara, M., Casero, G.: Enabling NFC Technology for Supporting Chronic Diseases: A Proposal for Alzheimer Caregivers. In: Aarts, E., Crowley, J.L., de Ruyter, B., Gerhäuser, H., Pflaum, A., Schmidt, J., Wichert, R. (eds.) AmI 2008. LNCS, vol. 5355, pp. 109–125. Springer, Heidelberg (2008)

A Novel Software Development Kit (SDK) to Foster Adoption of Health Informatics Standards in Personal Health Device (PHD) Communications

Miguel Martínez-Espronceda[1], Santiago Led[1],
Maciej Niegowski[1], Luis Serrano[1], and Luis Cabezas[2]

[1] Public University of Navarre, Pamplona 31006, Spain
miguel.martinezdeespronceda@unavarra.es
http://www.unavarra.es
[2] Life Quality Technology Accessibility and Innovation S.L.,
Noain 31110, Spain,
info@lqtai.com
http://www.lqtai.com

Abstract. As health care becomes distributed and wireless (home monitoring, M-Health, AmI), system interoperability becomes a challenge. The solution seems to be to use international health informatics standards. Among these, ISO/IEEE 11073 (X73PHD) is the best suited for interoperability of Personal Health Devices (PHDs). Nevertheless, given that low cost, wearable PHDs have limited hardware resources, it is required a deep control to adapt a base source code and generate a fully highly-optimized X73PHD-compliant device.

This article presents a novel Software Development Kit (SDK) that generates X73PHD source code for fully-optimized, X73PHD-compliant agents. The developer defines the objects of the Domain Information Model (DIM), its attributes, and the Finite State Machine (FSM) in the initial modeling phase. After that, the SDK automatically generates an optimized source code in additional phases: model checking, construction, transformation, optimization, and generation. Finally, during the integration phase, the developer manually incorporates the generated source code in its implementation. Given that the SDK follows the Patterns-based Methodology previously presented by the authors, the results are highly optimized in terms of processor usage (latency) and memory requirements (footprint). If the SDK was used by developers, it could accelerate the adoption of X73PHD.

Keywords: Ambient Intelligence (AmI), Health Informatics, Home monitoring, ISO/IEEE 11073 (X73), low cost wearable agents, Low-Voltage Low-Power (LV-LP), Patterns-based Methodology, Personal Health (P-Health), Personal Health Device (PHD), Point-of-Care (POC), Software Development Kit (SDK), standardization.

J. Bravo, R. Hervás, and M. Rodríguez (Eds.): IWAAL 2012, LNCS 7657, pp. 66–73, 2012.

1   Introduction

The decentralization of the Point-of-Care (PoC) promoted by the deployment of incipient Information Technologies (IT) is becoming a reality [1–3]. Its evolution to new balanced, user-centered designs could raise the efficiency of health care resources (human, mobiliary, medication, knowledge/learning, etc.) to deliver better quality to a broader number of subjects [4]. In the Ambient Intelligence (AmI) paradigm, smart sensors around the patient gather information continuously. The resulting data can be used in many different ways by the patient, familiars, or specialists [1,5].

An open issue in this paradigm is the lack of interoperability between heterogeneous systems. In order to overcome this situation several standards such as DICOM, MFER, FEF, EN13606, SPC-ECG and HL7 have been proposed. For Personal Health (P-Health), the best approach seems to be ISO/IEEE11073 for Personal Health Device (PHD) (X73PHD) [6]. This standard is an evolution of the classic ISO/IEEE11073 for PoC (X73PoC) focused in Intensive Unit Care (ICU) scenarios [7–10]. In this way, this new light-weight version simplifies the classic Domain Information Model (DIM) and Finite State Machine (FSM) of X73PoC, and incorporates new communication technologies: Universal Serial Bus (USB), Bluetooth and ZigBee [11]. During its development, X73PHD has gathered positive results [12]. Therefore, Continua Health Alliance, the leader private sector alliance that promotes the use of interoperability standards, adopts X73PHD for communications between PHDs of its interoperable ecosystem [13]. Nevertheless, this ecosystem has not fulfilled its expansion prospects. Several factors could be influencing. First, although its specifications have been simplified enormously, learning its details is still a time-consuming activity. Moreover, the optimization of the resulting implementation requires even further work and supplementary know-how. Furthermore, implementing a fully X73PHD-compliant device and passing conformance tests requires additional time.

The authors presented the Patterns-based Methodology previously in [14,15]. This methodology could allow implementing X73PHD-compatible agents using limited-resource microcontrollers (processor and memory) [16]. The methodology is based on two main points. First, the particularization of the implementation to a specific agent, and hence, a specific DIM configuration. Second, Application Protocol Data Units (APDUs) can be processed very efficiently using specialized analysis and synthesis algorithms based on decision trees (APDU-patterns). Nevertheless, this methodology is still difficult to implement [15]. This leads the authors to propose a novel Software Development Kit (SDK) to facilitate the whole process.

The novel proof-of-concept SDK presented in this work generates X73PHD source code following Patterns-based Methodology. The particularization of the Patterns-based Methodology principles to the SDK are explained in Section 2. Then, the SDK's 7-phase model is explained in Section 3. A discussion about the SDK is given in Section 4. Finally, the conclusions are drawn in Section 5.

2   Particularization of the Patterns-Based Methodology

The Patterns-based Methodology proposes the separation between state FSM and APDUs and associates them to the concepts of Kernel X73PHD and Patterns Library (APDU-patterns), respectively [15]. The SDK follows this proposal and adds the following particularities to the Patterns-based Methodology:

- Several approaches are available to implement the Patterns-based Methodology [17]. Although this SDK could produce code for all of them, the chosen strategy is to use dynamic memory to buffer APDUs. Among other things, it is easier to implement, easier to debug, and the results are slightly better than part-by-part processing for most of standard configurations that our research group is implementing.
- The target language is ANSI C (ISO/IEC 9899:1990) although compatibility with C99 and Embedded C++ is maintained. Most embedded SDKs support ANSI C and many of them support C99 and Embedded C++ so generating code in a 3-target language is fundamental in order to make the generated source code available to most embedded platforms.
- The SDK does not consider complete integration with hardware. Given that there are so many options, it is not viable to implement every possible driver. Alternatively, the source code provided by the SDK generates an interface and lets the job of linking this interface and the hardware layer to the developer.
- The SDK includes support for the Medical Device System (MDS), Numeric, Enumeration, Real Time (RT) Sample Array (RT-SA) and Scanner objects. Persistent Metric (PM) objects and PM segments are partially supported.

Moreover, the SDK maps the concepts of Kernel X73PHD and Patterns Library into three software modules, according to its role within the X73PHD stack. These are the following:

- **APDU-analyzer:** It analyzes incoming APDUs following APDU-patterns, and then transfers the results to the FSM module. It is implemented as a decision tree where different branches represent different APDU-patterns.
- **FSM module:** It changes X73PHD FSM states, handles events (including incoming APDU events from the APDU-analyzer), and manages the APDU-synthesizer (indicating which APDUs to synthesize). It is implemented as a decision tree where conditions match events and FSM states, and its leaves contain a selection of actions to execute when the conditions are matched.
- **APDU-synthesizer:** It synthesizes APDUs following APDU-patterns. It is implemented as a decision tree where different branches represent different APDU-patterns and the path determines an instance of APDU. This path is set by the FSM module and passed as parameter to the APDU-synthesizer.

3   Structure of the Software Development Kit (SDK)

The SDK takes the abstract model of the target X73PHD agent's configuration (standard or not), and generates the source code needed to manage the whole

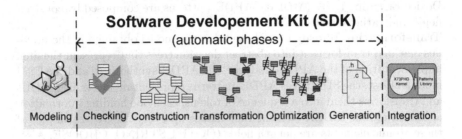

Fig. 1. Phases of the Software Development Kit (SDK)

X73PHD stack. Thus, details about X73PHD are hidden to the developer, whose role is limited to model the agent and to integrate the automatically generated X73PHD source code into the application layer. The source code generation process is divided into phases (Fig. 1). Every phase takes the model provided the previous one and makes some modifications to it, generating a new model representation as result. Each one gets the model closer (in representation) to the final target implementation. The phases are the following:

1. **Modeling phase:** The developer writes a file which represents the target agent's model. This model includes both, static information (such as objects and attributes, versions and configurations supported, association information) and dynamic behavior (such as service handling details, state changes). The model is made up of a hierarchy of objects, which are, in turn, made up of attributes and service descriptors. To define these objects, the developer uses an input configuration file that is passed to the SDK library. Many of the Abstract Syntaxis Notation One (ASN.1) structures provided by X73PHD are loaded into the library from an ASN.1 file (using an *ad-hoc* generator based on Another Tool for Language Recongnition (ANTLR) [18]). These structures are used to define attributes and some APDU-patterns (many APDU-patterns are automatically generated in the construction phase so there is usually no need to define additional ones). As an example, consider an weight scale (ConfigurationId=1500). Its DIM will contain a Numeric object with several static attributes (e.g. Type, Handle, Unit-Code, etc.) and dynamic attributes (e.g. Simple-Nu-Observed-Value, Absolute-Time-Stamp).

2. **Model checking phase:** The model defined by the developer in previous phase is analyzed for both consistency and compliance. Inconsistencies appear when the model defines unattainable implementations, such as the use of variables that have not been defined previously. Compliance fails are detected if the model does not conform to X73PHD.

3. **Construction phase:** It automatically completes some parts of the model provided by the developer. On one hand, this phase provides an abstract representation of the FSM that includes its states, substates, and state transitions (including conditions to execute the transitions, execution of code, etc.). On the other hand, this phase generates APDU-patterns for Medical

Device Encoding Rules (MDER). APDU-patterns are composed by constant fields and variable fields.

4. **Transformation phase:** This phase takes the model obtained in the previous one, and transforms it into abstract decision trees that represent the final implementation of the APDU-analyzer, the APDU-synthesizer, and the FSM module. First, the SDK takes APDU-patterns representing incoming APDUs and transforms them into a sequence of tokens, each one holding information about an atomic MDER element that makes up every APDU. Examples of these atomic elements are: length fields (OCTET STRING, CHOOSE, ANY DEFINED BY, etc.), variable fields (measurements, timestamps, attribute values, Invoke-Id, etc.), option CHOOSE fields, integer fields, etc. These sequences of tokens are then analyzed, and classified into APDU-analyzer's abstract tree. Something similar is done to obtain the APDU-synthesizer's decision tree. Finally, FSM events (e.g. assocReq, assocRelReq, startNoti-Fixed, etc.) and states (Connected, Associated, Associating, Configuring, etc.) are classified as *event-state* tuples and the actions to be taken for each one are determined. Then, these results are used to generate the FSM module's decision tree.

5. **Optimization phase:** This phase has been provided for future optimizations based on the intermediate abstract representation obtained in the previous phase. This phase optimizes some aspects that a regular compiler can be unable to perform due to information loss in the generation phase. Most C language compilers usually optimize better that what a programmer is able to. Nevertheless, based on the information of the abstract model it is possible to help the compiler with optimizations. For example, the transition phase generates a call for matching each byte at input sequence. Replacing repetitive calls with a loop or a function that matches a whole block of bytes may reduce the footprint in those cases.

6. **Generation phase:** This phase could be thought as a simplification phase. The generation phase transforms the whole abstract model representing the APDU-analyzer, APDU-synthesizer and the FSM module into real source code. StringTemplate (ST) is used to generate it [19]. For this proof-of-concept, a ST template file for C language has been defined. It is affordable to add many other output languages by including additional ST files.

7. **Integration phase:** After having obtained these source code files, the developer has to integrate them into its hardware platform as explained in [15]. The modules that the developer must develop manually include drivers to access measurements, user interface controller, interface with timer layer, and transport shim layer.

4 Discussion

A standard configuration weight scale (Configuration-Id=1500) was used to generate the X73PHD source code. Once generated, the source code was compiled for an ARM7TDMI based 32-bit microcontroller using a commercially available workbench for embedded systems. In this case, memory requirements are about 3600 bytes of Read-Only Memory (ROM) and 500 bytes of Random Access Memory (RAM). In order to check conformance, an interoperability test was carried out using an external manager provided by Dr. Clarke at Brunel University which was able to connect to the PHD and interchange data [9]. In terms of footprint, obtained results of this implementation are in the same order of magnitude of [15]. The differences between both implementations can be considerably reduced. As a proof-of-concept, some repetitive statements that correspond to constant blocks of bytes were replaced manually by loops. The results in this case were around 1900 bytes of ROM and 300 bytes of RAM, which are in the same order of magnitude to the presented in [15]. These relatively simple optimizations and others could be added in the optimization phase in the near future.

Regarding the programming language used for the definition of the input file, Java was chosen because its workbenches are very mature and advanced. After this first proof-of-concept, the authors are studying other programming languages such as Groovy, which offer easier ways to represent mappings and lists. Currently, the SDK generates source code in C programming language but it is quite easy to provide additional ST template files for others.

Regarding the applicability of the SDK to other protocols, it is not possible at the moment. There are still some points that are just defined for X73PHD, such as MDER part and model checking. Both programs have been hard-coded intrinsically within the SDK. For that reason, the SDK is tied to the X73PHD protocol and MDER. One open point being tackled is to remove these dependencies, providing a mechanism to load the encoding rules and the FSM from an external file which could allow using the SDK in other protocols.

Finally, the implementation of the transport shim layer has been left to the developer in order to maximize transport independence. Nevertheless, it would be possible to have some pre-built shim layers available for each transport layer option, and therefore the developer would be freed of this task. For example in the case of ZigBee, there could be different options as transport interface but usually these are limited to a few manufacturers. The same happens with Bluetooth. Once developed, the transport shim layer could be shared in many implementations.

5   Conclusions

The paper describes an X73PHD SDK based on the Patterns-based Methodology. The SDK generates the source code files needed to implement X73PHD within new or existing agents. Given an input file containing the model of an agent, the SDK generates automatically agent's source code for the APDU-analyzer, the APDU-synthesizer and the FSM module. The initial proof-of-concept weight scale implementation shows the SDK potential benefits: optimization of hardware usage, conformance to X73PHD, and ease of use. Some lessons learned during the development of the SDK, and later during its initial usage, suggest that further optimizations and improvements are possible. Given the low-memory and low-processor requirements of patterns-based implementations, implementing new X73PHD agents and upgrading existing non-X73PHD agents to be X73PHD-compliant is just a matter of upgrading software. The proposed SDK easies the development of new highly optimized X73PHD-compliant implementations. Thus, this SDK could foster the adoption of health informatics standards in PHD communications and reduce deployment costs.

A Acronyms

AmI	Ambient Intelligence
ANTLR	Another Tool for Language Recongnition
APDU	Application Protocol Data Unit
ASN.1	Abstract Syntaxis Notation One
DIM	Domain Information Model
FSM	Finite State Machine
ICU	Intensive Unit Care
MDER	Medical Device Encoding Rules
MDS	Medical Device System
PHD	Personal Health Device
P-Health	Personal Health
PM	Persistent Metric
PoC	Point-of-Care
RAM	Random Access Memory
ROM	Read-Only Memory
RT	Real Time
RT-SA	RT Sample Array
SDK	Software Development Kit
ST	StringTemplate
USB	Universal Serial Bus
X73PHD	ISO/IEEE11073 for PHD
X73PoC	ISO/IEEE11073 for PoC

References

1. Koop, C., Mosher, R., Kun, L., Geiling, J., Grigg, E., Long, S., Macedonia, C., Merrell, R., Satava, R., Rosen, J.: Future delivery of health care: Cybercare. IEEE Engineering in Medicine and Biology Magazine 27(6), 29–38 (2008)
2. Monteagudo, J.L., Moreno, O.: eHealth for Patient Empowerment in Europe. World Wide Web electronic publication (2009),
   http://ec.europa.eu/information_society/newsroom/cf/
   itemdetail.cfm?item_id=3448
   (last access: June 2012)
3. Paré, G., Moqadem, K., Pineau, G., St-Hilaire, C.: Clinical effects of home telemonitoring in the context of diabetes, asthma, heart failure and hypertension: A systematic review. Journal of Medical Internet Research 12(2) (2010)

4. Koch, S.: Home telehealth-current state and future trends. International Journal of Medical Informatics 75(8), 565–576 (2006)
5. Bonato, P.: Wearable sensors and systems. IEEE Engineering in Medicine and Biology Magazine 29(3), 25–36 (2010)
6. ISO/IEC/IEEE Health informatics–Personal health device communication–Part 20601: Application profile–Optimized exchange protocol. ISO/IEEE 11073-20601:2010(E), pp. 1–208, 1 (2010)
7. Gardner, R.: Development of medical informatics standards. Journal of the American Medical Informatics Association: JAMIA 1(1), 79–80 (1994)
8. Lutter, N., Norgall, T., Mell, J., Weigan, C., Schuettler, J.: Point of care: New connectivity standards and novel technologies in intensive care. International Journal of Intensive Care 12(4), 175–185 (2005)
9. Clarke, M., Bogia, D., Hassing, K., Steubesand, L., Chan, T., Ayyagari, D.: Developing a standard for personal health devices based on 11073. In: Annual International Conference of the IEEE Engineering in Medicine and Biology - Proceedings, pp. 6174–6176 (2007)
10. Galarraga, M., Serrano, L., Martinez, I., de Toledo, P., Reynolds, M.: Telemonitoring systems interoperability challenge: an updated review of the applicability of ISO/IEEE 11073 standards for interoperability in telemonitoring. In: Conference Proceedings: Annual International Conference of the IEEE Engineering in Medicine and Biology Society, vol. 2007, pp. 6162–6166 (2007)
11. Aragüés, A., Escayola, J., Martínez, I., Del Valle, P., Muñoz, P., Trigo, J., García, J.: Trends and challenges of the emerging technologies toward interoperability and standardization in e-health communications. IEEE Communications Magazine 49(11), 182–188 (2011)
12. Bogia, D.: Supporting personal health devices through standardization and collaboration, pp. 338–343 (2011)
13. Carroll, R., Cnossen, R., Schnell, M., Simons, D.: Continua: An interoperable personal healthcare ecosystem. IEEE Pervasive Computing 6(4), 90–94 (2007)
14. Martínez-Espronceda, M., Serrano, L., Martínez, I., Escayola, J., Led, S., Trigo, J., García, J.: Implementing ISO/IEEE 11073: Proposal of two different strategic approaches. In: Proceedings of the 30th Annual International Conference of the IEEE Engineering in Medicine and Biology Society, EMBS 2008 - Personalized Healthcare Through Technology, pp. 1805–1808 (2008)
15. Martínez-Espronceda, M., Martínez, I., Serrano, L., Led, S., Trigo, J., Marzo, A., Escayola, J., García, J.: Implementation methodology for interoperable personal health devices with low-voltage low-power constraints. IEEE Transactions on Information Technology in Biomedicine 15(3), 398–408 (2011)
16. Park, C.-Y., Lim, J.-H., Park, S.: ISO/IEEE 11073 PHD standardization of legacy healthcare devices for home healthcare services, pp. 547–548 (2011)
17. Martínez-Espronceda, M., Martínez, I., Serrano, L., Led, S., Trigo, J., Marzo, A., Escayola, J., Barrón, G., García, J.: Lessons learned implementing the ISO/IEEE11073 standard into wearable personal devices. In: Proceedings of the IEEE/EMBS Region 8th International Conference on Information Technology Applications in Biomedicine, ITAB (2010)
18. Parr, T., Quong, R.: ANTLR: a predicated-LL(k) parser generator. Software - Practice and Experience 25(7), 789–810 (1995)
19. Parr, T.: Enforcing strict model-view separation in template engines. In: Thirteenth International World Wide Web Conference Proceedings, WWW 2004, pp. 224–233 (2004)

Identification of Sounds and Sensing Technology for Home-Care Applications

Héctor Lozano[1], Inmaculada Hernáez[2], Javier Camarena[1], Ibai Díez[1], and Eva Navas[2]

[1] Tecnalia, Health Technologies Unit, Parque Tecnológico,
Edificio 202. E-48170 Zamudio (Bizkaia), Spain
{hector.lozano,javier.camarena,ibai.diez}@tecnalia.com
[2] Aholab Signal Processing Laboratory, University of the Basque Country (UPV/EHU),
ETSI, Alda. Urquijo s/n, E-48013 Bilbao (Bizkaia), Spain
{inma.hernaez,eva.navas}@ehu.es

Abstract. This article focuses on an analysis of the needs of Hearing Impaired People and on the development of a recognition of environmental sounds system in a typical home. Based on the extraction of acoustic characteristics (Mel Frequency Cepstral Coefficients, Zero Crossing Rate, Roll Off Point and Spectral Centroid) and their combination with data from presence sensors, an accuracy rate of 88.4% was obtained.

1 Introduction

The information transmitted by the acoustic medium has the potential of supporting an understanding of what happens in our environment [1]. The sound of a phone indicating that someone wants to contact us or a fire alarm warning of danger are examples of that. Providing information about what is happening to elder people, or people with hearing problems in general, can be a very important technology development within the field of Assistive Technology [2] [3]. Additionally, intelligent systems can further use this information to better adapt the environment to the user within the domain of Ambient Assisted Living (AAL) [4]. Recognition of a sequence of sound events (opening the fridge, sound of dishes, moving chairs, microwave beep,...) may help to infer activities (e.g.: the person is preparing food), which may enable the detection of changes in patterns that flag potential problems of cognitive impairments.

In this paper we analyse the needs of people with hearing disabilities in recognizing the environmental acoustic events. A statistical survey over 37 people provided conclusive data used to learn the most suitable characteristics in sound recognition systems. Based on this analysis, the implementation and evaluation of techniques developed to mitigate this problem using Gaussian Mixture Models and acoustic parameters extracted from the signal are presented.

Furthermore, within the AAL scenario of the European project RUBICON [5] that used different networks of sensors to infer activities of daily living, the combination of acoustic parameters along with other data from different sensors are analysed in detection and classification steps. The use of rules based on data coming from sensors

J. Bravo, R. Hervás, and M. Rodríguez (Eds.): IWAAL 2012, LNCS 7657, pp. 74–81, 2012.
© Springer-Verlag Berlin Heidelberg 2012

that indicate the presence of the user inside the house substantially improves the obtained results. Tests performed in a HomeLab obtained accuracy ratios of 88.4% working in real time, while without the information provided by the presence sensors the accuracy obtained was 82.4%..

2   Needs of Hearing Impaired People

In order to analyse the needs of persons affected by hearing impairment with respect to environmental sound recognition, a survey with 37 volunteers was conducted. For this work, we collaborated with several public and private institutions involved with the hearing impaired, to disseminate our hypothesis and to recruit participants.

97% of respondents have a moderate or total hearing loss. Therefore, we are dealing with people familiar with the sort of problems that hearing loss may cause in daily life.

To the question "what are the environments where you find more problems concerning non-speech sounds?", home environments showed to be most relevant to daily tasks performance. As it can be seen in figure 1, 34% of respondents rated the home as the most important environment, closely followed by work / study environments (30%). 20% and a 10% were indicated as important for street and vehicle, and 6% went to the group "Other" which, respondents reported as the theatre, film and entertainment in general.

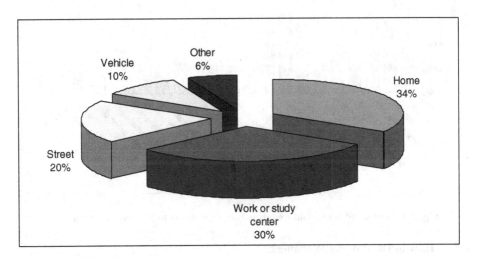

Fig. 1. Percentage distribution of environments where environmental sound recognition is considered relevant

Taking this information as a starting point for our work, the 'home environment' was chosen as target environment, and the kind of sounds that can be found there is the basis for the experimental work further described.

2.1   Sounds of Interest in the Home Environment

A list of 22 different sounds that can happen at a home environment was developed and presented to the participants. They were asked to choose most important 3 items for them. The results are shown in Figure 2. It can be deduced that the most important sound to recognize is the doorbell with a 13% rating followed closely by the alarm clock with an assessment of 12%. In this study, the television / radio and baby crying were considered to be closely linked to 'speech-like' sounds and were discarded. . In this way, the next four most important sounds considered by our participants are the intercom, the phone, knocks on the door and the sound of the faucet with percentages of 9%, 6.5%, 6.5% and 6.5% respectively. Of these 6 sounds that are ranked as the most important Non-Speech sounds, four of them (doorbell, alarm, intercom and tele-phone) are deterministic sounds. Their nature is highly dependent on the manufac-turer, model or user preferences, and in general they are well bounded in frequency.

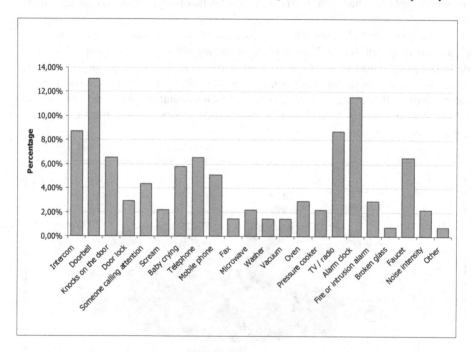

Fig. 2. Relevance of household sounds at home according to the performed survey

2.2   How to Display the Warning?

Based on a list of 7 options ("on my computer", "on my phone", "on the TV", "on a wrist watch", on the wall or ceiling", "on the device that was closer", "other"), the participants were asked to mark 2 devices that they considered most appropriate to receive the warning of the recognized sounds. Surprisingly, "on my mobile phone" was the most popular option with 32% of the scores, followed by "On the device that is closer to me" which reached 28% of the vote. The third choice was "in a wrist watch" with 16% as shown in the graph of the figure 3.

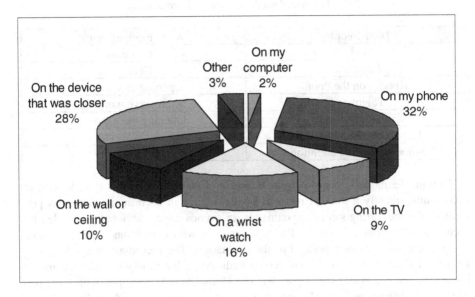

Fig. 3. Distribution of the preferred devices for the sound warning display

This fact shows the extended use of mobile phones by the group of people with hearing disabilities. These devices are widely used and well accepted by this community and, it can be seen as an excellent platform to implement technological advances that are emerging daily.

3   A Sound Recognition System for Assisted Environment

Having studied the needs of the group of hearing impaired people the next steps were the implementation and evaluation of techniques involved in automatic identification and classification of household sounds.

3.1   Environment and Sound Selection

For the experimental study a selection of 12 classes of sounds was performed taking into account the highest ranked types of sounds of the survey. Additionally, other sounds (chairs, dishes, cupboards,...) were incorporated that, despite of not having a character of "warning", are understood as important acoustic events to use in AAL systems for recognition of activities. A table with the evaluation of all selected sounds is shown below.

In order to train and validate the sound recognition system, it was essential to have a database with representative sound data.

Table 1. Selected sound in the experimental study

Deaf People	AAL Environment
Doorbell	Chairs noise
Intercom	Cutlery
Knocks on the door	Opening cupboards
Telephone	Microwave working
Faucet	Opening microwave
Microwave Final whistle	
Someone calling attention	

To train the models, samples were recorded of about 2 minutes for each class of event. Subsequently a manual removal of the silence in each audio track was performed. For the testing step, approximately 25 sounds were additionally recorded for each class (301 sounds in total). The test was done with continuous sounds so, environmental noise was incorporated to the evaluation. The recordings were done in a functional HomeLab of over 30m^2 with a bedroom, a living-room, a kitchen area, a bathroom, and a corridor (see figure 4). The HomeLab was equipped with a PC that had a multichannel audio card connected to 6 microphones located on the ceiling of the different areas / rooms.

Fig. 4. HomeLab with microphones in the ceiling

Additionally, presence sensors indicating in which room the user was during the tests were used in order to have more knowledge of the context and avoid false positives. The information of these sensors allows reducing the set of sounds in a certain time giving more probability to some sensors than others depending on the position of the user.

3.2   Acoustic Features Extraction

The audio signals were analysed using frames of 60 milliseconds. The acoustic characteristics extracted were the first 13 Mel Frequency Cepstral Coefficients (typically used in speech recognition), Zero Crossing Rate, Spectral Centroid and Roll Off Point (more frequent in the music recognition field) [6]. At the same time first and second differences - delta and delta-delta coefficients - were obtained for all parameters.

3.3   Classification Model

Not all classifiers offer the same performance in non-speech sounds recognition [7]. The chosen classifier, Gaussian Mixture Model (GMM) [8], is a simple model which can be described as a Hidden Markov Model (HMM) of a single state. Impulsive sounds which are difficult to separate into states are classified by observing the distribution based on the extracted parameters. Its implementation cost is low and it offers good properties for identifying short and impulsive events. Equation (1) defines the model, being K the number of Gaussians of the mixture, w_k the weight assigned to each Gaussian g of mean μ_k and covariance matrix Σ_k:

$$gm(x) = \sum_{k=1}^{K} w_k \cdot g(\mu_k, \Sigma_k)(x)$$

(1)

$$\sum_{i=1}^{k} w_i = 1 \quad \forall \quad i \in \{1,......, K\} \quad : w_i \geq 0.$$

For each class of sound a GMM was trained using 40 gaussians. Additionally, a non sound model was added to the sound list in order to work in real time and to be able to classify segments of environmental noise. To determine the starting and ending position of the events smoothing techniques were applied. A threshold was established and a sequence of frames was considered an event when a certain minimum number of consecutive frames were classified as coming from the same class.

4   Experiments and Results

The accuracy and reliability of the trained models were evaluated for each class initially using only acoustic information. The detection and classification tasks were performed in one step using expression (2) described in [9]. This equation returns the error of recognition based on the deleted items (D), new insertions (I) and substitutions (S) giving a measure to evaluate the detection and classification jointly.

$$\text{Error rate}(\%) = (D+I+S)*100/N°\text{Events}$$

(2)

The error rate obtained was 17.6%. In order to evaluate the improvement that the use of more sensors could contribute to the system, data coming from presence sensors were added to the sound recognizer. When a sound source was activated, information about the location of the person was also provided. Considering the designed environment, a small set of simple rules was defined (for example, for a positive doorbell detection it was necessary the presence of the user near the entrance area). This strategy helped to lower the number of false positives.

Using the data provided by the presence sensors rules the error percentage fell to 11.6% demonstrating the potential importance of the combination of other sensors for improved accuracy and reliability.

Previous experiments performed providing exact temporal location of the event to the classifier achieved a success rate of 97%. Thus, working in real time is one of the most challenging tasks in this research field.

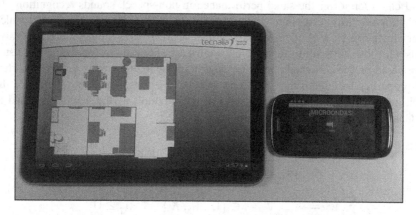

Fig. 5. Mobile phone and Tablet PC showing a detected sound

5   Conclusions and Future Lines

This work presented an analysis of a group of hearing impaired facing the handicap of "Non-Speech" sounds produced in the home. It offers a clear perspective of what are the sounds more relevant and the best devices where giving such information. We have here demonstrated the technical feasibility of achieving high ratios solution accuracy and reliability in the classification stage and in the detection, using probabilistic techniques and the combination of acoustic parameters and presence sensors. Applying the above described techniques, the recognition software was implemented to work in real time. Following the results of the surveys a mobile phone with Android operating system was used as interface. It was programmed with capabilities of vibrating when an event was detected and displaying their information graphically on the screen. Also the interface was implemented on a tablet PC simultaneously showing the icon of the sound in a map of the HomeLab.

Future areas of work include the use of more sensors installed in the home such as magnetic sensors, light, accelerometers, etc., to gain broader knowledge of the environmental context for the inference of the acoustic events. In addition, within the Rubicon Project, the sound could be evaluated and used for the detection and classification of daily live activities in an AAL environment. Information extracted from sounds together with data collected from autonomous wireless networks of sensors and actuators could be processed allowing higher classification level and an improvement in the accuracy and reliability.

Acknowledgements. The technologies and developments presented in this paper are partially supported by the European Union (7th Frame Programme ICT, project RUBICON, contract N. 269914, www.fp7rubicon.eu) and by the Basque Government through the grant IT537-10.

References

1. Cowling, M.: Non-Speech Environmental Sound Classification System for Autonomous Surveillance. Phd Thesis. Griffith University (2004)
2. Lozano, H., Hernáez, I., Picón, A., Camarena, J., Navas, E.: Audio Classification Techniques in Home Environments for Elderly/Dependant People. In: Miesenberger, K., Klaus, J., Zagler, W., Karshmer, A. (eds.) ICCHP 2010, Part 1. LNCS, vol. 6179, pp. 320–323. Springer, Heidelberg (2010)
3. Lozano, H., Hernáez, I., Navas, E., et al.: "Non-Speech" Sounds Classification for People with Hearing Disabilities. In: AAATE, pp. 276–280 (2007)
4. Ma, L., Smith, D.J., Milner, B.P.: Context Awareness using Environmental Noise Classification. In: Proceedings of Eurospeech, pp. 2237–2240 (2003)
5. Amato, G., Broxval, M., Chessa, S., et al.: Robotic UBIquitous Cognitive Network. In: 3rd International Symposium on Ambient Intelligence (ISAmI), Spain (2012)
6. Vacher, M., Istrate, D., Serignat, J.: Sound Detection and Classification Through Transient Models using Wavelet Coefficient Trees. In: EUSIPCO (2004)
7. Vacher, M., Istrate, D., Besacier, L., Serignat, J.F.: Life Sounds Extraction and Classification in Noisy Environment. In: IASTED'SIP, Honolulu, Hawaii, USA (2003)
8. Atrey, K., Maddage, C., Kankanhalli, S.: Audio Based Event Detection for Multimedia Surveillance. In: IEEE International Conference on ICCASP, pp. 813–816 (2006)
9. Temko, A.: Acoustic Event Detection and Classification. Phd Thesis. Universitat Politècnica de Catalunya (2007)

Modeling a Risk Detection System for Elderly's Home-Care with a Network of Timed Automata

Isabel Navarrete, José A. Rubio, Juan A. Botía,
José T. Palma, and Francisco J. Campuzano

Department of Information Engineering,
University of Murcia, Spain
{inava,joseantonio.rubio,juanbot,jtpalma,fjcampuzano}@um.es

Abstract. We address the problem of modeling a risk detection system oriented to elderly's home-care, which may cause the generation of an alarm if there is evidence of a serious problem. We have chosen a network of timed automata as a suitable formalism to solve the problem in a simple and elegant fashion. Our model is capable of representing the subject's environment, modeling his behavior dynamics, detecting several types of abnormal behavior patterns, and deciding whether they have enough evidence of being dangerous to generate an alarm. In addition, the formalism allows concurrent activity monitoring in different rooms, what is useful to determine if the person is alone at home, in order to avoid the generation of false alarms when the elder is supposed to be already under human care. We have verified critical properties of the model by using a model-checking engine.

Keywords: homecare, risk detection, activity recognition, timed automata, environment modeling and monitoring.

1 Introduction

Following the *Ambient Assisted Living* (AAL) initiative [1], the main concern of this paper is modeling a system for detecting potentially dangerous situations (risks) in which an elder may be involved at home when he/she is alone. *Activity recognition* is performed in real time in order to discover several abnormal behavior patterns, such as being too much time lying on the floor/bed, too much time moving or without leaving a given room of the house. To develop such a system, we assume that costs must be reduced as much as posible, and sensors used to capture information from the environment must avoid the elder feeling the sensation of being watched or uncomfortable. Thus, we suppose the home is equipped with simple wireless sensors for detecting movement, pressure and open door; cameras, microphones or wearable devices are discarded (see [2] for further details on the sensor infrastructure we consider).

Context aware techniques [3] represent the context in which a subject evolves and analyze his context dynamics by processing sensor data. When such data are given as a sequence of events, a risk detection system (RDS) of the type we

J. Bravo, R. Hervás, and M. Rodríguez (Eds.): IWAAL 2012, LNCS 7657, pp. 82–89, 2012.
© Springer-Verlag Berlin Heidelberg 2012

have pointed, may be considered as an event-driven system subject to timing constraints, in which activity dynamics in each room of the house can be seen as independently running processes that interact with the environment. For that reason, we have chosen a *network of timed automata* [4,5] as a suitable formalism to model the RDS. Such a network is the parallel composition of timed automata representing communicating processes, whereas a *timed automaton* is essentially a finite automaton extended with a set of variables modeling *clocks*. Models provide invaluable help in making important design decisions, prior to system implementation [6]. Thus, we believe this formalism may be useful for simple activity recognition problems in which timing constraints plays a important role.

Our proposal departs from a RDS home-monitoring platform [7] which has become a commercial product in the South-East of Spain. The RDS integrated in that framework gathers several techniques, such as handling an ontology, a decision rule set, a finite-state machine, and an inconsistency solver; the latter is mainly oriented to decide if the elder is alone. Our approach is intended to replace the mentioned techniques with a simple formalism, which, in addition, offers more information on the subject's activity-level over time, and on the cause of a risk alert. This way, the RDS, redesigned following the model proposed in this paper, gains in reliability, reaction time and ease of maintenance. Moreover, augmenting the system with the capability of adapting its behavior can be done without much effort following the technique proposed in [7]. Since our work suppose an evolution of the system in [7], we recommend the reader the related-work section showed there, in which a comparison with other approaches to elderly homecare is done. Just say that networks of timed automata have not been applied before to human activity recognition, to the best of our knowledge.

The rest of the paper is structured as follows. Section 2 introduces a brief overview of TA-networks. Section 3 is devoted to present the main domain-problem assumptions, the description of the model, and the process of model checking. Finally, section 4 outlines most important conclusions and future work.

2   Overview of Networks of Timed Automata

In this section we present a short overview of a *network of timed automata* (TA-network, for short). Formal definitions and a summary of the main topics of interest around the theory of timed automata can be found in [4,5]. Applications of timed automata are wide and varied, e.g., for designing communication protocols [8] or representing multi-agent systems [9].

A *TA-network* is the parallel composition of several timed automata representing concurrent or communicating processes, whereas a *timed automaton* (TA) is essentially a finite automaton extended with a set of real-valued variables modeling *clocks*. Clocks are initialized to zero when a TA starts, and then increase at same rate. As for the case of finite automata, a TA may also be described by means of an *state-transition graph*, in which nodes stand for *control states* (also known as *locations*) and labeled arcs represent *transition rules* (or *switches*). A TA allows the specification of simple linear *clock constraints* representing enabling conditions for transitions (*guards*) or conditions to stay in a given state

(*state invariants*, annotated next to the state-node in the graph). The *initial state* of a TA is marked by a double circle.

A number of simulation and verification tools have been developed for timed automata; we focus here on the well-known UPPAAL tool [10][1]. This tool extends the standard syntax and semantics of TA-networks with additional features, such as synchronization channels, integer variables and user defined functions. Transitions in UPPAAL have the following (possibly empty) labels: guard, sync, and update. A *guard* is a boolean expression combining clock constraints and side-effect free integer expressions. A *sync* label specifies a *receiving action*, marked with '?' or a *sending action*, marked with '!'; if this label is empty (denoted by ϵ), then the action is *internal*. The *update* label specifies a sequence of clock resets and/or integer-variable updates.

Initially, the TA-network starts running from the *initial state vector*, formed by all initial states of the network components. The network can perform either delay steps or action steps. A *delay step* only increments the value of all clocks with the same delay (thus, there is no change in the state vector), as long as the current clock values satisfy the conjunction of the invariants of the states in the state vector. In an *action step*, either (1) a *local-internal transition*, or (2) a *synchronized transition*, is fired. In case (1), one automaton fires, if possible, a transition on an internal action, which has no effect over the rest of the network. The meaning of a local-internal transition rule, such as $q \xrightarrow{g,\epsilon,u} q'$, is the following: if the current state of the TA is q, the current clock values and integer-variable values of the network satisfy both the invariant of q and the guard g, and the values modified according to u satisfy the invariant of q' (i.e, the transition is *enabled*), then the effect of firing such a transition is that the TA performs the update u and the state changes to q'. In case (2), if, for instance, one TA has an enabled transition on action $a!$ and another one has an enabled transition on the matching action $a?$, then the two automata synchronize, firing their corresponding transitions at the same time, while the others stay in their control states. If such a synchronization is not possible then a *deadlock* occurs.

3   Modeling the Risk Detection System in UPPAAL

First, we show the main *assumptions* we have considered to model the RDS. We suppose the subject lives alone, although he receives visits of variable duration. The subject's environment, relevant to the problem, is given by a house equipped with a wireless sensor network with at least one *move sensor* per room, one *press sensor* in each bed/armchair in which the subject may rest for a long period of time, and a magnetic *door sensor* at the entrance door. The RDS is aware of the evolution of the person's behavior by means of a sequence of *(abstract) sensor events* received from a driver connected to the base station of the sensor network. A sensor event provides meaningful information for activity recognition (hardware-status events are not considered in the model), namely:

---

[1] http://www.uppaal.org/

the *sensor identifier*, its *type*, and its *value* or state, which may be *on* if the sensor detects something or *off*, otherwise. A sensor event is generated only when its state *changes* from on to off and viceversa; moreover, spurious changes are suppressed [2] in order to avoid wasting energy and bandwidth resources.

Outline of the UPPAAL Project. We have used UPPAAL to build a project that allows us to simulate and verify the model. The person's environment can be represented throughout the declarations of the project. We define the numbers of rooms, the room codes, the number of sensors, and for each sensor, we provide its location (i.e., the room code) and its type. There may be more than one sensor of the same type in a given room. On the other hand, the dynamics of the person's behavior over time and the detection of abnormal behavior patterns is controlled by means of the states, the integer variables, the transition rules, and clock constraints of the TA-network. Our UPPAAL-project is composed of a *TA-template*, named RiskRoomDetector (see Fig. 1) and a *TA* named SystemMonitor ("monitor", for short; see Fig. 2), whose functionality is explained below.

3.1   RiskRoomDetector TA-Template

This template is a TA with parameters, which, once they are substituted by specific integer arguments in the system declaration, leads to one TA per room, which we refer to as "a detector"[2]. The actual values of the parameters are obtained by a priori knowledge on the domain and they are used as *timing thresholds* for discriminating between normal and anomalous person's states per room[3]. Proceeding like this, the model can be easily adapted to consider people with different lifestyles and living in houses of variable structure, since it is only necessary to change the declarations. This fact has a positive influence on the implementation of the model[4], such as in the ease of adaptability and maintenance. The parameters of RiskRoomDetector are the following: thisRoom, mtPresen, mtPassive, mtMov, mtPress, mtMvPr, where thisRoom is a valid room code, mtPresen stands for the maximum time of presence considered normal in the room, and the other ones represent, respectively, the upper bounds (timing thresholds) for the invariants of the states Passive, Moving, Pressing, and MovPress. These subject's states allow controlling different activity-levels subject to timing constraints, as we explain below.

Idle is the state in which the detector is waiting for a sensor event from the monitor. When a *move-on* (or *press-on*) event is received, the detector goes to Moving (or Pressing), and resets the clock cMov(or cPress) to start measuring

---

[2] For example, Lounge = RiskRoomDetector (0,300,15,30,200,70), declares a detector named Lounge, in which a time-unit may be a second.

[3] The timing thresholds are supposed to be different for different moments of the day, but this fact is not reflected in the model, for simplicity. We consider this as an implementation issue.

[4] Due to space limitation, we omit the details on the current model-based implementation and on experimental evaluation. Just say that each TA is a thread which behave independently from the others, unless there's synchronization involved.

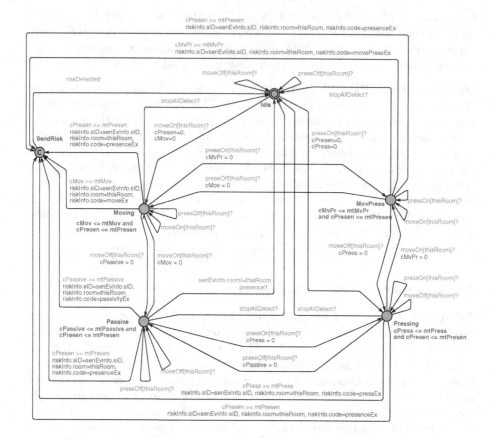

Fig. 1. `RoomRiskDetector`: recognizes activity and detects risks in some room

the elapsed time in the corresponding state; thereafter, the current state changes depending on the event received, as long as its invariant holds. Notice that if the room has not a press sensor then `Pressing` is not reachable. The abnormal behavior patterns are detected when: (1) the guard `cPresen>=mtPresence` is satisfied, what is considered a risk of type *total presence-time exceeded*, where `cPresen` is the clock that measures the total elapsed time since someone entered a room (with no evidence of presence) up to the moment; or (2) some of the guards `cPassive>= mtPassive, cMov>= mtMov, cPress>= mtPress, cMvPr>= mtMvPr`, becomes true, what is interpreted as, respectively, as: *passivity time exceeded* (too much time without moving or pressing any piece of furniture), *moving time exceeded* (too much time continuously moving but not pressing), *pressing time exceeded* (too much time pressing but not moving), and *mixed-activity time exceeded* (too much moving and pressing simultaneously). Here, risk levels are more precise than in the previous RDS, what leads to an increment of the reliability.

When a risk is detected, the automaton goes to state `SendRisk` and updates the record `riskInfo`, with useful information containing the sensor ID of the last

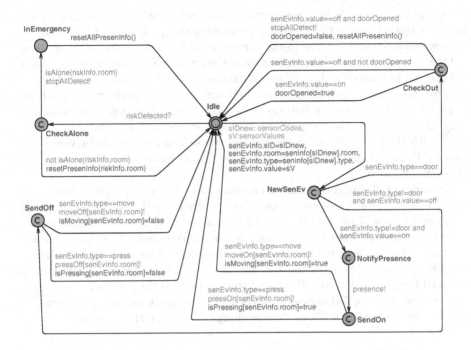

Fig. 2. SystemMonitor: process sensor events, receives risk alerts, and decides when to start the process of alarm generation

sensor-event received, the risk code, and the room code of the detector. Thereafter, the detector sends the action riskDetected! to the monitor, which must decide if the risk alert is not a false alarm, and if so it starts an emergency protocol. SendRisk (marked with C) is a *committed* state, implying that transition with riskDetected! must be immediately fired.

3.2   SystemMonitor TA

State Idle represents the situation in which the system receives a sensor event from the driver and forwards it to one of the detectors. Since UPPAAL only allows the modeling of *closed systems*, the interaction between the driver and the RDS is hidden. The local-internal transition from Idle to NewSenEv has an special *select label* that is used to non-deterministically generate a specific combination of sensor ID and sensor value, modeling the reception of a sensor event from the driver. After firing the transition, the senEvInfo record is updated with the sensor ID, location, type, and value, according to the event generated.

The risk-detection process must be automatically deactivated when the subject leaves the house and must be enabled again when he comes back. We suppose the subject is outdoors when a *door-on* event occurs, followed by an optional sequence of events and ending with a *door-off* event, and he is back when some sensor detects presence. Under this assumption, when the monitor detects that the subject is outside it broadcasts `stopAllDetect!` from state `CheckOut`, forcing all detectors return to `Idle`, thus preventing the generation of false alarms.

New sensor events are sent to the corresponding detectors via arrays of channel (e.g., `moveOn`). But, before sending an event, the monitor checks if the sensor value is *on*, in which case broadcasts `presence!` to all detectors, so they become aware of presence in some other room. This action may cause the transition from `Passive` to `Idle` in some room, since the subject may have left that room and may have moved to the room of the last sensor event. It is worth to mention that, with the type of sensors we consider, there is no way to differentiate between different people. The model just allows concurrent activity monitoring in different rooms.

We consider the system generate an alarm only when all people in the house are at risk (e.g., due to an escape gas fading); otherwise the subject is supposed to be under care. To decide if the subject is alone or not, the arrays `hasPress` or `hasMove` are used; for a given room, a true entry in any of the two arrays is an evidence that there is someone else in the house, whenever the given room is different from the one of the last sensor event. Hence, when a risk alert is received from some detector, the monitor first checks if the person is alone, and, if so, it goes to state `InEmergency`. This state represents the situation in which the RDS connects with a 3G modem in charge of alerting the caregivers.

3.3 Verification of the Model

UPPAAL provides automatic verification of TA-networks. We have verified a large number of reachability, safety and liveness properties [4,5] of the model, by formulating queries to UPPAAL model-checking engine, starting from a minimal configuration of the subject's environment[5]. It is not hard to prove that critical properties, such as those discussed below, also hold for an arbitrary infrastructure of the house, under the assumptions we have made, since detectors are independent of each other. We have checked that the model is deadlock-free and all control states are reachable. For example, reachability of *SendRisk* supposes the detector can send a risk alert; moreover, we have checked that a risk alert is sent to the monitor if and only if the invariants of the states representing activity levels are violated. That means a detector never asks for help, unless there is a true evidence of risk. These properties, among others we omit due to space limitation, assure the correctness of the RDS according to the requirements detailed in [7].

4   Conclusion

We have modeled a risk detection system for in-home elderly care, aimed to improve the RDS integrated in the home-monitoring platform described in [7].

---

[5] An apartment with a bedroom, with a move sensor and a press sensor, a bath with a move sensor, and a lounge with integrated kitchen, with a move sensor and a press sensor. The The entrance door, with a door sensor, leads directly to the lounge.

For that purpose, we have chosen a TA-network as a suitable formalism, resulting in a simple, but still powerful, model which can distinguish, for each room, several subject's activity-levels subject to timing constraints, with their corresponding abnormal activity-patterns (or detectable risks). Furthermore, this formal model allows us to verify the requirements of the system against the model. Hence, we believe it is worth re-design the existing RDS based on the model we propose. This way, the system gains in reliability, reaction time and ease of maintenance.

We have already developed a model-based implementation of the RDS and designed a tool to configure the system for a new subject easily. As for future work, we are working on an implementation that generate meaningful off-line logs in order to ease intelligent data analysis. Another interesting problem we are planning to address is providing adaptability to the system, in order to adjust the timing thresholds used for discriminating between normal and abnormal behavior patterns, so that the number of false alarms could be reduced.

Acknowledgments. This work has been partially supported by the Spanish MEC under grant TIN2009-14372-C03-01, TIN2011-28335-C02-02, Foundations for the Development of AAL Services and Applications, and through the project 15277/PI/10, funded by Seneca Agency of the Region of Murcia within the II PCTRM 2007-2010.

References

1. van den Broek, G., Cavallo, F., Odetti, L., Wehrmann, C.: Ambient assisted living roadmap. Technical report, AALIANCE (2009)
2. Fernández-Luque, F., Zapata, J., Ruiz, R., Iborra, E.: A Wireless Sensor Network for Assisted Living at Home of Elderly People. In: Mira, J., Ferrández, J.M., Álvarez, J.R., de la Paz, F., Toledo, F.J. (eds.) IWINAC 2009, Part II. LNCS, vol. 5602, pp. 65–74. Springer, Heidelberg (2009)
3. Loke, S.W.: Context-aware artifacts: Two development approaches. IEEE Pervasive Computing 5(2), 48–53 (2006)
4. Alur, R.: Timed Automata. In: Halbwachs, N., Peled, D.A. (eds.) CAV 1999. LNCS, vol. 1633, pp. 8–22. Springer, Heidelberg (1999)
5. Bengtsson, J., Yi, W.: Timed Automata: Semantics, Algorithms and Tools. In: Desel, J., Reisig, W., Rozenberg, G. (eds.) ACPN 2003. LNCS, vol. 3098, pp. 87–124. Springer, Heidelberg (2004)
6. Tripakis, S., Dang, T.: Modeling, verification and testing using timed and hybrid automata. In: Mosterman, P., Nicolescu, G. (eds.) Model-Based Design for Embedded Systems, pp. 383–436. CRC Press (2009)
7. Botía, J.A., Villa, A., Palma, J.T.: Ambient assisted living system for in-home monitoring of healthy independent elders. Expert Syst. Appl. 39(9), 8136–8148 (2012)
8. Tobarra, M.L., Cazorla, D., Cuartero, F., Pardo, J.J.: Modelling secure wireless sensor networks routing protocols with timed automata. In: Proceedings of PM2HW2N, pp. 51–58 (2008)
9. Hutzler, G., Klaudel, H., Wang, D.Y.: Towards Timed Automata and Multi-agent Systems. In: Hinchey, M.G., Rash, J.L., Truszkowski, W.F., Rouff, C.A. (eds.) FAABS 2004. LNCS (LNAI), vol. 3228, pp. 161–172. Springer, Heidelberg (2004)
10. Behrmann, G., David, A., Larsen, K.G.: A Tutorial on UPPAAL. In: Bernardo, M., Corradini, F. (eds.) SFM-RT 2004. LNCS, vol. 3185, pp. 200–236. Springer, Heidelberg (2004)

User Behavior Shift Detection in Intelligent Environments*

Asier Aztiria[1], Golnaz Farhadi[2], and Hamid Aghajan[3]

[1] University of Mondragon, Mondragon, Spain,
aaztiria@mondragon.edu
[2] Fujitsu Laboratories of America Inc., CA, USA
[3] Stanford University, Stanford, USA

Abstract. Identifying users frequent behaviors is considered as a key step to achieve real intelligent environments that support people in their daily lives. These patterns can be used in many different applications. An algorithm that compares current behaviors of the users with previously discovered frequent behaviors and detects shifts has been developed. In addition, it identifies the differences between both behaviors. Identified shifts can be used not only to adapt frequent behaviors, but also to detect initial signs of some disease linked to behavioral modifications, such as depression, Alzheimer's.

Keywords: Shift detection, Intelligent Environments, Disease detection.

1 Introduction

Ubiquitous Computing [12] refers to a paradigm in which a new type of relation between users and technology is established. This new relation demands recognizing the user, learning or knowing her/his preferences and acting according to the given current situation. Several systems have been developed for learning users frequent behaviors without disturbing them, i.e. in a transparent way. The Learning Frequent Patterns of User Behavior System (LFPUBS) [3], taking as a starting point the data collected from sensors, discovers users frequent behaviors and represents such patterns in a comprehensible way.

Once frequent behaviors of a user have been discovered, depending on the need and situation of that specific user, the patterns obtained can be used for many different purposes. An important application is behavior shift detection by comparing the current user's behavior with the previously discovered frequent behaviors. A shift from the frequent behaviors is not necessarily abnormal. This is because users can change their behaviors over time. Nevertheless, these shifts provide valuable information to the environment because they

- can show initial signs of some diseases (e.g. Alzheimer's disease, depression) or beginning of unhealthy habits.

---

* This work was done while Asier Aztiria and Golnaz Farhadi were at Stanford University, CA, USA.

J. Bravo, R. Hervás, and M. Rodríguez (Eds.): IWAAL 2012, LNCS 7657, pp. 90–97, 2012.

- can be very helpful to confirm diseases diagnoses. The environment can record historical data about shifts, so that experts in the domain can use them as additional information.
- can show change of preferences. Users can change their frequent behaviors for several reasons.

This paper develops an algorithm that compares the current behavior of a user with previously discovered frequent behaviors and identifies shifts. In addition, the proposed algorithm determines the criticality of different shifts for certain users and specific applications.

2   Related Work

Understanding human behavior has attracted a significant number of researchers, and much work has been devoted to modeling human behavior in order to act accordingly. Mozer et al. [11] and Chang et al. [4] were amongst the first reports on applications for ambient intelligence environments where user patterns were considered. Based on residents' lifestyle, models for predict occupancy were created. The models then were used for lighting control. Several other methods for identifying users' patterns have been proposed [8,7]. Holistic approaches considering the special features of intelligent environments have been also investigated [3]. A survey of these methods is given in [2].

Due to the novelty and characteristics of intelligent environments, complex model-based applications have not been developed. Human behaviors have been analyzed in many domains such as web navigation and activity workflow. Shifts in human behaviors have been examined in these domains [10,1]. However, it is necessary to obtain a specific solution taking into account the special features of intelligent environments.

3   General Architecture

Identifying shifts involves several steps. The first step is environment monitoring for collecting data. This monitoring task should be carried out as unobtrusively as possible. The next step is to infer meaningful information from the collected data. The objective of the transformation layer is to identify actions defined as interesting. The set of actions to be identified is denoted by $A = \{a_i\}$. The output of this layer is stored in the observation matrix, X. The observation matrix represents the occurrences of different actions, $a_i \in A$, in different timestamps. Given the observation matrix, the learning layer discovers the set of frequent behaviors. Frequent behaviors are obtained using the LFPUBS method given in [3]. LFPUBS first discovers the set of actions that frequently occurs together and then it identifies the order of such actions, defining each frequent behavior as a Markov chain.

Let F denotes the set of frequent behaviors of a user. Then $f_i \in F$ is a set of actions, $\{f_{i_k} : f_{i_k} \in A\}$, that forms a Markov chain with initial probability, $P_0 = Pr(f_{i_0})$ and the transition matrix $P = [P_{k,j}]$ where $P_{k,j} = Pr(f_{i_j}|f_{i_k})$.

The following scenario exemplifies the common behavior of a user. *On week-days Michael's alarm clock goes off ('Alarm,on') few minutes after 08:00AM. Approximately 10 minutes after getting up he usually steps into the bathroom ('Bathroom,on'), and sometimes he takes a shower ('Shower,on') and some other timer he does not. Then, he goes to the kitchen ('Kitchen,on') and after having breakfast ('Breakfast,on') he takes his daily pill ('Pill,on').*

Michael's morning behavior is discovered by the learning algorithm and represented as a Markov chain as shown in Figure 1. The transition probabilities shown in the chain indicate the frequency of that relationship.

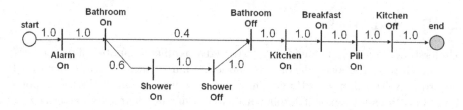

Fig. 1. Michael's morning ritual represented in a Markov Chain

Finally, the application layer allows the development of applications that can benefit from the discovered frequent behaviors. This paper proposes an algorithm for shift detection in user behavior.

4   Calculating Shifts

In order to calculate shifts in user behaviors, this paper develops an algorithm that compares the current set of observed actions from the user, $C = \{c_i : c_i \in A\}$, with all frequent behaviors, $f_i \in F$, obtained in the learning layer. If the current behavior matches any of the frequent behavior, the algorithm returns a likelihood value. Otherwise, the algorithm calculates the shift of the current behavior, C, from all frequent behaviors and determines the criticality of these differences.

Algorithm. CalculateShifts (F, C)

Input: Set of frequent behaviors F and current behavior C.
Output: Likelihood (LL), number of modifications, and criticality.

for each $f_i \in F$ compute $LL(C|f_i)$
    if $LL(C|f_i) \mathrel{!}= 0$ then return $LL(C|f_i)$
    else
        $calculateAllPosiblePaths(f_i)$
        for each path $\rho_{ij} \in f_i$
            $calculateNecessaryModifications(\rho_{ij}, C)$
            return $numberModification, modificationsCriticality$

4.1 Calculating Likelihoods

Given the current behavior, C, the first step is to determine if that behavior is part of user frequent behaviors, F. This requires comparing the current behavior with all previously discovered frequent behaviors $f_i \in F \; \forall i$. Recall that each frequent behavior f_i is represented as a Markov chain. Then, the likelihood is obtained as

$$LL\,(C|f_i) = \prod_{k=1}^{|C|-1} Pr\,(c_k \rightarrow c_{k+1}) \tag{1}$$

where $|\cdot|$ denote the cardinality of the set and $Pr\,(c_k \rightarrow c_{k+1})$ is given by the transition probability matrix for the frequent behavior f_i. In general, if for an $f_i \in F$, $LL(C|f_i) \neq 0$, the likelihood value implies the frequency of that behavior. On the other hand, having $LL(C|f_i) = 0 \; \forall f_i \in F$, indicates the current behavior is not frequent.

For example, consider the following three current behaviors and the transition matrix defined by the likelihoods shown by Figure 1.

C_1 = 'Alarm,on', 'Bathroom,on', 'Shower,on', 'Shower,off', 'Bathroom,off' 'Kitchen,on', 'Breakfast,on', 'Pill,on', 'Kitchen,off'

C_2 = 'Alarm,on', 'Bathroom,on', 'Shower,on', 'Shower,off', 'Bathroom,off' 'Kitchen,on', 'Breakfast,on', 'Kitchen,off'

C_3 = 'Alarm,on', 'Bathroom,on', 'Shower,on', 'Shower,off', 'Bathroom,off' 'Kitchen,on', 'Pill,on', 'Breakfast,on', 'Kitchen,off'

Then, $LL(C_1|f_1) = 0.6$, $LL(C_2|f_1) = LL(C_3|f_1) = 0$.

4.2 Calculating Paths

In order to be able to identify how different a current behavior from a frequent behavior is, all the possible behaviors that can be represented by the frequent behavior should be obtained. Possible paths included in a frequent behavior $f_i \in F$ are obtained using the depth-first search algorithm [6]. In addition, the likelihood of each path serves as a criterion to discard all the behaviors whose likelihoods are below a certain threshold. This condition is necessary because loops or self loops in the Markov chain can lead to infinite number of paths. Let $\rho_{ij} = \{\rho_{ij_k} : \rho_{ij_k} \in A\}$ denote the set of actions over the jth path for the ith frequent behavior, $f_i \in F$. Then, the likelihood of the path is given by

$$LL(\rho_{ij}) = \prod_{k=1}^{|\rho_{ij}|-1} Pr\left(\rho_{ij_k} \rightarrow \rho_{ij_{k+1}}\right) \tag{2}$$

where $Pr\left(\rho_{ij_k} \rightarrow \rho_{ij_{k+1}}\right)$ is given by the transition probability matrix for the frequent behavior f_i. Recall Michael's morning frequent behavior, f_1. It consists of two sequences of actions:

ρ_{11}: 'Alarm,on','Bathroom,on','Bathroom,off','Kitchen,on','Breakfast,on','Pill,on', 'Kitchen,off'

ρ_{12}: 'Alarm,on','Bathroom,on','Shower,on','Shower,off','Bathroom,off','Kitchen,on', 'Breakfast,on','Pill,on','Kitchen,off'

4.3   Calculating Modifications and Criticality

Recall that for $LL(C|f_i) = 0, \forall f_i \in F$, the algorithm should obtain the minimum number of modifications that matches the current behavior with any $f_i \in F$. For each $f_i \in F$, the algorithm compares the current behavior, C, with all the paths, ρ_{ij}, and obtains the set of modifications as well as the corresponding criticality values.

Identifying Modifications. The process to identify modifications is an adaptation of the Levenshtein distance [9]. Given two sequences of actions, C and ρ_{ij}, it calculates the set of modifications in C to get ρ_{ij}. In intelligent environments, the set of all possible modifications denoted by H is the union of:

- $H1 = \{insert(a_i) : \forall a_i \in A\}$: Insertion of an action if the user forgets to do an action.
- $H2 = \{delete(a_i) : \forall a_i \in A\}$: Deletion of an action if the user does an extra action.
- $H3 = \{subs(a_i, a_j) : \forall a_i, a_j \in A\}$: Substitution of action a_i with action a_j if the user does action a_j instead of a_i.
- $H4 = \{swap(a_i, a_j) : \forall a_i, a_j \in A\}$: Swapping of two action if the user does the actions in reverse order.

The algorithm for identifying modifications is based on the constructing of *distance matrix*, $D = [d_{m,n}]_{|C| \times |\rho_{ij}|}$, is constructed as follows:

Algorithm. ConstructDistanceMatrix (C, ρ_{ij})

Input: C and ρ_{ij}
Output: distance matrix (D) and number of modifications

```
for m = 0 to m = |C|
     for n = 0 to n = |ρij|
          if C(m) == ρij(n) then
               dm,n = dm−1,n−1 // no modification needed
          else
               dm,n = minimum(
               dm−1,n + 1 // insertion
               dm,n−1 + 1 // deletion
               dm−1,n−1 + 1 // substitution
               if((C(m − 1) == ρij(n − 2))&(C(m − 2) == ρij(n − 1)) then
                    dm−2,n−2 + 1 // swap
               )
return D, d|C|,|ρij|
```

The number of modifications is given by the value of $d_{|C|,|\rho_{ij}|}$. In addition, the construction of the distance matrix allows to identify the set of modifications $M_{ij} = \{m_{ij_k} : m_{ij_k} \in H\}$. For each value, the distance matrix records what modification(s) has/have been considered. The set of modifications is identified using the algorithm as identifyModifications $(D, |C|, |\rho_{ij}|)$:

Algorithm. IdentifyModifications (D, m, n)

Input: D and H
Output: set of modifications M_{ij}

if $(m, n)! = (0, 0)$ then
    if modificationsToConsider $(d_{m,n})$ == *empty* then
        modificationsToConsider $(D, m - 1, n - 1)$
    if modificationsToConsider $(d_{m,n})$ == $H1$ then
        $Mij.add(insertion)$; modificationsToConsider $(D, m - 1, n)$
    if modificationsToConsider $(d_{m,n})$ == $H2$ then
        $Mij.add(deletion)$; modificationsToConsider $(D, m, n - 1)$
    if modificationsToConsider $(d_{m,n})$ == $H3$ then
        $Mij.add(substitution)$; modificationsToConsider $(D, m - 1, n - 1)$
    if modificationsToConsider $(d_{m,n})$ == $H4$ then
        $Mij.add(swap)$; modificationsToConsider $(D, m - 2, n - 2)$
return M_{ij}

For example, the distance matrix for Michael's current behavior C_2 and his frequent behavior ρ_{11} is given by 2. In this case, 3 modifications are needed, specifically *deletion ('Shower,on')*, *deletion ('Shower,off')* and *insertion ('Pill,on')*. Figure 2 shows how the set of modifications is identified. The current behavior C_2 needs only one modification, *insertion ('Pill,on')*, for the path ρ_{12}. The current behavior C_3 requires 3 modifications for the path ρ_{11}, while it needs only 1 modification, *swap('Pill,on','Breakfast,on')*, for the path ρ_{12}.

	Alarm on	Bathroom on	Shower on	Shower off	Bathroom off	Kitchen on	Breakfast on	Kitchen off
Alarm on	0 ( )	1 (H2)	2 (H2)	3 (H2)	4 (H2)	5 (H2)	6 (H2)	7 (H2)
Bathroom on	1 (H1)	0 ( )	1 (H2)	2 (H2)	3 (H2)	4 (H2)	5 (H2)	6 (H2)
Bathroom off	2 (H1)	1 (H1)	1 (H3)	2 (H1/H2)	2 ( )	3 (H2)	4 (H2)	5 (H2)
Kitchen on	3 (H1)	2 (H1)	2 (H1/H3)	2 (H3)	3 (H1/H2/H3)	2 ( )	3 (H2)	4 (H2)
Breakfast on	4 (H1)	3 (H1)	3 (H1/H3)	3 (H1/H3)	3 (H3)	3 (H1)	2 ( )	3 (H2)
Pill on	5 (H1)	4 (H1)	4 (H1/H3)	4 (H1/H3)	4 (H1/H3)	4 (H1/H3)	3 (H1)	3 (H3)
Kitchen on	6 (H1)	5 (H1)	5 (H1/H3)	5 (H1/H3)	5 (H1/H3)	5 (H1/H3)	4 (H1)	3 ( )

Fig. 2. Generated distance matrix and identification of the set of modifications

Identifying Criticality. The importance of each modification is different. In Michael's example, the consequence of not taking the pill is far more important than forgetting to take the shower. Depending on each environment and the knowledge collected from experts, relatives, etc., a criticality value can be assigned to each possible modification. Let g define a mapping from set H to a set of all possible criticality values $V = \{v_i = g(h_i) : \forall h_i \in H\}$. Then, the criticality for a set of modifications, M_{ij}, is obtained as

$$Cr(M_{ij}) = \prod_{k=1}^{|M_{ij}|} g\left(M_{ij_k}\right). \tag{3}$$

For example, given the following criticality mappings (the lower the value, the more critical):

$$insert(shower, on) \xrightarrow{g} 0.9; \qquad\qquad insert(shower, off) \xrightarrow{g} 0.9$$

$$insert(pill, on) \xrightarrow{g} 0.2; \qquad swap((breakfast, on), (pill, on)) \xrightarrow{g} 0.4$$

we have $Cr(M_{12}) = 0.2$ and $Cr(M_{12}) = 0.4$ for the current behaviors C_2 and C_3, respectively. For a set of observed actions, C, the algorithm can consequently determine the behavior risk factor defined as:

$$\phi_i = \max_{\rho_{ij}} \frac{LL(\rho_{ij})}{Cr(M_{ij})} \tag{4}$$

for all $f_i \in F$. If ϕ_i is greater than a certain threshold, the current behavior C is declared as an anomalous behavior.

5   Conclusion

Intelligent environments suggest a new paradigm where environments adapt their behaviors based on preferences and habits of users instead of the other way around. For that, environments must learn users frequent behaviors. But, at the same time, users will not always behave in accordance with those patterns. On the one hand, users modify their habits over time. On the other hand, some other factors (e.g. age-related diseases) may influence the behavior.

This paper developed an algorithm that compares user's current behaviors with his/her frequent behaviors and identifies possible shifts. If user's current behavior is frequent, the algorithm determines its frequency. Otherwise, the algorithm identifies the shifts. Generally, such shifts can be used to adapt patterns. These shifts can also be used to detect early signs of diseases. In this case, the algorithm determines the criticality of a shift.

This algorithm is being validated using different datasets. Initial validations have been done using the dataset collected from Washington State University (WSU) Smart Apartment environment [5] which represents participants performing the same five ADLs (Activities of Daily Living) in the apartment: make a phone call, wash hands, cook, eat, and clean. Although, the participants had to perform the same five ADLs, performed set of actions could vary depending on each participant.

In order to validate the proposed algorithm, an adapted 10-fold cross validation process is performed. A simple 10-fold cross validation validates the frequent behaviors obtained using LFPUBS algorithm. Adapted cross-validation validates if the algorithm identifies shifts from frequent behaviors. The experiment verifies that the proposed algorithm was able to identify the likelihood when it matched a path, as well as identifying modifications to be done when needed.

References

1. Adams, M., Edmond, D., Hofstede, A.: The applicationso of activity theory to dynamic workflow adaptation issues. In: 7th Pacific Asia Conference on Information Systems, PACIS 2003 (2003)
2. Aztiria, A., Izaguirre, A., Augusto, J.C.: Learning patterns in ambient intelligence environments: A survey. Artificial Intelligence Review 34, 1–31 (2010)
3. Aztiria, A., Izaguirre, A., Basagoiti, R., Augusto, J.C.: Learning About Preferences and Common Behaviours of the User in an Intelligent Environment. In: Behaviour Monitoring and Interpretation-BMI-Smart Environments, Ambient Intelligence and Smart Environments, pp. 289–315. IOS Press (2009)
4. Chan, M., Hariton, C., Ringeard, P., Campo, E.: Smart house automation system for the elderly and the disabled. In: Proceedings of the 1995 IEEE International Conference on Systems, Man and Cybernetics, pp. 1586–1589 (1995)
5. Cook, D., Schmitter-Edgecombe, M.: Activity profiling using pervasive sensing in smart homes. IEEE Trans. on Information Technology for Biomedicine (2008)
6. Cormen, T.H., Leiserson, C.E., Rivest, R.L., Stein, C.: Introduction to Algorithms. MIT Press and McGraw-Hill (2001)
7. Doctor, F., Hagras, H., Callaghan, V.: A fuzzy embedded agent-based approach for realizing ambient intelligence in intelligent inhabited environments. IEEE Transactions on Systems, Man and Cybernetics 35, 55–65 (2005)
8. Jakkula, V.R., Cook, D.J.: Using temporal relations in smart environment data for activity prediction. In: Proceedings of the 24th International Conference on Machine Learning (2007)
9. Levenshtein, V.: Binary codes capable of correcting deletions, insertions, and reversals. Soviet Physics Doklady 10, 707–710 (1965)
10. Madhuri, B., Chandulal, A., Ramya, K., Phanidra, M.: Analysis of users web navigation behavior using grpa with variable length markov chains. International Journal of Data Mining and Knowledge Management Process 1(2), 1–20 (2011)
11. Mozer, M.C., Dodier, R.H., Anderson, M., Vidmar, L., Cruickshank, R.F., Miller, D.:The neural network house: an overview. In: Current Trends in Connectionism, pp. 371–380. Erlbaum (1995)
12. Weiser, M.: The computer for the 21st century. Scientific American 265(3), 94–104 (1991)

A Hybrid HMM/ANN Model for Activity Recognition in the Home Using Binary Sensors

Fco. Javier Ordóñez, Andrés Duque, Paula de Toledo, and Araceli Sanchis

Universidad Carlos III de Madrid
{fordonez,aduque,mtoledo,masm}@inf.uc3m.es

Abstract. Activities of daily living are good indicators of the health status of elderly, and activity recognition in a smart environment is a well-known problem that has been previously addressed by several studies. This paper presents a hybrid model based on ANN (Artificial Neural Network) and HMM (Hidden Markov Modeling) techniques in order to tackle the task of activity recognition in a home setting. The output scores of the ANN, after processing, are used as observation probabilities in the model. We evaluate our approach comparing it with classical probabilistic models using three datasets obtained from real data streams. Finally, we show how our approach achieves significative better recognition performance, at a confidence interval of 95%, in several features spaces, proving the hybrid approach to be better suited for the addressed domain.

1 Introduction

Over the last years, due to the increasing burden of healthcare on society, the need for automated, ambient monitoring systems is becoming more predominant [19]. It is important to find effective ways of providing care and support to the elderly at home, and automatic health monitoring systems are considered a key technology in this challenge [12].

Monitoring human activities of daily living (ADL), in order to assess the cognitive and physical wellbeing of elderly, is considered a main aspect in building intelligent and pervasive environments [16]. Systems that recognize ADL from sensor data are now an active topic of research, and wireless sensor networks are emerging as a particularly popular solution due to their flexibility, low cost and rapid deployment [8].

Previous approaches have shown how simple binary sensors have solid potential for solving the ADL recognition problem in the home [15], and can be applied in human-centric problems such as health and elder care [18]. In [11], binary sensors measuring the opening or closing of doors and cupboards, the use of electric appliances, as well as motion sensors were used to recognise ADLs of elderly people living on their own. Indeed, this kind of sensors is considered one of the most promising technologies to solve key problems in the ubiquitous computing domain, due to their suitability to supply constant supervision and their inherent non-intrusive characteristics.

J. Bravo, R. Hervás, and M. Rodríguez (Eds.): IWAAL 2012, LNCS 7657, pp. 98–105, 2012.

In different studies, several probabilistic models have been used to deal with the activity recognition problem, such as hidden Markov Models (HMM) [11], Conditional Random Field (CRF) [17] or Bayesian Networks [18]. But recognizing human activities has to cope with several challenges: each human performs each activity differently, the length of the activities is usually unknown and sensor data are noisy. However, temporal probabilistic models provide a good framework to handle the uncertainty caused by these issues. Specifically, the HMM has been successfully applied in many sequential data modeling problems, and has been shown to perform well in this domain [13].

HMM can be effectively used for recognizing human activities, but modeling the emission probabilities when observable variables are defined by a collection of binary values reach a high degree of complexity. Strong model assumptions, as the complete independence of every feature, must be applied. In this paper we postulate that the combination of the discriminative capabilities of artificial neural networks (ANN) and the superior dynamic time warping abilities of HMM's can offer better results for the dynamic pattern recognition task addressed in this domain. We have employed a hybrid HMM/ANN algorithm which exceed performance of the same HMM system using standard statistical approaches to estimate the emission probabilities.

This paper is organized as follows: Section 2 gives an overview of the type of data used in this study. Section 3 details the structure of the model employed in this work. 4 describes the experimental setting and experimental results obtained. Finally, Section 5 presents our conclusions and future work.

2   Binary Sensor Streams

In this paper we have employed datasets generated by a set of simple state-change sensors installed in several home settings. Each dataset is composed by binary temporal data from a number of sensing nodes that monitored the ADLs performed in a home setting by a single inhabitant. These datasets are publicly available for download from [1] and have been broadly employed in previous studies [2].

To provide a proper temporal format, the timeline is discretized into a set of time slices: measurements of the binary sensors taken at intervals that are regularly spaced with a predetermined time granularity Δt. Sensor events are denoted as x_t^i, indicating whether sensor i fired at least once between time t and time $t + \Delta t$, with $x_t^i \in \{0, 1\}$. In a home setting with N state-change sensors a binary observation vector $\vec{x}_t = (x_t^1, x_t^2, \ldots, x_t^{N-1}, x_t^N)^T$ is defined for each time slice.

In the employed data representation each time interval corresponds to a single data instance. The class of each data instance is defined by the activity label of the corresponding time segment. The activity at time slice t is denoted with y_t, so the classification task is to find a mapping between a sequence of observations $\mathbf{x} = \{\vec{x_{t1}}, \vec{x_{t2}}, \ldots, \vec{x_T}\}$ and a sequence of labels $\mathbf{y} = \{y_{t1}, y_{t2}, \ldots, y_T\}$ for a total of T time intervals (see Fig 1).

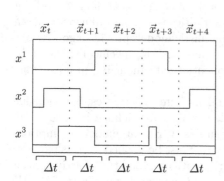

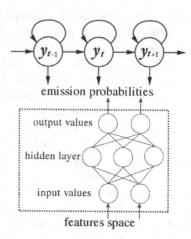

Fig. 1. Temporal segmentation and relation between sensor readings x^i and time intervals Δt

Fig. 2. HMM/ANN model structure

3　The Hybrid HMM/ANN Approach

The HMM/ANN model is a combination of a HMM and an ANN. Activities' temporal characteristics are modeled by the HMM state transitions while the HMM states probability distributions are represented by the ANN. A diagram of the HMM/ANN approach is shown in Fig 2.

The neural networks we used in this work are Multi-Layer Perceptrons (MLP) trained with the error back-propagation algorithm in order to maximize the relative entropy criterion. Hybrid MLPs systems have successfully been applied to speech recognition [3], time series prediction [14], handwritten text recognition [4] and digit recognition [7] problems. Several studies have shown that incorporating the classification power and discriminating capabilities of MLPs with the temporal segmentation power and statistical modeling of HMMs results in a system that is better than either MLPs or HMMs [5]. The benefits arising from using ANN as emission probability estimators are:

- They provide discriminant-based learning, supressing incorrect classification.
- They do not need to treat features as independent. There is no need of any particular assumptions about independence of input features and statistical distributions.
- They are robust against under-sampled training data, meaning that statistical pattern recognition can be achieved over an under-sampled pattern space.

In a hidden Markov modeling approach the emission probability density $p(\vec{x}_t|\mathbf{y}_t)$ must be estimated for each state $\mathbf{y}_t$ of the Markov chain. In previous studies with binary sensors each feature is modeled by an independent Bernoulli distribution

[11]. However, since in the presented model the emission probabilities are provided with a neural network, we took advantage of an important property of MLP, which is that outputs of such ANNs are estimates of posterior probabilities when trained for pattern classification. When the MLP contains enough parameters, the optimal output values are estimates of the probability distribution over classes conditioned on the input:

$$g_k(\vec{\mathbf{x}_t}) = p(\mathbf{y}_t|\vec{\mathbf{x}_t}) \tag{1}$$

where $g_k(\vec{\mathbf{x}_t})$ is the ouput value for unit k (associated with state $\mathbf{y}_t$) given $\vec{\mathbf{x}_t}$ at the input. Posterior probabilities like $p(\mathbf{y}_t|\vec{\mathbf{x}_t})$ can be transformed into *likelihoods* by Bayes' rule for use as emission probabilities required by HMMs:

$$p(\vec{\mathbf{x}_t}|\mathbf{y}_t) = \frac{p(\mathbf{y}_t|\vec{\mathbf{x}_t})p(\vec{\mathbf{x}_t})}{p(\mathbf{y}_t)} \tag{2}$$

At each time slice, the model transforms the MLP classification result to a class posterior probability, estimating the emission probabilities needed for the HMMs with better discriminating properties and without any hypotheses on the statistical distribution of the data.

4   Experimental Setup and Results

To properly evaluate the presented approach, we carry out the following experiments. In the first experiment, we define the feature space only as the binary values generated by the sensors, and compare the performance of the proposed approach with two models that have shown to perform well in this domain: HMM and CRF [10]. In a second experiment, we augment the feature space to evaluate the capability of ANNs to incorporate multiple constraints, including a new feature modeled by a different probability distribution: time. The performance of the hybrid model with both feature space configurations is compared. During the experimentation process and in the results presentation we have followed the recomendations stated in [6].

This section is organized as follows, we first give a description of the dataset and provide details of our experimental design. Then, we present the results and discuss the outcome.

4.1   Binary Sensors Datasets

The datasets used to validate the proposed approach were recorded using three different sensor networks. Each network was installed in a different home setting and was composed by a different number of sensors nodes.

Table 1 shows the different ADLs included as labels in the data and the number of separate instances per activity in each dataset. Time intervals with no corresponding activity are referred to as 'Idle'.

As previously mentioned, sensor data streams were divided in time slices of constant length. For these experiments, sensor data were segmented in intervals of lenght $\Delta t = 60$ seconds. This interval length is considered long enough to be discriminative and short enough to provide good accuracy labelling results [11].

Table 1. Percentage of instances per class for each dataset

Activity	HouseA	HouseB	HouseC
Leaving	49.74%	54.36%	46.27%
Toileting	0.65%	0.27%	0.62%
Showering	0.7%	0.6%	0.6%
Sleeping	33.42%	33.53%	28.46%
Breakfast	0.23%	0.52%	0.62%
Dinner	1.0%	0.42%	1.26%
Drink	0.1%	0.07	0.11%
Idle	14.12%	10.12%	21.97%

4.2   Experimental Design

The raw data streams generated by the sensors networks can either be used directly, or be preprocessed into a different representation form. In this work we have experimented with different feature representations, employed in other approaches [10]. The sensor streams have been employed using three different representations:

- Raw: The raw sensor representation uses the sensor data in the same way it was received from the sensors network. The value is 1 when the sensor is active and 0 otherwise.
- ChangePoint: The change point representation indicates the moment when a binary sensor changes its value. That is, the value is 1 when a sensor state changes from zero to one or vice versa, and 0 otherwise.
- LastSensor: The last sensor representation indicates which sensor fired last. The sensor that changed state last continues to give 1 and only changes to 0 when another sensor changes its value.

During the experimentation these feature representations were used standalone and combined. Combining the feature representations was done by concatenating the feature matrices.

As can be noticed in Table 1, datasets suffer from a severe class imbalance problem due to the nature of the data. The class imbalance problem can be defined as a problem encountered by inductive learning systems on domains for which some classes are represented by a large number of examples while others are represented by only a few [9]. In learning extremely imbalanced data, the overall classification accuracy is considered not an appropriate measure of performance. A trivial classifier that predicted every instance as the majority class could achieve very high accuracy. In our case, rare classes are of interest, therefore we evaluate the models using F-Measure, which can be calculated from the precision and recall scores [9].

The models were validated splitting the original data into a test and training set using a leave one day out approach, retaining one full day of sensor readings for testing and using the remaining sub-samples as training data. The process is then repeated for each day and the average performance measure reported. Significance testing is done at a confidence interval of 95% using a two-tailed student t-test and using matching paired data.

4.3   Results

In the first experiment we wish to determine which model gives the best results in activity recognition when the feature space is defined by binary values representing sensor events (as shown in Fig 1). Table 3 shows the F-Measure values for the three different models compared using this feature space. Each major column shows the different datasets (House A, House B and House C) and is subdivided into experiments with a different model: Hybrid model, HMM, and CRF.

Table 2. Experimental results (Hybrid HMM/ANN vs HMM vs CRF). Average F-Measure (expressed in %). Values whose difference is statistically significant are highlighted.

Dataset	HouseA			HouseB			HouseC		
	Hybrid	HMM	CRF	Hybrid	HMM	CRF	Hybrid	HMM	CRF
Raw	52 ± 14	41 ± 20	57 ± 17	**57 ± 09**	39 ± 13	38 ± 15	**54 ± 11**	15 ± 08	13 ± 10
ChangePoint	46 ± 13	**72 ± 14**	70 ± 16	57 ± 10	51 ± 16	49 ± 09	52 ± 12	45 ± 08	36 ± 19
LastSensor	61 ± 11	61 ± 15	66 ± 15	**64 ± 13**	40 ± 17	47 ± 11	**67 ± 09**	46 ± 12	35 ± 17
Raw&CP	54 ± 12	51 ± 20	**73 ± 14**	**55 ± 10**	28 ± 10	32 ± 19	51 ± 08	46 ± 10	42 ± 14
Raw&LS	68 ± 10	69 ± 13	67 ± 14	**62 ± 14**	37 ± 12	30 ± 19	**61 ± 07**	46 ± 11	43 ± 14
CP&LS	68 ± 09	72 ± 15	73 ± 14	**69 ± 10**	44 ± 09	39 ± 17	**67 ± 08**	40 ± 16	51 ± 11
Raw&CP&LS	68 ± 09	70 ± 14	73 ± 14	**62 ± 14**	42 ± 10	30 ± 17	**63 ± 08**	47 ± 12	46 ± 12

It can be noticed how the hybrid HMM/ANN method outperforms the other models, particularly for HouseB and HouseC, where the increase in F-measure is considered to be statistically significant, at a confidence interval of 95%, in almost all the cases. However, for HouseA most of the differences in the results can not be considered to be significant. But, in general terms, the performance of the proposed model improves the results over a non-hybrid approach when a feature space defined by binary values is employed.

The goal of the second experiment is to evaluate the performance of the hybrid model using two different feature spaces. The original binary feature space is augmented in order to evaluate the capability of ANNs to find optimal combination of multiple constraints for classification. An additional feature representing the time of each instance (time slice) is included as a continuous value.

Table 3. Experimental results (Original feature space vs Augmented feature space). Average F-Measure (expressed in %). Values whose difference is statistically significant are highlighted.

Dataset	HouseA Time Features	HouseA Standard Features	HouseB Time Features	HouseB Standard Features	HouseC Time Features	HouseC Standard Features
Raw	**58 ± 09**	52 ± 14	58 ± 10	57 ± 09	53 ± 13	54 ± 11
ChangePoint	**62 ± 12**	46 ± 13	**66 ± 08**	57 ± 10	**59 ± 08**	52 ± 12
LastSensor	63 ± 09	61 ± 11	66 ± 08	64 ± 13	69 ± 08	67 ± 09
Raw&CP	**64 ± 10**	54 ± 12	60 ± 08	55 ± 10	51 ± 09	51 ± 08
Raw&LS	**74 ± 08**	68 ± 10	62 ± 10	62 ± 14	63 ± 05	61 ± 07
CP&LS	**74 ± 08**	68 ± 09	68 ± 11	69 ± 10	71 ± 07	67 ± 08
Raw&CP&LS	**76 ± 07**	68 ± 09	**68 ± 08**	62 ± 14	66 ± 08	63 ± 08

Table 3 shows how the performance of the model increases in almost every experiment. Features addition gives the model more information for distinguishing activities. For Houses B and C, the performance of the model is slighty better when using the augmented feature space, although those improvements are not statistically significant in most cases. However, for HouseA the performance of the hybrid model using the augmented feature space can be considered significantly better.

5   Conclusions

In this paper we have shown how a hybrid HMM/ANN model can be effectively employed for activity recognition in a home setting. Using a MLP to estimate the emission probabilities of the HMM, we compared the proposed approach with other models that have shown to perform well in our domain. Comparing such models in terms of F-measure show a significative better performance of the hybrid method at a confidence interval of 95%, proving hybrid approach to be suited for the addressed problem. A second experiment on the features space dimension show how the hybrid approach capability to incorporate multiple constraints improves its performance when time is included as an additional feature. Furthermore, the HMM/ANN model do not require to apply model assumptions and can estimate the emission probabilities with better discriminating properties and without any hypotheses on the statistical distribution of the data, showing how the proposed system is a proper approach to deal with the addressed problem.

Acknowledgement. This work has been partially funded by the Ambient Assisted Living Programme (Joint Initiative by the European Commission and EU Member States) under the Trainutri (Training and nutrition senior social platform) Project (AAL-2009-2-129).

References

1. Datasets for Activity Recognition, http://sites.google.com/site/tim0306/ (accessed February 09, 2012)
2. Atallah, L., Yang, G.Z.: The use of pervasive sensing for behaviour profiling a survey. Pervasive and Mobile Computing 5(5), 447–464 (2009)
3. Bengio, Y.: A connectionist approach to speech recognition. IJPRAI 7(4), 647–667 (1993)
4. Bengio, Y., Lecun, Y., Nohl, C., Burges, C.: Lerec: A nn/hmm hybrid for on-line handwriting recognition. Neural Computation 7, 1289–1303 (1995)
5. Bourlard, H.A., Morgan, N.: Connectionist Speech Recognition: A Hybrid Approach. Kluwer Academic Publishers, Norwell (1993)
6. Brush, A., Krumm, J., Scott, J.: Activity recognition research: The good, the bad, and the future. In: Pervasive 2010 Workshop How to do Good Research in Activity Recognition (2010)
7. Cosi, P.: Hybrid hmm-nn architectures for connected digit recognition. In: IEEE - INNS - ENNS International Joint Conference on Neural Networks 5, p. 5085 (2000)
8. Jafari, R., Encarnacao, A., Zahoory, A., Dabiri, F., Noshadi, H., Sarrafzadeh, M.: Wireless sensor networks for health monitoring. In: MobiQuitous, pp. 479–781 (2005)
9. Japkowicz, N., Stephen, S.: The class imbalance problem: A systematic study. Intell. Data Anal. 6(5), 429–449 (2002)
10. van Kasteren, T.L.M., Englebienne, G., Kröse, B.J.: An activity monitoring system for elderly care using generative and discriminative models. Personal Ubiquitous Comput. 14, 489–498 (2010)
11. van Kasteren, T.L.M., Noulas, A., Englebienne, G., Kröse, B.J.: Accurate activity recognition in a home setting. In: Proceedings of the 10th International Conference on Ubiquitous Computing, UbiComp 2008, pp. 1–9. ACM, New York (2008)
12. Milenkovic, A., Otto, C., Jovanov, E.: Wireless sensor networks for personal health monitoring: Issues and an implementation. Computer Communications 29, 2521–2533 (2006)
13. Patterson, D.J., Fox, D., Kautz, H., Philipose, M.: Fine-grained activity recognition by aggregating abstract object usage. In: Proceedings of the Ninth IEEE International Symposium on Wearable Computers, pp. 44–51 (2005)
14. Rynkiewicz, J.: Hybrid hmm/mlp models for time series prediction. In: ESANN 1999, pp. 455–462 (1999)
15. Tapia, E.M., Intille, S.S., Larson, K.: Activity Recognition in the Home Using Simple and Ubiquitous Sensors. In: Ferscha, A., Mattern, F. (eds.) PERVASIVE 2004. LNCS, vol. 3001, pp. 158–175. Springer, Heidelberg (2004)
16. Turaga, P., Chellappa, R., Subrahmanian, V.S., Udrea, O.: Machine Recognition of Human Activities: A Survey. IEEE Transactions on Circuits and Systems for Video Technology 18(11), 1473–1488 (2008)
17. Vail, D.L., Veloso, M.M., Lafferty, J.D.: Conditional random fields for activity recognition. In: Proceedings of the Conference on Autonomous Agents and Multi-agent Systems, AAMAS 2007, pp. 235:1–235:8 (2007)
18. Wilson, D.H., Atkeson, C.: Simultaneous Tracking and Activity Recognition (STAR) Using Many Anonymous, Binary Sensors. In: Gellersen, H.-W., Want, R., Schmidt, A. (eds.) PERVASIVE 2005. LNCS, vol. 3468, pp. 62–79. Springer, Heidelberg (2005)
19. Zola, I.K.: Living at Home: The convergence of aging and disability, pp. 25–39. Baywood Publishing, Amityville (1997)

3D Object Reconstruction Using Convex Hull Improved by a Peeling Process

Ruben Machucho[1], Jorge Rivera-Rovelo[2], and Eduardo Bayro-Corrochano[1]

[1] CINVESTAV del IPN, Unidad Guadalajara
{rmachuch,edb}@gdl.cinvestav.mx
[2] Division de Ingenieria, Universidad Anahuac Mayab
jorge.rivera@anahuac.mx

Abstract. Several methods (discrete and continuous) for surface reconstruction have been proposed over the past years. Convex hull is one of them, which is the minimal convex envelope for a set of points X in a real vector space V. We present a method to 3D surface reconstruction which refines the convex hull by means of a peeling process with an adaptive radius. Tests with points of different objects, some of them from the AimatShape Project, were carried out, showing a better approximation than the one using traditional convex hull, and a little reduction in number of points used and computer time elapsed.

1 Introduction

Surface reconstruction is a problem that has been largely studied in computer graphics and vision. As a result, a variety of methods have been suggested to accomplish it. Such methods can be categorized as discrete, or continuous. Discrete methods take a set of points and compute combinatorial structures such as the Delaunay tetrahedrization or Voronoi diagram. Continuous methods take the set of points and deform a base shape (surface or function) until it fits the points. The function fitting can be local or global. Some approaches for surface reconstruction are: a) **Balloon fitting**, in which a surface S is iteratively grown by increasing its internal pressure; similar to 2D region growing but in 3D. The problem is that finding a seed surface automatically is not an easy problem. b) **Ball pivoting** [1], where a surface S is constructed from the set of triangles constructed from three distinct points in a set P, which can form a ball of radius ρ without containing any other points from P. c) **Power crust** [2], which reconstructs a surface S by making the observation that a surface can be represented by its medial axis, or skeleton, which is the set of all points that are equidistant to two or more points on S. d) **Fast level set**, where given an arbitrary initial γ surface, an energy function $E(\gamma)$ is defined using a distance function $d(x)$ and the energy flow is used to evolve the surface toward a better approximation of S. e) **RBF**, which tries to find F, an approximation of the signed distance function of the surface, given a set of points. F is represented as the weighted sum of the radial basis function $F(x) = \sum w_i \phi(x - c_i)_{i=1}^N$, where c_i is a constraint center, w_i is a weight, and $\phi(x)$ is a function that has global

J. Bravo, R. Hervás, and M. Rodríguez (Eds.): IWAAL 2012, LNCS 7657, pp. 106–110, 2012.

support. f) **Wavelets** [3], which uses a similar approach as FFT method, computing the indicator function from an oriented point set using Stokes' theorem. However, instead of using the Fourier basis, this method uses an orthogonal wavelet basis with compact support. A different approach consists of obtaining the **Convex Hull** for a set of points (the convex hull or convex envelope for a set of points X in a real vector space V is the minimal convex set containing X). Several problems can be reduced to the convex hull, for example, half-space intersection, Delaunay triangulation, Voronoi diagrams, and power diagrams. [4] describes applications of these structures in mesh generation, cluster analysis, crystallography, cartography, image processing, statistics, and sphere packing, among others.

2   3D Reconstruction: Convex Hull and Peeling Process

We modify the traditional convex hull (C.H.) algorithm in order to be faster. The method comprises the following steps: a) reduce the quantity of points to be processed (to get a fast approximation to the true C.H.); b) to use divide-and-conquer techniques and clustering to get the final C.H. of the surface S.

Reducing the Quantity of Points to Be Processed. This step quickly approximates to the true C.H. for S and is effective for degenerate cases; for example when data are unstructured, or when more than three of the selected points lie on a plane. In order to eliminate useless points, we do (see Fig. 1) first define a regular grid G with dimension $M \times N$ squares in the x and y directions, respectively, and with constant height (z direction). Then, for each square S_i in the grid, if S_i belongs to the boundary it is ignored (Fig 1.b; otherwise, if S_i has two or fewer points we keep the points undeleted; but if S_i has more points, we find the points with the higher and lower z-coordinate inside S_i (say, p_h and p_l respectively, as in Fig. 1.c), and then compute $\delta = min(M * K, N * K)/min(M, N)$ (K is the width/height ratio of S_i). Then we compute the distance of each point in S_i to p_h and p_l (say d_h and d_l), and compare: if $d_h > \delta$ and $d_l > \delta$, we eliminate the point.

To calculate the C.H. for the remaining points we use divide-and-conquer techniques and clustering.

Divide-and-Conquer and Clustering. The space is continuously divided in faces and a list of visible points is assigned to each one of the faces [5]. A point p is visible from a face f (plane, triangle) if p is above f, so the signed distance between p and f is calculated. To do this, a reference frame is chosen. Then the three points of f and p are represented with respect to this frame. After that step, the equation for the plane f and the normal n for this plane are calculated, and, finally, to get the signed distance between p and f, the inner product between p and n is computed. The center of an initial tetrahedron t_0, which is used as the initial convex hull, was chosen as the reference frame. Clustering the points for a list of visible points is done in order to choose the group that has the greater quantity of points to be processed in each step. A very efficient clustering method

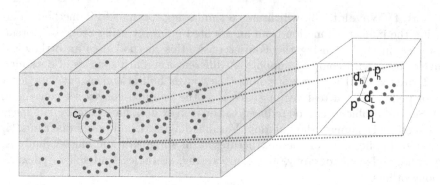

Fig. 1. Illustration of the process to eliminate useless points to calculate the convex hull

for points in 3D has been used, and only three groups are calculated for each list of visible points to be processed. Clustering the points is done if the quantity of elements on the list is greater than η. The algorithm for clustering used is k-means++ [6], and a value of $k = 3$ in step (c) has been used.

Refining the Convex Hull. Start by computing the Delaunay tessellation. The Delaunay tessellation for a set of points S consists of building a tetrahedrization T from S. The flips required to do the Delaunay tessellation are made with the tetrahedrons that do not satisfy the empty sphere criterion [7]; that is, they are not locally Delaunay. The flips could be required when a new point p is added to T. The number of required flips is variable, and there are of two types of flips: triangle flip and edge flip. **Triangle flip** consists in the replacement of two tetrahedrons t_1 and t_2, which are not locally Delaunay by three new tetrahedrons. The triangle flip is done if the union of the tetrahedrons t_1 and t_2 is convex. The union of two tetrahedrons is convex if one point p has only one visible face from p to t_2, where $p \in t_1$, $p \notin t_2$. **Edge flip** consists in the replacement of three tetrahedrons that are not locally Delaunay by two new tetrahedrons. To do the edge flip, an edge of degree 3 must be identified, that is, an edge shared by the three tetrahedrons. The geometric tests are computationally expensive. Therefore, it is better first to check if there exists an edge of degree 3 to do an edge flip; else, if the union of tetrahedrons is convex, a triangle flip is possible, otherwise, no flip is achieved. The candidate tetrahedrons for flipping are only those that participate when a new point p is added to T.

The Peeling Process. This paper proposes an adaptive peeling radius, and the process is as follows: first build a 3D regular grid B and sort the points inside each block. For each block, compute the number N of items inside it, and if $N > m$ (m is a user defined parameter, usually set to 20) get a point of the block as the cluster center. Then, for each point p, find the closest cluster C_c and assign to it. Then compute the adaptive radius and the average distance between the cluster centers and the points belonging to that cluster. Finally, for each tetrahedron t and its closest cluster, if the radius of the circumsphere of t is greater than d_i (average distance of such cluster), mark t as part of the final object; otherwise, eliminate the tetrahedron.

3 Results

The resulting method was applied to 10 different point sets, representing different objects (ranging from points of a banana, to points of a human heart). Figure 2 show the results obtained with one object (we show the point cloud, the ground truth surface, the convex hull, and the result with our approach with an adaptive radius). Also, we compare our results against the traditional convex hull results, comparing the number of points and tetrahedrons used to represent the surface, and the time consumed computing the 3D model. We find that on average we can eliminate 10 percent of useless points; the number of tetrahedrons obtained is almost the same with both approaches, but the time elapsed computing the 3D model was lower. However, it takes several seconds when the point set is dense, limiting the use of the method in real time systems. Some problems occurred when the surface defined by the set of points contained some irregularities. Currently, we are defining a topological measure which can help us to quantify how good/bad is the (topology of the) surface obtained.

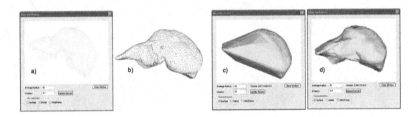

Fig. 2. Testing the proposed approach with points from a liver; it is shown the original set of points (a); the ground truth surface (b); the convex hull (c); and the result of the proposed approach (d)

Acknowledgments. The authors would like to thank to CINVESTAV Unidad Guadalajara and CONACYT, for supporting this work. They also like to thank the Visible Human Project team, for the cloud points repository free of charge available for research.

References

1. Bernardini, F., Mittleman, J., Rushmeier, H., Silva, C., Taubin, G.: The ball pivoting algorithm for surface reconstruction. IEEE Trans. on Vis. and Computer Graphics 4(4), 349–359 (1999)
2. Amenta, N., Choi, S., Kolluri, R.: The power crust, unions of balls, and the medial axis transform. In: Computational Geometry: Theory and Applications, pp. 127–153 (2000)

3. Manson, J., Petrova, G., Schaefer, S.: Streaming surface reconstruction using wavelets. Computer Graphics 27(5), 1411–1420 (2008)
4. Aurenhammer, F.: Voronoi Diagrams A Survey of a Fundamental Geometric Data Structure. ACM Computing Surveys 23(3), 345–405 (1991)
5. Barber, C., Dobkin, D., Huhdanpaa, H.: The quickhull algorithm for convex hulls. ACM Trans. Math. Softw. 22(4), 469–483 (1996)
6. Arthur, D., Vassilvitskii, S.: k-means++: the advantages of careful seeding. In: Proceedings of VIII ACM-SIAM Symposium on Discrete Algorithms (1), pp. 1027–1035 (2007)
7. Liu, Y., Snoeyink, J.: A comparison of five implementations of 3d delaunay tessellation, vol. 52, pp. 439–458 (2005)

emHEALTH: Online-Platform with Telecare Services to Promote Healthy Lifestyle for People with Multiple Sclerosis

Gonzalo Eguíluz, Begoña García Zapirain, and Amaia Méndez

DeustoTech LIFE Unit, University of Deusto, Bilbao, Spain
{geguiluz,mbgarciazapi,amaia.mendez}@deusto.es

Abstract. This paper presents a work of telecare and online monitoring of people with Multiple Sclerosis. The goal of our work is to support face-to-face sessions performed by patients one day per week with exercises at home the rest of the week through the online platform. In order to develop the system, we have used WEB technologies and multimedia technologies. All the tests have been checked by specialists. Initial results are very encouraging, not only for patients but also for their relatives.

Keywords: multiple sclerosis, telecare, online tool, web technologies.

1   Introduction

Spinal Cord Injury (SCI) and Traumatic Brain Injury (TBI) are two of the most important causes of neurological disability. The magnitude of the problem and its impact on health and social systems are two critical aspects. According to the Multiple Sclerosis International Federation [1], over 2.500.000 people suffer Multiple Sclerosis (MS) around the World and 400.000 in Europe. [2] In Spain, the incidence of SCI is estimated at $12\text{-}20/10^6$ inhabitants per year. The average cost for each patient is ~55.000 €/year [2], but vary substantially based on education, severity of injury and pre-injury employment history. If we value Disability-Adjusted Life Year (DALY) [3], the importance of rehabilitation in these people becomes even more pronounced, because it affects a large segment of young population with heavy reliance on family.

2   Methods

Our system is modular-designed, and each feature is represented by a module. Joomla, a Content Management System, acts as the infrastructure for data and modules handling. The data storage is powered by MySQL. Finally, the system runs with Apache server. To create these modules, we used WEB technologies like PHP[1],

---

[1] PHP is a widely-used Open Source general-purpose scripting language that is especially suited for Web development and can be embedded into HTML.

J. Bravo, R. Hervás, and M. Rodríguez (Eds.): IWAAL 2012, LNCS 7657, pp. 111–114, 2012.

JavaScript[2] and AJAX[3] and some multimedia technologies like Red5[4] and Adobe Flex[5]. Web technologies allow us to develop all the necessary modules based on the needs of users and multimedia technologies provides us the necessary to build online communication modules. We chose Adobe Flex instead of another Web technology like HTML5 because HTML5's necessary APIs for multimedia treatment (videoconference and recording) can't run properly on some web browsers like Internet Explorer 6, 7 and 8 or Firefox 3.x and above [4].

3   System Design

Figure 1 describes the system architecture of the telecare tool. The system was designed module-based (see Figure 2), so it can be configured in many ways, adding or removing modules based on specific needs.

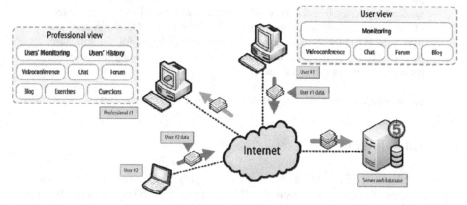

Fig. 1. System architecture

The system is web-based so it is only needed a PC or Mac with Internet and with a webcam. We have developed two views, one for the doctors/physiotherapist (in short professionals) and one for the users. Both views offer different elements and access level. Professional's view contains everything necessary to ensure efficient monitoring as well as all the necessary to provide content to the system. To add content, the professionals have several modules: exercises, questions, repository, forum, blog and users' management. Finally, to monitor users, the professionals have the monitoring module, which will be explained later, and the history module, which acts like the monitoring module but with the opportunity to select dates. The users' view offers a personalized monitoring module and a forum and a blog modules. Professionals and

---

[2] JavaScript is a dynamic scripting language supporting prototype based object construction.

[3] AJAX is a web development technique for creating RIAs running on the client's browser, maintaining asynchronously communication with the server in the background.

[4] Red5 is an Open Source server for presenting stream contents in Adobe Flash using RTMP.

[5] Adobe Flex allows programmers to rapidly develop cross-platform applications and their layouts using MXML and ActionScript language.

users have at their disposal two online communication tools: chat and videoconference. Both tools offer one-to-one communication. With the chat and with the video-conference users can communicate, without leaving home, easily and comfortably, while the professional manages times better and more efficient.

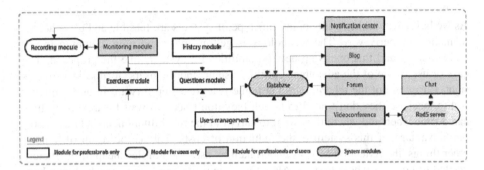

Fig. 2. Block diagram

The most important part of the system is the **monitoring module** in both professionals' and users' view. This module offers a day-by-day users' monitoring to the professionals, showing the carried out exercises, answered questions and comments. It also offers to the users their own monitoring, showing their day-by-day monitoring. The user's monitoring module offers a recording tool, so the users can record themselves carrying out the exercises. These recordings can help the professionals because they see the way the users carry out the exercises. Together with these recordings, the professionals assign questions, related with the exercises. These questions act like a questioner based on the carried out exercises, so the professionals can decide if the exercises are good or not.

4   Results

Concerning the technical area, we have developed a web-based rehabilitation tool, which offers all the necessary to get personalized treatments. The entire system was designed to be as efficient and user-friendly as possible, and we designed it together with ADEMBI (Asociación De Esclerosis Múltipe de Bizkaia) and EM (Fundacion Esclerosis Múltiple Eugenia Epalza), both related to the topic of MS. Moreover, the system was filled with all the material developed by ADEMBI and EM: videos, photos and texts divided into five main application areas: Speech Therapy, Physiotherapy, Neuropsychology, Occupational Therapy and Yoga, based on the needs of ADEMBI and EM. Thanks to the modularity of the system, each association/hospital/medical center may use their data without traumatic modifications. The system was tested with users and physiotherapists from ADEMI during three month, some of them inexperienced with computer. We chose two groups of age: 0-30 and 31-60, both male and female, making a total of 8 sub-groups. In order to estimate objectively, we developed some questionnaires for both professionals and users, based on the System Usability

Scale (SUS) [5]. We obtained an average score of 73, and according to SUS scale, a score over 68 is considered above average, so this system can be considered valid.

5   Conclusions

As we have seen in the results point, this type of systems are feasible and users accept them in a properly way. The technology is getting more and more common in our daily routine, and this opens up new possibilities for systems like the proposed. The ease of use is one of the advantages of this system, and the users' feedbacks prove us right. Carrying out the rehabilitation at home is a great step forward in users' quality of life, because they don't need to travel, they don't need to wait for treatment, they can decide when and where they want to carry out the rehabilitation, etc. Other important advantage of this system is the reduction of costs. This is the result of, among other things, the reduction of trips undertaken by users and of the cheap infrastructure needed to host the whole system. Also, the system fits any computer which can handle Adobe Flash properly, so this will not be an extra cost for the users, if they have a computer with that feature. Now, we are working on a hardware part to be connected with the system: a sensor blanket. This blanket will enable the professional to inform users' caregiver how long the users stay in the same position, avoiding the risk associated to the immobility, i.e., pressure sores. This blanket will be connected via Zig-Bee with the controller and the controller will send the data to the server over Internet. The data will be shared with the professionals in the users' monitoring part, monitoring in real time the position of the users and acting accordingly.

Acknowledgements. The authors wish to acknowledge the University of Deusto, which kindly lent infrastructures and material for this project. We would also like to express our gratitude to ADEMBI and EM for their work and finally, we want to express our gratitude to BIZKAILAB initiative of the Biscay Council and the Basque Country Department of Education, Universities and Research for their support.

References

1. Multiple Sclerosis (Internet) (2012), http://goo.gl/1ponq (cited June 2012)
2. Van den Berg, M.E., Castellote, J.M., Mahillo-Fernandez, I., et al.: Incidence of spinal cord injury worldwide: a systematic review. Neuroepidemiology 34(3), 184–192 (2010)
3. Metrics: Disability-Adjusted Life Year (DALY) (Internet) (2012), http://goo.gl/ds7ub (cited June 2012)
4. HTML5 Graphics & Embedded Content (Internet) (2012), http://goo.gl/rvFwo (cited September 2012)
5. Bangor, A., Kortum, P.T., Miller, J.T.: An Empirical Evaluation of the System Usability Scale. International Journal of Human-Computer Interaction 24(6), 574–594 (2008)

Pathological Vocal Folds Quantitative Parameters Exchange Using HL7 Standard

Amaia Méndez Zorrilla and Begoña García Zapirain

DeustoTech-Life Unit. Deusto Institute of Technology,
University of Deusto,
Avda. de las Universidades,24. 48007 Bilbao, Spain
{amaia.mendez,mbgarciazapi}@deusto.es

Abstract. This paper presents a proposal for the vocal folds objective parameters exchange according to HL7 standard. The authors, using digital processing techniques to image, process the previously recorded images by otolaryngologist in his office and extract information on each of the folds related to the amount of movement or size or if the patient has an abnormal vocal folds' morphology. Previous features are critical to study the patient's evolution, validate the treatment and contrast the diagnosis between different specialists. To ensure the access to all the information extracted from the vocal folds images, OBX HL7 messages are used, inserting additional fields which will be contained by hospitals' databases.

Keywords: Vocal folds, HL7, Vocal pathologies, Information Exchange.

1 Introduction

The abnormal production of voice or hoarseness may become a chronic health problem, in some cases. Dysphonia has individual and social consequences, affecting mainly the communication. To give chronic patients support, and in general, to all who suffer vocal pathologies, it is important to define objective parameters to measure and compare the state of their vocal folds in different periods of time. In addition, it is essential that everyone involved in the diagnosis, treatment and vocal rehabilitation, (such as otolaryngologist or speech therapists) have a common base of information that is provided by all.

Therefore, the main objective of this paper is to provide a message format where it can be introduced objective information in a specific way within an interoperability framework named HL7. Secondary objectives are described below:

- Identify which objective parameters of vocal folds images are interesting for treatment and rehabilitation evaluation.
- Establish OBX messages needed to set parameters within HL7 messages "unsolicited report" and enable interoperability between various specialists.
- Extract the parameters of vocal cord images by digital image processing.

J. Bravo, R. Hervás, and M. Rodríguez (Eds.): IWAAL 2012, LNCS 7657, pp. 115–118, 2012.
© Springer-Verlag Berlin Heidelberg 2012

2   Proposed Design

This section mainly describes the interoperability standard HL7 and digital image processing techniques necessary to extract the objective parameters of the vocal cords.

2.1   HL7 Standard

Health Level 7 (HL7) is a Standards Developing Organization accredited by the American National Standards Institute to author consensus-based standards representing a broad view from healthcare system stakeholders [2]. HL7 Defines a generic reference information model in which other standards are based. It aims to solve the communication between systems using XML messaging, but HL7 main goal is to enable interoperability between heterogeneous systems. Literature and actual implementations show us that to achieve interoperability between health systems it have been adopted DICOM [1], PACS and HL7 [2] standards. But mainly, it is HL7 the one which more affects to the ENT (ear, nose, and throat) specialty. Otolaryngology is not widespread because specialists tend to keep their evidence or laryngoscopy recordings on their own PC, and because in this specialty subjectivity plays an important role.

2.2   System Design

The proposed system consists of three distinct parts, and they are replicated in specialists' offices: capture devices, application that processes the images and the database.

Capture devices may vary in brand and features, but primarily equipment is characterized by the frequency of frames acquisition. In this paper we work with low speed recordings (25-30 frames per second). We use the heterogeneous *databases* which exist in hospitals, usually based SQL Server or Oracle. The *application* to process the images does not work in real time and it is installed in specialists' offices.

ENT Office has in-situ the stroboscope and installed the image processing application. Having described the main elements of the system we will focus on the two main elements to meet the targets: application to extract objective parameters and HL7 messages definition.

2.3   Vocal Folds Quantitative Parameters Extraction

The application stages to extract quantitative parameters are described in Figure 1. The quantitative parameters related to diagnosis and extracted thanks to the application are: movement measurements (variance and standard deviation), pathology size area (if it is exists), or angles in each fold, and glottal space area.

   A. Pre-Processing Stage. This stage is basic to unify the characteristics of the
       recorded images.

B.   Segmentation Stage. Main objective of this stage is the segmentation of glottal space to study later the edge of each fold [3].

C.   Movement Detection Stage. In this stage, the movement of each cord is studied to decide if one or both of the folds are paralyzed. To obtain these results block matching algorithms are applied.

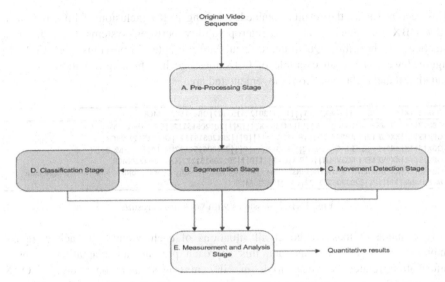

Fig. 1. Image processing application main stages

D.   Classification Stage. To carry out this classification, the Principal Component Analysis (PCA) –also known as the Eigenfaces Technique- is applied [4].

E.   Measurement and Analysis Stage. The last stage receives all the quantitative parameters and decides what diagnosis is the most appropriate according to the results.

2.4   HL7 Messages Definition

In this approach, we decide to insert the vocal folds measurements in HL7 Observation Segments (OBX). This kind of segments are used to carry key clinical results reporting information within report messages, which must be transmitted to the requesting system, to another otolaryngologist system, or to the medical record system. In this case, as usually, OBX segment is part of an ORU message (Observation Report- Unsolicited), but we insert between 4 and 8 new OBX segment with vocal folds quantitative parameters. The fields in the OBX segment can be reviewed in [2], but the exact fields where we introduce information are:

-   **ObservationIdentifier.** In this field, the description referred to each vocal fold is inserted, such as, "VF right" or "VF left" and the parameter: area, angle or movement.

-   **Units.** Here we write the unit in which will be measured the quantitative parameter: area in pixels, angles in degrees, or movement in percentage.

- **ReferencesRange.** This field permits us to indicate the normality range for analyzed parameter.

3   Results and Conclusions

This section shows the results obtained, resulting in the inclusion of information in HL7 OBX messages to achieve interoperability between systems from different practices and hospitals. Quantitative results are presented in previous work [3-4]. In figure 2 we can see an example of OBX message in which information has been added: left and right vocal cord movement and area.

```
OBX|1|TX|XX^TYPE^LN||0|PIX|0 - 1||||P|||201206151127|ORL^15421^MCR
OBX|2|TX|XX^VF RIGHT AREA^LN||0|PIX|10 - X||||P|||201206151127|ORL^15421^MCR
OBX|3|TX|XX^VF LEFT AREA^LN||0|PIX|10 - X||||P|||201206151127|ORL^15421^MCR
OBX|4|TX|XX^VF RIGHT MOV^LN||0|PIX|0 - 1||||P|||201206151127|ORL^15421^MCR
OBX|5|TX|XX^VF LEFT MOV^LN||0|PIX|0 - 1||||P|||201206151127|ORL^15421^MCR
OBX|6|TX|XX^COMENNTS^LN||Results: The patient has healthy vocal folds, and his progression in
favourable||||||P|||201206151127|ORL^15421^MCR
```

Fig. 2. HL7 messages with vocal folds results

HL7 standard does not cover all situations of each country or each complete implementation. Due to this fact, this approach presents an adaptation to insert information related to vocal folds in HL7 messages, and concretely, in OBX segments. To measure quantitative parameters is not also usual due to the quality of the images (sometimes bad) and the subjectivity of the diagnosis in otolaryngology.

The proposed scenario is not very common, because the otolaryngologists usually work in their offices alone, but during rehabilitation they have to exchange information with other specialists and it is essential. The insertion of data in previously explained segments suppose a great innovation in ENT area, because the standard HL7 has been centered in other medical areas, such as, pharmacy, radiology, etc.

Acknowledgements. This work was partially supported by the Basque Country Department of Education, Universities and Research. Also special thanks to Alexander Alonso DeustoTech Life researcher for his support.

References

[1] Mildenberger, P., Eichelberg, M., Martin, E.: Introduction to the DICOM standard. Eur. Radiol. 12(4), 920–927 (2002)
[2] Dolin, R., Alschuler, L., Boyer, S., Beebe, C., Behlen, F., Biron, P., Shvo, A.: HL7 Clinical Document Architecture, Release 2. J. Am. Med. Inform. Assoc. 13, 30–39 (2006)
[3] Méndez, A., García, B., Ruiz, I., Iturricha, I.: Glottal Area Segmentation without Initialization using Gabor Filters. In: Proc. of ISSPIT 2008, Sarajevo (December 2008)
[4] Méndez, A., Lopetegi, E., García, B.: FLDA and PCA classification supported by an adapted block matching algorithm to diagnose vocal folds paralysis. In: Proc. of Biomed. 2012 (February 2012)

MonAMI: Mainstream on Ambient Intelligence. Scaled Field Trial Experience in a Spanish Geriatric Residence

Alejandro Ibarz, Jorge L. Falcó, Esteban Vaquerizo, Luis Lain,
Jose Ignacio Artigas, and Armando Roy

Grupo de Investigación Tecnodiscap, I3A, Universidad de Zaragoza,
María de Luna 1, 50018 Zaragoza,
{aibarz,jfalco,evaquerizo,llain,jiartigas,armanroy}@unizar.es

Abstract. The MonAMI project was aimed to investigate the feasibility of the deployment of open platforms for Ambient Assisted Living (AAL) services provision and to test user acceptance and the usability of the services. The services were designed to give support in the areas of environmental control, security, and leisure. These services were installed and evaluated in a Spanish geriatric residence. The participants included elderly persons with disabilities, care staff and informal carers. The concept of the open platform proved to be satisfactory for the provision of the services. Furthermore, the usability of the technology was viewed positively and the overall result indicates that this system has the potential to prolong independent living at home for elderly people with disabilities.

Keywords: AAL, ambient intelligence, assistive technology, e-inclusion, elderly, mainstream technology.

1 Introduction

The increases in life expectancy and ongoing growth of the older adult population have led to new models of aging that empower people to have fulfilling lives in the residence of their choice. Independence is a critical issue not only for older adults but also people with disabilities who wish to remain at home and increase their quality of life.

The use of assistive technology is a successful strategy to help promotion of independence and maintenance of health [1-2]. Despite these positive outcomes, access to assistive technology is very restricted in developing countries. Availability of assistive technology is achieved by ensuring that infrastructure, personnel, products and materials are available. Appropriate assistive technology should meet users' needs and environmental conditions with services sustained, at the most economical and affordable price.

The European Commission has set up several activities under the 6th Framework Programme (FP), which have been continued under the 7th FP to initiate a Europe-wide dialogue among all parties working for an accessible and inclusive information society. MonAMI: Mainstreaming on Ambient Intelligence [3] is a 5 years long

J. Bravo, R. Hervás, and M. Rodríguez (Eds.): IWAAL 2012, LNCS 7657, pp. 119–126, 2012.

project, funded under the 6th Framework Programme by the European Commission, with 14 European partners and a budget of 13 M€.

2   Objectives

MonAMI [4-5] focus on:

- capitalizing on Ambient Intelligence (AmI) technologies to ensure that the services can be used without behavioral change
- building on top of mainstream devices and services such as TV based internet, nomadic devices, etc.
- doing initial experimentation in Feasibility and Usability centres and subsequent large-scale validation in Validation centres in five countries
- addressing economic viability and long term sustainability of such services in large communities in different Member States

MonAMI selects bouquets of services in the areas of comfort applications, communication/information, health, safety and security. It builds, tests and deploys these services and demonstrates that they can be economically brought through the future mainstream ambient intelligence technologies.

MonAMI focuses on services, platforms and usability: The technology platform is derived from mainstream technology. Usability requirements are identified, an evaluation methodology is selected and usability analyses are carried out.

The objective of the MonAMI project is to demonstrate that accessible, useful services for elderly and disabled persons living at home can be delivered in mainstream systems and platforms. This was done in close cooperation with users and by involving key mainstream actors throughout the whole process.

This report describes the work carried out at the living scale field trial (LSFT) site in Zaragoza Spain to test the MonAMI services and technologies in a living environment. It is intended to contribute to the body of knowledge concerning the testing and usefulness of ambient assisted living (AAL) services and technologies for persons with disabilities, elderly persons, their family and friends who care for them and care staff. Main findings are a positive proof of concept of open architectures for service provision for the elderly with impact on the exploitation and marketability, on the service update and new functions development and a potential support for improvement of quality of life for the final user and caregiver. It has shown potential as alternative and complementary solutions for dependency and its associated social cost and affection to quality of life.

3   Methodology

3.1   Technical Development

The technology base for delivering the MonAMI services is the MonAMI platform developed from mainstream, open-source components with a touch screen computer as the central element. Other parts are a Universal Control Hub as the user interfaces server, wireless sensor networks and a remote service management function. The total is a platform flexible enough to deliver a wide range of different services and facilitate future development and addition of services in a cost-effective manner. The services developed by MonAMI have been grouped into five packages: AMiSURE for safety and security, AMiCASA for home control, AMiVUE for home status information, AMiPAL for time management and AMiPLAY for games.

The selected services were first tested in six Feasibility and Usability centres with user tests in lab-like conditions. The centres have different profiles and address different user groups. For example, the Slovak centre [6-9]focused on analysing and enhancing the integration of inclusion services based on mainstream technologies in new EU Member States.

Once the services and applications were found to be feasible, usable and appropriate to user needs, a living-scale field trial was carried out at sites in Slovakia, Spain and Sweden. Many users tried the services in their homes and the impact and consequences have been analysed. The economic viability and long term sustainability of the services has been addressed in order to facilitate real mainstream implementation.

3.2   Living Scaled Field Trial

The LSFT in Zaragoza was carried out in a sheltered home owned and managed by the local government. This site was chosen to gain an insight in the deployment of AAL services in this scenario as well as to provide information concerning usability and acceptance of ICT support services for independent living.

There is an identified "independent living gap" that makes a difference in quality of life and social expenses in the transition of people from their own homes to shelter homes. MonAMi has set pilots in both sides of the gap: in the homes of elderly

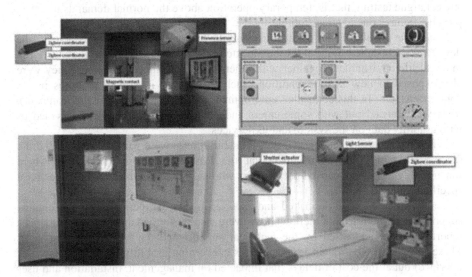

Fig. 1. Installation. The pictures show some of the sensors integrated into the LSFT as well as the Human Machine Interface device and a screenshot of the MonAMI system user interface.

persons living independently in their own apartments/homes in Sweden and Slovakia and in shelter homes in Spain for elderly persons. As such, the LSFT in Spain intended to provide insight on the acceptance, usability of AAL services by people at the least autonomous side of the gap.

The selection of participants was user-centred. The participants in the trial were 15 elderly persons with disabilities (users) living in the Romareda residential home (sheltered home) in Zaragoza, their carers (2) and care staff (7, from 12 recruited).

The MonAMI Living Scale Field Trial (LSFT) was the culmination of much of the work of the MonAMI project and provided the opportunity to field-test services developed within the project at three European sites. It was designed as one pilot project implemented in varying infrastructures at different locations in different configurations around the core set of MonAMI services to provide information for a coherent analysis with the additional potential for the comparison across geographically and culturally separate contexts.

4   Technical Experiments and Experiences

We had carried out various reliability and functionality test to ensure that the system is ready to be installed in the home environment. The tests were carried out in our laboratories, by qualified staff and all incidences have been recorded. After studying the test reports we identified the issues to be addressed and modifications that were necessary before continuing to the next set of tests. The actions taken depended on the relevance of the issue, and the possibility to modify within the project scope (e.g. limited time and resources). The tests were carried out on the integrated system as it would be installed in the home environment.

After this internal verification of the system, the device was put under stress/fatigue testing, that is, temporary operation above the normal demands to detect possible failures due to stress/fatigue.

When the result of this first stress/fatigue testing was found satisfactory, the devices were installed in the pilot flats located in Valdespartera, where they were run in a real life environment together with other devices. In this environment they were also exposed to new factors/conditions such as changes in voltage, failures in net connections, etc. In this controlled environment (yet closer to real life environment), trials were carried out with some carers and potential users. The trials provided us with usability data on the system and its services.

When the reliability, functionality and usability tests were passed, we installed the services in real home environments at the Residential Home Romareda where functionality tests were carried out by users who used the system and its services for a specified time.

Reliability tests were described and reported by the partners providing technical support for the field trial. Functional tests were also performed and several incidences reported to and addressed by the technical support and the LSFT technical staff. These tests led to significant improvements concerning usability (especially the user interface) but at the cost of delays that impacted on management, installation and user training.

The devices had to be adapted to the real conditions at the Residential Home Romareda where the users who are participating in the field trial live. There is a limited and defined physical space (placing of equipment, electricity, connections...) and time available for the trial. Also, the trial must not cause disturbances in the sheltered home.

Therefore, we carried out three types of testing in the trial:

- testing with care staff in the users' unit
- testing with care staff from the entire home
- testing with residents, carers (informal) and users.

Four main factors were considered in the selection of services to be tested in the LSFT:

- Results of the feasibility and usability testing, final reliability testing.as well as consultation exercise with external experts concerning their evaluation of how services could affect the different evaluation dimensions.
- Adjustment to project goals as framed by evaluation design to facilitate collection of information in evaluation dimensions that is comparable over the three LSFT sites (e.g. feasibility of larger numbers, using scenarios with carers or not, sheltered homes or private dwelling, etc.)
- Budget: Ability to comply with available budget for the project.
- Local needs: Taking into account individual LSFT sites and stakeholders' resources and expertise.

4.1   Gathering Evaluation Data

The MonAMI architecture is prepared to use a log mechanism to store and report log messages generated by the MonAMI platform and each of the services. The log entries are used to detect issues for debugging (reported to the service providers itself) and to analyse the usage of the services. The OSGi system and the respective service providers implemented a common log mechanism.

Each of the log entries is stored locally on the user gateway. They can be consulted in real-time using the web console. For off-line analysis, a MonAMI service takes the log entries and sends them periodically by e-mail. The period and the e-mail address are configurable and were configured by the installer.

Each LSFT site had a data repository for the log of service use. This log was developed such that each time a MonAMI service is employed in each home, data on the time and exact service are transmitted and filed back at the site. The log only records the User ID, so that the participant's identity is unknown to the staff member collecting the log data.

The purpose of the log is to record usage of a particular service. Any issues can subsequently be addressed either through re-configuration or removal of the service (at the users' request). The log is also designed to investigate any sustained periods of under-use or user-abandonment of the service. The log is a quantitative measure which can be used to support the users' self-assessed, anecdotal acceptability (or non-acceptability) of the services.

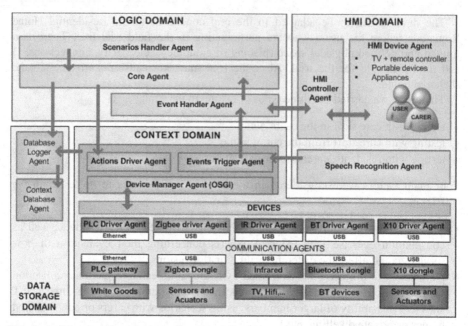

Fig. 2. Architecture. Description of technical implementation u based on OSGi architecture. The picture shows different technologies integrated into the system: PLC, Bluetooth, Zigbee, Lonworks or Infrared.

5   Results and Significance

We consider that the proof of concept of deployment of the technological architecture of the system has been a success, mainly due to its modularity and interoperability, and its potential to lower costs of equipment by introducing mainstreaming technologies. Awareness of the importance of the value chain, open platforms, interoperability, modularity and mainstreaming has been raised by a large extent.

Facility to change or add services has been a large advantage of current technological system. Anyhow, further development is needed to reach an off-the-shelf solution with more mainstreaming options.

We consider that the proof of concept of deployment of the system has been a success, searching and linking the elements of the provision chain ready to perform the experiment, integrating it in the environment of the shelter home, and proving and that the open platform is viable and potentially much very powerful in service provision, mainly due to its modularity and interoperability.

We have succeeded in raising awareness of the importance of the value chain, open platforms, interoperability, and modularity among the local stakeholders (government, organisations, industry) in Zaragoza. Having gained the interest and support of the stakeholders we are now making a number of national proposals to continue the work of MonAMI, to develop new services and to extend benefits to other groups (e.g. to demonstrate the extent independent living can be supported by ICT, to demonstrate the economic impact ICT services can have on the cost for support).

We identified several local stakeholders such as local public/private institutions and user organisations who could potentially be interested in the MonAMI services in various sectors. We held meetings with these stakeholders to check the possibility for integration of the services in schools, sheltered homes and homes for persons with disabilities and training/counselling institutions.

- *Compatibility of the platform with other existing and necessary platforms for service delivery (i.e. health and social services)*: This is clearly an advantage that the MonAMI open platform offers. Moreover, in the frame of Spanish national projects we are linking medical diagnostic devices for the home to this same platform.
- *Demonstrate the flexibility of the MonAMI system to add and update services efficiently (both convenient and with significant cost reduction)*: local institutional stakeholders we have worked with are convinced of these advantages of the MonAMi system.

Local government is considering the provision of an institutional framework and a budget to pursue actions concerning these suggestions with the Tecnodiscap research group, University of Zaragoza. The local government has demonstrated their interest in this work through their collaboration in the LSFT (e.g. involvement of the care staff, monitoring and registration of generated alerts, assistance with the recruitment and training of residents).

During the MonAMI project we contacted majority of user associations in our region, and had continual collaboration with the largest ones. With this action, we have promoted the concept of an open platform for delivery of AAL service provision based with focus on interoperability and mainstreaming, and culture of cooperation in finding new solutions integrating capacities and perspectives of implied stakeholders. During the MonAMI, a small local AAL community was created, which acted as a reference group, supervising and suggesting changes in services, validation methods, scenarios, timing, etc.

The combination of increased awareness of the importance of horizontal actions with a vertical market and a local AAL community are major achievements that the MonAMI project has reached on the local level. This may stimulate AAL services in the community and support more horizontal and standardisation actions in the future.

We consider the LSFT trial positive as a proof of concept of open architectures for service provision in a stakeholder ecosystem which implies the elements of the service provision chain and the primary stakeholders (carers and beneficiaries) and the quaternary stakeholders (political institutions). The raising of awareness and the creation of a local AAL community centred in the development of services and deployment of the LSFT have been important successes.

Acknowledgement. This work was supported by the EU under MonAMI (IST-5-035147).

References

1. Corchado, J.M., Bajo, J., Abraham, A.: GerAmi: Improving Healthcare Delivery in Geriatric Residences. Intelligent Systems 23(2), 19–25 (2008)
2. AAL Research Roadmap, http://www.aal-europe.eu/news-and-events/aaliance-presents-aal-research-roadmap/
3. MonAMI, http://monami.info/
4. Fagerberg, G.: Home services over a flexible platform. In: Gelderblom, G.J., Soede, M., Adriaens, L., Miesenberger, K. (eds.) Everyday Technology for Independence and Care – AAATE. Assistive Technology Research Series 29. IOS Press (2011)
5. Fagerberg, G.: Mainstream Services for Elderly and Disabled People. In: Emiliani, P.L., Burzagli, L., Como, A., Gabbanini, J., Salminen, A. (eds.) Home Assistive Technology from Adapted Equipment to Inclusive Environments. IOS Press (2009)
6. Simsik, D., Galajda, P., Galajdova, A., Alrabeei, S.A., Siman, D., Bujnak, J.: Ambient technology and social services for seniors. In: 2010 IEEE 8th International Symposium on Applied Machine Intelligence and Informatics (SAMI), pp. 287–292. IEEE Press, New York (2010)
7. Simsik, D., Galajdova, A., Siman, D., Andrasova, M., Krajnak, S., Onofrejova, D.: MonAMI platform, trials and results. In: 2012 IEEE 10th International Symposium on Applied Machine Intelligence and Informatics (SAMI), pp. 325–328. IEEE Press, New York (2012)
8. Balog, R., Szerdiova, L., Simsik, D., Galajdova, A., Onofrejova, D.: Intelligent rehabilitation devices and user interfaces. In: 2012 IEEE 10th International Symposium on Applied Machine Intelligence and Informatics (SAMI), pp. 359–364. IEEE Press, New York (2012)
9. Galajdová, A., Šimšík, D., Andrášova, M., Bujňák, J., Krajňák, S.: Socio-economical aspects of ICT based services for seniors in Slovakia. In: Gelderblom, G.J., Soede, M., Adriaens, L., Miesenberger, K. (eds.) Everyday Technology for Independence and Care – AAATE. Assistive Technology Research Series 29 (2011)

MonAMI: Economic Impact of Mainstream AAL Open Platform in Home Care

Alejandro Ibarz, Jorge L. Falcó, Esteban Vaquerizo, Luis Lain,
Jose Ignacio Artigas, and Armando Roy

Grupo de Investigación Tecnodiscap, I3A, Universidad de Zaragoza,
María de Luna 1, 50018 Zaragoza
{aibarz,jfalco,evaquerizo,llain,jiartigas,armanroy}@unizar.es

Abstract. The MonAMI project was aimed to investigate the feasibility of the deployment of open platforms for Ambient Assisted Living (AAL) services provision and to test user acceptance and the usability of the services. The services were designed to give support in the areas of environmental control, security, and leisure. The concept of the open platform proved to be satisfactory for the provision of the services. The usability of the technology was viewed positively and the overall result indicates that this system has the potential to prolong independent living at home for elderly people with disabilities. Furthermore, business opportunities in environmental control and security are shown.

Keywords: AAL, ambient intelligence, assistive technology, e-inclusion, elderly, mainstream technology, economic impact, business opportunity.

1 Introduction

The increases in life expectancy and ongoing growth of the older adult population have led to new models of aging that empower people to have fulfilling lives in the residence of their choice. Independence is a critical issue not only for older adults but also people with disabilities who wish to remain at home and increase their quality of life.

The use of assistive technology is a successful strategy to help promotion of independence and maintenance of health [1-4]. Despite these positive outcomes, access to assistive technology is very restricted in developing countries. Availability of assistive technology is achieved by ensuring that infrastructure, personnel, products and materials are available. Appropriate assistive technology should meet users' needs and environmental conditions with services sustained, at the most economical and affordable price.

With regard to individual, economic and social challenges by demographic trends, it is clearly stated that ICT can make key contributions to an independent living of elderly people. This refers to the following points in particular:

- ICT can reduce high expenses for health and care services
- ICT has the potential to provide individual solutions and hence to meet individual needs

J. Bravo, R. Hervás, and M. Rodríguez (Eds.): IWAAL 2012, LNCS 7657, pp. 127–134, 2012.
© Springer-Verlag Berlin Heidelberg 2012

- ICT has the potential to improve living standards
- ICT opens new business opportunities.

The European Commission has set up several activities under the 6th Framework Programme (FP), which have been continued under the 7th FP to initiate a Europe-wide dialogue among all parties working for an accessible and inclusive information society. Mainstreaming on Ambient Intelligence [5] is a 5 years long project, funded under the 6th Framework Programme by the European Commission, with 14 European partners and a budget of 13 M€.

2   Objectives

MonAMI focus on:

- capitalizing on Ambient Intelligence (AmI) technologies to ensure that the services can be used without behavioural change
- building on top of mainstream devices and services such as TV based internet, nomadic devices, etc.
- doing initial experimentation in Feasibility and Usability centres and subsequent large-scale validation in Validation centres in five countries
- addressing economic viability and long term sustainability of such services in large communities in different Member States

MonAMI selects bouquets of services in the areas of comfort applications, communication/information, health, safety and security. It builds, tests and deploys these services and demonstrate that they can be economically brought through the future mainstream ambient intelligence technologies.

MonAMI focuses on services, platforms and usability: The technology platform is derived from mainstream technology. Usability requirements are identified, an evaluation methodology is selected and usability analyses are carried out.

The objective of the MonAMI project is to demonstrate that accessible, useful services for elderly and disabled persons living at home can be delivered in mainstream systems and platforms. This was done in close cooperation with users and by involving key mainstream actors throughout the whole process.

3   Technical Development

The technology base for delivering the MonAMI services is the MonAMI platform developed from mainstream, open-source components with a touch screen computer as the central element. Other parts are a Universal Control Hub as the user interfaces server, wireless sensor networks and a remote service management function. The total is a platform flexible enough to deliver a wide range of different services and facilitate future development and addition of services in a cost-effective manner.

Once the services and applications were found to be feasible, usable and appropriate to user needs, a living-scale field trial was carried out at sites in Slovakia, Spain and Sweden. Many users tried the services in their homes and the impact and consequences have been analysed. The economic viability and long term sustainability of the services has been addressed in order to facilitate real mainstream implementation.

The MonAMI Living Scale Field Trial (LSFT) was the culmination of much of the work of the MonAMI project and provided the opportunity to field-test services developed within the project at three European sites. It was designed as one pilot project implemented in varying infrastructures at different locations in different configurations around the core set of MonAMI services to provide information for a coherent analysis with the additional potential for the comparison across geographically and culturally separate contexts.

4   Economic Viability

Guidelines were provided to assist the sites to establish service specifications consistent with social inclusion, commercial gain and the observation of public sector and legislative responsibilities and to ensure coherent deployment and evaluation methodologies.

Services to be evaluated in the LSFT were selected from those tested at the six MonAMI Feasibility and Usability Centres and had to fulfill criteria based on:

- expected improvement in cost efficiency, both private and public
- expected marketability of services

Experience from the feasibility and usability testing was taken into account, including

- mainstreaming ability
- economical viability
- European benefit
- potential innovative nature
- business opportunit

The objective is to promote awareness and interest in the continuation of the provision of the MonAMI services by local stakeholders. This was pursued among stakeholders in the various stakeholder groups. The stakeholders include those in the care and service for elderly persons sector as well as in other sectors such as education for persons with disability and independent living. In addition, its objective is to promote AAL community building locally, to involve a complete set of stakeholders to promote ICT services delivery via an open platform.

We have addressed the feasibility of the service provision chain, identifying and contacting local organisations/stakeholders who may:

- become service provider,
- take care of installations,
- take care of configuration and updates,
- provide/sell the devices that services require,
- provide maintenance.

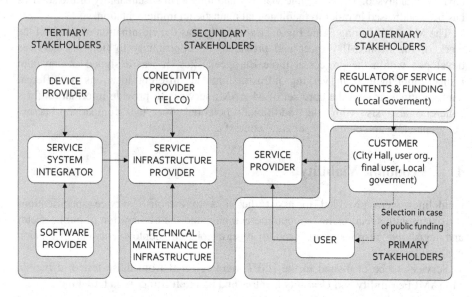

Fig. 1. AAL stakeholder categories, value chain and actors. This picture shows the different actors that are involved in the implementation of an AAL system. AAL stakeholder categories are based on AAL roadmap.

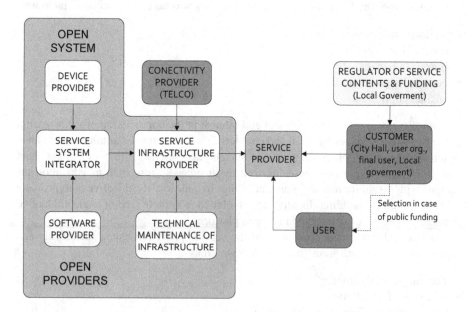

Fig. 2. This picture shows the AAL service value chain involving the system openness. This would include open providers that would lead to creating business opportunities.

4.1   Vertical vs. Horizontal Markets

In the AAL Joint Programme key thematic areas, which constitute promising markets ("quick wins"), should be identified in which R&D funding should have priorities. These „low hanging fruits" are service solutions based on existing technologies, standards and infrastructures. This will encourage SME and service/care provider participation and give necessary insights about user motivation and raise awareness. In these areas products/services, business models, markets intelligence, value chains and networks should be explored with combined resources from the public and private sector [1].

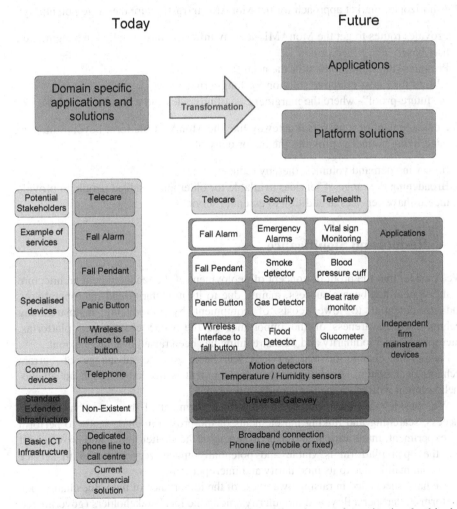

Fig. 3. Vertical vs. horizontal markets. The picture shows the transformation involved in the selected AAL services due to MonAMI implementation. A commercial monitoring domain application (column) become an open and flexible system with a great variety of technology providers involved.

Furthermore, no long-term results regarding the cost and labour saving effects of AAL technologies are available at the moment. These effects and their relation to the costs of AAL applications must to be identified. But firstly, a cost estimation of AAL system and services is necessary to quantify the cost-effectiveness of a particular AAL service considering the current ICT infrastructure.

Our goal in this part is to analyze some AAL developments done in the MonAMI European project based on mainstream technologies and open interoperable platforms from an economical perspective. This point of view represents another trend that unifies economics with technology and fosters to create cost-effective assistive technology for the home that the average user can buy, install, and monitor.

A horizontal market approach for the MonAMI infrastructure therefore potentially:

- Provides routes to get the MonAMI gateway infrastructure installed in a significant user base
- Provides "the right product for the need"
- Allows for a cost-effective solution for long-term care
- Is "future-proof"- where the marginal cost of upgrades and expansions are low

The development of a universal gateway like the MonAMI platform beyond the pure assisted living boundary provides the opportunity of:

- Increasing demand volumes, thereby reducing cost
- Broadening the range of services available for older and disabled people to provide nice-to-have services in addition to essential services

5   Results and Significance

We consider that the proof of concept of deployment of the technological architecture of the system has been a success, mainly due to its modularity and interoperability, and its potential to lower costs of equipment by introducing mainstreaming technologies. Awareness of the importance of the value chain, open platforms, interoperability, modularity and mainstreaming has been raised by a large extent.

Facility to change or add services has been a large advantage of current technological system. Anyhow, further development is needed to reach an off-the-shelf solution with more mainstreaming options.

We consider that the proof of concept of deployment of the system has been a success, searching and linking the elements of the provision chain ready to perform the experiment, integrating it in the environment of the shelter home, and proving and that the open platform is viable and potentially much very powerful in service provision, mainly due to its modularity and interoperability.

We have succeeded in raising awareness of the importance of the value chain, open platforms, interoperability, and modularity among the local stakeholders (government, organisations, industry) in Zaragoza.

We identified several local stakeholders such as local public/private institutions and user organisations who could potentially be interested in the MonAMI services in various sectors. We held meetings with these stakeholders to check the possibility for integration of the services in schools, sheltered homes and homes for persons with disabilities and training/counselling institutions.

Interest shown by these stakeholders is centered among Quality of life, help to the caregiver and improvement of cost-benefit regarding economical terms. In general, user associations are more opened to the way this benefits are assessed, while institutions have more specific requirements prior to their support for this system in service provision, as we have been gathering through the various meetings we have had with them:

- *Comparative study of MonAMI services with other similar services on the market*: main advantage of MonAMi system compared with market is the open architecture that allows for integration of different components without forcing the system to be limited to proprietary solutions. Local government have recognized through MonAMi LSFT that MonAMi system has the potential to give similar and superior services as the ones now in the market, in a more flexible and cheaper way, with the possibility to customize them to local singularities.
- *Demonstrate economic impact related to savings in the public and private expenditure with regard to the installation and maintenance of the system versus the cost of caring for the person without MonAMi system or with alternative solutions*: Also economical impact has gone out of the scope of the project as it is explained in evaluation study limitations and scope. This dimension will also be taken into consideration in next steps. For this we have made agreements of collaboration with socio-economic research groups and are starting to design new simplified models to tray and raise some evidences in medium term studies, which may later be verified by longer term studies. Still, simple inferences have been done together with local government staff in which the potential for this savings are recognized when associated to longer independent living at home.

Reader may appreciate that some crucial institutional local requirements, mainly cost benefit and assessment of user dependency improvement are still to be assessed. This pending work is necessary to have institutional promotion of MonAMi system for service provision and will be addressed in next steps. MonAMi has provided a starting point with technology and an initial set of services with an assessed evidence of acceptance and usefulness.

The combination of increased awareness of the importance of horizontal actions with a vertical market and a local AAL community are major achievements that the MonAMI project has reached on the local level. This may stimulate AAL services in the community and support more horizontal and standardisation actions in the future.

We consider the LSFT trial positive as a proof of concept of open architectures for service provision in a stakeholder ecosystem which implies the elements of the service provision chain and the primary stakeholders (carers and beneficiaries) and the quaternary stakeholders (political institutions). The raising of awareness and the creation of a local AAL community centered in the development of services and deployment of the LSFT have been important successes.

Acknowledgement. This work was supported by the EU under MonAMI (IST-5-035147).

References

1. AAL Research Roadmap, http://www.aal-europe.eu/news-and-events/aaliance-presents-aal-research-roadmap/
2. Europe is Facing a Demographic Challenge Ambient Assisted Living Offers Solutions, http://www.aal-europe.eu/Published/reports-etc/Final%20Version.pdf
3. Placencia-Porrero, I.: The information society in demographically changing Europe. Gerontechnology 6(3), 125–128 (2007)
4. Fuchsberger, V.: Ambient assisted living: elderly people's needs and how to face them. In: Proceedings of the 1st ACM International Workshop on Semantic Ambient Media Experiences (SAME 2008), pp. 21–24. ACM, New York (2008)
5. MonAMI, http://monami.info/

Authentication and Authorization in Ambient Assisting Living Applications: An Approach for UniversAAL

Pablo Antón, Antonio Muñoz, and Antonio Maña

University of Malaga - E.T.S.I.Informatica, 29071 Malaga, Spain
{panton,amunoz,amg}@lcc.uma.es

Abstract. In recent years the number of Ambient Intelligent systems is growing steadily, especially several fields such as domotic and remote teaching are practical applications of AmI. A relevant characteristic of these systems is sharing a double goal, comfort and simplicity of final users. However, the adoption of these scenarios lacks of a security basis. We defend that security is an essential feature to deploy in any kind of system. Security in conventional systems is a currently unsolved challenge and new attacks and vulnerabilities of systems arise everyday, in AAL systems the problem is even more complex since whether security challenges are hard in homogeneous solutions these escalate when moving to highly dynamic and heterogeneous systems. Several technical solutions have been proposed for specific security components in AAL systems, but the problem to solve the security of the whole system is still open. We address this problem providing a security architecture for the universAAL infrastructure. Among all the different security properties (trust, authenticity, integrity, confidentiality and accountability) we focus on the authorization and authentication, this paper presents a semantic based access control model for universAAL.

1 Introduction

A general consensus exists among computer scientists that in the future we will see an increase of open and distributed systems, and in the connectivity among these systems. Therefore this will encourage the need for rich and dynamic interaction between heterogeneous and open systems. An important aspect to consider is the convergence between fixed and mobile environments and the emergence of ubiquitous computing and communication, leading to the concepts of Ambient Intelligence (AmI)[1] and Ambient Assisting Living (AAL)[2]. Ubiquity is therefore considered to play a central role in the future of computing and communications. AAL and AmI emphasize on greater user-friendliness, more efficient services support, and support for human interactions. In this vision, people will be surrounded by intelligent and intuitive interfaces embedded in everyday objects and an environment recognizing and responding to the presence of individuals in an invisible way.

J. Bravo, R. Hervás, and M. Rodríguez (Eds.): IWAAL 2012, LNCS 7657, pp. 135–142, 2012.

Besides that, another essential concept for AAL environments is semantic information, which allow many heterogeneous applications to interoperate and we envisage that it will gain even more importance. Semantic information is being employed in different areas of computer science to support interoperability, ranging from artificial intelligence to agent oriented systems, semantic web, software engineering, knowledge management, and data management. However, the use of semantic information has been mostly limited to closed systems and has been provided mainly in a static and centralized way, based on predefined trust relationships, which is not appropriate to support the future of open computer-based systems.

Other element that increases interoperability and connectivity among different systems is AAL platform, which allows AAL applications and technologies be based on a middleware, which works as an intermediate layer between the operating system and the application itself[3]. In fact, in last few years, several projects have developed different platforms to deal with AAL environments. This paper deals with the authentication and authorization for a particular AAL platform, namely universAAL, which aim is to establish exactly such a cross application platform for AAL, health, home automation, entertainment, energy efficiency applications and services. Thus, we propose a global security architecture for universAAL fully compatible with the current specification, in such a way that the integration of security in UniversAAL does not imply drastic changes. However, the main contribution is the description of a semantic based access control.

The remain of this paper is structured as follows, section 2 makes an overview of the different AAL projects, their security mechanisms and different access control solutions. Section 3 describes our proposal for universAAL Security Architecture. In section 4 and 5 we present a scenario and mechanisms for authentication and authorisation. Finally, section 6 summarizes the most significant results of our discussions and describes some ongoing work.

2   Progress beyond the SOTA

The combination of heterogeneity, mobility, dynamism, sheer number of devices, along with the growing demands placed on software security in Ambient Assisting Living solutions, makes the provision of security increasingly difficult to achieve with existing security mechanisms and tools. Some approaches such as Shibboleth[4], PAPI (developed in TERENA workgroup), PERMIS [5], Radius[6], the Session Initiation Protocol (SIP)[7], iAccess[8], and the Lightweight Directory Access Protocol (LDAP)[9] (within the X.500 standard) are not tailored for particular features of AAL real scenarios. Thus, we advocate for a AAL tailored access control approach. Due to there are a certain number of heterogeneous devices with different capabilities and playing different roles, the most suitable solution is a semantic based approach since opposed to traditional schemes, the attributes required to access a resource may depend on the semantic properties of the resources. The allocation of the policy corresponding to a resource is not based on the storage structure of the resources but on the semantic properties of the resources. Besides, a semantic based Access Control (AC) can be tailored to interoperate with different directory services and universAAL spaces. Some approaches apply semantics to enhance authorization interoperation across semantically heterogeneous systems[10,11].

Currently, a certain number of projects have developed different AAL platforms, among them we highlight SOPRANO[1], Oasis[2], Amigo[3], MPOWER[4] and PERSONA[12] projects.

We could assume that security in SOPRANO depends on the developer and his knowledge of OSGi[5] and Java2 Security Architecture [13]. OASIS makes a great effort to create a hyper-ontological framework, helping communication and interaction of different services. Secure connection between devices and Oasis client application is out of the scope of Oasis, and this should be done by each service developer. In AMIGO [14] the authentication property is provided by means of a Kerberos based solution [15], and the authorization is managed using a Role Based Access Control (RBAC) approach [16]. MPOWER platform includes a middleware Security Service building blocks, which manages authentication and authorization of users and system components. Both AMIGO and MPOWER do not include semantic information, but they give services to deal with authentication and authorization. Persona nodes communicate through buses and data transmitted are encrypted using DES algorithm [17] with a pre-installed shared secret key. Several problems arise from Persona security solution, by extension universAAL inherits them from Persona. Some of the most relevant are that both authentication, authorization and confidentiality are not guaranteed [18].

3   Global Security Architecture

This section presents an overview of universAAL architecture with the security add-on modules. Before to expound the details, let us introduce some concepts that are important to understand universAAL platform. The core of universAAL platforms is its middleware, an instance of the middleware is an universAAL node, this instance is related to the AAL Space concept. AAL spaces are smart environments centred on human users. The devices embedded in such environments operate collectively using information and intelligence that are distributed in the infrastructure connecting the devices, this connection is done through a set of abstract buses that links all nodes in the same space.

After this brief description, we can describe in deep security architecture for universAAL. Security definition is given by a set of different properties as confidentiality, non-repudiation, integrity, etc. Affording all security properties is beyond the scope of this paper since it is a huge and unrealistic challenge. Therefore, we focus on security modules to provide authentication and authorization

---

[1] http://www.soprano-ip.org/
[2] http://www.oasis-project.eu/
[3] http://www.hitech-projects.com/euprojects/amigo/
[4] http://www.sintef.no/MPOWER
[5] http://www.osgi.org/Main/HomePage

properties for intra-space areas within the universAAL. Intra-spaces areas entails interactions among nodes belonging to some AAL Space, or the inclusion of a node in an AAL Space.

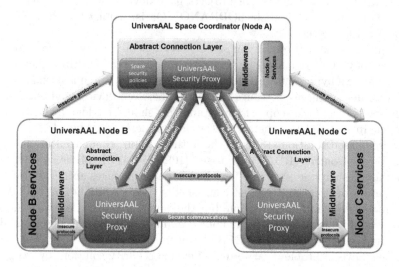

Fig. 1. Secure universAAL Architecture

The initial approach is based on the use of the universAAL security proxy module to perform secure communications, as we can see in Figure 1. Services are unaware of the security issues, then the same protocols are used in secure and insecure communications. In this way communications are carried out transparently, keeping the compatibility with current universAAL implementations, to achieve that goal two different communications (secure/insecure) are offered.

Figure 1 shows nodes playing different roles. UniversAAL defines that AAL nodes act with specific roles, such as AAL Space Gateway, AAL aware node or AAL Space Coordinator. The latter is in charge of creating a space and managing the configuration of it according to the pre-established profile. AAL Space Coordinator will be responsible to configure secure communications, to manage security policies and to perform the secure peering between the coordinator and nodes.

As it was aforementioned, the peering phase can rely on insecure basis (i.e. by using already available protocols like the set of UpnP), or can rely on the secure architecture (blue box in figure 1). In this case, the secure peering includes a negotiation procedure based on an interactive and privacy-enhanced exchange of credentials between the coordinator and node. According to the policy specifications and credentials provided, the secure peering can be successfully established (granted secure access to the AAL space), allowing nodes to use subsequent secure communication with the space through the buses.

4   Semantic Based AC Scenario

Once we have overviewed the global security architecture of universAAL, let us analyse the most relevant security requirements of this platform through a real world scenario.

As we previously mentioned in Section 3, universAAL works using the space concept, let us introduce the following scenario that includes two different spaces, namely "Bob Home Space" and "Alice Home Space". It is important to consider that spaces are user-centric areas administered by a person with special privileges (Space Manager).

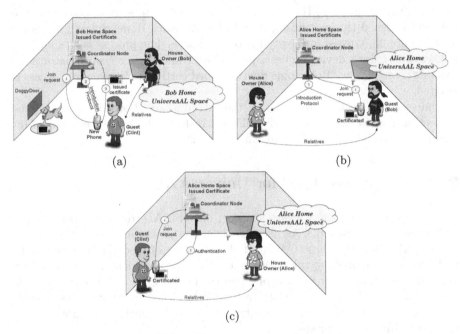

Fig. 2. Home space scenarios

Figure 2a shows the "Bob Home Space" scenario. We assume that there is a universAAL Space (Bob Home universAAL Space) created and managed by a Coordinator Node, which plays the role of Certificate Authority in this space. In order to describe the working process, let us show the case in which a new device (node) joins the space. Firstly, a new node (Clint cellphone) discovers "Bob Home Space". Secondly, it sends a "join" request. Then, "join" request is processed by the Coordinator, which starts an introduction protocol, which includes certificates distribution, since the new node is unknown. Once that Bob approves the introduction of Clint's new device in the space, a certificate is issued and sends to the Clint's device. From this point Clint will be able to use his cellphone in the space as a certified node with the privileges granted by the manager.

Figure 2b depicts the introduction of Bob in "Alice Home space" using the certificate issued by "Bob Home Space". The process is as follows, Bob's device sends a join request to space coordinator. Then, space coordinator requests a certificate and the certificate issued by "Bob Home Space" is given. Due to the fact that this certificate is not issued by "Alice Home Space", it is necessary that the Coordinator starts an introduction protocol, which allows the manager (Alice in this case) to add "Bob Home Space" CA in the list of trusted authorities. We highlight the fact that Alice trusts in this CA since Alice and Bob are relatives and she decided to add Bob's certificate CA in her space list of trusted CAs.

To show the most interesting appeal of our approach, figure 2c depicts how Clint (guest in "Bob Home space") requests access to the "Alice Home Space", for this purpose the "Bob Home Space" issued certificate is used. Once that the CA, which issued this certificate, is included in "Alice Home Space", as shown in the figure 2b, trusted authority list of this space. The process is as simple as follows, first Clint's device requests join, "Alice Home Space" coordinator node requests a certificate, "Bob Home Space" issued certificate is given and access is granted.

The scenarios security depends on the Introduction Protocols used to issue credentials (certificates). Currently, different technologies use the concept of Introduction Protocols to easily pair entities [19,20].

5   Semantic Based AC for UniversAAL

As we showed in section 4, every space in universAAL contains a list of rules that includes the trusted CAs. Nevertheless, the potential of our approach is given by the fact that these CAs are linked to a set of credentials according to preferences configured by this space manager. These credentials are based on semantic descriptions for the use of resources in the space. In this way, a node that is introduced in our space with a certificate issued by "My brother space" has access for using resources, in contrast to a similar device with a certificate issued by "My neighbour space".

Let us describe the process of inserting a trusted CA in the list of a particular space. This procedure is carried out through a set of semantic rules that are defined by the manager of the space. A solution based on the creation of a list of rules (i.e. SAML [21]) to be checked for granting access to the resources can be adopted, then we have a set of rules describing the certificate needed for every service defined. The main drawback is that a list of public keys of the authorities who signed those certificates is needed. Another strategy is based on a list of the authorities public keys, it is needed the public key of my space together with a list of all authorized keys. This includes a certificate and all delegated certificates. The main drawback of this strategy is in its management since the control over the delegation chain is not easy to handle when the number of authorities increases.

An advanced strategy is based on the fact that every authority declares a repository to include all semantic equivalences for accessing a resource (i.e. implemented by URL). The flexibility of this strategy allows different kind of equivalences (i.e. in service based environments, by means of web service description language WSDL; or in a LDAP environment, by the LDAP itself). The global idea is that every space contains a list of authorities, we notice that every authority in the list has an associated flag to set whether equivalent certificates are allowed in order to establish a delegation chain. The implementation of this strategy allows the storage of a short list that includes only one-hop delegation hierarchy. This strategy is flexible and can be implemented using any kind of existing attribute certificates, it is not restricted to a particular standard or an implementation. Subsequently, this approach can be used both for authentication and authorization purposes, allowing anonymous authorization, which can be highly interesting in some cases. Additionally, the space manager can create his own Authority Certification or use an existing one, which provides a higher level in flexibility terms. Particularly, in the context of universAAL, the consortium can define a set of Authorities according to the requirements for every real case scenario.

6 Conclusions and Ongoing Work

Many of the most important efforts in Ambient Assisting Living platforms fail in their lack of the appropriate security mechanisms, one of the most recent platforms in this area is universAAL. Security entails many properties with a huge number of challenges to afford. Evidently, addressing all of them is out of the scope of this work. However, we focus on the access control. This paper proposes a semantic based access control mechanism tailored for the universAAL platform. Ongoing work on this approach is the provision of an ontological semantic approach to information security. For this purpose, the creation of an ontology to establish an interoperable AC between different spaces in universAAL is under research.

Acknowledgments. Authors would like to thank Prof. Francesco Furfari for its comments and advice on the initial versions of this work and the universAAL consortium. This work is funded by the projects **DESEOS** (TIC-4257, **D**ispositivos **E**lectrónicos **S**eguros para la **E**ducación, **O**cio y **S**ocialización and **ICES** (TIC-6799, **I**dentificación y **C**ertificación de **E**lementos **S**oftware.

References

1. Aarts, E., Harwig, R., Schuurmans, M.: Ambient Intelligence, pp. 235–250. McGraw-Hill (2002)
2. Costa, R., Carneiro, D., Novais, P., Lima, L., Machado, J., Marques, A., Neves, J.: Ambient Assisted Living. In: 3rd Symposium of Ubiquitous Computing and Ambient Intelligence, Berlin, Heidelberg. AISC, vol. 51, pp. 86–94 (2009)
3. Hanke, S., et al.: universAAL - An Open and Consolidated AAL Platform. In: Wichert, R., Eberhardt, B. (eds.) Ambient Assisted Living, pp. 127–140 (2011)

4. Shibboleth Consortium. Shibboleth, http://shibboleth.net/
5. Chadwick, D.W., Otenko, A.: The PERMIS X.509 role based privilege management infrastructure. In: Proceedings of the Seventh ACM Symposium on Access Control Models and Technologies, SACMAT 2002, pp. 135–140 (2002)
6. Rigney, C., Willens, S., Rubens, A., Simpson, W.: Remote Authentication Dial In User Service (RADIUS). Technical Report 1645, Network Working Group (2000)
7. Rosenberg, J., Schulzrinne, H., Camarillo, G., Johnston, A., Peterson, J., Sparks, R., Handley, M., Schooler, E.: SIP: Session Initiation Protocol. Technical report, RFC 3261 (2002)
8. Koshutanski, H., Massacci, F.: Interactive access control for autonomic systems: From th eory to Implementation. ACM Transactions on Autonomous and Adaptive Systems 3(3), 1–31 (2008)
9. OpenLDAP Foundation. Lightweight Directory Access Protocol (LDAP): Technical Specification Road Map. Technical report, Network Working Group (2006)
10. Spyns, P., Oberle, D., Volz, R., Zheng, J., Jarrar, M., Sure, Y., Studer, R., Meersman, R.: OntoWeb - A Semantic Web Community Portal. In: Karagiannis, D., Reimer, U. (eds.) PAKM 2002. LNCS (LNAI), vol. 2569, pp. 189–200. Springer, Heidelberg (2002)
11. Jacek, K., Vitvar, T., Fensel, D.: D3.4.3 MicroWSMO and hRESTS (2008)
12. Tazari, M.-R., Furfari, F., Ramos, J.-P.L., Ferro, E.: The PERSONA Service Platform for AAL Spaces. In: Nakashima, H., Aghajan, H., Augusto, J.C. (eds.) Handbook of Ambient Intelligence and Smart Environments, pp. 1171–1199. Springer US, Boston (2010)
13. Gong, L., Ellison, G., Dageforde, M.: Inside JavaTM 2 Platform Security: Architecture, API Design, and Implementation, 2nd edn. Prentice Hall (2003)
14. Ahler, M., Grinewitschus, V., Ressel, C., Miranda, J.M., Ramos, Á., Mevissen, R., Tobies, S.: Detailed Design of the Amigo Middleware Core Security & Privacy, Content Distribution, Data Storage. Technical report (2005)
15. Miller, S.P., Neuman, B.C., Schiller, J.I., Saltzer, J.H.: Kerberos authentication and authorization system. In: Project Athena Technical Plan, pp. 1–32 (1987)
16. Ferraiolo, D.F., Kuhn, D.R.: Role-Based Access Controls. In: 15th National Computer Security Conference, vol. 2, pp. 554–563. Artech House Publishers, Baltimore (1992)
17. National Institute of Standards and Technology. Data encryption standard (des) (1999)
18. Kelly, S.: Aruba Networks. Security Implications of Using the Data Encryption Standard (DES). Technical report, Network Working Group (2006)
19. Scarfone, K., Padgette, J.: Guide to Bluetooth security. NIST Special Publication, 800:121 (2008)
20. Wi-fi Alliance. Wi-Fi Protected Setup Specification, pp. 1–110 (December 2006)
21. OASIS Security Services TC. SAML 2.0 (2005)

Could Virtual Reality Be an Effective Tool to Combat Obesity and Sedentariness in Children? Results from Two Research Studies

Jaime Guixeres[1], Ausias Cebolla[2], Julio Alvarez[3], Juan Francisco Lison[4],
Laura Cantero[3], Patricia Escobar[2], Rosa Baños[2], Cristina Botella[2], Empar Lurbe[3],
Javier Saiz[1], and Mariano Alcañiz[1]

[1] I3BH (Labhuman), Polytechnic University of Valencia, Spain
{jguixeres,jsaiz,malcaniz}@i3bh.es
[2] Universitat Jaume I, Ciber Fisiopatologia de la Obesidad y la Nutrición (CIBEROBN), Spain
{acebolla,botella}@labpsitec.uji.es, banos@uv.es
[3] Obesity and Cardiovascular Risk Unit, Pediatric Department, HGUV, CIBEROBN, Spain
alvarez_jul@gva.es, empar_lurbe@uv.es
[4] CEU Cardenal Herrera University
Valencia, Spain
juanfran@uch.ceu.es

Abstract. Virtual Reality (VR) could be interesting tool to combat obesity and sedentariness in children. Objective is to study possibilities of VR during aerobic exercise in children obese and normal weight . Physiological (cardiovascular and metabolic response with biomedical sensors (smart fabrics TIAS)) and psychological responses have been collected. First study (n=90), a commercial platform was tested as support to aerobic exercise in a treadmill. Results showed more physiological effort by obese group and limitations to measure effort perception with Borg scale especially in obese group. In second study (n=126) a new VR platform was developed (VREP) and tested ,all the boys completed both conditions (same Aerobic exercise with/without support VR). 59.5% felt more effort in the traditional condition The vast majority of the participants liked the idea of combining physical activity with VR as a form of treatment to increase physical activity.

Keywords: Virtual Reality, Children Obesity, Smart Fabrics, Physical Activity, Physiological Response, Active Gaming.

1 Introduction

1.1 Physical Activity as Obesity Treatment

Physical inactivity has been identified as the fourth leading risk factor for global mortality (6% of deaths globally). Overweight and obesity are responsible for 5% of global mortality.

J. Bravo, R. Hervás, and M. Rodríguez (Eds.): IWAAL 2012, LNCS 7657, pp. 143–150, 2012.
© Springer-Verlag Berlin Heidelberg 2012

The prevalence of overweight/obesity (OW/OB) among children and adolescents, which has significantly increased by 30% in recent decades, has become a serious public health concern in all industrialized countries [1].

PA in addition to dietary changes has proven to be beneficial to improving body composition, blood pressure levels, lipid profile, insulin sensitivity, self esteem, neurocognitive function and cardio-respiratory fitness (CRF) [2] . The impossibility to perform the kind of PA usually recommended (type, duration, frequency and intensity), the lack of a clear statement about its specific goal and the fact that the prescribed physical activity is not enjoyable, are some of the reasons to explain the low compliance and efficacy of paediatric obesity treatment programmes [3].

It is necessary to explore new ways to prescribe PA as part of the treatment of obesity in children and adolescents that takes into account the orthopedic, fitness and behavioral particularities of these populations. It is believed that technology could present new possibilities in this area.

1.2   Virtual Reality

Virtual reality technology allows the creation of three-dimensional environments, within which people can interact and be motivated, recorded, and measured, thereby offering possibilities for clinical assessment and intervention that are not possible with traditional methods [4].

As regards children and adolescents, the use of VR technology in these populations is less common. It has been employed in children with disabilities (autism, brain damage, motor impairment) [5], psychological phobias and behavioral disorders [6] and teaching, but it has been mainly used for entertainment purposes. One the most important ideas around the benefits of virtual reality is the manner in which a person becomes more engaged in a test, treatment, or training activity if he/she is motivated to participate by some form of digital gameplay embedded in a VE.

More recently, work has been done on the use of VR in rehabilitation and as a motivator of physical activity [7].Its effectiveness in these areas is based on the assumption that the user becomes immersed in an environment that simulates beneficial, familiar or novel audio/visual stimuli [8].

The two studies presented have been designed to test the acceptance and the physiological influence of VR during physical activity in children (obese and normal weight). In the first study, a commercial platform was employed and in the second study a new VR platform developed by our group was tested (VREP).

This article focuses on the comparison of traditional aerobic exercise with and without the support of virtual reality with the aim of testing **three main hypotheses**:

1. Smart shirt will be enough as biofeedback monitoring tool during VR with aerobic exercise
2. There will be no significant differences in physiological response to and possible influence of virtual reality during aerobic exercise.
3. The patients' acceptance of making aerobic exercise will increase with VR support.

2   Study 1

2.1   Methods

The objective of this study is to analyse the impact of the use of a commercial VR exergaming platform (WII Fit) to support the practice of traditional exercise, such as brisk walking, on physiological and psychological variables in two different populations of children and adolescents (normal weight (NWG) and obese (BMI > 97th per) or overweight (BMI > 85th per) (OWOG)).

A total of 90 children with ages ranging from 9 to 13 years participated in this study.

After anthropometric measurements, the children were fitted with physiological sensors. The protocol consists of a Brisk Walking on a treadmill at two different speeds (4.2 km/h & 5.7 km/h) (5 minutes on each stage). One randomized group with VR support and the other group without VR support). After exercise psychology instruments were answered.

The instruments employed were:

Physiological Measurement

- A smart shirt developed by our group was integrated into the VR platform to monitor the physiological response Therapy Interface Activity Sensor (TIAS) s a multi-parameter wireless electronic shirt that records the physiological response and movement of the patient [9]
- FitMate PRO indirect calorimeter (Cosmed, Rome, Italy)

Questionnaires

- Physical Activity Enjoyment Scale (PACES for children) (Fernandez, 2008)
- Sports Habits: used to assess the participants' sport-playing habits (Kowalski, 1997)
- Computer Game Habits
- Acceptability questions
- Borg's Perceived Exertion Scale (Borg, 1982)

2.2   Results

Descriptive Data

Eighty-seven participants were included in the data analysis (45 male). The mean BMIz was -0.03 (SD=.86) for the NWG and 2.44 (SD=.71). There were no significant differences in BMI regarding conditions (F=.700) or gender (F=.277). Most participants spend more than half an hour playing sports or doing physical activity two days per week (37.8%; no significant differences between groups (NS) X2=.173).

Almost all participants had a video-game console or computer at home (95.5%; (NS) X^2=.586), and liked to play computer games (90.9%; (NS) X^2=.09). The majority of them (64.4%) had an active video game console (WII or Kinect), and played it at least one day a week ((NS) X^2=.967). Regarding the PACES scale, the average score was 17.5 (SD=1.5). A one-way ANOVA analysis did not show significant differences between groups or conditions.

Acceptability

The acceptability questionnaire shows that 85.7% of the participants agreed with the idea to use a VR exergaming platform as a clinical tool prescribed by a clinician (M=5.4 (max: 7); SD=1.6). 82.2% agreed with the idea of coming back and repeating the exercise (M=5.6; SD=1.6). There were no significant differences in the responses between NWG and OWOG.

Physiological Measures

In order to analyze the effect of a VR exergaming platform on physiological measures, an ANCOVA analysis with two between-group levels 2 (group: NWG vs. OWOG.) x 2 (condition: Traditional vs. VR Exergaming) was applied. PACES scores, PA habits, video gaming habits and age were used as covariables.

The descriptive data is shown in table 2. The results of the ANCOVA over HR show a significant effect between groups [F(1.83)=11.939; p<.001; η2=.12], with OWOG scoring than NWG. But there are no differences between condition (Traditional vs VR) or interaction. Regarding VO2 and METS, the results are similar, showing a significant effect between groups [VO2. F(1.75)=5.187; p<.05; η2=.06; METS. F(1.76)= 2.147; p<.05; η2=.05], with OWOG scoring more than NWG. There is no significant effect over condition (Traditional vs VR) or interaction. There are no significant effects according to BR and ACC, neither condition, group nor interaction. Regarding Borg's perceived Exertion, results shows that there is a significant effect of interaction between both groups [F(1.76)= 27.367; p<.05; η2=.05].

Table 1. Mean and Standard Deviations (SD) for physiological measures and self-report exertion in Study One

		NWG	OWOG
		M (SD)	M (SD)
HR	Traditional	120.7 (9.2)	136.4 (14.4)
	VR	126.3 (13.8)	134.4 (17)
VO^2	Traditional	16.4 (2.4)	15.3 (4.4)
	VR	17.8 (2.6)	14.4 (4.6)
MET	Traditional	4.5 (.78)	3.8 (1.4)
	VR	4.9 (.71)	4.2 (1.3)
BR	Traditional	32.2 (4.1)	31.8 (7.3)
	VR	34.6 (6.7)	33.7 (6.1)
ACC	Traditional	.37 (.06)	.37 (.04)
	VR	.41 (.06)	.39 (.08)
RPE	Traditional	13.3 (3.2)	13.1 (3.1)
	VR	11.4 (1.4)	13.7 (2.4)

NWG= Normal weight group; OWOG= Overweight and obese group; HR= Heart rate; VO2= Oxygen volume consumed; MET: metabolic equivalent of task; BR: breath rate; CC=accelerometry; RPE= Rated perceived exertion.

3 Virtual Reality Exercise Platform (VREP)

A new VR platform to overcome the limitations identified by study one was developed. The Virtual Reality Exercise Platform (VREP) attempts to leverage virtual environments during aerobic exercise with children. VREP has been developed to lead children through aerobic activities by introducing a virtual space that encourages the child to continue with the planned activity and is parameterized by a clinical professional. The platform model is composed by a three-dimensional (3D) virtual environment projected, a software that control VE and let design session on a computer, an aerobic apparatus (in this case a treadmill) and a monitoring Smart Shirt (TIAS) which monitors the physiological response and movement of the patient during PA.

VREP features a set of characteristics that differ from commercial platforms:

- Programmable messages showed on screen which allow a psychologist to stimulate children by sending messages in real time or as part of a pre-programmed session
- The ability to configure VREP sessions; (aesthetics, opponents, camera view and the speed and timing intervals during the race)
- Input of effort and emotional perception during navigation integrated in VE
- The ability to add cognitive tasks during navigation inside VE.
- Integrate and synchronize data wirelessly from a Smart Shirt (TIAS)

4 Study 2

4.1 Methods

The objective of the study was to study and compare the cardiovascular and psychological response of NOB and OWOG children to aerobic Physical Activity with and without the support of a VR environment (VREP)

This study involved 126 child participants whose age ranged from 10 to 14 years, divided between NWG (n=91) and OWOG (n= 35).

A calorimeter was not used as in study one. HR was a good enough indicator of physiological outcome and the use of a calorimeter would have been uncomfortable for the participants. In difference to study one, VREP was used as VR support tool and groups performed both exercises (with/without VR) and not only one condition.

The instruments employed were:

Questionnaires

- PACES, Sport Habits & Computer Game Habits (previously described in study 1)
- Acceptability scale: 9 questions where developed to measure the VR acceptability

Physiological Measurement

- TIAS: Cardiac signal and movement (previously described in study 1).

4.2   Results

One hundred and fifteen participants (63 female) were included in the study. BMIz of the NWG was 0.14 (.71) and the OWOG was 1.74 (.36). Most participants spent more than half an hour playing sports or doing PA five days per week (37.8%; (NS) X^2=.173).

All participants had a video-game console or computer at home (97.8%; (NS)X^2=,586), and liked to play computer games (93.2%; (NS)X^2=.09). The majority of them (78.8%) had an active video game console (but there were significant differences between groups, X^2=.11, normal weight group contained more children with these technologies at home (n=57) than overweight group (n= 40)), and played with them at least two days a week (no significant differences between groups, X^2=.967).

Regarding the PACES scale, a one-way ANOVA analysis showed significant differences between the NWG (X=17.5; SD=1.5) and OWOG (X=18.2; SD=2.1) (F(1.122)=12.258; p<.05; η2=.03). Obese participants showed lower scores on enjoyment related to physical activity and sports.

Physiological Results

In order to analyse the effect of the VREP support platform on physiological measures, a repeated measures ANCOVA analysis with two between-group levels 2 (group: NWG vs. OWOG.) x 2 (condition: Traditional vs. VREP) was applied. PACES scores, PA habits, video gaming habits and age were introduced as covariables.

The descriptive data can be seen in table 1. The results of the ANCOVA over HR and percentage of HR reserve, a measurement correlated with oxygen consumption (Swain & Leutholtz 1997) (heart rate reserve is defined as the difference between the maximum heart rate minus the resting heart rate) did not show any significant differences between groups (NWG and OWOG) or conditions (TRAD and VREP), with no interaction effect present.

Table 2. Mean and Standard deviations (SD) for physiological response in Study Two

	NWG	OWOG	F
HR TRAD	120.9 (15)	127.6 (19.9)	.272
HR VR	128 (13.1)	124.5 (11.5)	
%HR TRAD	29.6 (12.3)	37.3 (14.7)	.278
% of HR VR	32 (9.6)	37.8 (11.9)	

NWG= Normal weight; OWOG= Overweight and Obese group;

Acceptability Analysis

58% reported that if the clinician were to recommend some additional exercise, they would prefer the VR exercise over traditional exercise. 59.5% felt that they had to exert more effort in the traditional condition, compared to 40.5% who reported that they had to exert more effort in the VR exergaming condition. 66% felt more tired in the traditional exercise, compared to the VR exercise. 74% thought that VR was a better method to encourage people to do physical activity compared to traditional methods. Regarding emotions, children reported being happier (60.7%), less sad (65%), having more fun (80.6%) and being less bored (74.3%) in the VR condition compared to traditional methods. 63.5% of participants also stated that they would be more interested in repeating the VR condition over the traditional condition. There were no significant differences between NWG and OWOG in any of these questions.

5   General Discussion and Conclusion

In the first study, our hypothesis was that when faced with the same physical activity of moderate intensity (MET 3–6), the level of effort of the obese participants would be greater than that of the normal weight participants, but that the use of a commercial VR platform could attenuate the subjective sense of effort and therefore increase adherence [10].

Despite the constant speed and similar physiological response, there was a reduction of RPE in the NWG that was not seen in the OWOG. One possible explanation of why the significant differences in RPE was only seen in the NWG is that the instrument used to measure the subjective fatigue was not adapted for children. Another reason could be that the commercial VR platform used was designed as a recreational platform and not with the intention of promoting physical activity.

One of the possible limitations of the study when analysing the positive effects of the VR was that the children only performed one of the two activities and they could not compare the aerobic exercise with and without the VR. This limitation was addressed in the second study presented below.

Because of this we decided to continue exploring the issue and to carry out a second study in which we tried to address the limitations identified in the first study as well as developing our own VR platform, VREP.

The hypotheses at the second study were VREP will improve adherence and TIAS would be enough to monitor physiological response given the uncomfortableness of the calorimeter.

The analysis of physiological measures showed that the activity supposed a similar effort in all conditions studied and only TIAS provide similar information as calorimeter in study one.

Furthermore the VREP system, in contrast to commercial systems, allows the adaptation of the exercise to the special needs of obese children and also allows clinicians to introduce questions during the VR scenario. This helps to measure the children's mood states and thoughts as they occur.

In regard to physiological responses, the use of VR does not produce relevant changes in cardiac and metabolic response during aerobic exercise, however future studies should test different kinds of exercises and different levels of exertion to support this hypothesis.

The use of TIAS on this platform has been proven as an ideal physiological monitoring system for biofeedback during clinical VR sessions. E-textiles can be worn during physical activity in VR sessions where currently available electronic devices or other biomedical monitoring systems, such as calorimeters, would hinder or perhaps embarrass the user.

Regarding to the acceptability, the vast majority of the participants liked the idea of combining physical activity with the VR platform as a form of treatment to increase physical activity. They were also willing to return a second time to do the same activity again.

After these studies, VREP is going to be included in two clinical aspects:

Adding VREP to an intervention program: VREP can be designed to address specific hypotheses, and it is possible to collect detailed data on the participant's response to the intervention without additional intrusion. Also, the capability to distribute identical virtual environments across multiple locations and platforms gives a new meaning to the concept of multisite data collection & intervention.

Adding VREP as a effort testing tool at the Hospital: The accurate measurement of maximal effort in children is known for its difficulty. [12] VREP will reinforce and motivate the child to achieve these maximal effort levels and assure that clinical tests obtain the results intended.

References

1. Janssen, I., LeBlanc, A.G.: Systematic review of the health benefits of physical activity and fitness in school-aged children and youth. The International Journal of Behavioral Nutrition and Physical Activity 7(06), 40 (2010)
2. Janssen, I.: Physical activity guidelines for children and youth. Applied Physiology Nutrition and Metabolism 32(S2E), S109–S121 (2007)
3. Pavey, T.G., Taylor, A.H., Fox, K.R., Hillsdon, M., Anokye, N., Campbell, J.L., Foster, C.: Effect of exercise referral schemes in primary care on physical activity and improving health outcomes: systematic review and meta-analysis. Bmj 343(nov04 2), d6462 (2011)
4. "Skip" Rizzo, A., Lange, B., Suma, E.A., Bolas, M.: Virtual reality and interactive digital game technology: new tools to address obesity and diabetes. Journal of Diabetes Science and Technology Online 5(2), 256–264 (2011)
5. Strickland, D.: A virtual reality application with autistic children. PresenceTeleoperators and Virtual Environments 5(3), 319–329 (1996)
6. Bouchard, S.: Could virtual reality be effective in treating children with phobias? Expert Review of Neurotherapeutics 11(2), 207–213 (2011)
7. Mestre, D.R., Dagonneau, V.: Does virtual reality enhance exercise performance, enjoyment, and dissociation? an exploratory study on a stationary bike apparatus. Presence Teleoperators and Virtual Environments 20(1), 1–14 (2011)
8. Der-Karabetian, A., Stephenson, K., Poggi, T.: Sex differences in exercise motivation and body-image satisfaction among college students. Perceptual and Motor Skills 83(2), 723–732 (1998)
9. Guixeres, J., Zaragoza, I., Alcaniz, M., Gomis-Tena, J., Cebolla, A., Zaragozá, I., Alcañiz, M.: A new protocol test for physical activity research in obese children (etiobe project). Stud. Health Technol. Inform. 144, 281–283 (2009)
10. Meyer, L.J.: The impact of virtual reality-enhanced exercise equipment on adherence to daily step goals. ProQuest Information & Learning (2009)
11. Bar-Or, O., Rowland, T.W.: Pediatric exercise medicine: from physiologic principles to health care application, p. xviii, 501 p. Human Kinetics, Champaign (2004)

Metaphorical Design of Feedback Interfaces in Activity-Aware Ambient Assisted-Living Applications

Daniel Pinske[1], Benjamin Weyers[2], Wolfram Luther[2], and Torsten Stevens[1]

[1] Fraunhofer Institute for Microelectronic Circuits and Systems, Finkenstr. 61,
47057 Duisburg, Germany
{daniel.pinske,torsten.stevens}@ims.fraunhofer.de
[2] University of Duisburg-Essen, Forsthausweg 65,
47057 Duisburg, Germany
{weyers,luther}@inf.uni-due.de

Abstract. This paper presents a new way of motivating the elderly to correct misbehavior without confronting them directly about it. This is done by reversing the usual human-computer interaction concept, so that the computer-based process influences the human user. By processing data on individuals' activity recognition system (ARS), the behavior of the elderly is rated by comparing it to expected behavior. Presenting visual or physical metaphors then motivates individuals to behave well in order to affect the appearance of the metaphor by achieving a given goal, such as making a flower flourish by brushing their teeth.

Keywords: ambient assisted living, metaphor, human-computer interaction.

1 Introduction

Today's society is changing. People are getting older; their life spans are increasing due to improvements in medical care. Thus, home care tasks and supporting the daily life routines of the elderly are becoming more and more challenging. Due to the growing number of tasks involved in daily elder care, ambient assisted-living (AAL) concepts and applications have grown in relevance. AAL systems are systems with embedded modern technology, e.g., ambient sensors and appropriate interfaces with social life to enrich quality of life [1].

Human-computer interaction (HCI) takes a central role in the development and implementation of AAL systems concerning research into human communication with technical systems. Without adequate user interface (UI) design, the efficient and effective implementation of AAL systems would not be possible. To centralize the role of HCI in AAL systems, we will propose a further step in UI development in AAL research that inverses the roles of technical system and user, i.e., the system senses a human process and reports the state of task completion by using metaphors. This concept views the user as being influenced by the system, in contrast to the normal definition of HCI, where the human controls the system.

J. Bravo, R. Hervás, and M. Rodríguez (Eds.): IWAAL 2012, LNCS 7657, pp. 151–158, 2012.

In this new research context, formal descriptions and metadata sets for modeling this reversal in roles must be developed for AAL systems. Human behavior needs to be measured and direct feedback returned in order to make an adjustment in behavior possible. To this end, we propose modeling linguistic metaphors as XML-based formal data models that can be algorithmically transformed to visual, animated representations displayed on a screen as part of a UI or technically reproduced in a physical model. A use case in daily elder care provides an initial look at possible integration into a real scenario. The proposed metaphor is realized as a physically implemented flower showing a certain aspect of a daily routine. This routine has been formerly identified through an automatic ARS, which has been developed in cooperation with Munstermann [5] at the Fraunhofer inHaus Center in Duisburg. The main purpose of this metaphorical feedback is to show directly the extent to which the user's daily activities correspond to desired normal behavior in a simple and easily understandable way. This simplification of abstract information like "the detected daily routine is aberrant" to a metaphor, such as a flower withering if the user forgets to brush his or her teeth, transforms abstract concepts into daily life representations. The association of "brushing teeth" and "flower withers" can be easily learned by the user as a withered flower perks up again as soon as the user starts brushing his or her teeth. The idea here is to exchange the motivation for the desired behavior, so that the main goal of brushing teeth is not having healthy gums and clean teeth (which the elder has most likely abandoned as a desirable goal), but to take care of the displayed metaphor.

To give a deeper insight into the methodologies used, this contribution will begin with a short introduction to related work followed by a closer look at the system developed for activity identification and recognition, and the use of linguistic metaphor concepts for the feedback channel in the form of a flower. Since it reports on an ongoing study in medical care and the use of metaphorical UI design, this paper gives a short overview of the project without addressing detailed implementation and evaluation issues.

2   Related Work

Automated behavioral monitoring systems (ABMS) are used mainly in daily care settings, i.e., AAL environments, or for products that seek to promote an improved lifestyle.

In [8] an ABMS is presented, which generates alerts for caregivers and shows a visual chart displaying trends in behavioral changes. This information is of a solely indicative character for the caregivers and is not automatically processed. However, the authors emphasize that it is important for the ABMS to be invisible to the person being monitored. This clearly implies that no direct input should be required of that person. Furthermore, to avoid the feeling of being observed, the ABMS should monitor objects in the environment instead of the individual.

Studies like [6] have shown the feasibility of behavioral changes in participating subjects by encouraging them to drink more water. The Playful Bottle acts as a sensing device monitoring its water level and calculating the amount of water ingested. By drinking, the user is also watering a virtual tree displayed on a mobile phone. The study focuses on social components, relying on mutual monitoring of the participants.

All ABMSs have in common that they need sensors to perceive certain aspects of reality. Many ABMSs rely on simple sensor inputs, as they monitor a simple measurable variable such as the amount of water removed from a cup. In this approach we focus on behavior as a pattern of high-level activities. To do this, an activity recognition system (ARS) is required. There have been several approaches, which differ mainly in used sensors and methods for interpreting sensor signals. Systems that require sensors to be worn by the person being monitored are not addressed here, as they do not conform to our requirement that all sensors be undetectable and not involve the user directly.

Activity recognition methods using static classification analyze the sensor signal stream by using a floating time frame to create attribute vectors, which are classified by a classifier like the naïve Bayes classifier (e.g., [9]) or decision trees (e.g., [10]). The performance of such a system directly depends on the chosen attributes and the quality of the training set used to train the classifier model. One weakness is the dependence on a fixed time frame, which is especially problematic for activities with high variance in duration. Another issue appears when concurrent activities result in patterns in the attribute vector, which cannot be assigned to any pattern learned in the classifier model. Furthermore, an activity is only recognizable as a whole and, therefore, cannot be rated in terms of correctness of execution. As it might be necessary to observe complex behavior, e.g., when a collection of activities has to be rated, we have chosen a temporal method for activity recognition.

Temporal methods use state-based models, organizing various states in chronological order to meet the temporal constraints provided by the model. In contrast to static classification methods, they can determine how far an activity has progressed. Examples of such methods are hidden Markov models (e.g., [11]), conditional random fields (e.g., [12]) and Petri nets (e.g., [5]). The potential ability to rate an individual's execution of an activity and performance of concurrent activities make temporal methods the better choice for an ABMS.

3   Activity Aware Feedback System

An activity aware feedback system (FS) is a system that generates feedback in the form of a metaphor in response to the outputs of any ARS, as long as these results are assignable to a specific resident. An ARS perceives its environment by using physical sensors distributed in the living environment of the resident being monitored. To meet the requirements of an AAL environment, these sensors are located such that the resident will not notice them.

As shown in Figure 1, the FS processes activity data to control the metaphor, and the resident interprets the metaphor and changes his or her behavior accordingly. The whole is assembled as a control loop, in which the FS is the controller, the output is the manifestation of the metaphor, and the ARS senses the controlled variable (i.e., the resident's behavior). In contrast to usual HCI systems, the user is influenced by the system—not vice versa—through the adjusted metaphor.

3.1 Sensors

For observing behavior, sensors are used to perceive the environment in which the activities take place. The sensor design needs to be adapted to specific situations, so that all relevant activities are recognizable. In our example, the use of toothbrush, water tap, and toothpaste can be indirectly detected by ambient sensors to give strong evidence that the resident is currently maintaining dental hygiene. If the resident has fixed places for toothbrush and toothpaste, a small magnet can easily be attached to these objects, creating an inexpensive, but effective reed contact, which will be detected by a microcontroller. By assuming that the objects will be in use when removed from their places and put back after that, the microcontroller will generate events called atomic actions, e.g., "toothpaste in use" or "toothbrush not in use". The same is possible with the water tap, depending on the opening mechanism, or other objects relevant for the activity to be detected. In other circumstances, the use of RFID transponders could be necessary to detect the presence and/or movement of relevant objects.

Instead of equipping objects with sensors, we recommend using "smart" devices able to report their use, which will speed up the system's deployment.

3.2 Activity Recognition System

The goal of activity recognition is to infer higher-level activities from a sequence of atomic actions. Especially if more than one activity needs to be detected, the atomic actions of one activity will not necessarily appear consecutively as activities can be

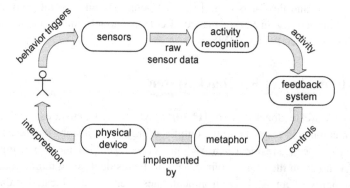

Fig. 1. The feedback system monitors the resident's behavior and adjusts the metaphor it displays

executed concurrently. To do so, the ARS needs to be able to detect a specific activity even when there is sensor noise (from the activity's point of view), generated by concurrent execution of other activities by the resident.

The ARS used [5] exploits predefined procedural knowledge modeled as Petri nets to directly monitor the executed activity as long as it continues. If an activity is detected as fully completed, the corresponding output is passed to the activity FS, which analyzes the resident's behavior according to a predefined rule set.

3.3   Feedback System

The rule set needs to be defined beforehand to meet the requirements of individual situations. The desired behavior is represented in the rules, as are the consequences of potential wrong behavior.

In health care settings, the rule set is worked out by the nurses in charge of the resident's care. They define which activities need to be addressed in a specific time period and how this behavior should affect the metaphor's outcome (see below). In contrast, this can be handled automatically by detecting abnormal behavior on the part of a resident [5], which then needs further investigation to see exactly what is going wrong.

Determining what constitutes abnormal behavior and defining an individual rule set is key to a successful application of the FS. Desired behavior needs to be specified, as does the extent to which it affects the metaphor, as this directly depends on the resident's abilities. It is essential not to overburden the resident with challenges he or she can never achieve, but, at the same time, not to make the tasks too easy; either of these situations may fail to prompt the hoped-for change in behavior.

Rules consist of constraints and reactions. Constraints are premises like "activity = taking medicine", "time = 10:00", "duration = 3 minutes" or how often an activity is to be executed. If all constraints are met, reactions affect an arbitrary number of output dimensions to control the subsequent metaphor. An output dimension controls a specific aspect of a metaphor, e.g., the color or the size of a plant, which can be used to distinguish between certain aspects of daily routine, like hygiene or amount of social contact.

3.4   Metaphorical Design

Metaphors are well known from linguistics as ways of transporting information based on pre-knowledge shared by the sender and the recipient. Lakoff and Johnson [2] define metaphors as follows: "The essence of metaphor is understanding and experiencing one kind of thing in terms of another." Among the three groups of metaphors they identify are ontological metaphors, which simplify abstract concepts, for example, linking "Forgetting to brush one's teeth is bad for one's health" to an everyday experience, like "A flower withering is bad for the plant." Thus, metaphorical designs in FS are a promising way of conceptualizing well-known approaches, like the Playful Bottle, to a representation as a metaphor and transfering it to other AAL application scenarios.

We have developed a formalization of metaphors based on the semiotic triangle suggested by Peirce [3] via an XML markup language where a metaphor is modeled as a set of possible visual or aural symbols (*representatives*) embedded in a certain context (*referent*) and a set of *interpretations* that are associated via IDs with several contexts defined separately in a global manner. The XML-based representation is fur-

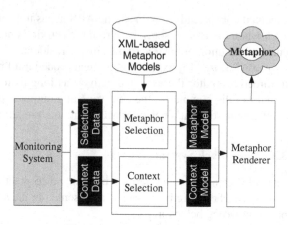

Fig. 2. Metaphor rendering system

ther extended by a metaphor classification presented by Lakoff et al. [7] called the "Master Metaphor List". Here, metaphors are grouped in four classes: event structure, mental events, emotions, and others. These classes are represented as MetaphorClass nodes in the XML representation. These classes also contain more specific groups of metaphors, represented as MetaphorGroup nodes. For instance, the class "event structure" contains groups like "states" or "event objects", etc. This type of classification and grouping makes a more reliable creation of a XML-based database possible, which includes various types of concrete metaphor models.

Using an implementation for rendering metaphors makes it possible to instantiate every metaphor for a given context based on the XML-based model applied. Furthermore, using selection rules associated with the XML representations of a metaphor, metaphors can be selected by the rendering system based on information from the monitoring system as described above. Thus, a rendering system for metaphors can be modeled and implemented as shown in Figure 2. Here, context and selection data are first derived from the monitoring system. This system observes the surrounding world using various sensors (cf. the preceding section). This data is then used to select the relevant metaphor model from the XML-based dataset, as well as the relevant context model describing how the metaphor is to be instantiated. Both models are passed to the metaphor renderer, which generates a concrete visual representation of the instantiated metaphor model selected or controlling data for a physically implemented metaphor, such as the inBloom described below. To do this, the context information is used to select the appropriate representation of the metaphor defined in the XML file. This description of the metaphor further defines which representations are possible (visual, audio, mechanical) and which values have to be used to instantiate the specific representation.

The interpretation part (also represented as an XML node) of the metaphor model can also be used for extended selection. Considering a user model and the situation, the system can also instantiate the formally described interpretation part of the metaphor model and check whether the current metaphor will be understood by the user or not. By using a user model, this validation of the metaphor choice can be raised to a semantic level. To do this, a selected interpretation that defines the semantic concept of a metaphor in a given context is associated with a specific representation in the XML that is then selected and instantiated by the renderer as described above. The concrete formal description format of interpretations for formal metaphor models will be addressed in future research.

3.5   Application Scenario

Studies evaluating ambient lifestyle FSs have shown an increasing motivational effect if subjects have established an emotional relationship with the metaphor shown [1]. This is why we developed a tangible physical device, described in [4], which assembles a mechanical flower capable of withering and blooming in accordance with the subject's behavior. The desired effect is a sense of responsibility for keeping the flower flourishing. The so-called "inBloom" is modeled loosely on the designs of Carl Smith (http://www.coroflot.com/carlsmith/Portfolio1). The flower can appear in the states shown in Figure 3, as well as in any state in between to represent the current rating of the subject's behavior.

For the study in [6], all participants were directly instructed as to how a certain behavior would affect the "hydration games" being introduced. As the measurement and the output device were one and the same, participants could easily make the causal connection between their behavior and the resulting effects. In our example, the flower is placed in the bathroom to give direct feedback to the resident. Assuming the flower is withered and the resident brushes her or his teeth, the positive effect (i.e., the flower flourishing) should be immediately visible, so that the resident can establish a causal connection between his or her actions and the state of the flower. In contrast, it is difficult to see why the flower withers when there is apparently no direct connection to abnormal behavior, which is most likely not recognized by the resident anyway. This is why it should be explained to residents what aspect of their behavior affects the condition of the metaphor.

Fig. 3. Current rating of behavior represented by a mechanical flower

4   Conclusion and Future Work

By using metaphors, the correction of undesirable behavior in elderly people is achieved without confronting the resident directly with his or her mistakes. Instead, analogies are composed which are familiar to the individuals, reducing learning effort.

Modeling these metaphors is done by a newly developed XML-based markup language. The selected scenario uses a withering/ flourishing mechanical flower. Whether the positive effect on the resident's behavior is supported over a longer period still needs to be examined in a systematic evaluation with residents, caregivers and UI designers. This evaluation will take place in nursing homes. The whole system will be deployed to a number of accommodation units to observe specific misbehavior, which has been identified in advance by caregivers. To investigate the effect of a metaphor on daily routine behavior, the metaphor system will be activated and potential change in behavior compared to the initial results.

First, however, the effect on behavior will be evaluated separately from daily care scenarios, relying on activity recognition, in a study at the University of Duisburg-Essen. Students will be tested through a series of exams following the lessons of a university lecture. Based on the students' performance, a metaphorical representation of the learning effort will provide feedback through changes in its appearance. So as to neutralize any effect from the intrinsic motivation simply to perform well on exams, a control group will not be shown the metaphor. We want to know whether the students who see the metaphor learn faster as a consequence of having the extrinsic motivation of taking care of it. In this initial study, in order to minimize the effects of possibly misreading the control variable, an ARS is not in use.

References

1. Hiroaki, K., Nakajima, T.: Applying Smart Objects for Persuading Users to Change Their Behavior. Int. J. of Multimedia and Ubiquitous Eng. 4(3), 21–36 (2009)
2. Lakoff, G., Johnson, M.: Metaphors We Live By, Chicago/London (1980)
3. Peirce, C.S.: A Syllabus of Certain Topics of Logic. EP 2, 258–330 (1903)
4. Weber, K.: A System for Rating Activities and Monitoring Behavior in Ambient Assisted-living Environments. Diploma thesis, University of Duisburg-Essen (2012) (in German)
5. Munstermann, M., Stevens, T., Luther, W.: A Novel Human Autonomy Assessment System. Sensors 12, 7828–7854 (2012)
6. Chiu, M.-C., Chang, S.-P., Chang, Y.-C., Chu, H.-H., Chen, C.C.-H., Hsiao, F.-H., Ko, J.-C.: Playful bottle: A Mobile Social Persuasion System to Motivate Healthy Water Intake. In: Proc. of the 11th Int. Conf. on Ubiquitous Computing, New York, pp. 185–194 (2009)
7. Lakoff, G., Espenson, J., Schwartz, A.: Master Metaphor List, Second Draft Copy. University of California at Berkeley (1991)
8. Glascock, A.P., Kutzik, D.M.: The Impact of Behavioral Monitoring Technology on the Provision of Health Care in the Home. Journal of Universal Computer Science 12, 59–79 (2006)
9. Tapia, E.M., Intille, S.S., Larson, K.: Activity Recognition in the Home Using Simple and Ubiquitous Sensors. In: Ferscha, A., Mattern, F. (eds.) PERVASIVE 2004. LNCS, vol. 3001, pp. 158–175. Springer, Heidelberg (2004)
10. Lombriser, C., Bharatula, N.B., Roggen, D., Tröster, G.: On-Body Activity Recognition in a Dynamic Sensor Network. In: 2nd Int. Conf. on Body Area Networks (2007)
11. Brand, M., Oliver, N., Pentland, A.: Coupled Hidden Markov Models for Complex Action Recognition. In: Computer Vision and Pattern Recognition, vol. 199, pp. 994–999 (1997)
12. Hu, D.H., Yang, Q.: CIGAR: Concurrent and Interleaving Goal and Activity Recognition. In: Proceedings of the 23rd AAAI Conference on Artificial Intelligence (AAAI 2008), Chicago, Illinois, USA, pp. 1363–1368 (2008)

Common-Sense Knowledge for a Computer Vision System for Human Action Recognition*

Maria J. Santofimia[1], Jesus Martinez-del-Rincon[2],
and Jean-Christophe Nebel[3]

[1] Computer Architecture and Network Group, School of Computing Science,
University of Castilla-La Mancha, Spain
[2] The institute of Electronics, Communications and Information Technology (ECIT),
Queens University of Belfast, BT3 9DT, UK
[3] Digital Imaging Research Centre, Kingston University, London, KT1 2EE, UK
MariaJose.Santofimia@uclm.es, j.martinez-del-rincon@qub.ac.uk,
J.Nebel@kingston.ac.uk

Abstract. This work presents a novel approach for human action recognition based on the combination of computer vision techniques and common-sense knowledge and reasoning capabilities. The emphasis of this work is on how common sense has to be leveraged to a vision-based human action recognition so that nonsensical errors can be amended at the understanding stage. The proposed framework is to be deployed in a realistic environment in which humans behave rationally, that is, motivated by an aim or a reason.

Keywords: Common-Sense Reasoning, Action Recognition, Computer Vision.

1 Introduction

Different approaches have been devised to tackle the problem of human action recognition from the computer vision perspective, just to name a few [1][2][3][4]. However, few works combine video-based strategies with anthropological aspects or knowledge about human and social behaviour[5]. The reason for that is also the same reason for autonomous and intelligent systems lack of success, as known: replicating human intelligence is a task that requires an extremely large amount of knowledge. However, it is neither expert nor specific knowledge that needs to be improved in these systems. On the contrary, the focus should be placed at collecting everyday knowledge, also known as common sense. For example, Cyc [6] has been gathering for over 25 years all common-sense knowledge held by humans.

In this sense, this work is intended to prove the hypothesis that computer vision systems for human action recognition could be enhanced with common-sense knowledge overcoming the occurrence of nonsensical recognized actions.

---

* This research was supported by the Spanish Ministry of Science and Innovation under the project DREAMS (TEC2011-28666-C04-03).

J. Bravo, R. Hervás, and M. Rodríguez (Eds.): IWAAL 2012, LNCS 7657, pp. 159–166, 2012.
© Springer-Verlag Berlin Heidelberg 2012

This work places the focus on the role that common-sense knowledge plays on the overall task of human action recognition. Although expert knowledge has been applied to many fields and applications, here we concentrate on common sense, understood as the everyday knowledge that describes how the world works.

Two main difficulties have to be overcome in order to verify the working hypothesis: on the one hand, to date, computer vision systems are not yet capable of recognizing whichever human action performed in video sequence recorded from real scenarios [7]; and, on the other hand, collecting the relevant common-sense knowledge held by humans is far from being a feasible task. These two constraints require reducing the number of considered human actions and assuming a reduced amount of available knowledge for reasoning.

It can be tempting to think that hand-crafted representation of expert knowledge can, at some point, replace the role of common-sense knowledge. In fact, the following quotation, extracted from [6], discusses this issue:

> " It is often difficult to make a convincing case for having a consensus reality knowledge base, because whenever one cites a particular piece of common sense that would be needed in a situation, it's easy to dismiss it and say "well, we would have put that into our expert system as just one more (premise on a) rule." For instance, in diagnosing a sick twenty-year-old coal miner, the program is told that he has been working in coal mines for 22 years (the typist accidentally hit two 2s instead of just one). Common sense tells us to question the idea of someone working in a coal mine since age -2. Yes, if this sort of error had been foreseen, the expert system could of course question it also. The argument is, however, that we could keep coming up with instance after instance where some additional piece of common sense knowledge would be needed in order to avoid falling into an inhumanly silly mistake."

Obviously, a more careful representation of information could take into consideration that the age of a person cannot be a bigger number than the number of years the same person has been working in coal mines. However, the work presented here is more concerned with describing the knowledge that would allow the system to achieve that conclusion on its own. The counterpart is that the amount of information required to do so is huge. For that reason, the approach followed by this work consists in minimizing the common-sense knowledge involved in the recorded scenario by constraining the context in which actors can perform. However, these constrains should not be equated to the approach followed by expert systems.

According to Davidson [8], the reason that motivates an action also rationalizes it. Consequently, if motivations could be heuristically guided and restricted, types of performed actions would also be limited. This approach pursues a twofold aim: first, avoiding rule-based and expert system strategies; and second, minimizing the directions given to actors. The Davidsonian theory of actions and events provides a theoretical justification for the proposed approach. The two pursued aims can be achieved by creating the appropriate atmosphere that makes actors prone to perform certain actions but allowing them, at the same time, to behave in a rational manner.

The limited number of actions that can be recognized by computer vision systems justifies the need for a set up scenario. There, actors are surrounded by suitable elements that encourage them to perform a predefined and expected set of actions such as punch or kick a punching-ball or read a book. The negligible probability of an actor performing those activities without the presence of interactive objects for fighting or reading makes them neccesary for capturing the actions of interest.

This article is organized as follows. Section 2 describes the semantic model proposed here to enable the integration of common-sense knowledge and computer vision. Section 3 describes the implementation details and some additional aspects of the proposed framework. Finally, Section 4 summarizes the most relevant conclusions drawn from this work.

2 Knowledge Modeling

Human action recognition is a task that should not be tackled in isolation from the context in which that actions are taking place. However, despite the importance of the notion of context, this concept has not yet been universally formalized. On the contrary, the fact that this concept is a relevant issue for different fields of knowledge such as natural language understanding, linguistics, context-awareness, or knowledge representation among others, makes it difficult to provide a common and unique definition of what context is.

Fig. 1. Knowledge modeled using Scone

The concept of context is here understood as the set of facts or propositional knowledge that describes a specific state of the world, in the same way that J. Allen refers to the concept of world in [9]. This concept is represented by a set of descriptions of both the static and dynamic aspects of the world, therefore modeling what is known about the past, present, and future.

Additionally, these propositions need to be semantically enhanced by associating a meaning to each of them. However the meaning of these propositions is unavoidably associated to the context in which they are being considered. In this sense, meaning is expected to be something more elaborate than just mere conventions about what other concepts state their significance to be.

The philosophical theory of *possible worlds* has tackled the problem of associating different meanings or truth value to the same proposition without worrying about inconsistencies or incongruousness. This theory has been successfully translated into a computational model by means of what S. Fahlman has come to call *multiple-contexts* [10].

The need for the multiple-context mechanism, for the purpose that concerns us here, is justified as a way of maintaining parallel action sequences. The multiple-context mechanism is provided as an essential feature of the Scone Knowledge-Base system[11]. As for the possible world theory, the multiple context mechanism allows the representation of different states of affairs, which simultaneously co-occur in the same knowledge-base, without leading to inconsistencies.

The proposed video based system relies on a primary classification of the actions being recognized, as depicted in Fig. 1, according to visual clues.This initial classification is then provided as an input to the knowledge system that reasons about the rationality of the recognized actions. Rather than yielding just one action, the computer vision system provides an ordered list of actions (the optimum number of actions will be discussed later on this paper). The similarity of actions such as wave or check the watch might lead the computer vision system to an erroneous identification. For that reason, actions ranked after the first one are not discarded, but on the contrary, are considered true in parallel contexts. In this sense, the multiple-context mechanism provides a way of holding the propositional knowledge that, *a priory* should have been discarded.

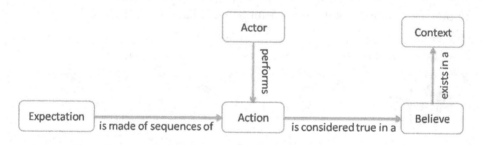

Fig. 2. A semantic model for video-based human action recognition

Since different contexts contain propositional knowledge about different plausible situations, an additional mechanism is therefore required to determine which context is considered true at a specific moment in time. Whenever a new action is recognized by the system, it outputs a ranked list of plausible actions. Each possibility is therefore asserted to a given context. Whenever the system is asked for the sequence of actions that describe the actor behaviour, only one context and its inherent propositions, should be active. Context activation is determined by the occurrence of action events that provides the most rational explanation. Explanations are considered here as the propositional knowledge contained in a given context. For example, it is more rational or it makes more

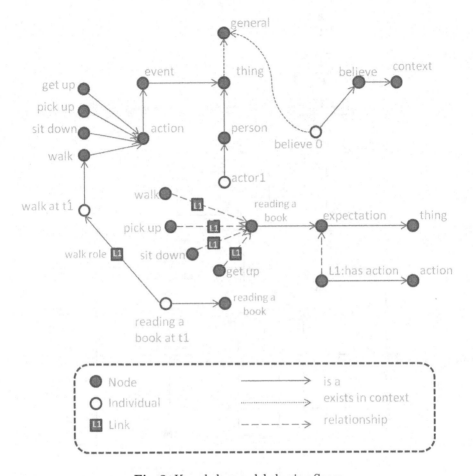

Fig. 3. Knowledge modeled using Scone

sense to pick up a book for reading it than for throwing it overhead, although both of them might be plausible.

After having justified how common-sense knowledge should be handled in order to be combined with a computer vision system for human action recognition, a more formal description of the semantic model is provided. Fig. 2 depicts the semantic model for visual-based human action recognition whereas Fig. 3 presents the implementation of such semantic model using Scone and its multiple-context mechanism.

3 Implementation Details and Validation

The main contribution of this work consists in leveraging common-sense capabilities to a computer vision system. Fig. 1 depicts the different modules involved in the proposed framework.

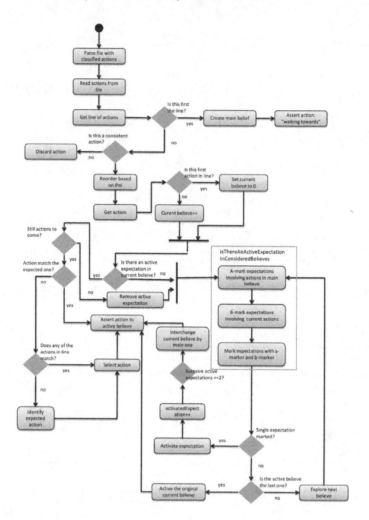

Fig. 4. Activity diagram for the proposed reasoning system

Although many existing datasets are commonly used to evaluate video based action recognition systems, their artificial nature made them unsuitable for testing the proposed system. First, actions had to be performed for a reason whereas actors are told what to do in the artificial scenarios. Moreover, actions have to be part of a comprehensive story, so that performed actions make sense with regard to the aims or the reasons that motivate actors to behave like they do. Finally, the most compelling reason to produce a new dataset[1] was the exiting dissociation among the IXMAS [12] actions used to trained the system and existing datasets.

---

[1] WaRoll dataset available at
www.arco.esi.uclm.es/~mariaj.santofimia/puff/videos.zip

Video sequences are provided to a Bag Of Words framework that outputs an ordered list of several actions, printed in a text file, in which each line contains the ranked list of actions. The empirically estimated optimum number of actions is five. Then, the propositional knowledge involved in that action events is modeled using the semantic model proposed in previous section and asserted to the knowledge base according to the algorithm outlined in Fig. 4.

There are some common-sense aspects that enable the system to make corrections without having to consider the output provided by the classifier. For example, given the fact that the set up scenario reproduces a waiting room, actors are expected to enter and leave the waiting room. In this sense, first and last actions are expected to be the *walking towards* action.

The proposed system performance has been assessed in [13] in which a comparison analysis shows how the proposed approach considerably improves results obtained by computer vision systems under realistic scenarios, in which humans are rationally motivated.

4   Conclusions

This paper presents a novel knowledge management approach that enables common-sense capabilities to be incorporated to a computer vision system for human action recognition. In order to do so a semantic model for human action recognition is proposed.

This work was motivated by one of the most intrinsic features of humans: their actions are rationally motivated. The incorporation of common-sense knowledge and reasoning capabilities can reduce errors introduced by computer vision systems that, to human observers, simply do not make any sense. Simple errors such as the fact that to throw away an object you need to hold that object prevents the system from identifying an action as throwing away an object if previously an object have not been picked up. Recall that this approach consists in providing the knowledge base system with the required information to achieve that conclusion on its own, rather than providing it with a basic rule of the type *"if you do not have an object you cannot throw it away"*.

Finally, it can be concluded that human action recognition performed under realistic scenarios can greatly benefit from incorporating common-sense capabilities to correct computer vision system mistakes committed due to similarities in movements defining different actions, such as waving and scratching your head, and variability between humans performing the same action.

References

1. Vezzani, R., Baltieri, D., Cucchiara, R.: HMM Based Action Recognition with Projection Histogram Features. In: Ünay, D., Çataltepe, Z., Aksoy, S. (eds.) ICPR 2010. LNCS, vol. 6388, pp. 286–293. Springer, Heidelberg (2010)

2. Martinez-Contreras, F., Orrite-Urunuela, C., Herrero-Jaraba, E., Ragheb, H., Velastin, S.A.: Recognizing human actions using silhouette-based hmm. In: Proceedings of the 2009 Sixth IEEE International Conference on Advanced Video and Signal Based Surveillance, AVSS 2009, pp. 43–48. IEEE Computer Society, Washington, DC (2009)
3. Laptev, I., Marszalek, M., Schmid, C., Rozenfeld, B.: Learning realistic human actions from movies. In: CVPR. IEEE Computer Society (2008)
4. Zhang, J., Gong, S.: Action categorization with modified hidden conditional random field. Pattern Recogn. 43(1), 197–203 (2010)
5. Baker, C.L., Saxe, R., Tenenbaum, J.B.: Action understanding as inverse planning. Cognition (2009)
6. Lenat, D.B., Guha, R.V.: Building Large Knowledge-Based Systems; Representation and Inference in the Cyc Project. Addison-Wesley Longman Publishing Co., Inc., Boston (1989)
7. Nebel, J.-C., Lewandowski, M., Thévenon, J., Martínez, F., Velastin, S.: Are Current Monocular Computer Vision Systems for Human Action Recognition Suitable for Visual Surveillance Applications? In: Bebis, G., Boyle, R., Parvin, B., Koracin, D., Wang, S., Kyungnam, K., Benes, B., Moreland, K., Borst, C., DiVerdi, S., Yi-Jen, C., Ming, J. (eds.) ISVC 2011, Part II. LNCS, vol. 6939, pp. 290–299. Springer, Heidelberg (2011)
8. Davidson, D.: Actions, reasons, and causes. The Journal of Philosophy 60(23), 685–700 (1963)
9. Allen, J.F.: Towards a general theory of action and time. Artif. Intell. 23, 123–154 (1984)
10. Fahlman, S.E.: Marker-Passing Inference in the Scone Knowledge-Base System. In: Lang, J., Lin, F., Wang, J. (eds.) KSEM 2006. LNCS (LNAI), vol. 4092, pp. 114–126. Springer, Heidelberg (2006)
11. Fahlman, S.E.: The Scone knowledge-base project (2010), http://www.cs.cmu.edu/~sef/scone/ (retrieved on February 8, 2010)
12. Weinland, D., Boyer, E., Ronfard, R.: Action Recognition from Arbitrary Views using 3D Exemplars. In: International Conference on Computer Vision, Rio de Janeiro, Brazil, pp. 1–7. IEEE (2007)
13. Martinez del Rincon, J., Santofimia, M.J., Nebel, J.C.: Common-sense reasoning for human action recognition. Under Review Process (2012)

Residential Care Home Awareness

Juan Enrique Garrido Navarro[1], Victor M.R. Penichet[2], and Maria-Dolores Lozano[2]

[1] Computer Science Research Institute, University of Castilla-La Mancha,
02071, Albacete, Spain
juanenrique.garrido@uclm.es
[2] Computer Systems Department, University of Castilla-La Mancha,
02071, Albacete, Spain
{victor.penichet,maria.lozano}uclm.es

Abstract. The evolution of technology has resulted in important advances in health computing. Nowadays, health environments are able to use sophisticated systems by which users can reduce efforts and make their actions more efficient. Additionally, health systems allow avoiding typical human errors by means of automated processes. An important parameter of health systems is awareness as it can be considered as collaborative. It can be defined as the information that users need about the environment. In this way, this paper presents an awareness analysis of a specific health environment: Residential Care Homes. We consider that scenario due to the importance of improving the quality of life of the residents by helping employees in their tasks.

Keywords: Awareness, Healthcare, Context-awareness, Collaboration, Coordination, Cooperation, Communication, Ubiquity.

1 Introduction

During the last years, health computing has changed due to the evolution of technology [1]. In this way, related research groups analyze how technology can facilitate users´ tasks in health systems. Additionally, reducing human errors is an important objective, which can be critical in health domains, e.g. medical stats, data capture, tasks reminder. Healthcare employees need information about the environment state which will help them to perform some tasks. They need to know the availability of resources, other workers who can help them, workmates tasks information, etc. Therefore, collaboration is a critical approach in healthcare which will improve working conditions. Any system applied in a healthcare center (e.g. hospitals, residential care homes, clinics, etc.) has to consider collaboration fundamentals: cooperation [2], communication [3], coordination [3] and information sharing [4]. In addition, a key concept to allow collaboration is awareness [5] because it implies to provide information about environment state.

In this paper, the awareness of health environments is analyzed in a specific scenario: Residential Care Homes (RCH). The concept of awareness has been emphasized as it is a fundamental element in collaborative, ubiquitous [6] and context-aware [7]

J. Bravo, R. Hervás, and M. Rodríguez (Eds.): IWAAL 2012, LNCS 7657, pp. 167–170, 2012.

environments, where users access to information and functionality required, regardless of location and time. Endsley [5] defined awareness as "knowing what is going on"; in other words, it is the user's perception of their workmates' activities and the state of resources. Such information is essential to complete any collaborative task. Consequently, we have identified a new type of awareness when analyzing our specific environment: RCH awareness. This new awareness can be defined as the information needed to complete RCH collaborative tasks: workmates tasks, resources location, tasks evolution, etc. RCH awareness is necessary in a RCH system because it provides essential information on the environment by clarifying users which part of the environment state affects their current tasks. For example, if a nurse is shown that a resident has fallen in her zone, she needs to call a workmate to help her. The nurse needs information about the workmates that could go to that point allowing her to select the most adequate one. The selection consists of searching the nearest workmate in the best conditions (performing low urgency level tasks). In this way, authors have developed a collaborative, ubiquitous and context-aware prototype [9] suitable for geriatric environments in which RCH awareness is an essential element. The prototype allows employees to access to needed information and functionality based on their current context (e.g. location and current task) at anytime and anywhere.

The rest of the paper is organized as follows: Section 2 describes the RCH awareness with its categorization. And following, Section 3 presents conclusions and future works.

2   RCH Awareness

The following analysis is based on the awareness study made by Greenberg [8] applied in a domestic scenario: the home. Greenberg described interpersonal awareness, which defines the information that people wish to maintain for their family and friends.

We have centered our awareness analysis in a health-related workplace scenario: Residential Care Homes. Each employee may be aware of specific information in relation with the tasks he has to perform: information about workmates´ tasks, information about residents and the state of the resources to be used. Workers usually compile the information they need by observation and interacting with the environment. For example, if a nurse has to take the temperature of a resident and give him some medication, the nurse will check if the needed medication is available, as well as a thermometer. In this way, we present a new awareness type representing the necessity to be aware of the above mentioned information: RCH awareness. This RCH awareness can be defined as the information about workmates and resources needed by RCH employees to perform their tasks.

In RCH, collaborative tasks present specific foundations, which are the underlying guiding principles. Specifically, the employees have to establish for each individual task the next key data to its performance: the related workmates´ tasks in the same shift, the existing relationships, the employees' locations, the state of the resources (whether used or not), etc. That information (categorized in users, tasks, location and resources) implies four different needed data sources that make up the four subtypes in which RCH awareness can be divided: *users´ awareness, tasks awareness, location awareness* and *resources awareness*. Each subtype indicates and implies different needs for information in RCH. A collaborative system, deployed in the environment where our analysis is focused, should offer users the possibility to be aware about information which satisfies their needs.

Users´ awareness represents the necessity to know the people present in the RCH (workmates, residents and external people). Employees may need information on the location of people in the environment in case they need someone to help with a specific task. In case an employee has a query or needs to solve a problem or communicate with someone to consult on any procedure, the adequate person can be easily found. That possibility allows employees to obtain a correct way to collaborate and information on the state of related workmates. The state will indicate if somebody can be interrupted and therefore can be useful in a concrete time. Using this information they can decide if the request should be sent.

Tasks awareness provides information on the state of performance of a specific task. Users have many different collaborative tasks in RCH; the main reason is that a great number of tasks when taking care of the residents will be interdependent. This dependence is due to two causes: on the one hand, employees make use of a set of common shared resources so their tasks depend on the state of the said resources (whether in use or not). For example, if an employee needs to use a blood pressure meter, he needs to know its availability. On the other hand, some tasks may require other tasks´ results performed by other workmates. For example, a doctor may need to check whether a nurse has made some medical measurement (previously ordered) to a specific resident.

Location awareness allows employees in RCH to get information about workmates´ location. This information is a key data for each employee. Users need to know where workmates are when they need to find them. An employee location will allow other workmates who need help to solve doubts about their current tasks. If a user knows other´s location, he can go there and get some help. Moreover, information on location allows users to imagine which is the workmate´ state. This information can provide implicit data. For example, if an employee is in a rest zone, that means he is taking a break. Then this can be considered as a good situation to be asked for help.

Resource awareness is essential to complete some tasks. Users need information on resources availability to be able to perform some tasks. If a user knows that a resource is available and its location, he can get it and perform the task. However, if any resource is not available, the employee may need to find alternatives or may start a pending task.

Each employee in a RCH may need different information. Some employees may need more detailed information and others simply do not need information to perform their tasks. Thus, in a RCH we have to distinguish the type of user when offering awareness. In RCH we can classify users in four main social groups: employees, residents, external users and the system itself.

3   Conclusions and Future Work

This paper presents an analysis of awareness in Residential Care Homes: RCH awareness. This new awareness type is the information needed by RCH employees about the environment to be able to perform their tasks. That information can be defined as part of the environment state. RCH awareness can be divided into four types: users awareness, information about who is in the environment; task awareness, information about who is doing each task and its development; location awareness, information about users´ location; and resources awareness, information (quantity, location and availability) on the resources available in the environment.

As future work we are improving a related prototype, by adding more collaborative capabilities, such as the creation of a synchronous and asynchronous communication system. Additionally, we are considering the possibility to create automatic advice notes which will create collaborative situations when solving emergencies.

Acknowledgments. We would like to acknowledge the project CICYT TIN2011-27767-C02-01 from the Spanish Ministerio de Ciencia e Innovación and the Regional Government: Junta de Comunidades de Castilla-La Mancha PPII10-0300-4174 and PII2C09-0185-1030 projects for partially funding this work.

References

1. Arnrich, B., Mayora, O., Tröster, G.: Pervasive Healthcare, Paving the Way for a Pervasive, User-Centred and Preventive Healthcare Model. Methods of Information in Medicine 1, 67–73 (2010)
2. Poltrock, S., Grudin, J.: Computer Supported Cooperative Work and Groupware. In: Plaisant, C. (ed.) Conference Companion on Human Factors in Computing Systems, CHI 1994, pp. 255–356. ACM Press, New York (1994)
3. Poltrock, S., Grudin, J.: CSCW, groupware and workflow: experiences, state of art, and future trends. In: CHI 1999 Extended Abstracts on Human Factors in Computing Systems, pp. 120–121. ACM Press, New York (1999)
4. Penichet, V.M., Lozano, M.D., Gallud, J.A., Tesoriero, R.: Requirement-based Approach for Groupware Environments Design. Journal of Systems and Software, JSS (2011) ISSN: 0164-1212
5. Endsley, M.: Toward a Theory of Situation Awareness in Dynamic Systems. Human Factors 37(1), 32–64 (1995)
6. Weiser, M.: The computer for the 21st century. Scientific American 265(3), 94–104 (1991)
7. Bricon-Souf, N., Newman, C.R.: Context-awareness in health care: A review. International Journal of Medical Informatics 76, 2–12 (2007)
8. Greenberg, S., Neustaedter, C., Elliot, K.: Awareness in the Home: The Nuances of Relationships, Domestic Coordination and Communication. In: Makopulos, P., De Ruyter, B., Mackay, W. (eds.) Awareness Systems: Advances in Theory. Kluwer Academic Publishers (2009)
9. Garrido, J.E., Penichet, V.M., Lozano, M.D.: UBI4HEALTH: Ubiquitous System to Improve the Management of healthcare Activities. In: Pervasive 2012, Newcastle, UK (2012)

An Ubiquitous Game for Providing Emotional Support to Hospitalized Children

Ramon Cruzat[1], Sergio F. Ochoa[1], and Luis A. Guerrero[2]

[1] Computer Science Department, University of Chile
{ramon.cruzat,sochoa}@dcc.uchile.cl
[2] CITIC Research Group, School of Computer Science and Informatics,
Universidad de Costa Rica
Luis.Guerrero@ecci.ucr.ac.cr

Abstract. Kids under treatments that involve long stays at a hospital or health center tend to get bored or depressed because of the lack of social interaction with family and friends. Such a situation also affects the evolution and effectiveness of their treatments. This article presents a mobile ubiquitous game called *MagicRace*, which allows hospitalized kinds to interact socially with one another, without putting to risk their sensitive health conditions. The game does not require a communication infrastructure at the hospital, but instead, it uses a mobile ad hoc network composed of the handhelds used by the kids to play.

Keywords: Ubiquitous game, children's emotional support, healthcare.

1   Introduction

Kids requiring long-term health treatments (e.g. for cancer, organ transplants, severe burns or chronic kidney disease) are located in special rooms, often in isolation. Their compromised health condition increases the risk of being infected by others whom which they are in contact. Usually, physicians and nurses working in these areas, and also personal caregivers, are the only people in contact with these children. Many children experience severe boredom, and often become depressed. As many have to spend a long time in bed, the problem is exacerbated and challenging. It is well-known that the patient's mood affects their immunological system, in turn, affecting their ability to take well to a treatment and their illness in general [1]. In this scenario, promoting a good mood and feelings of well being seems to be the best practice.

Several studies support the idea that social networks and social interactions may enhance the quality of life of older adults and also children [2, 3, 4]. Some social applications have shown to be useful at addressing the isolation and anxiety that some feel when they are undergoing long treatments in hospitals and also at home. An example of these applications is MEK (Mobile Exchange of Knowledge), a software tool that helps detect, in a ubiquitous way, patients or relatives with similar interests [5]. Another example is ePortrait -- an ambient display that allows family members to

J. Bravo, R. Hervás, and M. Rodríguez (Eds.): IWAAL 2012, LNCS 7657, pp. 171–174, 2012.

share pictures [1]. Sharing pictures, family members help boost the elder's mood, positively affecting their overall mental health condition.

Trying to deal with the stated challenge this article presents an ubiquitous game called *MagicRace*, which embeds collaborative features as a way to allow social interactions among kids, and thus, improve their mood.

Next section introduces the *MagicRace* application and its main components. Then, Section 3 presents the conclusions and the future work.

2   MagicRace

The game runs on handheld devices (particularly PDAs and smartphones) and uses a Mobile Ad hoc Network (MANET) [6] to support the communication among these devices. Since the communication is wireless, the patients can interact with each other from their rooms, thus avoiding risk of possible contagious contact.

This game involves several players and several stages depending on the drivers' expertise. The players can participate as independent drivers and also in teams. When they play in teams, each player receives points according to his/her final position in the race. The team members points obtained in the race are computed as part of the team score and the team that obtains the highest score is the winner. Therefore, it is important that the participants have a team strategy to race, thus, increasing their chances of winning the race.

Four teams were predefined in the game and they were identified by the color of the cars (teams blue, green, red and orange). Each team may have many participants. All cars participating in the race start the competition with a certain amount of energy, and as the car moves it can gain or lose energy depending on the driver's actions. For example, every time the car goes off the road or moves in the opposite direction, it loses energy. On the contrary, if the driver does not make mistakes for a certain time period, the energy of his/her car increases until reaching the maximum. The amount of energy determines the maximum speed that a car can reach.

During the different stages of a race, certain "magic objects" appear on the circuit. When the car passes over one of these objects, its behavior changes. Therefore, these objects can help or harm, not only the player, but also the team. The game considers four types of magic objects depending on the effect these objects produce: personal positive, personal negative, team positive and team negative. Objects in the first two categories affect just one player and those in the last two categories affect the whole team. Figure 1 shows the positive personal magic objects.

Fig. 1. Magical objects in the "positive personal" category

The stars increase the speed of the car. The ghost makes the player invisible to other players for five seconds. The fruits allow a car to recover part of the lost energy.

The first-aid kit lets you recover all lost energy. These magic objects appear randomly during the race, therefore making every race different from the previous one, even if the same circuit is used. The objects appear more frequently in later stages of a race, and in particular, the positive ones appear more frequently than the negative ones. The current prototype has 30 different scenarios or circuits. Figure 2 shows an example of the interface of the prototype.

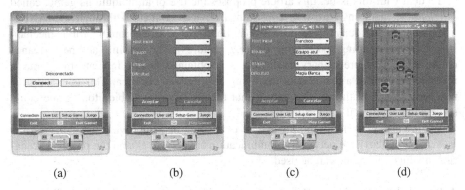

|(a)|(b)|(c)|(d)|

Fig. 2. The MagicRace game interface

The game user interface includes four tabs that are shown at the bottom area of that interface: *connection, users list, setup game, play*. These tabs group functionality or services provided by the game.

The first tab (Fig. 2.a) includes the functionality that allows potential players to connect to a MANET. The MANET represents the shared space where the users can see each other and interact via a chart to organize the racing teams, agree to circuit use in a race and discuss racing strategies with teammates.

The second tab of the game user interface shows a kind of "buddy list", where all users currently connected to the MANET appear. The buddy list also indicates the quality of the connection between the local user and the rest of the people. Such quality is determined by the number of hops required to reach a certain user. Through the buddy list the users can perform point-to-point interactions and also share files.

The parameters of the game can be configured using the functionality shown in the third tab (Fig. 2.b and 2.c); e.g. the teams that participate, the stages involved in the game, and the complexity level of the game. The last tab (Fig. 2.d) is for starting the game. In that screenshot we can see two teams participating in a race, and the white square indicates which car is being controlled by the local user.

The position of a player during the race is updated as it passes through certain checkpoint. The checkpoints are represented by orange cones. Each race consists of several laps around the circuit. The difficulty of the game is directly related to the speed at which cars move.

The first user who joins a particular race becomes the host of that race. The rest of the users connected to the MANET can choose to create a new race or join an existing one. The host user is the only one able to configure the race.

3   Conclusions and Future Work

Hospitalized kids are usually affected by changing moods due to their social isolation produced by treatments; particularly when these treatments are drawn out over time, or the kids must be remain in his/her room. Their mood affects body defenses, hence the importance of promoting healthy mood boosting environments.

To deal with this issue, this article proposes the use of an ubiquitous game, called *MagicRace,* that runs hardware constrained devices connected through a MANET. The game allows social interactions among hospitalized kids through various mechanisms: playing, chatting and sharing file (e.g. pictures). The usability and performance of the game was preliminary evaluated. The obtained results indicate the game is ready to be used in a real setting involving hospitalized children. This is exactly the next step of this initiative. We expect that this collaborative ubiquitous game could serve as an emotional support for these kids.

We are also continuing the process of evaluating and improving the game performance; particularly the network communication support, to extend the physical scenarios in which this game can be used.

Acknowledgments. This paper has been partially supported by FONDECYT (Chile), grant 1120207 and by LACCIR, grant R1210LAC002, and also by the CITIC-UCR (Centro de Investigación en Tecnologías de la Información y Comunicación de la Universidad de Costa Rica).

References

[1] Cordove, M.J., Giese-Davis, J., Golant, M., Kronnenwetter, C., Chang, V., McFarlin, S., Spiegel, D.: Mood disturbance in community cancer support groups: The role of emotional suppression and fighting spirit. Journal of Psychosomatic Research 55, 461–467 (2003)

[2] Giles, L.C., Glonek, G.F., Luszcz, M.A., Andrews, G.R.: Effect of social networks on 10 year survival in very old Australians: the Australian longitudinal study of aging. J. of Epidemiology and Community Health 59(7), 574–579 (2005)

[3] House, J.S., Landis, K.R., Umberson, D.: Social relationships and health. Science 241(4865), 540–545 (1988)

[4] Joinson, A.N.: Looking up or 'Keeping up with' people? Motives and Uses of Facebook. In: Proc. of CHI 2008, pp. 1027–1036. ACM Press, New York (2008)

[5] Monclar, R., Tecla, A., Oliveira, J., Souza, J.: MEK: Using spatial-temporal information to improve social networks and knowledge dissemination. Information Sciences 179(15), 2524–2537 (2009)

[6] Rodríguez-Covili, J.F., Ochoa, S.F., Pino, J.A., Messeguer, R., Medina, E., Royo, D.: A Communication Infrastructure to Ease the Development of Mobile Collaborative Applications. Journal of Network and Computer Applications 34(6), 1883–1893 (2011)

A Wearable Electrocardiogram Recorder (ECG) Using ISO / IEEE 11073 Interoperability Standard

Santiago Led[1], Miguel Martínez-Espronceda[1], Javier Redondo[1], Alfonso Baquero[1], Maciej Niegowski[1], Luis Serrano[1], and Luis Cabezas[2]

[1] Public University of Navarre,
Pamplona 31006, Spain
Santiago.Led@unavarra.es
http://www.unavarra.es
[2] Life Quality Technology Accessibility and Innovation S.L.,
Noain 31110, Spain
info@lqtai.com
http://www.lqtai.com

Abstract. Emerging technologies enable new health delivery services based on Ambient Intelligence (AmI) concepts, Ubiquitous Health (U-Health) paradigm, and patient empowerment. However, these services show several drawbacks, being the lack of standardization one of the most important. The under development ISO/IEEE 11073 for Personal Health Devices (X73PHD) has substantially evolved during the last years. It defines the interface between agents and managers. Nevertheless, this standard has not been broadly tested. This paper presents a proof-of-concept implementation of a Electrocardiogram (ECG) recorder used in a real U-Health service. The functional model of this agent proposes several solutions to problems that, being out of X73PHD scope, were found during the implementation process. The hardware architecture describes four blocks: ECG acquisition and conditioning, storage, Bluetooth communication, and microcontroller. This paper also describes the Domain Information Model (DIM) used to model the agent and its objects. One of them is the Medical Device System (MDS). It provides general information about the agent. Another one is the ECG waveform object which represents the acquired ECG signal. In addition, the Device Status object indicates events related to malfunction. The last object defined is the periodic scanner which gathers observations and reports them to the manager. In addition, the service and communication models are also described. The former implements mandatory object access procedures. The latter defines association procedures and transport profiles, including Bluetooth Health Device Profile (HDP). The ECG recorder is integrated into a U-Health interoperable service using Android 4.0 smartphones and X73PHD.

Keywords: Ambient Intelligence (AmI), Bluetooth, Electrocardiogram (ECG), Health Device Profile (HDP), Health Informatics, Interoperability, ISO/IEEE 11073 (X73), Low-Voltage Low-Power (LV-LP), Personal Health (P-Health), Personal Health Device (PHD), smartphone, smart sensors, stroke, wearable.

J. Bravo, R. Hervás, and M. Rodríguez (Eds.): IWAAL 2012, LNCS 7657, pp. 175–182, 2012.
© Springer-Verlag Berlin Heidelberg 2012

1   Introduction

During the last years, there has been an astonishing development of new health delivery applications and services based on Information Technology (IT). These suppose a mean to improve life quality of patients (Patient Empowerment) [1]. In a general Ubiquitous Health (U-Health) context, smart sensors transparently allow tracking of people in their environment, impacting minimally on their daily activities. Classic processes evolve to new application scenarios such as health and wellness, aging independently, and chronic disease management. In the latter scenario, Electro Cardiogram (ECG) monitoring services for patients may have a especial impact due to the high prevalence of cardiovascular diseases in modern society [2].

U-Health services are based on Ambient Intelligence (AmI) concepts and consist of wearable remote monitoring systems among others [3, 4]. These systems allow controlling the biomedical status of a individual and his/her environment by sending relevant information to a hospital or referral center. Once there, data can be post-processed to provide the appropriate feedback to specialists [5, 6]. The potential of these platforms is evident, but there are also some drawbacks. One of the most important is the lack of standardization. It is essential to have end-to-end standard-based communications to get maximum returns [7, 8]. In this sense, the main standardization bodies have developed various standards (DICOM, HL7, ISO/EN 13606), although their implementation is not trivial. For this reason, organizations such as Integrating Healthcare Enterprise (IHE) and Continua Health Alliance are significantly boosting development in order to establish interoperable personal health systems [9].

In terms of AmI, the ISO/IEEE 11073 family of standards has evolved substantially during the last years to adapt the newest wireless technologies and use cases. Originally it was focused on the Point-of-Care (PoC) with its classic version (X73-PoC). The emerging use cases in U-Health have boosted its development toward a simplified version for portable and wearable medical devices, called ISO/IEEE11073 for Personal Health Device (PHD) (X73PHD) [10]. Today, this family of standards is under development, but many medical device specializations are available. These include weight, blood pressure or glucometer, among many others. Especially, one of the latest documents to be adopted has been the X73-10406 specialization [11]. It is aimed at basic ECG devices (1-3 lead ECG). This paper presents a novel implementation of a ECG recorder implementing X73PHD.

This paper is organized as follows. In Section 2, the functional model of the ECG recording agent is presented, showing some decisions taken around initial set-up procedures that are out of X73PHD scope. Later, the hardware architecture is presented, showing the blocks that made up the agent. Then, the X73PHD stack implementation is shown in Section 3, indicating the options chosen in the Domain Information Model (DIM), the Service model and the Communication model. Finally, conclusions are drawn in Section 4.

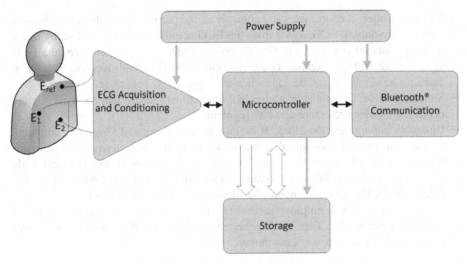

Fig. 1. Hardware architecture

2   Functional Model

The functional model defines how to work with this agent. The agent has a hidden reset button that enables to configure it. The reset button is hidden in the casing but it can be accessed using a punch. When it is pressed for no more than 10 seconds, the agent is put into configuration state. In that state, the agent enables Bluetooth module for one minute to listen to connection requests from managers (allowing paging and setting connectable). If other manager connects, the agent starts the association. If the association successes, the agent firstly stores manager's network address as the default manager address and then disconnects and disables listening. Whenever the agent is disconnected, the agent connects to the default manager, sending its data. If the reset button is pressed for more than 10 seconds, the agent additionally resets all settings to factory. The agent is protected by a Bluetooth Personal Identification Number (PIN) which is set in factory. The manager needs to know the PIN in order to connect to the agent, even in configuration state.

The agent is usually configured by the technician. Once the agent is configured, the agent will automatically connect to the manager, so the manager can begin gathering ECG waveform from the agent. If there are disconnections, the agent will retry to connect to the manager (once per minute).

3   Hardware Architecture

Front end's hardware architecture, shown in Fig. 1, consists of the following blocks:

— ECG acquisition and conditioning. This analog block acquires a single lead ECG (lead II) using three electrodes. It amplifies and filters the ECG waveform.

— Microcontroller. It coordinates and controls all the peripherals of the agent. First, it converts the analog ECG signal from the ECG acquisition and conditioning block using an internal Analog to Digital Converter (ADC). Second, it stores the ECG signal in the storage module. Third, it controls the Bluetooth module. Finally, it manages power status and decides when to trigger a low-battery-level alert.
— Storage module. It is made of non-volatile memories (32Mb) that are used to store persistent metrics (PM-store and PM-segment).
— Bluetooth communication block. It is implemented using and Original Equipment Manufacturer (OEM) module that provides Bluetooth connectivity. It implements Multi-channel Adaptation Protocol (MCAP) and the part of Health Device Profile (HDP). The OEM module incorporates an Operating System (OS) that is controlled externally via Universal Asynchronous Receiver-Transmitter (UART).
— Power management. It employs several DC/DC converters and a rechargeable Li-Po battery (650mAh). This block generates voltages to all the blocks. It is very optimized to improve agent's autonomy.

The Bluetooth communication block incorporates a WT12 module (Class II). The WT12 supports Bluetooth 2.1 and Enhanced Data Rate (2.1 + EDR). The WT12 provides the iWrap OS, a proprietary solution of Bluegiga. The iWrap OS implements the MCAP. This protocol is needed in order to implement HDP. The MCAP allows establishing multiple channels between the so-called sink (manager) and source (agent). MCAP defines two types of transports:

— Reliable: Data transmitted over these channels arrive in the same order. No packet is lost, unless the connection is lost.
— Best effort: Packets are lost if they are delayed in excess.

The communication between the microcontroller and the WT12 module is carried out through the UART and using an own command-based protocol. The high level Application Programming Interface (API) of this protocol simplifies the operation of the microcontroller module.

4   X73PHD Implementation

The agent implements the ISO/IEEE 11073-10406 "Simple ECG" specialization [10, 11]. It provides an extended configuration that allows operating in Real Time (RT) monitoring. It is implemented using a periodic scanner. When the scanner is enabled, it sends ECG signal waveform continuously.

4.1   Domain Information Model

The DIM represents the information in the agent, using an object oriented and structured representation. Objects are organized in a hierarchy where the root object is the Medical Device System (MDS). Each DIM configuration has its own set of objects. The objects that make up the DIM configuration is shown in Fig. 2.

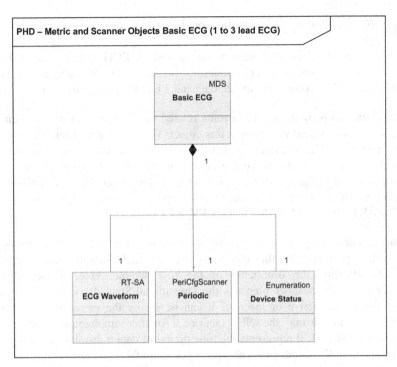

Fig. 2. Domain Information Model (DIM)

MDS Object. The MDS object represents generic features of the agent. Among other features, the MDS object indicates the type of device by the System-Type-Spec-List attribute with the values {MDC_DEV_SPEC_PROFILE_ECG, 1} and {MDC_DEV_SUB_SPEC_PROFILE_ECG, 1}. Since the agent only supports relative time stamp references, the Mds-Time-Info attribute contains the value agent-support-relative-time. With regards to the power supply features, the MDS object implements Power-Status and Battery-Level attributes. The Battery-Status attribute indicates that the agent is powered by batteries using setting it to the "onBattery" value. The Battery-Level attribute is used to indicate the level of battery available at any time (in percentage). Other features include serial number, model, etc.

ECG Waveform Object. The ECG Waveform object is a RT Sample Array (RT-SA) and models the acquired ECG signal. The Type attribute is set to {MDC_PART_SCADA, MDC_ECG_ELEC_POTL_II} to indicate the acquisition of ECG lead II. The ECG data is reported in the Simple-Sa-Observed-Value attribute. Several attributes are needed to interpret the data reported in the Simple-Sa-Observed-Value attribute:

— Sample-period. This attribute contains the 0x28 value according to a sample rate of 200 samples per second.
— Scale-and-Range-Specification. This attribute contains the values {-3, 3, 0, 4095} indicating the absolute voltage range of ECG (-3V and 3V) and the quantification

levels (0 and 4095). The quantification levels correspond to the 12 bit ADC resolution.
— Sa-Specification. This attribute has the number of ECG samples stored by the object and its numerical representation. In this case, 50 samples at 16 bit resolution; 12 bits correspond to real data and 4 bits are padded to zero.

Device Status Object. It indicates events related to the operation of the agent. An enumeration class is used to represent this object. The events that it represents are the reduction of the ECG recording quality due to bad electrode contact, or the total contact loss. These conditions are represented in the Enum-Observed-Value-Bit-Str attribute activating flags (leadwire-loss, leadsignal-loss, leadwire-loss-first-lead, and leadsignal-loss-first-lead). The attribute Type of this object is set to {MDC_PART_PHD_DM, MDC_ECG_DEV_STAT}.

Periodic Scanner Object. It reports the observations in the ECG waveform object. Each event report sent by this object contains 50 ECG samples and a temporal reference indicating the timestamp of the first sample. One of the attributes implemented by the scanner object is the Operational-State. Its value indicates the state of the object, active or inactive. It can be set by the manager to enable the reporting of data using the SET service. Another implemented attribute is the Reporting-Interval. It represents the time period of data transmission. In this case, its value is 250 milliseconds (4 event reports per second).

4.2   Service Model

The agent implements mandatory object access services defined by X73PHD. Not all services are allowed in every object. Thus, only the MDS and the Scanner provide object access services in the DIM implemented.

The MDS object implements three services. First, the MDS-Configuration-Event is used to transmit the configuration to the manager during the association. Second, the MDC-Dynamic-Data-Update-Fixed is used to report attribute change sets in the MDS but also in the Device Status object. Finally, the GET service is provided. It implements the all MDS attributes request (an empty list of attributes). The GET service allows the manager polling the MDS. It is useful to get general information of the agent, such as serial number, detailed specifications, manufacturer, model, etc.

Moreover, the Scanner object implements the Buf-Scan-Report-Grouped service to report ECG Waveform data. This service is the best option to minimize the amount of bytes to send. Scanner object event reports are sent over reliable channels. In this way, the whole ECG signal is received unless connection loss. Delays in the ECG signal visualization in the manager due to the use of reliable channels are negligible compared to the use of best effort channels. These delays could be reduced should the RT-SA used more frequent reporting (a shorter Simple-Sa-Observed-Value), although it goes against efficiency.

Fig. 3. ECG recorder

4.3   Communication Model

The data exchange between agent and manager is based on a point to point communication. According to the Communication model, the agent uses an interface with the iWrap module to manage MCAP and HDP. This interface implements a Type 1 transport profile with reliable and best effort communication channels. The ECG recorder agent firstly establishes a reliable control channel for MCAP management. Then, the reliable data channel for exchanging X73PHD Application Protocol Data Units (APDUs) is opened using the control channel.

An initial association process is required to establish association parameters such as association protocol, exchange protocol, encoding rules, and nomenclature versions. These parameters have the following values in the ECG recorder implementation:

— Association protocol: version 1 (assoc-version1).
— Exchange protocol and version: X73-20601-2010a (data-proto-id-20601) and version 2 (protocol-version2).
— Encoding rules: Medical Device Encoding Rules (MDER).
— Nomenclature codes: X73-10101 version 1 (nom-version1).

5   Conclusion and Future Work

This paper presents a proof-of-concept ECG recorder agent implementing the X73PHD interoperability standard (Fig. 3). The agent uses Bluetooth technology and the HDP. The MCAP is implemented in an external OEM module while the application layer is implemented in a 16-bit microcontroller. The decisions taken outside of the scope of X73PHD are exposed. These include the initial set-up of the agent. The solution adopted was to use a reset button that put the agent in discoverable and connectable state. The DIM of this agent contains the MDS object, a Device Status enumeration object, an ECG Waveform RT-SA object, and a Periodic

Scanner object. The Service model provides the needed operations to access DIM objects remotely. The Communication model defines the association procedures, and transport profile used. Only one reliable data channel is needed for APDU exchange. An ECG acquisition and conditioning block is needed to adapt the ECG signal levels. Moreover, an external storage block is integrated in the agent which is not required for this proof-of-concept application. However, it will be needed for a future store-and-forward version using permanent metric objects (PM-stores and PM-segments). This future version will be able to operate in two modes: real time and store-and-forward. The agent is integrated into an interoperable service based on X73PHD. The service core is an Android 4.0 smartphone. Currently, the smartphone analyzes the ECG signal in real time, providing the patient with real time information (arrhythmia and Atrial Fibrillation (AF)). In addition, the smartphone sends the ECG data to a HealthCare Information Server (HCIS) where the specialist may diagnose illness.

References

1. Monteagudo, J.L., Moreno, O.: eHealth for Patient Empowerment in Europe. World Wide Web electronic publication (2009),
   http://ec.europa.eu/informationsociety/newsroom/cf/itemdetail.cfm?item_id=3448 (last access: June 2012)
2. Donnan, G., Fisher, M., Macleod, M., Davis, S.: Stroke. The Lancet 371(9624), 1612–1623 (2008)
3. Remagnino, P., Foresti, G.: Ambient intelligence: A new multidisciplinary paradigm. IEEE Transactions on Systems, Man, and Cybernetics Part A: Systems and Humans 35(1), 1–6 (2005)
4. Rodriguez, M., Favela, J., Preciado, A., Vizcano, A.: Agent-based ambient intelligence for healthcare. AI Communications 18(3), 201–216 (2005)
5. Bonato, P.: Wearable sensors and systems. IEEE Engineering in Medicine and Biology Magazine 29(3), 25–36 (2010)
6. Teng, X.-F., Zhang, Y.-T., Poon, C., Bonato, P.: Wearable medical systems for p-health. IEEE Reviews in Biomedical Engineering 1, 62–74 (2008)
7. Kun, L.: Interoperability: The cure for what ails us (government affairs). IEEE Engineering in Medicine and Biology Magazine 26(1), 87–90 (2007)
8. Martínez-Espronceda, M., Martínez, I., Serrano, L., Led, S., Trigo, J., Marzo, A., Escayola, J., García, J.: Implementation methodology for interoperable personal health devices with low-voltage low-power constraints. IEEE Transactions on Information Technology in Biomedicine 15(3), 398–408 (2011)
9. Continua Health Alliance, http://www.continuaalliance.org (last visit: October 2010)
10. ISO/IEC/IEEE Health informatics-Personal health device communication-Part 20601: Application profile-Optimized exchange protocol. ISO/IEEE 11073- 20601:2010(E), pp. 1–208, 1 (2010)
11. Health informatics-Personal health device communication Part 10406: Device specialization-Basic electrocardiograph (ECG) (1- to 3-lead ECG). IEEE Std 11073-10406-2011, pp. 1–73, 30 (2011)

Ubiquitous Tele-monitoring Kit (UTK): Measuring Physiological Signals Anywhere at Anytime

Carlos Marcos Lagunar[1], Carlos Cavero Barca[1], Ana María Quintero Padrón[1],
Xavier Planes[2,3], Federico Simmross Wattenberg[4], Carlos Alberola López[4],
Marcos Martín Fernández[4], Noelia Martín Hernández[4], Enric Calderón Oliveras[5],
Javier Corral Herranz[6], Antonio González Martínez[6],
Jordi Huguet[7], and Rosalia Aguilar[7]

[1] ATOS, Albarracín 25, 28037 Madrid, Spain
{carlos.marcos,carlos.cavero,ana.quintero}@atosresearch.eu
[2] Networking Biomedical Research Center on Bioengineering, Biomaterials and
Nanomedicine (CIBER-BBN), Barcelona, Spain
[3] Universitat Pompeu Fabra, Barcelona, Spain
xavier.planes@upf.edu
[4] Universidad de Valladolid, Spain
{fedsim,caralb,marcma}@tel.uva.es, nmarher@lpi.tel.uva.es
[5] Cetemmsa Technological Center, Mataró, Spain
ecalderon@cetemmsa.com
[6] RGB Medical Devices, 28037 Madrid, Spain
{jcorral,agonzalez}@rgb-medical.com
[7] UDIAT Diagnostic Center, 08208 Sabadell, Barcelona, Spain
{jhuguetn,raguilar}@tauli.cat

Abstract. The Ubiquitous Tele-monitoring Kit (UTK) is aimed at helping the clinician in acquiring, managing and normalizing information coming from the patients at home and storing the data in a distributed system. This approach aims to reduce costs in the healthcare system and alleviate the inherent problems to chronic patients who usually may visit the doctors. The proposed system closes the tele-monitoring loop; wearable and ergonomic sensors integrated in the textile, automatic detection and storage of the information coming from the sensors in a common platform (XNAT) and processing and visualization of the retrieved physiological signals presenting the data treated to the clinician to optimize the continuum of care and the decision-making.

Keywords: ubiquitous, tele-monitoring, remote, person-centric, individual atlas, population atlas, signal simulation, alarm generation, XNAT.

1   Introduction

Chronic diseases, such as heart disease, stroke, cancer, chronic respiratory diseases and diabetes, are by far the leading cause of mortality in the world, representing 63% of all deaths [1]. The quality of life of such patients is severely affected by complications and continuous visits to hospitals to monitor physiological parameters increasing thus healthcare and social costs.

J. Bravo, R. Hervás, and M. Rodríguez (Eds.): IWAAL 2012, LNCS 7657, pp. 183–191, 2012.
© Springer-Verlag Berlin Heidelberg 2012

Another key issue is the increasing healthcare cost: according to World Bank figures, public expenditure on healthcare in the EU could jump from 8% of GDP in 2000 to 14% in 2030 and continue its growth beyond that date. The overriding concern of Europe's healthcare sector is to find ways to balance budgets and restrain spending. Unless that is done, the funds to pay for healthcare will soon fall short of demand [2]. The tele-monitoring allows easing the patient's life reducing hospital visits and time of hospitalization thus increasing the personal welfare and decreasing healthcare costs.

The tele-monitoring term mainly deals with two factors: functionality and volume of information. Functionality of an ubiquitous monitoring system firstly requires ergonomic sensors (usability) which is critical when the monitoring is done during long periods of time and secondly continuous storage of the data. The integration of the sensors into textile allows using them in a comfortable way. The utilization of non-invasive sensors integrated into textile permits the acquisition of relevant physiological parameters in a comfortable way without bothering the patient.

Data management covers communication with the sensors, data storage and normalization in a distributed system and signals processing. Physiological signals management in a scenario where acquisition is ubiquitously and securely performed requires the definition of a framework for the transmission and storage of collected data under a significantly flexible and simple format and also for efficiently enabling its posterior querying and exploitation in post-processing and data analysis tasks.

Similar existing tools as Fitbit, Adidas miCoach, and Nike Fuelband are popular between consumers but they are mainly focused on activity monitor. Other software available from Garmin, Suunto and Polar are more cardiovascular oriented but lack of ergonomics, standardization and medical analysis. UTK is a clinical oriented solution which provides ergonomics sensors integrated into textile, data normalization compliant with European health standards and physiological signal treatment.

The architecture contains four components:

Sensors and Textiles. The sensors used to obtain the cardiovascular physiological signals with an ergonomic and wearable system are:

- Intelligent T-Shirt with the sensors integrated.
- Wearable hardware modules with wireless transmission.

Gateway. This module permits the automatic detection of the sensors, data normalization and connection with the distributed system to store the information.

Data Management. This component provides data structure and integration with XNAT [3] platform and GIMIAS [4].

Post-processing. The last element permits the processing for the signal delineation obtaining new parameters and showing them to the clinician using GIMIAS software which also allows images treatment.

The general schema of the architecture developed is shown in Fig 1.

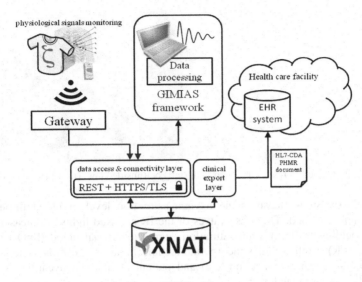

Fig. 1. UTK Architecture

2   Sensors and Textiles

Electrocardiogram (ECG) and Pulse oximeter (SpO_2) sensors have been integrated into a fabric garment to continuously monitor cardiovascular physiological data. The wearable intelligent garment is a T-Shirt with short sleeves with a zipper front opening. It has an adjustable belt with two internal lateral pockets where the acquisition modules are settled.

The pulse oximeter is an ear clip sensor. Because of its location the integration of the wiring begins on the neck going down through the lateral right frontal of the garment until the acquisition module interface on the belt. For comfortable reasons, the wire is guided through an inside build fabric tunnel which simultaneously hides it.

The ECG sensor consists of four electrodes of conductive fabric integrated as horizontal strips in direct contact with the body and located in the arms and waist. Two of them are placed on the superior side of the each sleeve which in has a Velcro strip flap. The two waist electrodes are located on the inferior lateral sides. Once the T-shirt is worn, the garment will be adjusted by the user to properly fix the electrodes and assure their contact with the body (see fig. 2).

The intelligent T-shirt also incorporates the electronic modules with the signal treatment and analysis of the textile ECG electrodes and SpO_2 sensor. Additionally, these modules have Bluetooth technology which allows the real time connection with the Gateway for transmitting the measured and processed data.

The ECG module is an electrocardiograph which records the electrical activity of the heart through the mentioned electrodes providing the derivations I, II, III, aVR, aVF y aVL. The different derivations are sampled at 200Hz, and after applying an algorithm for the QRS complex detection, the module is able to calculate the heart rate (HR) and some types of arrhythmias. To avoid ECG saturation by the mobility of electrodes, the derivations are sampled with 15 bits resolution in 32 mV range.

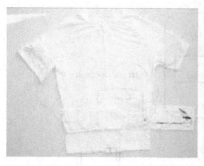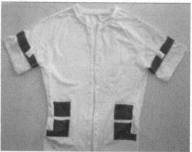

Fig. 2. ECG and SpO$_2$ sensors integrated, (left) belt inside view; (right) frontal view

The module of SpO$_2$ measures the oxygen saturation level of blood through the pletismography method. The pulse waves of the IR and Red lights are measured and analyzed yielding to the oxygen saturation degree of arterial blood (SpO$_2$) and the Pulse Rate (PR). Both modules incorporate technical alarms detection systems (level of the battery, sensors connection, etc) and patient alarms (Tachycardia, Asystole, Bradycardia, out of range levels, etc).

3   Gateway

The Gateway is a pc, laptop, Smartphone or server in charge of automatically collecting the information coming from the devices. It allows locally storing the data normalized in a standard format and sending the physiological signals to the distributed system.

For the tele-monitoring purposes a smartphone with Android platform (Samsung Galaxy II) is used as the gateway in order to easily adapt the gateway in the textile (with the multiple sensors integrated). Future versions will cover iOS and Windows mobile applications. The protocols covered are ZigBee and Bluetooth because of energy efficiency and high performance. The Gateway is aimed to be 11073 set of standards compliant.

There is a first stage of sensor discovering, where the whole Bluetooth spectrum is scanned looking for compatible devices, then a hand-shake protocol between the Gateway and each sensor and finally the transmission phase, when the sensor Bluetooth can be sent to sleep mode to save battery: when it has collected the specified amount of data, it wakes up and transmit it to the Gateway. These cycles are dependent of the kind of patient that is being monitoring and are completely configurable from the Gateway.

To store the data, it must be firstly normalized to a common format, since a variety of sensors information, like oxygen saturation, non-invasive pressure or heart rate is received by the Gateway. The communication with the sensors follows a RFCOMM schema, where the frames received are bytes-based. This is converted inside the Gateway into a XML file and uploaded to XNAT. The XML-schemas developed are meant to be scalable as new sensors (and kind of measures) are added to the system. The gateway not only receives clinical data from the sensors, but also Control Data like "sensor disconnected", "not enough light from the diode", "movement of the patient" or the level of charge of the sensors batteries warning the patients if some error condition happens and assessing them about how to better solve the problem. Concerning the security, the communication works under a Legacy Pairing mechanism, common for Bluetooth v2.0, although an upgrade to SSP (Secure Simple Pairing) is under study. The communication Gateway - XNAT is made over HTTP protocol with Basic Authorization, which is enough for research purposes. The upgrade to HTTPs over SSL is also straightforward and thus suitable for future development of the platform.

For the cvREMOD project XNAT was used as the data storage but the gateway is also prepared to comply with ISO EN13606 (even hl7) in order to provide the semantic interoperability to the Hospital Information System (HIS).

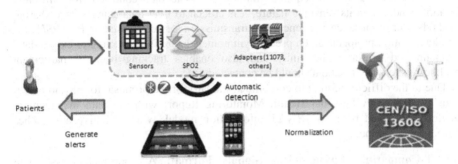

Fig. 3. Gateway

4   Data Management

To our knowledge, physiological signals are nowadays stored using many diverse existing data formats, but none of them has been established as a '*de facto*' format [5]. This issue complicates interoperability between systems in the exchange of data and also makes the hereby presented work a challenging and novel task. The objectives of having such a platform are to:

- Stimulate scientific research focused on stored data in order to generate new knowledge on cardiovascular diseases.
- Evaluate the integrative costs of propagating such physiological information in health records information systems.

Among the possible existing solutions studied, the Clinical Document Architecture (CDA) specification is of particular relevance, being part of the informatics standards for healthcare information management HL7, HL7-CDA specifies a document structure for the exchange of generic persistent clinical information [6] based on XML markup format. CDA includes a representation for health-related sensor data known as Personal Health Monitoring Report (PHMR). Although it is still in draft version, PHMR presents a promising solution for managing tele-health information [7].

The storage system proposed aims to archive in a structured manner biomedical signals from different devices and sensors in conjunction with meta-data affecting such acquired physiological signals. Furthermore, it is part of a heterogeneous data management platform, a repository of biomedical information related to cardiovascular pathologies deployed in the framework of Spanish project cvREMOD [8]. Such platform manages archived and processed information (multi-modal medical imaging, physiological signals, clinical and measured data, demographics and derived processed data) in a patient-centric linked manner, having different data sources combined together to provide additional and useful information in the diagnostic stage, treatment selection and prevention planning. The system deployed is based on XNAT framework [3], (eXtensible Neuroimaging Archive Toolkit). XNAT offers a highly flexible platform for research image-base archival, allowing the definition of customized data structures (e.g. biomedical variables or measures) to be stored.

A connectivity component has been developed using a common set of tools for searching, archiving, retrieving, processing and linking data in a harmonized framework. Such a system requires granting access to data collected from different locations and, given its sensitive nature, it is crucial to treat data using secure sharing methods. Our proposal ensures encrypted transmission services (based on HTTPS/TLS), de-identification protocols and a pseudonym nomenclature infrastructure to export data, maintain and preserve anonymity and also enables tracking back to participant healthcare site when a patient should be contacted.

Due to the difficulty found to combine a standard format proposal for physiological data as HL7-CDA Personal Health Monitoring Report with the data management platform deployed based on XNAT information model, two alternative approaches have been developed:

XNAT-Compatible Physiological Signals Format. A coordinated task-force established between clinicians, researchers and technologists in the formal definition and model of complex data types based on XNAT framework that reflect the required information entities present in cvREMOD project.

Interoperable HL7-CDA PHMR Format Approach. An effort to encode data measured and recorded by the biomedical sensors in standard HL7-CDA format using XML-based transformations.

5   GIMIAS

GIMIAS [4] is a workflow-oriented environment focused on biomedical computational image and simulation. The open source framework is extensible through plug-ins and provides a single research platform where different tools and algorithms are integrated to build clinical software prototypes ready to be transferred into clinical environment. GIMIAS has been successfully used to develop clinical prototypes in the fields of cardiac imaging and simulation, angiography imaging and simulation, orthopedics and neuroimaging.

BSD license has been chosen for GIMIAS, providing a very permissive use of GIMIAS for commercial and non-commercial purposes. All third parties used are also flowing BSD or LGPL license, like for example VTK, ITK or wxWidgets.

Three GIMIAS plugins are used in the context of this use case:

- **MITK plugin [9]** provides standard visualization and interaction features for medical imaging software, like for example the visualization of orthogonal views or selection of landmarks
- **XNAT plugin [10]** allows connecting to a remote XNAT database to transfer images, signals or any other kind of biomedical data.

- **Signal Viewer plugin [11]** extends the framework with the possibility to visualize and process signals, always synchronized with the rest of the patient data. For example an EEG can be visualized in synchronization with the fMRI images acquired synchronously. Furthermore, the plugin allows managing annotations, visualization of multiple channels or changing visualization properties.

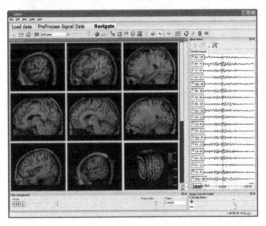

Fig. 4. Synchronous visualization of fMRI images and EEG signals

6   Post-processing

The post-processing pipe-line covers several physiological signals, such as ECG (electrocardiograms), PPG (photo-plethysmographic) signals, respiratory signals and so forth, which are processed in order to obtain individual atlases both for control subjects and for patients. Several steps are carried out: (1) the cardiologist gets data previously stored on XNAT platform using the Clinical data load plugin. This plugin facilitates the search allowing the general practitioner to filter out the information by age, sex and so on. Once selected the patient, there are two options: either download the data from XNAT or visualize they if they have been previously downloaded to our PC. In both cases Clinical data load plugin will show the next step depending on the signal being used. (2) preprocessing, such as filtering, base-line wandering correction, and so on; (3) signal delineation, in order to obtain representative signal points (labels); (4) time and amplitude normalization (warping) using the labels found in the delineation step; (5) statistical modeling of the label time series, which is performed by means of a non-linear, non-stationary stochastic model; and finally, (6) statistical modeling of the signal residue (waveform) by means of cyclo-stationary time series modeling. The parameters of all modeling steps give rise to what we called "individual atlas".

Statistical atlases of electro-physiological signals allow designing signal simulation by means of re-synthesizing waveforms using the parameters given by individual atlases. An atlas is constructed taking into account signal variability along time, so several simulations of the individual give rise to different signals sharing statistical similarities but, allowing statistical differences as if several samples of the same patient would have been acquired (see fig. 5). The atlas permits:

- To summarize patient properties in a reduced set of parameters.
- To simulate patient evolution by simply changing model parameters.
- To complete missing epochs in failed acquisitions.
- To compare different patients and construct automatic diagnostic aid systems.

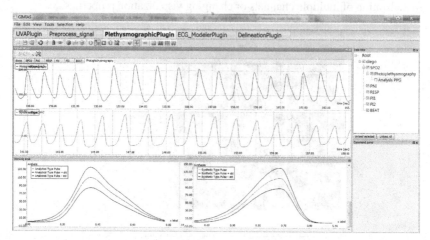

Fig. 5. PPG individual atlas estimation and re-synthesis after parameter modification

Population atlases for a set of individuals sharing some common properties such as, same cardio-pathology, same gender, same age range, same medication, same diet, and so on, can be built in order to simulate individuals within the population. They also allow to automatically triggering an alarm whenever a specific individual atlas gives rise to parameters out of range. This can be eventually performed in real-time making the ubiquitous system activate clinical procedures to send emergency units directly to patient home.

Post-processing has been prototyped in Matlab and migrated to GIMIAS platform. The migration, however, is not straightforward due to the very different programming philosophies followed by Matlab (a prototyping language) and GIMIAS (written in C++ and based upon a production-oriented framework).

7   Conclusion

The UTK system aims to design a robust, simple and scalable system to provide the automatic detection of the sensors which permits the connection of multiple devices simultaneously with a cost effective energy management in order to maximize the time of use of the batteries. Another objective is to implement a platform to transmit the information stressing the time throughput without losing the versatility. The gateway is the place where all the physiological signals coming from the wearable sensors are automatically and transparently retrieved, normalized and stored in a distributed system (XNAT).

The physician or nurse can configure the system and assign the T-shirt and smartphone to the patient, so the physiological signals will be associated to an anonymous id. The user does not know anything about the connection of the devices, because once configured the complete process is carried out in an automatic and transparent way.

The UTK provides the clinicians with the 24 hour patient monitoring, increasing the data to manage, and facilitates the decision making and the diagnosis. Finally the automatic connection between XNAT and GIMIAS allows the doctors to process and visualize the physiological signals discovering possible abnormalities in the patient health status almost immediately.

Acknowledgments. The research described in this paper was carried out in the cvREMOD project (Convergencia de tecnologías médicas para la gestión integral del Remodelado Cardiovascular). The project is co-funded by the CDTI (Centro para el Desarrollo Tecnológico Industrial) (2009 - 2012) by Spanish authorities.

References

1. World Health Oganization, Chronic Diseases,
   http://www.who.int/topics/chronic_diseases/en/
   (visited, September 11, 2012)
2. The future of healthcare in Europe. A report from The Economist Intelligence Unit, Page 1, Foreword (2011), http://es.scribd.com/doc/97648309/EIU-Janssen-Healthcare-Web-Version (visited, September 11, 2012)
3. Marcus, D.S., Olsen, T., Ramaratnam, M., Buckner, R.L.: The Extensible Neuroimaging Archive Toolkit (XNAT): An informatics platform for managing, exploring, and sharing neuroimaging data. Neuroinformatics, 11–34 (2007)
4. Larrabide, I., Omedas, P., Martelli, Y., Planes, X., Nieber, M., Moya, J.A., Butakoff, C., Sebastián, R., Camara, O., De Craene, M., Bijnens, B.H., Frangi, A.F.: GIMIAS: An Open Source Framework for Efficient Development of Research Tools and Clinical Prototypes. In: Ayache, N., Delingette, H., Sermesant, M. (eds.) FIMH 2009. LNCS, vol. 5528, pp. 417–426. Springer, Heidelberg (2009)
5. Schlögl, A.: An Overview on Data Formats for Biomedical Signals. In: Dössel, O., Schlegel, W.C. (eds.) WC 2009. IFMBE Proceedings, vol. 25, pp. 1557–1560. Springer, Heidelberg (2009)
6. Dolin, R.H., et al.: HL7 Clinical Document Architecture, Release 2. Journal of the American Medical Informatics Association, 30–39 (2006)
7. Wolf, K.-H., et al.: Representing Sensor Data Using the HL7 CDA Personal Healthcare Monitoring Report Draft. Medical Informatics in a United and Healthy Europe (2009)
8. Convergencia de tecnologías médicas para la gestión integral del Remodelado Cardiovascular, http://www.cvremod.com (visited, September 11, 2012)
9. SSD Team, CISTIB-UPF, MITK (October 05, 2011),
   http://www.gimias.org/gimias-extensions?sobi2Task=sobi2Details&sobi2Id=25
   (visited, September 11, 2012)
10. SSD Team, CISTIB-UPF/UDIAT, XNAT (October 05, 2011),
    http://www.gimias.org/gimias-extensions?sobi2Task=sobi2Details&sobi2Id=32
    (visited, September 11, 2012)
11. SSD Team, CISTIB-UPF, Signal Viewer (September 30, 2011),
    http://www.gimias.org/gimias-extensions?sobi2Task=sobi2Details&sobi2Id=2
    (visited, September 11, 2012)

Modular Hardware Design and Realization for Vital Signs Monitoring

Jan Havlík[1], Lenka Lhotská[2], Jakub Parák[1], Matouš Pokorný[1],
Jan Dvořak[1], and Zdeněk Horčík[1]

[1] Department of Circuit Theory, Faculty of Electrical Engineering,
Czech Technical University in Prague, Technická 6, CZ-16627 Prague 6
[2] Department of Cybernetics, Faculty of Electrical Engineering,
Czech Technical University in Prague, Technická 6, CZ-16627 Prague 6
xhavlikj@fel.cvut.cz

Abstract. Remote vital signs monitoring is attracting more and more attention as the population in developed countries is aging, and as the chronic diseases appear more frequently in the population. Smart mobile technologies and miniaturization in electronics have enabled fast development of systems for remote monitoring of vital signs. This paper presents a hardware solution of a mobile device for remote monitoring and shows that the mentioned issues can be addressed and efficiently solved. The project focused on long term measurement of heart rate and the Intelligent Primer Nurse project are introduced in the paper.

Keywords: telemedicine, telemonitoring, assistive technologies, heart rate, electrocardiography, plethysmography.

1 Introduction

Information and communication technologies have become inevitable and almost inseparable parts of our lives. One of the fast developing areas is remote patient monitoring that uses devices to remotely collect and send data to a monitoring station for interpretation. Such "home telehealth" applications might include a specific vital sign, such as blood glucose or heart ECG or a variety of indicators for homebound patients. Such services can be used to supplement the use of visiting nurses. This area attracts more and more attention as the population in developed countries is ageing. Especially in this area we can find a lot of mobile applications based on wearable sensing systems (wearable sensors, body area networks, etc.). They enable measuring and collecting vast amount of data of individuals. This multi-parametric data may include physiological measurements, medical images, biochemical data, and other measurements related to a person's activity, lifestyle and surrounding environment. There will be increased demand on processing and interpreting such data for accurate alerting and signalling of risks and for supporting healthcare professionals in their decision making, informing family members, and the person himself/herself.

J. Bravo, R. Hervás, and M. Rodríguez (Eds.): IWAAL 2012, LNCS 7657, pp. 192–199, 2012.

Although many issues have been successfully solved and introduced either in applied research or in development of prototypes or final products there are still many problems on the waiting list. Nowadays we can measure relatively unobtrusively many physiological parameters on a human body: electrocardiogram (ECG), heart rate, breathing rate, body temperature, blood pressure, energy output, etc. [1]. There have been performed many clinical trials, e.g. [2,3] assessing the usefulness and efficiency of telemonitoring systems. However the task of data processing and especially evaluation and interpretation remains still challenging. It has many reasons, especially if the signals are recorded while the persons perform their daily activities in standard environment and not in a noise free laboratory. The data contains noise and artefacts, both from the body itself (movements, worse contact of sensors to body) and environment. Thus the task of noise and artefact removal is not yet fully solved and remains open for the future research and development. Another challenging and open issue is standardization of data formats (i.e. the ECG, electroencephalography, and other medical devices measuring biological signals generate proprietary data formats which are usually not publicly known thus it is impossible to integrate such devices into larger systems because the signals can be processed only by software delivered by the device producer), data transfer protocols; security and data privacy. Recently there have been published many papers analyzing these problems, comparing existing standards and recommending future standardization activities, e.g. [4]. In [5] there has been proposed a general architecture of this type of systems respecting existing standards in communication between individual modules. It covers the whole chain from data acquisition / measurement over data collection, identification, transformation up to evaluation and storage in an EHR system. To allow the "plug-and-play" approach the interfaces must be based on well defined standards. We have in mind especially following categories: ISO units for measurement of physical quantities, ISO IEEE standards in communication, standard file formats in software area, HL7 standards on the side of information systems.

2   Hardware Design and Realization

General concept of the presented telemedicine system is based on several requirements. The most important ones are:

- system modularity
  One of the most important requirements is to have a modular system. This concept presents a possibility to make quick and easy changes of the system design.
- and easy-to-use system.
  Another requirement is to have an easy-to-use telemedical kit. It is very important, because it enables to rebuild the system for new applications with low effort.

The presented system is modular and could be divided into three main parts – input modules, control unit and telecommunication modules (see Fig. 1). The

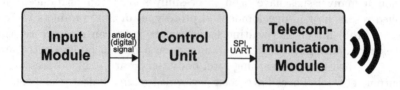

Fig. 1. General concept of the system

main task of the system is to sense several vital signs like electrocardiograph (ECG), blood pressure (NIBP) or oxygen saturation (pulse oxymetry, SpO2), to process acquired signals and to communicate them to a PC based system (desktop PC, laptop or computer network access point) using any type of standardized wireless technologies such as Bluetooth, WiFi or GSM. The choice of vital sign monitored by the system and the choice of wireless technology used for data transfer are based on the intended application of the system.

Input modules transduce measured biosignals to electrical value, especially analog voltage (however any type of digital data as input value is also possible). The output of these modules could be one or more dimensional signal. It means the control unit behind the input module has to be able to process more signals at the same time, for example leads I to III for ECG signal processing or red and infrared signals for pulse oxymetry measurement.

The control unit is a core of the whole system and has to perform more tasks simultaneously. The most important ones are:

- to acquire input analog signals and to convert them to digital data;
- to process these signals and/or to parameterize them;
- to prepare data packets according to defined communication protocol;
- to control the communication line (handshaking the line) and to send the data;
- and to provide the user interface of whole system.

Communication modules are the last part of the system. The main task of these modules is to support the signal transmission between the control unit and PC based system on the level of the physical layer. The handshaking of the line is controlled by the control unit and/or PC based part of system.

The communication interfaces between the modules are strictly defined, the modules are reciprocally inter-changeable. It means it is possible to choose measured signal (for example ECG, NIBP, SpO2) and the type of connection (Bluetooth, WiFi, GSM), choose appropriate modules and set-up the user-defined system quickly and easy. The data format is well defined and satisfies the basic requirements on interoperability [6].

All modules are realized using standard components mixed on surface mount and through-hole technologies. The PCBs are designed as four layer boards, with two signal layers and two layers for power supply and shielding.

The hardware realization of the telemedical system is supplemented by software libraries in our design. The prepared software libraries include code libraries for control unit, pre-prepared firmware set-ups for communication modules and software application for the desktop PC. This application serves as a basic gateway from the system to the PC based platform and provides easy way to set-up parameters of transfer and initial visualization of received data. The role of prepared software libraries is to support users in developing their own project without detailed knowledge of registry implementations in each module and assembler coding and also without additional requirements on time and effort.

3   Applications

The designed and realized telemedical system could be used as a basic platform for many applications in the field of assistive technologies, telemonitoring of vital signs, as a supervision system at home and institutialized care for the sick, disordered or elderly people etc.

The system is also able to transfer the raw data and the aggregated data. Based on the application demands it is possible to choose the communication protocol and the method of data processing.

3.1   Long Term Measurement of Heart Rate

A long term measurement of heart rate (HR) is the most common method of vital signs monitoring. A lot of cardiac abnormalities could be diagnosed from the long term record of the heart activity. For these reasons the long term recording of heart activity is used not only for medical purposes, but also during psychical and physical stress testing. During the physical stress tests the recordings of acceleration and heart rate are frequently performed.

There are a lot of methods how to obtain and process the ECG signal and how to compute the HR from the signal. Unfortunately, only few methods are implementable in small portable devices due to the lack of computational performance in these devices. For that reason the method for processing of ECG signal with very small computational demands was designed and implemented in our project. The raw ECG signal is normalized firstly and the mean value is removed. After the normalization the 50 Hz filtering is applied using the biquad band stop and also the filtering of breathing activity artefacts is applied using the 0,5 Hz Butterworth high pass filter. Finally, the signal preprocessing is completed with the R–peaks filtering using the Butterworth band pass filter with passband 15 Hz to 20 Hz.

After the signal preprocessing, the energy of ECG is computed. This operation enhances the R peaks in the signal. Finally, the integrator filter is applied to the signal. The filter smooths the signal and highlights the R-peaks. After this operation the R-peaks are localized by the thresholding and the HR is computed from the R–R intervals. The signal smoothed by integrator, the localized R-peaks and the computed HR are shown in Fig. 2.

The realized device was evaluated during the stress test containing running, walking and idle standing in the park. The professional HR meter Polar F7 [7]

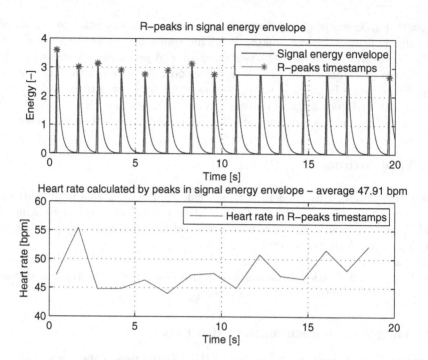

Fig. 2. The smoothed ECG signal, localized R-peaks and the computed heart rate

was used as a reference device for the evaluation. The comparison of results from the own developed and Polar F7 is shown in Fig. 3.

The results from the realized device are fully sufficient, the main advantage of the device is the possibility to store signals for future processing on a SD card or to transfer them to a superordinate system.

3.2   Intelligent Primer Nurse

This particular application focuses on the design and development of the device for monitoring vital activity. The realized device is able to monitor vital signs continously and to activate alarm if the signs are not in the specified range. It means the device is something like a personal and portable vital signs monitor similar to the monitors in intensive care units. The target group of users are chronically diseased, elderly and other threatened persons.

The device is based on the EvoPrimer [8] development kit, the new version of STM32 Primer2 kit. The electrocardiography (ECG) and photopletysmography (PPG) signals are acquired by the device described above and then they are sampled and processed by the software in the control unit. The signals are displayed on the screen in real time. The behaviour of the signals is supplemented with the actual value of heart rate.

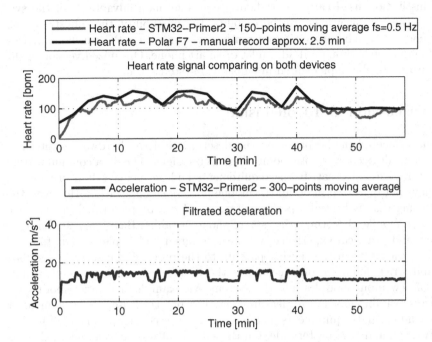

Fig. 3. Comparison of the signals from our device based on STM32-Primer2 with the signal from Polar F7 during running, walking and idle standing

The heart rate alarm, which detects low and high heart rates is implemented in the device. The thresholds, which activates alarm are 50 bpm (beats per minute) and 100 bpm. The alarm informs the user about probable heart rate problem, which may cause life threatening situation.

Another alarm that is implemented is the activity alarm. The alarm starts when the sensed user has no activity for a long time interval. This alarm works like vigilance button in the locomotive. The user has to move, or to click primer button after every 30 seconds to deactivate the alarm. The movements are detected by the build-in accelerometer.

The information about heart rate with time marks are logged on a flash card every 4 seconds. If the device is connected to a computer via Bluetooth, the heart rate, selected signal and alarm flags are visualized by a special software on the PC in real time.

3.3   General Features and Future Applications

The presented applications are not the only possible ones. There are many other applications in the field of assistive technologies, telemonitoring of vital signs and telemedicine where the realized system could be used. For example, the system is easily applicable for vital signs monitoring and classification of urgent states, falls detection and alarms and also as a surveillance system in home and institutionalized care, smart homes etc. The main advantages of the system in these applications are the mobility, the portability, the robustness and the modularity. The processing currently performed on a PC can be relatively easily implemented on an iPad, tablet or smart phone. Optimized version of the algorithms can be implemented in embedded systems, too.

4   Discussion and Conclusion

We have focused in the paper on the description of the hardware solution of the mobile device for remote monitoring of vital signs. The data communication and storage in a PC satisfy the requirements laid on medical data privacy [9]. We have not discussed in detail the mobile processing application. However, the processing that is basically performed on a PC can be performed in the same way on a mobile platform, either smart phone or tablet. Based on the literature review and practical experience, we have designed and implemented standard communication from the sensing part up to the processing modules. Modularity and strict definition of interfaces is the basic requirement for implementation of new input modules into the system. An example of planned modules is transthorasic bioimpedance measurement. For practical use, the system must satisfy additional requirements, namely small power consumption, small in size, lightweight, and long battery life. On the side of software development, there is necessary to design new more efficient signal processing methods, filtration and classification techniques that will be implementable in embedded systems. The measured data is in bit format, accompanied with the information about type of the data (ECG, blood pressure, FCG, etc.), sampling frequency, and other information if required. The software libraries support development of applications. Interfaces of software modules are also standardized. Thus the output of the processing module can be easily sent to an information system or EHR system. We have in mind that correct mapping of acquired data onto a data model that describes electronic patient record is a very important issue, especially with respect to future development and possibility to sense and store far more larger volumes of heterogeneous physiological parameters at a single patient. Interoperability may significantly influence effectivity both of design and development of an integrated system and of its routine operation. It will become more and more important with the development of telemedicine, home care and possibility of remote monitoring of patient state. As the technology is developing very quickly we have to assume that new types of sensors and devices will appear. The newly designed and developed systems must be necessarily created as open modular systems allowing direct connection of the new sensors and devices without any need of modification of the communication and data input. Possibly new data processing module will be added. Integrating information acquired from different sources and implementing it with knowledge discovery techniques allows medical and social actions to be appropriately performed with reliable information, in order to improve quality of life of patients and care-givers.

Acknowledgment. This work has been supported by the grant No. F3a 2122/ 2011 presented by the University Development Foundation.

This work has been also supported by the research program of the Czech Technical University in Prague No. MSM 6840770012 (sponsored by the Ministry of Education, Youth and Sports of the Czech Republic).

References

1. Xiao-Fei, T., Yuan-Ting, Z., Poon, C., Bonato, P.: Wearable medical systems for p-health. IEEE Reviews in Biomedical Engineering 1, 62–74 (2008)
2. Martín-Lesende, I., Orruño, E., Cairo, C., Bilbao, A., Asua, J., Romo, M., Vergara, I., Bayón, J., Abad, R., Reviriego, E., Larrañaga, J.: Assessment of a primary care-based telemonitoring intervention for home care patients with heart failure and chronic lung disease. the telbil study. BMC Health Services Research 11(56) (2011)
3. Kraai, I., Luttik, M., de Jong, R., Jaarsma, T., Hillege, H.: Heart failure patients monitored with telemedicine: Patient satisfaction, a review of the literature. Journal of Cardiac Failure 17(8), 684–690 (2011)
4. van Broeck, G. (ed.): Policy paper on standardisation requirements for AAL. AALIANCE (2009)
5. Lhotská, L., Štěpánková, O., Pěchouček, M., Šimák, B., Chod, J.: ICT and eHealth projects. In: 2011 Technical Symposium at ITU Telecom World (ITU WT), pp. 57–62. IEEE, Piscataway (2011)
6. Lhotská, L., Burša, M., Huptych, M., Chudáček, V., Havlík, J.: Standardization and interoperability: Basic conditions for efficient solutions. In: The 5th European Conference of the International Federation for Medical and Biological Engineering, pp. 1140–1143. Springer Science+Business Media, Berlin (2011)
7. Polar F7 (February 15, 2012),
   http://www.polarusa.com/us-en/products/earlier_products/F7
8. EvoPrimer for STM32F103VE (February 15, 2012),
   http://www.stm32circle.com/resources/stm32Eprimer.php
9. Gilbert, K., Valls, A., Lhotska, L., Aubrecht, P.: Privacy preserving and use of medical information in a multiagent system. In: Advances in Artificial Intelligence for Privacy Protection and Security - Intelligent Information Systems, vol. 1, pp. 165–193. World Scientific, London (2010)

An Study on Re-identification in RGB-D Imagery

Javier Lorenzo-Navarro, Modesto Castrillón-Santana,
and Daniel Hernández-Sosa*

Instituto Universitario SIANI
Universidad de Las Palmas de Gran Canaria
Campus de Tafira, 35017 Las Palmas, Spain
mcastrillon@iusiani.ulpgc.es

Abstract. Re-identification is commonly accomplished using appearance features based on salient points and color information. In this paper, we make an study on the use of different features exclusively obtained from depth images captured with RGB-D cameras. The results achieved, using simple geometric features extracted in a top-view setup, seem to provide useful descriptors for the re-identification task.

Keywords: re-dentification, surveillance, RGB-D.

1 Introduction

There has been an enormous growth in CCTV systems for surveillance in the last fifteen years. The management of the large amount of data acquired justifies the development of automatic surveillance systems that leverage human operator monitoring overload, i.e. the system costs.

Current human monitoring applications focus on non-overlapping camera networks to perform behavior analysis, and automatic event detection. Thus, people detection and tracking approaches are currently being applied in this context aiming at developing automatic visual surveillance systems [1]. A recent application, particularly in automatic monitoring assistance, is the need to re-identify individuals in scenarios with thousands of users (e.g. malls) during a post-analysis of the sequence, after a criminal act, or a dissapearing episode has taken place. Those systems must determine if an individual has been seen in a Time of Interest (TOI) within the camera network.

Facial and clothing information have already been used to re-identify individuals in photo collections and tv video [2]. However, the face pattern presents low resolution in most surveillance systems. Clothing descriptors alone are certainly weak, but can help to locate people with similar appearance, that may be later confirmed by a human. Indeed the human vision system employs external features for person description, body contours, hair, clothes, etc., particularly in low resolution images [3].

---

* Work partially funded by the Spanish Ministry of Science and Innovation funds (TIN 2008-06068), and the Departamento de Informática y Sistemas at ULPGC.

J. Bravo, R. Hervás, and M. Rodríguez (Eds.): IWAAL 2012, LNCS 7657, pp. 200–207, 2012.

Recent literature on the problem of re-identification is mostly focused on appearance based models. Among the appearance cues used for this problem, interest points, structural information and color have deserved researchers attention so far [4,5,6]. Proving that 2D visual information extracted from RGB images is a valid data source to solve, at least partially, the problem.

However, different authors state the implicit advantage of using depth information to reduce certain ambiguous situations. Thus the design of stereo pair based approaches [7] has been proposed to reduce the inherent illumination problems. But their performance keeps being affected by bad or changing illuminations conditions, as the correspondence map is based on visual information.

Nowadays the Kinect sensor provides affordable rough depth information coupled with visual images. This sensor has already been successfully used to detect individuals, and estimate their body pose. As stated by Harville [8], depth devices: 1) are almost insensitive to shadows and illumination changes, 2) provides additional 3D shape information, 3) include occlusion data, 4) add new types of features to the feature space, and 5) add a disambiguating dimension.

Top view cameras, have already been used in surveillance applications [9], avoiding in many cases an accurate calibration step. This top view configuration has the advantage of being privacy preserving because the face is never grabbed by the camera, being therefore suitable for applications with those restrictions. However, depth information provides new features easy to extract. They lack the distinctiveness to identify uniquely an individual, but provide some evidence that can be used to support or discard a given hypothesis. In our experimental setup, the objective is not to identify precisely any identity, but assist human operators to locate similar individual(s).

In this paper, we study the possibilities to re-identify individuals within the camera network, including depth information in the loop. We claim that current consumer depth cameras can contribute to improve the identity description in the re-identification task.

2 Detection

The aim of this paper is at re-identifying individuals in RGB-D images acquired from a top view setup installed in an entrance door. Individuals are detected based exclusively on the depth cue, using the individual trajectory information to build his/her model.

2.1 Background Modeling

Background subtraction is a common technique used to detect objects in surveillance systems. This technique requires a robust background model to be reliable. The solution is particularly simplified if the camera and lighting conditions are fixed, but the model must be robust enough to handle illumination changes. Different approaches to background modeling have been proposed due to its inherent complexity. However, in our scenario, the use of depth information simplifies the segmentation step [8], since considering the top view setup, walking people are clearly salient in the acquired depth images.

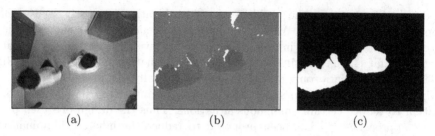

(a)   (b)   (c)

Fig. 1. (a) RGB image, (b) depth image and (c) foreground mask obtained

We have adopted the background subtraction method proposed by Zivkovic and van der Heijden [10]. According to their approach, a pixel-level background model is built from a Gaussian mixture model (GMM) defined as:

$$p(\boldsymbol{x}|\mathcal{X}_T, bg) \approx \sum_{m=1}^{B} \hat{\pi}_m \mathcal{N}(\boldsymbol{x}; \hat{\boldsymbol{\mu}}_m, \hat{\sigma}_m^2 I) \tag{1}$$

where T is the time window used to estimate the background/foreground model, $\mathcal{X}_T = \{x^{(t)}, \ldots, x^{(t-T)}\}$ is the training set (initial frames), $\hat{\boldsymbol{\mu}}_1, \ldots, \hat{\boldsymbol{\mu}}_B$ are the mean estimations, $\hat{\sigma}_1, \ldots, \hat{\sigma}_B$ are the variance estimations, and I is the identity matrix. For each component in (1), its weight is given by $\hat{\pi}_m$, so if they are sorted in descending order, the number of components B is obtained as:

$$B = \arg\min_b \left(\sum_{m=1}^{b} b\hat{\pi}_m > (1 - c_f) \right) \tag{2}$$

where c_f controls the amount of the data that can belong to foreground objects without influencing the background model. Indeed, the number of components in the GMM is not fixed as in other GMM based methods [11].

Observing that depth images are less sensitive to shadows and illumination changes, we experimentally determined a value $c_f = 0.2$. The reason for this is that the background model computed for the depth imagery will be much more stable than for RGB images. Given the background model in (1), a pixel belongs to the foreground if the Mahalanobis distance from the pixel value to some component is less than three standard deviations. Otherwise a new component centered in the pixel is generated. Figure 1 shows the background subtraction results for a sample frame along with its corresponding color and depth images.

Thus, according to (1) a pixel $depth(i,j)$ is classified as foreground using the following formula that makes use of a threshold c_{thr} (minimum person height).

$$fg(i,j) = \begin{cases} depth(i,j) & \text{if } p(depth(i,j)|bg) < c_{trh} \\ 0 & \text{otherwise} \end{cases} \tag{3}$$

2.2   Tracking

Figure 1c depicts the segmentation results for a sample image based on the depth information. Large connected components in the foreground image are

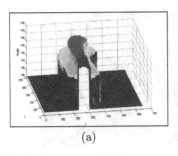
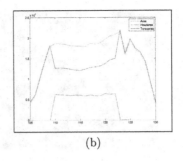

(a)   (b)

Fig. 2. (a) 3D trajectory virtual volume. (b) Area (blob and sub-blobs) related features (in pixels) extracted during a blob tracked trajectory (frames 105-120).

associated to blobs. Given a foreground image fg, the set of m valid blobs is $B = \{b_1, b_2, ..., b_m\}$.

We have adopted a tracking-by-detection approach, based not just on the object bounding box, but its silhouette. Resulting detections are connected in terms of trajectories defined by the tracking.

Tracking is simplified in this top view scenario as occlusions are hardly ever present. As the system is able to acquire and segment on the fly, the blob tracking in frame i can be reduced to test the overlap in consecutive frames of current frame blobs, $B_i = \{b_{i_1}, b_{i_2}, ..., b_{i_m}\}$, and previous frame blobs, $B_{i-1} = \{b_{i-1_1}, b_{i-1_2}, ..., b_{i-1_n}\}$. A new trajectory is considered each time a blob appears in the scene and not suitable matching is found. The trajectory life is then described in terms of its initial and final frames, and the geometric features of its blob and sub-blobs (head and non head, see section 3) components.

3   Modeling

Depth sensors provide a simple mechanism to obtain features that are not trivially computed from the visual cue. As stated before, in this paper we focus on the advantages derived from the use of top view depth images.

Given a foreground image fg, let's define the set of m valid blobs it contains as $B = \{b_1, b_2, ..., b_m\}$. In the case that a blob, b_p, corresponds to a walking human, generally the closest blob point to the camera (lowest gray value), lies on the head. The closest point location and value are useful cues in depth images to split the blob in two parts corresponding to the head and non head areas by a simple in-range operation [9]. Thus, for a given blob, its minimum is defined as:

$$b_{p_{min}} = \min(fg(i,j); \forall fg(i,j) \in b_p) \tag{4}$$

and the head and non head areas as:

$$head_p(i,j) = \begin{cases} fg(i,j) \in b_p \ \wedge \ b_{p_{min}} \leq fg(i,j) \leq b_{p_{min}} \times 1.1 \\ 0 \quad \text{otherwise} \end{cases}$$
$$nohead_p(i,j) = \begin{cases} fg(i,j) \in b_p \ \wedge \ fg(i,j) > b_{p_{min}} \times 1.1 \\ 0 \quad \text{otherwise} \end{cases} \tag{5}$$

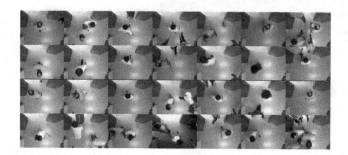

Fig. 3. Middle frame of a subset of the trajectories automatically selected

The head/no-head split is done whenever the blob container is not too close to the image border. In those situations, the head may be partially or totally out of the field of view and the process leads to erroneous calculations.

Other features may be extracted estimating the individual volume according to the scenario floor. To estimate the floor depth, $depth_{floor}$, it is assumed that that most of the visible area corresponds to the reference floor, i.e. a plane surface. The mean depth image, $\overline{depth}$, is calculated as the average of the k first depth images (assuming that no individual is present) as:

$$\overline{depth}(i,j) = \frac{\sum_{l=1}^{k} depth^{(l}(i,j)}{k} \tag{6}$$

where $depth^{(l}(i,j)$ is the pixel (i,j) of the $l-th$ depth image from the sequence.

On the resulting $\overline{depth}$, we calculate the mean pixel value to estimate the floor depth, $depth_{floor}$, that is useful to compute the volumetric descriptors:

$$depth_{floor} = \frac{\sum_{i=1}^{height} \sum_{j=1}^{width} \overline{depth}(i,j)}{width \times height} \tag{7}$$

Figure 2a depicts the trajectory of a 3D virtual volume built by means of the successive combination of its tracked blobs. Remember that the depth is given for each pixel, therefore the projected volume can be easily estimated.

After describing the blob subparts and the rough estimation of the scene floor depth, a set of features is defined. For a given set of blobs segmented from the depth image, we have selected the following simple and fast to compute features:

- **Blob height**: Given by the closest to the camera blob point.
- **Blob areas**: The blob and sub-blobs areas (head and non head, if obtained).
- **Blob projected volume**. The blob and sub-blobs (head and non head, if obtained), are projected to the floor. For a blob, b_p, containing $npixels$ pixels, its blob projected volume is computed adding the height value of each blob pixel and subtracting the floor height, $depth_{floor}$, multiplied by the number of blob pixels, i.e. $volume_{b_p} = \left(\sum^{fg(i,j) \in b_p} depth(i,j) \right) - npixels * depth_{floor}$

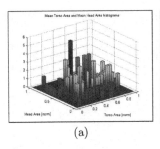 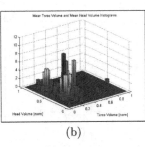 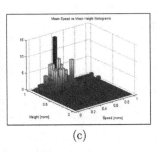

(a)   (b)   (c)

Fig. 4. Normalized projection of (a) the area features, (b) the volume features, and (c) the speed and height features for the analyzed trajectories

The blob tracking defines a trajectory in time. The trajectory features evolve, see for example the area related features shown in Figure 2b. Observe that the head area is not always greater than zero, indeed its value is zero at the beginning and at the end of the trajectory. This effect is due to the fact that when a person enters or leaves the scene, he/she is not completely inside the field of view. Indeed, the head and non head split is only performed when the blob is completely inside the field of view, i.e. its blob container does not "'touch"' the image border. During the trajectory "'middle life"', when the head area is not zero, its features present a fairly constant behavior.

4   Results

To test the features for re-identification we have collected data using a camera located in the upper frame of a door entrance. The resulting continuous video has been manually annotated, containing around 14200 frames with more than 250 crossing actions with no restrictions imposed to the number of individuals simultaneously present in the field of view, their speed, clothing, etc.

4.1   Trajectory Statistics

We have removed those trajectories of individuals not completely visible during the crossing action, so the total number of trajectories analyzed in the experiments is 211. Figure 3 depicts the middle frame of a subset of the total number of trajectories automatically detected by the system. The reader may observe that there are different crossing configurations and illumination conditions.

Histogram based representations of the different features used to describe each trajectory are presented in Figure 4. Each trajectory feature is computed as the mean of the values observed during its "'middle life"', i.e. when the blob could be separated in head and non head sub-blobs.

Figures 4a-b suggest that area and volume information are not coupled. Indeed, two blobs with the same area may project different volumes due to the height difference of the individuals to which the blobs corresponds to. Another consideration should be done related to the speed feature, see Figure 4c. In

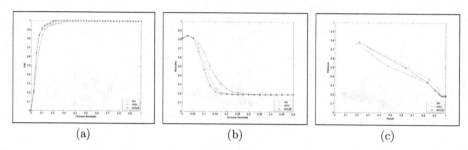

(a)   (b)   (c)

Fig. 5. (a) Recall, (b) accuracy, (c) precision vs recall

the experiments, some trajectories present particularly high speed. They likely reflect a running crossing action.

4.2   Re-identification

For our re-identification results, each trajectory is compared with the rest in a single-shot approach. This means that we have performed an experiment considering that the training set is composed by a single trajectory features, while the test set contains the rest of trajectories. Thus, the experiment is repeated 211 times for each proposed trajectory representation. The normalized euclidean distance is computed for each test trajectory in relation to the model trajectory. Different feature vectors have been used to describe a trajectory:

- **AH**: Only the area (head and torso) and height features are used.
- **AHV**: The area (head and torso), height and volume (head and torso) features are employed.
- **AHVS**: The area (head and torso), height, volume (head and torso) and speed features are employed.

The lower the distance, the larger the similarity between two trajectories. For each classification problem, the decision threshold defines if a classification is correct or not attending to the distance. The performance evaluation is done using the recall, accuracy and precision. The receiver operating characteristic (ROC) curve is computed for the Nearest Neighbor (NN) classifier considering different decision threshold values. The summarized results are depicted in Figure 5.

As expected, increasing the decision threshold increases the recall or true positive rate, but reduces almost simultaneously the accuracy. The use of more features to describe the trajectory seems to improve the recognition rates. However, the inclusion of the speed feature ($AHVS$ variant) introduce a bias. Certainly, if an individual modifies his speed in different observations, the descriptor is not valid to re-identify him/her.

The results indicate that apparently simple features, provide useful information to re-identify individuals. We can conclude that even using such a simple and weak descriptors the individual re-identification performances are promising. Focusing for instance in Figure 5c, if the decision threshold is set to 0.05

the precision is close to 50% and the recall to 64%. Observe that no appearance based descriptor has been used in the experiments.

5 Conclusions

We have made use only of depth information to detect, track and describe individuals crossing a monitored area. The top view configuration eases the task and makes simple to extract different trajectory features.

No appearance information is used to described the individuals, just geometric descriptors extracted from the blob. Their discriminative power has provided promising results in the experiments.

A set of features has been selected attending to its computational cost. An experimental setup has been carried out in an entrance door scenario, where more than 14000 frames and 250 crossing events have been manually annotated. The selected depth images based features have proven to be useful to detect outliers, and seem to be significant as soft biometrics cues.

References

1. Dollár, P., Wojek, C., Schiele, B., Perona, P.: Pedestrian detection: An evaluation of the state of the art. IEEE Transactions on Pattern Analysis and Machine Intelligence 34(4), 743–761 (2012)
2. Everingham, M., Sivic, J., Zisserman, A.: Taking the bite out of automated naming of characters in tv video. Image and Vision Computing 27, 545–559 (2009)
3. Jarudi, I., Sinha, P.: Relative roles of internal and external features in face recognition. Technical Report memo 225, CBCL (2005)
4. D'Angelo, A., Dugelay, J.L.: People re-identification in camera networks based on probabilistic color histograms. In: Proc. SPIE, vol. 7882 (2011)
5. Lo Presti, L., Sclaroff, S., La Cascia, M.: Object Matching in Distributed Video Surveillance Systems by LDA-Based Appearance Descriptors. In: Foggia, P., Sansone, C., Vento, M. (eds.) ICIAP 2009. LNCS, vol. 5716, pp. 547–557. Springer, Heidelberg (2009)
6. Muñoz Salinas, R., Aguirre, E., García-Silvente, M.: People detection and tracking using stereo vision and color. Image Vision Computing 25(6), 995–1007 (2007)
7. Yahiaoui, T., Khoudour, L., Meurie, C.: Real-time passenger counting in buses using dense stereovision. J. Electron. Imaging 20 (July 2010)
8. Harville, M.: Stereo person tracking with adaptive plan-view templates of height and occupancy statistics. Image and Vision Computing 22(2), 127–142 (2004)
9. Englebienne, G., van Oosterhout, T., Krose, B.: Tracking in sparse multi-camera setups using stereo vision. In: Third ACM/IEEE International Conference on Distributed Smart Cameras, ICDSC (2009)
10. Zivkovic, Z., der Heijden, F.: Efficient adaptive density estimation per image pixel for the task of background subtraction. Pattern Recognition Letters 27, 773–780 (2006)
11. Stauffer, G.: Adaptive background mixture models for real-time tracking. In: IEEE Computer Society Conference on Computer Vision and Pattern Recognition, pp. 246–252 (1999)

Offline and Online Activity Recognition on Mobile Devices Using Accelerometer Data

Andrés Duque, Fco. Javier Ordóñez, Paula de Toledo, and Araceli Sanchis

Universidad Carlos III de Madrid
{aduque,fordonez,mtoledo,masm}@inf.uc3m.es

Abstract. This paper presents a process for extracting knowledge for physical activity recognition, from accelerometer data provided by mobile devices. Starting from a dataset collected by three different users, knowledge discovery is performed through a phase of feature extraction from raw data, minimizing the number of statistical features and optimizing the classification process. The development and comparison of classifying models over this new dataset, using both offline and online algorithms, is also described. Phases of data acquisition, pre-processing and classification are detailed, and experimental results for different machine learning algorithms are provided. For these results, different evaluation criteria are used, and the best algorithm is selected according to these criteria. Final results show success rates around 98%, while other similar works offer rates around 87%.

1 Introduction

Activity recognition on mobile devices is currently a widely explored field in data mining and artificial intelligence, due to the large range of technical possibilities that these devices offer to users and developers. The different types of sensors embedded into these devices, such as accelerometers, GPS, light and temperature sensors, and audio and image recorders, together with their small size and their computing power, make mobile devices one of the best tools for ubiquitous computing [11].

There are a large number of real applications for activity recognition in small mobile devices, such as patient monitoring [12], video surveillance [13] or smart-homes development [10].

In this work, a set of six different physical activities, regularly performed on a daily basis, is proposed to be classified, namely sitting, standing, walking, running, ascending stairs and descending stairs. For this aim, accelerometer from Android-based mobile phones will be used for recording data, since this sensor offers robust and reliable measurements for determining body-position and posture-sensing [7].

This paper is organized as follows: section 2 provides a discussion of the current state of the art, describing the previous work that has been developed in this field and the difference with the work presented in this paper. Section 3

J. Bravo, R. Hervás, and M. Rodríguez (Eds.): IWAAL 2012, LNCS 7657, pp. 208–215, 2012.
© Springer-Verlag Berlin Heidelberg 2012

describes the materials and methods, detailing the acquisition of data, the structure of the dataset used for classification, and the different algorithms and techniques evaluated. Section 4 details the proposed evaluation criteria, and provides the obtained experimental results. Finally, conclusions and future work are presented in section 5.

2   Related Work

Many sensor-based activity recognition systems have been presented in the past years. However, the sensing process for obtaining data for classification can be performed in many ways. In [1], five different accelerometers are located in different body parts (ankle, knee, elbow, wrist and hip). [8], [5], [15] and [17] also propose approaches involving several sensors to cover up the maximum possible data from the environment, while [18] and [14] use ad-hoc designed sensors for receiving data. In this work, a reduction in the number of sensors is proposed, in order to take advantage of the wide extension of smart phones all over the world, which allows the development of applications that can be used by several millions of people.

Regarding the techniques for extracting information from raw data obtained by an accelerometer, most of the previous works on this topic propose feature extraction for knowledge discovery. However, the number of different statistical features used for creating data instances is usually high, such as in [11], where 6 different statistical markers are extracted, or in [20], where 22 features are initially extracted, and then reduced via feature selection algorithms. The use of a reduced set of statistical features (mean and standard deviation) proposed in this work, could lead to a lower consumption of resources from the mobile phone, a desirable condition due to the limitations of these devices.

In relation to the algorithms and techniques used in other works, most of the approaches propose supervised machine learning techniques, such as decision trees [5], Naive Bayes [18] or Nearest Neighbor algorithms [1], as well as artificial neural networks [11], although some approaches explore Hidden Markov Models [17] and SVM [9] for obtaining classifying models. In this work, a comparison between well known machine learning techniques is presented, and one of the algorithms is finally selected. Moreover, a comparison between the results from this work and those from similar works such as [11] and [20] will be performed.

Although some works treat the online classification approach [6], due to the nature of data used for activity recognition, and the characteristics of the data acquisition itself, comparison between offline and online classification is needed, in order to determine whether models regarding only a fixed number of past measurements are able to offer the same classification results as offline techniques.

3   Materials and Methods

This section introduces the proposed approach for activity recognition, dividing the development process into three different phases: data acquisition, related to the collection and labeling of data that will be used for training the different classifying models, data pre-processing, regarding the process of formatting the data in order to obtain reliable results, and data classification, this is, selection of the different algorithms and techniques used for recognizing activities.

3.1   Data Acquisition

For this purpose, an Android labeling application has been developed. In this application, the user can select, from a set of six different activities (sitting, standing, walking, running, ascending stairs and descending stairs), the activity he is going to perform, and then start recording data from the accelerometer. Thus, once the user has selected the activity, the acceleration experienced by each of the three axis of the mobile phone is stored into the database, as well as the class representing the type of activity being performed.

However, before data is collected by this application, two previous assumptions have to be taken into account:

- The mobile phone will be located inside the user's pocket.
- Frequency of sensing will be one second, i.e., every second the application will record a piece of data from the accelerometer.

The aim of the first assumption is to determine a concrete location and position of the device when data is being collected, in order to assure the congruence and robustness of the data used for classification. The sensing frequency is selected in order to reduce the consumption of resources from the mobile device, since the final classification model that will be developed in this process is thought to be implemented inside a mobile application for activity recognition.

3.2   Data Pre-processing

In this point of the knowledge discovery process, the problem to be solved is a sequential classification problem, which can be transformed into a classical classification problem through the use of a sliding window [4]. The size of the window will be 20 measurements, enough to capture activity intervals of 20 seconds, in which useful cycles and characteristics for classification could exist. Therefore, the window is slid along the data stream and every time that the 20 measurements inside the window belong to the same class, a new instance is extracted for classification.

A selection and extraction of statistical features is performed over data from the sliding-window. The extraction of statistical characteristics from the original instances is an important step for obtaining accurate classifiers in patter recognition problems [16]. Although the number of features that can be calculated is high, in order to maintain the aim of reducing the consumption of resources, in this work only two widely used statistical markers are extracted: mean and standard deviation [19], [1]. The difference of values between two consecutive data inside the window, in each of the three axis of the accelerometer, is also taken into account. Therefore, for each instance of the sliding window, an instance suitable to be used for classification is generated. This final instance is denoted by:

$$(M_x, M_y, M_z, M_{\Delta x}, M_{\Delta y}, M_{\Delta z}, SD_x, SD_y, SD_z, SD_{\Delta x}, SD_{\Delta y}, SD_{\Delta z}, Class)$$

It contains 12 attributes and the class representing the physical activity to which it refers, can be observed. M_x, M_y, M_z refer to the means of the values from the three axis (X, Y and Z) of the accelerometer, $M_{\Delta x}$, $M_{\Delta y}$, $M_{\Delta z}$ represent the means of the values of two consecutive measurements for the three axis, SD_x, SD_y, SD_z refer to the standard deviations of the values from the three axis, and $SD_{\Delta x}$, $SD_{\Delta y}$, $SD_{\Delta z}$ are the standard deviations of the values of two consecutives measurements, for the three axis.

3.3   Data Classification

Algorithms used for offline classification are divided into three main types, inside the field of supervised classification: lazy algorithms (K-Nearest Neighbor, with K=3, 5 and 11, and Nearest neighbor with generalization, NNge), decision trees (C4.5) and decision rules (RIPPER). Using 10-fold cross validation, these six algorithms have been tested over the dataset.

Online classification is performed using the same six algorithms, and 10-fold cross validation. However, some of the algorithms do not provide an incremental implementation, this is, the classifying model is not directly updateable, so a non-incremental approach is implemented to perform the online classification, building the complete classifying model each time a new instance is loaded from the training set, instead of updating the model.

4   Evaluation and Results

Data acquisition process was carried out by three different users, and 6.523 measurements were retrieved. After data pre-processing, a total of 5.714 instances are available for training the classifying models.

Table 1. Number of instances per class

	Sit	Stand	Walk	Run	Ascend	Descend	Total
Raw	767	346	1969	2804	321	316	6523
Final	677	308	1722	2636	188	183	5714

Table 1 shows the number of raw and final instances per class. It can be clearly observed that data used for classification are unbalanced, this is, there exists a high difference between the number of instances from classes "Standing", "Ascending stairs" or "Descending stairs", with less than a 10% of total instances, and classes "Walking", with 30% of the instances, and "Running", with almost half of the instances.

4.1   Evaluation Criteria

Success rate and Kappa coefficient [3] are used for evaluating the performance of the different algorithms over the dataset. However, since original data are unbalanced, success rate is not the most appropriate measure of performance. F-Measure is defined as a harmonic mean of precision (measurement of purity in retrieval performance) and recall (measurement of completeness in retrieval performance) [2], and will be used for testing the algorithms taking into account minority classes. Significance testing between algorithms is done at a confidence interval of 95% using a two-tailed student t-test and using matching paired data.

Differences between offline and online algorithms are also useful for understanding the problem. In this case, online experiments will show the performance of the algorithm as the size of the training dataset increases, over the same test dataset, while the size of the training dataset used by offline algorithms to build the model is always the same.

4.2   Offline Results

Table 2 shows the results for offline classification performed by the six algorithms. The algorithm that presents the best classification results, in terms of all the proposed evaluation criteria, is K-Nearest neighbor, with K = 3. The t-test also confirms that the difference between this algorithm and the rest is statistically significant in almost all cases. However, t-test indicates that 3-NN and 5-NN are equivalent in this case.

Table 2. Results for Offline Classification (expressed in %). Best results appear in boldface type.

	3-NN	5-NN	11-NN	NNGE	C4.5	Ripper
Success	**99.14±0.45**	98.95±0.40	98.20±0.53	98.08±0.39	98.16±0.45	97.58±0.79
Kappa	**98.73±0.67**	98.44±0.60	97.32±0.80	97.14±0.57	97.28±0.66	96.41±1.18
Precision	**97.87±1.71**	97.43±1.28	96.56±1.56	96.66±1.50	95.27±1.60	94.11±2.49
Recall	**96.19±1.94**	95.34±1.61	92.33±1.90	91.76±1.87	93.74±2.04	91.36±2.82
F-Measure	**97.02±1.72**	96.37±1.38	94.40±1.49	94.14±1.41	94.49±1.73	92.71±2.47

Table 3. Confusion Matrix for 3-NN Offline

	Inferred					
True	Sit	Stand	Walk	Run	Ascend	Descend
Sit	68	0	0	0	0	0
Stand	0	31	0	0	0	0
Walk	0	0	171	0	0	0
Run	0	0	0	264	0	0
Ascend	0	0	1	0	17	1
Descend	0	0	1	0	1	16

Table 3 shows the confusion matrix for the test set of algorithm 3-NN. It can be observed that the overall performance of the algorithm is quite good for all the classes.

4.3 Online Results

Table 4 shows the results of the online algorithms (both incremental and non-incremental). The percentages are slightly lower than for offline classification, although the algorithm that presents the best results is 3-NN again, except for precision. In this experiment, there is a statistically significant difference between 3-NN and the rest of the algorithms in all cases.

Table 4. Results for Online Classification (expressed in %). Best results appear in boldface type.

	Incremental				Non-Incremental	
	3-NN	**5-NN**	**11-NN**	**NNGE**	**C4.5**	**Ripper**
Success	**97.58±2.50**	97.09±3.39	96.07±4.15	96.57±2.14	96.33±3.21	95.26±3.75
Kappa	**96.38±3.83**	95.61±5.55	94.04±7.10	94.85±3.29	94.55±4.83	92.90±5.99
Precision	94.53±3.84	94.18±4.13	92.84±4.67	**94.97±2.00**	90.94±4.83	89.54±5.01
Recall	**89.77±8.02**	87.77±8.96	83.71±10.23	85.96±7.24	88.46±7.51	85.17±9.05
F-Measure	**92.00±6.25**	90.73±6.93	87.81±7.96	90.10±5.06	89.62±6.35	87.16±7.25

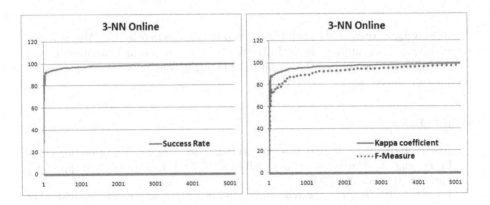

Fig. 1. Online Classification Performance for 3-NN

Fig 1 shows the evolution of the performance of algorithm 3-NN as the number of instances used for training the model increases. Convergence is fast, and success rate, Kappa coefficient and F-Measure reach acceptable values around instance 1000.

5 Discussion

In this work, a method for acquiring accelerometer data from mobile devices has been proposed. The data pre-processing includes the use of a sliding-window and feature extraction, allowing the transformation of a sequential classification problem into a classical classification problem. However, this feature extraction has been reduced to the minimum amount of statistical characteristics (mean and standard deviation), in order to minimize the consumption of resources of mobile devices. Future lines of work should cover the real impact of this reduction of statistical features, by implementing the classification model into a mobile device and extracting information about the use of resources. Several machine learning algorithms, such as K-Nearest Neighbor, C4.5 or RIPPER have been tested and their performance compared. After this comparison process, algorithm 3-NN has shown the best results for both offline and online classification, providing statistically significant differe nces with the other evaluated algorithms. New algorithms such as artificial neural networks could be applied to the dataset, and their performance compared to those already evaluated.

Regarding a direct comparison between different works, in [20] the experiments are performed over a dataset retrieved by four different users, and success rates of around 87% for the best algorithm (decision trees) are obtained, while [11] achieves 91.7% of success using the multilayer perceptron, over a dataset retrieved by twenty-nine users. The approach proposed in this work uses a dataset collected by three users, and obtains more than 99% of success through a 3-NN offline algorithm, and more than 97% through the online version of the same algorithm.

Acknowledgement. This work has been partially funded by the Ambient Assisted Living Programme (Joint Initiative by the European Commission and EU Member States) under the Trainutri (Training and nutrition senior social platform) Project (AAL-2009-2-129).

References

1. Bao, L., Intille, S.S.: Activity Recognition from User-Annotated Acceleration Data. In: Ferscha, A., Mattern, F. (eds.) PERVASIVE 2004. LNCS, vol. 3001, pp. 1–17. Springer, Heidelberg (2004)
2. Buckland, M., Gey, F.: The relationship between recall and precision. Journal of the American Society for Information Science 45(1), 12–19 (1994)
3. Cohen, J.: A Coefficient of Agreement for Nominal Scales. Educational and Psychological Measurement 20(1), 37–46 (1960)
4. Dietterich, T.G.: Machine Learning for Sequential Data: A Review. In: Caelli, T.M., Amin, A., Duin, R.P.W., Kamel, M.S., de Ridder, D. (eds.) SPR 2002 and SSPR 2002. LNCS, vol. 2396, pp. 15–30. Springer, Heidelberg (2002)
5. Ermes, M., Pärkka, J., Mantyjarvi, J., Korhonen, I.: Detection of daily activities and sports with wearable sensors in controlled and uncontrolled conditions. IEEE Transactions on Information Technology in Biomedicine: a Publication of the IEEE Engineering in Medicine and Biology Society 12(1), 20–26 (2008)

6. Ermes, M., Parkka, J., Cluitmans, L.: Advancing from offline to online activity recognition with wearable sensors. In: Conference Proceedings of the International Conference of IEEE Engineering in Medicine and Biology Society, pp. 4451–4454 (2008)
7. Foerster, F., Smeja, M., Fahrenberg, J.: Detection of posture and motion by accelerometry: a validation study in ambulatory monitoring. Computers in Human Behavior 15(5), 571–583 (1999)
8. Gyrbr, N., Fbin, k., Homny, G.: An activity recognition system for mobile phones. Mobile Networks and Applications 14(1), 82–91 (2008)
9. He, Z., Jin, L.: Activity recognition from acceleration data based on discrete consine transform and SVM. In: 2009 IEEE International Conference on Systems, Man and Cybernetics, pp. 5041–5044. IEEE (October 2009)
10. Hong, X., Nugent, C., Mulvenna, M., McClean, S., Scotney, B., Devlin, S.: Evidential fusion of sensor data for activity recognition in smart homes. Pervasive and Mobile Computing 5(3), 236–252 (2009)
11. Kwapisz, J.R., Weiss, G.M., Moore, S.A.: Activity recognition using cell phone accelerometers. In: Proceedings of the Fourth International Workshop on Knowledge Discovery from Sensor Data, pp. 10–18 (2010)
12. Lau, S.L., Knig, I., David, K., Parandian, B., Carius-Dssel, C., Schultz, M.: Supporting patient monitoring using activity recognition with a smartphone. In: The Seventh International Symposium on Wireless Communication Systems (ISWCS 2010) (September 2010)
13. Lin, W., Sun, M.T., Poovendran, R., Zhang, Z.: Human activity recognition for video surveillance. In: ISCAS, pp. 2737–2740. IEEE (2008)
14. Maurer, U., Rowe, A., Smailagic, A., Siewiorek, D.: Location and Activity Recognition Using eWatch: A Wearable Sensor Platform. In: Cai, Y., Abascal, J. (eds.) Ambient Intelligence in Everyday Life. LNCS (LNAI), vol. 3864, pp. 86–102. Springer, Heidelberg (2006)
15. Minnen, D., Starner, T.: Recognizing and discovering human actions from on-body sensor data. In: Proc. of the IEEE International Conference on Multimedia and Expo., pp. 1545–1548 (2005)
16. Nanopoulos, A., Alcock, R., Manolopoulos, Y.: Feature-based classification of time-series data. International Journal of Computer Research 10, 49–61 (2001)
17. Olgún, D.O., Pentland, A.: Human activity recognition: Accuracy across common locations for wearable sensors. In: Proc. 10th Int. Symp. Wearable Computers, pp. 11–13 (2006)
18. Ravi, N., Dandekar, N., Mysore, P., Littman, M.L.: Activity recognition from accelerometer data. In: Proceedings of the Seventeenth Conference on Innovative Applications of Artificial Intelligence(IAAI. pp. 1541–1546. AAAI Press (2005)
19. Wang, S., Yang, J., Chen, N., Chen, X., Zhang, Q.: Human Activity Recognition with User-Free Accelerometers in the Sensor Networks, vol. 2, pp. 1212–1217 (2005)
20. Yang, J.: Toward physical activity diary: Motion recognition using simple acceleration features with mobile phones. Data Processing, 1–9 (2009)

Human Activity Recognition on Smartphones Using a Multiclass Hardware-Friendly Support Vector Machine

Davide Anguita[1], Alessandro Ghio, Luca Oneto,
Xavier Parra[2], and Jorge L. Reyes-Ortiz[1,2]

[1] DITEN - Università degli Studi di Genova, Genoa I-16145, Italy
{davide.anguita,alessandro.ghio,luca.oneto}@unige.it
[2] CETpD - Universitat Politècnica de Catalunya, Vilanova i la Geltrú 08800, Spain
xavier.parra@upc.edu, jorge.luis.reyes@estudiant.upc.edu

Abstract. Activity-Based Computing [1] aims to capture the state of the user and its environment by exploiting heterogeneous sensors in order to provide adaptation to exogenous computing resources. When these sensors are attached to the subject's body, they permit continuous monitoring of numerous physiological signals. This has appealing use in healthcare applications, e.g. the exploitation of Ambient Intelligence (AmI) in daily activity monitoring for elderly people. In this paper, we present a system for human physical Activity Recognition (AR) using smartphone inertial sensors. As these mobile phones are limited in terms of energy and computing power, we propose a novel hardware-friendly approach for multiclass classification. This method adapts the standard Support Vector Machine (SVM) and exploits fixed-point arithmetic for computational cost reduction. A comparison with the traditional SVM shows a significant improvement in terms of computational costs while maintaining similar accuracy, which can contribute to develop more sustainable systems for AmI.

Keywords: Activity Recognition, SVM, Smartphones, Hardware-Friendly.

1 Introduction

Since the appearance of the first commercial hand-held mobile phones in 1979, it has been observed an accelerated growth in the mobile phone market which has reached by 2011 near 80% of the world population [2]. This shows that in a very short time, mobile devices will become easily accessible to virtually everybody. Smartphones, which are a new generation of mobile phones, are now offering many other features such as multitasking and the deployment of a variety of sensors, in addition to the basic telephony. Current efforts attempt to incorporate all these features while maintaining similar battery lifespans and device dimensions.

J. Bravo, R. Hervás, and M. Rodríguez (Eds.): IWAAL 2012, LNCS 7657, pp. 216–223, 2012.

The integration of these mobile devices in our daily life is rapidly growing. It is envisioned that such devices will seamlessly keep track of our activities, learn from them, and subsequently help us to make better decisions regarding our future actions [3]. This is one key concepts in which AmI relies on. In this paper, we employ smartphones for human Activity Recognition with potential applications in assisted living technologies. We take into account current hardware limitations and propose a new alternative for AR that requires less computational resources to operate.

AR aims to identify the actions carried out by a person given a set of observations of itself and the surrounding environment. Recognition can be accomplished, for example, by exploiting the information retrieved from inertial sensors such as accelerometers [4]. In some smartphones these sensors are embedded by default and we benefit from this to classify a set of physical activities (*standing, walking, laying, walking, walking upstairs* and *walking downstairs*) by processing inertial body signals through a supervised Machine Learning (ML) algorithm for hardware with limited resources.

This paper is structured in the following way: The state of the art regarding previous work is depicted in Section 2. The description of the adopted methodology is presented in Section 3. There, the experimental set up for capturing the data and the mathematical description for the proposed Multiclass Hardware Friendly Support Vector Machine (MC-HF-SVM) are explained. Experimental results and conclusions of this research are described in Sections 4 and 5.

2 Related Work

The development of AR applications using smartphones has several advantages such as easy device portability without the need for additional fixed equipment, and comfort to the user due to the unobtrusive sensing. This contrasts with other established AR approaches which use specific purpose hardware devices such as in [5] or sensor body networks [6]. Although the use of numerous sensors could improve the performance of a recognition algorithm, it is unrealistic to expect that the general public will use them in their daily activities because of the difficulty and the time required to wear them. One drawback of the smartphone-based approach is that energy and services on the mobile phone are shared with other applications and this become critical in devices with limited resources.

ML methods that have been previously employed for recognition include Naive Bayes, SVMs, Threshold-based and Markov chains [6]. In particular, we make use of SVMs for classification as it was also used in [7] and [8]. Although it is not fully clear which method performs better for AR, SVMs have confirmed successful application in several areas including heterogeneous types of recognition such as handwritten characters [9] and speech [10].

In ML, fixed-point arithmetic models have been previously studied [11,12] initially because devices with floating-point units were unavailable or expensive. The possibility of retaking these approaches for AmI systems that require either low cost devices or to allow load reduction in multitasking mobile devices has nowadays become particularly appealing. Anguita et al. in [13] introduced the concept of a Hardware-Friendly SVM (HF-SVM). This method exploits fixed-point arithmetic in the feed-forward phase of the SVM classifier, so as to allow the use of this algorithm in hardware-limited devices. In this paper, we extend this model for multiclass classification.

The SVM algorithm was originally proposed only for binary classification problems but it has been adapted using different schemes for multiclass problems such as in [9]. In particular, we have chosen the One-Vs-All (OVA) method as its accuracy is comparable to other classification methods as demonstrated by Rifkin and Klautau in [14], and because its learned model uses less memory when compared for instance to the One-Vs-One (OVO) method. This is advantageous when used in limited resources hardware devices.

3 Methodology

3.1 Experimental Setup

The experiments have been carried out with a group of 30 volunteers within an age bracket of 19-48 years. Each person performed the six activities previously mentioned wearing the smartphone on the waist. The experiments have been video-recorded to facilitate the data labeling. The obtained database has been randomly partitioned into two sets, where 70% of the patterns has been used for training purposes and 30% as test data: the training set is then used to train a multiclass SVM classifier which is described in the following section. A Samsung Galaxy S2 smartphone has been exploited for the experiments, as it contains an accelerometer and a gyroscope for measuring 3-axial linear acceleration and angular velocity respectively at a constant rate of 50Hz, which is sufficient for capturing human body motion.

For AR purposes, we have developed a smartphone application based on the Google Android Operating System. The recognition process starts with the acquisition of the sensor signals, which are subsequently pre-processed by applying noise filters and then sampled in fixed-width sliding windows of 2.56 sec and 50% overlap. From each window, a vector of 17 features is obtained by calculating variables from the accelerometer signals in the time and frequency domain (e.g.

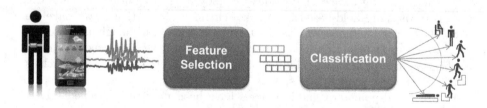

Fig. 1. Activity Recognition process pipeline

mean, standard deviation, signal magnitude area, entropy, signal-pair correlation, etc.). Fast Fourier Transform is used for finding the signal frequency components. Finally, these patterns are used as input of the trained SVM Classifier for the recognition of the activities. The entire AR process pipeline is as shown in Figure 1.

3.2   The Multiclass HF-SVM Model

Consider a dataset consisting of l patterns where each one is a pair of the type $(\boldsymbol{x}_i, y_i) \forall i \in [1, ..., l]$, $\boldsymbol{x}_i \in \Re^m$, and $y_i = \pm 1$. A standard binary SVM can be learned by solving a Convex Constrained Quadratic Programming (CCQP) minimization problem which is given by the following formulation [13]:

$$\min_{\alpha} \quad \frac{1}{2}\boldsymbol{\alpha}^T Q \boldsymbol{\alpha} - \boldsymbol{r}^T \boldsymbol{\alpha} \tag{1}$$

$$0 \leq \alpha_i \leq C \;\; \forall i \in [1, ..., l], \tag{2}$$

$$\boldsymbol{y}^T \boldsymbol{\alpha} = 0, \tag{3}$$

where C is the regularization parameter, $r_i = 1 \; \forall i$ and Q is the symmetric positive semidefinite $l \times l$ kernel matrix where $q_{ij} = y_i y_j K(\boldsymbol{x}_i, \boldsymbol{x}_j)$.

After solving this CCQP problem, the $\alpha_i \; \forall i \in [1, ..., l]$ values can be found and used to predict the class of any new pattern using the Feed-Forward Phase (FFP) formulation of the SVM:

$$f(\boldsymbol{x}) = \sum_{i=1}^{l} y_i \alpha_i K(\boldsymbol{x}_i, \boldsymbol{x}) + b, \tag{4}$$

where b is the bias term and is obtained by using the method proposed in [15]. Clearly, this output is not valid for use in a fixed-point arithmetic approach as these α_i values are by default real numbers ranging between zero and C. Hence a normalization procedure is proposed that will not affect the sign of the classifier output but only its magnitude, maintaining the performance of the SVM as it is known that the class is only determined by the feed-forward function sign. The HF-SVM described in [13] proposes a new vector $\boldsymbol{\beta}$ and it is defined as:

$$\beta_i = \alpha_i \frac{2^k - 1}{C}, \tag{5}$$

where k is the number of bits and $\beta_i \in \mathbb{N}^0$. Also the bias term b of the FFP formulation is removed with the purpose of having a complete integer parameter prediction. The modified formulation is:

$$\min_{\boldsymbol{\beta}} \quad \frac{1}{2}\boldsymbol{\beta}^T Q \boldsymbol{\beta} - \boldsymbol{s}^T \boldsymbol{\beta} \tag{6}$$

$$0 \leq \beta_i \leq \frac{2^k - 1}{C} \;\; \forall i \in [1, ..., l], \tag{7}$$

where $s_i = \left(2^k - 1\right)/C \ \ \forall i \in [1,...,l]$. Note that the cost function keeps unchanged but Eq. 3 disappears. This is consistent because we use an RBF kernel such as the Laplacian that has infinite VC dimension and the bias b becomes unnecessary [16].

Lastly, to hold true the assumption of having a FFP with only integer values, the kernel $K\left(\cdot,\cdot\right)$ and the input vector x are also represented with u and v bits respectively [13]:

$$0 \leq K\left(x_i, x\right) \leq 1 - 2^{-u} \ \ \forall i \in [1,...,l], \tag{8}$$

$$0 \leq x_i \leq 1 - 2^{-v} \ \ \forall i \in [1,...,m]. \tag{9}$$

The modified FFP formulation with the β vector is:

$$f\left(x\right) = \sum_{i=1}^{l} y_i \beta_i K\left(x_i, x\right). \tag{10}$$

We opted for a Laplacian kernel, instead of the more conventional Gaussian kernel, as it is more convenient for hardware limited devices because it can be easily computed using shifters:

$$K\left(x_i, x_j\right) = 2^{-\gamma \|x_i - x_j\|_1}, \tag{11}$$

where $\gamma > 0$ is the kernel hyperparameter and the norm is expressed as $\|x\|_1 = \sum_{i=1}^{m} |x|$.

The complete learning process for each SVM consists of performing grid search model selection of the C and γ hyperparameters that converge with the minimum validation error. A k-fold cross validation with $k = 10$ is employed for each hyperparameter pair.

The output of the FFP varies depending on each learned SVM model as these are not normalized. Our extension of this binary problem for the multiclass case employs the OVA method in which each class c is compared against the other classes. This evidently requires a method to allow comparability between the output of each SVM. For this reason, we have opted to compute probability estimates for each SVM $p_c\left(x\right)$ and choose the one with the highest probability as the actual class c^* of each test pattern.

We have developed the following approach using the J.Platt's method for estimating probability estimates [17]. The training dataset and the learned SVM model are employed to fit the output of the FFP $f\left(x\right)$ with a sigmoid function of the form:

$$p\left(x\right) = \frac{1}{1 + e^{(Af(x)+B)}}, \tag{12}$$

in which $p\left(x\right)$ is the probability estimate, and A and B are function parameters which are properly fitted on the available learning samples.

Taking into account that we have the fixed-point arithmetic restriction, the sigmoid function cannot be directly applied on $f\left(x\right)$. To solve this, we have designed a method based on Look-Up-Tables (LUTs). By defining a fixed number

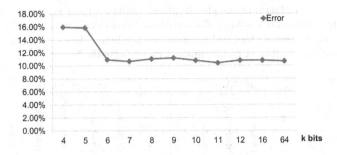

Fig. 2. Comparison between the MC-SVM and the MC-HF-SVM: Classification test error for the MC-HF-SVM with different values of k against the MC-SVM which is represented with $k = 64$ bits

of bits t, it is possible to map the probability estimates $p(x)$ given $f(x)$ without requiring floating-point arithmetic. It has been observed that $t = 8$ is suitable for this application and it only requires a LUT with 256 elements.

4 Experimental Results

For evaluating the performance of the MC-HF-SVM, a set of experiments were carried out using the AR dataset described in this paper. They consisted of learning SVM models with different number of bits k for β estimation and then comparing their performance in terms of test data error against the standard floating-point Multiclass SVM (MC-SVM). The results of this comparison are depicted in Figure 2.

The experiment shows that for this dataset $k = 6$ bits are sufficient for achieving a performance comparable with the MC-SVM approach that uses 64-bit floating-point arithmetic. The test error remains stable (around 1% variation) for k values from 64 to 6 bits, but it increases noticeably to 15% when it reaches 5 bits. Moreover, it is also seen from the graph that some values of k produced smaller errors than the one obtained with the MC-SVM. This finding coincides with that in [18] and then in [19]. Thus, suggesting that these methods can exhibit a lower generalization error. We believe that the truncation of the model parameters could be producing a regularization effect.

The classification results of the MC-SVM and the MC-HF-SVM with $k = 8$ bits for the test data are depicted by means of a confusion matrix in Table 1, where estimates of the overall accuracy, recall and precision are also given. 789 test samples were evaluated with approximately equal number of samples per class. Both confusion matrices show similar outputs varying slightly in the classification accuracy of the activities *walking downstairs* and *walking upstairs*. They also expose some false predictions mostly in the dynamic activities. Static activities instead perform better, particularly the *laying* activity which obtained an accuracy of 100%.

Table 1. Confusion Matrix of the classification results on the test data using the traditional floating-point MC-SVM (Left) and the MC-HF-SVM with $k = 8$ bits (Right). Rows represent the actual class and columns the predicted class. The diagonal entries (in bold) show the number of test samples correctly classified.

Method	MC-SVM							MC-HF-SVM $k = 8$ bits						
Activity	Walking	Upstairs	Downstairs	Standing	Sitting	Laying	Recall %	Walking	Upstairs	Downstairs	Standing	Sitting	Laying	Recall %
Walking	**109**	0	5	0	0	0	95.6	**109**	2	3	0	0	0	95.6
Upstairs	1	**95**	40	0	0	0	69.8	1	**98**	37	0	0	0	72.1
Downstairs	15	9	**119**	0	0	0	83.2	15	14	**114**	0	0	0	79.7
Standing	0	5	0	**132**	5	0	93.0	0	5	0	**131**	6	0	92.2
Sitting	0	0	0	4	**108**	0	96.4	0	1	0	3	**108**	0	96.4
Laying	0	0	0	0	0	**142**	100	0	0	0	0	0	**142**	100
Precision %	87.2	87.2	72.6	97.1	95.6	100	**89.3**	87.2	81.7	74.0	97.8	94.7	100	**89.0**

5   Conclusions

In this paper, we proposed a new method for building a multiclass SVM using integer parameters. The MC-HF-SVM is an appealing approach for use in AmI systems for healthcare applications such as activity monitoring on smartphones. This alternative that employs fixed-point calculations, can be used for AR because it requires less memory, processor time and power consumption. Moreover, it provides accuracy levels comparable to traditional approaches such as the MC-SVM that uses floating-point arithmetic.

The experimental results confirm that even with a reduction of bits equal to 6 for representing the learned MC-HF-SVM model parameter β, it is possible to substitute the standard MC-SVM. This outcome brings positive implications for smartphones because it could help to release system resources and reduce energy consumption. Future work will present a publicly available AR dataset to allow other researchers to test and compare different learning models.

Acknowledgments. This work was supported in part by the Erasmus Mundus Joint Doctorate in Interactive and Cognitive Environments, which is funded by the EACEA Agency of the European Commission under EMJD ICE FPA n 2010-0012.

References

1. Davies, N., Siewiorek, D.P., Sukthankar, R.: Activity-based computing. IEEE Pervasive Computing 7(2), 20–21 (2008)
2. Ekholm, J., Fabre, S.: Forecast: Mobile data traffic and revenue, worldwide. In: Gartner Mobile Communications Worldwide, pp. 2010–2015 (July 2011)

3. Cook, D.J., Das, S.K.: Pervasive computing at scale: Transforming the state of the art. Pervasive and Mobile Computing 8(1), 22–35 (2012)
4. Allen, F.R., Ambikairajah, E., Lovell, N.H., Celler, B.G.: Classification of a known sequence of motions and postures from accelerometry data using adapted gaussian mixture models. Physiological Measurement 27(10), 935 (2006)
5. Rodríguez-Molinero, A., Pérez-Martínez, D., Samá, A., Sanz, P., Calopa, M., Gálvez, C., Pérez-López, C., Romagosa, J., Catalá, A.: Detection of gait parameters, bradykinesia and falls in patients with parkinson's disease by using a unique triaxial accelerometer. World Parkinson Congress, Glasgow (2007)
6. Mannini, A., Sabatini, A.M.: Machine learning methods for classifying human physical activity from on-body accelerometers. Sensors 10(2), 1154–1175 (2010)
7. Ravi, N., Dandekar, N., Mysore, P., Littman, M.L.: Activity recognition from accelerometer data. In: Proceedings of the Seventeenth Conference on Innovative Applications of Artificial Intelligence, IAAI, pp. 1541–1546. AAAI Press (2005)
8. Kwapisz, J.R., Weiss, G.M., Moore, S.A.: Activity recognition using cell phone accelerometers. SIGKDD Explor. Newsl. 12(2), 74–82 (2011)
9. LeCun, Y., Jackel, L., Bottou, L., Brunot, A., Cortes, C., Denker, J., Drucker, H., Guyon, I., Mller, U., Sckinger, E., Simard, P., Vapnik, V.: Comparison of learning algorithms for handwritten digit recognition. In: International Conference on Artificial Neural Networks, pp. 53–60 (1995)
10. Ganapathiraju, A., Hamaker, J., Picone, J.: Applications of support vector machines to speech recognition. IEEE Transactions on Signal Processing 52(8), 2348–2355 (2004)
11. Wawrzynek, J., Asanovic, K., Morgan, N.: The design of a neuro-microprocessor. VLSI for Neural Networks and Artificial Intelligence 4, 103–107 (1993)
12. Anguita, D., Gomes, B.A.: Mixing floating- and fixed-point formats for neural network learning on neuroprocessors. Microprocess. Microprogram. 41(10), 757–769 (1996)
13. Anguita, D., Ghio, A., Pischiutta, S., Ridella, S.: A hardware-friendly support vector machine for embedded automotive applications. In: International Joint Conference on Neural Networks, IJCNN 2007, pp. 1360–1364 (August 2007)
14. Rifkin, R., Klautau, A.: In defense of one-vs-all classification. Journal of Machine Learning Research 5, 101–141 (2004)
15. Keerthi, S.S., Shevade, S.K., Bhattacharyya, C., Murthy, K.R.K.: Improvements to platt's smo algorithm for svm classifier design. Neural Comput. 13(3), 637–649 (2001)
16. Vapnik, V.N.: The nature of statistical learning theory. Springer-Verlag New York, Inc., New York (1995)
17. Platt, J.C.: Probabilistic outputs for support vector machines and comparisons to regularized likelihood methods. In: Advances in Large Margin Classifiers, pp. 61–74. MIT Press (1999)
18. Anguita, D., Sterpi, D.: Nature Inspiration for Support Vector Machines. In: Gabrys, B., Howlett, R.J., Jain, L.C. (eds.) KES 2006. LNCS (LNAI), vol. 4252, pp. 442–449. Springer, Heidelberg (2006)
19. Neven, H., Denchev, V.S., Rose, G., Macready, W.G.: Training a binary classifier with the quantum adiabatic algorithm. Arxiv preprint arXiv08110416 (x) 11 (2008)

Gait Quality Monitoring Using an Arbitrarily Oriented Smartphone

Oscar Ambres and Gracian Trivino

European Centre for Soft Computing
Mieres, Asturias, Spain

Abstract. Gait sensing by means of accelerometers yields quasi-periodic signals that can be analyzed in order to extract useful information. This paper introduces a method based on a Fuzzy Finite State Machine with temporary restrictions for tracking and recognizing the different states of human walking. Such operation is a mandatory task prior to perform a subsequent analysis on gait quality. Besides, the method described here allows to achieve this recognition when the sensing device, i.e. a smartphone, is being carried by the user in arbitrary orientations related to his/her body's natural axes.

1 Introduction

Human gait analysis and the development of practical applications with the extracted information represent a huge challenge for engineers, physical therapists and doctors alike. This is partly because human walking is an extremely complex process that changes from a given person to another, but also change for the same person walking under different physical —surface, footwear— or psychological conditions.

However, gait analysis is a valuable source of knowledge about the health condition of a patient. It might be a key part in clinical assessment of several pathologies, ranging from those merely physical to complex diseases like Parkinson [1] or, most notably, cerebral palsy [2]. Unfortunately this often requires a considerable amount of resources —professionals, laboratory time, expensive equipment, etc— and the monitoring scope is limited. In addition it is a well-known fact that people under a test environment do not behave in the same way as they would normally do [3].

Recent efforts have been made to apply intelligent systems to gait analysis in order to cope with some of these drawbacks, specially the need for a passive, long-term monitoring system. Computer vision [4] is one of these techniques, however it introduces other disadvantages in the shape of high complexity, limited spatial scope and, most importantly, privacy issues.

Another option is the acceleration-based gait sensing. This technique is able to record the human walking with an acceptable degree of accuracy and therefore to extract meaningful —although limited— information about its quality in a long-term tracking period. Previous researches in this field have opted to use a

J. Bravo, R. Hervás, and M. Rodríguez (Eds.): IWAAL 2012, LNCS 7657, pp. 224–231, 2012.

triple axis accelerometer attached to the user's body to measure gait quality [5], so the directions of those axes are aligned with the natural axes of the person. This represents a considerable setback when the goal is to design systems in order to be as less obtrusive as possible. In these systems users are forced to constantly take care of the position of the device because the system would not work if it is not properly placed.

The approach taken in this paper, by contrast, is to explore the possibility of monitoring the gait quality of the user without any condition regarding the orientation of the device, and therefore without significantly change his/her habits or behaviors. An important role in this vision is the device itself. Nowadays many people in the western countries —where also fast population ageing is becoming an important concern— carries some sort of mobile device, namely a smartphone or a PDA, for long periods of time each day. These gadgets usually have a built-in accelerometer, good computational performance and internet access capabilities, so they are potentially very interesting tools for the purpose of monitoring human activity.

Section 2 describes briefly our approach to Fuzzy Finite State Machines; section 3 describes how to apply this concept to model the human gait; section 4 presents a way of defining the gait quality; section 5 describes a basic experimentation and finally, section 6 contains the conclusions.

2   Fuzzy Finite State Machine with Temporary Restrictions

Once the acceleration data is acquired, the question that remains is how to effectively treat it to be able to identify the different states of gait. Many possibilities arise, being Hidden Markov Models maybe the most common method due to its extensive and successful employment in gait recognition [6]. Our approach on this matter, however, diverges from machine learning solutions and it is inspired instead by the concept of Linguistic Fuzzy Modeling [7].

Linguistic Fuzzy Modeling allows to describe a system from a qualitative point of view by means of linguistic variables, i.e. variables whose values are taken from natural language, and by the relations between these variables in the shape of conditional fuzzy statements. Given that variables and relations are established by an expert designer based on his/her knowledge and experience, the models tend to be reliable yet conceptually easy to understand, which is a desirable feature when dealing with complex processes like human gait.

Another feature of gait is that it produces quasi-periodic signals when magnitudes like acceleration are measured. This means that these values roughly repeat in time under a period that may not be constant either. Given such conditions —complexity and quasi-periodicity—, a suitable linguistic model that has already been successfully applied in previous works [8][9] is the Fuzzy Finite State Machine (FFSM). Here, a refinement of this type of model is proposed taking into account that human walking is a process subject to some obvious physical limitations. This means that additional knowledge can be added to the model in the form of "intuition" about what will happen next. We call this model Fuzzy Finite State Machine with temporary restrictions and it is defined by the following tuple:

$$\{Q, S, S', U, Y, f, g\}$$

where:

- Q is the set of states defined by the designer based on his/her perceptions about the behavior of the system.
- S is a vector that contains the degree of activation of each state at a given moment.
- S' is a vector that contains the predicted degree of activation of each state at given moment. It also relies on the designer's interpretation of phenomena.
- U is a vector containing the numerical values of the input variables.
- Y is the output vector of the system.
- f is the transition function that yields the next activation vector given the input and the current and predicted degrees of activation. $S[t+1] = f(S[t], S'[t+1], U[t])$.
- g is the output function: $Y[t] = g(S[t], U[t])$.

The key part of the model is the transition function which is defined through a set of fuzzy conditional statements. There is potentially one statement per each possible change of state and these statements operate over inputs as linguistic variables. The number of statements and their content are up to the designer but, generally, a rule for changing from state i to state j is shaped as follows:

$$R_{ij} = R_k : \text{ IF } (S[t] \text{ is } Qi) \text{ AND } (C_{ij}) \text{ AND } (S'[t+1] \text{ is } Qj)$$
$$\text{THEN } S[t+1] \to Q_j$$

Where C_{ij} is the set of fuzzy statements that evaluates to what degree the input variables meet the criteria of the given transition.

After assessing the antecedent of every rule, a set of firing degrees $\{w_k\}_{k=1}^{N}$ is obtained. Each degree represents the likelihood of transition to a given state and the combination of all of them yields $S[t+1]$.

3   A Human Gait Model

As said before, the approach proposed here needs a designer, who, using his experience and knowledge, has to choose the parameters of the FFSM. The most relevant are, perhaps, the number of considered states and their meaning because they define how the system is expected to behave.

Human gait can be explained as a cyclic process involving several phases. The most widely accepted models consider up to 7 different states for each leg [10], which, in addition, overlap in time. To avoid such complexity, we propose a simpler model that has only two states, namely *double support* and *swing*. *Swing* refers to the leg that moves forward. By contrast, if the leg in contact with

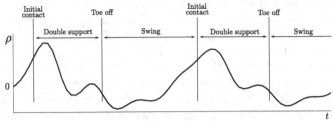

Fig. 1. Human gait model

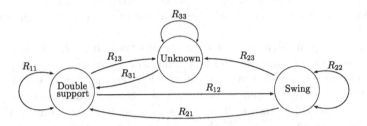

Fig. 2. States and transitions of the FFSM

the ground is considered, the state should be called *double support*. This way of defining states is slightly based on the former models, but it is also backed up by the orientation-independent resultant acceleration signal ($\rho = \sqrt{a_x^2 + a_y^2 + a_z^2}$), in which both states can be easily recognized (Figure 1).

Double support starts when one of the legs is finishing its swinging state and the heel is about to make the initial contact. As the hit happens, the acceleration becomes greater until it reaches a maximum and then, the person starts to move his/her body weight towards the forward leg. The state ends when the back foot takes off and the forward foot lays flat. This produces an slightly upwards thrust —spotted as the second local maximum— that will lift the body on the following swing phase, leading it to reach its highest point on the cycle. While the acceleration is kept low, the back leg starts to move forward until the heel hits the ground again and a new cycle starts.

On the other hand, an additional state has to be added in order to build a practical FFMS that takes into account the case in which the acceleration signal doesn't meet the double support nor the swing state conditions. When the user starts an activity other than walking, the sensed signal has nothing to do with the typical gait signal. Therefore, the FFSM has to acknowledge this situation and transition to the referred unknown state.

Once the states are defined, the connections between them have to be established —again from the designer's experience and knowledge—. In this case the scheme chosen is shown in Figure 2. There is a transition from each state to the rest, except for the case of the unknown state, in which it is only possible to go to the double support state, considered as the start of the cycle. This decision has been made in order to make the system simpler and more robust.

The inputs considered are the above-mentioned resultant acceleration signal, ρ, and its successive derivatives, ρ' and ρ''. All signals are axes independent and thus they are suitable for the proposed goal of modeling human gait irrespective of the orientation of the sensing device. These signals are previously low pass filtered in order to get rid of the spurious accelerations that appear at high frequencies and are not naturally produced by the human gait. A fair cut off point could be 5 Hz as it is unlikely that a person is able to perform movements with a period lower than 200 ms. Sampling frequency in cutting edge smartphones is around 60 Hz —i.e. way more than twice the considered bandwith of 5 Hz— so capturing every meaningful movement is assured. In addition, the gravity influence is canceled and the signal is normalized in order to ease and simplify the FFSM.

An important issue that has not been tackled yet is how the predicted state vector, S', is built. In this case, the first thing to do is estimate the step period (T_{step}). This can be achieved by performing a Fast Fourier Transform (FFT) on the resultant acceleration and subsequently detecting its dominant frequency. Once the step period is known, it is necessary to split it according to the percentage of time spent in each of both gait states. Based on previous experience, a reasonable balance might be 30% for double support and 70% for swing.

$S'[t + T_{step}]$ is then constructed by chaining two fuzzy membership functions that represent the expected lasting time of each state. This has to be done every time the FFSM transitions to double support state at time t.

Figure 3 shows how the FFSM is able to recognize the temporal evolution of the gait while it is shifting between the two states.

4   Gait Quality Parameters

Taking into account the obvious limitations of dealing with just the resultant acceleration, four quality parameters are proposed: Double Support Symmetry (DSS), Swing Symmetry (SS), Double Support Homogeneity (DSH) and Swing Homogeneity (SH). Here, this vector of four parameters can be considered the output Y of the FFSM.

The first step is to segment the total walking signal using the FFSM. Once the segmentation is done, three values are extracted for each k set and state: average acceleration ($\bar{\rho}_k$), duration (Δt_k) and peak acceleration ($max(\rho_k)$ or $min(\rho_k)$) (Figure 3). Comparing these values across different sets of samples will allow to obtain the above-mentioned parameters.

4.1   Symmetry

Symmetry aims to capture how balanced the gait is by comparing two set of acceleration samples that belong to the same state. These two sets of samples have to appear one after another so they represent different legs. Duration and acceleration values are then computed for each couple (Figure 4) through a function that yields a value between 0 and 1, with 1 meaning a total match between sets.

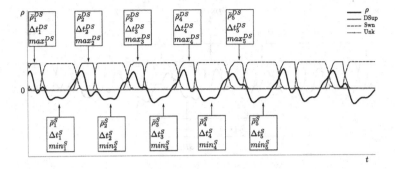

Fig. 3. State segmentation and comparing values

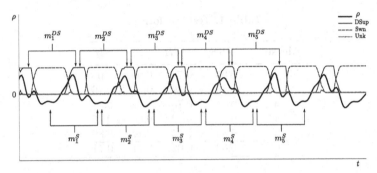

Fig. 4. Symmetry

At the end, two vectors, $\mathbf{m}^{DS}$ and $\mathbf{m}^S$, are obtained, with their lengths depending on how long the total walking signal is. Symmetry's parameters, DSS and SS, can be then calculated as:

$$DSS = mean\left(\mathbf{m}^{DS}\right) \in [0,1], \qquad SS = mean\left(\mathbf{m}^S\right) \in [0,1]$$

4.2 Homogeneity

Homogeneity focuses on the similarity of sets of acceleration samples that are not successive —specifically, that have another set of the same state between them— (Figure 5), and therefore represent the same leg.

Again, $\bar{p}_k$, Δt_k and $max(\rho_k)$ —or $min(\rho_k)$— are considered, so a vector for each parameter, leg and state is built. These vectors are computed through a function that produces a value between 0 and 1 for each state and leg: DSH_A, DSH_B, SH_A and SH_B. It is not possible for the method to tell if the leg is the right or the left one, so the notation of A/B is used to refer to each leg.

Finally, homogeneity's parameters, DSH and SH, are calculated as:

$$DSH = \frac{DSH_A + DSH_B}{2} \in [0,1], \qquad SH = \frac{SH_A + SH_B}{2} \in [0,1]$$

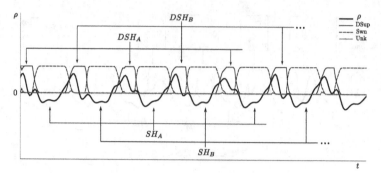

Fig. 5. Homogeneity

Table 1. Tests performed

Measure	DSS	DSH	SS	SH
1	0.86	0.76	0.90	.80
2	0.88	0.80	0.87	0.76
3	0.85	0.75	0.82	0.81
4	0.85	0.72	0.86	0.76
5	0.84	0.75	0.87	0.80
6	0.63	0.62	0.71	0.71

5   Experimentation

The experimentation process has been carried out with an Android smartphone running a custom application to gather the gait signals from the built-in triple-axis accelerometer. This simple program can perform measures for several hours while being executed in the background. The user assigns a name and starts the measure. When he/she decides to stop it, the application produces a *.csv* file in the local storage media —e.g. the SD Card— with all the data recorded.

The device can be arbitrarily oriented, but it has to be placed attached to the trunk of the person. Placing it on a limb —e.g. in a trouser's pocket— may produce different accelerations for opposite steps and therefore inaccurate symmetry scores. In this case, the phone was introduced in a backpack in order to be completely orientation-free, but it can be carried, for instance, in a shirt's pocket.

In order to easily test the proposed method, five measures were taken for a healthy young male walking under normal conditions, namely, flat surface, normal footwear and medium speed. Additionally, another measure was taken for the same person, but this time, while carrying a weight in one of his hands with the purpose of introduce some degree of dissymmetry.

As expected, the quality parameters have decreased for the sixth measure (Table 1) proving that the method properly acknowledge the lack of symmetry —and potentially the lack of homogeneity— in human gait. By contrast, the parameters for the rest of the measures show a remarkable similarity, indicating that the system is also consistent.

6 Conclusions and Future Work

We have described a solution to model human gait quality from the accelerations registered by an arbitrarily oriented smartphone. It successfully tracks the different states of walking and produces consistent quality measures under different conditions.

Further and intensive experimentation has to be done to fully test the system for longer periods of time, specially on ill patients. However, as shown, the method is already a considerable step forward regarding other methods that cope with gait quality by means of accelerometers, as it overcomes the drawback of having to place the device under a given orientation.

Acknowledgment. This work has been funded by the Spanish Government (MICINN) under project TIN2011-29827-C02-01.

References

1. Blin, O., Ferrandez, A.M., Serratrice, G.: Quantitative analysis of gait in Parkinson patients: increased variability of stride length. Jour. Neur. Scie. 98, 91–97 (1990)
2. Lee, E.H., Goh, J.C., Bose, K.: Value of gait analysis in the assessment of surgery in cerebral palsy. Arch. Phys. Medi. Reha. 73, 642–646 (1992)
3. Moe-Nilssen, R.: Test-retest reliability of trunk accelerometry during standing and walking. Arch. Phys. Medi. Reha. 79, 1377–1385 (1998)
4. Gavrila, D.M.: The visual analysis of human movement: a survey. Comp. Visi. Imag. Unde. 73, 82–98 (1999)
5. Alvarez, A., Trivino, G.: Linguistic description of the human gait quality. Engi. Appl. Arti. Inte. (to appear, 2012)
6. Nickel, C., Busch, C., Rangarajan, S., Mobius, M.: Using hidden markov models for accelerometer-based biometric gait recognition. In: IEEE 7th Inte. Collo. Sign. Proc. Appl., pp. 58–63 (2011)
7. Zadeh, L.A.: Outline of a new approach to the analysis of complex systems and decision processes. IEEE Tran. Syst. Man Cybe. SMC-3, 28–44 (1973)
8. Alvarez, A., Trivino, G.: Comprehensible model of a quasi-periodic signal. In: Nint. Inte. Conf. Inte. Syst. Desi. Appl. (2009)
9. Alvarez, A., Trivino, G., Cordon, O.: Human gait modeling using a genetic fuzzy finite state machine. IEEE Tran. Fuzz. Syst. 20, 60–65 (2012)
10. Whittle, M.W.: Gait analysis: an introduction, 4th edn., pp. 52–53. Elsevier (2007)

Ambient Sensor System for Freezing of Gait Detection by Spatial Context Analysis

Boris Takač[1,2], Andreu Català[2], Daniel Rodríguez[2], Wei Chen[1], and Matthias Rauterberg[1]

[1] TU/e - Eindhoven University of Technology,
Industrial Design Department, Den Dolech 2, 5612 AZ Eindhoven, The Netherlands
b.takac@tue.nl
[2] UPC - Universitat Politècnica de Catalunya,
Technical Research Centre for Dependency Care and Autonomous Living (CETpD)
Neàpolis, Rambla de l'Exposició, 59-69, 08800 Vilanova i la Geltrú, Spain

Abstract. Freezing of gait (FoG) is one of the most disturbing and least understood symptoms in Parkinson's disease (PD). One of the specificities of FoG is its dependency on the context of the patient, such as current location or a task at hand. Recent advances in assistive technology have strived towards the realization of personal health systems able to prolong independent living capability of people experiencing the symptom. So far, only solutions based on wearable sensing exist, but these systems do not take advantage of the external context for FoG detection. We present the concept and the laboratory prototype of an ambient sensor system designed to enhance its companion FoG wearable monitoring system through precise localization and active mapping of the environment.

1 Introduction

Freezing of Gait (FoG) is a temporary, involuntary inability to initiate or continue movement lasting just a few seconds or, on some occasions, several minutes [1]. FoG is experienced by approximately 50 % of patients with advanced Parkinson's disease (PD). FoG depends on the walking situation. It often occurs on turns, start of walking, upon reaching the destination and in open spaces [2]. It can also occur when people approach narrow spaces, such as doors, and in crowded places [3]. In a home environment, freezing episodes are reported by patients to occur on the same location every day. Other factors that can elicit freezing are set-shifting deficits [4], increased cognitive load such as dual-task, stress, anxiety and depression. Freezing of gait, irrespective of what caused it, is mostly characterized by a decrease in stride length, an increase in stepping frequency preceding the episode and the presence of a highly abnormal frequency of leg movements during the episodes [5].

Some of the patients developed different ways to deal with FoG on their own. This involves various techniques for solving start hesitation like lateral swaying, stepping over someone's foot and stepping over lines on the floor. Observation of

J. Bravo, R. Hervás, and M. Rodríguez (Eds.): IWAAL 2012, LNCS 7657, pp. 232–239, 2012.

these techniques led to the research of cueing. Evidence was found that external "cues" (visual, auditory) may be able to compensate for the defective internal "cueing system" for initiating and maintaining movement, usually facilitated by dopamine [6]. Freezing episode can happen suddenly, particularly when walking, which makes it one of the main causes of falls in PD. Bigger risk of falling causes people to lose their independence [7], aggravates activities of daily living (ADLs) and can have substantial impact on their quality of life.

The research of cueing techniques lead to the development of a few commercial products intended to help patients to improve their gait performance (laser cane, PD Glasses, GaitAid). Disadvantage of current existing products is that they are not adaptable to the walking rhythm of each patient, offering permanent stimulation not useful in most FoG episodes. Recent findings suggest that active monitoring technology [8] has potential to alleviate FoG through timely episode detection and sensory stimulation.

One of the main challenges for adoption of wearable assistants for FoG is to achieve high level of usability, through reliable detection and minimal wearable sensor footprint. We expect that information about patient's external context, like location and orientation during FoG, will be able to improve detection reliability. To obtain this contextual information, we propose the use of ambient visual sensors, hoping that this task could later be implemented as one of the services in vision systems in the homes of the future.

The paper is structured as follows: in section 2, the concept and description of components of the hybrid wearable-ambient system for FoG monitoring are given, in section 3 the laboratory prototype of the ambient system with focus on sensor setup and tested tracking algorithm is presented, while section 4 offers a short conclusion.

2   Ubiquitous Monitoring System for FoG

In our concept for ubiquitous FoG monitoring system, wearable inertial sensor system is used as the main gait monitoring device through the day. Gait monitoring device coupled with a cueing device allows for the treatment of the patient at the point of need at any time. Sensing capacity of the wearable system is expanded with a network of visual sensors installed in the patient's home environment. Use of visual sensors is targeted for non-private areas of a home, such as living room, kitchen and hall. Components of the hybrid system shown in Figure 1 are wearable subsystem running independent FoG detection algorithm, and vision subsystem composed of software modules for image based tracking, environment mapping and context inference that are running on a dedicated server. The remainder of this section gives description of system components and modules.

2.1   REMPARK Wearable System

REMPARK (Personal Health Device for the Remote and Autonomous Management of Parkinson's Disease) is an ongoing three and half year project funded

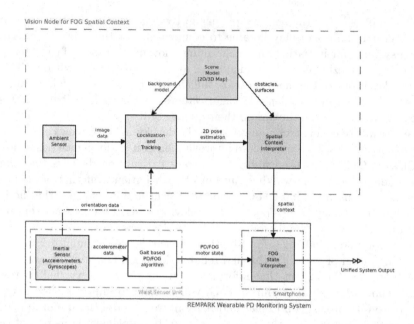

Fig. 1. Ubiquitous Monitoring System for FoG. Wearable system independently detects FoG based on IMU data (blue rectangle), except when in home areas covered with vision sensor system (red rectangle), where users spatial context is also considered.

by the European Commission [9]. The ultimate goal of the project is to develop Personal Health System (PHS) with closed loop detection, response and treatment capabilities for management of PD patients. An important part of the final solution is the possibility to detect and act on FoG episode.

Sensing components of the wearable monitoring system include two inertial sensor units, on a waist and around a wrist. Waist sensor is used for the identification of basic movement related parameters such as posture, stride length and gait speed. The task of the wrist sensor is to detect symptoms of tremor and dyskinesia. Possible actuators are injection pump for drug delivery, the auditory cuing system and Functional Electrical Stimulation (FES) system. FES actuator can be used both as a haptic cueing system, and as a step initiating device in the case of detected FoG episode.

Smartphone is acting as the main control and communication unit of the whole Body Area Network (BAN). Furthermore, smartphone is used as the main input device for collecting patient's input about medication intake and non-motor symptoms. Wearable sensor fixed around the waist is not very valuable for precise indoor localization on its own. However, we expect to be able to utilize this sensor for improved orientation tracking and long term identification in congruence with visual tracking system. Algorithms that run on wearable sensor unit and smartphone are part of the future work and they will not be discussed in this paper.

2.2   Vision System

Vision system has three main tasks: a) identification and tracking of the patient (*Tracking module*), b) automatic analysis of the observed scene (*Scene Model module*), and c) inference about how current location influences the FoG state of the user (*Context Interpretation module*). Output value of the visual system operation is the estimation of probability of FoG based on current location of the patient.

Application driven top-down analysis of requirements of each task determines visual system in terms of the type and spatial distribution of vision sensors.

Tracker Requirements. To infer spatial context in FoG, we are primarily interested in the locomotion behaviour of the patient, addressing the question of how he changes his location over time. Examples from the literature, show that usually two-dimensional (2-D) point representation involving floor map is sufficient for this kind of task [10]. We extracted situations and contextual triggers of FoG that could be identified from two-dimensional motion in a robust and efficient way under realistic conditions. These are turns, start of walking, approach to destination, narrow spaces and locations where FoG occurs every day. For some situations, like turning, 2-D point representation is not sufficient, so we propose 2-D pose (position and orientation) as the minimal representation that should be used in the tracking algorithm.

Scene Analysis Requirements. In their home environment PD patients are likely to encounter narrow passages, such as doorways or dynamically changing spaces created by other people and movable objects. When the space is perceived to be very narrow for the dimensions of their body, adaptive postural changes during locomotion may be necessary to achieve collision-free passage [11]. Experiments with PD patients show that there might be a direct correlation between the width of the narrow space and tendency for FoG episode [12]. If we want our system to be able to use this direct correlations on a dynamically reconfigurable scene, it is necessary to use a floor map with metric values.

Sensor Selection. The need for geometrical relations and real world measurements eliminates the possibility of using monocular color cameras, because they can only do tracking in the image plane, and they are unable to infer distances on the scene. The solution is in the scene recovery by the means of 3-D perception for which there are two possible vision system setups. The first possibility is to use a set of multiple overlapping color cameras per room, which are able to achieve scene reconstruction through joint calibration and solution of the correspondence problem. The second possibility is to use cameras that can sense both color and range data (RGB-D), and which are able to directly recover scene geometry. RGB-D cameras can be installed in non-overlapped mode, focusing only on particular areas in a home. For the laboratory prototype development, we chose to work with the second option.

Context Inference Process. In the case of multiple non-overlapped sensors, context inference process will be done for each RGB-D camera using the concept shown on Figure 1.

Scene Model (SM) module contains 3-D point cloud of the observed scene maintained through periodic updates from the vision sensor. Scene point cloud is updated every few minutes, on occasions when there are no tracked people in the field of view. SM module has dual role in the system. First, updated depth image of the scene is used in the background subtraction process of the vision node tracker. Second, SM module does the planar segmentation and hull extraction of the horizontal and vertical elements, which are obtained from floors, walls and pieces of furniture, and sends them to the Spatial Context Interpreter (SCI) module for further processing.

SCI projects extracted hulls on the floor plane and obtains updated 2-D metric map of the scene (direct geometric representation). Next, SCI analyses the properties of extracted hulls, such as their height, area, relation of vertical and horizontal and tries to infer the meaning of the places on the map, i.e. door or table corner (semantic level representation). Furthermore, SCI employs database, with the history of tracks of the patient and state observations made (historical representation). Combining the set of rules over all three representations, along with the current pose given by the tracker, SCI infers contextual probability of FoG episode. This probability is then published over wireless network and read by FoG State Interpreter (FSI) module running on smartphone device of REMPARK BAN. FSI conducts high level probabilistic fusion of ambient and wearable detector information and produces final system output.

3   Laboratory Prototype

We are currently developing laboratory prototype of the vision system. The prototype development has two main objectives: 1) to prove feasibility of the concept of patient tracking and identification using non-overlapped RGB-D sensors, 2) to establish a way for simple acquisition of video and geometrical data of ADL of PD patients in their home environment.

In our development process, we use one MS Kinect connected with a notebook PC running Linux. The programming is done in C/C++ using *Open Source Computer Vision Library* (OpenCV) and *Point Cloud Library* (PCL) for Kinect data processing, and using *Qt* application framework for user interface design.

3.1   Sensor Properties and Setup

In the laboratory, we use Kinect in the overhead position at a height between 2.2 and 2.4 m and with a downward angle between 20-30 degrees from the horizontal. Although, the nominal operation range of Kinect's range sensor is 0.8 - 3.5 m, we apply it in the extended range of up to 6 m in order to enlarge floor area under observation. Described positioning and the parametric setup of the Kinect sensor, result in the active floor area having trapezoidal shape and size of approximatively 15 m2 (Figure 2.).

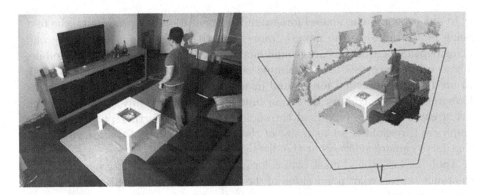

Fig. 2. Left, image of Context Lab at TUE Department of Industrial Design. Right, visualization of the tracking algorithm. Active tracking area has trapezoidal shape (green line). Tracked position of the person is marked by the red rectangle on the floor plane. Coordinate frame shown in the right down corner is *camera base* frame.

3.2   Scene Analysis and Tracking

Plan-view tracking is a computer vision approach which combines geometric analysis, appearance models and probabilistic methods to track people on the 2-D floor plane [13]. The main prerequisite for the successful implementation of any *plan-view* tracking algorithm is to define camera in relation to the floor plane. For our application, we developed a semi-automatic procedure which can detect the floor plane with the minimal input from the user when setting up the system. The procedure is based on planar segmentation by the means of *Random Sample Consensus* (RANSAC) method, and the presumption that the floor plane is among the dominant horizontal planes in the field of view. Two main parameters used during segmentation are the estimate of the camera height in meters, and a minimal number of points for the floor plane.

The procedure takes point cloud of the visible scene as the input, and after applying voxel grid filtering and planar segmentation, it calculates planar equations and hulls of potential candidates for floor plane and visualizes them in the user interface of the application. User can then choose a hull which is the best fit for the floor plane. Usually, only one or two options are offered. After the user input, the axes of the *camera image* frame are vertically projected on the floor plane. Projected axes form an independent vector base for a new reference frame called *camera base* frame. *Camera base* frame is set in exactly under the camera, with X and Y axes spanning the plane of the floor and Z axis pointing up towards camera. This frame is the main frame of reference for tracking in floor plane.

Our adaptation of the the *plan-view* tracking algorithm for the Kinect sensor is based on the work of Munoz [14]. Significant changes were made in the first two stages of the algorithm, foreground segmentation and point projection, to take into account for the specificities of our hardware configuration (different resolution; 640x480 vs. 320x200, different calibration), different software libraries and the role of the tracker towards the rest of the system.

B. Taka et al.

In our version, image-based foreground segmentation has two inputs, the first being depth image of the newest frame from the range sensor and the second being depth image in the background model maintained by Scene Model module. These images are used in the simple subtraction and binary threshold step, to produce unsegmented foreground image. After morphological erosion on the foreground image, contour detection function is applied. Only contours of area size greater than the empirical threshold are kept for further processing. The empirical threshold is set as a size of the upper body half of the grown human that faces camera sideways at the distance of 6m.

Applying foreground mask over color image, and using intrinsic parameters of the range sensor, color point cloud of the foreground is built. This point cloud is transformed into *camera base* frame using the transformation matrix that was calculated during camera setup process. After the transformation, points of the foreground cloud are projected vertically onto the floor plane. From this stage onward, representation maps, people detector and particle filter implementation are done accordingly to [14], so we point the reader to the referenced work for the detailed description. The example of the tracker under operation, as can be seen inside our application, is given at the right of Figure 2.

Preliminary, qualitative tests of the tracker in the laboratory conditions, confirmed that it is able to deal well with the occlusions of the lower extremities produced by the furniture, and that it is able to keep track of the people with sub-meter precision, which are both important properties for our intended purpose. Using non-optimized code with visualization on dual-core P4 2.2 Ghz, we were able to get operation at around 5 Hz.

4   Conclusions and Future Work

In this paper we presented the concept for ubiquitous monitoring system for detection of FoG in PD patients. The concept combines wearable system for gait monitoring with ambient visual sensors for context analysis. In the spatial context analysis, we go beyond localization, as we are also trying to take into account changing characteristics of the surrounding home environment. The focus of the presented practical work is on the implementation of a laboratory prototype of vision system for human tracking. Preliminary results showed that it was possible to adapt chosen tracking algorithm to work with Kinect, and that the algorithm was well suited for handling occlusions in a simulated home environment. The wearable system was presented in terms of sensing components and desired functionality, but none of its algorithms were discussed in this work.

Future work on ambient sensor system will be done in the direction of tracker improvements and scene analysis algorithms. Existing tracker needs to be expanded with the ability of orientation tracking and long-term identification. In scene analysis, we will focus on automatic planar segmentations of 3D scene models and on-line 2-D map building.

Acknowledgement. This work was supported in part by the Erasmus Mundus Joint Doctorate in Interactive and Cognitive Environments, which is funded by the Education, Audiovisual and Culture Executive Agency under the FPA 2010-0012, and in part by the REMPARK project: FP7-ICT-2011-7 287677, Personal Health Device for the Remote and Autonomous Management of Parkinsons Disease.

References

1. Fahn, S.: The freezing phenomenon in parkinsonism. Advances in Neurology 67, 53–63 (1995)
2. Schaafsma, J.D., Balash, Y., Gurevich, T., Bartels, A.L., Hausdorff, J.M., Giladi, N.: Characterization of freezing of gait subtypes and the response of each to levodopa in parkinson's disease. European Journal of Neurology 10(4), 391–398 (2003)
3. Bloem, B.R., Hausdorff, J.M., Visser, J.E., Giladi, N.: Falls and freezing of gait in parkinson's disease: A review of two interconnected, episodic phenomena. Movement Disorders 19(8), 871–884 (2004)
4. Naismith, S.L., Shine, J.M., Lewis, S.J.: The specific contributions of set-shifting to freezing of gait in parkinson's disease. Movement Disorders 25(8), 1000–1004 (2010)
5. Vercruysse, S., Spildooren, J., Heremans, E., Vandenbossche, J., Levin, O., Wenderoth, N., Swinnen, S.P., Janssens, L., Vandenberghe, W., Nieuwboer, A.: Freezing in parkinson's disease: A spatiotemporal motor disorder beyond gait. Movement Disorders 27(2), 254–263 (2012)
6. Burleigh-Jacobs, A., Horak, F.B., Nutt, J.G., Obeso, J.A.: Step initiation in parkinson's disease: Influence of levodopa and external sensory triggers. Movement Disorders 12(2), 206–215 (1997)
7. Giladi, N., Hausdorff, J.M.: The role of mental function in the pathogenesis of freezing of gait in parkinson's disease. Journal of the Neurological Sciences 248(12), 173–176 (2006)
8. Bachlin, M., Plotnik, M., Roggen, D., Maidan, I., Hausdorff, J., Giladi, N., Troster, G.: Wearable assistant for parkinson's disease patients with the freezing of gait symptom. IEEE Transactions on Information Technology in Biomedicine 14(2), 436–446 (2010)
9. http://www.rempark.eu
10. Vieilledent, S., Kerlirzin, Y., Dalbera, S., Berthoz, A.: Relationship between velocity and curvature of a human locomotor trajectory. Neuroscience Letters 305(1), 65–69 (2001)
11. Higuchi, T., Cinelli, M., Greig, M., Patla, A.: Locomotion through apertures when wider space for locomotion is necessary: adaptation to artificially altered bodily states. Experimental Brain Research 175, 50–59 (2006)
12. Almeida, Q.J., Lebold, C.A.: Freezing of gait in parkinson's disease: a perceptual cause for a motor impairment? Journal of Neurology, Neurosurgery, and Psychiatry 81(5), 513–518 (2010)
13. Harville, M.: Stereo person tracking with adaptive plan-view templates of height and occupancy statistics. Image and Vision Computing 22(2), 127–142 (2004)
14. Muñoz Salinas, R.: A bayesian plan-view map based approach for multiple-person detection and tracking. Pattern Recogn. 41(12), 3665–3676 (2008)

Multiple Structured Light-Based Depth Sensors for Human Motion Analysis: A Review

Kyis Essmaeel[1,2,3,*], Luigi Gallo[1], Ernesto Damiani[2],
Giuseppe De Pietro[1], and Albert Dipandà[3]

[1] Institute of High Performance Computing and Networking, Italian National Research Council,
Via Pietro Castellino 111, Naples, Italy
{kyis.essmaeel,luigi.gallo,giuseppe.depietro}@na.icar.cnr.it
[2] Department of Computer Technology, University of Milan, Via Comelico 39-41, Milan, Italy
ernesto.damiani@unimi.it
[3] Laboratoire LE2I (CNRS-UMR 5158), Aile des Sciences de l'Ingénieur,
Université de Bourgogne, 9 Avenue Alain Savary, BP 47870-21078 Dijon Cedex, France
adipanda@u-bourgogne.fr

Abstract. Human motion analysis is an increasingly important active research domain with various applications in surveillance, human-machine interaction and human posture analysis. The recent developments in depth sensor technology, especially with the release of the Kinect device, have attracted significant attention to the question of how to take advantage of this technology in order to achieve accurate motion tracking and action detection in marker-less approaches. In this paper, we review the benefits and limitations deriving from the adoption of structured light-based depth sensors in human motion analysis applications. Surveying the relevant literature, we have identified in calibration, interference and bias correction the challenges to tackle for an effective adoption of multi-Kinect systems to improve the visual analysis of human movement.

Keywords: Human Motion Analysis, Multiple depth sensors, Calibration, Interference.

1   Introduction

Human motion analysis [1] is a vast research domain concerned with providing efficient tools to detect and track people, identify human actions and more generally interpret human motion from a set of images. The process of human motion analysis can be divided into different subsections, like human body modelling, pose estimation and tracking. Each of these subsections can represent a whole research area in itself. There have been several attempts to provide a well-defined taxonomy for the components of human motion analysis. Nonetheless, the boundaries between these components are not clear with even the possibility of excluding one or more components depending on the application [2], [3].

---

* Corresponding author.

J. Bravo, R. Hervás, and M. Rodríguez (Eds.): IWAAL 2012, LNCS 7657, pp. 240–247, 2012.
© Springer-Verlag Berlin Heidelberg 2012

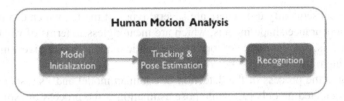

Fig. 1. Human Motion Analysis Pipeline

In human motion capture and analysis we can identify two main approaches, marker-based and marker-less. The marker-based approach relies on sensors attached to the human body; a receiver processes the signals from these sensors to reconstruct the shape of the body and detect its movements [4], [5]. Even though these kinds of system are capable of delivering an accurate estimation of the human body and of tracking efficiently its movement, they are expensive and cumbersome to install and use; these drawbacks and many others prevent the marker-based approach from being applied on a wide scale. Unlike the marker-based approach, the marker-less approach uses affordable, unobtrusive devices ranging from a web-cam and DSLR to video recorders. However, marker-less approach-based systems are usually lacking in accuracy and require computationally intensive techniques to recognize human motion from images because of the insufficiency in depth information in 2D projections.

Depth measurement using multiple camera views is a practical solution to increase the accuracy of such systems. However, this requires multiple computationally expensive steps, and is dependent on scene illumination and on surface texturing. This factor has led to an increasing use, among light wave-based techniques, of time-of-flight (ToF) and laser scan devices, especially in human motion analysis applications. However, with the arrival of the Kinect [6] in 2010, a novel 3D measurement device became available, and many aspects of this new device caught the attention, like the cheap price and the reliable measurements it can provide. In a short time, there have been many interesting applications build around the device, which shows the wide range of application domains that Kinect may be involved in. In this paper we describe some of the benefits and limitations of using multiple Kinects for human motion analysis, by considering hardware and software solutions to provide accurate, reliable 3D sensing data.

2   Human Motion Analysis

Following several previous surveys and taxonomies on human motion analysis we can identify three main components that describe the whole process, in which each component depends on the previous one (see Fig. 1).

Human body modelling [7] is the process of defining a model that simulates the structure of the human body. Even though there is the possibility of omitting this step and following a model-free approach, it is still preferable to build such a model, which would guide the work in the following steps more exactly. In general, the definition of the human body model depends on the level of detail the application aims to capture and subsequently use. There are several types of model, which can be categorized into appearance/shape models, which are meaningless in terms of what the pose of the subject is, and the more appropriate kinematic models, which give a meaningful understanding of the human body structure [8].

Tracking is the process of the detection of a human model and its association with previously detected models [9], while pose estimation is the process of estimating the configuration of the underlying kinematic structure of the human body [10]. These two processes are highly dependent on the previously defined human body model. This step faces several challenges including the large variation in poses, occlusion and the loss of depth information in 2D image projection [10]. The loss of such information can affect the whole process and significant effort is spent to resolve this problem using multi-camera systems or depth sensors like ToF cameras or structured light-based sensors, like the Kinect.

The levels of recognition can vary from detecting primitive actions to interpreting complex actions, taking into consideration the environment and the application scenario, which can sometimes be considered as behaviour analysis, a higher level of human motion analysis [11]. The robustness of recognition is related to the precision and level of detail actually captured. This should adapt the variation in action speed and should take into consideration the fact that in the real world humans perform composite actions [12].

3　Depth Sensors in Multi-camera Set-Up

One of the major limitations of RGB cameras is the loss of depth information of the scene. This limitation has been commonly tackled by building large systems that comprise several devices. With the recent developments in imaging hardware, depth sensors like ToF cameras and Kinect have begun to overcome this limitation. Whereas ToF-sensors are still expensive, the Kinect is a low cost device that provides RGB and depth information with a reasonable precision and performance. Even though the Kinect has only recently been released, it is already considered to be the primary 3D measurement device for plenty of applications in several fields like robotics [13], human motion analysis [14] and human-computer interaction [15]. This has suggested an analysis of the performance of the Kinect in more detail and a comparison with its main competitors, which are stereo camera systems and ToF sensors.

The Kinect is a composite device consisting of an IR projector, an IR camera and an RGB camera. The IR camera captures the pattern projected onto the scene by the IR projector; then, by using triangulation, the position of the points in the 3D space is recovered. The RGB camera is then used to recognize image content and texture 3D points. In a recent study [12] a comparison of the accuracy measurement of the Kinect with an SLR stereo camera system and an SR-4000 ToF sensor has shown that the Kinect outperforms the ToF sensor and is close in performance to the SLR stereo systems.

The Kinect suffers from the same limitations as other depth measurements devices: the measurements are restricted to objects facing the device. In situations where it is important to achieve a complete 3D scene reconstruction, it becomes necessary to build multiple sensor systems that cover the whole scene and retrieve the maximum possible information about the subject.

While the performance of a single Kinect has been well assessed, there have been only a few studies on the possibility of combining multiple Kinects together and on a consideration of to what extent we can exploit the capability of the device in such a system. A multiple Kinect system will have to handle the common challenges already found in a multi-camera system (e.g., calibration), and new ones related to the nature of the device and the way it works (e.g. the interference with the projected IR pattern).

3.1   Calibration

Multiple camera calibration is a problem that has been well addressed with many methods providing good and reliable solutions. The most frequently adopted method of calibrating multiple cameras is by using a reference object which is seen by all of the cameras. Such a method can be used to calibrate the RGB sensor in each Kinect. The challenge remains of how to calibrate the depth sensors simultaneously together with the other RGB sensors.

The most common solution adopted to date has been to use the capability of the Kinect driver to register the depth image to the RGB image, and then to perform only calibration on the RGB cameras using any of the already provided methods. This solution is easy to implement but is not suitable for applications that require a high level of accuracy. Another solution is to follow the conventional procedure of relying on a reference object seen by all of the devices. However, this object needs to have special characteristics that make it possible to provide distinguishable values in the depth image. Following this approach, [16] uses a material that deflects the emitted light of the depth sensor, thus making it invisible, and another material that diffusely reflects it.

3.2   Interference

One of the major problems in multiple Kinect systems is interference. When two or more Kinect view fields overlap, this causes a high level of noise and missing data, so decreasing the performance of each Kinect and of the whole system. The few existing approaches to tackle this problem can be divided into hardware and software solutions.

Hardware Solutions. Time multiplexing is a suggested solution to solve the problem of interference [16] by installing a set of shutters over each IR projector, so making it possible to cover the scene by allowing only one projected pattern at any time. The main drawback of such a method is the reduction of the frame rate and of the amount of light available for the IR camera depending on the speed of the shutter.

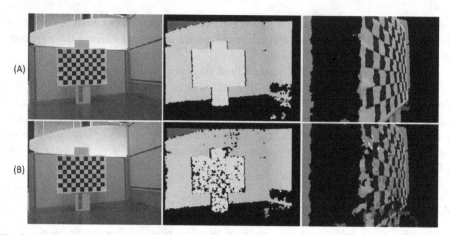

Fig. 2. Interference in multi Kinect systems - RGB, depth map and 3D reconstructed image (A) from a single Kinect (B) from a single Kinect, but with a second active Kinect with overlapping view

Another method recently proposed is IR filtering, but the peak-to-peak range of the wavelength is too close to be practically filtered [17]. Another approach is to apply a small amount of movement onto each device using an electronic motor attached to the device [18]. Such motion will blur the projected pattern relative to the other devices, while it can still be captured by the reference device. However, the device motion blurs also the RGB camera, so requiring a time-consuming image post processing step.

Software Solutions. Software solutions provide an alternative way of handling interference and overcoming some of the limitations of the hardware solutions. Such solutions take into consideration the characteristics of the interference. In [17], a hole filling algorithm based on a median filter is described. This solution results from the fact the Kinect returns no data when interference occurs causing relatively small holes on the surfaces. Such a solution can also be helpful in situations where small regions on the surfaces reflect infra-red light. An additional smoothing filter, the Bilateral Filter, can be applied to help keep the continuous surfaces consistent with each other.

Fig. 2 depicts the interference problem, where two Kinects with an overlapping view field are set up about 0.8 meter from the chessboard target. The interference between the Kinects causes small holes in the depth image. Fig. 3 illustrates the different software solutions proposed in [17]: in the first step a hole filling algorithm is applied resulting in removing most of the holes in the image; then, a bilateral filter, a smoothing algorithm, is applied; finally, a temporal noise suppression is applied in order to reduce the jittering effect.

The temporal noise suppression simply thresholds the new depth values: if the difference from the old values is greater than a distance-based threshold, the new value is accepted. This filter produces good results, but at the cost of filtering out all the slow movements performed far from the camera. No variable gain approach, like the one proposed in [19], has been applied to tackle this problem so far.

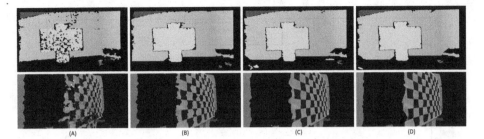

Fig. 3. Software solutions to the interference problem: depth map and 3D reconstructed image (A) unfiltered; (B) hole filling method; (C) hole filling and bilateral filter; (D) hole filling, bilateral filter and temporal noise suppression

4   Lessons Learnt and Ongoing Challenges

The variety of potential applications the Kinect may be involved in is vast, and although only in its first generation the Kinect is already considered to be an important breakthrough in the development of more efficient 3D measurement devices. While a lot of research has been carried out on integrating the Kinect into different systems, less interest has been given to assessing the device capability taking into consideration the distinctiveness of the application domains.

In [14], the authors show that the Kinect can be used for postural control assessment. The Kinect device has been compared to a marker-based multiple-camera 3D motion analysis system and, even though the result was not as accurate as the result from the multiple-camera system, the Kinect still has the advantage of being markerless, cheaper and portable. Another demonstration of the usability of the Kinect from a different domain is shown in [17], where multiple Kinects have been used to build a telepresence system. In this work, the authors also introduce new algorithms to handle interference and noise while maintaining a good level of performance. Besides the previous examples of the usability of the Kinect, we can read about many other attempts to exploit the benefits of the Kinect. The most notable advantages of the Kinect are its affordability, portability and speed of measurements. Additionally, multiple Kinects can be set up to work together as several previous publications have demonstrated [16], [17].

On the other hand, there are several drawbacks relating to the usability of the Kinect. In [17], the authors show that the measurements returned by the Kinect are biased, and the bias increases linearly with distance (see Fig. 4). Multiple-Kinect calibration remains an open challenge, too. The calibration procedure usually follows that of the OpenCV camera calibration, like in the RGB Demo project [20]. However, the distinctive features of the Kinect should be considered, like the shift between the infra-red and depth image [21], and the geometrical model [12]. Furthermore, in a multiple Kinect system interference becomes a serious problem. Whereas hardware solutions are effective but cause a decrease in the system performance, software solutions are less effective but do not decrease the performance of the system in terms of frame rate processing (see Table 1). Another drawback of the Kinect is the relatively short depth range, from 0.5 to 3 meters, which makes it unsuitable for use in an outdoor environment.

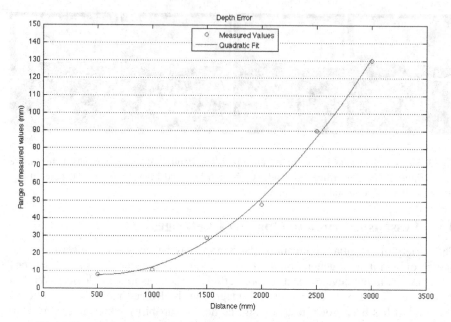

Fig. 4. The relationship between distance and depth precision of the Kinect sensor

Table 1. Reported FPS of sw and hw interference solutions

Method	# Kinects	FPS
Hole Filling & Smoothing	5	48
Time Multiplexing	2	15

Therefore, calibration, interference and bias correction seem to be the major problems to be solved in the building of reliable and accurate multiple Kinect systems. An analysis of current solutions suggests that, to design non-error calibration models and interference-free multi-Kinect systems, research needs to be carried out to further investigate the specific characteristics of structured light technology and to tailor the techniques to the application scenario considered.

References

1. Aggarwal, J.K., Cai, Q.: Human motion analysis: a review. Comput. Vis. Image Underst. 73(3), 428–440 (1999)
2. Moeslund, T.B., Granum, E.: A Survey of Computer Vision-Based Human Motion Capture. Comput. Vis. Image Underst. 18, 231–268 (2001)
3. Wang, L., Hu, W.: Recent developments in human motion analysis. Pattern Recognition 36(3), 585–601 (2003)

4. Herda, L., Urtasun, R., Fua, P.: Hierarchical Implicit Surface Joint Limits to Constrain Video-Based Motion Capture. In: Pajdla, T., Matas, J(G.) (eds.) ECCV 2004. LNCS, vol. 3022, pp. 405–418. Springer, Heidelberg (2004)
5. Cerveri, P., Pedotti, A.: Robust recovery of human motion from video using Kalman filters and virtual humans. Human Movement Science 22(3), 377–404 (2003)
6. Microsoft. Kinect for X-BOX 360 (2010), http://www.xbox.com/en-US/kinect
7. Poppe, R.: Vision-based human motion analysis: an overview. Comput. Vis. Image Underst. 108(1-2), 4–18 (2007)
8. Kehl, R., Van Gool, L.: Marker-less tracking of complex human motions from multiple views. Comput. Vis. Image Underst. 104(2), 190–209 (2006)
9. Ji, X., Liu, H.: Advances in view-invariant human motion analysis: a review. Trans. Sys. Man Cyber Part C 40(1), 13–24 (2010)
10. Moeslund, T.B., Hilton, A., Kruger, V.: A survey of advances in vision-based human motion capture and analysis. Comput. Vis. Image Underst. 104(2), 90–126 (2006)
11. Wang, L., Hu, W., Tan, T.: Recent developments in human motion analysis. Pattern Recognition 36(3), 585–601 (2003)
12. Smisek, J., Jancosek, M.: 3D with Kinect. In: 2011 IEEE International Conference on Computer Vision Workshops, pp. 1154–1160. IEEE Press, New York (2011)
13. Hartmann, J., Forouher, D., Litza, M., Klüssendorff, J.H., Maehle, E.: Real-time visual SLAM using FastSLAM and the Microsoft Kinect Camera. ROBOTIK (2012)
14. Clark, R.A., Bryant, A.L.: Validity of the Microsoft Kinect for assessment of postural control. Gait & Posture (2012)
15. Gallo, L., Placitelli, A.P., Ciampi, M.: Controller-free exploration of medical image data: experiencing the Kinect. In: 24th IEEE CBMS, pp. 1–6. IEEE, Los Alamitos (2011)
16. Berger, K., Ruhl, K.: Markless capture using multiple color-depth sensors. In: 2011 Workshop on Vision, Modeling, and Visualization, pp. 317–324. Eurographics Association (2011)
17. Maimone, A., Fuchs, H.: Enhanced personal autostereoscopic telepresence system using commodity depth camera. Computers & Graphics (2012)
18. Maimone, A., Fuchs, H.: Reducing interference between multiple structured light depth sensors using motion. In: 2012 IEEE Virtual Reality Workshops, pp. 51–54. IEEE Press, New York (2012)
19. Gallo, L., Minutolo, A.: Design and comparative evaluation of Smoothed Pointing: a velocity-oriented remote pointing enhancement technique. Int. J. of Human-Computer Studies 70(4), 287–300 (2012)
20. Burrus, N.: RGB Demo project (2011), http://labs.manctl.com/rgbdemo
21. Konolige, K., Mihelich, P.: Technical description of Kinect calibration. Tech. Rep., Willow Garage (2011),
    http://www.ros.org/wiki/kinect_calibration/technical

YOAPY: A Data Aggregation and Pre-processing Module for Enabling Continuous Healthcare Monitoring in the Internet of Things

Antonio J. Jara, David Fernández, Pablo López, Miguel A. Zamora, Leandro Marin, and Antonio F.G. Skarmeta

Clinical Technology Lab (CLITech)
Research Institute for Oriented ICT (INTICO)
Computer Sciences Faculty, University of Murcia, Murcia, Spain
Regional Campus of International Excellence "Campus Mare Nostrum"
{jara,david.f.r,p.lopezmartinez,mzamora,leandro,skarmeta}@um.es

Abstract. Wireless transmissions of continuous vital signs are gaining importance for providing rich patient-care data in ambient assisted living environments, these monitoring systems are moving towards the Internet of Things, which offers a global and end-to-end connectivity with technologies such as 6LoWPAN. This work analyzes the requirements to transmit the continuous vital sign from an electrocardiogram to a remote server. Specifically, this presents the impact from the security in the performance, in issues such as overload, latency, and power consumption i.e. patient monitoring system lifetime, for different cryptographic primitives. For that reason, a pre-processing module is also proposed, denominated YOAPY, to reach a trade-off among the requirements from the continuous vital signs data transmission, security/privacy level, and lifetime.

Keywords: Keywords-Internet of Things, e-Health, 6LoWPAN, Security, Ubiquitous Integrated Clinical Environments.

1 Introduction

E-Health was created by the Information and Communication Technologies (ICT) to reach a cost-effective and secure use of the patient-care data in order to improve the performance and quality of the health services [1]. The adoption of e-Health in AAL environments creates huge opportunities to enrich the patient-care data and allow more sophisticated care solutions, incentive management programs and treatments, but currently, some challenges still need to be resolved to build an efficient, secure and reliable platform/network.

The Future Internet of Things (IoT) [2] allows the evolution of consumer devices and communications to smart devices that offers new capabilities allowing a new dimension for the exploitation of data captured. These new devices enables new interaction methods depending on the environment in which they are to be used through

J. Bravo, R. Hervás, and M. Rodríguez (Eds.): IWAAL 2012, LNCS 7657, pp. 248–255, 2012.

three main technologies, NFC, Bluetooth Low Energy 4.0 and 6LoWPAN. Each of them are useful in different environments and uses, through them is possible identify and connect all the people, devices, and things that are surrounding us.

Extensive research on using this concept in different areas such as building automation and health care is being conducted. For example, its potential for mobile health applications has been recently reported [3]. Other example of this application's capabilities is displayed through chronic disease management and is presented in the solution for diabetes found in [4]. This presents a solution for remote monitoring of discrete data from the glucometers. However, no research studies to date present an evaluation of 6LoWPAN capabilities for secure integration of sensors for continuous vital signs monitoring. The current work is too focused on the application layer, and it has not yet been addressed or evaluated in respect to the communications impact and performance security, nor to the protocols in the different kinds of clinical sensors used in an integrated clinical environment.

Hence, this work is focused on carry out a complete communication evaluation of continuous patient monitoring through 6LoWPAN (IPv6 over Low Power Area Networks) to transmit the ECG of a patient in real time.

2   Ubiquitous Integrated Clinical Environments

This work presents how to employ the IoT capabilities to build secure protocols for personalized healthcare and therapy in the patient´s environment i.e. from hospital to the patient environment i.e. patient´s home, in order to reach what we have denominated Ubiquitous Integration of Clinical Environments. Figure 1 presents the scenario deployed under our work, that it's explained in next page.

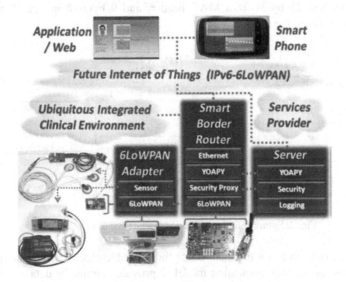

Fig. 1. Ubiquitous Integrated Clinical Environment scenario

The scenario is composed of three parts, the **Future Internet of Things network**, that offers the capability to reach global addressing and connectivity in order to identify the devices connected over IPv6; The **Ubiquitous Integrated Clinical Environment** that is the Patients' environments such as patients' homes or hospitals, where a connected set of clinical sensors, such as the presented wearable electrocardiogram (ECG). This is connected through the:

- *6LoWPAN adaptor*: Clinical sensors are connected to the network through 6LoWPAN technology. For this purpose, an adaptor has been developed to translate from native protocol to 6LoWPAN. It is carried out with the *YOAPY* module, which is described in the Section V.
- *Smart Border Router*: This connects the local network based on 6LoWPAN with the Future Internet of Things Network based on IPv6.

And finally, the **Service Provider** that presents a centralized server for logging the monitored information for the Personal Health Record, Health Status Monitoring Services, Patient Alarm Proxy for detection of anomalies, and Communication Services with patients, specialists, and caregivers.

3   Communication Model

The communication model used in this work is based on UDP traffic type over IPv6 adapted following the last 6LoWPAN specification, i.e. RFC 6282. This defines an optimized header compression for global addressing based on contexts. 6LoWPAN presents with the header compression version 6, which is the available in the Contiki OS 2.5, a payload of 92 bytes, which is the result of 127 bytes from IEEE 802.15.4 MAC frame, less 25 bytes from MAC header, and 9 bytes from the IP and UDP compressed headers, see Fig. 2.

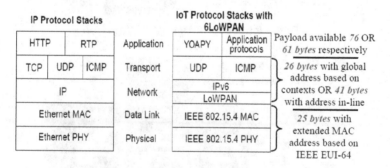

Fig. 2. Future Internet of Things stack (IPv6 & 6LoWPAN)

This work is focused on the analysis of the wearable electrocardiogram (since its requirements for the communication model to provide continuous data and the capabilities to process and protect the collected data are the largest) with the EG 01000 module from Medlab, which provides one channel data. This has a native protocol with a monitoring speed equal to 300 samples/sec, a high resolution mode (1mv signal are 150 steps), what offers a total of χ bytes for the ECG trace of a pulse.

The sample frequency (ω) is set to 300 Hz. Therefore, considering an ECG trace with a beat rate (β) of 76 BPM. This requires χ to equal to 236 bytes/sample, following eq. 1.

$$60* \omega/ \beta = \chi \tag{1}$$

4   Security Issues and Performance Metrics

The nature of the presented solution requires the guarantee of security, patients' privacy, integrity and patient confidentiality. Two levels of security has been considered in this work to satisfy the metioned requirements, on one hand, **AES-CCM-128 Link Layer Security** based on Symmetric Key Cryptography (SKC). It is natively supported by the 6LoWPAN microprocessor and offer MAC code such as encryption for privacy and authentication. SKC is suitable to offer local solutions, but since the security needs to support end-to-end communication, a second security level considers Public Key Cryptography (PKC). Specifically, our 6LoWPAN adapter offers a suitable security stack based on **Elliptic Curve Cryptography (ECC),** which has been optimized for embedded IoT devices [5]. **ECDSA** is implemented for digital signature based on ECC, which allows the authentication of the involved parties and ensures data integrity and confidentiality.

The performance metrics are focused on both the trade-off between power consumption (in wireless monitoring patient systems, one of the imposed requirements in order to reach a proper usability is to reach a suitable lifetime), and security/privacy level and with the evaluation of latency (in certain contexts such as health, the additional latency incurred by the additional tasks derived from the operation is unacceptable) incurred by the protocols in function of security level and impact in lifetime.

5   YOAPY Module to Optimize Communications

RAW data from ECG can be transmitted directly to the monitored information, where approximately 250-300 bytes are transmitted for each sample (this means more of an IEEE 802.15.4 frame for a single sample). For that reason, it's proposed a *YOAPY* compression module in order to reduce the size and to be able to transfer more than a sample by packet. YOAPY carries out a simple pre-processed to reach a representation of the waveform based in the amplitude and times of each one of the significant points from the curve [7], i.e. P, Q, R, S and T points, since it is really the relevant information, thereby the majority of the values such as the closer to the baseline can be removed. Fig 3 presents the significant points from the curves, which are transmitted when it is considered the use of compression.

The format presented in Table 1 consumes 10 bytes/sample to represent the wave, which means that 5 samples are transmitted in a frame. In addition, this pre-process makes the development of health status monitoring solutions easier, such as the Knowledge Based System presented in [7].

Table 1. Format for pre-processed samples (in red examples)

0	1	2	3	4	5	6	7
BPM	P	Q	R	S	T	S_TP	S_PQ
68	132	121	185	122	144	151	9
0x44	0x84	0x79	0xB9	0x80	0x90	0x97	0x09
S_Q S	S_ST	S_RS	Other samples … (until a total of 5 samples, it is a fix number to avoid counters)				
32	3	71					
0x20	0x03	0x47					

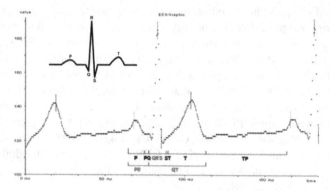

Fig. 3. Representation of the pre-processed trace. Top corner is the reference. Points are P:green, Q:yellow, R:pink, S:blue, and T:dark blue.

6   Evaluation

Performance evaluation of YOAPY scheme (Section V) with respect to the native communication model (Section III) it is composed of an evaluation of power consumption with an oscilloscope in conjunction with a mathematical modeling to calculate the device lifetime, and a practical implementation for the evaluation of the latency and overhead introduced by the security level.

6.1   Power Consumption

The power consumption of the 6LoWPAN module is measured for the different operations. In normal conditions, the 6LoWPAN module enters sleep mode for the sake of power saving, and the power consumption from the board is 0,72mA from a mere 0.06uA from the transceiver. When the sensor module wakes up, due to an abnormal event or periodical tasks, the 6LoWPAN module enters a CPU doze mode, where consumption varies between 41mA and 48mA. UARTs are used for this mode, one for debugging and one for the clinical sensor. Finally, receiving and transmitting 6LoWPAN packets varies between 44m and 56mA. Power consumption is summarized in Table 2. Power consumption to transmit a 6LoWPAN packet is presented in the Fig. 4, where this spends 34,2ms. It could be considered that for a frame of the maximum length i.e. 127bytes should spend a total time of 4,064ms (250kbps bandwidth).

Table 2. Power/Radio characteristics in module JN5139

Power/Radio Mode	Datasheet (D) and Application Note (AN) references [5]	Empirical value from oscilloscope
Deep sleep current	1.6uA from D and 0.06uA from AN	0,72mA for any sleep mode, it is the lowest consumption.
Sleep current with wake up (I/O and Timer)	2.8uA from D and 3,5uA from AN	
Active Processing, i.e. CPU Mode	2.85 + 0.285 per MHz, i.e. 7,41mA for 16Mhz CPU	41mA to 48mA, we are considering the maximum value equal to 48mA
Active CPU and transceiver idle (CPU doze)	27,3mA from AN	
Radio transmit current	37mA from D and 38mA from AN	44mA to 56mA, we are considering the maximum value equal to 56mA
Radio receive current	37mA from D and AN	
UART (Sensor connection)	Additional current of 0.095mA for each o3wne from AN	

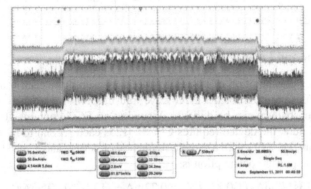

Fig. 4. Power analysis for the transmission of a 6LoWPAN packet carried out with the Tektronix DPO 7104C and a shunt resistance of a low value (10 Ω ± 0.5%). It is presented V: yellow, I:blue, and Power: orange.

However, this consumes 30ms more because the time required to turn on the transceiver and the application of CSMA/CA algorithm to access the radio medium, i.e. Clear Channel Assessment (CCA), is performed to determine if the channel is currently in use. CCA takes 8 symbol periods (0.128 ms) to complete a assessment. Once the channel is assessed to be free, this sends the packet. After, it waits around 1.3ms, and then it switches again to the radio transceiver to receive the corresponding acknowledgement (ACK message). In conclusion, the relation between total transfer time and payload time is highly unbalanced (4ms/34ms). Therefore, our goal is to reduce the number of total frames.

6.2   Overload and Payload Size

The overload is reduced by YOAPY where an ECG trace of 257 bytes is reduced to 10 bytes (see Table I). Therefore, considering the available payload of 76bytes (see Fig. 2); 6 frames are required per sample in the original format. The new format allows the inclusion of 5 samples in a single frame. Specifically, as presented in Section IV, it is considered to have two security levels. These levels are ECDSA, which requires a field of 16bytes for the digital signature, and AES-CCM-128 Link Layer Security, which requires 21bytes. They offer integrity and confidentiality, and an additional timestamp is considered to ensure freshness. Overload is summarized in Table 3.

Table 3. Overload evaluation by security levels & YOAPY

Security Level	Security Overload + Timestamp	Available Payload	#frames with RAW data	#samples in a frame with YOAPY less 1 packet per sample
AES-CCM 128bits Layer Security	23bytes + 2bytes = 25bytes	76bytes – 25bytes = 51bytes	257/51 ≈ 6 packets for a sample	(51-1)/10 ≈ 5 samples in one packet
ECDSA 160bits based on ECC	16bytes + 2bytes = 18bytes	76bytes -18bytes = 58bytes	257/58 ≈ 5 packets for a sample	(58-1)/10 ≈ 5 samples in one packet

6.3   Lifetime and Latency from Security

Once the power consumption of a sensor node is measured for each frame, then the number of frames required for the ECG wave transmission is estimated, and the lifetime for a given battery can be derived. Assuming an ECG contains 70bpm, i.e. 70 samples per minute, the device requires CPU 0,3125s each second to receive the data from the sensors, i.e. ECG with a sample frequency of 300Hz and a speed of 9600bps. Hence, the basic power consumption is:

$$0,313s*48mA+(1-0,313s- \zeta s)*0,72mA = (15,5-0,72\zeta)*mAs \qquad (2)$$

This also requires the consumption during the time ζ, which is the required to encrypt and transmit the packet. The encryption time depends on the security level.

The time it takes AES-CCM-128 to encode 51bytes from payload (64bytes, since 16bytes multiple is required) is 61ms. This is not suitable for the RAW data, since it only can transfer 16 frames per minute and 420 frames are required. But, it is suitable with the 14 frames per minute required after YOAPY module pre-processing. The time for the digital signature with the optimized ECC stack, based on shifting primes [8], is 765ms. This latency makes ECDSA unsuitable for the continuous monitoring, but it can be used to establish the end-to-end communication (i.e. set up / bootstrapping), and transfer packets for events.

$$14*(0,034s*56mA+0,061s*48mA)=67,8mAM = 1,13mAs$$
$$\zeta=1,3328s \text{ for each minute} = 0,022s \text{ for each second} \qquad (3)$$
$$\text{Total consumption} = 15,5-0,72*0,022+1,13*0,022=15,51mAs$$

The battery capacity is measured in milliamps hours (mAH). This device has 2 x AAA batteries with 800mAH drive to continuously transmit packets for more than 100 hours (AES-CCM-128 security and YOAPY pre-processing).

$$\text{Lifetime}=2*800*3600/15,51=371373s=4\text{days } 7\text{hours } 10\text{min} \tag{4}$$

7   Conclusions and Future Work

This work presents an evaluation of the impact of the security for the continuous vital sign transmission. It has been concluded that PKC is only suitable for discrete events, and SKC is suitable for continuous monitoring, only when it data compression is carried out with the proposed YOAPY module. Lifetime with the proposed optimizations is over 4 days. Ongoing work is focused on reaching a higher compression, extending YOAPY to other sensors such as patient monitors with oxygen saturation, and finally reducing the time required by the ECDSA algorithm.

Acknowledgments. This work has been made possible by the means of the Excellence Researching Group Program (04552/GERM/06) from Foundation Seneca, FPU program (AP2009-3981) from Education and Science Spanish Ministry, and finally in the framework of the IoT6 European Project (STREP) from the 7th Framework Program (Grant 288445).

References

1. Rengarajan, R., Croslin, D., Barroso, C.: R&D Best Practices for Medical Device Innovation: A Cross Industry Perspective (2011)
2. Atzori, L., Iera, A., Morabito, G.: The Internet of Things: A survey. Computer Networks 54(15), 2787–2805 (2010)
3. Istepanian, R.S.H., Jara, A., Sungoor, A., Philips, N.: Internet of Things for M-health Applications (IoMT). In: AMA IEEE Medical Tech. Conference on Individualized Healthcare, Washington (2010)
4. Jara, A.J., Zamora, M.A., Skarmeta, A.: An internet of things–based personal device for diabetes therapy management in AAL. Personal and Ubiquitous Computing 15(4), 431–440 (2011)
5. Marin, L., Jara, A.J., Skarmeta, A.F.G.: Shifting Primes: Extension of Pseudo-Mersenne Primes to Optimize ECC for MSP430-Based Future Internet of Things Devices. In: Tjoa, A.M., Quirchmayr, G., You, I., Xu, L. (eds.) ARES 2011. LNCS, vol. 6908, pp. 205–219. Springer, Heidelberg (2011)
6. Istepanian, R.S.H., Petrosian, A.A.: Optimal zonal waveletbased ECG data compression for a mobile telecardiology system. IEEE Trans. Infor. Tech. in Biomedicine 4(3), 200–211 (2000)
7. Jara, A.J., Blaya, F.J., Zamora, M.A., Skarmeta, A.: An ontology and rule based intelligent information system to detect and predict myocardial diseases. Inf. Tech. App. in Biomedicine (2009)
8. Jennic, "Application Note: JN-AN-1001 - Calculating JN5139-JN5148 Power Consumption" and "Data Sheet: JN5139-001" (2010)

Multiprotocol Android Application for Smart Control and Monitoring in Buildings

Jesús Ángel Heras, Guillermo del Campo, César Gómez, Iris Galloso,
and Carmen Lastres

Universidad Politécnica de Madrid (UPM) - CeDInt
Madrid, Spain
{jheras,gcampo,cgotero,iris,clastres}@cedint.upm.es

Abstract. This paper presents a multiprotocol mobile application for building automation which supports and enables the integration of the most representative control technologies such as KNX, LonWorks and X-10. The application includes a real-time monitoring service. Finally, advanced control functionalities based on gestures recognition and predefined scenes have been implemented. This application has been developed and tested in the Energy Efficiency Research Facility located at CeDInt-UPM, where electrical loads, blinds and HVAC and lighting systems can be controlled.

Keywords: Building Automation, Android, Multiprotocol, Monitoring Service.

1   Introduction

Traditional building management systems (BMSs) have evolved quickly in the last years. Currently, both proprietary systems and non-proprietary ones are available in the market. As a consequence, many different control technologies and device manufacturers co-exist. The main disadvantage of commercial BMSs is that they do not allow the intercommunication between subsystems using different technologies.

Most developments on similar mobile applications for home automation work only with a specific technology such as X-10 [1] or KNX [2]. Advanced services are currently being integrated in some of these applications. For instance, interfaces based on 3D virtual world [3] or security such as video-surveillance to avoid burglary [1] or to prevent from failures of the systems causing destruction [4].

As a solution to this issue, this paper introduces the development of a user - friendly and configurable mobile application that integrates the control of different systems, regardless of the technology they use. A mobile application is proposed, in order to provide more dynamism to control. Although the application has been implemented for Android devices, it could also be easily ported to other mobile platforms. This application has been developed and tested in the Energy Efficiency Research Facility (EERF) located at CeDInt-UPM, where electrical loads, blinds and HVAC (Heating, Ventilation and Air Conditioning) and lighting systems can be controlled [5]. The application also includes a monitoring service, a set of predefined scenes and advanced control functionalities such as the gestures recognition.

J. Bravo, R. Hervás, and M. Rodríguez (Eds.): IWAAL 2012, LNCS 7657, pp. 256–260, 2012.

2   System Architecture

The architecture proposed for the control and monitoring application is based on a client-server structure. The client program is installed on the mobile device. It sends the control requests from the user to a Java server program that runs on a remote computer. Figure 1 illustrates the structure of the Java server program.

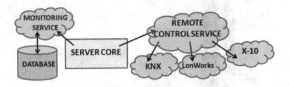

Fig. 1. Server structure

The structure of the Java server program is divided into two different parts: one related to the communication with the technologies installed in the EERF (KNX [6], LonWorks [7] and X-10 [8]) and the other one linked with the monitoring service.

Each controllable device or system can be operated using several technologies (KNX, DALI, LonWorks or BACnet), only one at a given moment. The Calimero-KNXnet/IP library [9] allows the platform to communicate directly with KNX devices, with no need of a KNX-IP gateway. LonWorks technology uses an ilon-350 router with a web server which provides the control and monitoring functions. The X-10 technology requires an USB interface to connect the server computer to the home power grid. Finally, regarding the monitoring service, an external MySQL database stores all the parameters received from the sensors of the different technologies.

3   Client Application

The graphical interface of the application has been developed using Android graphic libraries. The functionalities of the client application are described below:

3.1   Remote Control Service

The mobile application allows the control of different systems installed in the EERF, such as HVAC, lighting, blinds and electrical loads, using different control technologies and enabling the commutation between them:

HVAC system. It is controlled using KNX. The application recommends the user a range of convenient temperatures for summer and winter, according to IDAE (Institute for Energy Diversification and Saving) recommendations [10].

Lighting system. The lighting system supports KNX and LonWorks technologies. It is possible to regulate separately different areas of the EERF.

Blinds system. Blinds can be opened, closed and regulated to a specific aperture percentage using KNX or LonWorks. Figure 2a shows a screenshot of the application that allows the user to control blinds individually.

Electrical appliances. On/off control over electrical loads is considered using KNX, LonWorks and X-10 technologies.

Fig. 2. Blinds control screen (a). Photovoltaic generation monitoring screen (b).

3.2   Monitoring Service

A building monitoring service has been implemented in order to show users interesting parameters such as comfort parameters (temperature and brightness level), presence, windows contact state, photovoltaic generation (generated power, irradiance and cell temperature) (Fig. 2b) and meteorological parameters (outside temperature, wind speed, precipitation, etc.). These parameters are received from wireless and wired sensors of different technologies and a KNX meteorological station.

3.3   Predefined Scenes

There are some situations frequently repeated in the EERF. Thus a set of scenes have been defined, each of them corresponding to a specific scenario. The scenes implemented are:

Working scene. The purpose of this scene is to create a pleasant atmosphere in the working area with an optimum level of brightness and temperature, according to national legislation [11], avoiding sun glares.

Guided tour scene. The purpose of this scene is the automation of a set of actions when the EERF is used as a showroom for guided visits. It entails the creation of an appropriate atmosphere around the projection screen area, where the demonstrators and infrastructures are explained to visitors.

Empty room scene. The aim of this scene is to switch off every system and devices in the EERF, when the user leaves the room.

Programming by demonstration (PbD). PbD is an end-user development technique that simplifies programming process by providing examples of the intended interactions between the user and the application, rather than using a textual notation [12]. In this case, PBD is used to define a personalized scene according to user preferences.

3.4   Gesture Recognition

The Android application can recognize some gestures performed by the user in order to carry out some home automation actions, according to the gesture in question. This is possible thanks to the integration of a Java library developed at CeDInt-UPM that allows sampling the movements and turns detected by the accelerometer of the smartphone. The library implements a gesture recognition algorithm based on Temporal Fuzzy Automata [13].

In addition, the management of user profiles is also available. Two types of users are identified in the application: basic and advanced. The only difference between them is that only advanced users are allowed to commute control technologies.

4   Conclusions

The multiprotocol mobile application for building automation presented in this paper supports and allows the integration of the most representative control technologies (KNX, LonWorks and X-10), which makes it suitable for multiple environments.

The application allows the management of different subsystems within a building such as HVAC, lighting, blinds or electrical appliances and enables the centralized control of all the infrastructures. Furthermore, the application proposed offers advanced control possibilities making use of specific components of smartphones, like the accelerometers. This application has been developed and tested in the Energy Efficiency Research Facility located at CeDInt-UPM, where electrical loads, blinds and HVAC and lighting systems can be controlled.

The interface of the application presents a user-oriented design, characterized as intuitive, flexible and easy to use. The application was tested by 40 users and results were quite satisfactory. The simplicity and the range of functionalities were especially well-evaluated by the users.

References

1. Das, S., Chita, S., Peterson, N., Shirazi, B., Bhadkamkar, M.: Home Automation and Security for Mobile Devices. In: IEEE International Conference on Pervasive Computing and Communications Workshops, Seattle, WA (2011)
2. Bittins, B., Sieck, J., Herzog, M.: Supervision and Regulation of Home Automation Systems with Smartphones. In: Fourth UKSim European Symposium on Computer Modeling and Simulation, Pisa (2010)
3. Han, J., Yun, J., Jang, J., Park, K.-R.: User-Friendly Home Automation based on 3D Virtual World. IEEE Transactions on Consumer Electronics 56, 1843–1847 (2010)
4. Mandurano, J., Haber, N.: House Away: a Home Management System. In: IEEE Long Island Conference on Systems, Applications and Technology Conference, Farmingdale, NY (2012)
5. Martínez, R., Gómez, C., Cuevas, A., Montoya, E., Galloso, I., Lastres, C., Feijoo, C., Santamaría, A.: Building Automation and Control Multi-technology System (2010)
6. KNX, http://www.knx.org
7. LonWorks (Echelon), http://www.echelon.com

8. European Distributor of Home Automation X10 Devices, http://www.eurox10.com
9. Malinowsky, B., Neugschwandtner, G., Kastner, W.: Calimero: Next Generation. Automation Systems Group. Institute of Automation, Vienna University of Technology (2007)
10. Instituto para la Diversificación y Ahorro de la Energía (IDEA),
    http://www.idae.es
11. Boletín Oficial del Estado, RD 1826/2009,
    http://www.boe.es/boe/dias/2009/12/11/pdfs/
    BOE-A-2009-19915.pdf
12. McDaniel, R.G., Myers, B.A.: Getting More out of Programming-By-Demonstration (1999)
13. Bailador, G., Triviño, G.: Pattern Recognition using Temporal Fuzzy Automata. Fuzzy Sets and Systems 161, 37–55 (2010)

I *Feel* You: Towards Affect-Sensitive Domotic Spoken Conversational Agents

Syaheerah Lebai Lutfi[1,*], Fernando Fernández-Martínez[2],
Andrés Casanova-García[1], Verónica López-Ludeña[1],
and Juan Manuel Montero[1]

[1] Speech Technology Group, Universidad Politécnica de Madrid, Madrid, Spain
[2] Departamento de Teoría de la Señal y Comunicaciones
Universidad Carlos III de Madrid
Avda. de la Universidad, 30, Leganés, Madrid, 28911, Spain
{syaheerah,ffm,acasanova,veronicalopez,juancho}@die.upm.es,
fernando.fernandez.martinez@uc3m.es
http://www-gth.die.upm.es/

Abstract. We describe the work on infusion of emotion into limited-task autonomous *spoken conversational agents* (SCAs) situated in the domestic environment, using a Need-inspired task-independent **Emo**tion model (NEMO). In order to demonstrate the generation of affect through the use of the model, we describe the work of integrating it with a natural-language mixed-initiative HiFi-control SCA. NEMO and the host system communicates externally, removing the need for the Dialog Manager to be modified as done in most existing dialog systems, in order to be adaptive. We also summarize the work on automatic affect prediction, namely frustration and contentment from dialog features, a non-conventional source, in the attempt of moving towards a more user-centric approach.

Keywords: Spoken Conversational Agents, affect prediction, domotic applications, Affective HiFi SCA, frustration, contentment, conversational features, satisfaction judgment.

1 Introduction

Emotion is quintessential for intelligence, to the point that psychologists and educators have re-defined intelligence to include emotion and social skill. With the mass appeal of computer-mediated agents, computers are no longer viewed as machines whose main purpose is to complete tasks, rather they are required to have the social abilities that humans naturally demonstrate in their daily interactions.

* The work leading to these results has been supported by INAPRA (MICINN, DPI2010-21247-C02-02), TIMPANO (TIN2011-28169-C05-03) and ITALIHA (CAM-UPM) projects. Authors also thank all the other members of the Speech Technology Group for the continuous and fruitful discussion on these topics. The first author thanks University Science of Malaysia and the Malaysian Ministry of Higher Education for the PhD funding. Authors also thank all the other members of the Speech Technology Group for the continuous and fruitful discussion on these topics.

J. Bravo, R. Hervás, and M. Rodríguez (Eds.): IWAAL 2012, LNCS 7657, pp. 261–269, 2012.
© Springer-Verlag Berlin Heidelberg 2012

Thus the developments of conversational agents typically move towards including socio-emotion content, which upgrades them to being socially intelligent.

This paper concerns the incorporation of a recently developed task-independent emotional model into a voice-only social domotic agent. Using this model, the generation of emotion is driven by *needs*, inspired by human's motivational system, hence called NEMO (Need-inspired EMOtion Model). The intention is to incorporate NEMO into existing SCAs in order to enable them to be affect-sensitive. This is accomplished by predicting user affective states and responding to them with appropriate affective responses, through an emotional text-to-speech system. The focus of the paper is not on NEMO in itself (which has been described elsewhere [13]), but how this model will be used in non-adaptive applications, in order to make them more adaptive to the users' emotion. Though NEMO is a generic and task-independent architecture, actual events and situations are required in a specific domain in order to run this model. Therefore to demonstrate affect sensing and generation through the use of this model, we describe the work of integrating this model with a natural-language mixed-initiative High-Fidelity-control spoken dialog (henceforth 'HiFi-NEMO') towards the goal of a socially intelligent HiFi agent. Specifically, this part is described in the first part of the paper. The second part focuses on building a real-time automatic detection of affect, as robust automatic detection is vital to any affect-sensitive system.

2   Infusing Emotions into the HiFi Agent

We attempt to infuse emotions into an existing HiFi agent using NEMO. The baseline (non-adaptive version) HiFi system is a proprietary system developed by Grupo Technología del Habla (GTH), (see details in [8]). As mentioned earlier, NEMO is a need-inspired system, whereby the agent elicits an emotion that is coherent with the situation *in view* of its different needs. One of the most influential needs for the agent's emotion modification, is the Success need. Therefore, this section focuses on the Success need. The Success level is influenced by various events that are related to different tasks. Previously this was done by updating a predefined percentage of an individual event (values differ according to events). For example, in the previous prototype of NEMO that was put to test with a domotic robot, Groucho, whose main tasks are to manage various domestic appliances (see [13,14][1]), an event detected by sensory inputs such as user touching or caressing the agent's face might have a fixed value of 0.5, indicating a medium success level or winning a game might have a fixed value of 0.7, a high success level. In integrating NEMO with the HiFi spoken conversational agent though (henceforth 'HiFi-NEMO'), we moved a step ahead by adopting a more user centric approach, using machine learning to *automatically predict* the said values by learning from past evaluation's data using a trained classifier, described later in Section 3. An interaction event is predicted as good or bad (and also of *how* good or bad) and the corresponding values will then be taken to compute the Success need.

---

[1] A couple of demos showing applications of different domains used to test this model can be acessed here:http://www.syaheerah.com/?page_id=789

2.1   Architecture of HiFi-NEMO

Most spoken dialog systems have an architecture that is similar to the HiFi SCA, as shown on the left side of Figure 1. The user utters a sentence and the Speech Recognizer captures the sounds from the user's speech, matches the recognized words against a given set of vocabulary. Then the matched words are passed to the Language Understanding module to extract the concepts (semantic information) of the sentence. A series of concepts are then passed to the Dialog Manager to activate dialog goals. The Dialog Manager decides both the actions to be taken and the feedback to the user for the current dialog turn, and passes the semantic information to the Natural Response Generator module to generate a suitable textual response to the user. The text-to-speech (TTS) module then synthesizes the message and speaks to the user. The original non-adaptive HiFi SCA version used a non-emotional commercial TTS. A detailed architecture of the non-adaptive system is given in [8]. In converting the HiFi SCA into

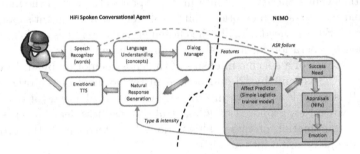

Fig. 1. The architecture of HiFi-NEMO

an affect-adaptive system, its existing components were *not* modified. Instead the HiFi SCA communicates *externally* with NEMO. The interaction between the system's modules and NEMO is shown in Figure 1. The information flow is similar as described previously, but this time, the Dialog Manager additionally passes certain dialog features that are significant predictors of the user emotional state to the Affect Predictor. The Affect Predictor classifies the emotion state of the user following a Simple Logistics trained model. The classification result is then passed on to the need module to update the agent's Success need. Consider a user having a few bad dialog turns – perhaps the HiFi SCA failed to completely understand the user request and repeatedly asks the user to provide new information and extends the otherwise short dialog. In this case, the Dialog Manager sends certain relevant features (request turns, contextual information etc.) to the Affect Predictor. Based on these features, the Affect Predictor predicts that the user is frustrated. This information is then updated to the need module, which modifies the agent's Success need. The agent now perceives the user as being frustrated and therefore its Success need is low. The dynamicity of the need level also depends on the situations of the previous turns; consecutive or continuous prediction that the user is frustrated causes the agent's Success need satisfaction to decrease rapidly, and so when a good event (turn) appears right after, (and the user is now predicted to be in a positive emotion), the agent will not immediately change its state to a joyful one, but rather surprised or neutral, depending on the situation. Conversely, if the agent is in a joyful state for sometime, and continues with turns that are perceived as good (user predicted to be satisfied in consecutive turns), the drive to gratify its Success need will not be as significant as in the other case, and so its joyful state reaches its maximum and starts decaying into a a neutral state, though it continues to perceive the ongoing events as positive ones.

It should be noted however that the Dialog Manager receives dialog features only when the Speech Recognizer is successful in *detecting* the user's words. When a speech recognition failure occurs, the failure event updates the agent's Success need directly, bypassing the Dialog Manager (as indicated by the dotted arrow in Figure 1). A failure message is passed to the need module which decreases the agent's Success satisfaction level.

Next, the agent's Success need information updates the rest of the modules in NEMO and to generate an emotion that is coherent with the agent's assessment of its current Success need. Finally the chosen emotion matches against the natural response generation for a suitable response content and is synthesized into a speech response of a specific intensity of the chosen emotion by an Emotional TTS. This TTS is built by [2] and is used in replacement of the original neutral one. It is capable of generating speech in various colourings of the Big Six emotional categories, proposed by [6]:neutral, joy, sadness, fear, anger, surprise and also a combination of these. This is done by interpolating the prosodical variation of one emotion into another.

3   Automatic Detection of Affect

Real time automatic detection of emotion is vital to any affect-sensitive system. In this section we describe the method used to automatically predict the agent's Success need value of HiFi-NEMO, that will subsequently update the cognitive appraisals' module in order to generate a suitable affective response. As mentioned previously, in HiFi-NEMO's context, the success rate of an interaction modulates the agent's need, particularly its Success need. An interaction is deemed successful when the *user* is content with the agent's performance. Thus a fundamental challenge in converting a non-affective HiFi agent (or *any* systems in general) into an affective one is robust automatic detection of user affect. A highly satisfied user also satisfies the agent's success need, hence user-agent satisfactions have a positive linear relationship. User affect can be reflected in the user *satisfaction* judgment [1,5,12] and the relationship of affect and satisfaction judgment have been empirically proven in [10,11] and also in our work, which will be further described. To model user affect, we used *satisfaction rating* as the target and *conversational features* as predictors, obtained from a corpus collected in a past evaluation [7]. What makes our approach different from others is that we used target and predictor variables whose potentials are often ignored to model affect. While many studies focus on numerous channels for affect detection, very few have explored dialog as a potential source [4]. User affect could be mined from conversational elements, which are always cheaper and are usually obtained with little or no computational overhead. However, since the focus of this paper lies on modeling affect in the HiFi agent, we limit this section into summarizing the method and the outcome of the experiments carried out in automatic affect detection using the data from two studies that will be described shortly.

We also focus on discriminating affect between two classes: *contentment* and *frustration*, two types of emotions that are known to be prevalent within spoken HCI. These two categories of affect represent positive and negative user emotional state and their varying intensities (e.g., at the end of an interaction, a particular user might have felt intensely contented with the system when the user gave a score of 5 or 'excellent' (in a 5-point scale), and rather frustrated when he or she gave a score of 3)[2]

3.1   User and Annotator Studies

To model affect by predicting user satisfaction, we used the HiFi-AV2 corpus [9], collected during a *user* study. HiFi-AV2 consists of audiovisually recorded information of real, non-acted interactions (N=190 interaction sessions) between user and non-adaptive version of the HiFi agent. In this study, users interacted with the HiFi agent hands on and at the end of each interaction, they rated the HiFi agent by providing a score between 1-5 Likert point (1 being very poor to 5, very good). Later, we used a reduced version of the same corpus to obtain satisfaction and affect-labelled data from several independent *annotators*. The corpus was reduced to 10 speakers that were chosen randomly (N=100 sesions) to downsize manual labelling efforts. This study was similar to the first one, except that the annotators *also* perceived user emotion in each interaction - the annotators were given a set of full recordings (from the start until the end of an interaction) and they were free to label as many defined emotions (the nuances within the six basic emotions proposed by [6]) detected throughout the whole interaction. It is important to note that the annotators were asked to rate the agent based on the perspective of the *user*, and were naïve on real-users ratings - in other words the annotators put themselves in the users' shoes and rated the system as how the users should have rated the system. Thus we could view both datasets as that of users' actual ratings and targeted ratings (by annotator). Additionally we also now have *affect-labelled* data by annotators.

3.2   Affect Classification from Conversational Features

In order to obtain a model of user affect, we conducted two experiments; Experiment I was evaluated on the satisfaction-labelled data from both user and

---

[2] Depending on the model that was chosen - different models have different groupings of scores, elaborated later in Section 3.3. A score of 3, for example, may either represent a low-intensity frustration (category Three version 2) or slight contentment (category Three version 1).

annotator subject group. Experiment II involved the emotion-labelled data by annotators. In both types of experiments, we applied standard classification techniques in which several classifier schemes were utilized with the intention of comparing the performance of the various classification techniques, apart from determining which technique(s) yield the best performance. The Waikato Environment and Knowledge Analysis (WEKA) [15] was used for these purposes. One or more classification algorithms were chosen from different categories including rule-based classifiers (ZeroR as baserate and OneR), functions (SimpleLogistic, SMO), meta classification schemes (Multischeme, MultiBoost, AdaBoost) and trees (J48). A 10-fold cross validation technique was used for all the classification tasks.

3.3   Data Redistribution

All satisfaction-labelled datasets were first resampled in order to obtain a more uniformed distribution; samples with similar outcomes were grouped together, and this was repeated five times to satisfy all combinations of classification problems as shown in Table 1. This way we were also able to determine which clusters obtained optimized classifications.

4   Summary of Results and Discussions

4.1   Experiment I (Model 1)

Table 2 presents the statistically significant improvements of classification results over baserate in percentage accuracy for Experiment I. Results revealed that there was a significant effect of the subject type: $F(1,40)=83.07$, p<.001, partial $\eta^2=.68$. Classifiers evaluated on user data mostly revealed worse results than baserate with exception to SMO, whilst at least three classifiers that were evaluated on an-

Table 1. Datasets re-clustered according to similarity of score points into all possible combinations of classes

Category	Label				
	very poor	poor	satisfactory	good	excellent
Five (original class)	1	2	3	4	5
Four	-	1,2	3	4	5
Three (version 1)	-	1,2	3	4,5	-
Three (version 2)	-	1,2,3	-	4	5
Two (version 1)	-	1,2,3	-	4,5	-
Two (version 2)	-	1,2	-	3,4,5	-

notator data show significant improvement (at p<.001) over baserate in each category, with exception to category 3V2 and 2V2. This indicates that most classifers were able to predict satisfaction from dialog features based on the *annotator* data, suggesting that annotators were more impartial when judging the HiFi agent. Classification evaluated on annotator data however yielded interesting result and is more suitable to be used for user affect modeling. Thus we now focus on the results from annotator data. The chart in Figure 2 illustrates the interactions between the factors that obtained the best classification improvements for *annotator* dataset, that are statistically significant.

4.2   Experiment II (Model 2)

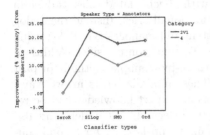

Fig. 2. Summarized interaction chart for annotators dataset

Experiment II involved classification evaluated on the emotion-labelled data based on inter-annotator agreement. The computation that derive such agreement was adopted from [3]. Results revealed that the SMO scheme yielded the best statistically significant (at p<.01) improvement of classification over baserate, with improvement of 13.2%, followed by the Ordinal and Simple Logistics schemes, with 9.8% and 9.2% improvements respectively, both statistically significant at p<.05.

Both satisfaction and emotion-agreement data are significantly correlated (Pearson r=.29, at p<.01) but provide complementary information to model user affect. The data used for Model 1 involved users providing a satisfaction score at the end of each interaction; a global average score that represented the user's opinion of the agent - that could also be considered as the best representation of score for each turn, should we have to rate the system on a turn basis. Thus this information is suitable to be used to predict user affect on a *turn* basis. On the other hand, Model 2 involved annotators perceiving user emotion at different locations of a particular interaction, when the emotions displayed were most obvious. However the information on the exact locations within the interaction was not noted. Hence this kind of prediction is suitable to be performed at the end of the whole interaction, in order for the agent to be alerted that the user has been frustrated at some point during the interaction.

Table 2. Comparisons of significant improvements in classification accuracies in detecting satisfaction score from conversational features (for both *user* and *annotator* datasets)

Category	Base rate		SiLog		SMO		Ord	
	U	A	U	A	U	A	U	A
Five	38.0	36.0	-	49.3	-	44.6	-	51.3
Four	38.0	36.0	-	53.1	-	43.4	-	52.0
Three (version 1)	71.0	47.0	-	64.0	-	61.1	-	62.5
Three (version 2)	38.0	53.0	-	-	50.7	-	-	-
Two (version 1)	71.0	53.0	-	75.0	-	74.4		69.4
Two (version 2)	93.0	83.0	-	-	-	-	-	-

SiLog=Functions.SimpleLogistics,
SMO=Functions.SMO,Ord=Meta.Ordinal.
U=User data, A=Annotator data.
Results were truncated to display only the best statistically significant classification improvements (at p<.05)

5   Conclusions, Current and Future Directions

We propose an approach of incorporating emotions into spoken dialog systems using NEMO. We demonstrated this by describing the integration on a proprietary baseline system, a non-adaptive HiFi agent.

Our main contribution is to show that the Dialog Manager of the baseline system were neither modified nor hardwired with affect-related rules as done in most existing dialog systems, in order to be emotionally rich. Instead the dialog manager communicates with the emotion system and manages the dialog using the emotionally-relevant features provided by the emotion classifier. Additionally, the emotion classifier is based on a learning-by-example method (of past data), not an imperative, hand-crafted one. These minimize costs in two ways; first, not only the requirement for domain-specific expert knowledge can be reduced, but the adaptation is also more user centric. Second, this model could also be re-used in new but similar domains, with minimum labour.Our second contribution is to show empirically that conversational features, a non-conventional source, could be used as a single source to model user affect reliably by predicting satisfaction ratings, however within a limited-task domestic domain. The conversational features were the predictors and the satisfaction judgments were the target. For this task we used an annotation method that is less sophisticated (such as the use of untrained judges to rate both satisfaction judgments and emotions) and smaller array of features for classification tasks. Nevertheless, emotion classification improvements achieved statistically significant results over baserate.

We have implemented the emotion classifier into the emotion model, and the latter is incorporated into the HiFi agent to make it more affective. We have also developed a suitable response generation model according to the various intensities of the predicted user frustration and contentment. Future work involves a series of cross evaluations that will be conducted between users and adaptable/non-adaptable versions of the agent to compare the findings.

References

1. Bailey, J.E., Pearson, S.W.: Development of a tool for measuring and analyzing computer user satisfaction. Management Science 24, 530–545 (1983)
2. Barra-Chicote, R., Yamagishi, J., King, S., Montero, J.M., Macias-Guarasa, J.: Analysis of statistical parametric and unit selection speech synthesis systems applied to emotional speech. Speech Commun. 52(5), 394–404 (2010)
3. Callejas, Z., López-Cózar, R.: On the Use of Kappa Coefficients to Measure the Reliability of the Annotation of Non-acted Emotions. In: André, E., Dybkjær, L., Minker, W., Neumann, H., Pieraccini, R., Weber, M. (eds.) PIT 2008. LNCS (LNAI), vol. 5078, pp. 221–232. Springer, Heidelberg (2008)
4. D'Mello, S.K., Craig, S.D., Witherspoon, A., McDaniel, B., Graesser, A.: Automatic detection of learner's affect from conversational cues. User Model User-Adap. Inter. 18, 45–80 (2008)
5. Doll, W.J., Torkzadeh, G.: The measurement of end-user computing satisfaction. MIS Quarterly 12, 259–274 (1988)
6. Ekman, P., Friesen, W.: The Facial Action Coding System: A technique for the measurement of facial movement. Consulting Psychologists Press (1978)
7. Fernández-Martínez, F., Blázquez, J., Ferreiros, J., Barra-Chicote, R., Macias-Guarasa, J., Lucas-Cuesta, J.M.: Evaluation of a spoken dialog system for controlling a hifi audio system. In: Proceedings of the IEEE Workshop on Spoken Language Technology, Goa, India (2008)

8. Fernández-Martínez, F., Ferreiros, J., Lucas-Cuesta, J.M., Echeverry, J.D., San-Segundo, R., Córdoba, R.: Flexible, robust and dynamic dialogue modeling with a speech dialogue interface for controlling a hi-fi audio system. In: Proceedings of the IEEE Workshop on Database and Expert Systems Applications (DEXA 2010). Springer, Bilbao (2010)
9. Fernández-Martínez, F., Lucas-Cuesta, J.M., Chicote, R.B., Ferreiros, J., Macías-Guarasa, J.: HIFI-AV: An audio-visual corpus for spoken language human-machine dialogue research in Spanish. In: Proceedings of the Seventh Conference on International Language Resources and Evaluation (LREC 2010), European Language Resources Association (ELRA), Valletta, Malta (May 2010)
10. Gelbrich, K.: Beyond just being dissatisfied: How angry and helpless customers react to failures when using self-service technologies. Schmalenbach Business Review 61, 40–59 (2009)
11. Kernbach, S., Schutte, N.S.: The impact of service provider emotional intelligence on customer satisfaction. Journal of Services Marketing 19(7), 438–444 (2005)
12. Locke, E.A.: The nature and causes of job satisfaction. Consulting Psychologists Press, Palo Alto (1976)
13. Lutfi, S., Barra-Chicote, R., Lucas-Cuesta, J., Montero, J.: Nemo: Need-inspired emotional expressions within a task-independent framework. In: Proc.of Brain Inspired Cognitive Systems (BICS), Madrid, Spain (July 2010)
14. Sanz-Moreno, C., Lutfi, S., Barra-Chicote, R., Lucas-Cuesta, J., Montero, J.: Desarrollo de un asistente domótico emocional inteligente. In: XIX Jornadas Telecom I+D, Madrid, Spain (November 2009)
15. Witten, I.H., Frank, E.: Data Mining: Practical machine learning tools and techniques. Morgan Kaufmann, San Francisco (2005)

Evaluation of Emerging Audio Description Systems for Broadcast TV

Anna Vilaro, Aitor Rodriguez-Alsina, Pilar Orero, and Jordi Carrabina

CAIAC, Universitat Autònoma de Barcelona, Spain
{anna.vilaro,aitor.rodriguez,pilar.orero,
jordi.carrabina}@uab.cat

Abstract. Following EU directives on Media Access and Ambient Assisted Living, the broadcasting industry needs to introduce new services in order to guarantee access to all citizens. The article and its conclusions are part of the EU project DTV4ALL, which focuses on some possible broadcasting scenarios for achieving barrier-free television for those with visual impairments. Five enhanced Audiodescription (AD) scenarios were proposed and evaluated: 1) Live streaming Internet TV with AD, 2) AD reception in a group situation, 3) Video on demand over a set-top-box, 4) Video on PC and 5) Podcasts. User evaluation concerning usefulness, quality and usability of the services was assessed using questionnaires. Results of the user evaluation show that not only are AD emerging services technically viable but they are also positively rated by users. Implementation of these services will provide improved access to content, making TV accessible for all.

Keywords: accessibility, audio description, emerging services, user evaluation, ambient assisted living, elderly.

1 Introduction

Ambient Assisted Living (AAL) defines the solutions for the enhancement of the quality of life of older people based on the information and communication technologies. The home environment is a significant space for the family conciliation and, while the technology of the consumer electronics for the home environment is evolving rapidly, the risk of exclusion of elderly people increases. Some of this barriers concern to the accessibility of multimedia content and, in particular, to audiovisual content. In this context, technology must be especially designed taking into account the user needs rather than in the technology itself [1].

People who are blind or partially sighted need audio description (AD) to be provided with a television program if they are to fully appreciate the context of what they hear. Nowadays, an AD track is broadcasted within the TV stream as a separated audio track [2] [3] that users can select using the remote control. AD track contains the original audio content mixed with a voice-over track giving further explanation about what is happening on the screen [4]. This service is provided in some countries such as the UK, where the rate of AD has been raised to 20% in recent years. This

J. Bravo, R. Hervás, and M. Rodríguez (Eds.): IWAAL 2012, LNCS 7657, pp. 270–277, 2012.
© Springer-Verlag Berlin Heidelberg 2012

rate varies across Europe [5], with some countries not offering any AD, and some beginning to raise their content to 10% of total output - the share recommended by the Spanish Government [6]. This is the case for Television of Catalonia (TVC).

TV broadcasters have also been deploying their content on different distribution networks such as the Internet or IPTV in order to enhance user engagement and user benefit from the new features they can offer. Since IPTV promotes a user-centric model of content broadcasting, it should provide suitable and improved accessibility services to ensure universal access for people who are deaf or visually impaired [7] as well as elderly people [8]. However, AD for video content seems to be less wide-spread in IP networks compared to broadcast systems, due to technical limitations of some distribution formats. These limitations require a higher implementation effort that has to be assumed by each content producer. In order to facilitate the provision of access services on TV, the European Union funded the project Digital Television for All (DTV4All) where TVC along with UAB undertook this study.

- The first objective is to identify significant emerging AD access services to cover all possible situations in a domestic environment. These services have to address the needs of disabled people and deliver services that are not yet on the market but are expected to become available in the near future. In this article we introduce five emerging AD scenarios for receiving AD. The scenarios simulated different audiovisual consumption situations and were aimed at evaluate the services.
- The second objective is to evaluate the users' perceived value of the proposed services. Specially, how attractive the new service is (its Usefulness), how easy it is to interact with the system (its Usability), and the general quality of the content received (its Quality). The results presented here are the first stage in the validation process of the services. We wanted to assess as many aspects of the services as possible. In particular, the quality of the broadcasted image and audio. This approach requires ensuring that users did not present any visual or hearing impairment. For this reason, people with visual or hearing impairments were not included in the participants' group in this stage. Taking into account that the target users of AD services are visually impaired people, a second stage of user evaluation will be carried out in the future involving visually impaired participants and an improved version of the services in order to evaluate specific aspects concerning its use by visually impaired users.

2 Evaluation Methodology

Fourteen participants were recruited as volunteers. Audio described content was provided by TVC. TV series named "La Riera", which is broadcasted using DTT signal, was used as the reference content in terms of quality of service.

Five questionnaires were specially designed to evaluate each scenario. Three features concerning the scenarios were evaluated: usefulness, usability and quality. The usability scale was adapted from Lewis questionnaire "post-study system usability questionnaire" [10]. Different types of questions were used: (1) Likert scale questions consisting of seven alternative responses ranging from "strongly disagree" to "completely agree". A normalization procedure was applied in the results in order to present the ratings in a 0-10 scale, (2) Comparative questions were presented in order to rank the features of the new system against those of the current system, and (3) Open-answer questions concerning the pros and cons of the system, as well as space for comments and suggestions.

Information about the tests and the objectives of the session were provided in written mode. Users were asked to carry out a specific task for each scenario and individually answer the corresponding questionnaire. A training phase was conducted to familiarize participants with the equipment and the assessment procedure.

3   Evaluation

According to the project plan, TVC delivered 5 prototypes of AD emerging services to address different user needs. The evaluated service descriptions and the user evaluation results are detailed below.

3.1   Service Description and Results

- Service 1: Live Streaming of Internet TV

This service emulates Digital Terrestrial Television (DTT) broadcasting by means of Internet (figure 1). Audio described content is transmitted in live mode via streaming from media servers located at TVC facilities. The signal emitted includes a high quality video signal and a minimum of two audio signals: a stereo Catalan audio channel and a mono AD channel, which is a mix of the normal audio and the AD created by the broadcaster. The content is encoded and packaged at the origin with the same quality as (DTT). The end-user will need a properly configured set-top-box to receive and decode the content instead of the current DTT air signal.

Fig. 1. Live Streaming of Internet TV

Participants watched the TV program 2-3 minutes using DTT signal first and using Internet TV afterwards. Their task was to activate the AD track with the remote control.

Results show that, in general, the system was rated by participants as being "very useful". The rating included functionality and satisfaction attained. For example, the statement "In general, I think the service is useful" obtained a mean value of 8.8 points out of 10. Similarly, "The system has all the features and capabilities I expect" and "In general, I am satisfied with the service" both received a mean rating of 8.1.

Quality was assessed by means of four Likert scale questions concerning image and audio quality as well as velocity to access the service. It was positively evaluated by participants. For example, users were very satisfied with the speed with which they could access the service (mean rating of 8.5). However, there are aspects of the service that need to be improved regarding Internet connection. Providing a constant and sufficient Internet bandwidth will guarantee good image quality. The global mean value for usability was 9.1. Users highlighted the ease of use and the quick access to the service as well as the cleanness of the graphic interface. Regarding the open-answer questions, users mentioned the system's usefulness for people with visual disabilities. They also pointed out "clarity of command" and that it "is friendly and easy to use". This latter aspect was highlighted by the majority of the users. Some suggestions were made regarding the incorporation of information about the content provided. For example, the inclusion of an audio described synopsis of the films will make the service more accessible.

- Service 2: AD reception in a group situation

This service proposes a solution for consuming television in group or family situations when one member of the group suffers from a visual impairment and requires AD. Figure 2 depicts the proposed service.

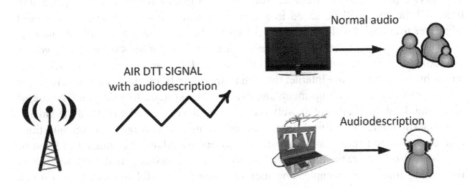

Fig. 2. AD Reception in a Group Situation

The proposed service allows different users to watch the same TV screen together while the disabled user receives the AD channel individually through headphones connected to a laptop with a DTT tuner. It deals with simultaneous reception of media content both with and without AD. We wanted to test feasibility of the service and ensure that it does not involve problems with audio synchronization. The user received the AD through headphones connected to a laptop while other people received the standard audio channel. As this scenario focuses on the audio reception, only usefulness and quality were evaluated. Participants were told to answer having in mind that the question referred to the situation where a visually impaired person is watching the audiovisual contents together with the participant.

Usefulness questions were presented as follows: 1) In general, I think this service is useful; 2) I would like to have this service; 3) If I had the service, I would use it; and 4) In general, I am satisfied with the system. In addition, participants were asked three open-answer questions regarding pros, cons and suggested improvements. The system was evaluated as very useful (gaining a mean rating of 8.6 in question 1) since it allows visually impaired people to have AD individually. To evaluate the quality of image and sound, users answered a question concerning the overall quality rating in terms of: bad, mediocre, satisfactory, good or excellent. They also answered five Likert scale questions about quality: 1) The audio quality of my headphones is good; 2) The sound does not experience cuts or breaks; 3) The audio from my headphones and the audio from the TV are presented at the same time; 4) No mismatches occur between the headphones and the TV; and 5) After selecting the service, access to content is quick. The overall quality was rated as "Good" by most users (64%), with 22 % considering it "Excellent". The mean rating for the Likert scale questions was 8.9. The positive evaluation validates this service as a possible solution for family conciliation in cases where a person suffers a visual impairment. Its acceptance has been demonstrated both in the technical aspect and in its application.

- Service 3: Video on Demand to a Set-Top-Box.

The service permits to choose a recorded program from a list (i.e. 'catch-up') at any time. All the files will be saved in a repository and will be available to be served whenever users ask for them. The hybrid set-top-box used in the test allows the user to access the website to choose the video content he or she wishes to watch, as well as the audio he or she wants to listen to: either a standard Catalan or AD channel. Content is broadcasted via the Internet through a streaming IP channel. Task was to select a program from the catch-up menu and evaluate the system, focusing on the ease of achieving the desired content as well as evaluating the perceived quality of the video.

A questionnaire with five Likert scale questions and two open-answer questions regarding pros and cons was administered. Service usefulness was rated as 8.9 out of 10. Users also highlighted the fact that access is instantaneous (streaming), so there is no waiting time. For example, one user mentioned as useful the fact that you can "access at any time to your favorite program without waiting" or "do not need to download and save the chapter". All these features make video on demand to a set-top-box a very attractive solution for AD reception. Figure 4 shows the selection menu screens for Video on demand system. Image and sound quality were evaluated through a question with five alternative answers. Most users declared that the quality was "Good" (64%), whereas 29% declared that it was "Satisfactory" and 7% said it was "Excellent". The usability assessment included questions concerning "ease of use" and "graphic interface". Data from the questionnaire showed that both aspects of usability obtained a good rating. The global mean rating for system usability was 9.2. Regarding the pros of the system, users emphasized the ease and speed of access to the video on demand service with AD. They also highlighted the temporal flexibility provided by the availability of chapters at any time and the possibility of watching a program more than once. Furthermore, some suggestions were made for improving the service. For example, users pointed out that there is no access to a time bar to advance or rewind the content.

- Service 4: Downloading videos on the PC.

This service allows the user to download media files on a PC so that these can be played on the same PC or on another multimedia device. The user will be able to download the content by accessing a web page with links to the AD programs. Participants' task was to browse the menu and select a program to download. The content was played on the computer using the VLC playback software [11].

Users rated the general usefulness as 9.1 out of 10. The possibility to play AD content on mobile devices was also appreciated by users. General quality was rated as "satisfactory" by 50% of users, as "good" by 36%, and as "excellent" by 14%. Image quality was rated as 8.4. Users emphasized the fact that the service guarantees excellent picture and sound quality as the service is provided directly by the broadcasters. However the time needed to download the files obtained the lowest value (6.7). The implementation of a more efficient download manager that allows the user to manage multiple files simultaneously would be an improvement. The system usability was highly appreciated by the users, with a global mean rating of 8.7 out of 10. This score indicates that the tasks were performed satisfactorily. Some of the comments collected to evaluate the graphic interface indicated that it could be improved in some ways. At the same time, participants suggested that the introduction of auditory information in the application menus would increase the usability and accessibility of the system.

- Service 5: Downloading of AD podcast.

The podcast service allows the users to download audio files and listen to them on a PC or a portable media device. These files only contain the AD audio channel of the selected programs. Once the files are downloaded, they can be copied to the portable audio player devices so that users can access the content wherever they want. The participants´ task was to access the website, select and then play the podcasts. One of the goals of the evaluation was to find out whether there is a need for end-users to access podcasts of the programs they have previously missed.

Service usefulness was rated with a mean score of 8.3 out of 10. In the questions regarding the positive aspects, users highlighted the time and location flexibility provided by podcasts. For example, one user said "if you are following a TV series, you can hear it in the car or while doing other things". Similarly, users stated that "podcasts might be very useful for blind people". The quality questionnaire comprised four Likert scale questions as well as one 5-alternative question regarding general quality. Quality was rated as "good" by most respondents, 64%, and "excellent" by 29% of users. Similarly, in terms of their level of satisfaction, the system was rated very favorably by users, with a rating average of 8.4. Users evaluated all aspects concerning usability very positively. Almost all the questions were rated at 9 out of 10 or higher, indicating an excellent level of usability. The global average rating for usability was 9.1 points. These scores indicate that the system is easy to use when performing a podcast download. However, it is important to note that the question regarding the pleasantness of the graphic interface obtained a lower score (7.6 points), suggesting that the appearance of the display should be improved.

4   Conclusions

Five emerging services for AD were proposed and evaluated. Users evaluated the usefulness, quality and usability of each service through questionnaires. Ratings and comments about the services were reported and analyzed. The project DTV4ALL has shown that it is technically feasible for IPTV and video on demand to incorporate AD emerging services. Figure 3 summarizes the results achieved for all the scenarios.

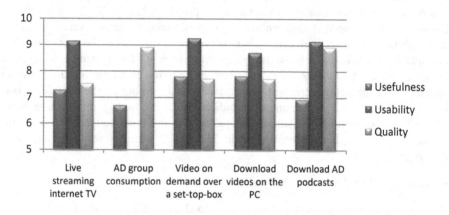

Fig. 3. Summary of results for all the evaluated scenarios

The usefulness of AD services has been validated by the users, not only as a tool to make content more accessible, but also as a means of reconciling the family. Evaluation showed that some attention should be paid to improving quality in order to enhance the experience of the user. Finally, usability has been clearly validated with respect to the ease of use and proposed improvements of the graphic interface.

Although each AD scenario focuses on a specific use case, two main conclusions are extracted from the study: (1) users especially appreciate the fast access to video contents, and (2) the downloading of content for offline consumption is a common practice among users because of the spread of smart devices. This last point is of particular importance for people who really need AD for understanding audiovisual contents. Mobile content providers should take that into account for providing accessible audiovisual content to anyone besides to make it accessible anywhere and anytime.

We can conclude that the proposed services are widely accepted by users as an accessibility service, highly regarded as a social tool, and have the expected quality to encourage their deployment. The user evaluation process provided valuable information and feedback from participants. The results obtained at this stage will be compared with those obtained in the next evaluations, when more tests involving visually impaired users provide the necessary information to validate the current results.

Acknowledgements. This research is supported by the grant from the Spanish Ministry of Science and Innovation FFI2009-08027, Subtitling for the Deaf and Hard of Hearing and Audio Description: objective tests and future plans; and also by the Catalan Government funds2009SGR700.

References

1. Kleinberger, T., Becker, M., Ras, E., Holzinger, A., Müller, P.: Ambient Intelligence in Assisted Living: Enable Elderly People to Handle Future Interfaces. In: Stephanidis, C. (ed.) UAHCI 2007 (Part II). LNCS, vol. 4555, pp. 103–112. Springer, Heidelberg (2007)
2. Tanton, N.E., Ware, T., Armstrong, M.: Audio Description: what it is and how it works, BBC White paper (2006),
   http://www.bbc.co.uk/rd/pubs/whp/whp051.shtml
   (accessed November 2011)
3. Oliveira, R., Ferraz de Abreu, J., Almeida, A.M.: An approach to identify requirements for an iTV audio description service. In: Proceedings of 9th European Conference EuroITV 2011, Lisbon, pp. 227–230 (June 2011)
4. Braun, S.: Audiodescription Research: state of the art and beyond. Translation Studies in the New Millennium 6, 14–30 (2008)
5. Orero, P.: Sampling audio description in Europe. In: Díaz Cintas, J., Orero, P., Remael, A. (eds.) Media for All: Subtitling for the Deaf, Audio Description and Sign Language, pp. 111–125. Rodopi, Amsterdam (2007b)
6. Orero, P.: Audio Description: Professional Recognition, Practice and Standards in Spain. Translation Watch Quarterly 1(Inaugural issue) (December 7-18, 2005b)
7. Springett, M.V., Griffiths, R.N.: Accessibility of Interactive Television for Users with Low Vision: Learning from the Web. In: Cesar, P., Chorianopoulos, K., Jensen, J.F. (eds.) EuroITV 2007. LNCS, vol. 4471, pp. 76–85. Springer, Heidelberg (2007)
8. Boyle, H., Nicolle, C., Maguire, M., Mitchell, V.: Older Users' Requirements for Interactive Television. In: Clarkson, J., Langdon, P., Robinson, P. (eds.) Designing Accessible Technology, pp. 85–92. Springer (2006)
9. Digital Television For All (DTV4All), http://www.psp-dtv4all.org/
10. Lewis, J.R.: IBM computer usability satisfaction questionnaires: Psychometric evaluation and instructions for use. International Journal of Human-Computer Interaction 7(1), 57–78 (1995)
11. VLC media player (1.1.11). The VideoLan Project, http://www.videolan.org/ (accessed November 2011)

Implementing Shared Displays: A Tool for Smooth Integration of Large-Screen TVs and Mobile Devices

Christian Berkhoff[1], Sergio F. Ochoa[1], José A. Pino[1], Jesús Favela[2], Jonice Oliveira[3], and Luis A. Guerrero[4]

[1] Department of Computer Science, Universidad de Chile, Santiago, Chile
{berkhoff,sochoa,jpino}@dcc.uchile.cl
[2] Department of Computer Science, CICESE, Ensenada, Mexico
favela@cicese.mx
[3] Universidade Federal do Rio de Janeiro, Rio de Janeiro, Brazil
jonice@ufrj.br
[4] CITIC Research Group, School of Computer Science and Informatics,
Universidad de Costa Rica
luis.guerrero@ecci.ucr.ac.cr

Abstract. One of the keystones of vision of AmI is the ability of multiple devices to seamlessly communicate within themselves. To this end, this article presents a mobile computer application which is able to smoothly connect via WiFi to large-screen TVs and mobile computer devices. Thus the application allows implementing shared displays with minimal effort and cost. These shared displays have shown to be useful to support meetings and informal encounters in various scenarios, such as at home, hospitals or business settings. The application was tested in real scenarios with encouraging results.

Keywords: Shared displays, resource sharing, encounters, meetings, large-screen TV, mobile computing devices.

1 Introduction

The recent widespread availability of mobile devices (such as smartphones, slate devices and notebooks) has energized the development of novel mobile and ubiquitous applications. Although these devices have improved their computing and storage capacity and also their power autonomy, their small screen constrains their use in several scenarios, particularly in meetings where information needs to be shared by multiple participants.

Typically, connecting a smartphone or laptop to a projector or a LSTV involves connecting and disconnecting cables which usually interrupts the fluidity of the meeting, distracts participants and reduces the meeting's effectiveness. In some cases it is possible to count on meeting rooms equipped for such purpose, which eases the meeting activity but they are not always available and their cost may be high.

If we take into account that many meetings are not necessarily formal activities, we realize that many meeting types (such as the social encounters) have little or no

J. Bravo, R. Hervás, and M. Rodríguez (Eds.): IWAAL 2012, LNCS 7657, pp. 278–286, 2012.

support; e.g. an encounter of grandsons and grandparents to see pictures of the last vacation, or a group of friends that meets to plan a fishing trip for the next weekend.

In many of these informal meetings and social encounters many people try to look at a computing device screen because they have no projector or special cables to connect a mobile device to a LSTV. Although many meeting sites (including homes) have a LSTV (e.g. a LCD or LED TV device), people are not able to take advantage of it due to the burden involved in connecting the device.

In this paper we present a software tool named Clairvoyance that allows a smooth integration of LSTV and mobile devices. Since this integration is based on a WiFi communication channel, people do not need to use cables or directly manipulate the LSTV device. Thus, this application enables any room with a LSTV to become a potential meeting room with projection capabilities.

Fig. 1 shows the Clairvoyance basic working scenario. The application is also able to locate available and busy LSTVs in a certain area, as a way to guide interested people towards a free resource.

Clairvoyance has a client application running in the mobile device (e.g. a laptop or smartphone) and a server application running in a micro-component (a nettop) that is connected to the LSTV.

Fig. 1. Clairvoyance interaction scenario

The system has been tested in a real scenario and the obtained results are highly positive. The next section presents the related work. Section 3 describes the Clairvoyance application and its main components. Section 4 presents the experimentation scenarios and the obtained results. Finally, Section 5 presents the conclusions and future work.

2 Related Work

LSTV's and HD projectors are becoming ubiquitous. They are usually available in meeting rooms and increasingly so in corridors, near elevators and other office spaces. Many meetings and informal encounters are currently supported by audiovisual equipment. The LSTVs (measuring 32" and up) are commonly used often in several rooms.

LSTVs can also be installed outside the meeting room being used to show contents. If these devices have some intelligence, they also can support interactions with people [2]. Several researchers have studied the role played by these devices as public screens. In particular, they can be used to provide information to passers-by [3, 4], and also as mechanisms to support casual meetings [5, 6].

LSTVs may become ubiquitous in the near future and smartphones may be the input devices to interact with them. In a certain sense, smartphones could be considered the future universal remote controls for several other devices.

Various techniques have been proposed to allow computing devices to interact with LSTVs. However most of them require considerable effort to set up (e.g. cables or adapters). Jeon et al. [7] present, e.g., several techniques that could be used to deploy images and video/animations on a LSTV, but they do not address the connection process between devices or the communication issues among them.

Cornejo et al. [8] provide a solution that allows users to show pictures in LSTV using hand gestures. Such gestures are captured and recognized by a Kinect sensor which sends particular orders to a computer controlling the LSTV. Although such a solution is interesting, it requires additional infrastructure and for the user to be familiar with the gestures understood by the device.

Although the previous works are interesting, in most cases the contents to be shared must be stored in the server controlling the LSTV, which jeopardizes the ubiquity of this sharing process and the privacy of the shared resources.

3   Clairvoyance

Clairvoyance allows mobile devices to connect to a LSTV on demand using a Mobile Ad hoc network (MANET). The application uses the HLMP API [1] to detect mobile devices and LSTVs in the vicinity, and also to automatically form a MANET among them. In order to make the LSTV visible for mobile devices a small nettop needs to be plugged to the smartTV. The nettop is a micro-computer with WiFi, processing and storage capabilities. The application has a client-server architecture.

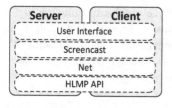

Fig. 2. Basic Architecture

The server module runs in the nettop and the client runs in the mobile devices used to interact with the LSTV (Fig. 2.). The client and the server modules have four components: the HLMP API, the net component, the screencast and the user interface. They are briefly described below.

3.1   User Interface

When the user of a mobile computing device wants to connect to a LSTV, the Clairvoyance client application scans the environment and detects all LSTVs within one or more hops of distance. Fig.3.a shows the process result indicating that just one LSTV (named WindBox) is available. If the user selects such a screen and connects to it, then the mobile device displays the features of the connection. (Fig. 3.b). While the link is active, any application or resource deployed in the client device is shown also on the LSTV (Fig. 3.c). Depending on the resource size, the user could perceive that this deployment is done in real-time.

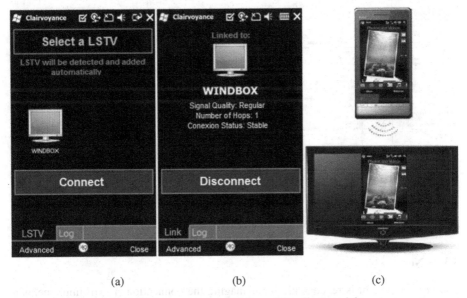

(a)   (b)   (c)

Fig. 3. Clairvoyance user interface of the client module

If other users are participating in the meeting, all of them are able to scan the environment and detect the presence of the WindBox screen (i.e. the LSTV). Since they know that the WindBox screen is busy (i.e. linked to another device), the connection button will appear as disabled until the current user frees the LSTV.

3.2   Screencast

According to the architecture shown in Fig. 2, this component is divided in a client and a server module. The *screencast* client is in charge of compressing and packing the user interface of the client device connected to a LSTV, and the server module is the counterpart; i.e. it is in charge of unpacking and decompressing such information when it is received by the nettop connected to the LSTV (Fig. 4). The server module makes available this information to the upper layer components (i.e. those managing the LSTV user interface) to allow thus the image deployment on the screen.

From the client side, the *ICompressionStrategy* class is in charge of selecting one of two currently available compressions strategies: simple or BDS compression. Fig. 4 shows the classes (i.e. *SimpleCompressor* and *BSDcompressor*) that are responsible of performing such a compression. The information to be compressed is a screenshot of the client device, which is captured by the *ScreenShooter* class.

From the server side we have almost the same classes than in the client side, except the *ScreenShooter*, which does not make sense in the server.

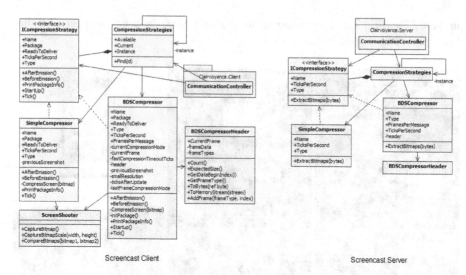

Fig. 4. Structure of the *screencast* component

3.3   Net

The *net* component is responsible for managing the connection (i.e., it implements a session link) between a client device and a LSTV. Like the *screencast* component, this one is also implemented through a client and a server module (Fig.5). From the client side, the *CommunicationController* interface allows access to the services provided by the class with the same name. That class is in charge of configuring and managing the communication link between a client device and a LSTV using the *Protocol* class. The *Constants* class is used by the *Protocol* class to identify the devices participating in the meeting session.

The *CommunicationController* uses the *ScreenEmitter* class which allows a Clairvoyance client to build the messages containing the graphical information (i.e. *ScreenMessage*). In order to perform this operation the *ScreenEmitter* uses interfaces to the *ICompressionStrategy* and *CompresssionStrategies* classes that belong to the *Screencast* component.

The *net* client module also implements the interfaces to access the services and message types provided by the HLMP (High-Level MANET Protocol) [1]. HLMP implements the MANET that allows interactions among devices participating in the meeting. Each of these devices shares control information with the rest of the nodes by using the *UserDataAdmin* class. The shared information includes the type of device (e.g. smartphone, slate, laptop or LSTV) and its status (e.g. available or busy). Thus, it is possible to identify LSTVs available in the area. A HLMP service indicates the distance (in terms of hops) between a client device and the available LSTV.

The *Linker* class encapsulates the task of linking a client device and a LSTV. In the client side this class implements a blocking call to the server module that returns a boolean value. *True* indicates the linking process was successful, and *false* means that it failed (typically by the server unavailability or timeout). To perform this task the *Linker* uses the *Protocol* and *LinkMessage* classes.

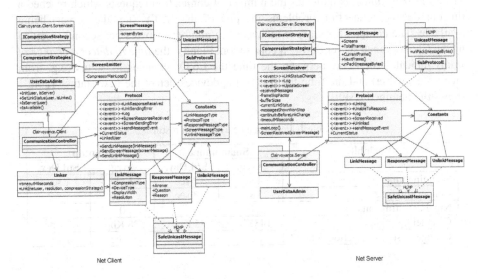

Fig. 5. Structure of the *net* component

The *LinkMessage*, *UnlinkMessage* and *ResponseMessage* message types implement the *SafeUnicastMessage* interface, since they require a more reliable delivery than the one used for regular messages. From the server side the *net* structure is similar to the client. However the server by default is passive and just reacts to the requests sent by the client devices.

Finally, the HLMP API is the component that automatically creates a MANET among computing devices that are physically close, and manage it appropriately depending on the movements of the users [1]. This middleware manages the mobile nodes connection and disconnections, and messages passing and routing. HLMP provides the developers with an abstraction layer to manage the messages passing through the MANET without the need to address the low-level details involved in this type of networks.

4   Experimental Results

Two types of evaluation processes were performed to assess Clairvoyance performance and usability. The performance evaluation used 30 instances of the same test. Half of the tests were done using a smartphone as client device and the rest used a laptop. The following variables were measured in each test: scanning time, connection time, number of timeouts, channel throughput between client and server, and time to detect a change of status. The *scanning time* indicates the time spent by a Clairvoyance client to sense the environment and determine which devices are present. Similarly, the *connection time* measures the time required by a client device to connect to a LSTV. That period goes from the time that the linking request is sent, until the instant at which the link between the client and server is available for use. The *number of timeouts* indicates the number of connection requests which reached a timeout due to connection problems in spite of the LSTV (i.e. the server) being available. The *channel throughput* indicates the number of bytes per second received by the Clairvoyance server during a connection. Finally, the *time to detect a change of status* indicates the delay between the time the LSTV changes its status (e.g. from busy to available) and the time the rest of the devices detect the new status. Table 1 shows the obtained results.

Table 1. Performance evaluation results

Variable	Smartphone		Laptop	
	Avrg.	Std.Dev.	Avrg.	Std.Dev.
Scanning time	4 sec	2 sec	3 sec	1 sec
Connection time	8 sec	3 sec	6 sec	1 sec
Number of timeouts	0	-	0	-
Channel throughput	143Kbps	35 Kbps	228 Kbps	42 Kbps
Change of status detection delay	8 sec	3 sec	5 sec	2 sec

The obtained results are quite consistent and within the expectable values. We observe the interaction between the LSTV and powerful client devices (i.e. a laptop) achieves a better performance than the case of a smartphone being used as client. The throughput of the communication channel is limited by the HLMP API implementation. Although the throughput values could seem relatively low, they are comparable to those obtained by well-known MANET implementation infrastructures [1]; e.g. Optimized Link State Routing (OLSR).

We performed usability evaluation with twelve participants in order to determine whether this performance was acceptable for end-users. Three of them were between 10 and 15 years old, four between 18 and 25, three between 42 and 45, and two over 55 years old. People received a basic instruction (2 or 3 minutes), and then they used the application to complete a sketch of actions consisting of 3 connections, 3 disconnections, 2 scans and deployment of 5 images and one video on the LSTV.

A random device (between smartphone and laptop) was assigned to each user. Five of them used a laptop and seven people used a smartphone. All participants were able to complete the sketch. The main difference among them was the time spent to complete the sketch. The fastest in completing the sketch were the youngest participant, with an average time of 7 minutes using a smartphone and 8 using a laptop. The slowest users were the oldest participants with a time of 16 minutes using a laptop and 22 minutes using a smartphone. These numbers are not enough to get definitive conclusions, but they provide some hint about the Clairvoyance usability.

After using the system the users completed a survey using a 5-point scale to rate each item: good (5), acceptable (4), neutral (3), deficient (2), and unacceptable (1). Table 2 shows the obtained results.

Table 2. Usability evaluation results

Variable	Smartphone		Laptop	
	Avrg.	Std.Dev.	Avrg.	Std.Dev.
Response time	3,9	0,69	4,6	0,55
Understandability	4,3	0,76	4,4	0,55
Usefulness	4,6	0,53	3,8	0,45
Reliability	4,7	0,49	4,6	0,55

Seven participants asked us for a copy of the software to try to use it in their own homes. Although the results are preliminary, they offer some evidence that Clairvoyance is usable and useful for most users.

5   Conclusions and Future Work

This article presents a middleware named Clairvoyance, which allows a smooth integration between large-screen TVs and mobile devices. The main goal of this application is to help people to share visual resources during formal meeting or social encounters. The solution uses a wireless link between a micro-computer connected to the LSTV and the mobile device used to deploy the visual information. No infrastructure-based communication networks are required in the environment where this solution is used, since Clairvoyance automatically creates and manages the communication links required to perform the operations.

After evaluating the usability and performance with real users, the obtained results were quite good for most people. Particularly young people were highly enthusiastic of using the application. The system performance is appropriate to support this type of information sharing; however, it is still not good enough to reproduce real-time video or large images (e.g. weighting more than 20 MB). Provided the Clairvoyance user interface is simple, an ample range of people were able to use it successfully.

Acknowledgements. This work has been partially supported by Fondecyt (Chile), grant N° 1120207 and LACCIR, grant N° R1210LAC002.

References

1. Rodríguez-Covili, J.F., Ochoa, S.F., Pino, J.A., Messeguer, R., Medina, E., Royo, D.: A Communication Infrastructure to Ease the Development of Mobile Collaborative Applications. J. of Network and Computer Applications 34(6), 1883–1893 (2011)
2. Scanlon, J.: If walls could talk, streets might join in. New York Times (September 18, 2003)
3. Churchill, E., Nelson, L., Denoue, L.: Multimedia Fliers: Information Sharing With Digital Community Bulletin Boards, pp. 97–117. Kluwer Acad. Pub., Palo Alto (2003)
4. Greenberg, S., Boyle, M., LaBerge, J.: PDAs and Shared Public Displays: Making Personal Information Public, and Public Information Personal. Personal Techn. Springer (1999)

5. McCarthy, J.: Using public displays to create conversation opportunities. In: Proc. of the ACM 2002 Conf. on Computer Supported Cooperative Work (CSCW 2002), New Orleans (2002)
6. Russell, D.M., Drews, C., Sue, A.: Social Aspects of Using Large Public Interactive Displays for Collaboration. In: Borriello, G., Holmquist, L.E. (eds.) UbiComp 2002. LNCS, vol. 2498, pp. 229–236. Springer, Heidelberg (2002)
7. Jeon, S., Hwang, S., Kim, G.J., Billinghurst, M.: Interaction Techniques in Large Display Environments using Hand-held Devices. In: Proc. of the ACM VRST 2006, Cyprus (2006)
8. Cornejo, R., Hernández, D., Favela, J., Tentori, M., Ochoa, S.F.: Persuading older adults to socialize and exercise through ambient games. In: Proc. of the Workshop of Wellness and HCI, PervasiveHealth, San Diego California, May 21-24 (2012)
9. Mejia, A.D., Favela, J., Moran, A.L.: Understanding and Supporting Lightweight Communication in Hospital Work. IEEE TIT in BioMedicine 14(1), 140–146 (2010)

User Experience of Elders and Relatives in a Collaborative Cognitive Stimulation Tool

Alberto L. Morán and Victoria Meza-Kubo

Universidad Autónoma de Baja California, Ensenada BC 22860, México

Abstract. Aiming at improving the design of cognitive stimulation (CS) applications for elders, we have conducted studies that allowed us to gain an understanding of the nature of CS activities, and to envision how we might support them using pervasive technologies. One such support is InTouchFun, a CS application that allows for the integration of remote social family network members into an elder's CS activities. Although the results of a TAM-based usability evaluation provided evidence that the tool was perceived as useful, easy to use, and generating pleasurable user experiences, we did not have insights into which were the application's features that fostered these results. In this paper, we present and discuss the results of a further evaluation centered on the analysis of the interactions observed during a CS session, and which provide evidence to determine the features that fostered reaching goals such as engagement, satisfaction, enjoyment and a low anxiety level.

Keywords: user experience evaluation, cognitive stimulation, elderly.

1 Introduction

The increase of age-related diseases (e.g., dementia) as a consequence of global population aging, has made more evident the need for approaches that allow to cope with cognitive decline (CD). Although there are no treatments to cure some of these diseases (e.g., the Alzheimer's disease) [1], there are pharmacological approaches, such as cognitive stimulation (CS), that when conducted frequently and properly, reduce the risk of suffering from the disease, or improve the cognitive state of the affected elder [2,3].

Furthermore, according to [4], the lack of social contact is a factor that contributes to accelerate CD. Thus, it is necessary to develop strategies to favorably modify the conditions in which elders are living in order to prevent the onset or progression of CD. One way to do this is to involve members of the elder's social family network (SFN) as participants in his/her daily activities, including CS activities. We believe that the introduction of Ambient Assisted Living (AAL) technology is promising in terms of making CS interventions more accessible to both elders and their SFN members.

In order to address this opportunity area, we developed InTouchFun, a pervasive CS collaborative system that provides support for CS at the elder's home,

J. Bravo, R. Hervás, and M. Rodríguez (Eds.): IWAAL 2012, LNCS 7657, pp. 287–294, 2012.

and that allows the integration of remote SFN members [5]. Initially InTouch-Fun was evaluated using subjective techniques, through the use of questionnaires and interviews, to gather the participants' perception regarding the application's usefulness, ease of use and user experience (UX). In this work we present the results of a second evaluation that gathers evidence on more specific UX aspects of the application. To do so, we performed a further analysis on the use of InTouchFun, identifying the interactions that occurred during a session of actual use, and determining whether they support different UX aspects, such as enjoyment, satisfaction, and engagement.

The paper is organized as follows: Section 2 presents related work on UX and its evaluation, while Section 3 describes InTouchFun, the proposed CS system. Section 4 describes the evaluation process, and the observed interactions. Section 5 discusses whether and how the observed interactions support the different UX aspects. Finally, Section 6 presents our conclusions and directions of future work.

2   User Experience and Its Evaluation

Assessing the UX of applications and other products is an important research topic for the HCI community [6]. Understanding and evaluating UX, however, has not yet been established given the myriad of parameters that can be used to determine whether the use of a product can be considered as a successful UX. Among others, parameters depend on the people involved (e.g. children, older adults, people with disabilities), the type of product (e.g. production, entertainment, education) and on other social and cultural factors [7].

Different techniques have been used to capture UX, depending on the specific context and population in which it is being evaluated [8].

Self-report techniques are employed in settings where verbally expressing emotions can be difficult [9]. Techniques used include Self Assessment Manikin and pictograms, which include cards with faces expressing emotions.

Observation techniques have been used to analyze subjects' nonverbal expressions, as these inform about their emotions; including those about experiences participants may be unaware of during the evaluation [7]. Additionally, the techniques used include interviews with participants, which sought information about the participant's past experience, current emotions, and about application's aspects such as mobility, adaptability and context of use.

Finally, psychological techniques infer emotions during the use of technologies, with devices to measure respiration rate, electrocardiograms, galvanic skin response and electromyography [10].

3   InTouchFun: A Pervasive Collaborative CS System

InTouchFun is a collaborative pervasive system that provides support for CS sessions and that allows for the integration of members of the elder's SFN during these CS activities [5].

3.1   System Description

The InTouchFun system has two main client interfaces: The elder client and the SFN member client interfaces. These interfaces are depicted in Fig. 1.

The elder client interface allows elders to perform their CS activities in a more natural way as they are more used to directly manipulate physical objects instead of indirectly manipulate digital objects using the mouse. The main elements of the interface include (see Fig. 1a): the shared digital board or work area that is projected on the tabletop, the tangible objects and their digital representation (TUI), an exercise selection and solution menu, the SFN member picture and status, and a tele-pointer for the remote SFN member user.

The SFN member client interface basically replicates the elder client interface and gathers gesture and audio information to be sent to the elder's client side. The main difference is the absence of the TUI physical objects. It includes (see Fig. 1b), the shared digital board or work area, the digital representation of the objects, and the exercise selection and solution menu. The current prototype

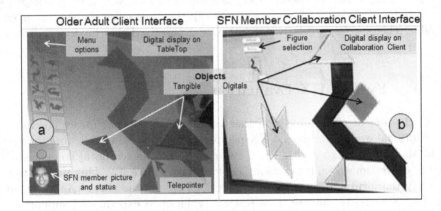

Fig. 1. System Prototype: A) TUI-based elder client interface on a tabletop multitouch surface computer. B) GUI-based SFN member client interface on a laptop computer.

system integrates functional versions of these clients. The elder client interface introduces the use of tangible objects and a multitouch tabletop surface computer using a Reactivision server for the recognition of the Tangram pieces, and the TUIO protocol for communication with the actual computer application [11]. The SFN member client interface presents a traditional GUI-based interface. Event communication between the elder client and the SFN member client is implemented using a client-server architecture (C#, socket-based, custom XML protocol), which basically replicates a subset of events from the local client to the remote client using an Internet connection. Audio communication between the elder client and the SFN member client was implemented using an off-the-shelf audio application.

3.2   The System Usability Evaluation

In order to determine the ease of use of the proposed system and its usefulness by allowing the members of the elder's SFN to participate during the CS activities as informal caregivers, in our previous work [5] we carried out a usability evaluation of the system. Participants in this evaluation were 6 elders with no apparent CD, and a close relative (SFN member, e.g., child).

The evaluation consisted of three steps: 1) Video scenario projection; 2) CS activity; and 3) On-exit questionnaire. In step 2, they performed two different activities: i) A Cognitive Activity, the elder assembled four figures using the Tangram puzzle, while his relative observed and provided help and motivation; and ii) An Entertainment Activity, which consisted on playing one of the available board games (Tic-tac-toe, and Checkers). In this case the elder and his relative competed against each other. In step 3, we inquired the participants about their general perception on the application's ease of use and usefulness by using TAM-based questionnaires [6].

The TAM-based evaluation provided the following results: All participants perceived the system as useful (6.40, on a 7-point Likert scale); all participants perceived the system as easy to use (6.61/7); they perceived the system as enjoyable (elders, 6.92/7; relatives, 6.33/7), and perceived that anxiety regarding system use was low (2.33/7).

4   The System UX Evaluation

With the aim of performing a further validation of the system, we conducted an addtional evaluation from a UX perspective. We used indirect observational analysis techniques to gather data, and coded gestures, corporal language and verbal expressions from interactions as a rich data source [12]. This allowed us to identify the form and function of interactions among the participants engaged in the CS activity, and use it as further evidence to explain and support the usability and UX results of the previous evaluation.

4.1   Process

We analyzed the videos of the six elder-relative couples while they executed the activities. A facilitator assisted them during the session. Each session lasted about 18 minutes, which resulted in a total of 106 minutes of recorded video. We analyzed the interactions that occurred in these sessions to identify the functions they served. We also looked at their interaction with materials and other behaviors they externalized.

4.2   Actor-Actor Interactions identified during the CS Session

We identified a set of interactions that occurred among the participants, as well as some of the functions of these interactions (see Table 1). These include:

- *Elder - Relative interactions.* These interactions occur between an elder and his/her relative, with the elder starting it. Identified functions include: Request for help, and Social communication.
- *Relative - Elder interactions.* These interactions also involve the elder and the relative, but the latter initiates it. Identified functions include: Provide feedback or Encouragement to the older adult when required.

Table 1. Actors, interaction types and their functions and frequencies in a CS Collaborative session

Actors involved	Interaction functions	Frequency
Elder – Relative (32.35%)	Request help	48.48%
	Social communication	51.52%
Relative – Elder (67.65%)	Provide feedback to elder	26.09%
	Encourage elder	23.19%
	Provide help to elder	23.19%
	Give instructions to elder	13.04%
	Social Communication	14.49%

After identifying the different types of interactions, we quantified them based on the actors involved, and based on the functions they served. During the six sessions (106 minutes in total), there were 102 interactions among the participants. From these 102 interactions, 33 (32.35%) were Elder-Relative interactions, and 69 (67.65%) were Relative-Elder interactions. As expected, relatives were the most active during the session, given their role as facilitators and motivators. Furthermore, from the 33 Elder-Relative interactions, 16 (48.48%) were to Request help, and 17 (51.52%) were for Social communication. In the case of the 69 Relative-Elder interactions, 18 (26.09%) were to Provide feedback, 16 (23.19%) were for encouragement, 16 (23.19%) were to provide help, 10 (14.49%) were for social communication, and the remaining 9 (13.04%) were to Give instructions.

4.3 Externalized Emotions Observed during the CS Session

All participants externalized different emotions while executing the activities.

Enjoyment. Almost all elders (5/6) externalized behaviors that denoted that they were having fun during the execution of the activities. They were making jokes, laughing, and telling stories about when they used to play with their younger relatives when they were children. Relatives denoted their having fun laughing and making jokes, and complementing and sharing their parts of the stories told by elders.

Surprise. Some of the participants externalized their being surprised about their performance on the execution of the activities. On the one hand, some elders (3/6) expressed that although they did not know how to play the game (the

Tangram in particular), they were able to easily and successfully complete or win the games. On the other hand, relatives (3/6) were surprised about their elder relative being able to complete the puzzle or win the game.

Concentration. All participants (both elders and relatives) externalized their being focused on the activity by humming, singing, asking for some time to think, or scratching their heads while determining their next move.

The only participant that did not externalized any enjoyment emotions was elder 6, whom remained serious and silent, focusing on the execution of the activities. She commented that she did not know how to play Checkers, the Tic-tac-toe, or the Tangram game. Although at the end she was able to complete the four Tangram puzzles, and three Tic-tac-toe games, she was the elder that required most feedback (3), encouragement (7), instructions (6) and help (6) interactions from her relative.

4.4   Discussion of the UX Evaluation Results

To determine whether the use of the system generated a pleasurable UX on the participants in the collaborative CS, we considered the participants' involvement in the activity. We took into account the type and frequency of the actor-actor and actor-materials interactions, as well as some of the behaviors and emotions externalized during activity execution. We considered the following UX goals: engagement, enjoyment, satisfaction and anxiety or frustration.

Engagement. Participants were immersed in the activity regardless of their being in different sites. Elders were the focus of feedback, help and motivation interactions from their relatives (67.65%), and they even generated some interactions to ask for help and socialize (32.35%). On the one hand, cognitive activities provided an opportunity for elders to solve a challenge, while giving their relatives an opportunity to assist them on achieving it. Both participants assumed their roles, and all elders (6/6) were able to solve the 4 Tangram puzzles presented to them. On the other hand, entertainment activities provided them with an opportunity to compete against each other.

Satisfaction. Participants were able to achieve their goals, either by solving a challenge, or providing help, or winning a game. Regarding the cognitive activity, and as mentioned earlier, elders were able to solve all of the proposed cognitive activities (4 tangram puzzles) regardless of their being novices to the activity (none of them reported on having previous experience with the Tangram), and relatives were able to assist them regardless of their being remotely located. This generated a sense of pride and teamwork in them. Concerning the entertainment activity, some participants (3/6) were particularly satisfied about their being able to win some of the Tic-tac-toe and Checkers games, which resulted in a surprise to both the elder and his/her relative.

Enjoyment. Evidence from this observation analysis backs up the information gathered with the TAM-based questionnaires. Elders and their relatives enjoyed executing the activities. This was denoted by the behavior exhibited during their performing the activities. As stated earlier, elders made jokes, told stories about when they used to play with their younger relatives when they were children, and laughed about it. Relatives denoted their having fun also by making jokes, complementing and sharing parts of the funny stories told by elders, and laughing along with them. Furthermore, participants celebrated the achievements of the other, either as a teammate as in the cognitive activity, or as an opponent as in the entertainment activity.

Anxiety or frustration level. Participants denoted low anxiety or frustration during the execution of their activities. On the beginning, the TUI interaction modality generated some anxiety on the elders, as they were novel to its use. However, after interacting with it for a while they understood the metaphor and use it in a relaxed and efficient manner. Also, being remotely distributed put some pressure on participants because of the novelty of the setting for them. However, after interacting through the provided elder (TUI + voice channel) and relative (GUI + voice channel) interfaces and getting used to them, they interacted in a known and natural manner. Further, they were able to develop protocols to perform coordination tasks such as help provision and turn-taking indications and to interact in a social manner during the proposed activities (17 interactions, 26.47%). Finally, given the nature of activities, some of the elders felt as being evaluated or urged to win, which resulted in low anxiety (2.33 on a 7-point Likert scale) as reported by them in the on-exit questionnaire.

Although it was clear from the results of the first evaluation [5] that participants perceived InTouchFun as a useful and easy to use tool, which generated enjoyable and low anxiety user experiences, we did not obtained evidence enough as to pinpoint which aspects of the application and of the proposed activities were responsible for these results. The use of the resulting multi-method approach, involving an indirect observation technique (i.e. analysis of observed interactions) and the self-report technique (i.e. TAM-based questionnaires) used in [5], allowed us to generate a richer picture without increasing the work load on the evaluation's participants, as suggested by [8].

5   Conclusions

In this work, departing from a pervasive collaborative application that promotes the CS of various cognitive functions, and the integration of SFN members into the CS activity, we assessed the UX of this application through an analysis of the actor-actor and actor-materials interactions that occurred during an ensemble of distributed CS sessions. These results provide evidence that the tool favors interaction among the elderly and their remote relative, and fosters feedback, motivation, help and social interaction among them. Also, results provide evidence that the proposed TUI (elder) and GUI+Mouse (relative) interfaces promoted easy and natural interactions with the materials and the activity. These kind of actor-actor interactions provide evidence about the UX achieved by participants during a CS session, and allows users to have fun, be satisfied about its use and engaged in the activity, while lowering anxiety and avoiding frustration. These results also highlight the role of the relative as feedback and instructions provider to support the proper execution of CS activities even in a remote manner.

References

1. Stevens, L.M., Lynm, C., Glass, R.M.: Alzheimer disease. JAMA: The Journal of the American Medical Association 286(17), 2194 (2001)
2. Wilson, R.S., Mendes de Leon, C.F., Barnes, L.L., Schneider, J.A., Bienias, J.L., Evans, D.A., Bennett, D.A.: Participation in cognitively stimulating activities and risk of incident alzheimer disease. JAMA: The Journal of the American Medical Association 287(6), 742–748 (2002)
3. Ball, K., Berch, D.B., Helmers, K.F., Jobe, J.B., Leveck, M.D., Marsiske, M., Morris, J.N., Rebok, G.W., Smith, D.M., Tennstedt, S.L., Unverzagt, F.W., Willis, S.L.: Effects of cognitive training interventions with older adults. JAMA: The Journal of the American Medical Association 288(18), 2271–2281 (2002)
4. Orrell, M., Sahakian, B.: Education and dementia. BMJ (British Medical Journal) 310(6985), 951–952 (1995)
5. Meza-Kubo, V., Morán, A.L., Rodríguez, M.: Bridging the gap between illiterate older adults and cognitive stimulation technologies through pervasive computing. Universal Access in the Information Society (in press, 2012)
6. Väänänen-Vainio-Mattila, K., Roto, V., Hassenzahl, M.: Now let's do it in practice: user experience evaluation methods in product development. In: CHI 2008 Extended Abstracts on Human Factors in Computing Systems, CHI EA 2008, pp. 3961–3964. ACM, New York (2008)
7. Arhippainen, L., Tähti, M.: Empirical evaluation of user experience in two adaptive mobile application prototypes. In: Proceedings of the 2nd International Conference on Mobile and Ubiquitous Multimedia. Linkping Electronic Conference Proceedings (2003)
8. Vermeeren, A.P.O.S., Law, E.L.C., Roto, V., Obrist, M., Hoonhout, J., Väänänen-Vainio-Mattila, K.: User experience evaluation methods: current state and development needs. In: Proceedings of the 6th Nordic Conference on Human-Computer Interaction: Extending Boundaries, NordiCHI 2010, pp. 521–530. ACM, New York (2010)
9. Isomursu, M., Tähti, M., Väinämä, S., Kuutti, K.: Experimental evaluation of five methods for collecting emotions in field settings with mobile applications. International Journal of Human-Computer Studies 65(4), 404–418 (2007)
10. Mandryk, R.L., Inkpen, K.M., Calvert, T.W.: Using psychophysiological techniques to measure user experience with entertainment technologies. Behaviour & Information Technology 25(2), 141–158 (2006)
11. Kaltenbrunner, M., Bovermann, T., Bencina, R., Costanza, E.: Tuio: A protocol for table-top tangible user interfaces. In: Proc. of the 6th Intl. Workshop on Gesture in Human-Computer Interaction and Simulation (2005)
12. Sanderson, P.M., Fisher, C.: Exploratory sequential data analysis: Foundations. Human Computer Interaction 9(3-4), 251–317 (1994)

Discovering the Social Interaction Patterns of Younger and Older Facebook Users

Darren Quinn[*], Liming Chen, and Maurice Mulvenna

School of Computing and Mathematics, University of Ulster, Jordanstown. Northern Ireland
quinn-d15@email.ulster.ac.uk, {l.chen,md.mulvenna}@ulster.ac.uk

Abstract. Increased use of social networking applications has resulted in an explosion of user generated content; however the online interactions and differences in behaviour of younger and older users have not yet been fully explored. Traditionally, social network analysis has had a macro level focus, with little attention paid to individual behaviours. Interaction analysis is an emerging social behaviour analysis approach, investigating issues at a more micro level, providing an enriched capability to understand and contrast individual and group behaviour(s). In this study we test if age is a factor underlying the behaviour of users within Facebook. Data was gathered from 500 users, composed equally of younger and older users. To determine behavioural patterns, user data was analysed on a daily and weekly basis, detailing the day and hour of each user interaction. Results showed that distinct behavioural characteristics are identifiable between the cohorts, concluding age is a determining factor.

Keywords: Interaction Analysis, Social Networking, Online Interactions, Behavioural Patterns.

1   Introduction

The rise in popularity of Online Social Networking (OSN) applications such as Facebook and Twitter has created enormous amounts of User Generated Content (UGC), which provide a unique opportunity to understand the behavioural habits of its users [1]. Traditionally OSN has been studied through the discipline of Social Network Analysis. The focus of much research has had a macro level approach, observing issues such as community structure [2] with little attention paid to the behaviours of individual users. Interaction analysis is an emerging social behaviour analysis approach which aims to understand the online patterns and characteristics of each individual, investigating issues at a more micro level such as the frequency and modality of engagement.

As users of all ages engage, interaction analysis provides an enriched capability to understand and contrast individual and group behaviour(s). Within the world's largest OSN site of Facebook, younger users are recognised as the core demographic and

---

[*] Corresponding author.

J. Bravo, R. Hervás, and M. Rodríguez (Eds.): IWAAL 2012, LNCS 7657, pp. 295–303, 2012.

conversely older users are the minority [3]. Due to reasons such as retirement, bereavement, reduced mobility or increasingly dispersed family networks, older people are acknowledged as being vulnerable to an increased risk of social isolation [4]. Given that the core aim of OSN is to increase opportunities for connectivity, it has the potential to play a role in alleviating the burden of any increased isolation. At first glance it would appear that the technology of OSN and older people are an ideal match, providing an approach that may help reduce the burden of social isolation. For example, OSN can allow them to connect to those who share a common interest (e.g. family member, hobby, university etc.) [5], stimulating their social network. Nevertheless, factors such as access, technical ability, usability and privacy concerns [6, 7] have posed as just some of the barriers hindering older users from fully exploiting the potential within OSN, resulting in a large disparity between younger and older user engagement levels [8]. If OSN is indeed an approach to assist older users, we must understand how users are employing these technologies, providing a foundation to comprehend the varying adoption rates that have been observed for both groups [1].

In this study we aim to contribute knowledge by advancing the understanding, detailing specifics about precise user interactions within two age groups. As such, we report upon the behavioural patterns of the core demographic of younger users and those older users who may stand to benefit from OSN. We study the social interactions of 500 users in Facebook to test the hypothesis that age is a factor underlying the changes in behaviour of younger and older users. By analysing weekly and daily patterns of social interactions gleaned from the UGC of two disparate cohorts, we assess if unique characteristics are attributable between the two user groups. The primary motivation is that in detailing precisely how users engage; we can not only begin to fully reason the variances, but also quantify the value engagements hold in later works. The remainder of the paper is organised as follows: Section 2 discusses the concept and methodology exploring in greater detail the chosen social network, and the associated stages involved within the study. Section 3 describes data collection along with the analysis and methods approach. Section 4 presents the results. Section 5 presents the findings, with a discussion on the observed patterns. The paper is concluded within section 6, with a summary of current work and future work.

2   Concept and Methodology

The primary objective of this study is to investigate the micro-level patterns of engagement of user social interactions on an hourly and daily basis. Studies were designed to quantify individual interaction activities, providing an understanding into how the behaviour of two age groups compare. Understanding how individuals act allows us to know what is representative collectively. Analysis was subsequently applied to categorise behaviour into specified ranges which could be applied for a cross comparison of the cohorts. It is expected that results (particularly contrasting ones) of engagement and intensity will not only provide flat behavioural data in terms of metrics, but also reveal trends and disparities in the adoption rates of younger and older users. In addition, the research results will be used to help establish if real world social activity maybe indicated within the online interactions of users, i.e. does a decrease in online activity mean an increase in real world activity?

2.1 Methodology

To conduct the study the first thing is to decide the source where social interaction data can be acquired. There are a number of social networking applications, e.g. Twitter, LinkedIn and MySpace etc., each of which provides different functions and features. After a review and evaluation we chose Facebook as the OSN site for our study. *"Facebook is a social utility that connects people with friends and others who work, study and live around them. People use Facebook to keep up with friends, upload an unlimited number of photos, post links and videos, and learn more about the people they meet"* [9]. The rationale for our decision is as follows: firstly, it was and still is the world leader, with 901 million monthly active users [9]. Facebook contained large-scale data for both cohorts, who had equal access and opportunity for the use of application features. Secondly, as an application it provides rich features for its users that enable subsequent measures of activity and network contribution. Users engage through their profile 'Wall', a facility which controls and contains UGC (e.g. for the posting of comments to other users). As a user makes contributions, a chronicle of interactions becomes amassed, a history which is viewable from within the users profile. Privacy settings control what information is disclosed to other Facebook users. Information set to *'everyone'* is classed as public. It was only these profiles with which the study was concerned.

Once the data source is determined, the study is undertaken in four principal stages. The first stage is to identify appropriate users, suitable for the purpose of the study. It was required within the study that a user's age is either stated or could be determined. The age of a user was not always explicitly provided. However, provided certain character information was available it became possible to determine the age of a user (within a close proximity), in one or more of three ways, either by university, school leaving year or date of birth. The second stage involved specifying which interactions were to be assessed. We reviewed a comprehensive array of potential Facebook interactions for inclusion and decided to focus on the core functionality of user comments and replies and their corresponding metadata of date and time. All non-user elements (e.g. non-user comments or replies) were omitted. Following user selection, UGC was acquired at source code level, and processed through a bespoke parsing program, designed specifically to measure Facebook user engagement. Finally, UGC data was subsequently analysed providing metrics for every individual with respect to each identified interaction. An analysis process applied firstly at individual and then at group level, provided overall engagement statistics. This process enabled a direct comparison to be drawn of all user data.

3 Data Collection and Analysis Methods

This section describes data collection and analysis processes. To collect user interaction data, a user profile was firstly created through the standard Facebook sign up process, following which the '*find classmates*' tool was employed with a seeding point of local universities. Based on predefined profile attributes (age, gender, etc.), a listing of potential friends was identified by Facebook. User suitability for inclusion in the study was determined on the following two criteria: firstly, a user's wall must be publicly viewable. Secondly, the age of the user must be identifiable. Profiles of each suitable user's 'friends' were then assessed employing the same approach. The process was repeated until a sufficient amount of users for each group and gender was acquired. By applying the above process to both groups, a total of 500 full user profiles were obtained (125 younger males, 125 younger females, 125 older males and 125 older females) in a two month period from December 2010. The collected UGC data consisted of the entire wall history for each user, with walls exhausted until posts were no longer available. Younger users were set from the earliest possible age of 15 ranging to 30 years. Older users were assessed as being any users from 50 years with no upper limit imposed. User age data was determined on a user's '*info*' page, and extracted in conjunction with wall data. As a group, the mid age range of users (i.e. 31 - 49) was omitted as the aim was to focus on contrasting the most socially active, against those declared as vulnerable. Given the data collection requirement and that they are not vulnerable, the mid range are outside the scope of this particular study.

To analyse the behavioural characteristics of a user's social interaction, it was decided to observe the engagement patterns of users at two levels of abstraction, namely on a '*daily*' and '*weekly*' basis, which we believe can disclose a user's social interaction habits at the micro level. Daily usage provided a detailed understanding into the specific hours each cohort engaged throughout the course of a day. Weekly usage was also investigated, determining what bias and patterns occur (if any) as a result of each cohort's social engagement on each day. The analysis is carried out in the following process. We first isolated all relevant user activities, and defined where appropriate the activity type and date/time (time, hour and week day) for all interactions. As users will have joined Facebook at different times, the collected UGC for each user would therefore represent datasets over a different period of time. As such, a normalisation process was duly implemented to derive the percentage value each activity had in relation to overall activity volume. In calculating daily activity, each day was divided into 24 one-hour slots in which to allocate interactions (e.g. a user comment occurring at 22:45:00, allocated to the hour of 22hr, counter +1). In calculating weekly activity, each event was allocated into the day of occurrence. For example, a user reply occurring on the date '06/11/2010' will be allocated to the corresponding day of Tuesday. As a result, the above processes for daily and weekly activity enabled discrete measures for each interaction, e.g. User 'A' had 23 comments on a Tuesday in the hour of 22hr. The analysis methods described above were first applied to all individual users. Following this, individual user data was combined for each group to calculate the same daily and weekly metrics at group level. All analysis methods were applied for their ability to evaluate and statistically qualify a testable hypothesis.

4   Analysis Results

We apply the above analysis method to the datasets of each user group respectively. The results are presented in the two sections below.

4.1   Daily Activity (by hour)

Fig.1 shows the distribution of social interaction activity throughout the course of a day, whereby the totals are an aggregation of the mean values for each hour irrespective of day, illustrating the behavioural differences for both groups.

Younger Users - Daily Activity: Out of 250 users only 1 user contained no user activity (i.e. no user comments or replies). Results demonstrated younger users as having a mean of 7.82 activities per hour, with a median value of 9.27. Peak values were observed between 22:00hrs - 23:00hrs accounting for 8.38% of all activity, translating into a mean value of 15.71 and a median value of 9.00. The maximum value was 130 interactions in any one hour by a single user and occurred between 20:00 - 21:00. In relation to minimum values, all hours for younger users were observed as containing a NIL value for at least one user. The overall STDEV of younger users was 6.28. Results for the top 5 hours for activity (accounting for 37.76% of all activity) occurred in the order of 22:00, 21:00, 18:00, 19:00 and 20:00 respectively.

Older Users - Daily Activity: Out of 250, 109 older users contained no user activity. Results demonstrated older users as performing a mean of 1.27 activities per hour with a median of 0.00, due largely to the volume of NIL values. Peak values were observed between 13:00hrs - 14:00hrs accounting for 8.78% of all daily activities. Results equate to a mean of 1.27 activities. A maximum value of 94 occurrences was observed between 13:00 - 14:00, whilst all hours for older users were observed as containing a NIL value. The STDEV was 2.45 for older users, peaking within 13:00 - 14:00 with a value of 11.30. Results show the top 5 hours for activity occurred in the order of 13:00, 22:00, 21:00, 17:00 and 14:00, accounting for 35.93% of all activity.

Cohort Comparison - Daily Activity: It is noted that 43.60% of potential older users contained no user activity, compared directly to 0.4% of younger users. The daily mean of 7.82 (younger) and 1.27 (older) represents a significant difference in the hourly contributions, with younger users engaging at a rate 6.19 times that of older users. Activity between the hour of 22:00 – 23:00 is noted as highly important for both groups with values of 8.39% (younger) and 8.00% (older). Within both cohorts NIL values were recorded for all hours. However, the standard deviation contrasted heavily with younger users' mean value (6.28) being 2.8 times that of older users (2.58). As can be seen from Fig.1 older users were shown to display a daily pattern of spikes (e.g. 08:00, 13:00, 17:00 etc.) and troughs. Younger users conversely showed a more steady engagement. Declines in use also contrasted, in that older users decline more rapidly when compared to younger users, with the latter shown to engage later into the early hours. Contrasts were also noted in the distribution values of the two groups with younger users having greater extended ranges.

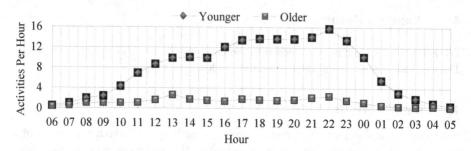

Fig. 1. Daily Activity Line Graph: Average Number of Activities per Hour

4.2   Weekly Activity (by day)

In the case of both cohorts, mean interaction values were acquired on a per day basis and subsequently normalised to a percentile of weekly behaviour. A pre-study assumption was declared that all days were to be equal for user activity, with a baseline value of 14.29% (i.e. 1/7th of activity) associated upon which to gauge activity and represent average daily behaviour. Activities were further analysed in terms of weekday and weekend percentages (see Table 1.).

Younger Users - Weekly Activity: Results demonstrated the day of most activity is a Monday, accounting for 15.56% of activity with a real world value of 29.19 interactions. Thursdays were the 2nd highest day with 15.53%. The day of least activity is a Saturday with 12.02%. Weekday (Mon-Fri) behaviour accounts for 73.65% of all activities, with the remaining 26.35% attributed to weekend behaviour. 54.38% of weekend behaviours were attached to Sundays in contrast to 45.62% on Saturdays.

Older Users - Weekly Activity: Results revealed the most active day is a Friday accounting for 15.77% of all activity, translating into a value of 4.82 activities. Thursdays were the 2nd highest day at 15.52%. The day of least activity is a Saturday with 13.05%. Weekday behaviour accounted for 73.64% of all older users' activities, with 26.36% attached to weekend behaviour. 50.49% of weekend behaviours were associated with Sundays, with 49.51% on Saturdays.

Cohort Comparison - Weekly Activity: In contrasting the cohorts, noticeable variances were apparent. As demonstrated, younger users peak post weekend on a Monday (15.56%) with a similarly strong value attached to Thursdays (15.53%). Older users peak more prominently on a Friday (15.77%) with a strong value attached to the previous day of Thursday (15.52%). Younger users were seen to decline on Tuesday and Wednesday before activity rises again on a Thursday. The pattern for older users is similar only with a minor dip occurring on Tuesdays. Both cohorts were observed as declining to a weekly activity low on Saturday, while younger users were seen to decline earlier with a drop in activity from Thursday, whereas older users decline more markedly. Both cohorts share a strongly similar rise in activity from Wednesday to Thursday to where both values were within 0.01%. Notably, contrasts occurred on a

Friday when the younger users' activity is shown to decline, whereas older behavioural patterns were to the contrary with a rise in activity to a weekly peak. Both cohorts were seen to increase on Sundays which continues into the new week.

Table 1. Weekly Activity Table

	Younger	%	% of weekday or weekend	Older	%	% of weekday or weekend
Monday	29.19	15.56%	21.13%	4.42	14.48%	19.67%
Tuesday	27.65	14.74%	20.01%	4.23	13.84%	18.79%
Wednesday	27.33	14.57%	19.78%	4.28	14.02%	19.04%
Thursday	29.12	15.53%	21.08%	4.74	15.52%	21.08%
Friday	24.86	13.25%	18.00%	4.82	15.77%	21.42%
Saturday	22.55	12.02%	45.62%	3.99	13.05%	49.51%
Sunday	26.88	14.33%	54.38%	4.06	13.31%	50.49%

5   Finding and Discussion

By comparative studies of the UGC relating to the daily and weekly patterns of two cohorts, a number of findings have been discovered, which are discussed below.

Daily Usage: In evaluating daily usage, younger users were shown to perform on average 7.82 activities per hour. Older users however were shown to perform a significantly lower amount of 1.27. Results reveal that OSN applications are of a greater significance for younger users in relation to their chosen modalities for communication. This view is further supported by the contrasts in profiles which contained UGC, in particular the significant number of older users which held no data. Results showed that both cohorts observed high volumes between 22:00 and 23:00, witnessing the highest and second highest volumes of user activity. A time late in the evening such as this is viewed as a reflection of the role Facebook plays within a user's day. The doing of activities (work, socialising etc.) is carried out throughout the course of a user's day, with activity posted in the late evening in reflection. As an application designed to facilitate social engagement, users were viewed as forming habits, engaging at defined daily periods, with time consciously set aside for the maintenance of a user's social network. The recording of descriptive statistics such as maximum, minimum, mean and median values illustrated the breadth of usage by individuals within each cohort. Younger users were seen to comprise a broad range of participants with high hourly usage levels (i.e. Max of 130 activities), whilst also recognising the minority of low volume users. Older users were seen to have less of a variance in usage, as would be expected from a group with a lower daily consumption. Conclusions that younger users are a more varied cohort are supported by the observed standard deviation values. Analysis indicates younger users as being consistent and active engagers throughout the day. Older users however were seen to be more sporadic, behaviour which is viewed as being more targeted and specific, engaging during set times with what appears to be a more focused approach. In contrast, it is less likely that each of the many contributions made by younger users were of a focused nature.

Weekly Usage: The patterns of weekly usage were based on the assumption that all days (without prior knowledge) should theoretically be equal for all users within each cohort, with a relevant baseline value attributed. As a sub-study the engagement of weekday / weekend patterns was observed, motivated by trying to understand if a relationship is identifiable between real world and online activity, i.e. low volumes of online weekend activity when the majority of real world engagement is assumed to occur. The activity (or more precisely the lack of activity) for both cohorts strongly indicates real world activity maybe indicated through the monitoring of activity levels. However, quantitative work with end users is required to confirm any such hypothesis. As detailed within Table 1, notable declines were seen to occur from a Thursday, reducing on Friday and then to the low of a Saturday. Results indicate users were engaging in real world activities, particularly visible on a Saturday, with activity increasing on Sundays. It appears (particularly younger) users update on Mondays from the weekend events whilst making plans on Thursdays. Older users' weekly engagement portrays both similarities and disparities. Firstly the similarities; activity dips to a low on Saturdays (as with younger), rising on Sundays and furthermore on a Monday with a dip in activity on Tuesday. Thursdays for both groups were noted as sharing an almost identical value, varying by 0.01%. The key disparity in behaviour observed by older users is that at the low of Saturday, is preceded by a peak in activity on a Friday. Also engaging on a Monday does not appear as important, with activity increasing throughout the rest of the week.

6   Conclusion

This study carried out an observational examination of 500 users and their interactions in Facebook, quantifying the weekly and daily patterns of two age cohorts (Younger and Older). Wall profiles containing the comments and replies of each subject were analysed to provide insights into the social interaction patterns at both individual and group level. We presented the analysis results and visualisation to depict the trends and differences of social interaction patterns. Results illustrated that there exist distinguishable variances in the behavioural patterns between the two groups. This proved age is a predetermining factor. Contributions not only quantify current engagement levels and patterns of behaviour, but also have wider implications such as the design of future systems. To evaluate the research findings, future work will focus on engaging with users to obtain their views regarding online social activities. Furthermore, future work will investigate how users view the use of such technologies in relation to their overall impact upon well being.

References

1. Quinn, D., Chen, L., Mulvenna, M.: An Examination of the Behaviour of Younger and Older users of Facebook. In: Proceedings of the 4th ICST International Conference on eHealth, Malaga, Spain, pp. 9–16 (2011)

2. Porter, M.A., Onnela, J.P., Mucha, P.J.: Communities in Networks. Notices of the American Mathematical Society 56, 1082–1097 (2009)
3. Corbett, P.: Facebook Demographics and Statistics Report 2010 – 145% growth in 1 year (2010),
   http://www.istrategylabs.com/2010/01/facebookdemographicsands
   tatisticsreport2010145growthin1year/
4. Fokkema, T., De Jong Gierveld, J., Dykstra, P.A.: Cross-National Differences in Older Adult Loneliness. The Journal of Psychology 146(1-2) (2012)
5. Cheung, C.M.K., Chiu, P., Lee, M.K.O.: Online social networks: Why do students use facebook? Computers in Human Behavior 27(4), 1337–1343 (2011)
6. Age Concern 2009: Only 1 in 6 older people embrace social networking and Age Concern wants more (2009),
   http://www.ageconcern.org.uk/AgeConcern/
   socialnetworking-release-130309.asp
7. Selwyn, N.: The information aged: A qualitative study of older adults' use of information and communications technology. Journal of Aging Studies 18, 369–384 (2004)
8. Pfeil, U., Arjan, R., Zaphiris, P.: Age differences in online social networking – A study of user profiles and the social capital divide among teenagers and older users in MySpace. Computers in Human Behavior 25, 643–654 (2009)
9. Facebook 2012. Facebook press room, about facebook (2012),
   http://newsroom.fb.com/content/default.aspx?NewsAreaId=22

Adapting Social and Intelligent Environments to Support People with Special Needs

Xavier Alamán[1], Francisco J. Ballesteros[2], Zoraida Callejas[3], Javier Gómez[1],
Estefanía Martín[2], Sara de Miguel[3], and Alvaro Ortigosa[1]

[1] Universidad Autónoma de Madrid, Madrid, Spain
{xavier.alaman,jg.escribano,alvaro.ortigosa}@uam.es
[2] Universidad de Granada, Granada, Spain
zoraida@ugr.es
[3] Universidad Rey Juan Carlos, Madrid, Spain
nemo@lsub.org, estefania.martin@urjc.es

Abstract. In this paper we describe ASIES, a project funded by the Spanish Minsterio de Economía y Competitividad, that seeks to provide technologies to support independent living for people with special needs, while broadening the use of these technologies by integrating their capabilities with that of Social Networks. This integration supplies a social dimension, traditionally used in supporting daily activities and training, to the possibilities of Adaptive Hypermedia and Ambient Intelligence.

Keywords: Ambient Intelligence, Special needs, Ambient Assisted Living, Natural Language Interfaces, Social Interfaces, Emotion Aware Systems.

1 Introduction

This paper describes the ASIES project, which is funded by the Plan Nacional de I+D+i (TIN2010-17344), and that is focused on supporting the daily activities of collectives with special needs. The main target population is that of people with cognitive disabilities: Down's syndrome (primary trisomy and mosaicism), Turner's syndrome, autism, cerebral palsy and encephalopathy with non-specific etiology (50 < IQ < 70). The project is developing solutions for helping these collectives in their daily activities that can be generalized to other populations with special needs.

People with cognitive disabilities have difficulties with everyday tasks such as money management, travel, daily routines and social relationships. ASIES tackles the problem of independent living through the support of daily routines in three different domains: home, work and transport, while also developing innovative methods and tools to provide ubiquitous training to the target collectives.

ASIES project deals with several aspects of this problem. In the following sections we will present briefly these different aspects.

2 ASIES Middleware

To support the various pervasive tools of the ASIES project we have continued the development of the Octopus system for personal pervasive environments [1]. For

J. Bravo, R. Hervás, and M. Rodríguez (Eds.): IWAAL 2012, LNCS 7657, pp. 304–311, 2012.

example, Octopus software can be used to integrate emotional processing with mail applications and to control the real world environment using the voice, among other things.

The goal of a personal pervasive environment is to provide a single system image: a per-user virtual computer composed by the personal, disperse resources, including data, devices, and applications, and other services imported from a smart space, such as a context data infrastructure, storage, sensors, actuators, computing facilities, etc.

To support that, the Octopus provides services and mechanisms for event delivery, reconfiguration and adaptation, service discovery, protection, among others.

It makes writing new applications on the pervasive space extremely simple, because in the octopus all services are accessed using a file interface. Resources are represented by the servers as tiny synthetic file systems exported through the network, and are accessed by the client through the file handling system calls (mostly open, read, write, and close). All such file systems are usually mounted on a per-user name space (reconfigured at run time to consider changes in the environment).

For example, a light switch in the Octopus is handled by using a file that represents the switch. Of course, there is no such file, the file is an invention of the software that drives the switch. However, reading the file reports as text either the string "on" or the string "off", depending on the switch state, and writing it (with the same strings) updates the switch state. The same is done for other resources: for example a voice synthesis device is just a file that can be written to speak the written text.

Being able to use all resources as if they were files, and interoperating with them just by reading and writing files, greatly simplifies the interoperability and portability of the components. This is very useful on a heterogeneous project such as ASIES. That is, the Octopus technology simplifies things for the rest of the project, as stated in [2, 3].

3   Natural Language Interfaces for People with Special Needs

Most speech-based tools currently available to help people with disabilities are based on displaying images or synthesizing voice from a textual input. Those which accept spoken input have to address the challenge of developing a speech recognizer that obtains acceptable recognition rates with users who suffer from speech disorders. Usually, this has been done by specializing in a certain pathology, which allows optimizing the acoustic features employed by the recognizer [4].

We are particularly interested in comparing different corpora that can be used to train speech recognizers for cognitive disabled people, covering a varied range of the pathologies and communication levels. In order to do this, we have used two corpora of average Spanish speakers, and we are currently collecting a new corpus with cognitive impaired people.

The first corpus we used was Albayzín [5], the Spanish reference corpus that consists of a total of 6800 balanced elocutions that were recorded by 304 speakers. In second place we obtained ourselves a new corpus from a call center, which consists of 200 sentences and a reduced grammar on the routing of calls within our Department.

It has been used for comparison purposes, as it was recorded with lower quality than Abayzín. In third place, we are currently collecting in collaboration with different associations a corpus of recordings of people with cognitive disability. The initial collected corpus contains recordings by 15 persons (4 women and 11 men) arranged in three groups attending to their verbal communication level (low, medium or high) and is comprised of 1965 recordings. We have finalized a first collection stage in which we were interested in recording words that could be used as commands for a simple speech-based system. The participants recorded a list of 131 words related to their daily activities.

Our experimental results show that speech recognition of people with a low communication level might benefit from resources collected from speakers with different levels of communication. In general, for the high-level communication group better results were obtained when the recognizer was trained only with recordings made by this group, obtaining worse results when adding recordings from the other groups (1,89% less accuracy). For the medium-level communication group, the results obtained for the recognizer trained with all corpora were similar to those obtained training it just with the speech samples from this group. Finally, for the low-level communication group, better recognition rates (2,59% improvement in accuracy) were obtained when adding all corpora rather than building a recognizer specifically trained with the recordings made by this group.

Thus, we believe that there is a relevant opportunity for academia and industry to build on the previous efforts in order to developed speech-based tools for more diverse target users.

4   Interfaces for Socialization

Multitouch surfaces are physical spaces suitable for collaboration and socialization that enable face-to-face interaction [6,7]. It is not surprising that multiple studies have appeared in recent years describing the potential pedagogical benefits of these devices [8], in particular for socialization skills [9]. However most of the existing projects are based on bespoke multitouch applications. This prevents teachers to easily modify the structure of the learning activity or to incorporate new contents.

We propose to create authoring tools that will allow teachers to become instructional designers using multitouch technologies. Teachers will either create new learning activities or modify existing ones in an easy way. Our main efforts were focused on facilitating the design of traditional learning activities for the cognitive disabled that will run on top of a physical shareable interface.

With this goal in mind we developed in cooperation with the Down Syndrome Foundation of Madrid (http://www.downmadrid.es/) two complementary tools: DEDOS-Editor and DEDOS-Player [10]. The first one is an authoring tool and the second one is a run-time multitouch learning activities player.

The authoring tool takes advantage of teacher's prior knowledge on existing authoring tools. For doing so, we studied which are the most used learning activities and adapted them to the multitouch environment. The teacher uses direct manipulation for selecting and connecting the different elements of the activity. The design process is independent of the number of players and their physical location. The elements can be grouped on the player's area or on a common area: DEDOS-Player automatically replicates the player's area as many times as there are student (see Fig. 1). Additionally, DEDOS-Player allows customizing on the fly different aspects of the execution of the learning activity.

Both tools are based on our FLING framework [11]. FLING is a functionality layer which adds multi-touch capabilities to Adobe Flash and Air applications using ActionScript. Its main functionality is a two-fold transformation. Touch events are transformed into gestures, and these are converted into higher level events (ex. resize, rotate, move, etc.) that are fed into the application.

These tools are currently used as part of the Down Syndrome Foundation Programme on educational innovation. We are also performing several ongoing studies of the educational benefits of these technologies on Down's syndrome population.

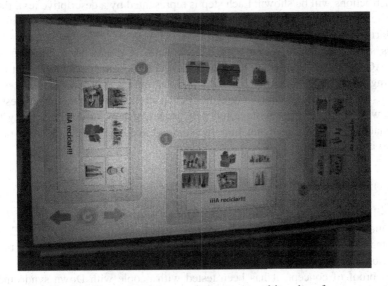

Fig. 1. A learning activity running on top a multitouch surface

Fig. 1 shows an activity that has been configured for three players situated on left, right and the bottom side of the tabletop. The goal is to drag and drop player's garbage card into the correct recycle bin. These bins are placed in the common area and are shared by all the players.

5   Assisting the Cognitive Disabled at Work

One of the problems that people with cognitive disabilities have to face at is the lack of personal autonomy [12]. Even in the case of people whose disability is not very prominent, they may have some difficulties to find and keep a job, thus it is harder for them to get economic independence: to fulfil their personal autonomy they must find a job. We think that some of the problems they could find at the working place could be addressed using Ambient Intelligence technologies.

For this purpose we have developed two systems: aQRdate and QRUMBS. Both of them are based on the use of mobile devices and QR Codes to provide assistance to people with cognitive disabilities, but in two different ways. The first one, aQRdate, provides adaptive manuals to guide the user while doing an activity. The second one, QRUMBS, provides guidance to physically find resources at the working place.

5.1   aQRdate

This tool provides step-by-step instructions to perform an activity [13]. To do that, the working place has to be tagged with QR Codes that represent the different activities to be done. The user can scan one of them with her mobile phone and a set of step-by-step instructions will be shown. Each step is represented by a descriptive text, that can be read aloud automatically, and an image. This way, the user is provided with guidance during the whole activity.

This system has been tested with patients with acquired brain injury from the CEADAC (Spanish Reference Centre of Acquired Brain Injury Attention) but instead of giving help for the working place, as initially intended, we decided to test it in activities of their daily living, as this fits better in their rehabilitation process. The results we obtained were encouraging: patients learnt how to do the activity to the point that, at the end of the evaluation, they did not need the mobile phone to perform the activity.

5.2   QRUMBS

This tool gives guidance to people with cognitive disabilities to navigate the physical space and find resources at the working place. It is based on the use of QR Codes as visual marks that have to be followed and scanned with a mobile phone until the user arrives to the resource or place she was looking for.

As a proof of concept, it has been tested with people with Down syndrome at a building that they were not familiar with. During the process all the activity was stored and at the end of the tests users were asked to complete some questionnaires about their experience. Up to day we have only analysed the questionnaires and we can conclude that users found the guidance clear enough to be understood. We are currently working on the activity log to extract objective data about timing and navigation patterns.

6   Emotion Aware Systems

The use of adaptation methods and techniques allows the development of personal assistants able to guide each user according to her particular needs [14]. However, personalized assistance is possible only when information about each individual, such as her features, needs, preferences, behaviour or emotional state, among others, is available [15]. According to the experts on training cognitive impaired people, the user emotional state an interesting feature to be considered for adaptation purposes. Our research deals with obtaining this information as automatically as possible, yet without compromising its reliability. At ASIES we have explored two ways to obtain emotional states so far: from messages written by users spontaneously in Facebook, and from student writings, using natural language processing techniques.

6.1   Emotion Detection through Facebook Messages

Nowadays there are more than nine hundred million active users on Facebook and more than half of them use it daily. Therefore, we have explored the possibility of extracting information about user emotions by analyzing their Facebook messages, as a non-intrusive potential source of information. In order to do so, we have developed a Facebook application called SentBuk (SENTiment faceBUK) that obtains the messages written by the users on their Facebook wall and applies sentiment analysis to them [16]. It comprises a sentiment classifier that follows a lexicon-based approach that employs a dictionary of words annotated with their semantic orientation (positive/negative sentiment polarity) and detects additional language features such as positive interjections (i.e. laughs), negative interjections, emoticons, misspells and negation (polarity shifter). The resulting classes, with their respective Linguistic Inquiry and Word Count (LWIC) categorization [17] were: positive (positive emotions, positive sentiment, optimistic) and negative (negative emotions, anger, sadness, death, to swear). The process for assigning a positive/negative polarity to the messages written by the users is described in detail in [16].

SentBuk presents wall messages annotated according to the score calculated for each of them. It allows the user to report when a message appears to be wrongly classified. The results of the first uses of SentBuk, as reported in [16], show that messages were quite correctly classified (95,63% of success for positive messages, and 79.33% for negative ones, when classifying 1000 messages and leaving out those written in another language but Spanish).

6.2   Emotion Detection from Writings

Provided the good results obtained from the emotion detection in Facebook entries, we considered analyzing longer texts in which more information could be processed in order to detect specific emotions and their development. Therefore, we worked with essays already written by students to check whether it was possible to get information about the author level of joy, anger, sadness and fear when writing these texts, following the emotion classification proposed in [18]. In this direction, we tested two approaches. The first one is based on the use of an emotion dictionary, as the one used in Chat-SEE [19]. The second one employs word spotting techniques, looking for words related to those four basic emotions. Twelve essays (from 614 to 3139 word long each) written by a student along her first semester in college, related to Anthropology, were analyzed.

Some interesting relationships were found in this study. We found that the greatest anger score was obtained just in the two essays that the student had highlighted as the most significant for her [20]. The emotions gathered in this study, reflected on each essay, were not directly related either to the topic of the essay or to the interest of the student regarding the subject. They seemed to be more related to the author's emotions when developing each essay. Although more experiments are needed, these first results suggest that this non-invasive emotion detection technique can be used for getting information about the user emotion from his writings.

7   Conclusions and Future Work

In this paper we have presented a wide picture of an ambitious project on using Ambient Intelligence and pervasive technologies to help the cognitive impaired in their daily activities. Several technologies are being developed, including an innovative middleware, natural language interfaces adapted for the cognitive impaired, multitouch interaction, tools for guidance at work of the cognitive impaired and emotion aware computing. All of these technologies are being integrated in several demonstrators that will be tested by cognitive impaired people.

Acknowledgements. We want to thank all the members of the project that have contributed to the work presented in this paper: Linda Barros, Rosa M. Carro, Manuel Freire, Manuel García-Herranz, Miguel Gea, Gorka Guardiola, Pablo Haya, Dolores Izuzquiza, Ramón López-Cózar, José M. Martín, Juan Mateu, Germán Montoro, Miguel Mora, Roberto Moriyón, Pilar Rodríguez and Enrique Soriano.

The work described in this paper was funded by the Spanish National Plan of I+D+i (TIN2010-17344).

References

1. Ballesteros, F.J., Soriano, E., Guardiola, G.: Octopus: An Upperware based system for building personal pervasive environments. J. Syst. Softw. 85, 1637–1649 (2012)
2. Ballesteros, F.J., Guardiola, G., Soriano, E.: Upperware: Bringing Resources Back to the System. In: 8th Annual IEEE International Conference on Pervasive Computing and Communications, pp. 511–516. IEEE Press, New York (2010)
3. Ballesteros, F.J., Guardiola, G., Soriano, E.: Personal Pervasive Environments: Practice and Experience. Sensors 12, 7109–7125 (2012)
4. Kain, A.B., Hosom, J.P., Niu, X., Van Santen, J.P.H., Fried-Oken, M., Staehely, J.: Improving the intelligibility of dysarthric speech. Speech Communication 49, 743–759 (2007)
5. Casacuberta, F., García, R., Llisterri, J., Nadeu, C., Pardo, J.M., Rubio, A.: Development of Spanish corpora for speech research (ALBAYZIN). In: Workshop International Cooperation Standarization Speech Databases Speech I/O Assessment Methods, pp. 26–28 (1991)
6. Yuill, N., Rogers, Y.: Mechanisms for collaboration: A design and evaluation framework for multi-user interfaces. ACM Trans. Comput.-Hum. Interact. 19, 1–25 (2012)

7. Rogers, Y., Lindley, S.: Collaborating Around Large Interactive Displays: Which Way is Best to Meet? Interacting with Computers 16, 1133–1152 (2004)
8. Rogers, Y., Lim, Y.K., Hazlewood, W.R.: Extending Tabletops to Support Flexible Collaborative Interactions. In: TABLETOP 2006, pp. 71–78. IEEE Computer Society (2006)
9. Piper, A.M., O'Brien, E., Morris, M.R., Winograd, T.: SIDES: A Cooperative Tabletop Computer Game for Social Skills Development. In: 20th Anniversary Conference on Computer Supported Cooperative Work, pp. 1–10. ACM Press, New York (2006)
10. Martín, E., Haya, P.A., Roldán, D., García-Herranz, M.: Generating adaptive collaborative learning activities for multitouch tabletops. In: Computer Assisted Learning (2011)
11. Llinás, P., García-Herranz, M., Haya, P.A., Montoro, G.: Unifying Events from Multiple Devices for Interpreting User Intentions through Natural Gestures. In: Campos, P., Graham, N., Jorge, J., Nunes, N., Palanque, P., Winckler, M. (eds.) INTERACT 2011, Part I. LNCS, vol. 6946, pp. 576–590. Springer, Heidelberg (2011)
12. Kirsh, B., Stergiou-Kita, M., Gewurtz, R., Dawson, D., Krupa, T., Lysaght, R., Shaw, L.: From margins to mainstream: What do we know about work integration for persons with brain injury, mental illness and intellectual disability? Work: A Journal of Prevention, Assessment and Rehabilitation 32, 391–405 (2009)
13. Gómez, J., Montoro, G., Haya, P.A., Alamán, X., Alves, S., Martínez, M.: Adaptive manuals as assistive technology to support and train people with acquired brain injury in their daily life activities. Personal and Ubiquitous Computing, 1–10 (2012)
14. Brusilovsky, P.: Adaptive hypermedia. In: Kobsa, A. (ed.) User Modeling and User Adapted Interaction, Ten Year Anniversary Issue, vol. 11, pp. 87–110 (2001)
15. Kobsa, A.: Generic User Modeling Systems. In: Brusilovsky, P., Kobsa, A., Nejdl, W. (eds.) Adaptive Web 2007. LNCS, vol. 4321, pp. 136–154. Springer, Heidelberg (2007)
16. Martín, J.M., Ortigosa, A., Carro, R.M.: SentBuk: Sentiment analysis for e-learning environments. In: XIV Simposio Internacional de Informática Educativa (2012)
17. Ramirez-Esparza, N., Pennebaker, J., Garcia, F., Suria, R.: La psicología del uso de las palabras: Un programa de computadora que analiza textos en Español (The psychology of word use: A computer program that analyzes texts in Spanish). Revista Mexicana de Psicología 24, 85–99 (2007)
18. Zinck, A., Newen, A.: Classifying emotion: a developmental account. Synthese 161, 1–25 (2008)
19. Bueno, C., Rojo, J.A., Rodriguez, P.: An Experiment on Semantic Emotional Evaluation of Chats. In: 5th International Conference on Advances in Semantic Processing, pp. 116–121 (2011)
20. Rodriguez, P., Ortigosa, A., Carro, R.M.: Extracting Emotions from Texts in E-learning Environments. In: 2nd International Workshop on Adaptive Learning via Interactive, Collaborative and Emotional approaches (2012)

The Impact of Introducing Therapeutic Robots in Hospital's Organization

Cecilia Yu Chung Chang, Marta Díaz, and Cecilio Angulo*

CETpD. Centre Estudis Tecnòlogics atenció Dependència i Vida Autònoma
UPC. Universitat Politècnica de Catalunya · BarcelonaTech
08800 Vilanova i la Geltrú, Spain
ceciliayu.chung@alumni.esade.edu, {marta.diaz,cecilio.angulo}@upc.edu
http://www.upc.edu/cetpd

Abstract. The introduction of robots in health and wellbeing services could mean a great improvement in patients' life, but also implies a huge change in hospital's organization. This work introduces a empirical study that investigates the factors influencing the process of adoption of robots in hospitals. Interviews have been completed in a health organization leading this change. Learned lessons lead to define a balance of facilitators and barriers that should help to apply the innovation. This process has been completed from Kotter's leading change approach, since it would be the roadmap for the whole procedure.

Keywords: technological change, therapeutic robot, hospital.

1 Introduction

The introduction of robots in health and wellbeing services could mean a great improvement in users' life, and there is a great amount of investigation related to this topics. Their introduction implies a huge change not only in the patient's personal life, but also in the way doctors, nurses, therapists and psychologists work. The impact in the first group of people's life is clear and has been documented in several papers, but the impact of robotics in the workplace is not well stablished yet.

Craig Brod defines *technostress* [2] as "a modern disease of adaptation caused by an inability to cope with the new computer technologies in a healthy manner". It could happen in two types of people: the ones who do not want to accept computer technology, and the ones who over-identificates with it. This work introduces a empirical study that investigates the factors influencing the process of adoption of robots in hospitals. It expands the topic of robotics from a management - human resources point of view [7] by using Kotter's Leading Change theory [4]. Factors influencing this adaption/rejection are firstly studied based on interviews with professionals leading this change in a real institution (Kotter's approach was not employed), then facilitators and barriers are defined from learned lessons. Finally, some conclusions and future work lines are summarized.

* Research supported by the Spanish Ministry of Science and Education through the project SOFIA (TIN2011-28854-C03-01,03).

J. Bravo, R. Hervás, and M. Rodríguez (Eds.): IWAAL 2012, LNCS 7657, pp. 312–315, 2012.
© Springer-Verlag Berlin Heidelberg 2012

2   Introducing a Technological Change

It is reported in [5] that the introduction of computers in the workplace did have an effect of stress among 18% workers because of the need of learning a new skill. On the other hand, computers at work also contributed to make it more interesting, as 60% of the people stated. An even more curious figure is that only a 4% thought computers made work less interesting. Lessons learned from this kind of studies can be easily linked with the Kotter's theory about Leading Change [4]. Accordingly, a number of steps are recommended and required in order to manage changes and transformations in an organization: (1) Establish a sense of urgency; (2) Form a powerful guiding coalition; (3) Create a vision; (4) Communicate the vision; (5) Empower others to act on the vision; (6) Plan for and create short-term wins; (7) Consolidate improvements and produce more change; and (8) Institutionalize new approaches.

In order to apply the Kotter's theory to the introduction of robotics in hospitals, this study investigates the factors that could influence in its adaptation or rejection. Initial hypothesis will be set about facilitators and barriers to adopting robots in the organization [1], then they will be checked and revisited after having interviews with different profiles of professionals.

3   Methodology

For this study, information about introducing robotics in hospitals have been collected based on the Technology Adoption Model approach [3]. The main instruments used were interviews of 45 minutes long and semi-open questions on different topics related to the introduction of robotics in a hospital. Participants were professionals recruited from the Hospital Sant Joan de Déu (HSJD), Barcelona, Spain. Interviewed people were four: a doctor from the Research and Innovation Department; two professionals from the Psychology Department were also asked for support through interviews on their opinions towards the introduction of robots at their workplace; finally, a doctor of the Pediatric department was also interviewed.

3.1   Revisiting Facilitators and Barriers

Some phases were completed in the HSJD before starting experimentation with robots. In the first place, they read a lot about robotics therapeutic applications until they decided to give it a chance. Next, it was important to determine which kind of robot and what department of the hospital were going to be selected. Taking this consideration into account, robots were finally introduced in the Psychology department with the treatment of children with autism, cerebral deficit, and traumatism. In the Director of Innovation's words: "you look for open-minded people, we did not chose any department for using the robot, but the one we knew that would accep it". After three months and several sessions, the group of therapists and engineers were satisfied with the results: the robot became a source of motivation for the children, and it also became a catalyst of the relationships between these children, as they had a common interest.

Through the focus groups analyses, we concluded that professionals envisaged two conflicting perspectives: on the one hand, professionals would foster the use of robotics if they do feel it is useful and benefits patients. On the other hand, the perceived effort related to learning new skills and the fear of depersonalization in the professional-patient relationships leads people to refuse these new technologies. This is one reason why all new changes have to overtake a slower period of adaptation at the beginning, same as with products there is a group called "early adopters". Only those doctors and healthcare professionals who have seen it work before will feel safe and apply robotics with their patients; we can observe that the phase in which we are now is the "early adopters" one.

3.2   A Modified Balance of Facilitators and Barriers

Factors were finally grouped in: *Usefulness*, i.e., how likely the robot will really help the patient and his/her disease, though interviewed professionals agreed they did not expect robots to solve the whole problem. Robots can show emotions depending on their environment, so that they seem to be alive and create more engagement with the child, it is to say, robots enhance the sense of social presence.

Previous success is a second 'in favor' factor. It is important for doctors because it is a risk minimizer. It will be great help if doctors who have experience with robots would write reports or publish articles in specialized magazines so that the medical community would be more used to listen the word "robot" related to their business [6]. This would create a comfort around the topic, and would make inexperienced doctors easier to reach.

The third element is that organization's own *vision and values* are also critical in anticipating whether it is going to accept robots or not. Hospitals are, in the end, companies, so they have a vision and values that determine its personality.

On the other side, high *costs* attached to the implementation of robots and their maintenance could make managers and also doctors more reluctant to apply the new technology. This effect can be easily neutralized in the near future, as the utility will counter the costs, and the costs will be lower in any case.

The *effort needed* for learning new skills is a second adverse factor, because it can also back away the efforts. However, in the case of health practitioners, the lifelong training is naturally accepted as a professional requirement.

The third factor is the fear of *depersonalization* when using robots with patients. Many professionals guess that using robots will replace, at least in part, their daily visits and direct contact with patients. This barrier is probably the most difficult obstacle to overcome because it is not related to a tangible characteristic of robots, but an intangible idea that many people have in mind.

Finally, there is a lack of people who know about both healthcare and robotics fields. Hence, an implicit difficulty in the introduction of therapeutic robots is the joint work of healthcare professionals together with technicians. Even though the healthcare professional could use the robot, technician help might still be needed. A professional both, controlling the robot and studying the patients, is very likely to feel overwhelmed by the activity, as our interviewed psychologist manifested. This fact was initially ignored, as the study was more focused on how professionals should learn the skills needed to work with robots but forgot in part how difficult and important their actual work is.

4 Conclusions and Further Research

The introduction of robots in health and wellbeing institutions implies a huge change in these organizations. This work introduces a empirical study that investigates the factors influencing the process of adoption of robots in hospitals. Methodology to obtain this information includes interviews with professionals in a health organization leading this change, the HSJD. Learned lessons from early experiences lead to define a balance of facilitators and barriers thant should help to apply the innovation. This process has been completed from the Kotter's leading change approach. Since the institution is decided to apply therapeutic robots in its daily activity, further research includes to plan a roadmap for the whole procedure.

Acknowledgments. The authors appreciate the collaboration of the professionals interviewed from the Hospital Sant Joan de Déu.

References

1. BenMessaoud, C., Kharrazi, H., MacDorman, K.F.: Facilitators and barriers to adopting robotic-assisted surgery: Contextualizing the unified theory of acceptance and use of technology. PLoS ONE 6(1), e16395 (2011)
2. Brod, C.: Techno Stress: The Human Cost of the Computer Revolution. Addison-Wesley (1984)
3. Díaz, M., Català, A., Font, A., Narvaiza, L., Rodríguez-Molinero, A.: Factors influencing acceptability of ambulatory telemonitoring systems: A qualitative approach of physicians' views as end-users and prescriptors. Gerontechnology 7(2) (2008)
4. Kotter, J.P.: Leading Change: Why Transformation Efforts Fail. Harvard Business Review 37(3), 59–67 (1995)
5. Lin, Z., Popovic, A.: The effects of computers on workplace stress, job security and work interest in canada. Tech. rep., Applied Research Branch, Human Resources Development Canada (2002)
6. Lo, A.C., Guarino, P.D., Richards, L.G., Haselkorn, J.K., Wittenberg, G.F., Federman, D.G., Ringer, R.J., Wagner, T.H., Krebs, H.I., Volpe, B.T., Bever, C.T., Bravata, D.M., Duncan, P.W., Corn, B.H., Maffucci, A.D., Nadeau, S.E., Conroy, S.S., Powell, J.M., Huang, G.D., Peduzzi, P.: Robot-Assisted Therapy for Long-Term Upper-Limb Impairment after Stroke. New England Journal of Medicine 362(19), 1772–1783 (2010)
7. Senge, P., Kleiner, A., Roberts, C., Ross, R., Roth, G., Smith, B., Guman, E.C.: The dance of change: The challenges to sustaining momentum in learning organizations. Performance Improvement 38(5), 55–58 (1999), http://dx.doi.org/10.1002/pfi.4140380511

Evaluation of an Inclusive Smart Home Technology System

Judit Casacuberta[1], Fausto Sainz[2], and Jaisiel Madrid[2]

[1] CETpD Technical Centre for Dependency Care and Autonomous Living, Barcelona Tech
Neàpolis Rbla. Exposició, 59-69 08800 Vilanova i la Geltrú, España
[2] Fundosa Technosite S.A., Albazans, 16 3ª planta B1 28037 Madrid, España
{judit.casacuberta}@upc.edu,
{fsainz,jmadrid}@technosite.com

Abstract. A prototype for an accessible home control system was tested for usability and accessibility appropriateness. A comprehensive subjective user-centred design evaluation methodology was used to validate the system accessibility and usability. The paper makes a contribution in terms of validating the developed evaluation approach on one side and the perceived usefulness of system and devices on the other. It also provides information regarding devices and results from the evaluation of the interfaces.

Keywords: accessibility, multimodal interaction, ubiquitous interfaces.

1 Introduction

The main objective of the research presented in this paper was to develop an enabling technological environment that creates accessible and pervasive interaction and communication channels to be used by everyone, especially disabled and elderly people, thus helping to communicate with the surrounding devices and services. The project[1] objectives highlight the importance of technology becoming a tool to improve people's quality of life [1]. The system conveys the appropriate interface according to the user's functional capabilities and the device at use and allows multi-device access to the home automation arrangement. Thus this paper presents the results from the system evaluation phase where the interfaces where tested on different devices by a group of elderly people in a home simulated environment. Elderly people benefit more from ambient intelligent environments than mid-aged non-disabled people [2] testing the system with this group seems suitable. Human factors that influence the interaction with different household items, such as are trust [3] were explored during the evaluation stages. The prototype evaluated allowed the control of the different elements of the home such as: heating, lights, blinds and doors. The interface presents home's devices in the living room, bathroom, kitchen bedroom and outside. Inside

---

[1] Research supported by the Spanish CDTI's project INREDIS (CEN-2007-2011), under the INGENIO 2010 programme.

J. Bravo, R. Hervás, and M. Rodríguez (Eds.): IWAAL 2012, LNCS 7657, pp. 316–319, 2012.

each room the elements of the home are presented through icons, which indicate the operating condition of the elements (switch on/off).

2   Methodology and Evaluation

The evaluation methodology is based on the Extended Technology Acceptance Model [4] -based on Technology Acceptance Model [5] and *The Diffusion of Innovation* theory [6] - and People Lead Innovation referential [7], that includes the citizen in the innovation processes.

The validation of the home environment involved evaluating the home control and monitoring system as well as the devices to control the system, thus supporting the ideas of universal access. For each home system component (devices and interfaces) different dimensions were defined and adapted to evaluate the degree of technology acceptance, and the compliance degree with P.L.I.. Among these were usability indicators -efficiency, effectiveness, usefulness, safety, easy learning and retention [8]- as well as accessibility, information transmission, navigation, configuration, training, fitness requirements, ethics and privacy.

The information to asses the home control and monitoring system was gathered through questionnaires considering the following dimensions:

-    Technology acceptance: acceptance technology degree by users. Composed for: Perceived risk (PR), Cost (COS), Compatibility (COM), Perceived usefulness (PU), Perceived easy of use (PEU) and Behavioral intention to use (BIU)
-    Trust (T): degree to which a person perceives the system like a trust element,
-    Level of automation (LA): degree which a person perceives that have system control in order to level automation

The dimensiones adapted from the P.L.I. referential were: emotional approach (EA), functional ergonomics (FE), cognitive ergonomics (CE), familiarity (F), accesibility (A).

2.1   Tests

Twelve elderly people between 70 and 88 years of age (m=79.33) volunteered; three had previous experience in computer, two had previous experience in using internet and two participants had displacement problems and another one manipulation problems. Four devices were used: 1) a touchscreen mobile phone (iPhone), 2) a touchscreen tablet computer (iPad), 3) a touchscreen computer (Tobii P10 v2.4, 15 inches) and 4) a touchscreen computer (ASUS EeeTop ET1610PT and 15.6"). Users interacted with one portable and one fixed device. The platform allows users to know the status of such devices and to change them at will: it is possible to open or close a door remotely, or to know whether a light is on or off for a blind person. Experiments were carried out at the FEMPA home[2], divided in three fully equiped rooms, equiped with non-intrusive observation software: AXIS 212 PTZ-V camera. After training the following taks were performed: 1) project's system registration; 2) digital home tasks

---

[2] The Federation of Employers of the Metal from Alicante provided the metalTIC-digital home.

manipulation (manipulating home commodities), and 3) telecare tasks (consisinting on requesting, checking and canceling a doctor´s appointment). Quantitative and qualitative data was gathered: 1) Objective system performance variables through objectives (time and error measures) and subjective performance (questionnaire), 2) Users spontaneous comments and verbalizations 3) Observations and recording of participants behavior by experts, and 4) Assessment of system and control devices ease of use through questionnaires at different stages of the test protocol.

2.2   Results

Regarding effectiveness performance results with the iPad and Asus indicated that all users were able to perform the tasks, although sometimes only partially: the telecare use case tasks were successfully overcome by all participants using the iPad. On the other hand, performance results with the iPhone and Tobii indicate that all users have managed the registering task without difficulty. However only one user managed using the iPhone to partially complete the telecare task (request, view and cancel a doctor's appointment). A significant amount of difficulties caused by the device's functions were detected, rather than system problems. The task of controlling the home elements was completed successfully by 2 users and partially by 5.

In terms of behavior analysis it was observed a trend in older people not to assess negatively neither the devices nor the services, very few users suggested changes in the interface or the system even when they had important difficult during its use. Participants' comments showed that all "looks easy" but they "need to learn to use" better, so they self-perceived as people with little or nothing experience with the technology. Problems with the portable devices were detected: mainly with functionalities implemented on the browser –such as "copy" –, a traditional web interface element, like the URL box, unnecessary for the interface, disconcerted participants.

Table 1 shows the results from the device evaluation. Non-portables devices were better assessed confirming observations. Participants using iPad assessed appreciably better all dimensions evaluated than those using iPhone. Differences between participants using Tobii or normal touchscreen weren't significant. Regular Touchscreen was best assessed in emotional approach, which asked about the frustration, comfort and friendly interaction. Regarding cognitive ergonomics, about navigation and information distribution was the worst dimension assessed by those using Tobii.

Table 1. Results from Devices Questionnaire (1: "Strongly agree" , 5: "Strongly disagree")

	EA	FE	CE	F	A	Av.		EA	FE	CE	F	A	Av.
iPad	1.93	2.45	2.20	2.40	1.80	**2.16**	iPhone	2.33	2.36	2.29	2.19	2.24	**2.28**
ASUS	1.60	2.00	2.46	2.27	2.13	**2.09**	Tobii	1.81	2.21	2.53	2.21	1.9	**2.13**

The questionnarie about users perceptions on the home control and monitoring system results showed a correlation coefficient (r=-.058, p>0.05) between task completion rate and System Questionnaire, there isn't a relation between the level of satisfaction after using the system with the task completion rate: users perceived interaction with the system as satisfactory regardless of its effectiveness. In general results pointed at the cost (2.27) as a potential problem for the acquisiton of the tecnology, followed by compatibility (2.99), as some participants didn't perceive the system aproppiate to their needs. This results contradict the best assessed dimension: PU (1.93), which explored quality of life improvement. Even so, except for the COS dimension (2.27), there aren't other dimensions with values above 3 (neither agree nor disagree), so, as a whole, we can say that participants had a positive use experience.

3   Conclusions

The results pointed out at the benefits of a multi method approach when designing and testing the usability of inclusive systems and devices. It also signalled elderly people's acceptance of technology, and at economic concerns that hinder technology adoption. Assistive technology was seen as necessary in the future for those still able or presently for those with mobility problems. Users perceived the facilities as comfortable and adequate, accepting the technology experienced as a commodity by some participants and as necessary products and services by others. Verbalizations confirmed the perception of usefulness on the questionnaire and points at comfort and health issues as relevant concerns for this group. Users felt most confortable using the iPad and they express how conveninet was to be able to carry it around the house. The movile phone was not seen as easy to use as the tactile pad.

It would be interesting to think in a format that allows the spontaneous expression of negative or less candid comments, such as proposed by [9].

References

1. Freedman, V.A., Agree, E.M., Martin, L.G., Cornman, J.C.: Trends in the Use of Assistive Technology and Personal Care for Late-Life Disability, 1992–2001. The Gerontologist 46(1), 124–127 (2006)
2. Fellbaum, K.: The future: Communication in an ambient intelligence envi-ronment. Technology and Disability 20(2), 157–171 (2008)
3. Sandström, G.: Smart homes and user values: long term evaluation of IT-services in residential and single family dwellings. Doctoral Thesis (2009)
4. Wu, J.-H., Wang, S.-C.: What drives mobile commerce? An empirical evaluation of the revised technology acceptance model. Information & Management 42(5), 719–729 (2005)
5. Davis, F.D.: Perceived usefulness, perceived ease of use, and user acceptance of information technologies. MIS Quarterly 13(3), 319–334 (1989)
6. Rogers, E.M.: The diffusion of Innovation, 5th edn. Free Press, New York (2003)
7. I2BC, People Led Innovation. Reference of certification for solutions de-signed under the principles of technological effectiveness. I2BC Technical Report (2009)
8. ISO 9241-210:2010, Ergonomics of human-system interaction-Part 210: Human-centred design for interactive systems. ISO (2010)
9. Renaud, K., van Biljon, J.: Predicting technology Acceptance and adoption by the elderly: a qualitative study. In: Wilderness, S. A. (ed.) Proc. SAICSIT 2008, October 6-8, pp. 210–219 (2008)

Towards Ubiquitous User Modeling Interoperability for Dealing with Overweight and Obesity

María de Lourdes Guadalupe Martínez-Villaseñor[1,2] and Miguel González-Mendoza[2]

[1] Universidad Panamericana Campus México, Augusto Rodin 498,
Col. Insurgentes-Mixoac, México, D.F., México
[2] Instituto Tecnológico y de Estudios Superiores de Monterrey,
Carretera Lago de Guadalupe Km 2.5,
Atizapán de Zaragoza, Edo. de México, México
lmartine@up.edu.mx, mgonza@itesm.mx

Abstract. A major challenge for creating personalized diet and activity applications is to capture static, semi-static and dynamic information about a person in a user-friendly way. Sharing and reusing information between heterogeneous sources like social networking applications, personal health records, specialized applications for diet and exercise monitoring, and personal devices with attached sensors can achieve a better understanding of the user. But gathering distributed user information from heterogeneous sources and making sense of it to enable user model interoperability entails handling the semantic heterogeneity of the user models. In this paper we describe a flexible user modeling ontology to provide representation for a ubiquitous user model and a process of concept alignment for interoperability between heterogeneous sources to address the lack of interoperability between profile suppliers and consumers. We provide an example of how information of different profile suppliers can be used to enrich fitness applications and personalize web services.

Keywords: User modeling interoperability, ubiquitous user model, overweight and obesity, diet and exercise monitoring, web service personalization.

1 Introduction

According to the World Health Organization (WHO), overweight and obesity are serious public health challenges in the WHO European Region, and their prevalence is growing worldwide even in countries with low or middle income [1]. If a person consumes more calories than she/he expends, she/he will gain weight, resulting in overweight and obesity. Many personal factors must be taken into account when designing personal diet and exercise goals and plans. Basic demographic and anthropometric data, nutrition preferences, allergies and restrictions, medical conditions, activity patterns and preferences, cultural and religious factors, are some of them. In brief, static, semi-static and dynamic information is needed to succeed when develop personal goals and plans to deal with overweight and obesity.

J. Bravo, R. Hervás, and M. Rodríguez (Eds.): IWAAL 2012, LNCS 7657, pp. 320–328, 2012.
© Springer-Verlag Berlin Heidelberg 2012

Fitness applications and/or wearable personal training systems, provide training advice, encourage physical activity, and even try to change the user behavior with Web-based interventions. Nevertheless if the application is not used as intended, its effectiveness decreases [2]. Each application requires a lot of effort from the user to explicitly capturing some basic profile information, preferences and interests and daily records. Transferring data from personal devices that record activity with sensors is also needed. So a major challenge for creating personalized health applications is to gather the information needed for personalization in a user-friendly way avoiding repeated configurations.

People interact with social networking applications, semantic web technologies such as Friend of a Friend (FOAF), Personal Health Records (PHR) and personal gadgets. These are valuable sources of personal information that could be used to construct a ubiquitous user model and therefore a better understanding of the user. Sharing and reusing profile information from heterogeneous sources as those mentioned, can prevent the user from repeatedly capturing the same information in several applications and services; helps deal with "cold start" problem of new applications and services; and provides enrichment to existing user models. But gathering distributed user information from heterogeneous sources and making sense of it to enable user model interoperability entails handling the semantic heterogeneity of the user models [3]. In this paper, we address the lack of interoperability between heterogeneous sources. We describe a flexible user modeling ontology to provide representation for a ubiquitous user model and a process of concept alignment for interoperability between heterogeneous sources. User modeling interoperability facilitates the efficient use of fitness and health applications. We provide an example to illustrate how reusing and sharing profile information from heterogeneous sources can be done with the mediation of our ubiquitous user model and the process of concept alignment. In this example, we show how information of different profile suppliers can be used to enrich fitness applications and personalize web services.

The rest of the paper is organized as follows: in section 2 we present a short survey of the field of ubiquitous user modeling interoperability. We explain the U2MIO ontology and process of concept alignment for ubiquitous user model interoperability in section 3.We describe an example of sharing and reusing profile information in the scenario of dealing with overweight and obesity in section 4. In section 5 we briefly describe our demonstration and results. We conclude an outline our future work in 6.

2   Ubiquitous User Modeling Interoperability

From literature [4,5], we see that current research in ubiquitous user modeling has two major approaches: *(i) standardization based user modeling* based in semantic standardization of user model defining some common ontology and language; *(ii) mediation-based user modeling* using mediation techniques to build semantic bridges between representations.

In standardization-based user modeling approach, sharing and reusing user models is easier, but it requires all systems to adhere to a standardized ontology and representation [6-10]. Recently, it has become clear that developing a commonly accepted ontology to deal with sparseness of data and heterogeneity of sources in a multi-application environment is not a feasible solution.

The mediation approach consists in mapping different user model representation. Berkovsky et al.[4] explained that "Mediation deals with transferring user modeling data from one representation (for example, collaborative filtering) to another (for example, content based filtering) in the same domain, or across domains" Mediation can be done converting user models and integrating them into a single user model. This entails dealing with syntactic and semantic heterogeneity. We can mention [3,11] as representatives of this approach. The Generic User model Component (GUC) presented in [11] proposed to construct combined ontologies for exchanging user models between web-based systems. GUC allows the configuration of a distributed management of mappings between user models. The schema mappings were determined by a human and the possibility of automatic merging techniques was discussed but implemented requiring human effort. Carmagnola et al.[3] proposed a solution with high flexibility representing user models and providing semantic mapping of the user data from heterogeneous sources. However, to take part in the interoperability process every provider need to comply to a standard format for the exchange and maintain a sharable user model which includes the fragments of user model as RDF statements.

In summary, we need to provide a semantic representation of a ubiquitous user model that is not static in order to adapt itself to new profile suppliers and consumers, and we have to deal with semantic heterogeneity with the least intervention and effort of ubiquitous user modeling stakeholders.

3 Ontology and Process of Concept Alignment for Ubiquitous User Model Interoperability

In this section, we present an ontology based on Simple Knowledge Organization System (SKOS) [12] that provides semantic representation for a flexible ubiquitous user model. We also present a process of concept alignment that enables interoperability between profile suppliers/consumers and the ubiquitous user model by automatically defining semantic mappings. The user profile structure represented by the ontology is able to evolve over time because the process of concept alignment is capable of establish semantic mappings and determine if new skos:Concepts are to be added to the ontology. So we try to build a bridge between the two approaches described in 2 as suggested in [4,13] with a central ubiquitous user model that can adapt itself to changing multi-application environment, and a process of concept alignment that provides articulation between heterogeneous sources without any effort of profile suppliers or consumers. The ontology and process of concept alignment are part of a work-in-progress project of a user-adaptive system to share and reuse information from social networking applications, personal health records, FOAF and personal devices.

3.1 U2MIO Ontology

We briefly describe Ubiquitous User Modeling Interoperability Ontology (U2MIO) that:

- Provides semantic support for user model overcoming differences between concepts at knowledge level.
- Represents a flexible user profile structure, with domain independency which provides the possibility for the ubiquitous user model to evolve during time.
- Provides representation for new profile suppliers and consumers that take part in the interoperability process without effort of the provider or consumer system.

The ontology reuses SKOS ontology and it can be seen as an aggregation of concept schemes each one representing a profile supplier or consumer, and a central ubiquitous user model concept scheme. Semantic mapping relations are established between each supplier/consumer concept scheme and the ubiquitous user model concept scheme at concept level by the process of concept alignment in order to enable interoperability between user models.

The ubiquitous user modeling ontology was set-up with Facebook, FOAF, and one profile of a specialized web application to monitor person's diet and physical activity of one user. This demands the design of four concept schemes, one for each profile provider and the ubiquitous user model concept scheme.   Semantic mapping relations were established with SKOS properties. We used Protégé ontology Editor for the set-up process. A detailed description of U2MIO is given in [14].

3.2 Process of Concept Alignment

The interrelations between profile supplier/consumer and U2MIO are shown in figure 1. The adaptive system mentioned in section 3, deals with providers' transfer mechanisms and obtains sources documents *(sd)* in XML, JSON or RDF. If the source is new to the system, a corresponding skos:ConceptScheme *(C)* is designed and added to U2MIO. The process of concept alignment automatically determines semantic mappings for each source concept with the best suited concept in the ubiquitous user model concept scheme *(u2m)*. New skos:Concepts and skos:Collections can be added to *u2m* resulting of rule based decisions made by the process of alignment. A web service is considered as profile consumer in figure 1, since semantic mapping can also be found between the preferred values of Web services request and the *u2m* best suited concepts.

The process of concept alignment is based in a two-tier matching strategy. First an element level matching step finds a set of concept candidates for alignment for each concept in the source concept scheme. This task is performed combining three types of similarity measures: a) String similarity based in Dice [15] b) A simple distance of longest substring c) semantic similarity based on WordNet [16]. From this step in which we analyze the word similarity between each concept in the source with all concepts in *u2m*, we find a set of best suited concepts for alignment (or one best suited concept) in the target *(u2m)*. Next, the method looks for structure similarity.

The goal in the structure level matching step is to disambiguate the meaning of the word analyzing its context, this means analyzing the structure and meaning of the neighbor concepts in the same source document. In this step, the similarity between the neighbor concepts in the source and the neighbors of the best suited concept(s) in the target are calculated. After this step, a set of IF THEN rules are applied to determine one-to-one semantic mappings and recommendations of concept and collection additions. The process of concept alignment is described in detail in [17].

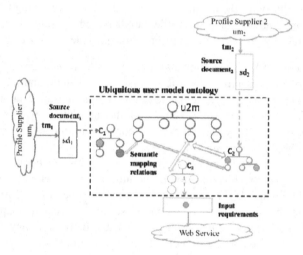

Fig. 1. Interrelations between profile supplier/consumer and the ubiquitous user modeling ontology

4   Application Scenarios

When trying to facilitate the use of devices and applications that help dealing with overweight and obesity, user modeling interoperability between multi-applications is very valuable. Information needed to build diet and/or exercise personalized plans and/or interventions is often scattered in different applications and devices. Sensors attached, or not, to personal gadgets have an important role in the collection of data about physical activity and training sessions. The data recollected with these devices can be transferred to its corresponding application, but interoperability between similar applications is painful or impossible. We provide an example to illustrate how the concept of reusing and sharing information in multiple user models can be done with the mediation of our ubiquitous user model and the process of concept alignment. We present a scenario where the user usually has to endure the pain of repeatedly setting new web applications explicitly capturing some basic demographic data and downloading again the valuable data of many training sessions, captured by some wearable devices that are not always compatible with the new web application.

4.1   Information Needed to Help Dealing with Overweight and Obesity

In order to help dealing with overweight and obesity, it is necessary to obtain user information of different nature in content, frequency of observation and measurement, and means of collection. Essential profile data needed to monitor overweight and obesity of a person are anthropometric indicators: Body Mass Index (BMI), waist circumference, height and weight. These parameters should be complemented with vital signs monitoring according to medical suggestions. Information about daily calorie intake and calorie burned in physical activity is also essential for checking the daily calorie balance. Other useful data when designing diet and activity goals and plans are basic demographic data, information about nutrition like allergies, food preferences and restrictions, and information about physical activity like disabilities, activity preferences and restrictions. Personal choices of food and activity are also influenced by cultural factors, religious beliefs, family structure and economic situation as well as for medical requirements and health status. It is very difficult from one application or service to gather a complete personal profile. Sharing these profile information can increase the success of a good diet or activity plan, because they contribute significantly to personalization and user-friendly usage. Table 1 shows possible sources where information can be extracted to deal with overweight and obesity.

Table 1. Sources of profile information to control overweight and obesity

Source	Data	Format
Social Networks	Basic demographic data (gender, religious believes, age, etc.), preferences and interests in sports and food.	JSON/XML
Personal Health Records (PHR)	Information about medical conditions, allergies, suggested diet, contraindications, vital signs, weight, goals.	XML
Specialized health sites and web applications to monitor a person's diet and physical activity	Daily activity records, calorie consumption and food diaries and corresponding summaries by period	XML
FOAF	Basic demographic data, interests.	RDF
Sensors attached or not to personal gadgets and mobile devices	Observations and results of physical activity and training session, fitness data and vital signs, burned calories.	XML

Each supplier has its own particular means, methods and policies that enable user profile data harvesting. If a system wants to gather this information, it has to deal with every transfer mechanisms, but it is always possible to obtain an XML, JSON or RDF document.

4.2   Example of Reusing and Sharing User Profile Information

Example: A user, considered as an active social network user, has already a fair populated user profile in some social network application. She/he is interested in improving her physical performance and getting fit. She/he has been using provider 'A' web application with the compatible wearing devices to monitor her/his progress. She/he has already configured the web site and bought compatible wearable and uploading devices. In spite of having the same information in her social network user profiles, she had to explicitly give some of this information again in web application 'A'. The same user has heard that provider 'B' web application has interesting services to monitor training sessions and nutrition software, and she wants to try them out. The drawback is the time she has to spend in explicitly setting some basic demographic data again and upload her training sessions again, with the inherent possible problems of device incompatibility with the new web application.

5   Demonstration and Results

For our demonstration we considered the integration of the training sessions of provider 'A', in this case the training sessions gathered with a Polar RS300X watch in addition with a Polar S1 foot pod, to the ubiquitous user model. Then we try to reuse some of the information of this profile supplier to personalize a Web service of provider 'B', in this case LogWeight Web Service from Training peaks [18]. In this manner, we show that enrichment of fitness applications is possible as well as web service personalization with our proposed solution. The outcomes of our experiments were the following: if an equivalent concept existed in the ubiquitous user model, the process was able to determine the exact match and homonyms were disambiguated; the concepts with very specific labels were added to the ubiquitous user model and the labels with in which the sense was not possible to determine were discarded. The process successfully found the correct data from the $u2m$ to populate the preferred values of the Web service. These results are encouraging but further research must be done because we cannot be sure that the values of exact match concepts are interchangeable without transformation. We also need to validate if the new concepts added were really necessary and essential to our purposes.

6   Conclusions and Future Work

We presented the U2MIO ontology that provides a dynamic representation for the ubiquitous user model and the process of concept alignment that could find the best suited concepts for alignment and established one-to-one semantic mappings. Recommendations of concept addition to the $u2m$ were given by the concept alignment in order to permit the evolution of the U2MIO ontology. We show that our solution can be used to allow the interoperability between fitness applications and web service request parameters can be populated from heterogeneous sources profile information. These results are encouraging but further experimentation and validation of the proposed approach is needed. We are planning intensive design of experiments with focus groups of various domains.

References

1. World Health Organization Regional Office for Europe. The challenge of obesity in the WHO European Region and the strategies for response for response, http://www.euro.who.int/document/E90711.pdf (accessed on June 24, 2012)
2. Kelders, S.M., Van Gemert-Pijnen, J.E., Werkman, A., Nijland, N., Seydel, E.R.: Effectiveness of a Web-based Intervention Aimed at Healthy Dietary and Physical Activity Behavior: A Randomized Controlled Trial About Users and Usage. J. Med. Internet Res. 13(2), e32 (2011)
3. Carmagnola, F.: Handling Semantic Heterogeneity in Interoperable Distributed User Models. In: Kuflik, T., Berkovsky, S., Carmagnola, F., Heckmann, D., Krüger, A. (eds.) Advances in Ubiquitous User Modelling. LNCS, vol. 5830, pp. 20–36. Springer, Heidelberg (2009)
4. Berkovsky, S., Heckmann, D., Kuflik, T.: Addressing Challenges of Ubiquitous User Modeling: Between Mediation and Semantic Integration. In: Kuflik, T., Berkovsky, S., Carmagnola, F., Heckmann, D., Krüger, A. (eds.) Advances in Ubiquitous User Modelling. LNCS, vol. 5830, pp. 1–19. Springer, Heidelberg (2009)
5. Viviani, M., Bennani, N., Egyed-zsigmond, E., Liris, I.: A Survey on User Modeling in Multi-Application Environments. In: Third International Conference on Advances in Human-Oriented and Personalized Mechanisms, Technologies and Services, pp. 111–116 (2010)
6. Heckmann, D.: Ubiquitous User Modeling. PhD thesis, Department of Computer Science, Saarland University, Germany (2005)
7. Kay, J., Kummerfeld, B., Lauder, P.: Managing Private User Models and Shared Personas. In: Proceedings of the Workshop on UM for Ubiquitous Computing, Pittsburgh, PA (2003)
8. Razmerita, L., Angehrn, A., Maedche, A.: Ontology-based user modeling for knowledge management systems. In: Brusilovsky, P., Corbett, A.T., de Rosis, F. (eds.) UM 2003. LNCS, vol. 2702, pp. 213–217. Springer, Heidelberg (2003)
9. Dolog, P., Schäfer, M.: A Framework for Browsing, Manipulating and Maintaining Interoperable Learner Profiles. In: Ardissono, L., Brna, P., Mitrović, A. (eds.) UM 2005. LNCS (LNAI), vol. 3538, pp. 397–401. Springer, Heidelberg (2005)
10. Mehta, B., Niederée, C., Stewart, A., Degemmis, M., Lops, P., Semeraro, G.: Ontologically-Enriched Unified User Modeling for Cross-System Personalization. In: Ardissono, L., Brna, P., Mitrović, A. (eds.) UM 2005. LNCS (LNAI), vol. 3538, pp. 119–123. Springer, Heidelberg (2005)
11. Van Der Sluijs, K., Houben, G.: A generic component for exchanging user models between web-based systems. International Journal of Continuing Engineering Education and Life-Long Learning 16(1/2), 64–76 (2006)
12. Miles, A., Pérez-Agüera, J.: SKOS: Simple Knowledge Organization for the Web. Cataloging & Classification Quarterly 43(3), 69–83 (2007)
13. Kuflik, T.: Semantically-enhanced user models mediation: Research agenda. In: Workshop on Ubiquitous User Modeling, in International Intelligent User Interface Conference, IUI 2008 (2008)
14. Martinez-Villaseñor, L., González-Mendoza, M.: Towards a Ontology for Ubiquitous User Modeling Interoperability. In: Proceedings of 4th International Conference on Knowledge Engineering and Ontology Development, Barcelona, Spain, October 4-7 (2012)
15. Dice, L.R.: Measures of the amount of ecologic association between species. Ecology 26, 297–300 (1945)

16. Fellbaum, C.: WordNet and wordnets. In: Brown, K. et al. (eds.) Encyclopedia of Language and Linguistics, 2 edn., pp. 665–670. Elsevier, Oxford (2005)
17. Martinez-Villaseñor, L., González-Mendoza, M., Gress-Hernández, N.: Towards a Ubiquitous User Model for Profile Sharing and Reuse. Sensors 12, 13249–13283 (2012)
18. Training Peaks LoGWeight Web Service,
    http://www.trainingpeaks.com/tpwebservices/
    service.asmx?op=LogWeight (accessed on: June 13th, 2012)

TURAMBAR: An Approach to Deal with Uncertainty in Semantic Environments*

David Ausín, Federico Castanedo, and Diego López-de-Ipiña

Deusto Institute of Technology, DeustoTech. University of Deusto,
Avda. Universidades 24. 48007 Bilbao, Spain
{david.ausin,fcastanedo,dipina}@deusto.es
http://www.morelab.deusto.es/

Abstract. Research community has shown a great interest in OWL on-tologies as a context modeling tool for semantic environments. OWL ontologies are characterized by its expressive power and are based on description logics. However, they have limitations when dealing with un-certainty and vagueness knowledge. To overcome these caveats, some approaches have been proposed. This work presents a novel approach to deal with uncertainty in semantic environments, called TURAMBAR.

1 Introduction

In Ambient Intelligence applications (AmI), context, could be defined as any data which can be employed to describe the state of an entity (an user, a rele-vant object, the location, etc) [1]. OWL ontologies are one of the most popular, employed and recommended ways to model context [2]. Several AmI projects model the context with ontologies, such as SOUPA[3], CONON[4] or CoDAMoS [5], to name a few.

However, previous approaches are not flexible enough to deal with inaccurate or incomplete information. Vagueness and uncertainty management has become a hot topic in AmI research. Several approaches have been tried to cope with this kind of uncertainties. Different approaches can be classified into probabilis-tic theory, possibilistic theory or fuzzy theory. But none of them has obtained enough popularity to turn them into an standard or common approach. So, it seems to be enough room for research and advance in this direction.

In this work, we present a novel approach that will try to combine OWL 2 expressibility and reasoning power with uncertainty through the use of Bayesian Networks with the goal to overcome well-known limitations of OWL. The aim of this work is to determine the main features that the framework will have and to explain some of the implementations options.

The structure of this article is as follows. The next section provides an overview of OWL Web Ontology Language and is relationship to Description logics. Be-sides, it includes a brief description of some OWL reasoners. Then section 3 gives

---

* This work is supported by the Spanish MICINN project TALIS+ENGINE (TIN2010-20510-C04-03).

J. Bravo, R. Hervás, and M. Rodríguez (Eds.): IWAAL 2012, LNCS 7657, pp. 329–337, 2012.
© Springer-Verlag Berlin Heidelberg 2012

a brief description of the OWL limitations and some of the proposed solutions. Section 4 describes the TURAMBAR proposal in the current initial state and some benefits. Finally, section 5 summarizes this work.

2   A Brief Introduction to OWL

The OWL Web Ontology Language, or simply OWL, was designed for representing knowledge by the World Wide Web Consortium (W3C). The current version of OWL, OWL 2 [6] was published in 2004. OWL 2 allows ontology engineers to describe the domain of an application. An advantage of modelling the knowledge with OWL 2 is that new knowledge can be inferred from the explicit knowledge, thanks to the use of semantic reasoners. However, OWL 2 does not specify how the inference is realized and only the correct answer is predetermined by the formal semantics. There are two versions of formal semantics: the Direct Semantics [7] and the RDF-Based Semantics [8]. The latter is a semantic extension of "D-Entailment". The former is based on Description Logics (DL) and it is in which we are interested on.

DL provides a formal logic-based semantics and the ability of reasoning as its most important features [9]. The more expressive a logic is, the more complex the reasoning process is. Due to this fact, there are several languages which try to balance the complexity of the inference and the expressive power. Under the direct semantics, OWL 2 can be viewed as an extension to the semantics of $\mathcal{SROIQ}$ [10]. The most remarkable features which are included in OWL and not in $\mathcal{SROIQ}$ are support for data types and punning.

However, there are some cases in which the efficiency of reasoning is more important than expressiveness. For those cases, OWL 2 *profiles* have been created. OWL 2 *profiles* establish expressive restrictions in order to guarantee an scalable reasoning. OWL 2 specification defines the following three *profiles* [11]: OWL 2 EL, OWL 2 QL and OWL 2 RL.

Ontology statements are called axioms and they are divided in the following three groups: (i) *ABox* are axioms which encode information about named individuals, (ii) *TBox* consists on axioms which define the terminology and (iii) *RBox* are axioms which describe relationship between roles.

An important characteristic of OWL, is that it follows the open world assumption. This means that if a fact is not explicitly stated, it is impossible to determine its truthfulness, in contrast to the closed world assumption in which every fact which are not explicitly defined as true are false.

2.1   OWL Reasoners

This subsection describes two of the most famous and widely employed OWL reasoners: HermiT and Pellet.

HermiT [12] is a description reasoner for $\mathcal{SROIQ}$, it is distributed under the terms of LGPL which can be accessed through OWLlink or OWL API. The main difference against other reasoners is the employed reasoning algorithm, which is based on the hypertableau calculus algorithm[13].

HermiT supports DL Safe SWRL rules, but it does not include built-in implementations. Therefore, rules that call built-in atoms can not be executed under HermiT.

Pellet [14] is an OWL 2 reasoner for Java under dual license terms: AGPLv3 for open source projects and a special one for closed source applications. Pellet can be accessed through Jena, OWL API or OWLlink.

It uses a a tableaux algorithm which is able to handle $\mathcal{SROIQ}(D)$ logic and includes several optimizations such as back-jumping, simplification or absorption. Pellet has also techniques for incremental reasoning, such as incremental consistency checking and incremental classification. Besides, it implements DL-Safe SWRL rules support. All the built-ins for SWRL rules described in [15] are provided, with the exceptions of built-ins for *List* and some built-ins for *date*, *time* and *duration*. Anyway, custom built-ins can be developed and registered into the reasoner in order to be called from SWRL rules.

3   Main Limitations of OWL

However, OWL is not perfect and has some limitations such as the management of uncertainty and vagueness [16] which have been tried to overcome by several approaches as we show below.

An uncertain statement is a statement which is true or false, but due to the lack of information it is no possible to ensure its value. In contrast to uncertainty, vagueness defines a statement which is true to a certain grade.

In general, modelled application domains contains uncertainty, vagueness or both at the same time. To cope with uncertainty, there are two popular approaches: the possibilistic theory and the probabilistic theory. *Possibilistic theory* define the possibility of an event as the most likely case in which the event occurs. In contrast, in *probabilistic theory* the probability of an event is the amount of favourable case in which an event occurs. Typical reasons which enforce developers to use uncertainty comes by: the requirement to determine the overlapping between classes of different ontologies, information retrieval tasks, handling inconsistency in ontologies or imprecise information about the context. On the other hand, vagueness describes the statement degree of truth. For scenarios in which vagueness is presented, fuzzy logic is usually applied. It has been applied for information retrieval, in medical domain or describing subjective context, to name a few.

Some approaches have appeared to solve these drawbacks, being the most important (grouped by category) the following ones:

– Probability based approaches to overcome OWL limitations
  BayesOWL [17]: translates OWL ontologies into a Bayesian Network acyclic graph. The translation process has two steps. First, a set of rules are applied to create the Bayesian Network. Then the conditional probability tables are calculated, applying the decomposed iterative proportional fitting procedure (D-IPFP) algorithm. BayesOWL can represent two different types of probabilities: (i) prior or marginal probability and (ii) conditional probability.

Pronto [18]: is a probabilistic OWL reasoner with P-$\mathcal{SHIQ(D)}$ logic support. Pronto allows to encode conditional constrains about TBox and ABox and they are expressed as OWL 2 annotations. One of its goals is to be an alternative to Bayesian approaches. Currently, Pronto's development is not completed and its performance is not quite good.

- Possibility based approaches to overcome OWL limitations

  PossDL [19]: is a possibilistic description logic reasoner. PossDL extends Pellet adding uncertainty reasoning. This reasoner relies on Pellet and OWL API [20].

- Fuzzy logics based approaches to overcome OWL limitations

  fuzzyDL [21]: is a description logic reasoner which supports fuzzy logic and fuzzy rough set reasoning. It includes support for "Zadeh semantics" and Lukasiewicz Logic.

  DeLorean [22]: is a fuzzy rough description logic reasoner, which is able to convert a fuzzy rough ontology into a OWL or OWL 2 ontology. Pellet reasoner, HermiT reasoner or any reasoner which supports OWLlink protocol can be employed with DeLorean.

4   TURAMBAR Approach

OWL follows the open world assumption, which defines that a non asserted fact is unknown. However, we believe that sometimes is possible to determine the probability that a fact were true via the relationships and influences that other facts have on this. So, TURAMBAR's main goal is to offer a mechanism to predict the probability that an unknown fact was true under certain conditions.

TURAMBAR proposes to enrich OWL 2 reasoning with a probabilistic extension to deal with uncertainty. To achieve this we pretend to extend the OWL API, adding new methods which allow developers to perform queries about facts which are uncertain. Developers could choose between using traditional reasoning services or extended probabilistic services to answer queries. In other words, TURAMBAR adds a new layer to current description reasoners, such as Pellet, enhancing them with new capabilities to cope with uncertainty via Bayesian Networks. A Bayesian Network is a graphical model that is defined as a directed acyclic graph. The nodes in the model represent the random variables and the edges define the dependencies between the random variables. Each variable is conditionally independent of its non descendants given the value of its parents. They offer a simple solution to describe the relationships between facts and how they influence each other.

In our approach, probability axioms are added via OWL 2 annotations. OWL 2 annotations offers an straightforward, cleaned way to add uncertainty to the ontology. The main advantage of annotations is that they offer an standard mechanism to add extra information about an axiom. Also, Bayesian Networks will be described by annotations.

The next example (1.1) aims to illustrate the advantages of this approach. It models a smart home which contains several sensors which detect user's activity and the location of the activity. In this example, we have defined the existing relationship between the probability of an individual classified as *EatingAction* which can be classified also as a subclass of it. As shown the figure 1, an individual which is a subclass of *EatingAction* is influenced by the time and place in which the action took place. The complete ontology of this example can be seen below.

Listing 1.1. Example of an ontology with probabilistic knowledge employed in TU-RAMBAR

```
Declaration(Class(p0:Action))
Declaration(Class(p0:Bathroom))
SubClassOf(p0:Bathroom  p0:Location)
Declaration(Class(p0:Bedroom))
SubClassOf(p0:Bedroom  p0:Location)
Declaration(Class(p0:BreakfastAction))
SubClassOf(p0:BreakfastAction  p0:EatingAction)
Declaration(Class(p0:DinnerAction))
SubClassOf(p0:DinnerAction  p0:EatingAction)
Declaration(Class(p0:EatingAction))
AnnotationAssertion(p0:talismanClassProbability
p0:EatingAction
"ID:  EatingAction
InitGraph
Time -> this;
Location -> this;
EndGraph
p0.BreakfastAction  :
0.125, 0.1, 0, 0, 0.9, 0.9, 0.6, 0, 0, 0, 0, 0;
p0.LunchAction  :
0, 0, 0, 0, 0, 0, 0, 0, 0.27, 0.2, 0.1, 0 ;
p0.DinnerAction  :
0.125, 0.1, 0, 0, 0, 0, 0, 0, 0.27, 0.2, 0.1, 0;
p0.SnackingAction:
0.75, 0.8, 1, 1, 0.1, 0.1, 0.4, 1, 0.45, 0.6, 0.8, 1;")
SubClassOf(p0:EatingAction p0:Action)
Declaration(Class(p0:Kitchen))
SubClassOf(p0:Kitchen  p0:Location)
Declaration(Class(p0:LaunchAction))
SubClassOf(p0:LaunchAction  p0:EatingAction)
Declaration(Class(p0:LivingRoom))
SubClassOf(p0:LivingRoom  p0:Location)
Declaration(Class(p0:Location))
Declaration(Class(p0:SnackingAction))
SubClassOf(p0:SnackingAction  p0:EatingAction)
Declaration(ObjectProperty(p0:atLocation))
AnnotationAssertion(p0:talismanPropertyProbability
p0:atLocation
"ID:  Location
p0.Kitchen  :    0.33;
p0.Bedroom  :  0.41;
p0.LivingRoom  :  0.166;
p0.Bathroom  :  0.083;")
FunctionalObjectProperty(p0:atLocation)
ObjectPropertyDomain(p0:atLocation p0:Action)
ObjectPropertyRange(p0:atLocation p0:Location)
Declaration(DataProperty(p0:time))
AnnotationAssertion(p0:talismanPropertyProbability
p0:time "ID: Time
>= 0 && <= 28800 : 0.333;
>= 28800 &&  <=57600 : 0.333;
>= 57600 && <= 86400 : 0.333;")
FunctionalDataProperty(p0:time)
```

```
DataPropertyDomain(p0:time p0:Action)
DataPropertyRange(p0:time xsd:double)
Declaration(AnnotationProperty(
p0:talismanClassProbability))
Declaration(AnnotationProperty(
p0:talismanPropertyProbability))
```

In the previous example, if a developer was interested to find out the kind of meal that a user is having, he would query the reasoner about the specific action. Then, two different options could take place. One of them is when the activity is correctly classified as a subclass of *EatingAction*. In this case, the developer does not have to employ the probabilistic extension because traditional reasoning (using first-order logic) is enough. However, if the activity is not classified as a subclass due to a lack of information (second case), the developer can be able to query TURAMBAR probabilistic extension to obtain the odds that the action was a *DinnerAction*, *BreakfastAction*, *SnackingAction* or *LaunchAction*. To answer the probabilistic query, a Bayesian Network and their corresponding conditional probability distributions must be defined (as shown in figure 1). In other words, TURAMBAR can run as an OWL reasoner or as uncertainty reasoner depending on the developer needs.

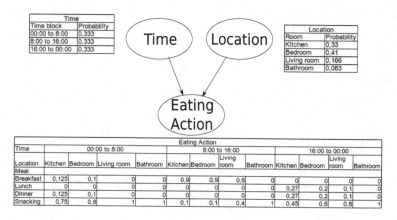

Fig. 1. An example of TURAMBAR Bayesian Network and their corresponding conditional probabilities tables

Constraints probabilities can be given in the ontology by the ontologist engineer or by the domain expert and will be updated according to historical data.

Two OWL annotations has been defined to describe an axiom probability: (i) *talismanPropertyProbability* and (ii) *talismanClassProbability*. The first one states the probability that an OWL individual with a property x has the value y. On the other hand, *talismanClassProbability* states the probability of an OWL individual which is classified as a member of a class x was also a member of its subclasses. Both annotations can be used to build a probabilistic graph which define the probabilities of an axiom. The annotation content is divided in three parts: (a) the identification, (b) the probabilistic graph definition and (c) the conditional probability distribution. The identification is the first line of a annotation and is mandatory. The probabilistic graph is defined between *InitGraph* and *EndGraph* tags and is optional. Each line between these tags describes a dependency between two variables. As an example, the *EatingAction* dependencies shown in figure 1 are modeled in this way:

```
Time -> this;
Location -> this;
```

In the example, the keyword *this* is used instead of *EatingAction* id to identify an *EatingAction* variable and its definition must appear before the conditional probability distributions. Lastly, the conditional probability distribution section is mandatory. It is possible to define a probability for a specific value or for a value range (only available for data properties whose ranges are numerics). When the variable depends on several variables, probabilities are expressed regarding to their graph description order. For example, in the previous graph definition, the probability of being an *EatingAction* and also a *BreakfastAction* is described as "*p0.BreakfastAction : 0.125, 0.1, 0, 0, 0.9, 0.9, 0.6, 0, 0, 0, 0, 0;*".

Another feature that TURAMBAR will offer is the creation of rules combining the probabilistic knowledge with the description logic knowledge. The idea behind this feature is to create a set of custom built-ins which can be called from SWRL rules. These features are not available in the previous probabilistic reasoners described. Among the different OWL reasoners, we honestly though that Pellet is the best one to be extended with a probabilistic layer. Besides, it offer a friendly own API interface to developers, the OWL API is chosen. This decision is based on experimental results from previous works [23] [24], where Pellet and OWL API combination has demonstrated to be a good choice to perform a fast reasoning.

One difference between TURAMBAR and BayesOWL is that variables are not binary constrained. In contrast to BayesOWL, TURAMBAR needs that the Bayesian Networks are defined, because it does not rely on the class hierarchy and its restrictions to determine the network and classify the concept. Instead, TURAMBAR assumes that there are relationships between individuals and their properties whose values may influence the probability of the existence of an assumption which has not been able to infer using traditional reasoning service. So, TURAMBAR not only could be used to classify instances, but it could also be used to predict if an individual has a property with a determined value.

5   Conclusion

In this work we present the initial state of a new probabilistic approach to handle uncertainty in AmI environments. The proposed approach combines OWL 2 reasoning with Bayesian Networks to offer new reasoning capabilities to the developers of AmI applications. One of the main advantages comes from its complementary behaviour with OWL 2 reasoning instead of replacing it. Besides, it proposes to extend a very well known API for developers (OWL API) with Bayesian Networks to complement OWL reasoning with probabilistic capabilities.

References

1. Dey, A.: Understanding and using context. Per. and ub. comp. 5(1), 4–7 (2001)
2. Strang, T., Linnhoff-Popien, C.: A context modeling survey (2004)
3. Chen, H., Perich, F., Finin, T., Joshi, A.: Soupa: Standard ontology for ubiquitous and pervasive applications. In: IEEE MOBIQUITOUS 2004, pp. 258–267 (2004)
4. Wang, X., Zhang, D., Gu, T., Pung, H.: Ontology based context modeling and reasoning using owl. In: Proceedings of the Second IEEE Annual Conference on Pervasive Computing and Communications Workshops, pp. 18–22 (2004)
5. Preuveneers, D., Van den Bergh, J., Wagelaar, D., Georges, A., Rigole, P., Clerckx, T., Berbers, Y., Coninx, K., Jonckers, V., De Bosschere, K.: Towards an Extensible Context Ontology for Ambient Intelligence. In: Markopoulos, P., Eggen, B., Aarts, E., Crowley, J.L. (eds.) EUSAI 2004. LNCS, vol. 3295, pp. 148–159. Springer, Heidelberg (2004)
6. Krötzsch, M., et al: OWL 2 web ontology language primer. Technical report, W3C (October 2009)
7. Patel-Schneider, P.F., Motik, B., Grau, B.C.: OWL 2 web ontology language direct semantics. W3C recommendation, W3C (October 2009)
8. Schneider, M.: OWL 2 web ontology language RDF-based semantics. W3C recommendation, W3C (October 2009)
9. Baader, F., Nutt, W.: Basic Description Logics. In: The Description Logic Handbook. Cambridge University Press (2002)
10. Horrocks, I., et al.: The even more irresistible sroiq. In: Knowledge Reasoning, 57–67 (2006)
11. Motik, B., et al.: OWL 2 web ontology language profiles. W3C recommendation, W3C (October 2009)
12. Shearer, R., Motik, B., Horrocks, I.: Hermit: A highly-efficient owl reasoner. In: Proc. of the 5th International Workshop on OWL: Experiences and Directions (OWLED), pp. 26–27 (2008)
13. Baumgartner, P., Furbach, U., Niemelä, I.: Hyper tableaux. In: Logics in Artificial Intelligence, pp. 1–17 (1996)
14. Sirin, E., et al.: Pellet: A practical owl-dl reasoner. Web Semantics: Science, Services and Agents on the WWW 5(2), 51–53 (2007)
15. Horrocks, I., et al: Swrl: A semantic web rule language combining owl and ruleml, 2004. W3C Submission (2006)
16. Lukasiewicz, T., Straccia, U.: Managing uncertainty and vagueness in description logics for the semantic web. Web Semantics: Science, Services and Agents on the WWW 6(4), 291–308 (2008)
17. Ding, Z., Peng, Y., Pan, R.: Bayesowl: Uncertainty modeling in semantic web ontologies. In: Soft Computing in Ontologies and Semantic Web, pp. 3–29 (2006)
18. Klinov, P., Parsia, B.: Pronto: Probabilistic ontological modeling in the semantic web. In: Proc. of International Semantic Web Conference, Posters Demos (2008)
19. Qi, G., Ji, Q., Pan, J.Z., Du, J.: PossDL — A Possibilistic DL Reasoner for Uncertainty Reasoning and Inconsistency Handling. In: Aroyo, L., Antoniou, G., Hyvönen, E., ten Teije, A., Stuckenschmidt, H., Cabral, L., Tudorache, T. (eds.) ESWC 2010, Part II. LNCS, vol. 6089, pp. 416–420. Springer, Heidelberg (2010)
20. Horridge, M., Bechhofer, S.: The owl api: a java api for working with owl 2 ontologies (2009)

21. Bobillo, F., Straccia, U.: fuzzydl: An expressive fuzzy description logic reasoner. In: IEEE Int. Conf. on Fuzzy Systems, pp. 923–930. IEEE (2008)
22. Bobillo, F., et al.: Delorean: A reasoner for fuzzy owl 2, 423 (2008)
23. Ausín, D., Castanedo, F., López-de Ipiña, D.: Benchmarking results of semantic reasoners applied to an ambient assisted living environment. In: ICOST
24. Ausín, D., Castanedo, F., López-de Ipiña, D.: On the measurement of semantic reasoners in ambient assisted living environments. In: IS (2012)

Intervention Tailoring in AAL Systems
for Elders with Dementia Using Ontologies

René F. Navarro[1], Marcela D. Rodríguez[1,2], and Jesús Favela[1]

[1] Computer Science Department, CICESE Research Center, Ensenada, Mexico
{rnavarro,favela}@cicese.edu.mx
[2] Computer Engineering School, UABC, Mexicali, Mexico
marcerod@uabc.edu.mx

Abstract. We present an approach for personalizing non-pharmacological interventions for people with dementia (PwD) using ontologies. A successful intervention requires an individualized approach that considers the evolving needs
of the PwD and the the caregiver. Person-centred models of dementia care focus
on addressing individual needs and emotional reactions. From an in situ intervention with persons suffering with Alzheimer's, we derived an ontological
model to allow an Ambient Augmented Memory System (AAMS) to personalize the planning and execution of interventions to address problematic
behaviors. Through an application scenario, we illustrate the flexibility of the
ontology to provide the AAMS system with contextual information to personalize an intervention to assist PwD who have problems recalling their medication.

Keywords: ambient assisted living, ontology, dementia, context awareness.

1   Introduction

Alzheimer's Disease (AD) is characterized by the loss of intellectual functions to the
extent that it interferes with daily activities. Disorientation in time and an impairment
of executive functions are also observed from the early stages of the disease [10]. For
the person with AD, memory difficulties can have a major impact on self-confidence
and can lead to withdrawal from activities, anxiety, and depression. Family caregivers
are also affected due to the practical impact of memory problems on everyday life and
to the strain of frustration that can result from it [15]. There is a growing agreement
that AD treatment should include non-pharmacological interventions to ameliorate
challenging behaviors. Interventions with a cognitive focus are frequently used parallel with approaches emphasizing the stimulation of the senses. For instance, reality
orientation (RO) aims to help people with memory loss and disorientation by reminding them of facts about themselves and their environment [4].

   We developed an Ambient Augmented Memory System (AAMS) to assist elders
with early AD by augmenting awareness of people, places and things with additional
information [12]. The system is inspired in RO interventions, and proposes the use of

J. Bravo, R. Hervás, and M. Rodríguez (Eds.): IWAAL 2012, LNCS 7657, pp. 338–345, 2012.

different electronic devices as external memory aids, to deliver useful information to reduce the burden of problematic behaviors in AD patients and their caregivers.

We extended the AAMS with an ontology of problematic behaviors derived from an intervention with 3 pairs of PwD and caregiver. With the ontology, the AAMS can be adapted to support problematic behaviors that are frequent for a particular PwD.

2   Caring for People with Dementia

People with dementia (PwD) need a great deal of support and assistance, and this need increases as the disease progresses. It is recognized that a number of common non-cognitive symptoms (challenging behaviors, neuropsychiatric symptoms of dementia NPS) are distressful not only for the PwD, but also for their caregivers. Behavioral and psychological symptoms of dementia (BPSD) include agitation, depression, repetitive behaviors, and aggressive behavior directed towards caregivers [13]. Repetitive questioning (RQ), whereby a person asks the same question over and over again to their caregiver, along with amnesic behaviors, have been reported as the most common complaint by family of persons with AD [7].

Interventions to address BPSD may include both pharmacological and non-pharmacological interventions (NPI). However, the effects of some classes of medications are generally modest and have severe side effects, which highlight the need for NPI alternatives for these symptoms [10,11]. NPI have been classified as [13]: a) cognitive/emotion-oriented (e.g. reality orientation, reminiscence therapy, simulated presence therapy); b) sensory stimulation (e.g. aromatherapy, light therapy, music therapy); c) behavior management techniques; and d) other psychosocial interventions such as animal-assisted therapy and exercise. A successful intervention needs to be based on person-centred models by addressing individual needs, emotional reactions, differences in progression and severity of symptoms [13]. Therefore, it is important to tailor the intervention to the specific circumstances of the persons with dementia, their caregivers, and their environment [4,10].

Reality orientation (RO) involves consistent use of orientation devices such as signposts, whiteboards, cards, and other external memory aids (EMA) [4]. Training PwD to use EMA, has shown a positive effect on memory related problems and repetitive behaviors [2]. The frequency of repeated verbalizations is decreased when caregivers are trained to direct PwD to read a memory book page (or written message on a memo board, or index card) when they asked a question repeatedly. Additionally, caregivers have expressed satisfaction with both their ability to redirect the person to an AME that answered the question, and the speed with which the person learned to use the AME independently [2,3].

3   A Field Study to Understand the Use of External Memory Aids

We are conducting a field study to evaluate in situ the usability and effectiveness of external memory aids. In this study participants are patient-caregiver dyads living in the same home. Inclusion criteria for the participants are persons over 65 years, living in their home, diagnosed in the early stages of AD (MMSE score 10-24), and manifestation of at least two BPSD (screening via Neuropsychiatric Inventory Questionnaire and the Revised Memory and Behavior Problems Checklist). Caregivers complete the Zarit Burden Interview to assess the distress caused by patient´s problematic behaviors. In the first phase of the study, participants are trained in the use of RO to address different challenging behaviors. To personalize the intervention we conducted a preliminary interview in which the caregiver completes two surveys: a) Personal Wants, Needs and Safety Assessment Form, and b) Memory Aid Information Form (Biographical information). During four weeks, caregivers are required to implement this interventions using traditional EMA (e.g. whiteboards, calendars, index cards), and to keep a diary of BPSD using a mobile phone logging application. We present two scenarios derived from interviews with the participants to illustrate the diversity of problematic behaviors that concern the caregivers.

Scenario 1: *Julia prepares breakfast for her mother Maria as she usually does every morning. Over the last two years, after suffering a diabetic coma, Maria's memory has deteriorated. Julia's main concern is that due to her diabetes and hypertension, her mother needs to take 7 different medications at different times of the day, and she has difficulties following her medication regime. After breakfast, Julia administers 30ml of insulin and asks her mother to take her medication for her pressure. Maria goes out of the kitchen and comes back asking Julia for her medication. She tells her that they are on her bedside table, and continues cooking since she needs to finish before going to work. Ten minutes later, Julia comes out of the kitchen and finds Maria, with a sad demeanor, sitting on the sofa in the living room. She asks her mother if she took her medication, to which she responds that she could not find them.*

Scenario 2: *Frida, a 82-year old women who was diagnosed with Alzheimer's five years ago (MMSE=10), watches TV on her living room with Rosa, a retired nurse who cares for her during the day. Suddenly, Frida walks to her room and starts taking cloth out of her closet. Rosa comes in, realizes that she is putting her cloth on a suitcase, and asks Frida why she is doing this. Frida replies that it is getting late and she needs to get back home. Rosa tells her that she is home, and that she is currently at her house, but Frida insists that her home is in another city, where she used to live 30 years ago. After several minutes discussing the issue, Rosa convinces Frida to stop trying to leave home by showing her some family photographs.*

For each of these scenarios there are several approaches and special circumstances to ponder before the caregiver applies a particular intervention. Subsequent stages of the study require the introduction of the AAMS in the participants' home. We propose a mechanism to allow the caregiver to apply a more suitable intervention according to the actual context, and considering previous interventions.

4 An Ambient Augmented Memory Systems

We developed an Ambient Augmented Memory System (AAMS) to leverage on the pervasiveness of technologies for augmenting awareness of people, places and things with additional information, in order to assist elders with early AD [12]. Our hypothesis is that providing situation awareness in an accessible manner can decrease stress in patients with AD and their caregivers. For PwD, having contextual external memory aids at hand provides them reassurance in ADLs, knowing they have a safety net of useful information to understand their environment and the support of their caregiver. For caregivers, allowing the elder to access the required information on their own may decrease the burden imposed by some BSPD.

The system implementation is based on two main components: AnswerBoard and AnswerPad. AnswerBoard is a public ambient display implemented with a touch screen LCD computer. Located in a common area within the PwD's home, it provides information of the person's activities for the current day, the current date, and time of day. Reminder messages are displayed on the AnswerBoard to prompt the patient on relevant events on his agenda, such medication. The caregiver may create reminder notes from scratch or select one of the predefined templates completing the required information. Through the AnswerBoard the caregiver adds activities and appointments to the patient's agenda. From a predefined set of events and activities, caregiver may select the one that fits her purpose and drag it to the elder's agenda.

AnswerPad is an application running on an Android mobile phone with touch screen. It includes different widgets aiming to offer the PwD time and place awareness, reminder notes, cues on his/her current activity, and to maintain the connection with his/her social network. Using an InCense [14] application AnswerPad recollects data from the mobile phone's sensors to feed the context engine. Additionally, caregivers may use AnswerPad to manage elder's daily activities, keep track of his/her whereabouts, create reminder notes, and keep a diary of patient's behavior using an application. The diary application uses RFID tags to record incidents of BPSD via the NFC reader in the mobile phone. For each incident, the caregiver completes a three-item survey to document the degree of burden imposed by this behavior, the perceived degree of affectation, and the specific signs shown by the patient. Figure 1 shows the architecture of the AAMS.

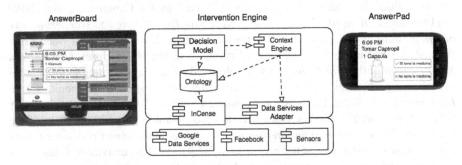

Fig. 1. AAMS Architecture and applications

Figure 1 also represents the Intervention Engine, which is a logical representation of the main components that support the functionalities of the AnswerPad and AnswerBoard. For instance, the InCense application, which is executed on the mobile phone, and other components that collaborate to tailor and suggest interventions for the PwD. These components are explained in the following sections.

5   Ontology-Based Ambient Assisted Intervention

An ontology is a formal representation of a set of concepts within a domain and the relationships between those concepts which can be used to reason about the properties of that domain [6]. Figure 2 shows the ontology we propose to represent the knowledge within the domain of BSPD and non-pharmacological interventions.

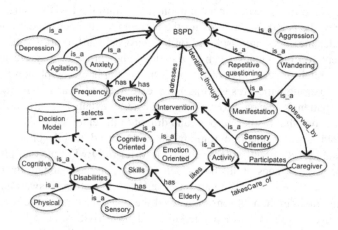

Fig. 2. Non-Pharmacological Interventions Ontology

5.1   Ontology for Problematic Behaviors and Interventions

The ontology represents the types of *BSPD* that a cognitive impaired elder may present, such as *Depression*, *Aggression*, *Agitation*, and *Wandering*. These can be identified through different *Manifestations* observed by the Caregiver. Some *BSPD* can be *Manifestations* of other *BSPD*, e.g. *Repetitive Questioning* and *Wandering* may be *Manifestations* of *Anxiety*. For instance, in Scenario 2, Rosa observed when Frida suddenly walked to her room and started taking cloth out of her closet, which was a *Manifestation* of the *Wandering* behavior observed by Rosa. According to the ontology, when a problematic behavior is identified by the *Caregiver*, she should use an *Intervention*, which can be based on *Cognitive Oriented*, *Emotion Oriented*, *Sensory Oriented*, or *Activities* that the elder likes to do or is able to do with the help of the *Caregiver*. Thus, Rosa used an *Intervention* consisting on showing Frida some family photographs since it is one of her preferred *Activities*. As Rosa convinced Frida of not trying to leave home by proposing her to do this activity, then this Intervention can be rated as successful.

The ontology also represents the *Burden* of the *Caregiver*, the *Frequency* of the *BSPD* and its *Severity*. That is, how much it emotionally distressed the *Caregiver*, how often it has occurred and how much it disturbed the older adult, respectively. The abovementioned are concepts that describe how seriousness was an elder's *BSPD*, which along with information regarding the elder's *Disabilities* and lost *Skills* can be used by a *Decision Model* to suggest an *Intervention* to the *Caregiver*. For example, in Scenario 1, Maria has lost *Skills* for following instructions to adhere to her complex medication regimen. This is a situation that moderately Distress Julia. A *Decision Model* may use this information to suggest Maria a *Cognitive Oriented* (e.g. external memory aids). Similarly, in Scenario 2, based on the fact that an Intervention, based on showing family photos to Frida was previously successful, the *Decision Model* may suggest to use this same *Intervention* to Rosa when future incidents of *Wandering* be present.

5.2   Intervention Tailoring

The ontology supports the tailoring of the AAMS services in two phases of its deployment: i) customizing the AAMS services for a PwD before deployment, and ii) providing a timely and adequate intervention when the caregiver is using the system.

Tailoring the AAMS Services for the Patient

For explaining this type of tailoring we revisit Scenario 1. Thus, to tailor the AAMS services for assisting Maria, we create an ontology instance with the information gathered from her caregiver in the preliminary survey and assessment instruments. For instance, the ontology initially describes the presence of Maria's amnesic behavior (BPSD), and that she usually (*Frequency*) is not able to follow her medication regime, which severely distresses (*Burden*) Julia. It also describes that Maria's Cognitive Disability is characterized by an MMSE=21 and that she has visual impairment (*Skills*). Based on this information, and along with the caregiver, we decide what interventions should be initially provided by the system by configuring the Intervention Engine components. That is, we register on the ontology a descriptor of the intervention to use based on providing medication memory aids through the AnswerPad. Then, we used the widgets provided by the Data Services Adapter to configure the set of medication notes that will be displayed on the AnswerBoard, and we made adaptation on colors, text and icons presented in the reminder and added audible prompts. Thus, the Decision Model, based on the ontology, will suggest using this intervention until the elders and caregiver conditions change (i.e the ontology content change).

Context-Based Tailoring of the Intervention

During the deployment, instances of the ontology are populated by integrating data from different sources (e.g. Internal system logs, incidents logged by the caregiver using AnswerPad), which allows the AAMS to access the PwD behavioral changes for intervention tailoring. To reach this end, the Intervention Engine uses the ontology, along with the contextual information collected through the AnswerPad logging application. Thus, the Intervention Engine recommends an intervention to apply based on information of previous manifestations of BPSD, current manifestations, and information on the actual context.

In order to illustrate how the AAMS works, we continue describing scenario 1. It is 7:00 hrs and the AnswerPad prompts a reminder. Maria looks at the reminder and goes to the kitchen where Julia is preparing breakfast. "It's time to take my insulin" she says. Julia administers the insulin, and asks her mother to take her medication for her pressure. Maria goes out of the kitchen and comes back asking Julia "Where is the *captopril*?". She tells her that it is on her bedside table. Since this has never happened before, using AnswerPad diary application, she registers the incident. Then, the ontology represents a new instance of the amnesic behavior with descriptors that depict the manifested problematic behavior, i.e. the information or instruction that Maria forget to follow. Afterwards the AnswerPad asks Julia if she would like a suggestion for an appropriate Intervention. Julia replies affirmatively. The AAMS looks up in the Intervention Engine (IE) for a suitable intervention for an amnesic behavior. The IE using the ontology and a rule based decision model, suggests her to create a reminder note. Julia decides to create one and goes to her mother's bedroom. Using AnswerPad she creates a new reminder taking a picture of the bedside table and adding the text "Captropil is at my bedside". Thus, if in the future Maria needs to know where her medication is, she may use this reminder.

6   Related Work

Several ontology-based architectures for specific domains have been proposed, which are of particular interest for our project. For instance, with the aim of enhancing the effectiveness of therapeutic treatments for persons with cognitive problems, the SOAD ontology captures the agitation experienced by PwD and the contextual conditions that have to be met to provide different intervention options, such as music therapy [7]. Similarly, the Mout Framework provides an ontology for modeling the treatment of persons with mental disorders (e.g. depression). A rule-based reasoning uses this ontology to identify the services that patients and professionals need to establish an online session for Cognitive behaviour therapy (CBT) [9]. On the other side, Biswas et al [1] proposes an ontology to provide assistance services to PwD through different devices; i.e. an instance of the ontology is needed to interface a device (e.g. IPTV, and mobile devices) with the assistance service. These works emphasize the utility of using ontologies to enable the adaptation of assistance systems according to contextual conditions. Thus, these works motivated us to design an ontology to enable the two levels of adaptation that we identified as relevant for facilitating the deployment of ambient assisted intervention systems.

7   Conclusions and Future Work

In this paper we propose an ontological representation model for problematic behaviors to personalize non-pharmacological interventions provided through AAMS services. We have already tailored the AAMS to be deployed in the home of the participants described in scenario 1. According to the caregiver, with the paper-based intervention the PwD is now much more engaged in activities of daily living, and spends more time awake during the day attending her memory aids. We plan to evaluate the effectiveness of the AAMS system with 3 dyads of PwD and caregivers during 8 weeks. Future work includes the implementation of a decision model to support the above-mentioned tailoring phases, since actual decision model is rule based which may not be suitable for reasoning about these complex behaviors which are characterized by contextual variables which are highly dynamic (i.e the distress of the caregiver may increase, or new BSPD manifestations may emerge). Therefore, we are considering using a Partially Observable Markov Decision Process (POMDP) [8].

References

1. Biswas, J., Mokhtari, M., Dong, J.S., Yap, P.: Mild Dementia Care at Home – Integrating Activity Monitoring, User Interface Plasticity and Scenario Verification. In: Lee, Y., Bien, Z.Z., Mokhtari, M., Kim, J.T., Park, M., Kim, J., Lee, H., Khalil, I. (eds.) ICOST 2010. LNCS, vol. 6159, pp. 160–170. Springer, Heidelberg (2010)
2. Bourgeois, M.S., et al.: A comparison of training strategies to enhance use of external aids by persons with dementia. Journal of Communication Disorders 36(5), 361–378 (2003)
3. Clare, L., Woods, R.T.: Cognitive training and cognitive rehabilitation for people with early-stage Alzheimer's disease: A review. Neuropsychological Rehabilitation 14(4), 385–401 (2004)
4. Douglas, S.: Non-pharmacological interventions in dementia. Advances in Psychiatric Treatment 10(3), 171–177 (2004)
5. Foo, V.S., et al.: An Ontology-based Context Model in Monitoring and Handling Agitation Behaviour for Persons with Dementia. In: Proc. of the International Conference on Pervasive Computing and Communications Workshops, Washington, DC, USA, 560
6. Gruber, T.R.: Toward principles for the design of ontologies used for knowledge sharing. International Journal of Human-Computer Studies 43(5-6), 907–928 (1993)
7. Hawkey, K., et al.: Requirements gathering with alzheimer's patients and caregivers. In: Proc. Assets 2005, pp. 142–149. ACM Press, Baltimore (2005)
8. Hoey, J., Yang, X., Quintana, E., Favela, J.: LaCasa: Location And Context-Aware Safety Assistant. In: Proc. Intl. Conf. on Pervasive Healthcare, San Diego (May 2012)
9. Hu, B., et al.: Ontology-based ubiquitous monitoring and treatment against depression. Wirel. Commun. Mob. Comput 10, 1303–1319 (2010)
10. Jalbert, J.J., et al.: Dementia of the Alzheimer Type. Epidemiologic Reviews 30(1), 15–34 (2008)
11. Mebane-Sims, I.: 2009 Alzheimer's Disease Facts and Figures. Alzheimer's and Dementia 5(3), 234–270 (2009)
12. Navarro, R., Favela, J., García-Peña, C.: An Ambient Augmented Memory System to Provide Situation Awareness to Elders with Early Alzheimer's Disease, In. In: Proc. of International Workshop of Ambient Assisted Living, IWAAL 2010, Valencia, Spain, pp. 25–34 (2010)
13. O'Neil, M., et al.: Non-pharmacological Interventions for Behavioral Symptoms of Dementia: A Systematic Review of the Evidence. VA-ESP Project #05-225 (2011)
14. Perez, M., Castro, L., Favela, J.: InCense: A Research Kit to Facilitate Behavioral Data Gathering from Populations of Mobile Phone Users. In: Proc. UCAmI, Cancun, Mexico, pp. 25–34 (2011)
15. Topo, P.: Technology Studies to Meet the Needs of People With Dementia and Their Caregivers: A Literature Review. Journal of Applied Gerontology 28(1), 5–37

Linguistic Description of Human Activity Based on Mobile Phone's Accelerometers

Daniel Sanchez-Valdes, Luka Eciolaza, and Gracian Trivino

European Centre for Soft Computing (ECSC)
Mieres, Asturias, Spain
{daniel.sanchezv,luka.eciolaza,gracian.trivino}@softcomputing.es

Abstract. Monitoring the physical activity of a person is used for many applications such as medical assistance, personal security, etc. We use the accelerometers embedded in current mobile phones to identify the physical activities and generate periodical linguistic reports which describe relevant information about the activities carried out, their intensities and trends. Based on the Computational Theory of Perceptions, we have developed an application able to generate these linguistic descriptions, presenting a simple demonstration of our contribution in this field.

Keywords: Linguistic summarization, Computing with perceptions.

1 Introduction

Activity recognition has captured the attention of several computer science communities due to its strength in providing personalized support for many different applications and its connection to many different fields of study such as medicine, human-computer interaction, or sociology.

Monitoring the body posture and the physical activity of a person can be useful for applications such as medical assistance, trying to identify falls or abnormalities in the course of daily activity. Until recently, the evaluation of a patient's health outside a doctor's office has been limited to questionnaires which were hindered by memory and patients' subjectivity. New technological devices are now providing information which was previously impossible to attain. Continuous health monitoring of a patient could lead to faster and better diagnosis of problems. It could also be used to gauge patient's progress during rehabilitation where medicines and physical treatments could be better controlled.

Using three axial accelerometers in order to recognize the body posture and activities of a person is a well-known area of study. The analysis of the personal physical activities is used to assess the health of a subject, taking into account that walking gives a good indication of the energy expenditure of an individual. However, so far the use of accelerometers has been limited to a lab setting and could not be used in continuous health monitoring.

In this paper, we analyze the physical activities performed by people along a period of time, typically one day, only by taking acceleration data from their mobile phones. Nowadays common use devices, such as mobile phones, allow

J. Bravo, R. Hervás, and M. Rodríguez (Eds.): IWAAL 2012, LNCS 7657, pp. 346–353, 2012.

acquiring data from a patient in an inexpensive way. The sensors embedded to these devices are very accurate, easy to use and non-intrusive for the patients.

We use natural language (NL) to describe patterns emerging in data by means of linguistic expressions, choosing the most adequate granularity degree in each circumstances, in the same way that humans describe their perceptions. Linguistic Description of Data (LDD) is intended in general for applications in which there is a strong human-machine interaction involving accessing and understanding data. Therefore, it is well suited for activity recognition and description purposes.

Fuzzy logic (FL) [1] and the Computational Theory Perceptions (CTP) [2] are the basic theories of our LDD approach. FL is widely recognized for its ability in linguistic concept modeling. FL evolved to CTP, which provides a framework to implement computational systems with the capacity of computing with the meaning of NL expressions, i.e. with the capacity of computing with imprecise descriptions of the world in a similar way that humans do it. In previous works [3][4][5][6], we have developed the architecture to implement CTP for the linguistic descriptions of complex phenomena.

This paper describes how to apply our approach for linguistic description of complex phenomena to recognize and report the daily physical activities of a person. We correctly identify activities as important as walking, standing, sitting, walking upstairs and walking downstairs. In addition, knowing the quantity of time spent in each activity, we can approximately calculate the user caloric expenditure.

This paper is organized as follows. Section 2 describes the architecture of a system able to create linguistic descriptions of phenomena while section 3 explains how to apply it in the field of activity recognition. Afterwards, section 4 shows the experimentation and validation carried out. Finally, section 5 provides some concluding remarks.

2   Architecture

The main processing modules of this computational system are, namely, the *Data Acquisition (DAQ) module*, the *Validity module*, and the *Expression module*.

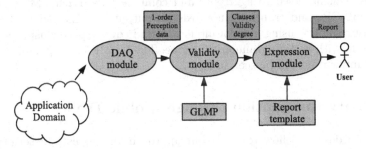

Fig. 1. Main components of the proposed computational system for linguistic description of data

Fig. 1 shows the architecture used for automatic report generation in the application case presented in this paper. The *DAQ module* could include either sensors or access to database information, representing the interface with the physical environment. This module provides the data needed to feed up the *Validity module*, which uses the linguistic model (GLMP) to generate a collection of linguistic sentences of the phenomenon with associated validity degrees.

Finally, the *Expression module* will combine all the information to choose the adequate linguistic clauses, in order to build a final linguistic report customized to the user's needs.

2.1   Granular Linguistic Model of a Phenomenon (GLMP)

The kernel of the report generator is the *Granular Linguistic Model of a Phenomenon* (GLMP). The designer creates the GLMP as a representation of his/her own perceptions of the monitored phenomenon, organized in several granularity levels.

A GLMP represents our approach to implement CTP [2] [7] [8] to linguistically describe phenomena. This approach represents any type of phenomena, describing its characteristics linguistically. These linguistic variables can be inter-related and the GLMP has to be designed attending to the questions that we want to answer. The linguistic description of a phenomenon evolving in time will have a big number of valid sentences. Each individual sample will represent a picture of the current state of the phenomenon and it will have associated sentences describing it linguistically.

Some of our previous works [3][4][5][6], show detailed definitions of the GLMP. These papers show examples such as the evaluation and descriptions of driving quality in simulators, the description of relevant features of the Mars' surface from satellite images, and the description of the traffic evolution in roads.

The main element of this structure is known as Computational Perception (CP), which is defined by the couple $(A, W) = \{(a_1, w_1), (a_2, w_2), \ldots, (a_n, w_n)\}$. A represents the set of NL sentences that linguistically describes the perception (i.e.: *"Walking speed is {slow | normal | fast}".*), and $W \in [0, 1]$ are the validity degrees of each sentence.

On the other hand, the GLMP is a network of Perception Mappings (PM), which are elements used to aggregate and combine CPs. Each PM receives a set of input CPs and transmits upwards an output CP. Each output CP is explained by the PM using a set of input CPs and covers specific aspects of the phenomenon with certain granularity degree. The GLMP corresponding to the practical application can be seen in Fig. 2.

3   Activity Recognition through Mobile Device

This section describes how to apply our approach for linguistic description of complex phenomena to the daily physical activities identification of a person. The relevant modules needed to produce the linguistic report are explained.

3.1 DAQ Module

To identify and report the daily physical activities of a person we have used the triaxial accelerometers embedded in current mobile phones. In particular, we have used *Android* based mobile phones as platform because it is a free and open-source operating system, easy to program. Acceleration data was acquired and stored by an Android application that we have created to run on these devices. Through our application we can control what data is collected as well as how frequently it is done (typically, 50 samples per second). The main idea of this acquisition process is that data are easily obtained and it does not represent an intrusive wearable device for the user. Since mobiles are not always in a fixed position and it is sometimes important to identify in which position the user is, in this paper, we have limited the analysis to the case that the mobile is placed into the trousers pocket. The mobile orientation can be determined using the accelerations module and the azimuth angle.

3.2 Validity Module

In our approach we analyze the accelerations produced in person's daily routine activities, such as walking, standing, sitting, etc. We also approximately calculate the caloric expenditure of each activity carried out. The application output consists of a linguistic summary report with all the relevant features of each daily activity.

Fig. 2 shows the GLMP designed to summarize and highlight the relevant aspects of the physical activities. It is based on first, second and top order CPs that linguistically describe different aspects of the physical activities, and PMs that aggregate and combine them.

The execution of the GLMP and the aggregation rules in its PMs generate the validity degrees of each CP at every instant. Table 1 shows the list of all the CPs used in our application.

Table 1. Table of CPs with the corresponding linguistic variables and labels

CP (y)	Linguistic Variables	Linguistic Labels (A_y)
$1 - CP_{Phi}$	Azimuth angle variance	{*small, big*}
$1 - CP_{MY'}$	Mean y'	{*low, high*}
$1 - CP_{Var}$	Variance y'	{*low, medium, high*}
$1 - CP_{MZ'}$	Mean z'	{*low, high*}
$2 - CP_S$	Initial State (Detect Azimuth step variations)	{*state 1, state 2*}
$2 - CP_{S1}$	State 1	{*sitting, standing*}
$2 - CP_{S2}$	State 2	{*sitting, traveling, standing, moving while standing*}
$2 - CP_U$	Up state	{*walking, going upstairs, going downstairs*}
$2 - CP_{S2_S}$ & $2 - CP_{U_S}$	Summary CPs	{*short time, some time, rather long time, too much time*} & corresponding labels
$2 - CP_{WS}$	Walking Speed	{*slow, normal, fast*}

At first, some mathematical operations were performed to calculate some relevant magnitudes needed as GLMP inputs. These inputs are represented as Z_1, Z_2, Z_3, Z_4, Z_5 and Z_6:

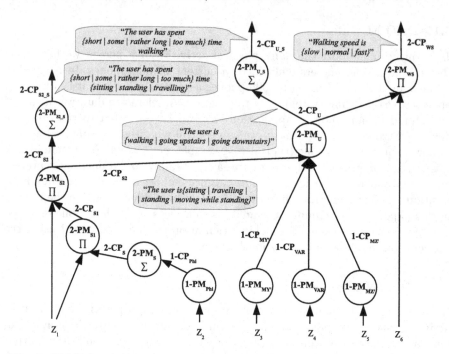

Fig. 2. GLMP for the linguistic description of the physical activities identification

Accelerations Module (AM) (Z_6) and Its Variance (Z_1): is calculated using the Pythagorean summing of the three axes values: $AM = \sqrt{x^2 + y^2 + z^2}$.

Azimuth Variance (Z_2): The polar coordinates and the azimuth are used in order to identify relevant changes in mobile orientation and determine mobile's flat and upright positions.

Accelerations y (Z_3, Variance Z_4) and z (Z_5) in terms of user axes (y' and z'): Once the flat and upright states of the mobiles are distinguished, the accelerations can be transformed into user axes (global coordinate axes).

The validity degrees of the first order perceptions (1-PM) which describe the sensor information ($Z_1, \ldots, Z_6$) are obtained by means of a set of uniformly distributed trapezoidal membership functions, forming strong fuzzy partitions.

The validity degrees of the second order perceptions (2-PM) are calculated by combining or aggregating the information of their input CPs. The symbol Π corresponds to combination functions based on fuzzy IF-THEN rules. The symbol Σ represents the aggregation of 2-PMs, where the validity of the quantified sentences have been computed using the α-cuts method proposed by [9].

3.3   Expression Module

Apart from the goal of obtaining suitable texts to be showed to users, the linguistic reports can be used by therapists with the aim of understanding physical changes, rehabilitation evolutions, patients' habits of life and so on.

The developed application provides two different types of linguistic description reports: a daily report that linguistically and graphically describes the physical activities, their duration and intensity throughout the day, and a periodical report that summarizes physical activity trends throughout a specific period of time (typically one week). In both cases it has been applied basic report templates. See in [5] an example of template that change the structure of the report depending on the validity degrees of the sentences.

The Expression module has the goal of answering the main questions that an expert want to know when he/she is going to design and elaborate a treatment program or giving medical assessment. The GLMP has to be capable to provide to the *Expression module* the information that it needs to answer these questions.

4   Experimentation

In order to validate the accuracy of the developed system we believed advisable to perform a series of test by contrasting the real activity sequences with the application output ones.

The first experiment consisted of developing 10 tests of approximately one hour. For each test, one user recorded the accelerations produced by his/her mobile phone and took note of the activities performed during the session (normal or routine activities were carried out, no specific ones). The matching between the performed and reported activities allows us to know the accuracy of the application in this task.

Table 2 shows the results of the experiment. First columns shows the name and times of the recorded sessions. Second columns counts the number of activities performed in each session. Columns 3 and 4 present the number of correctly and incorrectly classified activities respectively. Last column shows the percentage of time the activity identification is correct during the test. The percentage error calculation penalizes not only the fact of misclassification of an activity but also the amount of time this classification is wrong.

Table 2. Validation experiments and classification results

Test names & duration	Num. of activities	Correctly classified activities	Misclassified activities	% of time correctly classified
T-1 (58')	10	10	1 (1')	98.28
T-2 (96')	9	9	0	100
T-3 (45')	7	7	1 (1')	97.77
T-4 (65')	8	8	0	100
T-5 (58')	11	10	1 (1')	98.28
T-6 (40')	11	11	0	100
T-7 (63')	8	8	0	100
T-8 (48')	5	5	0	100
T-9 (38')	7	7	0	100
T-10 (63')	9	8	1 (1')	98.41

The average of correct classifications was equal to **99.27%**, which means a very high accuracy. Incorrectly classified activities typically corresponds to minor mistakes, mostly produced by strange accelerations or movements existing in the

Table 3. Example of validation experiment. Activities performed vs. Activities reported.

List of Performed Activities	Linguistic Report of Activities
"Start application with mobile phone on a table"	*"19:00 - 19:18 Out (✓)"*
"Introduce mobile into the pocket and stand for a few minutes"	*"19:18 - 19:19 Standing (✓)"*
"Walk some minutes at home"	*"19:19 - 19:21 Walking (✓)"*
"Go downstairs to the garage"	*"19:21 - 19:21 Down stairs (✓)"*
"Walk to the car"	*"19:21 - 19:22 Walking (✓)"*
"Stand beside the car keeping some things"	*"19:22 - 19:23 Standing (✓)"*
"Get in the car and start driving"	*"19:23 - 19:38 Traveling (✓)"*
"Arrive destination, leave car and walk some minutes"	*"19:38 - 19:41 Walking (✓)"*
"Walk upstairs several floors"	*"19:41 - 19:42 Climbing stairs (✓)"*
"Stand some minutes"	*"19:43 - 19:43 Standing (✓)"*
"Sit down, and stop application after some minutes"	*"19:43 - 19:49 Sitting (✓)"*

course of normal life. These minor mistakes are not relevant when producing a linguistic report of conclusions.

Table 3 shows an example of one test (T-6 in Table 2) used for the validation. It presents the list of performed activities annotated by the user and the corresponding linguistic report produced by the application. The state *'Out'* corresponds to the state when the mobile phone is not with the user.

The main feature of this work is that the application has the ability of providing a wide variety of reports, highlighting different characteristics of human activity. It will depend on the particular needs of the different users. For example, we could customize the output reports considering the amounts of time the user should be walking or sitting, as well as the quantity of energy he/she must spend. This configuration set could be done by an expert in order to advice patients on behalf of their activity levels. The generated reports could be similar to the following one:

"During these 40 minutes you walked for a short time and you were sitting most of the time. You have burned very few calories. In order to meet your objectives, you should increase your activity level."

The second experiment consists in obtaining the accelerations generated for a whole day over the whole week. Each daily recording period has consisted of 10 hours of continuous recording. The main goal of this experimentation resided in demonstrating that significant conclusions can be drawn from the observation of long periods of time by comparing results, trends and so on. The report obtained from the observation of 7 experimental days was the following:

"During this week you have consumed less energy than it was expected. The energy consumption has been very similar every day of the week."

"The day of the week you have walked less time was on Thursday, however, on Sunday you have been walking far longer than the other days."

"On Tuesday and Saturday, you have spent much more time standing than other days. In addition, you spend too much time sitting, so you should reduce as much as possible the time spent sitting."

5   Concluding Remarks

In this paper we have focused our efforts in the development of a GLMP which describes the most common physical activities of a person during a day. We have developed a practical application that lies in the use of current mobile phones to acquire and store user accelerations in an inexpensive and non-intrusive way. Experimentation allows us to demonstrate the viability of our approach to become a real commercial application.

In this paper we present a glimpse of our ongoing work devoted to generate linguistic descriptions of human activities, being a field constantly growing and with a great potential to be improved. Detecting falls, combining acceleration data with other sensors information, or incorporating the capability of interacting in social networks would be some of the improvements that we want to tackle in the future.

Acknowledgment. This work has been funded by the Spanish Government (MICINN) under project TIN2011-29827-C02-01.

References

1. Zadeh, L.A.: The concept of linguistic variable and its application to approximate reasoning. Information sciences 8, 199–249 (1975)
2. Zadeh, L.A.: From computing with numbers to computing with words - from manipulation of measurements to manipulation of perceptions. IEEE Transactions on Circuits and Systems 45 (1999)
3. Eciolaza, L., Trivino, G., Delgado, B., Rojas, J., Sevillano, M.: Fuzzy linguistic reporting in driving simulators. In: Proceedings of the 2011 IEEE Symposium on Computational Intelligence in Vehicles and Transportation Systems, Paris, France, pp. 30–37 (2011)
4. Eciolaza, L., Trivino, G.: Linguistic Reporting of Driver Behavior: Summary and Event Description. In: 11th International Conference on Intelligent Systems Design and Applications (ISDA), Córdoba, Spain, pp. 148–153 (2011)
5. Alvarez-Alvarez, A., Sanchez-Valdes, D., Trivino, G.: Automatic Linguistic Description about Relevant Features of the Mars' Surface. In: Proceedings of the 11th International Conference on Intelligent Systems Design and Applications (ISDA), Córdoba, Spain, pp. 154–159 (2011)
6. Alvarez-Alvarez, A., Sanchez-Valdes, D., Trivino, G., Sánchez, A., Suárez, P.D.: Automatic linguistic report about the traffic evolution in roads. Expert Systems with Applications 39, 11293–11302 (2012)
7. Zadeh, L.A.: A new direction in AI. Towards a Computational Theory of Perceptions of measurements to manipulation of perceptions. AI Magazine 22 (2001)
8. Zadeh, L.A.: Toward Human Level Machine Intelligence - Is It Achievable? The Need for a Paradigm Shift IEEE Computational Intelligence Magazine (2008)
9. Delgado, M., Sánchez, D., Vila, M.: Fuzzy cardinality based evaluation of quantified sentences. Int. Journal of Approximate Reasoning 23, 23–66 (2000)

Semantic Based Self-configuration Approach for Social Robots in Health Care Environments

Gorka Azkune[1], Pablo Orduña[2], Xabier Laiseca[2],
Diego López-de-Ipiña[2], and Miguel Loitxate[1]

[1] Tecnalia – Industry and Transport Division
[2] Deusto Institute of Technology – DeustoTech, University of Deusto

Abstract. Health care environments, as many other real world environments, present many changing and unpredictable situations. In order to use a social robot in such an environment, the robot has to be prepared to deal with all the changing situations. This paper presents a robot self-configuration approach to overcome suitably the commented problems. The approach is based on the integration of a semantic framework, where a reasoner can take decisions about the configuration of robot services and resources. An ontology has been designed to model the robot and the relevant context information. Besides rules are used to encode human knowledge and serve as policies for the reasoner. The approach has been successfully implemented in a mobile robot, which showed to be more capable of solving not pre-designed situations.

Keywords: e-health, AAL, social-robotics, semantic-web.

1   Introduction

As the proportion of the elderly people keeps increasing, programs such as Ambient Assisted Living[1] aim to enhance their quality of life taking advantage of the latest ICT technologies. The range of technologies used and target situations in the literature is wide [7,5], but they all attempt to reduce health care costs by providing a more independent life to patients through ICT solutions.

In this line, the use of robotics -in particular social robotics-, given the satisfying human-robot interaction [13], are being studied to achieve these goals, both at the health center [6] and at the patients home [9]. As section 2 of this contribution details, the motivation of this research is indeed based on a real experiment developed as part of the ACROSS[2] project, where a robot assisted healthcare providers in a health center by interacting with the patient and archiving the measurements taken to enable future analysis by therapists.

On this experiment, certain limitations arose during the deployment. Robots in general need to be aware of their context in order to perform tasks more effectively. However, social robots involved in a health environment, whether

---

[1] http://www.aal-europe.eu/
[2] http://www.acrosspse.com/

J. Bravo, R. Hervás, and M. Rodríguez (Eds.): IWAAL 2012, LNCS 7657, pp. 354–361, 2012.
© Springer-Verlag Berlin Heidelberg 2012

they are at the patient's home or at the health center, need to obey especially complex rules that may change with time and even depend on concrete patients. Therefore, a flexible solution to enable the robot to configure itself with complex and dynamic rules is particularly necessary in these environments.

The focus of this contribution is to explore a self-configuration solution for social robotics that enables their integration in health scenarios. On section 2, the initial scenario from which the contribution starts will be described, while scenario itself is beyond the scope of this paper. The proposed solution is described in section 3, outlining the developed techniques. Section 4 shows the related work and finally section 5 summarizes the outcomes and proposed solution advances the state of the art, pointing out possible future works.

2   Initial Scenario

As part of the ACROSS project, a joint effort between the ABAT hospital, M-Bot Solutions and the University of Deusto was developed to assist therapists[10]. While the scenario itself is outside the scope of this contribution, it is described here to show the required context.

The scenario was divided into two applications, both running in the robot. The first application was used by the patients themselves: the robot moved to the user and it showed a set of customized questions so as to check that the patient recalls correctly places where she had been living, pictures of her family, music that she may remember, etc. These questions were prepared by therapists, who additionally tagged the questions -e.g. visual, personal-. Figure 1(a) shows the patient answering in the robot. The robot will store in a Triple Space[3] information such as what questions were answered, how long took the patient answering, which questions were not answered, etc. The second application consumed the information stored by the first application, so therapists could see the results of the patient and the historic evolution in the quality of the responses for each tag.

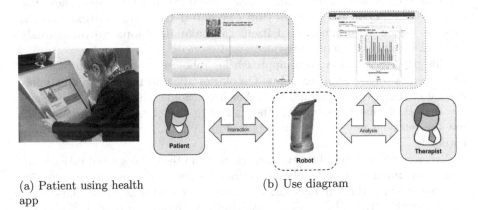

(a) Patient using health app

(b) Use diagram

Fig. 1. Initial scenario

Figure 1(b) summarizes the described interaction and the existing roles. However, the robot movement in the first application was controlled by a human. A target scenario aimed to be used in a group of patients in a room, and the robot had to go by itself from one patient to other, which is a challenge. Indeed, the next logical step would be moving in the health center from one room to other or even go with the patient to the room. This could be even scheduled by the therapist once a day, where therapist details to which rooms the robots should go at which times. All this type of movements become a special problem that must take into account the patient speed and problems that arise in the context.

Additionally, the inputs and outputs of the robot may need to be configured to enhance the user experience. For example, the level of sound depends not only on the person but on the room where the robot is. During the experimental session, the patient had problems pressing the tactile buttons, since she pressed them for longer than regular users, so the application should also configure itself for that type of user. In summary, as detailed in the introduction, a high level of flexibility was desirable in the scenario.

3   Robot Challenges in a Health Care Environment

The application requirements explained in section 2 can be enumerated from the point of view of robotics as follows: 1) flexibility in human-robot interaction: in the usage of the touch-screen, the volume of the speakers, how the messages are communicated, etc. 2) flexibility in task scheduling and execution: abort a patient guiding task when batteries are too low, give indications if a task has been aborted, change the scheduling when a task is taking too long, etc. 3) flexibility in resource management: switch all the interaction devices to stand-by if the battery is low and interaction devices are not needed, disable navigation if motors report an error, etc. 4) flexibility in software configuration: slow down navigation speed if a patient is a disabled person, change obstacle avoidance behaviour if the robot is surrounded, etc.

Those requirements can be met using **self-configuration** approaches. The robot, depending on the **information extracted from its context** and the **models** of the environment and itself, can **take decisions autonomously** about the configuration of its resources and services.

This paper presents a novel approach for robot self-configuration based on rule-extended ontological reasoning. Ontologies allow to model symbolic information of the environment and the robot itself. Some advantages of ontologies are that they enable reusability, they allow to model not only the concepts but the relations among the concepts and many reasoners can work on top of ontologies.

A reasoner is used to infer new information from the ontology and take advantage of the implicit rules of relations among concepts. The reasoner works also as a rule engine, where human knowledge can be encoded as rules. Those rules are the policies the robot uses to take decisions about the best configuration of services and resources depending on the situation modelled in the ontology.

Besides, rules have many practical benefits, such as flexibility to change them dynamically avoiding to re-compile the application and its logic, or the restrictions defined in rule engines that add consistency to the whole reasoning system.

As the reasoner has to be continuously updated with new information, a link between robot sensor-actuator and the reasoner is needed. This link is a robotic framework that makes possible to integrate sensor and actuator drivers with higher-level robot skills such as navigation or feature extraction. The framework selected for this paper is Robot Operating System (ROS) (see section 3). ROS allows the robot to grab information from the context, to update the reasoner and apply the configuration changes inferred by the reasoner to the robot.

Semantic Reasoning Challenges: The proposed system uses a semantic reasoning component based on the triple space computing (TSC) paradigm. TSC is a shared memory paradigm that stores data as RDF triples. This data store, called space, allows the system to query and share information easily among the nodes spread in the environment. More precisely, it allows the semantic reasoner to query/share information in the space and to subscribe to relevant incoming information.

Due to the semantic capabilities of TSC, an ontology has been designed to represent the information relevant for the self-configuration system. The self-configuration ontology describes: i) the robots' devices classified depending on their nature (sensor and/or actuator), their use (for navigation, interaction, etc.) and their status (unavailable devices), ii) the robots' skills (navigate, interact, etc.), iii) the tasks available (going to the dock, attending a patient, etc.) and iv) the robot status (location, devices, etc.).

The aim of the described semantic component is, depending on the status of the robot, to enable/disable robot skills and to perform some task (like going to dock station to charge batteries) to guarantee its correct and autonomous operation. In order to achieve that, the Jena semantic framework is been deployed over this component. Moreover, a set of rules has been developed to extend the information inferred by the semantic framework, such as the one shown in figure 2. This rule sets the *going-to-dock* task as current if the battery status is *very-low*.

Integration in ROS: ROS[3] is a software development framework for robots. Due to its extensive use by robot developers, ROS has a wide repository of software components such as sensor drivers, navigation systems or artificial vision algorithms. Besides, ROS is being actively supported by the *Open Source Robotics Foundation*[4]. Based on those features, ROS was selected for the developments presented in this paper.

The application described in section 2 demands autonomous navigation capabilities from the robot. Hence, the navigation stack[5] of ROS has been used.

---

[3] http://www.ros.org/

[4] http://www.osrfoundation.org/

[5] http://www.ros.org/wiki/navigation

```
[very_low_battery_causes_going_to_dock_task:
#0:
          (?robot rdf:type ac:Robot),
          (?bat rdf:type ac:Battery),
          (?robot ac:has_device ?bat),
          (?bat ac:battery_level "very low"),
          (?c_task rdf:type ac:Task),
          (?robot ac:current_task ?c_task),
          (?n_task rdf:type ac:Task),
          (?n_task ac:type ?n_task_type),
          (?c_task ac:type ?c_task_type),
          equal(?n_task_type, "GoingToDock"),
          notEqual(?c_task_type, "GoingToDock"),
          notEqual(?c_task_type, "Docking")
          ->
          drop(5),
          (?robot ac:current_task ?n_task)
]
```

Fig. 2. A self-configuration rule example

The navigation stack offers two main features to the robot: (i) the capacity to go from any point of the environment to any other point and (ii) the capacity to localise the robot respect to the map of the environment. In addition to the navigation stack, the *diagnostics* stack[6] is also used in this paper to centralize all the hardware status in a standard way.

The software architecture used to integrate the TSC middleware into ROS is depicted in Figure 3. All the communication between the ROS world and the Triple Space is centralized in a ROS node called *bridge_node*. This node subscribes to all the needed information from the robot and uses the *TS_API* to set and get information from the TSC middleware. This allows a very clean integration. Besides, the triple spaces are continuously updated with new context information and the reasoner can extract new conclusions and knowledge. Those conclusions are notified to the *bridge_node*, which has direct impact on the configuration of the robot services and behaviour.

Deployment of the Proposed Solution: The proposed solution works in a continuous loop with the following steps: (i) the robot extracts relevant information from the context, (ii) it updates the Triple Space, (iii) the reasoner processes the new information and checks the rules, (iv) the activated rules modify different aspects of the robot, (v) those changes are translated into ROS, which commands the involved actuators and software components.

Let us see the whole process with a simple example. There is a rule that states that if the battery level is very low, the robot has to go to the docking station, switching all the interaction devices to stand-by and limiting robot's maximum speed.

The process starts in the battery driver. When the battery measures charge levels that go below certain threshold, the battery driver publishes a *very low* level. This information is grabbed by the *bridge_node* (see Figure 3), which is

---

[6] http://www.ros.org/wiki/diagnostics

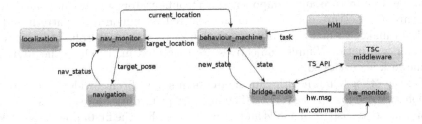

Fig. 3. Software architecture for TSC middleware integration into ROS; orange boxes are ROS nodes while the yellow box depicts the TSC middleware

the responsible of updating the Triple Space. The *bridge_node* uses the setting mechanisms of the Triple Space defined in the *TS_API*. Consequently, as new information has been set, the reasoner checks all the rules of the system. Particularly, the reasoner can infer that the touch-screen, the speakers and the microphone are interaction devices, so it changes their operating mode to *stand-by*. The reasoner also changes the scheduled task to *going-to-dock* and decreases the robot speed for navigation.

All those changes in the ontology are notified to the *bridge_node*, which publishes the new information to the involved components. For instance, the touch-screen is commanded to switch its operating mode to *stand-by*. The ROS driver of the touch-screen is prepared to receive this information and execute it. Hence, the loop closes and the rule is executed in the situation it should be executed. The same procedure applies to all the rules, which can be as complex as required by the functionality. The power of those rules becomes obvious when they are combined by the reasoner to generate suitable configurations in complex situations.

4   Related Work

Self-configuration is becoming a hot topic in robotics, where changing environments and high-level task specifications demand more flexible software and hardware architectures. Self-configuration research can be focused on hardware modules and robot design [14] or on robot software architectures and services. This paper fits in the second group.

Some researchers use self-configuration approaches to make robot teams configurable while operating. Based on ideas brought from the Semantic Web Services community, Gritti *et al* [4] present a framework for discovery and composition of functionalities which is used to make robot ecologies self-configurable.

However, self-configuration has also been studied for single-robot scenarios. Literature shows extensive work on dealing with dynamic software architectures that can self-configure depending on the task and the available resources. A good example can be found in [8] where authors develop a self-managed robot software framework called SHAGE. The framework uses ontology-based models to describe architecture and components, a reconfigurator, which can change the software architecture depending on the selected reconfiguration pattern and a decision maker to find the optimal solution of reconfiguring software architecture for a situation. Similar objectives are presented in [1] where the ROBEL framework is developed.

On the other hand, health care environments have been a widely used application scenario for service robots. The most frequent duties for service robots in hospitals are transport of goods and floor cleaning. For the first application Ozkil et al [11] present an extensive survey, analysing the benefits of introducing service robots for transportation. As a transport example, Carreira et al designed a service robot to deliver meals to patients [2], whereas Ozkil et al show the design of a fleet of robots for general transportation of goods [12]. Finally, a European project called IWARD[7] was devoted to introduce a self-configuring robot team for hospital cleaning, surveillance, drug delivery, environment monitoring and virtual consultancy, as described in [15].

5   Conclusions and Future Work

This contribution has presented a novel solution for addressing self-configuration in health care social robots. The impact of this contribution is not restricted to scenarios similar to the scenario detailed in section 2, but also to those scenarios where social robots are involved in a complex and dynamic scenario in which the robot must react. The solution proposed in section 3 uses the capabilities of semantic reasoners, adapted to the well known ROS framework, so as to solve complex situations. As detailed along the contribution, this solution enables developers to use a high degree of expressivity, which would have been very interesting during the development of the section 2.

Regarding future work, a deep evaluation in terms of flexibility when compared with the original work will be interesting. Several positive and negative factors have an impact, such as the learning curve when developers have low or no experience with semantic web and rule engines, the tools used and the development speed (e.g. IDEs will provide quicker feedback reporting an error during development than the rule engine), lines of code versus size of the few rules, and the number of unexpected situations covered. Additionally, at the moment the rules are manually defined by developers. However, it would be interesting to explore the implementation of certain degree of automation process in the development of the rules, so the robot itself may learn from the situations and dynamically generate its own rules and add them to the knowledge base.

References

1. Benoit, M., Guillaume, I., Malik, G., Ingrand, F.: Robel: Synthesizing and controlling complex robust robot behaviors. In: Proceedings of the Fourth Int. Cognitive Robotics Workshop, CogRob 2004, pp. 18–23 (2004)

---

[7] http://www.iward.eu/

2. Carreira, F., Canas, T., Silva, A., Cardeira, C.: i-merc: a mobile robot to deliver meals inside health services. In: IEEE Conf. on Robotics, Automation and Mechatronics, pp. 1–8. IEEE (2006)

3. Gómez-Goiri, A., López-de-Ipiña, D.: On the complementarity of triple spaces and the web of things. In: Proceedings of the Second Int. Workshop on Web of Things, WoT 2011, pp. 12:1–12:6. ACM, New York (2011)

4. Gritti, M., Broxvall, M., Saffiotti, A.: Reactive self-configuration of an ecology of robots. In: Proc. of the ICRA 2007 Workshop on Network Robot Systems, Rome, Italy, pp. 49–56 (2007), http://www.aass.oru.se/~asaffio/

5. Hervás, R., Garcia-Lillo, A., Bravo, J.: Mobile augmented reality based on the semantic web applied to ambient assisted living, pp. 17–24. Springer (2011)

6. Hu, J., Edsinger, A., Lim, Y.J., Donaldson, N., Solano, M., Solochek, A., Marchessault, R.: An advanced medical robotic system augmenting healthcare capabilities-robotic nursing assistant. In: IEEE Int. Conf. on Robotics and Automation (ICRA), pp. 6264–6269. IEEE (2011)

7. Jara, A.J., Zamora, M.A., Skarmeta, A.F.: An internet of things—based personal device for diabetes therapy management in ambient assisted living (aal). Personal and Ubiquitous Computing 15(4), 431–440 (2011)

8. Kim, D., Park, S., et al.: Shage: a framework for self-managed robot software. In: Proceedings of the 2006 international workshop on Self-adaptation and self-managing systems, pp. 79–85. ACM Press, New York (2006)

9. Kranz, M., Linner, T., et al.: Robotic service cores for ambient assisted living. In: 2010 4th Int. Conf. on Pervasive Computing Technologies for Healthcare (PervasiveHealth), pp. 1–8 (2010)

10. Laiseca, X., Castillejo, E., Orduña, P., Gómez-Goiri, A., López-de-Ipiña, D., González Aguado, E.: Distributed Tracking System for Patients with Cognitive Impairments. In: Bravo, J., Hervás, R., Villarreal, V. (eds.) IWAAL 2011. LNCS, vol. 6693, pp. 49–56. Springer, Heidelberg (2011)

11. Ozkil, A., Fan, Z., et al.: Service robots for hospitals: A case study of transportation tasks in a hospital. Statistics, 289–294 (August 2009)

12. Ozkil, A.G., Dawids, S., et al.: Design of a robotic automation system for transportation of goods in hospitals. In: Int. Symposium on Computational Intelligence in Robotics and Automation, CIRA 2007, pp. 392–397 (2007)

13. Robins, B., Dickerson, P., et al.: Robot-mediated joint attention in children with autism: A case study in robot-human interaction, vol. 5. John Benjamins Publishing Company (2004)

14. Stoy, K., Nagpal, R.: Self-reconfiguration using directed growth. In: In Proc. 7th Int. Symp. on Distributed Autonomous Robotic Systems, pp. 1–10 (2004)

15. Thiel, S., Habe, D., Block, M.: Co-operative robot teams in a hospital environment. In: IEEE Int. Conf. on Intelligent Computing and Intelligent Systems, ICIS 2009, vol. 2, pp. 843–847. IEEE (2009)

Context-Aware Generation and Adaptive Execution of Daily Living Care Pathways*

Inmaculada Sánchez-Garzón, Gonzalo Milla-Millán,
and Juan Fernández-Olivares

Department of Computer Science and A.I., University of Granada, Spain
{isanchez,gmillamillan,faro}@decsai.ugr.es

Abstract. Ambient Intelligence (AmI) can be of great support for the care of people with cognitive impairment. This people require effective treatment plans with clear goals, including pharmacological treatment, Activities of Daily Living (ADL) and assessment tests, all of them according to the recommendations specified in Clinical Practice Guidelines (CPGs) and centred on the patient. Moreover, these plans need to be adapted in a sensitive and responsive way to both the natural disease evolution and unexpected circumstances. This work presents an approach to automatically generate (from formal CPGs) and adaptively execute daily living care plans in the frame of a planning-based distributed architecture that allows for its application on AmI environments. This approach is based on temporal hierarchical planning and scheduling techniques, which allow for the context-awareness of the whole process.

Keywords: Personalized daily living care treatments, Architectures for developing AAL environments, Hierarchical Task Network planning.

1 Motivation

A core concept of Ambient Assisted Living (AAL) is the *aging-in-place* philosophy [4], the main goal of which is to help people living at home as long as possible, regardless of age, income or ability level. The idea of this philosophy is to provide highly personalized support for home-based healthcare, by offering guidance and decision support in the daily routine of the patient, including help for performing and monitoring both activities of daily living (ADL) as well as medication tasks. This objective requires both the generation and management of an effective treatment plan with clear goals for each specific patient. Formally, this treatment plan can be defined as a *daily living care pathway* (DLCP), i.e., a care plan that is composed by the timing and sequence of activities to be performed in order to assist the patient properly. Regarding the generation process of a DLCP, some issues must be taken into account. Firstly, this care plan

* This research work has been partially supported by the Andalusian Regional Ministry and the Spanish Ministry of Innovation under projects P08-TIC-3572 and TIN2008-06701-C03-02 respectively.

J. Bravo, R. Hervás, and M. Rodríguez (Eds.): IWAAL 2012, LNCS 7657, pp. 362–370, 2012.
© Springer-Verlag Berlin Heidelberg 2012

should be designed regarding the recommendations specified in Clinical Practice Guidelines (CPGs, [6]) that describe, for a specific disease, the decisions and procedures to be followed during the phases of diagnosis, therapy and follow-up. A CPG, which is commonly represented in a text-based format, is based on the best available medical evidence and it also contains temporal constraints for specifying the medication patterns or the periodicity of clinical assessments. Secondly, the specific patient profile (composed by clinical data, needs and preferences) must be also taken into account in order to create a personalized treatment plan. An important issue here is the consideration of the comorbid conditions of the patient since it is common that elderly people suffer more than one disease and undesirable effects, such as drug interactions, should be avoided. In addition, this treatment plan requires the involvement of clinicians and caregivers (at probably different places), so allocation of medical resources to activities should be also considered. Moreover, regarding the management process, a DLCP should be remotely monitored and responsively adapted according to the progression of the disease(s), the current health conditions of the patient as well as to the appearance of exceptional circumstances (or deviations). Finally, the adaptation process of a DLCP must also guarantee the adherence to CPG recommendations as well as the accomplishment of temporal constraints.

Due to the difficulty of generating patient-centred DLCP regarding all these requirements as well as dealing the exceptional circumstances that may occur in healthcare settings, we propose the use of temporal hierarchical task networks (HTN) planning and re-planning techniques [2, 5]. HTN paradigm is an enabling technology in this kind of knowledge-intensive domains since it allows the representation of CPGs, complex temporal constraints, patient profiles as well as medical resources. Moreover, a knowledge-driven planning process over these entities allows the automated generation and adaptation of DLCPs regarding the current health conditions of the patient and ensuring the adherence to CPG recommendations. For these reasons, in this work we propose an architecture (based on the HTN planning techniques) that provides support for the dynamic generation, the distributed monitoring and adaptive execution of DLCPs in sensitive environments. This architecture, which interleaves episodes of context perception, reasoning and acting, allows the collection of context data from different sources (like sensor data or electronic health records - EHR). These context data, which are continuously monitored and updated, are used to adapt the care pathway by a replanning episode if any deviation arises during its execution.

An experimental evaluation of the architecture has been carried out with DLCPs dynamically generated from an Alzheimer guideline. As a result, the proposed architecture seems to be an adequate context-aware and distributed system that provides support for both detecting deviations during DLCP execution and for reasoning about the current health status of the patient in order to offer the best guidance and decision support in the daily patient routing.

The next section describes the knowledge representation and plan generation techniques. Then, the distributed architecture and the experimental evaluation are explained. Finally, the related work and some conclusions are commented.

2   Context Modelling, Knowledge Representation and Generation of Daily Living Care Pathways

The knowledge representation[1] used in this work includes both a *Context Model* for representing the context data and an *Expert Knowledge Model* to encode the main ADL as well as the clinical decisions and procedures detailed in CPGs.

The Context Model (CM) is devoted to model clinical data, like patient clinical conditions (e.g., heart rhythm or disease severity) or information related to medical resources (e.g., time scheduling of caregivers). This model is based on five key UML concepts: *class* (to represent hierarchies of objects types), *attribute* (for object properties), *operation* (special attributes which need to be computed), *association* and *generalization* (relationships between classes).

The Expert Knowledge Model (EKM) is based on three basic concepts: *compound task* (or *goal*), *decomposition method* and *primitive task*. Compound tasks represent high-level processes or goals to be accomplished in possibly alternative ways depending on the context data. Decomposition methods are used to specify the alternative ways in which either a high-level process may be decomposed or a high-level goal may be achieved. Decomposition methods consist of (1) the applicability conditions that must hold in the context for the decomposition method to be applicable and (2) a partially ordered set of (compound or primitive) subtasks. If applicability conditions for a method m of a task t hold in a given context, then subtasks of m specify the way to decompose (or accomplish) the compound task (or goal) represented by t in that given context. Primitive tasks represent concrete actions (e.g., a medication activity) which consist of (1) the conditions that must hold in the context data for them to be applicable, and (2) the changes that their execution produces in the context data. Finally, the EKM can also represent complex temporal information [2] via: (1) start and end time intervals for the tasks, (2) duration of the primitive tasks and (3) temporal constraints among tasks at different levels of abstraction.

The generation of patient-tailored daily living care pathways is based on a knowledge driven, temporal hierarchical planning process[2] which receives as inputs: the CM, the EKM and a set of object instances, which both accomplish the UML specification of the CM and conform the context data on which the activities of the DLCP must be carried out. This generation process follows a state-based forward HTN planning algorithm that decomposes a set of top-level compound tasks (or goals)[3] in a set of only primitive tasks which make up

---

[1] The knowledge representation (KR) used in this work is based on a temporal HTN planning language developed by our research group [5, 6]. This KR has been extended with a graphical notation [10] and it conforms the core of *IActive Knowledge Studio* (download at http://www.iactiveit.com/tecnologia/studio-modelado-de-conocimiento-experto/), a Knowledge Engineering tool commercialized by our start-up *IActive Intelligent Solutions*, which has also been used in our experiments.

[2] This planner is described in detail in [2] and has been applied in several applications [5, 6, 2]. It has been extended as a commercial product called *Decisor*, currently property of *IActive Intelligent Solutions*.

[3] The top-level goal has the semantics: *"Obtain a daily living care pathway"*.

the plan. This is done according to the temporal constraints posed in the task network and the current context data, which are continuously updated by each primitive task, thus allowing for the context-awareness of the whole process. The output of this process is a patient-tailored DLCP, that is to say, a set of instantiated and temporally annotated primitive tasks which incorporate and integrate the concerned context data. This is the keystone for obtaining context-aware pathways, because all the object instances (representing the patient conditions, stage of the disease, resources availability, etc.) are incorporated natively into the care plan by the planning process.

Furthermore, deviations from the expected care pathway (e.g., changes in patient conditions, disease progression, unavailability of resources) which may arise during plan execution can be also represented and managed. The conditions to be monitored for detecting these deviations are natively included in the DLCP by the planning process. The response to the deviations is represented in the EKM as choices that must be done among different careflow alternatives (depending on the context data), implemented as applicability conditions of different decomposition methods for the same compound task (or goal). The execution-monitoring stage of the adaptive execution process explained in next section is in charge of continuously updating the context data and checking if any of these deviations arise. Thanks to this continuous update, the planning process is aware of what part of the expert knowledge (e.g. clinical guideline plus ADL) must be considered to respond to the just arisen situation. As a result, the DLCP is adapted according to the steps specified in the expert knowledge model following the same planning process, but in a re-planning episode. This responsive and adaptive reasoning process is interleaved with the appropriated acting processes that are explained in next section.

3   Adaptive Execution of Daily Living Care Pathways

Figure 1 depicts the approach for the adaptive execution of DLCPs. This approach is composed by the following elements:

(1) The *Patient Activities Model*, which encodes the expert knowledge model composed by the CPG recommendations, the pharmacological treatment, the ADL and information related to drug interaction and deviation management.

(2) The *Context Data*, which implements the UML-based context model integrating both resource data (i.e., availability) and patient data (i.e., demographic and clinical data, preferences, current medication, disease stage, evolution).

(3) The *Daily Living Care Pathway*, which includes all the activities (ADL, medication, clinical tests) in which the patient is involved. Every activity is annotated with temporal information about its *start* and *end* dates and the conditions that must hold in the context data during its execution.

(4) The *Conditions To Be Monitored*, which are annotated with the time that they are expected to hold in the context data (i.e., { *(Patient.visit-toilet Joseph)*, *9:00*} indicates that patient *Joseph* must have visited the toilet by nine o'clock in the morning). These conditions are the keystone for detecting deviations. The

system considers that a deviation arises when a condition is not held at the planned time in the context data (like the previous example) or when new items denoting unexpected deviations are detected ({*Patient.suffer Joseph Anxiety*}). The main processes of our methodology are: (1) a *Dynamic Generation* process, which is in charge of automatically generating the personalized DLCP regarding the patient data and the clinical knowledge encoded. This process is context-aware thanks to the use of the context data. (2) A *Variance Management* process, which extracts from the previously generated care pathway the conditions to be monitored during pathway execution; (3) a *Monitoring* process, which sends actions to execution, checks if any deviation from the expected course arises and manages it via a new *Dynamic Generation* process; and (4) an *Execution* process of the care tasks, which continuously update the context data making possible the context-awareness of the approach. Full access to up-to-date context data is ensured at any stage of the pathway execution management.

All these processes have been implemented as web services in a modular architecture based on continuous planning techniques called PELEA[7]. This is a domain-independent, component-based architecture able to perform planning, execution, monitoring and repairing in an integrated way, in the context of operator-based and HTN-based planning. PELEA follows a continuous planning approach, i.e., an ongoing and dynamic process in which planning and execution are interleaved but, unlike other approaches [9], it allows knowledge engineers to easily generate new applications by reusing and modifying the components. This way, the system can be distributed among different and appropriated locations and allowing for the ubiquitous management of the pathways. For instance: *Dynamic Generation*, *Variance Management* and *Monitoring* processes can be implemented in some server(s) inside the hospital. The physician responsible of giving the *Approval* can do it either at hospital or using a mobile application. The *Execution* process, in charge of changing the context data can be implemented as (1) a mobile application managed by the caregiver from home, (2) an institutional PC at a nursing home, (3) ubiquitous sensors placed at home.

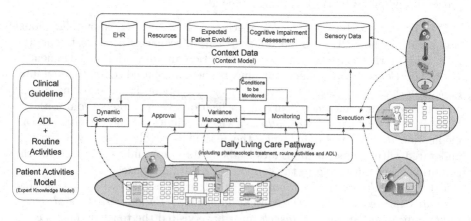

Fig. 1. Adaptive Execution of Daily Living Care Pathways

4 Experimental Evaluation

The experimental evaluation of the architecture here presented is based on DL-CPs for managing the Alzheimer's disease. As a result, a CPG related to this chronic disease[4] has been modelled in a computer interpretable format, as commented in section 2. The expert knowledge model and the context model encode the necessary items for defining both the CPG recommendations (pharmacological treatment, ADL[5], information related to drug interactions, interventions for handling some exceptional disorders, etc.) as well as the patient profile (demographic and clinical data, functional and cognitive status[6], preferences, additional medication, etc.) in a complete and precise way. Once represented the CPG, 2 patients with different profiles have been defined. Then, a personalized DLCP has been automatically generated, for each of them, by the Dynamic Generation process, as shown in section 3. The duration of these care plans is one week. In addition, a simulation process has been included in the architecture (between the execution process and the repository representing the context data) in order to simulate the appearance of deviations, as if it were a real healthcare environment. This process is in charge of generating deviations in a probabilistic way, but taking into account the set of possible exceptions that may occur at each step. For example, it may generate a deviation denoting a progression in the Alzheimer's disease of the patient after a cognitive test. This deviation, which is detected by the Variance Management process, produces a replanning episode performed by the Dynamic Generation process in order to adapt the DLCP regarding the CPG recommendations. Then, the DLCP resumes its execution.

Figure 2 shows the results obtained in the experimental evaluation. For the first patient, a care plan with 122 actions is automatically generated in 1.152s. The medication tasks of this care plan use the drug *galantamine* since this drug is compatible with the additional medication (*quimidine*) that the patient is receiving for treating other diseases. During the episode of plan execution, which lasts 35min 53s, 2 deviations are detected. The first one is related to the no confirmation of the completion of the bathing task, so a phone call is made for guaranteeing the patient safety. The second deviation is caused by low symptoms of depression. In this case, the Dynamic Generation process includes in the DLCP the proper medication (*nortriptyline*) for treating depression. This drug is taken at bedtime. For the second patient, the care plan is composed by 111 actions and it is generated in 0.918s. During the episode of plan execution, which lasts 32min 45s, 2 deviations are also detected. The first deviation is related to a disease progression (from *moderate* to *severe*). For this reason the Alzheimer's medication of the patient is changed (from *donepezil* to *memantine*). Both drugs are compatible with the additional medication of the patient (*paroxetine*). The second deviation is related to symptoms of high anxiety and it produces the

---

[4] Text-based clinical guideline : http://www.aafp.org/afp/2002/0615/p2525.pdf

[5] ADL are represented in a dual form, i.e., requiring or not the help of a caregiver according to the functional and cognitive status of the patient.

[6] The functional and cognitive evaluations of the patient are made by formal instruments like the Katz Index and the Mini Mental State Evaluation (MMSE).

inclusion of more medication tasks (*buspirone*) in the DLCP. As a result, the HTN planning techniques seem to be an enabling approach for promoting the dynamic generation and adaptive execution of daily living care pathways in AmI environments since the daily routine of each patient is monitored and every deviation is autonomously detected and managed according to the CPG recommendations.

Patient Profile	Statistics of care pathway generation	Deviations	Adaptation Steps
<2,MILD, Quimidine,false>	Total actions of plan = 122 Planning time = 1.152s Execution time = 35 min 53s Alzh. medication = Galantamine (8mg/day)	1. No confirmation bathing 2. Depression (low)	1. Make call phone 2. Take Nortriptyline 10mg/day bedtime
<9,MODERATE, Paroxetine,true>	Total actions of plan = 111 Planning time = 0.918s Execution time = 32 min 45s Alzh. medication = Donepezil (5mg/day)	1. Disease progression 2. Anxiety (high)	1. Change medication to Memantine 2. Take Buspirone 5mg/day

Fig. 2. Results of the experimental evaluation. The patient profile is represented by the tuple <Week of treatment, Disease status, Additional medication, If a monthly test is required>. The second column shows the number of actions, the planning time, the execution time and the Alzheimer's medication selected in the first plan generation process. The third and fourth columns summarize, respectively, the deviations detected during plan execution (by the Variance Management process) and the adaptation steps performed (by the Dynamic Generation process) in a replanning episode.

5   Related Work

Some relevant works may be identified in the different fields faced by this work. Focusing on the application of Computer Interpretable Guidelines (CIGs) in AmI environments, the project SAPHIRE [8] proposes an agent-based architecture where CIGs are represented using the well known GLIF formalism. The approach is centred on guideline execution, and does not address the generation of personalized care pathways neither their adaptation to evolving patient conditions. Our work uses a temporal HTN representation for CIGs that has proven to be as expressive as well-known CIG languages [6] and, additionally, provides support for the generation of personalized care pathways. In addition, SAPHIRE provides semi-automatic monitoring and execution processes that require a high involvement of human intervention, as opposed to the fully automated planning-based monitoring techniques used in our work. Considering the application of AI Planning in AmI environments, [11] is focused on Smart Homes applications, while [1] presents an agent-based architecture in the field of diabetic care, devoted to coordinate the operation of several devices. This work concentrates on planning and not on plan execution or plan repair, as opposite to our work. GerAmi [3] is an agent-based architecture devoted to provide support to clinical staff (doctors and nurses) in performing ADL for Alzheimer's patients. It is based on CBR techniques, and it allows for the representation and management of schedules of clinical resources and ADL. However, up to authors' knowledge, it does not provide support for encoding care pathways obtained from Alzheimer's clinical guidelines as the architecture here presented proposes.

6   Conclusions

A distributed architecture which makes use of HTN planning techniques has been proposed in order to leverage the dynamic generation and adaptive execution of daily living care pathways in AmI environments. The architecture rest on two pillars: a Dynamic Generation process, and a distributed and adaptive execution process. The first one is based on (1) a knowledge representation model that authors have prove in previous work [6] to be as expressive as common CIGs languages in order to represent formal clinical guidelines; (2) a temporal HTN planning process capable of generating patient-centred daily living care pathways (that integrate ADL, medication and assessment activities in order to check the disease progression of the patient) from this formal representation. The planning process is a context-aware process that contemplates context data, conforming to an UML-based model, coming from different sources of information. The second pillar is based on standard temporal planning techniques, which takes as input a previously generated care pathway and manages its execution by keeping track of the patient conditions to be monitored (already present in the pathway and automatically extracted from it). This process is capable of detecting deviations from the original pathway and adapting it adhering to the guideline recommendations, by using the Dynamic Generation process at a replanning episode.

Furthermore, an experimental evaluation of such architecture, which has been implemented using the planning infrastructure provided by PELEA[7], has been carried out in order to demonstrate its usefulness in the field of AAL. A clinical guideline for managing Alzheimer's disease has been encoded and, as a result, the approach presented in this work seems to be an adequate mechanism for automatically generating and adaptively executing daily living care pathways.

References

[1] Amigoni, F., Gatti, N., Pinciroli, C., Roveri, M.: What planner for ambient intelligence applications? IEEE Transactions on Systems, Man, and Cybernetics - Part A: Systems and Humans 35(1), 7–21 (2005)

[2] Castillo, L., Fdez-Olivares, J., García-Pérez, O., Palao, F.: Efficiently handling temporal knowledge in an htn planner. In: International Conference on Automated Planning and Scheduling (ICAPS), pp. 63–72 (2006)

[3] Corchado, J.M., Bajo, J., Abraham, A.: GerAmi: improving healthcare delivery in geriatric residences. IEEE Intelligent Systems 23(2), 19–25 (2008)

[4] Dishman, E.: Inventing wellness systems for aging in place. IEEE Computer 37(5), 34–41 (2004)

[5] Fdez-Olivares, J., Castillo, L., Cózar, J.A., García-Pérez, Ó.: Supporting clinical processes and decisions by hierarchical planning and scheduling. Computational Intelligence 27, 103–122 (2011)

[6] González-Ferrer, A., ten Teije, A., Fdez-Olivares, J., Milian, K.: Automated generation of patient-tailored electronic care pathways by translating computer-interpretable guidelines into hierarchical task networks. A.I. In Medicine (2012)

[7] Guzmán, C., Alcázar, V., Prior, D., Onaindía, E., Borrajo, D., Fdez-Olivares, J., Quintero, E.: Pelea: a domain-independent architecture for planning, execution and learning. In: ICAPS Workshop on Scheduling and Planning Applications woRKshop (SPARK), pp. 38–45 (2012)

[8] Laleci, G.B., Dogac, A., Olduz, M., Tasyurt, I., Yuksel, M., Okcan, A.: SAPHIRE: a multi-agent system for remote healthcare monitoring through computerized clinical guidelines. In: Agent Technology and e-health, pp. 25–44 (2008)

[9] Myers, K.: CPEF: a continuous planning and execution framework. AI Magazine 20(4), 63–69 (1999)

[10] Palao, F., Fdez-Olivares, J., Castillo, L., García-Pérez, Ó.: An extended htn knowledge representation based on a graphical notation. In: ICAPS Workshop on Knowledge Engineering for Planning and Scheduling (KEPS), pp. 126–133 (2011)

[11] Simpson, R.C., Schreckenghost, D., LoPresti, E.F., Kirsch, N.: Plans and Planning in Smart Homes. In: Augusto, J.C., Nugent, C.D. (eds.) Designing Smart Homes. LNCS (LNAI), vol. 4008, pp. 71–84. Springer, Heidelberg (2006)

EmotionContext: User Emotion Dataset Using Smartphones

Gonzalo Blázquez Gil, Antonio Berlanga, and José M. Molina

Applied Artificial Intelligence Group, University Carlos III, Colmenarejo, Spain
gbgil@inf.uc3m.es, {aberlan,molina}@ia.uc3m.es

Abstract. Mobile device's boom allows to researchers to step forward and design new applications and why not apps which can feel what user feels. This paper presents a smartphone architecture to retrieve user emotions context.

1 Introduction

Recently, increasing attention has been directed to the study of the human emotional state. Affective Computing (AC) is a branch of AI that deals with the design of systems and devices that can recognize, interpret process and reproduce human affective states. AC term was introduced by Rosalind Picard at MIT in 1997 [3].

AC is traditionally carried out through video systems [4] or through intrusive systems (wearable sensors) which make difficult to implement in real applications due to user's reluctance to wear devices across their bodies. Smartphones are particularly well-suited to accomplish this task. They are considered a wearable system and also they can operate during long periods of time sensing user activities, routines and the environment.

Moreover, smartphones are changing communication channels computer mediated communication (CMC). Typically, e-mail, social networks (asynchronous) sms, or even instant messaging (synchronous). New communication channels reduce personal contact between speakers to zero. For example, nowadays text messaging and social networks are the most popular way to communicate for teenagers. Taking the advantage of these new smartphone features [1] (Sensors, communication channels and so on), it is possible to create an application which gather user information in order to infer user emotional state.

To conclude this paper presents ContextCare, an architecture to obtain a user labeled emotion information using smartphones and rely on the user social networks posts. Since, these situations to recognize are known a priori, the problem can be tackled as a classification task.

2 EmotionContext: Architecture and Dataset Proposal

EmotionContext dataset is developed to satisfy a new wave in smartphones application research community. Nowadays, smartphones are not just a communication tool (telephone or internet), besides, they have embedded sensors which

J. Bravo, R. Hervás, and M. Rodríguez (Eds.): IWAAL 2012, LNCS 7657, pp. 371–374, 2012.
© Springer-Verlag Berlin Heidelberg 2012

may provide countless information about the user. Hence, smartphones can (at least theoretically) hear what you hear, see what you see and even read what you read. This section describes pros and cons to use smartphones sensors in order to obtain user emotion.

2.1 Emotion Representation

There exist two different Emotion representation models: Categorical and dimensional. Categorical model of emotion has its roots in the evolutionary theories which claims that emotions are biologically determined, discrete and belong to one of a few groups, these groups are consider fundamental or *basic*. According with [2] definition of affective state the basic emotions are considered: happiness, sadness, surprise, fear, anger and disgust.

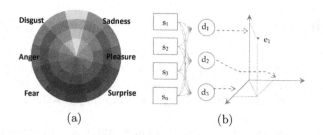

(a)   (b)

Fig. 1. Emotion representation: Categorical model (a) and Dimentional model (b)

In contrast to categorical model, dimensional models do not fix a finite set of emotions. Under this model, emotions are described in terms of three components or dimensions [5]. The three dimension approach is synthesized in figure (a) where a concrete emotion (e) is the result of the intersection between every different dimensions (d) whose values are determined by pattern of signals (s).

2.2 EmotionContext Architecture

The architecture of our framework is depicted in figure 2. ContextCare is a multimodal architecture which collects sensor information when the user is posting something on internet. The schema shows the three main modules: Smartphone app, SN server and the EmotionContext backend server.

Firstly, SN API's enable developers to access some of the core primitives of each SN including timelines, status updates, pictures, etc. This information is reachable through OAuth authentication protocol which grants access to user information to third-party applications. When users introduce their Facebook or Twitter credentials, they give back an access token, a string denoting a specific scope, lifetime, and other access attributes.

Secondly, EmotionContext smartphone app is developed in Android OS. Sensor module is an Android service which continuously gathers smartphone sensor

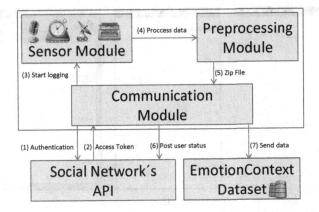

Fig. 2. EmotionContext requests authorization from the SN API using OAuth over HTTP Protocol (1). OAuth Authorization server sends an access token which grants access to user SN protected resources (2). At the same time, Sensor module start to log smartphone data (3). When users post their comment, sensor module sends raw information to the preprocessing module (4) which select the best samples and compress them (5). Finally, Communication Module sends .zip file to EmotionContext dataset via PHP (7).

information according to table 1. The preprocessing module transforms raw data to a vector features. MEMS data have been stored into a sliding window of 512 samples (approximately 5 seconds), 256 of which overlap with consecutive ones. Besides, the first and last 10% of windows stored are cropped in order to avoid outliners data, and finally stored in a plain text file.

Finally, EmotionContext Dataset server is a LAMP distribution (Linux, Apache, MySQL and PHP/Python). LAMP distribution support large file size (greater than 2 GB), bandwidth throttling to limit the speed of responses in order to not saturate the network and also provides Server-side scripting (PHP) to store every vector features in the MySql database. Figure 3 shows Emotion-Context Andorid app screen flow.

Table 1. EmotionContext Dataset Proposal: Matching between smartphone sensor and emotion recognition technique

Sensor	API Class	Tecniques	Emotions
Front Camera	MediaRecorder	Facial Expression	6 Basic & neutral
Microphone	MediaRecorder	Emotional Speech	6 Basic & neutral
Accelerometer	SensorManager	Hand movements	Happy & anger
Location	LocationManager	-	Happiness & Neutral
Typing	Sensing Module	Frequency	Anger & Neutral
SN status	Twitter API	Language Processing	6 Basic & neutral

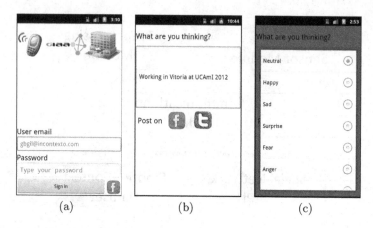

Fig. 3. Login screen (a), Post user status screen (b) and user emotion chooser (c)

3   Conclusion

This paper proposes a smartphone architecture and dataset (EmotionContext) which combines information from a smartphones embedded sensor. Emotion-Context dataset is developed to satisfy a new wave, human emotion recognition, in smartphones application research community.

Considering future works are to make a study of the extracted data from the smartphones and of course make an application able to discern the human emotional state. This kind of applications will be very useful in eHealth application, for example monitoring people with mental diseases and sending an alert when the patient is having a disorder.

Acknowledgment. This work was supported in part by Projects CICYT TIN2011-28620-C02-01, CICYT TEC2011-28626-C02-02, CAM CONTEXTS (S2009/TIC-1485) and DPS2008-07029-C02-02.

References

1. Blazquez Gil, G., Berlanga, A., Molina, J.M.: inContexto: A fusion architecture to obtain mobile context. In: 2011 Proceedings of the 14th International Conference on Information Fusion (FUSION), pp. 1–8. IEEE (2011)
2. Ekman, P., Friesen, W.: Facial action coding system: A technique for the measurement of facial movement (1978)
3. Picard, R.: Affective computing (1997)
4. Reilly, J., Ghent, J., McDonald, J.: Modelling, classification and synthesis of facial expressions. In: Affective Computing: Emotion Modelling, Synthesis and Recognition, pp. 107–132
5. Schlosberg, H.: Three dimensions of emotion. Psychological Review 61(2), 81 (1954)

A Model to Develop Frailty Diagnosis Tools through Mobile Devices and a Service-Oriented Approach

Jesús Fontecha[1], Ramón Hervás[1], José Bravo[1], and Fco. Javier Navarro[2]

[1] MAmI Research Lab, University of Castilla-La Mancha, Ciudad Real, Spain
{jesus.fontecha,ramon.hlucas,jose.bravo}@uclm.es
[2] Geriatric Services, Residencia Asistida de Ancianos, Ciudad Real, Spain
fjnavarroo@sescam.jccm.es

Abstract. Frailty is a health condition related to aging and dependence. A reduction or delay of frailty state can improve the quality of elderly life. However, providing a frailty assessment is difficult because many factors must be taken into account. Most of the time, measurement of these factors is performed in a non-centralized way, encouraging physician to make a wrong diagnosis or not as objective as it should be.

In this paper we propose a general model as a guideline to develop systems focused on elderly frailty assessment by using mobile phone capabilities and service-based approach. The proposed model uses a set of identified elements, facilitating the deployment of relevant services to support physicians in frailty decision-making. From this model, accelerometer sensors are entities used to get data of physical activity, while the mobile phone is responsible for service deployment.

Keywords: Frailty, elderly people, mobile phone, accelerometer, healthcare services.

1 Introduction

Human aging is a natural process characterized by a progressive loss of multiple abilities, including physical and cognitive ones. Normally, aging leads to a frailty state, and possibly a dependence condition. In 1988, Woodhouse [1] defined frail elderly people as those more than 65 years old who dependent on other people to perform their basic needs. Gillick [2] defined frail elderly people as "old debilitated individuals who cannot survive without substantial help from others", emphasizing the social consequences of frailty. Therefore, frailty is a condition which increases the risk of disability and dependency in the elderly.

In recent years, the concept of frailty has taken on a new topicality. Hamerman [3] shows its importance, due to the large number of parameters to be considered. In fact, detection and diagnosis of frailty must be studied on the following domains: medical, functional, socio-economic, cognitive and institutional. Functional domain have been classically appreciated to measure the independence

J. Bravo, R. Hervás, and M. Rodríguez (Eds.): IWAAL 2012, LNCS 7657, pp. 375–382, 2012.

level of a person. This includes the performance of activities of daily living (ADL) [4][5]. In this case, frailty is often equated with functional dependence in these activities, although frail elderly people are sometimes described in predominantly medical terms. However, it is difficult to standardize an operational definition of frailty taking into account this broad perspective.

Fried [6] proposes a phenotype of frailty according to the symptoms and signs from the clinical syndrome of frailty. Thus, Fried sets out five general criteria to decide whether an elder is frail or not.

Nowadays, the results for frailty detection and diagnosis are based on the following:

- Global scores from standard questionnaires filled by physicians.
- Overview of the elder and his environment.
- Measures from medical instruments.
- Analysis of lab reports from the elderly patient.

Moreover, doctors do not take into account all the previous items at the final assessment, but their decision is based only on some of them. Besides, the first two items depend on the physician viewpoint affecting the final result. For example, the assessment of gait and balance, one of the main indicators for frailty diagnosis, is obtained by several questionnaires. In this sense, the use of mobile phones with built-in accelerometers as a medical instrument during gait and balance activities, in combination with other factors, can be a useful method to generate more accurate and centralized results of frailty.

This paper is organized into 6 sections. Section 2 presents a set of relevant related work about frailty detection and diagnosis, including the use of new technologies for that. In section 3, we detail the risk factors for frailty diagnosis. Then, in sections 4 and 5 the proposed model is described in detail. Finally, section 6 presents the conclusions of our work.

2   Related Work

Study of frailty has been aided by the inclusion of new technologies, especially in the last decade. However, frailty detection and diagnosis is a complex process which takes into account many factors, as discussed above. In this sense, Martin [7] presents an overview of tools (tests and scales) used by relevant researchers in the field of frailty, studying the importance of each tool and the provided information. Jones [8] proposes a method to determine a frailty index from a detailed geriatric assessment which is focused on studying a set of variables including: balance, communication, cognitive state, nutrition, continence, ADLs and comorbidity among other. However, he says the best way to measure frailty remains unresolved. On the same line, Searle et al. [9] propose a quantification procedure for creating a fraility index from a dataset of variables. In this case, non-numerical variables were coded.

On the other hand, Gobbens et al. [10] define a conceptual framework to group the most important factors related to frailty, detected through an experiment.

These ones include cognitive factors, strength, balance, nutrition, physical activity and mobility; while social and psychological factors were less important.

Most authors agree that physical assessment is the most important domain in frailty analysis because it offers plenty of information about a person. The emergence of new technologies and the development of Accelerometry field, facilitates an objective analysis of the physical condition in the elderly. In this case, accelerometer sensors can provide much more information than current tests.

So far, accelerometer mechanisms have been used in activity recognition, falls detection and lately, in physical rehabilitation work. But studies of frailty detection from physical exercises are not so numerous. Tehou [11] performs a comparison between the use of different devices and frailty levels. This includes the use of the following: accelerometer device, heart rate monitor, portable electromyography unit, GPS[1] system and serveral questionnaires. When these devices are used in combination, provide important information about physical condition. However, in most of cases it is an unaffordable solution in daily work of health environments.

In recent years, the use of mobile devices in healthcare systems has increased significantly. In this sense, accelerometer sensors attached to the patient's waist are commonly used to measure simple parameters related to gait and other physical exercises. Auvinet [12] and Foerster [13] concluded the suitable use of a single accelerometer is sufficient and acceptable for general gait analysis. Today, growth of mobile phones capabilities allow us to improve certain tasks in healthcare environments not only related to physical activity monitoring, without using specific devices. In this case, a complete assessment of elderly frailty can be performed. In [14], Fontecha develops a mobile frailty detection architecture based on the model proposed in this paper.

3 Factors for Frailty Assessment

According to the state of art, there are a set of relevant factors to be taken into account when a physician carries out a frailty diagnosis. Espinoza [15] identifies a group of possible risk factors from the frailty phenotype and a sistematic review. Also, physical characteristics of frailty are presented. However, the importance of each one is not mentioned, at least in a quantitative way.

Clinical variables related to frailty come from the patient record. The score of tests and scales, results of lab reports, general information, etc., are stored by physicians to be studied as needed. Meanwhile, social and psychological indicators are not considered because they have not a direct relationship with the patient record. The most common indicators are associated with the following clinical groups (all these items can be quantified easily): *-Anthropometric and general data-* Including gender, age, size, weight, BMI, lean mass, fat mass, total water and drug number. *-Functional assessment-* Including Tinetti gait and balance score, Barthel index, Lawton&Brody score, Get-Up and Go score, need help in physical activities, etc. *-Independence in ADL-* Choosing an option from the following: independent, mild dependence, moderate dependence, great dependence

---

[1] http://www.gps.gov

or serious dependence. -*Geriatric syndromes*- Checking dementia, depression, incontinence, immobility, recurrent falls, polypharmacy, comorbidity, sensory deprivation, pressure ulcer, malnutrition and terminally illnes. -*Nutritional assessment*- Including results from total protein, serum albumin, cholesterol level triglycerides, blood iron, ferritin, vitamin B12, serum folic acid, serum transferrin, leukocytes, lymphocytes, hemoglobin, calcium, etc. -*Cognitive assessment*- Including Mini Mental Status MMS) score, CRP test, etc. -*Pathologies and diseases*- Chronic diseases can be divided into several groups. The number of diseases from each group provides important data about the patient.

New parameters can be identified to take part in the final assessment.

Functional assessment is the most important group to determine frailty and the first to be studied. In this sense, physician applies two gait and balance tests to assess several features: Tinetti test [16] and *Get-Up and Go* test [17]. The use of an accelerometer attached to the elderly waist during these activities collects relevant data about gait and balance. In [14], the following indicators were identified from the movement analysis as a accelerometry indicators: *arithmetic mean, standard deviation, absolute mean difference, acceleration mean, variance, amplitude and Pearson's coefficient of variation*. This new group of parameters is also considered part of the frailty assessment.

4   Conceptual Design

We have created a general model for supporting a frailty diagnosis based on the analysis of frailty risk factors, previously identified in section 3. The main goal of the model is to facilitate the implementation of an automated system to be run on mobile devices such as smartphones in order to get a centralized and objective frailty assessment. Obviously, the technology used to implement our model depends on developers.

4.1   Entities and Role Definition

The first step is to identify the set of entities which form our model. In this case, the mobile phone is the crux of the model and the most important entity. These entities have been grouped in four classes: *Devices, Users, Procedures/Services and Artifacts* (see table 1). Each entity is responsible for one or more actions (this is known as entity role).

Procedures and services are software components which must be previously implemented unlike tangible entities (from devices, users and artifacts). In section 5 the features of software services are described in detail.

4.2   Entity Relationship. Ontology-Based Model

The previous entities are related to each other in a mobility and ubiquitous domain. In this sense, the Fig. 1 shows a graphical representation of the model according to the Table 1 in which relations between entities represents the model assumptions and these are defined as follows:

Table 1. Model entities and roles

Class	Entity	Role
Device	Mobile phone	Service deployment, facilitating interaction, visualization, accelerometer data acquisition
	Accelerometer	Accelerometer data acquisition
	Server	Serve requests from mobile phone, process deployment
User	Elderly patient	Carry mobile phone / accelerometer to the waist during physical activity, provide the patient record
	Pysician	Assess frailty state of the elder, interact with mobile phone
Artifact	Questionnaires	Provide one or more measures for a general assessment based on clinical indicators from physician viewpoint (e.g. Barthel Index test)
	Medical instrument	Providing accurate measures of clinical indicators from clinical equipment (e.g. IMC scales)
Procedure^P/Service^S	Patient record (P)	Providing values of risk factors for frailty
	Patient stack (P)	Frailty data storage from studied patients
	Acquisition (S)	Acquisition services get data from the corresponding entities, including accelerometer data, patient record data and patient stack data
	Processing (S)	Analysis and processing of accelerometer data, patient record data and patient stack information
	Storage (S)	Data storage used by entities and processing tasks
	Result (S)	Creating a structure for visualization of frailty results on mobile phone screen

- Physician-*Treats to*-Elder. Physician is responsible for tretaing an elder.
- Elder-*has*-Patient record. The elder has a patient record.
- Elder-*carries*-Mobile device. The elder carries an accelerometer-enabled mobile device during gait and balance tests.
- Physician-*interacts*-Smartphone. The physician interacts with the smartphone to know the patient state.
- Accelerometer-*has*-Smartphone. The accelerometer can be integrated in the own smartphone.
- Smartphone-*provides*-Service. All identified services (acquisition, storage, result and processing) are provided by the smartphone.
- Service-*Request to*-Server. The service is requested to a server.
- Server-*Communicates with*-Mobile device. The server sends the corresponding result to the smartphone.
- Server-*obtains*-Patient record. Also the server obtain the patient record as a medical resource.
- Server-*stores*-Patient stack. The server stores the patient stack entity.
- Patient record-*stores*-Clinical parameter. Besides, the patient record stores a set of frailty clinical parameters.
- Artifact-measures-Clinical parameter. An artifact (questionnires and medical instruments) measures a clinical parameter.

So far, we have described *"Which"* elements are necessary (structure), but we have not discussed *"How"* these items work according to their roles (functionality).

5   Functional Design

To develop the procedures and services included in the model as software components, we propose a service-oriented approach. Thus, functionalities of proposed

380   J. Fontecha et al.

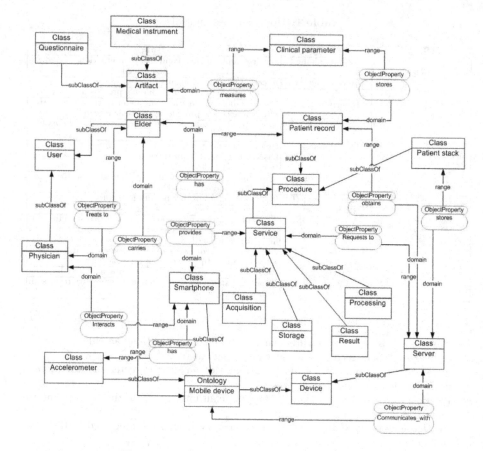

Fig. 1. Ontology. Representation of the model.

model are offered by means of software services. Their implementation features depend on the system and the used platform. In this section, we propose a guideline about services requirements and their functions.

Firstly, we have identified two kinds of services according to the running device: mobile and web services. The first one includes the internal services which can be deployed by the mobile phone or smartphone. The second one is related to services hosted in a server as web services. For that, a network connection (via wireless) between mobile device and server is needed.

Assuming a real scenario, the services are runned in order according to the table 2, with their inputs and outputs. Inputs represent needed objects or procedures for service running. And the outputs are the results provided by the services.

For example, the comparison procedure to get a *frailty assessment output* can include the use of data mining and classification algorithms, or mathematical formulas based on similarity and distance. In the same way, the *frailty assessment*

Table 2. Inputs and outputs of identified services

Service	Type	Description	Inputs	Outputs
Accelerometer data acquisition	mobile	Responsible for accelerometer data gathering and storage at run time, when elderly people perform a specific gait and balance test. This also includes mobile communication between smartphone and accelerometer sensor.	accelerometer signal	accelerometer values in x,y,z axes)
Accelerometer data processing	mobile	Responsible for carrying out accelerometer data handling through the data filtering and segmentation as well as accelerometry indicators calculation.	accelerometer values (x,y,z axes)	accelerometry indicators
Patient record extraction	web	It defines the mechanisms to obtain frailty risk factors from the patient record. The use of clinical standards could be necessary.	patient record, accelerometry indicators	frailty risk factors
Comparison procedure	web	This service is responsible for performing a comparison between frailty risk factors from the elderly patient studied and each of the patients stored into the patient stack	frailty risk factors, patient stack	frailty assessment
Setting up a built result	web	Parsing of comparison results in a formal language, easily readable by the mobile phone.	frailty assessment	frailty assessment formalized
Visualization of frailty assessment	mobile	Services which define the method for frailty results preparation and visualization on the smartphone screen, after receiving data from the server.	frailty assessment formalized	information, tips and charts for the physician
Storage into Patient Stack	web	Service related to the storage of the new patient data in the patient stack structure, increasing patient stack size and improving the accuracy for frailty assessment in the future.	risk factors from a new patient	patient stack with new patient

formalized output may consist of XML files, structures or programming objects. These are some ideas to develop the corresponding services, but that are not part of this work.

6   Discussions

In this work we have presented a model to support the elderly frailty diagnosis in a ubiquitous environment by using mobile devices such as mobile phones and accelerometers. Nowadays, physicians do not have a centralized method which provides a frailty assessment based on the results of existing tests and clinical information.

On the other hand, we can take advantage of smartphone features to develop frailty diagnosis tools. Accelerometer sensors and wireless communication capabilities are essential in our model which aims to lead the developer in implementing mobile software systems for frailty assessment based on services, providing a conceptual and functional frame.

Ongoing work is to evaluate the efficiency and usability of the model on a group of software developers considering the proposed entities and services. Besides, in the future, we would like to make a comparison between frailty assessment mobile tools which make use of our model and other systems that do not take into account.

Acknowledgment. This work has been partially financed by the TIN2010-20510-C04-04 project from Ministerio de Ciencia e Innovacion (Spain) and PII1I09-0123-2762 project from Junta de Comunidades de Castilla-La Mancha (Spain).

References

1. Woodhouse, K.W., Wynnie, H., Baillie, S., et al.: Who are the frail elderly? Q J. Med. 68, 505–506 (1988)
2. Gillick, M.R.: Long-term care options for the frail elderly. J. Am. Geriatr. Soc. 37, 1198–1203 (1989)
3. Hamerman, D.: Toward an understading of frailty. Ann. Intern. Med. 130, 945–950 (1999)
4. Spirduso, W., Gillam-Macrae, P.: Physical activity and quality of life in the frail elderly, pp. 226–255. Academic Press, New York (1991)
5. Berkman, B., Foster, L.W., Campion, E.: Failure to thrive: paradigm for the frail elder. Gerontologist 29, 654–659 (1989)
6. Fried, L.P., Waltson, J., Newman, A.B.: Frailty in older adults: evidence for phenotype. J. Gerontology 56(A)(3), 146–156 (2001)
7. Martin, F.C., Brighton, P.: Frailty: different tools for different purposes? Age and Ageing 37, 129–131 (2008)
8. Jones, D.M., Song, X., Rockwood, K.: Operationalizing a frailty index from a standardized comprehensive geritaric assessment. J. Am. Geriatr. Soc. 52, 1929–1933 (2004)
9. Searle, S.D., Mitnitski, A., Gahbauer, E.A., Gill, T., Rockwood, K.: A standard procedure for creating a frailty index. BMC Geriatics 8, 8–24 (2008)
10. Gobbens, R.J., Luijkx, K.G., Wijnen-Sponselee, M.T., Schols, J.M.: Towards an Integral Conceptual Model of Frailty. The Journal of Nutrition Health & Aging 14, 175–181 (2010)
11. Tehou, O., Jakobi, J., Vandervoort, A., Jones, G.: A comparison of physical activity (PA) assessment tools across levels of frailty. Gerontology and Geriatrics (2011) (article in press)
12. Auvinet, B., Chaleil, D., Barrey, E.: Accelerometric gait analysis for use in hospital outpatients. Rev. Rhum. Engl. Ed. 66(7-9), 389–397 (1999)
13. Foerster, F., Fahrenberg, J.: Motion pattern and posture: correctly assessed by calibrated accelerometers. Behav. Res. Methods Instrum. Comput. 32(3), 450–457 (2000)
14. Fontecha, J., Navarro, F.J., Hervás, R., Bravo, J.: Elderly Frailty detection by using accelerometer-enabled smartphones and clinical information records. Personal and Ubiquitous Computing Journal, doi:10.1007/s00779-012-0559-5
15. Espinoza, S., Fried, L.: Risk Factors for Frailty in the Older Adult. Clinical Geriatrics 15(6), 37–44 (2007)
16. Tinetti, M.E.: Performance-oriented assessment of mobility problems in elderly patients. Journal of the American Geriatrics Society 34(2), 119–126 (1986)
17. Matias, S., Nayak, U., Isaacs, B.: Balance in elderly patients: the "get-up and go" test. Arch. Phys. Med. Rehabilitation 67(6), 387–389 (1986)

Personal Ambient Intelligent Reminder for People with Cognitive Disabilities

Leila S. Shafti[1], Pablo Alfonso Haya[2], Manuel García-Herranz[3], and Xavier Alamán[3]

[1] Computer Science and Engineering Dept., Universidad Carlos III de Madrid
[2] IIC-Knowledge Engineering Institute, Universidad Autónoma de Madrid
[3] Computer Engineering Dept., Universidad Autónoma de Madrid

Abstract. The high number of people with Cognitive Disabilities (CD) is a serious social issue. A significant number of workers in the society provide care to family members with CD. The working caregivers either need to reschedule their working hours or spend less time with their elders. This article proposes PAIR, a Personal Ambient Intelligent Reminder that is designed to assist subjects with CD, their caregivers and the health professionals in an intelligent environment. Its goal is twofold: i) to create schedules that support complex temporal relationships between activities; ii) to generate a set of rules as a reminder agent to be included in an ambient intelligent environment in order to remind the patients and caregivers about the daily activities of the patient.

Keywords: Mental Disorder, Intelligent Reminder, Personal Environment, Event-Condition-Action Rules.

1 Introduction

In 2001 the World Health Organization reports that one in every four people develop one or more mental or behavioral disorders at some stage in life [1]. Although not all of them have difficulties in performing daily tasks without assistance, there are a significant number that do require some kind of external aid. Extrapolating from the 490 million citizens of the 27 Member States comprising the European Union, suggests that five to fifteen million citizens of the European Union are estimated to have an intellectual disability [2]. Other cognitive disabilities such as Alzheimer's Disease, Autism, or Traumatic Brain Injury require similar level of assistance.

Yet, each case of cognitive disability (CD) demands a particular treatment; there are requirements that are common to the most of them. The subject may forget the routine activities such as drinking or eating, taking medicines, calling a family member, or taking a bath. Besides, many intellectually disabled people could not live alone, or if they could, it was only for short periods [3]. In these cases, the subject may need some kind of occupational therapy to enhance the ability to perform daily activities. Occupational therapy consists of giving the subject a list of tasks to perform each day to keep them active. The caregiver

J. Bravo, R. Hervás, and M. Rodríguez (Eds.): IWAAL 2012, LNCS 7657, pp. 383–390, 2012.
© Springer-Verlag Berlin Heidelberg 2012

is responsible for supervising that the subject fulfills the assigned daily routine. Frequently, the caregiver is not a health professional but a family member. Thus, the actor that creates the task list is different from the actor that supervises it.

This paper describes PAIR and evaluates its user interface. It is organized as follows: next section compares PAIR with similar approaches. Sections 3 and 4 describe PAIR's user interface and ECA rule generations. Section 5 evaluates the interface and conclusions are given in Section 6.

2   Related Works

Several systems have been published in the literature to technologically support the Activities of Daily Living for people with CD. One of the earlier systems is Isaac system [4]. It is based on GPS-enabled hand-held devices with dialing and taking picture support. The main goal of the project is to increase the independence of subjects by enabling them to do more on their own and to decide themselves when they want to use the option of interacting with their caregivers. In order to provide such support, the subject is guided by sequences of images showed on the hand-held screen to perform the daily task. Additionally, the subject can decide to dial the caregiver who automatically receives visual and GPS information about the location of the subject. There are also commercially available systems [5,6,7,8] that share with the previous one the multimedia capabilities, but lack the communication ones. They provide scripting support to the caregivers for creating schedules for their users. However, these systems are limited because they cannot react to dynamic situations.

Carmien et al. [9] aimed to bridge the gap between the envisioned context by the caregivers and the actual context in which the action takes place. In so doing, they follow a distributed cognition approach that extends the caregivers capabilities instead of replacing it. The outcome of their endeavors is called MAPS-Line which includes a caregiver authoring, client prompting tools based on hand-held and remote monitoring tools for caregivers.

This article proposes PAIR, a Personal Ambient Intelligent Reminder that is designed to assist patients with CD and their caregivers in an intelligent environment. PAIR permits the caregiver or health professional to define the daily activities that the patient should perform and then translates this information to a set of Event-Condition-Action (ECA) rules using our rule language [10]. The rules generated by PAIR are used in the intelligent environment system as a reminder agent for two purposes. First, the agent in the intelligent system can provide the caregiver a list of activities for each day and remind him/her about the activity to be performed by the patient when the time is approaching. Second, the agent can be combined with an activity recognition module to supervise over the patient to check whether an activity in a specific time is performed. In case that the activity is performed earlier or later than when it was defined, the agent reminds the subject about it or alerts the caregiver. The main difference between PAIR and other similar systems is that due to using ECA rules to represent the activity schedules, the result of PAIR can be easily integrated into an intelligent system to make a connection with an activity recognition module.

3   PAIR Interface - Receiving Information

Previous approaches are based on the principles of creating a shared understanding between the caregivers and the subjects [11]. We pose a similar proposal but with three main differences. First, we deal with three different human actors: the subject, the caregivers and the health professional (usually an occupational therapist). Similar to other approaches, the schedule is executed by the subject, but its creation and monitoring can be performed by different actors. Second, previous approaches provide support for creating scripts which plan individual's activities. Their scripts are composed of a sequence of multimedia data representing the sequence of tasks to be performed. In our approach, a script describes a more complex temporal relationship. An activity in a schedule can be performed in relation to another activity or the time of the day. We aim to integrate several of the temporal relationships proposed by Allen in [12]. According to our own experience, health professionals are willing to manage more complex and powerful tools than previous proposals. Third, our system permits to convert the defined schedule to a set of ECA rules. These rules are easily added to an intelligent environment for monitoring patients.

PAIR consists of two main parts. The first part is a web-based user interface that permits the caregiver or health professional to define the daily activities that the subject should perform. The second part consists of generating a set of rules using our ECA rule language [10] which will be integrated later into an intelligent system for further use.

To prepare the reminder system, the occupational therapist or caregiver, as the user of the system, must enter a list of routine activities and time when they should be performed. This is done using the interface provided in PAIR. The user should first log in so that the system knows the identification of the patient, for example *phaya*. Then, the user enters the description of each activity into the system through the following four sessions.

Definition of Activity. In this part, first, the user determines the date from when the rules related to this activity must be fulfilled, for instance, start a medication from next week. Then, the user defines when during the day the activity must be performed. The time that an activity is performed can be in relation to an hour or another activity (see Fig. 1(a)). For example *starting from tomorrow, wake up at 10 am* or *starting from next week, take the medicine at least 15 minutes before lunch.*

Repetition of Activity. Here, the user determines the frequency of performing the activity, such as *each day, every 6 hours*, and so on, as shown in Fig. 1(b).

Termination of Activity. Activities might need to be repeated forever or till a certain time. This part helps the user to enter information about the termination time for an activity (see Fig. 1(c)).

Alert about Activity. This part asks the user to enter instructions (provided by occupational therapist) in case that the patient does not perform what s/he was supposed to do. The user has three options to choose as an alert, as shown in Fig. 1(d). The first option is to keep reminding the patient about the mistake until s/he corrects it. This option is selected for mistakes that do not cause any danger, such as forgetting to turn off the TV. The second option is to alert the patient about the mistake. This option is selected for activities that if not performed in a certain time are likely to cause a danger, for example, turning off the oven after cooking. The last option is to alert the supervisor (that is, the corresponding doctor or therapist) directly. This option is selected for activities that must be performed in a certain time otherwise cause a serious problem, like for example, taking a medicine earlier than when it was supposed to be taken.

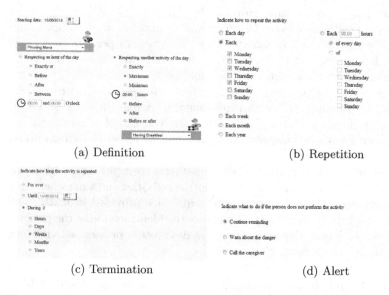

(a) Definition (b) Repetition

(c) Termination (d) Alert

Fig. 1. Pair Interface: activity entered as "start from 15/06/2012, Phoning Maria maximum 02:00 hours after Having Breakfast, and repeat it each Monday, Wednesday, Friday, during 2 weeks. In case of not performing the activity continue reminding.".

4　PAIR's Rule Generation

PAIR is designed to convert the definition of activities given by the caregiver to rules. The generated rules are then introduced to the ambient intelligent system as an agent to control the activities performed by the person with CD or to assist the caregiver to monitor the patient.

Considering Fig. 1(a), thirteen possible options are available for an activity: four options in case of "Respecting an hour" and nine options in case of "Respecting another activity". Thus, thirteen sets of rules can be generated. However, the

PAIR program is based on six fixed rules (five simple rules and one composed rule). All the thirteen sets of rules are generated by combining these six rules. The six rules are defined bellow, where A_1 and A_2 are activities and t is a time in milliseconds. Note that rules 2 and 3 say "when A_2 is performed after A_1". It doesn't mean that A_2 must always be performed after A_1.

1. after_act(A_2, A_1): A_2 must be performed after A_1 and not before.
2. atmost_act(A_1, A_2, t): when A_2 is going to be performed after A_1, there must be at most t milliseconds between them.
3. atleast_act(A_1, A_2, t): when A_2 is going to be performed after A_1, there must be at least t milliseconds between them.
4. after_t(A_1, t): A_1 must be performed after t and not before.
5. before_t(A_1, t): A_1 must be performed before t and not after.
6. exactly_at(A_1, A_2, t): when A_2 is going to be performed after A_1, it must be performed exactly t milliseconds after A_1. It is equivalent to say when A_2 is going to be performed after A_1, it must be started between t and t+EPSILON after A_1, where EPSILON is a short time defined in the program (by default, one minute). This is equivalent to say there must be at least t and at most t+EPSILON milliseconds between two activities, that is, atleast_act(A_1, A_2, t) and atmost_act(A_1, A_2, t+EPSILON).

Then the thirteen sets of rules obtained from PAIR's interface are defined as conjunction of the above fixed rules. For example, 'A_2 must be performed exactly t milliseconds after A_1' is equivalent to after_act(A_2,A_1) and exactly_act(A_1,A_2,t).

The six main rules are easily translated to ECA rules (see Fig. 2 for examples). In the implementation, it is considered that each activity has a property called status which can have the following values: UNDONE (when activity hasn't been started), ACTIVE (when it is started), INACTIVE (when it is paused), and DONE (when it is finished). The warning message of each rule is sent to the patient or the caregiver (this part is not implemented yet).

When rules are generated, they are integrated into the intelligent ambient as a reminder agent. The agent is activated at the date the caregiver indicated and deactivated by the date of termination of activity (Section 3). If the intelligent ambient has a module for activity recognition, this module detects when an activity's status is changed. When the status is changed, its corresponding rule in reminder agent is evaluated using rule agents and in case that something is done incorrectly the corresponding alert message is sent.

The generated rules are also used to provide a list of activities for the caregiver. Each activity in the list is associated with a time stamp that determines when it must be performed. Note that the performance time of some activities depends on the performance time of other activities, for instance, *taking the medicine at least 15 minutes before having lunch*. In this case the system calculates when the activity *taking the medicine* should be performed, knowing the time when *having lunch* will occur. If the user does not enter any information about *having lunch*, then the system uses predefined time associated to this activity by the administrator of the system (that is, usually the occupational therapist). The activities in the list are then ordered according to the time stamp.

```
Rule 1: after_act(A_2, A1)
A2:*:status::
    A2:$0:hasinvolved=person:phaya && A2:$0:status="ACTIVE" &&
    A1:*:hasinvolved=person:phaya && A1:$1:status!="DONE"
            => "warn:TOO_EARLY!!!";
Rule 2: atmost_act(A1, A2, t)
A1:*:status::
    A1:$0:hasinvolved=person:phaya && A1:$0:status="DONE" &&
    A2:*:hasinvolved=person:phaya && A2:$1:status!="ACTIVE"
        => TIMER t
            {A2:*:hasinvolved=person:phaya && A2:$0:status!="ACTIVE"
            => "warn:TOO_LATE!!!";}
            {}
Rule 3: atleast_act(A1, A2, t)
A1:*:status::
    A1:$0:hasinvolved=person:phaya && A1:$0:status="DONE" &&
    A2:*:hasinvolved=person:phaya && A2:$1:status!="ACTIVE"
        => TIMER t
            {}
            {A2:*:status ::
                A2:$0:hasinvolved=person:phaya && A2:$0:status="ACTIVE"
                => "warn:TOO_EARLY!!!";}
```

Fig. 2. Implementation of Rules

5   Evaluation of the Interface

As a primer phase of evaluation, PAIR has been introduced to 14 occupational therapists of the Care Center for Brain Injury in Spain (CEADAC) to evaluate the interface and utility of the system. These professionals work with persons with acquired brain injury. This disease is the result of damage in the structure of the brain that can provoke a wide variety of problems. Middleton defined in [13] three groups of after-effects that affect directly to the patient: physical effects, cognitive effects, and emotional and behavioral effects. The last one may affect their relatives as well. PAIR aims to enhance the life of such patients through guiding the patient to perform different activities.

For this evaluation, a list of 17 activities was given to each person to enter into PAIR. Definition of activities had different levels of difficulties, from very simple tasks such as *Get up at 10am* to more complex ones such as *Take*

Table 1. The evaluation results: the average amount of agreements in each aspect is calculated. Numbers between parentheses show the standard deviation.

PAIR Aspects	Interface	Usability	Ease of Use	Satisfaction
Average	3.3 ($\pm$0.7)	3.1 ($\pm$0.6)	3.1 ($\pm$0.8)	3.3 ($\pm$0.7)

the medicine Artane after 12 and at least 15 minutes before lunch. Then, the therapists were asked to fill out a form, answering 16 questions regarding four aspects of PAIR: Interface (whether it was clear and understandable), Usability (whether the system is useful), Ease of Use (how easy it was to use the system), and Satisfaction (whether the results were satisfactory). Answers were given by marking numbers one to four indicating the level of agreement: 1) Completely Disagree, 2) Not Agree, 3) Agree, 4) Strongly Agree. The result for each aspect of PAIR is summarized in Table 1.

In general the therapists did not have major difficulties in using the application. They were able to enter information into the system with almost no help of PAIR developers. Also, they showed satisfaction after testing the system, as it can be seen in Table 1. Their comments indicate that PAIR can be of great help for patients with mental disorders and their family members.

6   Conclusions and Future Work

PAIR is designed to enhance the life of people with CD, their caregivers and the health professionals. It permits to create a schedule of daily activities with complex temporal relationships and to remind the patient and the caregiver about the activities to be performed when the time is approaching. It should be noted that activity schedule creation and monitoring can be performed by both the caregivers and the occupational therapists.

This article described PAIR's rule generation and evaluated its user interface. The system allows therapists and caregivers to define complex activities easily. The defined activities are converted to a set of ECA rules. Six fixed rules are implemented in PAIR which provide the facility to generate more complex rules representing complex temporal relationships among activities. The set of rules are easily integrated into an intelligent system to be connected with an activity recognition module or assist the caregiver to monitor the patient. The ability to define activities in a non-sequential order permits a quick preparation of activities schedule. The therapists who evaluated the system believe PAIR provides a quick and efficient programming of activities and opens many possibilities for further enhancement of patient's life. In contrast with other approaches, we have shown that a more ambitious tool can provide more representation power to the professional end-user without affecting the usability.

The integration of PAIR in an ambient intelligent environment requires a challenging research for further progress. We are currently working in the integration of PAIR with aQRdate [14], a system that shows adaptive manuals for daily life activities for people with acquired brain injury using mobile devices. Other direction that we would like to explore is the integration of an activity recognition module. This module receives the list of activities with time stamps and checks whether an activity in a specific time is performed or not through analyzing the interactions of the patient with sensors and devices in the intelligent environment. In case that the activity is performed earlier or later than when it was defined, PAIR reminds the subject about it or alerts the caregiver.

Acknowledgments. This work was funded by ASIES (Adapting Social & Intelligent Environments to Support people with special needs), Ministerio de Ciencia e Innovación - TIN2010-17344, and it has been developed in conjunction with CEADAC (Centro Estatal de Atención al Daño Cerebral).

References

1. World Health Organisation Fact Sheet: Mental and neurological disorders (2001), http://www.who.int/whr/2001/media_centre/en/whr01_fact_sheet1_en.pdf
2. Pomona II project: Health indicators for people with intellectual disabilities (2008), http://www.pomonaproject.org/action1_2004_frep_14_en.pdf
3. Moonen, R., Kauppinen, S., Iyer, A., Ojasalo, K.: Methods and challenges for doing research with intellectually disabled people: an ongoing empirical study. In: Proc. UMADR, pp. 25–30 (2010)
4. Jönsson, B., Svensk, A.: Isaac - a personal digital assistant for the differently abled people. In: Proc. 2nd TIDE Congress, pp. 356–361 (1995)
5. Visions System, http://www.thevisionssystem.com/
6. AbleLink Technologies, http://www.ablelinktech.com
7. Meet PEAT: A life-changing mobile app for people with cognitive challenges, http://brainaid.com//
8. Davies, D.K., Stock, S.E., Wehmeyer, M.L.: Enhancing independent task performance for individuals with mental retardation through use of a handheld self-directed visual and audio prompting system. Education and Training in Developmental Disabilities 37(2), 209–219 (2002)
9. Carmien, S., DePaula, R., Gorman, A., Kintsch, A.: Increasing workplace independence for people with cognitive disabilities by leveraging distributed cognition among caregivers and clients. Computer Supported Cooperative Work 13(5-6), 443–470 (2004)
10. García-Herranz, M., Haya, P.A., Alamán, X.: Towards a ubiquitous end-user programming system for smart spaces. Journal of Universal Computer Science 16(12), 1633–1649 (2010)
11. Arias, E., Eden, H., Fischer, G., Gorman, A., Scharff, E.: Transcending the individual human mind-creating shared understanding through collaborative design. ACM Transactions on Computer Human Interaction 7(1), 84–113 (2000)
12. Allen, J.F.: Maintaining knowledge about temporal intervals. Communications of the ACM 26(11), 832–843 (1983)
13. Middleton, J.A.: Acquired brain injury. Psychiatry 4(7), 61–64 (2005)
14. Gómez, J., Montoro, G., Haya, P.A., Alamán, X., Alves, S., Martínez, M.: Adaptive manuals as assistive technology to support and train people with acquired brain injury in their daily life activities. Personal and Ubiquitous Computing (in press, 2012)

JeWheels: Kinect Based Serious Game Aimed at Wheelchair Users

Zelai Sáenz de Urturi, Amaia Méndez Zorrilla, and Begoña García Zapirain

DeustoTech Institute of Technology, DeustoTech-LIFE Unit
University of Deusto, Avda. Universidades 24, 48007 Bilbao, Spain
{zelai.saenz,amaia.mendez,mbgarciazapi}@deusto.es

Abstract. People who use wheelchairs tend to have lower leisure activity levels compared to the able-bodied population. This is due to several factors such as the feeling of not being capable or lack of accessibility. JeWheels is an exergame intended for wheelchair users, aiming to improve motor-skills and cognitive abilities as well as stimulate physical exercise while having fun. To achieve this, a Kinect based system intended for Windows have been developed using skeletal tracking to capture the body movements, enabling users to control and interact intuitively with the computer without any intermediary controller. Preliminary tests have shown an increase in the users' motivation while playing the game. Feedback was taken from physiotherapists' written observations and user experience questionnaires.

Keywords: Kinect, serious game, wheelchair, physical disability.

1 Introduction

People with physical disabilities have limitations in control and strength of motion, which in turn limits their ability to perform daily tasks. These individuals often require mobility aids such as wheelchairs, crutches or canes and consequently, they experience many changes in their lives, such as a decrease in leisure activities. This could be due to several factors including the feeling of not being capable, lack of accessibility and limited opportunities to participate [1]. Leisure is a health promotion strategy for all adults that also provides enjoyment, opportunity to develop a self-concept and opportunities to build and enhance social relationships. The numerous benefits that leisure offers justify its use as an intervention for them [2, 3].

The study by Coyle et al. [4] suggests that people with an active lifestyle feel more satisfaction with their life, are less depressed and have more reliable relations than non-active people. However, despite the importance and benefits of leisure for this population, many environmental, physical and psychological barriers exist, such as issues of accessibility, inadequate finances or lack of interest, which results in a reduction or a complete loss of participation in meaningful leisure activities [5].

Nowadays, one of the most common leisure activities to engage in is playing video games. Electronic games have become a major part in child and youth culture, to the extent of being socially accepted amongst adults. But they are the most challenging

J. Bravo, R. Hervás, and M. Rodríguez (Eds.): IWAAL 2012, LNCS 7657, pp. 391–398, 2012.
© Springer-Verlag Berlin Heidelberg 2012

applications concerning accessibility and usability for people with a physical impairment. Many of them find computer games difficult to control and those that suffer from tremor have difficulty in making accurate movements with their devices. These surface-dependent devices present challenges for those who use a wheelchair and have difficulties positioning their chair close enough to a table or desk so that they can operate the control device. Also, it has been identified in various studies [6-8] that with problems like these, users might become frustrated and demotivated and fail to benefit from the advantages of using virtual environments.

The rising popularity of serious games has seen a recent push towards the application of video game-based technologies to doing physical exercise and improving health.

A serious game can be defined as an interactive computer application, with or without a significant hardware component, that has a challenging goal, is fun to play and/or engaging and incorporates some concept of scoring [9]. Exergames are type of serious games that combine both play and exercise. One of the important factors in the generation of an exergaming system is the need to make the game attractive to players and at the same time effective as an exercise.

Here we provide preliminary details of the JeWheels project; a serious game aimed at people with a physical impairment, which is currently being developed. This project involves designing and developing a serious game using the Kinect for Windows sensor. Its designated audience is people with a wide range of physical disabilities, but must have at least one functioning arm to operate the system. This group includes wheelchair users with lower limb motor disabilities.

The overall objective is to make new technologies more accessible to individuals with physical disabilities, specially for those who use a wheelchair, stimulating the engaging in leisure activities, as well as making them perform physical exercise to improve mobility and health while still having fun.

This general approach can be broken down into several specific objectives, as described below:

- Design an interface that suits the needs of the population who use wheelchairs, making use of ICT, specifically through the use of the Kinect Sensor.
- Identify and evaluate a range of objective variables such as: the movements a user can made and the level of success measured by the caregivers or physiotherapists.
- Promoting e-inclusion: equal opportunities for access and participation of people with special needs in the Information Society.

The article is structured as follows: Section 2 describes the proposed system design and Section 3 summarizes the obtained results of the game. Finally, some concluding remarks are presented in the last section.

2 Proposed System Design

In this section the general architecture and the implementation of the game are described. Please refer to Figure 1 to see the general diagram of the system.

2.1 Architecture Description

The architecture used to develop the application is a three-layer one. The main goal of the architecture is the segmented design, which separates the logical layer from the business layer. This means that tasks can be divided in order to work comfortably by levels, abstracting some levels from others and coming up with improved scalability and modifiability. The three layers are described below:

Presentation Layer. The various interface elements making up the application are situated in this layer. They display and capture the user's information in order to deliver it to the business layer.

Gameplay. This layer houses the internal logical needed to provide core functionality of the game. Having an independent business layer provides great adaptability to the application because it allows the incorporation of new game levels to this Serious Game without compromising other application components. Here, information the sensor gathered in relation with the position of the user's hands is received. The resulting information is sent to be displayed in the presentation layer, on the computer screen, or to be used in concurrence with the database, to store all the data generated during the last session.

Database Layer. This layer is made up of the database manager, which will back up the business layer in the storing and data-obtaining processes. In the database some parameters will be stored like the name of the user, the scores, records, time needed to complete the level and game mode (play with one or both arms).

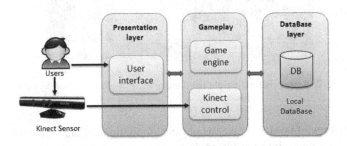

Fig. 1. JeWheel's architecture diagram

2.2 Implementation

The proposed game is based on Microsoft's Kinect sensor, which is a webcam-style add-on peripheral intended for Windows operating system. Kinect enables users to control and interact intuitively with the computer without any intermediary device, such as a controller, through a natural user interface using gestures. The increased physical activity from arm movement, could be a potentially useful exercise.

Kinect is a sensor set on a horizontal bar with a small base, to be positioned below the video display. It has an RGB camera and a depth sensor, which provide full-body 3D motion capture capabilities.

The design of the game consists mainly of three blocks: a pose recognition system, a set of options to configure the game and the main game.

Block 1. Pose Recognition: This part consist of the partial recognition of the body posture, which is limited to the upper trunk of the user, due to the game being aimed at people who use wheelchairs and taking into account that it is not physically possible for the users to move their legs and feet.

It processes the depth data obtained from the Kinect sensor to locate the users' body and captures 16 joints of the human body structure (head, hands, elbows, shoulders, spine, hip, knees and feet) to make the pose recognition part. With this, the JeWheels' recognition system is able to detect if a person is seated or standing up and also differentiates whether a user has his arms raised or not and which one of them (right or left) is currently being used, in order to obtain more accurate movements from the user. Please refer to Figure 2 to see the pose recognition system.

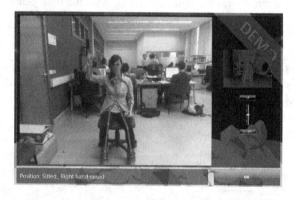

Fig. 2. A user rising the right hand using the Pose Recognition System

Block 2. Settings: In order to take the physical limitations of the users into account, a set of configuration options have been designed to make the game easier to play, such as the option of changing the angle of the camera (allowing the user to tilt the device up or down to get a better image or more complete view of the player) only moving one arm up and down, or the choice of a game mode: use the left hand, the right hand, or both.

If the users start playing and the sensor is not connected to the computer or does not fully function, various alert messages appear in the screen such as: "No Kinect device found" or "Plug my power cord in!". The objective is to provide the user with more information on why the sensor is not currently working.

Block 3. The Game: The objective is to collect coins that appear on the screen, utilizing the arms which will be represented as two pictures on the screen. The game controls the difficulty by specifying the number of coins to collect and the speed in which they need to be collected in order to pass the level. The score is related to the time elapsed, that is, the sooner the user catches a coin, the more points will be obtained.

The game has three different entities (images), which appear randomly on the screen (coin1, coin2 and a sack of money). Although only these three images are used, a user is able to distinguish four entities at any given time. When a coin is collected, a new coin will appear, making the user see four in total. This continues until a total of 50 entities have been processed.

Apart from the skeleton data the Kinect also gives a user index i.e. while the skeleton data gives you the position of various parts of the body, the user index gives you, after a little processing, the point-of-view that each user currently has. However in this case, if more than one player stands in front of the sensor only the closest user will be detected, showing a single-player game. This design decision was made due to the difficulty of placing two or more wheelchairs within the Kinect's field of vision.

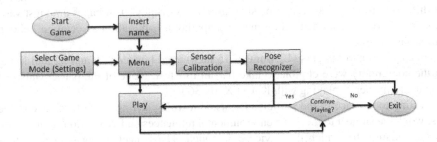

Fig. 3. JeWheels' flow Chart

3 Results

This section describes the results obtained in two facets: technical results and the feedback received from the user satisfaction questionnaires completed by the users and physiotherapists.

Technical Results. At the beginning of the game, the users will be asked to enter their name, which will be referenced in the scores. Then, the users have to calibrate the sensor in order to check their position. To achieve this, the users have to access the Pose Recognition menu and calibrate the sensor moving their hand up or down until they can fully see the body on the screen. In the right side of the Figure 2 the tilt option is shown and in the Figure 3 main flow chart is presented.

After the sensor's calibration, the user is now able to play the game. The Figures 4 and 5 shows the main menu and a user moving his hands around the screen in order to catch the coins and bags of money. This is the first level of the game but the authors are implementing more scenarios taking into account the users' and physiotherapists' feedback.

Fig. 4. JeWheels' Main Menu   **Fig. 5.** JeWheels' game first level

Satisfaction Survey. Permission to carry out the experiment was obtained from the Fekoor association and the IRB Committee. Participants provided prior informed consent and were approved by the IRB to participate in the test. Individuals with a variety of different disabilities (cerebral palsy, muscular dystrophy...) and ages amongst various ranges were recommended by the participating rehabilitation association Fekoor, our project partner.

Twenty seven volunteers (12 women, 15 men) aged between 20 and 52 and living in the community were eligible to take part in this test. None of the participants had previous experience playing with Kinect Xbox 360.

Testing took place in the participants' usual learning setting so performance in the test would be subject to the same environmental influences and distractions that prevail in the situation for which the device is intended. The Kinect sensor connected to a computer in a large television (32") was required to perform the test.

Each participant took part in an individual game session and immediately after it, a usability experience questionnaire was filled out by them. All questions were answered on a 5-point semantic rating scale from Strongly disagree (0 points) to Strongly agree (4 points). These questionnaires were designed based on the System Usability Scale. Table 1 shows the performed questionnaire during test sessions.

Table 1. System Usability Questionnaire

QUESTIONS
1. I think I would like to use this game frequently
2. I completely understand game instructions
3. I found it easy to play
4. I think I need help while playing
5. I know always exactly what I am doing
6. I know always exactly why I am doing things while playing
7. I am able to read all the options in the screen
8. I needed to learn a lot of things before I could get going with this system

Two physiotherapists from Fekoor with whom they perform their daily exercises and rehabilitation were present during the test. Their feedback was sought in a simple personal interview, in which they were asked the following questions, answered also on the same semantic rating scale. Please refer to Table 2.

Table 2. Experts' Survey

QUESTION	SCORE (points)
Is useful to use Kinect to do physical exercise or rehabilitation?	7.0
Did you like the game design?	6.0
Was the user interface easy to use for individuals who use wheelchairs?	5.0
It increases the leisure activity?	6.0
It promotes e-inclusion?	5.0

The results obtained from the survey reported an increase in the users' motivation while playing the game, forgetting that it focuses on physical exercises. The usability questionnaires' scores (72) proved that is a valid tool and the survey reported positive results (29/40 points) based on the physiotherapists' feedback. However, developers are taking into account the results and are continually adapting the application to the final users.

Additionally, the physiotherapists suggested that by adjusting the movements of the objects that appear on the screen to enable specific user movements, the system could then be used as a rehabilitation tool for patients.

4   Conclusions

Most physical disabilities prevent people from using the hardware needed to interact with, and thus effectively playing, a game. JeWheels game might solve these problems, due to its lack of needing a controller to play and the fact that a wheelchair does not have to be positioned near a table or desk. Being surface free and unobstructed by connecting cables makes it much easier to use, as well as refraining from making the user memorize complex button systems. Controllers can cause problems for an increasingly older population, because there is often a gradual loss of muscle tone (Parkison's disease e.g), making fine movements more difficult which can also affect the ability to control a game [10].

This game has been developed so that beyond the pure entertainment value, the user also performs physical exercise, which in future might be used for physiotherapists to make their patients rehabilitation more fun to do.

The results obtained from the physiotherapists questionnaire and observations the researchers took will be used to continue developing next levels of the game.

This paper reflects only the first results, but this game can be extended to other groups such as old people who use wheelchairs.

Acknowledgments. This work was partially supported by the Basque Country Department of Education, Universities and Research. The authors also want to thank the cooperation of FEKOOR (*Association of individuals with physical disabilities in Biscay*), 'Cátedra de Ocio Deusto' Researchers and BIZKAILAB Initiative of the Biscay Council. Also special thanks to Asier López and Gonzalo Eguíluz DeustoTech's Life researchers for their support.

References

1. Gabriel, W., Renate, S.: Work loss following stroke. Int. J. Disability and Rehabilitation 31, 1487–1493 (2009)
2. Farrow, S., Reid, D.: Stroke survivors' perceptions of a leisure-based virtual reality program. Technology and Disability 16, 69–81 (2004)
3. Cassidy, T.: All work and no play: A focus on leisure time as a means for promoting health. Int. J. Counselling Psychology Quarterly 9, 77–90 (1996)
4. Coyle, P., Shank, J.W., Kinney Hutchins, D.A.: Psychosocial functioning and changes in leisure lifestyle among individuals with chronic secondary health problems related to spinal cord injury. Journal of Therapeutic Recreation 27(4), 239–252 (1993)
5. Specht, J., King, G., Brown, E., Foris, C.: The importance of leisure in the lives of persons with congenital physical disabilities. American Journal of Occupational Therapy 56, 436–445 (2002)
6. Standen, P.J., Brown, D.J., Anderton, N., Battersby, S.: A systematic evaluation of current control devices used by people with intellectual disabilities in non-immersive virtual environments. Cyberpsychology & Behavior 9(5), 608–613 (2006)
7. Trewin, S., Pain, H.: Keyboard and mouse errors due to motor disabilities for interaction tasks. International Journal of Human-Computer Studies 50(2), 109–144 (1999)
8. Standen, P.J., Camm, C., Battersby, S., Brown, D.J., Harrison, M.: An evaluation of the Wii Nunchuk as an alternative assistive device for people with intellectual and physical disabilities using switch controlled software. Computers & Education 56(1), 2–10 (2011)
9. Bergeron, B.: Developing Serious Games. Charles River Media (2006)
10. Bartiméus Accessibility Foundation, http://www.game-accessibility.com (accessed: February 23, 2012)

AngryEmail? Emotion-Based E-mail Tool Adaptation

Rosa M. Carro[1], Francisco J. Ballesteros[2], Alvaro Ortigosa[1],
Gorka Guardiola[2], and Enrique Soriano[2]

[1] Computer Science Department
Escuela Politécnica Superior, Universidad Autonoma de Madrid,
Francisco Tomás y Valiente, 11. Campus de Cantoblanco,
28049 Madrid, Spain
{Rosa.Carro,Alvaro.Ortigosa}@uam.es
[2] Laboratorio de Sistemas
Universidad Rey Juan Carlos
Camino del molino s/n
28943 Fuenlabrada (Madrid), Spain
{nemo,paurea,esoriano}@lsub.es

Abstract. This paper presents AngryEmail, an e-mail tool that adapts its behavior according to the user emotional state. When a user finishes writing an e-mail and clicks the send button, the e-mail is automatically analyzed to get information about the emotions reflected on it, following a lexical-based approach. If a high level of anger is detected, then the e-mail program keeps the message unsent, waits for five minutes and, afterwards, notifies the user that the e-mail will be sent one minute later. This approach allows users to reconsider the convenience of sending certain e-mails when they are noticeably angry. This can be useful for all the people in general, but especially for those with cognitive limitations, for whom emotion control is harder.

Keywords: Emotion detection, Interface adaptation, Special needs.

1 Motivation

Daily, people are involved in a wide variety of activities, which can be easy to tackle for some persons and more difficult for others, depending on each one's capability. In particular, people with cognitive limitations usually have more difficulties to cope with daily routines or to take decisions, especially when unforeseen events happen. In this context, we are working on the development of tools to assist people with cognitive limitations, in the framework of the project ASIES ("Adapting Social & Intelligent Environments to Support people with special needs"). This project aims to enhance user independent living and focuses on providing training and supporting daily activities of people with special needs by means of adaptive systems [1].

One of the collectives for which our developments are intended are young people with cognitive limitations coming to the Universidad Autonoma de Madrid (UAM) to be trained (for two years) to achieve labor and social integration [2]. According to the

J. Bravo, R. Hervás, and M. Rodríguez (Eds.): IWAAL 2012, LNCS 7657, pp. 399–406, 2012.

expert trainers of this group, one of their main limitations relates to emotion identification and control. In fact, this is one of the main competences to acquire during their training. With the aim of contributing to this purpose, we are working from two different perspectives. The first one consists on providing computer-based scenarios in which they learn to identify emotions in different situations and how to cope with each of them. The second one focuses on providing emotion-based assistance to them. Our recent research deals with automatic emotion identification, which allows the adaptation of the applications that they use accordingly. In particular, we have developed an adaptive e-mail tool that considers the user emotions as transmitted in each e-mail. If a high level of anger is detected, then the application keeps the message unsent during some minutes, allowing the user to reconsider the convenience of sending the e-mail. This is especially useful for people with cognitive limitations, for whom controlling emotions is not easy at all, and makes it possible to avoid unnecessarily uncomfortable situations related to highly emotive e-mails transmitting anger. Since communicating by e-mail is a usual activity of daily life, the application presented in this paper can do its bit in the framework of assisted living.

This paper is organised as follows. Section 2 describes the foundations of this work: the emotion recognition approach as well as the basis of the e-mail tool before the adaptation. Section 3 presents the emotion-aware adaptive e-mail, including some examples of use. Finally, section 4 discuss about the conclusions and future work.

2   Basis

In order to check the feasibility of our emotion-based e-mail adaptation proposal, we started from an easily configurable e-mail tool already developed in previous works. This tool was converted, afterwards, into an adaptive e-mail manager able to work differently according to the emotions detected. Lexical-based techniques were used for extracting emotions from e-mails. This section describes the base for emotion detection as well as the characteristics of the e-mail tool used.

2.1   Emotion Detection

Regarding emotion recognition in texts, the methods developed in recent research on sentiment analysis have shown to be very reliable. Sentiment analysis refers to the computational study of sentiments in texts [3]. Although many works have centered on the analysis of reviews [4], these techniques can be applied to recognise the overall sentiment in other formats. For example, news headlines are analysed in [5]. Commercial products can also be found in this area, like SAS Sentiment Analysis [6], which claims to be able to analyze digital content in real time, in order to understand customers' opinions and priorities.

Theorists disagree on which the basic emotions are. Ortony and Turner [7] collated a wide range of research on identification of basic emotions. Later, Parrot categorised a bigger list of emotions into a short tree structure [8]. In our case, we have focused on getting information about the level of joy, anger, sadness and fear reflected on written texts, following the emotion classification proposed in [9]. In particular, our previous work deals with analysing essays written by students to check whether it is possible to get information about these emotions. The first results obtained from this lexical-based approach suggest the possibility of making use of it for emotion detection [10]. We followed the same approach for emotion recognition in pieces of news, also with promising results. Therefore, we have followed the same procedure here: We have employed word-spotting techniques. For each e-mail, the emotion-recognition module looks for words related to each of the four basic emotions. It compares the words appearing in the e-mail with those included in four lists of words systematically generated, each of them corresponding to words related to one of those four emotions. The results of analysing a set of e-mails with adaptation purposes are presented in section 3.

2.2   E-mail Tool

The e-mail tool used as starting point for this proposal has been generated in the Olive Environment for the Octopus system. The basis of Olive, as well as the e-mail functioning, is presented next.

The Olive Environment. Octopus is a system that has been in use for several years to build pervasive applications and to provide a general-purpose computing environment [11]. Olive is both a user-interface management system and a window system developed for Octopus. It aims at providing support for User Interfaces (UIs in what follows) for ubiquitous computing applications.

UI components (i.e., widgets of a high-level of abstraction) are implemented and exported by means of network file systems. A file hierarchy represents the hierarchy of UI elements found in a UI. UI file servers, which implement a set of widgets and permit their use through the file system interface, support graphical displays and other devices employed for UIs. As a result, the application can program and use its UI in the same way it uses regular files, and it can be mostly unaware of the actual set of devices used to deploy the UI. Furthermore, external programs can rely on the file interface to inspect and operate on existing UI components. This centralized approach permits to introduce new functionalities quite easily. For example, it is possible to process e-mails looking for emotional content without disturbing the mail application. All the applications rely directly on the file interface, as described next.

Editing Files and Executing Commands. Olive supports file editing, directory browsing, and command execution. Thus, it can be considered a shell for the system. For each file being edited, Olive creates a tag panel (single line of editable text, in bold face) and a text panel below the tag that shows the file. It initializes the tag to contain the name of the file being edited, along with some commands understood by the system, and space for the user to type further text. To help programs started by the user, Olive sets the variable $file to the path of the file being edited. This permits the creation of programs that operate on the file being edited. For example, lp $file prints the text shown in the panel.

A powerful consequence of both using files and mapping the interface elements to them is that general purpose tools can be built to operate on any UI considered.

Examples are countless: rm can be used to remove them, ls can list the panels used, chgrp can be used to donate screen space, etc. The applications may run unaware of any of the external commands used on them. No code must be included to provide support for these commands, because all that is needed is to be able to use files.

Email Reading. For e-mail processing, we also rely on a simple approach that leverages the Olive environment. We keep e-mail decoded and stored in the file system, as any other document would be. An e- mail including some text along with several PDF documents is not different from a note made on a file along with two PDF files. This is the format used by the e-mail tool described here.

The editor becomes a mail reader as soon as there is a convenient way of producing mail listings. That can be done using grep, for example, although it is more convenient to use a program built for such task. A mouse click on an e- mail name (an e- mail path) opens it for reading. The same happens to any attachment. Regarding e-mail sending, a similar approach is followed. A program may collect files written by the user into an agreed-upon directory. These files are simple text files in the format used by Mail. It should be noticed that any editor is able to compose e-mail for delivery, without requiring a specific tool, because the e-mail spooler (by convention) tries to deliver any such file as an e-mail.

We find this approach a good strategy for handling e-mails. It consists mostly on avoiding the need for software to handle e-mail. Since there is no software, it will hardly run slow or out of memory. Of course, this is feasible only after having decoded e-mail messages, which means that we require software for the task indeed. Its job is now to unpack a mailbox into an already decoded set of files.

A mailbox is a directory, usually under /mail/box/$user/, that contains one directory per month (e.g., 200603/ for mails processed on March 2006). In these directories there is one directory per message. The directory for a message contains at least two files: text and raw. The text file has the e-mail headers and body already processed for reading. Its contents are similar to what is shown in figure 1 for an e-mail being read. Any attachment in the e-mail is kept stored in a separate file ready to be used. That is, decoded. When the attachment is a mail, the message is stored in a subdirectory. For mails with attachments, the text file contains additional text indicating the relative path names (from the mail's directory) that can be used to open the attachments. This is convenient to open attachments using the mouse.

To send a new e-mail, a script called Reply takes the text from the text panel where the e-mail to reply to is shown (if any) and creates a new text panel that the user can edit to compose the new e-mail. Once it has been composed, another script, Send, renames the file to indicate, to the spooler program, that the e-mail should be sent:

```
#!/bin/rc
fname=`{awk '{print $1}' < /dev/time}
cd /mail/box/$user/out
mv $file  $fname && echo $file spooled for delivery
```

This program renames the file $file to a name containing just numbers, which means that it will be spooled for delivery.

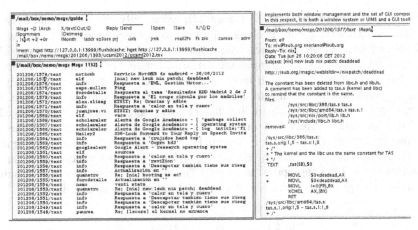

Fig. 1. Screenshot of the e-mail interface

3   Emotion-Aware E-mail

Figure 2 shows the general schema of this proposal. The user interacts with AngryEmail, the e-mail manager. When the user clicks on the send button, the Send script asks the emotion recognizer module to determine whether the e-mail reflects a high level of anger (isAngry?). The emotion recognizer analyses the e-mail following the lexical-based approach described above, and sends the response to the Send program. Then AngryEmail either send the message or postpone it accordingly. In the last case, it alerts the user so that he can discard the message. More details about how this is implemented are given next.

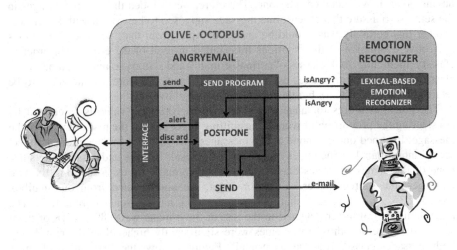

Fig. 2. General schema of emotion-aware e-mail management

In order to support the e-mail working adaptation, only the script Send must be modified, since this is the one in charge of asking the spooler program to send each e-mail. Before sending the message, Send calls the emotion recognition module. This one takes the e-mail text as an input and performs emotion recognition. If the result says that the text reflects a high level of anger, it sets the status of isAngry to success, which will be taken into account by the Send program. In such case, the program sleeps for 5 minutes, assuming that the user is angry and he might change his mind in a few minutes (regret having sent this e-mail). After 5 minutes, it notifies the user that the e-mail will be sent one minute later. Therefore, the user has still time to discard the message (by removing the corresponding file) if, on a second thought, he considers that it is not appropriate to be sent. The modified program to defer spooling when the message is considered to reflect a high level of anger is the following:

```
#!/bin/rc
fname=`{awk '{print $1}' < /dev/time}
cd /mail/box/$user/out
if( isangry $file){
   sleep 300
   echo $file spooled for delivery in 1 minute
   sleep 60
}
mv $file  $fname && echo $file spooled for delivery
```

A set of twenty five e-mails were processed to get information about the emotions reflected on them, in order to check whether our approach for emotion detection worked properly with texts from e-mails. They were chosen from our own mailboxes randomly, except two of them. One was remembered by us as inappropriate and, therefore, was directly selected from our mailbox. Regarding the other, we asked our colleagues to send us e-mails that they had sent when feeling anger and now regret having done it. We received only one. Therefore, we included these two messages in the set, just to assure that at least one message supposed to be written with anger, and another that certainly was, would be analysed. Apart from that, we made a previous subjective evaluation of the emotions transmitted in each of the e-mails, in order to classify them into two classes: "normal e-mail" and "angry e-mail". None of us classified any of the messages as "angry e-mail" (and, therefore, as candidate to be retained before been sent), but those two mentioned above.

The potential scores for anger range from 0 to 100. This value is calculated by considering the proportion of words transmitting anger against the rest of words in the message. It turned out that none of the messages, except those two mentioned above, scored more than 1 in the anger dimension. This result is quite understandable, since none of those messages was classified as "angry e-mail" by us. Regarding the two messages that scored higher values for anger, the one selected from our mailbox scored 2,35 while the one that our friend regret having sent scored 4,83. The maximum level of anger detected in the rest of the e-mails was 0,89 and 18 of them scored 0. Therefore, those two values were significantly higher than the rest, being both messages classified as "angry e-mail". Figure 3 shows the distribution of anger scores for this set of e-mails. According to the results obtained, the classification accuracy for that sample turned out to be 100%. We plan to repeat this study with a different and wider set of e-mails.

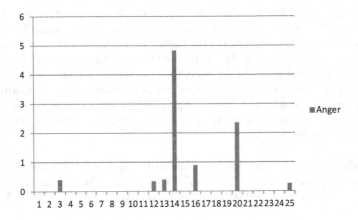

Fig. 3. Anger score distribution

4   Conclusions and Future Work

In this paper, we have presented AngryEmail, an emotion-aware e-mail tool that adapts its behaviour according to the emotions detected on each e-mail written. An automatic lexical-based approach has been used to identify emotions in e-mails, using a word-spotting technique. When a high level of anger is detected in an e-mail, AngryEmail keeps this e-mail unsent for five minutes and, after this time, notifies the user that the e-mail will be sent one minute later. This allows the use to reconsider the convenience of sending that e-mail.

The emotional analysis made to a set of e-mails already sent show that it is feasible to obtain information about the user emotions (in particular, anger) rather precisely by analyzing e-mail texts. From all the messages analysed, a high level of anger was detected in the two messages already identified as "inappropriate to be sent". In these cases, it might have been useful to give the senders the opportunity to rethink about sending the e-mail some minutes later.

We would like to explore the possibility of combining emotion e-mail analysis with that of messages written by users in the Facebook social network, as the one performed by SentBuk Facebook application [12]. In that work, positive/negative emotions are detected, as reflected on those messages written on Facebook walls. Furthermore, SentBuk detects high positive/negative changes on the user sentiment, with respect to the user "usual state". One possibility for improving AngryEmail would be to store, for each user, the usual level of anger reflected by the messages he writes. Then, AngryEmail could keep unsent for a second thought only those messages reflecting a significant emotional change in comparison with the user "usual level of anger". In other words, for a person whose messages always score 0 in anger, a message that scores, e.g., 2 can represent that he is angry. However, for a person that tends to write in an angrier or more aggressive style, the threshold to determine the convenience of keeping their e-mails unsent could be set higher.

In general, identifying the user emotions and incorporating this information in the user model can be very useful for intelligent and adaptive applications such as [13] or

[14]. Knowing the user emotion can contribute to identify his potential preferences or needs in different contexts. As it was stated before, this can be especially helpful in the context of assistive environments for users with cognitive limitations, since this collective have more difficulties to identify and control emotions [15]. However, we think that this proposal is useful for everybody, because sometimes it is difficult to control emotions (especially anger) and, in e-mail communication, it is probable to write inappropriate e-mails when feeling angry. In these situations, some users discard the message on time, while others feel better after sending it (and, in the end, they probably regret having done it).

Acknowledgments. This work has been funded by the Spanish Ministry of Science and Education, project ASIES (TIN2010-17344) and by Comunidad Autonoma de Madrid, projects CLOUDS (S2009/TIC-1692) and E-Madrid (S2009/TIC-1650).

References

1. Brusilovsky, P.: Adaptive hypermedia. In: Kobsa, A. (ed.) User Modeling and User Adapted Interaction, Ten Year Anniversary Issue, vol. 11(1/2), pp. 87–110 (2001)
2. Prodis Foundation, http://www.fundacionprodis.org/
3. Liu, B.: Sentiment Analysis and Subjectivity. In: Indurkhya, N., Damerau, F.J. (eds.) Handbook of Natural Language Processing, 2 edn. (2010)
4. Pang, B., Lee, L.: Opinion Mining and Sentiment Analysis. Foundation and Trends in Information Retrieval 2(1-2), 1–135 (2008)
5. Strappavana, C., Mihalcea, R.: Learning to identify emotions in text. In: Proc. of 23th ACM Symposium on Applied Computing (SAC 2008), pp. 1556–1560. ACM Press (2008)
6. SAS ® Sentiment analysis, http://www.sas.com/textanalytics/sentiment-analysis/
7. Ortony, A., Turner, T.J.: What's basic about basic emotions? Psychological Review 97, 315–331 (1990)
8. Parrott, W.: Emotions in Social Psychology. Psychology Press, Philadelphia (2001)
9. Zinck, A., Newen, A.: Classifying emotion: a developmental account. Synthese 161(1), 1–25 (2008), doi:10.1007/s11229-006-9149-2
10. Rodriguez, P., Ortigosa, A., Carro, R.M.: Extracting Emotions from Texts in E-learning Environments. In: Procs. of 2nd Int. Workshop on Adaptive Learning via Interactive, Collaborative and Emotional approaches, Palermo, Italy (July 4-6, 2012)
11. Ballesteros, F., Guardiola, G., Soriano, E.: Octopus: An Upperware Based System for Building Personal Pervasive Environments. Journal of Systems and Software 85(7), 1637–1649 (2012) ISSN 0164-1212
12. Martín, J.M., Ortigosa, A., Carro, R.M.: SentBuk: Sentiment analysis for e-learning environments. In: Proceedings of the XIV Simposio Internacional de Informática Educativa (SIIE 2012), Andorra (October 29-31, 2012)
13. Martín, E., Carro, R.M.: Supporting the Development of Mobile Adaptive Learning Environments: A Case Study. IEEE Trans. on Learning Technologies 2(1), 23–36 (2009)
14. Carro, R.M., Haya, P.A., González, A.: Where Should I Go? Guiding Users with Cognitive Limitations through Mobile Devices Outdoors. In: Proceedings of the International Conference Interaccion 2012, Elche, Spain, October 3-5 (2012)
15. Rojahn, J., Rabold, D.E., Schneider, F.: Emotion specificity in mental retardation. American Journal on Mental Retardation 99, 477–486 (1995)

New Approaches for Alzheimer's Disease Diagnosis Based on Automatic Spontaneous Speech Analysis and Emotional Temperature

Karmele López-de-Ipiña[1], Jesús B. Alonso[2], Nora Barroso[1], Marcos Faundez-Zanuy[3],
Miriam Ecay[4], Jordi Solé-Casals[5], Carlos M. Travieso[2], Ainara Estanga[4],
and Aitzol Ezeiza[1]

[1] System Engineering and Automation Department,
University of the Basque Country, Donostia 20008, Spain
karmele.ipina@ehu.es
[2] IDeTIC-DSC, Universidad de Las Palmas de Gran Canaria (ULPGC)
[3] Escola Universitària Politècnica de Mataró (UPC), Tecnocampus
[4] Neurology Department, CITA-Alzheimer Foundation
[5] Digital Technologies Group, Universitat de Vic

Abstract. Alzheimer Disease (AD) is one of the most common dementia and their socio-economic relevance is growing. Its diagnosis is sometimes made by excluding other dementias, but definitive confirmation must await the study post-mortem with brain tissue of the patient. According to internationally accepted criteria, we can only speak about probable or possible Alzheimer's disease. The purpose of this paper is to contribute to improve early diagnosis of dementia and severity from automatic analysis performed by non-invasive automated intelligent methods. The methods selected in this case are Automatic Spontaneous Speech Analysis (ASSA) and Emotional Temperature (ET). These methodologies have the great advantage of being non invasive, low cost methodologies and have no side effects.

Keywords: AD, Automatic Spontaneous Speech Analysis, Automatic Spontaneous Speech Analysis.

1 Introduction

Alzheimer's Diseases (AD) is the most common type of dementia among the elder people and it is characterized by progressive and irreversible deterioration of higher brain functions or cognition, with loss of memory, judgment and language. In some cases, during the early stages of the disease, it has symptoms of other mental non-cognitive disorders (psychosis, depression, anxiety, apathy, etc.) and of behavior changes (restlessness, irritability, etc). The disease prevents the execution of the tasks of daily life, giving rise to severe disability towards a full dependence. An early and accurate diagnosis of AD helps patients and their families to plan for the future and offers the best opportunity to treat the symptoms of the disease. Currently the only possible way to diagnosis the disease with absolute certainty is by exclusion of other dementias and making a post-mortem brain tissue analysis. Thus for the diagnosis of AD three distinctions are being used: possible, probable and definite [1, 2]. In the in

J. Bravo, R. Hervás, and M. Rodríguez (Eds.): IWAAL 2012, LNCS 7657, pp. 407–414, 2012.

life diagnosis, the accuracy is about 90% and it is based on a combination of several tests and examinations. This paper presents a new approach for early AD diagnosis based on two non-invasive and low cost automatic methods: the Automatic Spontaneous Speech Analysis (ASSA) and the Emotional Temperature (ET).

This paper is organized as follows: In the next section some aspects of Alzheimer disease diagnosis and speech features of the language are presented. Resources and methods used are presented in Section 3. In Section 4 we present the methodology, while in section 5 some experiments are detailed. Finally conclusions and future work are depicted in section 6.

2   Alzheimer Disease Diagnosis

Eight cognitive domains are most often damaged in AD [3, 4]: memory, language, perception, attention, constructional skills, counseling skills, problem solving and functional capabilities. The clinical diagnosis is usually based on [3, 4]: Tests of memory and other cognitive functions, behavioral changes analysis, Neuroimaging (CT, SPECT, PET), and the absence of other causes by other medical tests. The greater the number of tests used in the detection, the higher the reliability of the diagnosis. However, the cost may be too high in relation to the benefits. Nowadays the diagnosis takes place when the signs of the disease are very advanced and it is no possible to use any treatment to prevent its natural evolution. AD patients live, on average, after diagnosis, about eight years, although some of them may live for 20 years. The evolution of symptoms differs from person to person and in each stage (early, intermediate and advanced) develops gradually over several years.

Noninvasive Intelligent Techniques of diagnosis may become valuable tools for early detection of dementia and they can be used by non-technologists in the habitual environments of the patient without altering or blocking their abilities. ASSA and ET are some of them. On the one hand the patient does not perceive the spontaneous speech as a stressful test. On the other hand, the cost is really low, does not require extensive infrastructure or medical equipment available, fostering information easily, quickly and inexpensively.

3   Non-invasive Diagnosis techniques Based on Analysis of Speech and Emotions

After the loss of memory, one of the major problems of AD is the language. The loss of ability to express with language will affect two types or two aspects: difficulty to speak and difficulty to understand others, which difficult the natural communication process with the environment. This inability to communicate already appears in the previous phases. We can meet different communication deficits in the area of language, such as [5, 6]: Aphasia: difficulty in speaking and understanding; Anomia: difficulty for recognizing and naming things. The problems that the patients have for communicating according to the stage of the disease, and how it can help, would be: First Stage: Difficulty for finding the right word in the spontaneous speech. Often it is not detected. Second Phase: impoverishment of language and vocabulary for everyday use. Phase Three: Answers, sometimes are very limited and with very few words.

Moreover, the emotional response in Alzheimer's patients becomes impaired and seems to go through different states. In the early stages appears social and even sexual disinhibition, behavioral changes (be angry and not being able to perform common tasks, not to express or not remembering) [7, 8, 9]. However, the emotional memory remains, and they cry more easily to be aware that caregivers or stroke. They gratefully acknowledge the caresses, smiles and hugs. The Alzheimer's patient reacts aggressive on things that for healthy people are harmless. Perceives a threat or danger where does not exist. In more advanced stages of Alzheimer, patients often may seem shy and apathetic, symptoms that often are attributed to memory problems or difficulty for finding the right words. Some responses are likely to be magnified due to an alteration in perception. Other research suggests, moreover, that the patients in this progressive brain disorder, in advanced stages, may also have a reduced ability to feel emotions due to loss of memory, memories. Then it appears apathy and sometimes depression.

4   Methods

There are different elements that are part of social life, intellectual and personnel that constitute the individual, and one of the most important is spoken language. This allows us to speak, to communicate with others, share knowledge, express well with cultural and personal identity. Spoken language is the most spontaneous, natural, intuitive and efficient communication way among people. Therefore, the analysis by automatic methods of spontaneous speech, the freer and more natural expression of communication, could be a useful noninvasive way for early diagnosis by combining it with other methodologies. In this study we analyze spontaneous speech fluency through measures of voice segment length, pause length, speech development, libraries, short time energy and centroid [10].

Emotions arise from the need to face a changing and partially unpredictable world which makes necessary to any intelligent system (natural or artificial) the development of emotions to survive [11, 12, 13]. Emotions are closely linked to learning and understanding process. Emotions are cognitive processes related to the architecture of the human mind (decision making, memory, attention, etc.).

Human interaction includes emotional information about partners that is transmitted through language explicitly and implicitly through nonverbal communication. The nonverbal information, which is often spread by corporate-cultural gestures, attitudes, modulations of voice, facial expressions, etc., it essential in human communication as it has a high effect on the communication provision of the partners and on the intelligibility of speech [11,12,13]. Human emotions are affected by the environment, the direct interaction with the outside world but also by the emotional memory emerged from the experience of individual and cultural environment, the so called socialized emotion. Emotions use the same components subjective, cultural, physiological and behavioral that the individual's perception express with regard to the mental state, the body and how it interacts with the environment. The emotions, far from being an obstacle in understanding the universe, they describe it clearly.

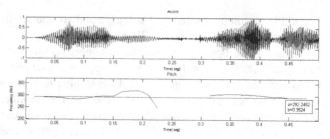

Fig. 1. Example of model of pitch curve with a polynomial function of first order

The proposed method estimates a measure to evaluate the degree of severity of the patients with Alzheimer. The measure is called "emotional temperature". This method proposes a new strategy based on a few prosodic and paralinguistic features set obtained from a temporal segmentation of the speech signal. Next it is described the steps to estimate the value of the measure "emotional temperature". The speech signal is windowed by a hamming window of 0.5 seconds overlapped 50% [14].

In each frame $\{x(n)\}$ the DC component is removed and the Z normalization is applied. Two prosodic features and four paralinguistic features related to the pitch and energy, respectively, are estimated from each frame. These features are chosen for several reasons: firstly their robustness in emotion recognition has been proven, secondly they are quickly and easily calculated, and finally, they are independent of linguistic segmentation, therefore problems in real time applications in real environments can be avoided.

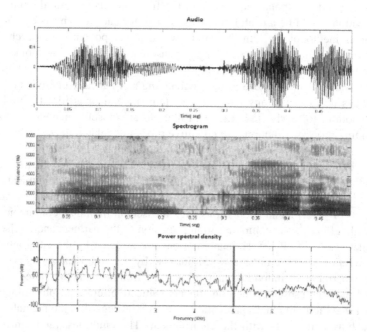

Fig. 2. Example of the spectral distribution in different frequency bands

For prosodic features, a voiced/unvoiced decision is made to each frame and two linear regression coefficients of the pitch contour $p(n)$ [15, 16, 17] are obtained:

$$MIN(a,b) = \sum_{i=1}^{n}(p_i(n) - a - bx_i(n))^2$$

where the coefficients a and b are computed using the method of least squares. In our implementation we use the pitch estimation algorithm called YIN [18].

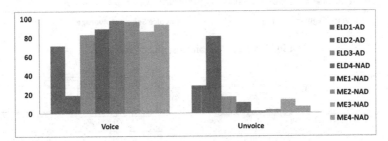

Fig. 3. Voiced/unvoicedd percentage in the spontaneous speech

For paralinguistic features, voice spectral energy balances [15] are calculated from each frame, being quantified using 4 percentages of energy concentration in 4 frequency bands (B_i where $i \in [0,3]$). For a sampling frequency greater or equal to $16\,\mathrm{kHz}$, the frequency bands are divided into the following ranges: $B_0 = [0\,\mathrm{Hz}, 400\,\mathrm{Hz}]$, $B_1 = [400\,\mathrm{Hz}, 2\,\mathrm{kHz}]$, $B_2 = [2\,\mathrm{kHz}, 5\,\mathrm{kHz}]$ and $B_3 = [5\,\mathrm{kHz}, 8\,\mathrm{kHz}]$, where theses bands were studied in previous research related to the phonatory system [19]. The percentage of energy in each frequency band E_{B_i} is obtained using the following expression:

$$E_{B_i} = \frac{\sum\limits_{f=B_i}|X(f)|^2}{\sum\limits_{f=0}^{8KHz}|X(f)|^2} \quad 0 \leq i \leq 3$$

Where $|X(f)|^2$ is a periodogram of the temporal frame $\{x(n)\}$.

5   Experimental Results

The database for the experimentation is composed by about 10 hours of Spontaneous Speech from videos where people tell enjoyable personal stories divided in about 30 minutes of people with AD diagnosis and about 9 hours of control people. The recording atmosphere is relaxed and noninvasive. The speech is divided into segments of 60 seconds. Finally it is obtained a database of about 600 segments of Spontaneous Speech. The database is multicultural and multilingual and with a wide range of ages. In this experimentation 4 control people of middle age (ME-NAD) (2 males and 2 females), 3 people with AD (ELD-AD) diagnosis and one elder person without pathology (ELD-NAD) will be used. The first set of tests consists of ASSA experiments.

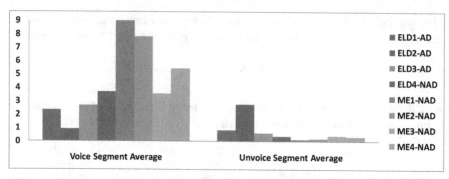

Fig. 4. Voiced/unvoiced segment average

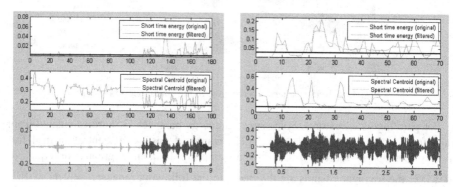

Fig. 5. Plots of Speech Signal, Short Time Energy and Spectral Centroid for a control person and a person with AD

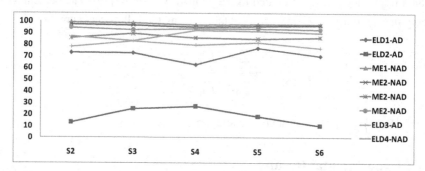

Fig. 6. The Spontaneous Speech Evolution with regard to the Speech Percentage along the time (consecutive segments (S2:S6)

Results (figures 3 ,4 ,5 and 6) show significant fluency loss in people with AD with regard to the voiced/unvoiced percentage in the speech (figure 3) and to the length of voiced/unvoiced segments (figure 4). Figure 5 shows lower Short Time Energy also for this people and lower Spectral Centroid for AD. The Spontaneous Speech Evolution with regard to the Speech Percentage (figure 6) along the time (consecutive segments (S2:S6) shows that people with AD disease tend to decrease the length of voice segments and the fluency by increasing the unvoiced segment number and decreasing the length of voice segments. Results show a decreasing slope in the evolution of Spontaneous Speech for people with AD.

The first set of tests, consist of experiments of Emotional Temperature. Support vector machines (SVM) [20] have been used to quantify the discriminative ability of the proposed measures. We have used a freely available implementation named LIBSVM [20] in our implementation, where a radial basis kernel function was used. Classification targets are: speakers without neurological pathologies and speakers diagnosisd with Alzheimer. To estimate the measure "emotional temperature", first of all, each temporal frame is classified using a SVM, (also using a threshold that is obtained from EER in the training step) and next, the percentage of temporal frame that are classify as no pathological is calculated, where this value is the "emotional temperature" measure. Besides, a normalization is made to the measure "emotional temperature", for that the measure "emotional temperature" has a value 50 in the threshold of EER estimated in the training step (figure 7).

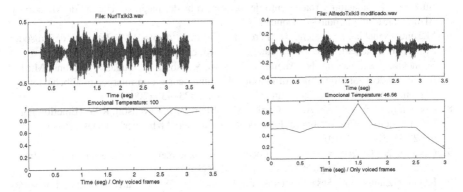

Fig. 7. Emotional Temperature for a control person and a person with AD in a segment of 3 seconds

6   Conclusions

In this paper new approaches for Alzheimer Disease diagnosis based on Automatic Spontaneous Speech Analysis and Emotional Temperature have been presented. The purpose of the work is to contribute to improve early diagnosis of dementia and severity from automatic analysis, performed by non-invasive automated intelligent methods. The selected methods in this case are, Automatic Spontaneous Speech Analysis (ASR) and Emotional Temperature. These methodologies have the great advantage of being non invasive, low cost methodologies and have no side effects. The research on multicultural and multilingual population shows some encouraging results both in terms of the ASSA and the Emotional Temperature, showing tendencies to explore with a broader population. In future work we will integrate the described methodologies with automatic analysis methods of drawing and handwriting as well as with automatic analysis of facial features. We will extend also the analysis population as well as the type of pathology.

Acknowledgment. This work has been partially supported by SAIOTEK from the Basque Government. Dr. Solé-Casals acknowledges support of the University of Vic under the grant R0904. Besides, this work has been partially supported by "Cátedra Telefónica ULPGC 2012" under reference e-VOICE.

References

1. Sociedad Española de Neurología, http://www.sen.es
2. Van de Pol, L.A., et al.: The effects of age and Alzheimer's disease on hippocampal volumes, a MRI study. Alzheimer's and Dementia (2005)
3. Morris, J.C.: The Clinical Dementia Rating (CDR): current version and scoring rules. Neurology 43, 2412b–2414b (1993)
4. American Psychiatric Association, Diagnostic and Statistical Manual of Mental disorders, 4th edn. Text Revision, Washington DC (2000)
5. Buiza, C.: Evaluación y tratamiento de los trastornos del lenguaje. Unidad de Memoria y Alzheimer. Matia Fundazioa. Donostia (2010)
6. Martinez-Sanchez, F., Garcia, M., Perez, E., Carro, J., Arana, J.M.: Patrones de Prosodia expresiva en pacientes con enfermedad de Alzheimer. Psicothema 24, 16–21 (2012)
7. Shimokawa, A., Yatomi, N., Anamizu, S., Torii, S., Isono, H., Sugai, Y., Kohno, M.: Influence of deteriorating ability of emotional comprehension on interpersonal behaviour in Alzheimer-type dementia. Brain and Cognition 47, 423–433 (2001)
8. Goodkind, M.S., Gyurak, A., McCarthy, M., Miller, B.L., Levenson, R.W.: Emotion regulation deficits in frontotemporal lobar degeneration and Alzheimer's disease. Psychol. Aging 25(1), 30–37 (2010)
9. Cadieux, N., Greeve, K.: Emotion processing in Alzheimer's disease. Journal of the International Neuropsychological Society 3, 411–419 (1997)
10. Faúndez Zanuy, M., Sesa-Nogueras, E., Monte-Moreno, E., Garre-Olmo, J., Lopez-de-Ipiña, K., Viñals, F., Puente, M.L.: Aplicaciones biométricas más allá de la seguridad. In: Proc. VI Jornadas de reconocimiento biométrico de personas, pp. 25–43 (2012)
11. Knapp, M.L.: Essentials of nonverbal communication. Holt, Rinehart & Winston (1980)
12. Cowie, E., et al.: Emotion Recognition in Human-Computer Interaction. IEEE Signal Processing Magazine 18(1), 32–80 (2001)
13. Plutchnik, R.: Emotion: A psychoevolutionary synthesis. Harper and Row (1980)
14. Pao, T.L., Chien, C.S., Yen, J.H., Chen, Y.T., Cheng, Y.M.: Continuous tracking of user emotion in mandarin emotional speech. In: Proceedings, 3rd International Conference on International Information Hiding and Multimedia Signal Processing, pp. 47–52 (2007)
15. Petrushin, V.A.: Emotion in speech: recognition and application to call centers. In: Proceedings, Conference on Artificial Neural Networks in Engineering, pp. 7–10 (1999)
16. Lee, C.M., Narayanan, S.: Emotion recognition using a data-driven fuzzy interference system. In: Proceedings, 8th ECSCT, pp. 157–160 (2003)
17. Kwon, O.W., Chan, K., Hao, J., Lee, T.W.: Emotion recognition by speech signals. In: Proc.8th European Conference on Speech Communication and Technology, pp. 125–128 (2003)
18. De Cheveigné, A., Kawahara, H.: YIN, a fundamental frequency estimator for speech and music. Journal of the Acoustical Society of America 111(4), 1917–1930 (2002)
19. Alonso, J., León, J., Alonso, I., Ferrer, M.A.: Automatic detection of pathologies in the voice by HOS base parameters. Journal on Applied Signal Processing 4, 275–284 (2001)
20. Chang, C.C., Lin, C.J.: LIBSVM: a library for support vector machines. ACM Transactions on Intelligent Systems and Technology 2(3), article 27 (2011)

Detection of Motion Disorders of Patients with Autism Spectrum Disorders

Antonio Coronato* and Giuseppe De Pietro

ICAR-CNR, Via P. Castellino 111,
Naples, Italy

Abstract. The autistic spectrum disorders (ASD) are behaviorally-defined developmental disorders of the immature brain which affect three domains of behavior: sociability and empathy; communication, language and imagination; and mental flexibility and range of interests. Main symptoms include motion disorders and stereotyped behaviors.

This paper presents an approach based on Artificial Intelligence techniques and Ambient Intelligence technologies for the detection of stereotyped motion disorders of patients with ASD. Specifically, monitoring is realized by means of tri-axis accelerometers applied to the patient's wrists. Signals obtained by accelerometers are pre-processed to obtain features that, in turn, are passed to classifiers that classifies the current observation in order to detect stereotyped motions. Results are under validation at the Department of Child Psychiatry at Children's Hospital Santobono-Pausilipon in Naples.

Keywords: Motion Disorders of Autistic Patients, Real-Time Monitoring.

1 Introduction

Autism is a group of developmental brain disorders, collectively called autism spectrum disorder (ASD). The term spectrum refers to the wide range of symptoms, skills, and levels of impairment, or disability, that children with ASD can have. Some children are mildly impaired by their symptoms, but others are severely disabled [1].

Thirty years ago autism was considered to be a rare childhood disorder most often associated with severe intellectual disabilities, lack of social awareness and the absence of meaningful expressive language [2]. Today, the spectrum of autistic disorders (or Autism Spectrum Disorder, ASD) is now recognized as a set of common developmental disorders, with an estimated prevalence of about 1 in every 110 children in the U.S. [3].

Symptoms of autism spectrum disorder (ASD) vary from one child to the next, but in general, they fall into three areas: 1) Social impairment; 2) Communication difficulties; and, 3) Repetitive and stereotyped behaviors [1].

---

* Corresponding author.

J. Bravo, R. Hervás, and M. Rodríguez (Eds.): IWAAL 2012, LNCS 7657, pp. 415–422, 2012.
© Springer-Verlag Berlin Heidelberg 2012

This paper focuses on the automatic recognition of repetitive and stereotyped behaviors, with a specific emphasis for motion disorders like hand flapping or hand hitting against ears, which are symptom of a status of anxiety or the tentative of isolation from the surrounding environment.

The proposed approach uses tri-axis accelerometers applied to patient's wrists to get motion information. In case of motion disorders signals caught from accelerometers reflects specific patterns. Thus, some features extracted from signals are used to classify the motion by means of classificators. Three types of classificators have been evaluated, Neural Networks, Naive Bayes and Bayesian Networks for the off-line classifications; whereas, Neural Networks have been adopted for the realtime monitoring having shown better results.

The rest of the paper is organized as it follows. Section 2 introduces some related work. Section 3 describes the proposed approach and reports some results. Finally, Section 4 concludes the paper.

2   Related Work

Different Artificial Intelligence techniques are adopted to detect human activities in smart environments [4]. Among the others, Hidden Markov Models and Neural Networks [5] are major solutions in case of gesture recognition.

To the best of our knowledge, there is only few papers on the automatic recognition of motion disorders of patients with ASD.

In [6], authors adopted accelerometers and pattern recognition algorithms to detect stereotypical motor movements in the classroom. In [6], instead, authors focused on motion disorders of children with autism, but they didn't compare with other approaches and worked with mimicked motions.

Other papers presents approaches adopted for other applications of gesture recognition by means of signals acquired by accelerometers. Here we report some related work.

Arce and Valdez [7] used the Nintendo Wiimote controller and built an artificial neural network to recognize five gestures: *Circle, Square, Trinangle* and the letters *S* and *Z*.

A similar approach has been adopted by Kim et al. [8] to design a dance game controller. Starting from a basic posture, the user can move her hands *Up, Down, Left* and *Right*.

Ahsan et al. [9] trained an artificial neural network with data extracted from electromyography signal in order to recognize hand motions for advanced human computer interaction mechanisms.

In this paper, we focus on four kinds of stereotyped motion disorders, namely *Hand hitting against the Ear (HE), Arm Flapping, (AF), Hand Rotation Up (HRU), Hand Rotation Down (HRD)*. These are typical motion disorders for a patient with autism who tries to isolate himself from the surrounding environment.

Fig. 1. TI eZ430-Chronos

3 Proposed Approach

3.1 Data Acquisition

In order to acquire motion data, we apply accelerometers to the patient's wrist. The device is shown in figure 1.

The eZ430-Chronos is an integrated, wireless development system that provides a complete reference design for developers creating wireless smart watch applications. Chronos is a reference platform for many applications, such as wireless watch systems, personal displays for personal area networks, wireless sensor nodes for remote data collection and other applications. It includes a 96 segment LCD display and provides an integrated pressure sensor and 3-axis accelerometer for motion sensitive control. The Chronos to act as a central hub for nearby wireless sensors such as pedometers and heartrate monitors. The eZ430-Chronos offers temperature and battery voltage measurement and is complete with a USB-based CC1111 wireless interface to a PC. The eZ430-Chronos watch may be disassembled to be reprogrammed with a custom application and includes an eZ430 USB programming interface.

Such a device comes with a DLL control driver; however, we used the RXTX library [10]. RXTX is a native lib providing serial and parallel communication for the Java Development Toolkit (JDK). All deliverables are under the gnu LGPL license.

Figure 2 shows the results of almoast one hour of continuous monitoring. Red circle denotes an episode of motion disorder of the type AF, which is also reported in figure 3.

3.2 Feature Extraction

Signals reported in figure 2 are pre-processed in order to extract features usefull for classificaiton. In particular, the following features are calculated:

Mean Absolute Value, which is obtained from the avarage of the absolute value of each signal.

$$MAV = \frac{1}{N} \sum_{n=1}^{N} |x_n|$$

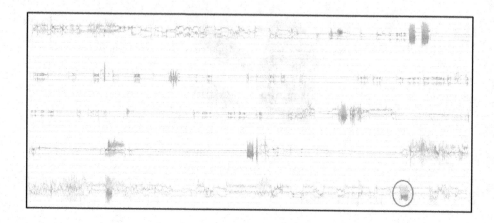

Fig. 2. Monitoring

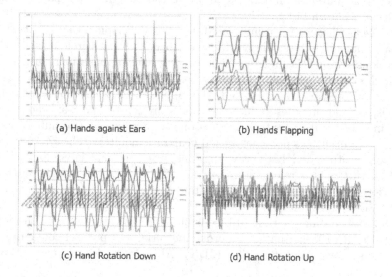

(a) Hands against Ears

(b) Hands Flapping

(c) Hand Rotation Down

(d) Hand Rotation Up

Fig. 3. Example of motion disorders

Root Mean Square RMS, which is also known as the quadratic mean, is a statistical measure of the magnitude of a varying quantity.

$$RMS = \sqrt{\frac{1}{N} \sum_{n=1}^{N} x_n{}^2}$$

Variance VAR, which is a measure of how far a set of numbers is spread out. It is one of several descriptors of a probability distribution, describing how far the numbers lie from the mean (expected value).

$$VAR = \sqrt{\frac{1}{N} \sum_{n=1}^{N} x_n{}^2}$$

Standard Deviation SD, which shows how much variation or "dispersion" exists from the average (mean, or expected value). A low standard deviation indicates that the data points tend to be very close to the mean, whereas high standard deviation indicates that the data points are spread out over a large range of values.

$$SD = \sqrt{\frac{\sum_{n=1}^{N} x_n{}^2}{N} - (\frac{\sum_{n=1}^{N} x_n}{N})^2}$$

Waveform Lenght WL, which is the cumulative lenght of the waveform over the time fragment. WL is related to the waveform amplitude, frequency and time.

$$WL = \sum_{n=1}^{N} |x_{n+1} - x_n|$$

Zero Crossin WZC, which is the number of times that the amplitude value of the signal crosses the zero y-axis.

All these features are computed for each (x,y, and z) signal. In addition to this, we have also computed covariances among such signals, which, however, have not shown to be relevant for classification.

3.3   Off-line Classificator

In order to identify motion disorders, we built threea classificators based on an artificial intelligence techniques: Neural Networks, Naive Bayes and Bayesian Networks. The system architecture was designed adopting KNIME [11], an open-source environment for data integration, processing, analysis, and exploration.

The architecture of the classificator is shown in figure 4. Data set is read by the *File Reader* component and successively shuppled by the *Shuffle* component. Next, all three classificators process the same set of data.

Experiemntal results have shown some better classification performances for the neural network, whereas other classificator show faster training. For the sake of brevity, we report only results related to the neural network. Its configuration parameters are shown in figure 5.

Cross validation has been performed with two values of K-Fold.

Figure 6(a) and 6(b) show the missclassification and percentage of errors while cross validating results with two different levels of paramerer K.

Figure 7, instead, reports best performance of the network empirically determined. In particular, it is possible to see that the neural network reports seven false negative and two false positive over one thousand samples. The resulting accuracy is over 99.

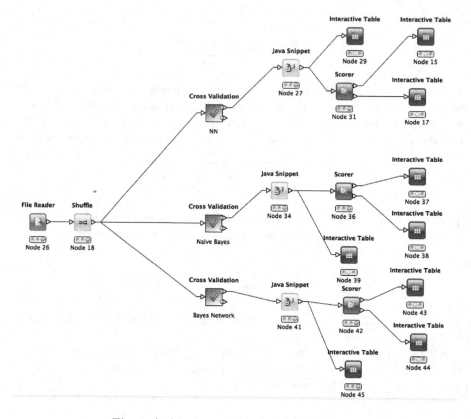

Fig. 4. Architecture of the off-line classificator

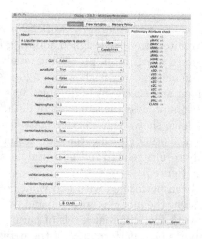

Fig. 5. Neural Network parameters

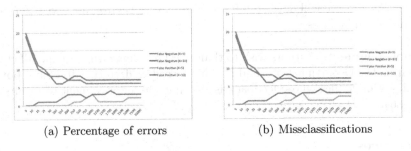

(a) Percentage of errors   (b) Missclassifications

Fig. 6. performance of the Neural Network

CLASS \ Wi...	NORM	ANOM
NORM	879	2
ANOM	7	143

Correct classified: Wrong classified: 9
Accuracy: 99,127 %   Error: 0,873 %

Fig. 7. Performance of the neural network classificator

3.4 On-line Classificator

Based on off-line results, we realized an on-line classificatore using WEKA libraries [12]. Weka components are the same adopted by the knime tool. For the on-line classification we set the software module that acquires data from sensors to collect 32 samples per second and considered temporal frames of 2 second for the classification.

4 Conclusion

In this paper we have presented an approach to detect stereotyped motion disorders in children with Autism Spectrum Disorders. We have compared the performance of three different classifators, based respectively on Neural Networks naive Bayes and Bayesian Networks. Neural Networks have show a slightely better performance during off-line motion disorder recognition. After that, we have realized an on-line recognition system.

Preliminary laboratory results have encouraged the adoption of such an approach in real case studies. For this reason, we are going to deploy the monitoring system at the Department of Child Neuropsychiatry at the Santobono-Pausillipon Children Hospital.

The final objective, however, is to realize a full context-aware environment [13], which should be able to detect patient anomalous behaviors and causes (e.g actions performed within the environment by the pationt or other users). To achieve this aim, we will develop a full context-aware enviromnent with activity recognition capabilities.

Acknowledgment. Authors wish to thank Dr Gianpina Grimaldi and all clinicians from the Department of Child Psychiatry at Children Hospital Santobono-Pausilipon in Naples whose feedback is enabling the improvement of results of this research activity.

References

1. A parents guide to autism spectrum disorder (2011)
2. Lotter, V.: Epidemiology of autistic conditions in young children. Social Psychiatry and Psychiatric Epidemiology 1, 163–173 (1967)
3. Autism and developmental disabilities monitoring network surveillance year 2006. In: Prevalence of autism spectrum disorders-Autism and Developmental Disabilities Monitoring Network. MMWR Surveillence Summary, Centers for Disease Control and Prevention (2006)
4. Ye, J., Dobson, S., McKeever, S.: Situation identification techniques in pervasive computing: A review. In: Pervasive and Mobile Computing (2011) (in Press, Corrected Proof)
5. Han, J., Kamber, M., Pei, J.: Data Mining: Concepts and Techniques, 2nd edn. The Morgan Kaufmann Series in Data Management Systems. Morgan Kaufmann (January 2006)
6. Albinali, F., Goodwin, M.S., Intille, S.S.: Detecting stereotypical motor movements in the classroom using accelerometry and pattern recognition algorithms. In: Pervasive and Mobile Computing, pp. 103–114 (2012)
7. Arce, F., Valdez, J.M.G.: Accelerometer-Based Hand Gesture Recognition Using Artificial Neural Networks. In: Castillo, O., Kacprzyk, J., Pedrycz, W. (eds.) Soft Computing for Intelligent Control and Mobile Robotics. SCI, vol. 318, pp. 67–77. Springer, Heidelberg (2010)
8. Kim, N., An, Y., Cha, B.: Gesture recognition based on neural networks for dance game contents. In: International Conference on New Trends in Information and Service Science, NISS 2009, pp. 1134–1139 (2009)
9. Ahsan, M., Ibrahimy, M., Khalifa, O.: Hand motion detection from emg signals by using ann based classifier for human computer interaction. In: 2011 4th International Conference on Modeling, Simulation and Applied Optimization (ICMSAO), pp. 1–6 (April 2011)
10. Rxtx library
11. Silipo, R., Mazanetz, M.P.: The knime cookbook: Recipes for the advanced user (2012)
12. Holmes, G., Donkin, A., Witten, I.H.: Weka: a machine learning workbench, 357–361 (August 1994)
13. Coronato, A., De Pietro, G., Esposito, M.: A semantic context service for smart offices. In: Proceedings of the 2006 International Conference on Hybrid Information Technology, ICHIT 2006, vol. 02, pp. 391–399. IEEE Computer Society, Washington, DC (2006)

eFisioTrack: A Telerehabilitation Platform for Monitoring Prescribed Therapeutic Exercises in Orthopaedic Injuries

Joaquín García[1], Daniel Ruiz[1], Antonio Soriano[1], Oscar Marín[1],
Sergio Hernández[2], and Segismundo Ferrairó[1]

[1] Department of Computer Technology, University of Alicante, Spain
{jdgarcia,druiz,soriano,omarin,segis}@dtic.ua.es
[2] Dept. Pathology and Surgery, Physiotherapy Area, University Miguel Hernández, Spain
sehesa@umh.es

Abstract. The aim of this work is to describe the specification and the current results of eFisioTrack, a new telerehabilitation platform for monitoring prescribed therapeutic exercises. Unlike previous telerehabilitation platforms we focused on keeping the low-cost feature as well as setting the elements to increase the adherence of patients to rehabilitation treatments. The platform consists of two sides. The server side is based on web services paradigm and the client side interacts with the user and is in charge of registering the movements of the rehabilitation exercises for its control and monitoring. To date, the platform has been deployed in a hospital and we conclude that eFisioTrack is appropriate and technically feasible to set new ways of taking rehabilitation monitoring to places other than the rehabilitation centers. Experimental protocols are currently being designed in order to extend the test and validation process to a major number of real patients.

Keywords: Ubiquitous monitoring, Telerehabilitation, Treatment adherence.

1 Introduction

Treatment adherence is a key concept in the area of rehabilitation. It is defined as how well a patient follows the physiotherapist's recommendations and includes aspects like completing the number of therapeutic exercises prescribed and the assistance in each of the scheduled exercise sessions [1]. The lack of adherence within rehabilitation programmes has been identified as one of the most important reasons for treatment failure in pathologies of the locomotor system [2], [3]. In other words, the patient implication in the rehabilitation programme generates an improvement in the treatment results, as well as avoids new injuries caused by miscarried treatment [4]. Other systems use similar technologies that we use [5], [6], [7], [8], however our design was focused in three main objectives: keeping the low-cost feature, being simpler than these other systems, and reducing discomforts for the patient by using an only wireless controller and by providing a more usable device.

J. Bravo, R. Hervás, and M. Rodríguez (Eds.): IWAAL 2012, LNCS 7657, pp. 423–430, 2012.
© Springer-Verlag Berlin Heidelberg 2012

Information and communication technologies could came to the aid of the field of rehabilitation, e.g. allowing the patient to perform the treatment outside the medical center being still monitored. These facts lead us to the hypothesis that the use of I.T. is feasible in the field of rehabilitation allowing to develop systems with a threefold objective: reducing costs due to waiting lists and the overload of work at public health centers, improving the quality of the treatment and monitoring programs while sharpening the efficiency of public health resources , and finally, giving to the patients the means needed to increase their adherence to rehabilitation programs.

In fact, telemedicine approaches have already been considered to improve rehabilitation treatments [9]. For instance Brennan et al [10] presented a system to improve arm function in stroke victims with mild to severe hemiparesis. Yongjiu et al [11] investigated a control system of a rehabilitation robot based on walking gait and other proposals like the work of Shi et al [12] advanced the field with the presentation of a lower limb rehabilitation robot. Others researchers implement virtual reality techniques like the work presented in [13], [14]. In fact most of the telemedicine approaches use virtual reality environments and robot machinery. The telerehabilitation platform presented in this paper is not the first one in the research field but it can be thought of as the first one aiming to increase rehabilitation treatment adherence by allowing remote monitoring. Our approach intends to improve the rehabilitation experience by not using a virtual environment and by using widespread motion capture devices. The feature of a low-cost system has been taken into account in every step of the implementation.

Our developed platform allows the performance of any type of rehabilitation exercise in the area of rehabilitation. From the patient point of view, the system interface provides an easy-to-understand way of allowing direct access to the rehabilitation routine. On the other hand, for physiotherapists, the application offers an ubiquitous interface to control and examine the evolution of the exercises that the patients perform in a place other than the rehabilitation center and the possibility to check some customized reports of patient's information.

2   System Specifications

2.1   Software

Software elements (Fig. 1) has been designed to fulfill the following main requirements: 24/7 connectivity; the use of low-cost motion capture devices; easy to use graphical interfaces; integration of different development platforms and operating systems; allowing physiotherapists to manage rehabilitation programmes from places other than the medical center. We have focused software development from the following viewpoints:

Database. The database is a key part of the platform since it provides the data structures for the main functionalities. Data structures have been refined since the first meeting with physiotherapists in order to offer them a complete experience like medical center consultation. The database contains data related to patients, medical records, assigned treatments, planned sessions, etc.

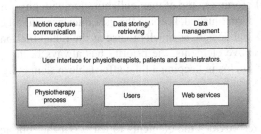

Fig. 1. Software elements

Web Services. The software developed in the server follows the fourth generation of web server paradigm using XML and WSDL interfaces with SOAP-based messaging. Web services have been deployed into a 2-tier architecture (database connectivity and web server). There are three kinds of web services which send and receive our own data types: insert, retrieve and modify.

Connectivity. eFisioTrack sends and receives data to the server through an Internet connection. Also, an offline connectivity mode has been implemented which can be activated by the physiotherapists in the application. Once it is turned on, rehabilitation programme data are stored in the patient computer so the user does not need to log into the application again. Data remain available in the application instead of retrieving them from the server. In the case of data about the performance of rehabilitation exercises, it can be stored on a USB flash memory or on a hard drive so it can be retrieved later.

Security Measures. Since the platform environment is related to healthcare, security controls must be used in order to protect patient data. The essential developed security measures are: to record user actions so that every step taken in the system is known, e.g. incorrect password in a login attempt; database structures have been designed so that database instances will not be associated with any of the patients nor the physiotherapist as required by law; communications are encrypted using SSL secure protocol. Other precautionary measures have been taken into account such as recording every unexpected application error or filtering IP address and port of the connections made to the application server.

Technology Integration. eFisioTrack is the result of an important effort integrating different technologies and platforms, in order to build up a sustainable and powerful system. The client side is a C# based standalone application. On the other side, the server is based in a Unix environment. The motion capture device and the application communicate using an open source library created for this purpose by Brian Peek [15].

Development Guidelines. During the development of the platform, agile software development methods have been used. Elaboration cycles have been centered in evolving functionalities over the time, as the meetings were held with physiotherapists in order to test parts of the platform. On top of that, collaboration with physiotherapist has been crucial to get the platform finished, keeping the user interface and other features such as usability, window layout design, as much precise as the rehabilitation treatment needs. Throughout all the above elements, the priority has always been to use open-source elements because this helps in keeping a final affordable system budget.

2.2 Hardware

eFisioTrack hardware provides the elements to carry out the remote monitoring task in places other than medical centers or hospitals. The platform consists of two distinct parts: (1) a central system to store, coordinate and analyze all platform data and (2) a pervasive application used by the patient (Fig. 2). The basis of the platform hardware can be understood also as formed by the following elements:

Motion Capture Devices. The platform uses one Wii Remote© controller as the device to capture the body movements of the rehabilitation exercises. This device provides a wireless and wearable low-cost motion capture device. It sends the data of the movements using a BCM2042 Broadcom Bluetooth chip.

Computers. eFisioTrack does not require any high performance computing resources. Both, server and client application can be deployed on common devices like laptops, desktop PCs or tablets. The hardware and computational scalability analysis made in the design phase, showed that there will not be a need to acquire any other equipment for the future once the system is deployed in the medical center, so the price of the overall system is not going to increase, remaining as a low-cost platform.

3 System's Use

3.1 Experimental Setup

eFisioTrack platform can manage any kind of exercise for any part of the body. The main scope of the platform is centered in orthopaedic injuries rehabilitation like Subacromial Impingement, Rotator cuff tendinopathy or Slap lesion. Specifically, the one

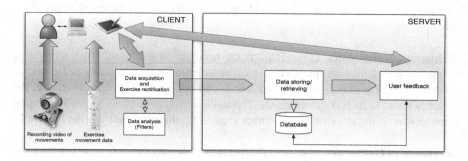

Fig. 2. Hardware architecture

Fig. 3. Experimental setup

depicted in Fig. 3 is a prescribed rehabilitation exercise for Subracromial impingement injury called active shoulder flexion where the patient application is executed on the tablet. Other deployed exercises are: supraspinatus eccentric, leg extension and mini-squad (quadriceps). For the exercises that can not be done grabbing the motion capture device, a velcro strip is supplied in order to attach the device to the associated part of the body correctly.

3.2 User Interfaces

The platform has three types of users based on the specific role they play: physiotherapists, patients and administrators. Each one of them access different parts of the client application, e.g. the administrator adds new physiotherapist to the platform, a physiotherapist user manages all the data regarding a physiotherapy process such as add new patient, add new rehabilitation exercise and so forth. Finally a patient user can access the physiotherapy process information to perform a rehabilitation exercise or look his scheduled elements of a specific day.

When a physiotherapist logs into the application, he can choose between patients data management or physiotherapy process remote monitoring (Fig. 4). In the first option, after the physiotherapist adds a new patient to the system, a new physiotherapy process can be created for that new patient. Then, the plan elements can be added to the physiotherapy process such as: rehabilitation exercise session and so forth. On the other hand, data about physiotherapy remote monitoring can also be managed and edited in order to delete one element from the schedule or to add new elements at the end of the treatment if the injury has not been cured giving some advice to the patient about their realization.

When a patient accesses the application, a menu shows the elements of the active physiotherapy process. Moreover, a rehabilitation exercise can be performed with the motion capture device and once the exercise is finished, resulting data is sent to the server. After that, the application shows the results to the user and suggests some tips to fix detected mistakes such as *remember to try staying in the same plane*. When an

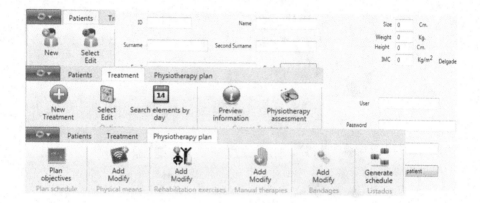

Fig. 4. Screens of the application

administrator logs into the application, a small option panel is shown that allows the administrator to add new users to the platform. It can add a physiotherapist or a new administrator since there could be the need for different administrators in the same medical center.

3.3   Remote Monitoring

The implementation of remote monitoring features allows the physiotherapist to totally personalize the rehabilitation program of the patient. First, a customized movement is recorded which is considered as the master movement for an specific patient and exercise. Then pattern matching techniques are applied to compare each exercise repetition done by the patient with the recorded master. In third place, the user knows if the exercise has been done right, and the physiotherapists has more information about the performance like how many repetitions have been done right or the reasons why a repetition is wrong. This means that the physiotherapist can quickly adjust intensity and duration of the rehabilitation exercises. Two main advantages have been found, the first one is that with tele-rehabilitation we intend to save expenses in the overall budget. The second one is contributing to the fact that the patient can perform rehabilitation exercises at home, in this way we avoid problems when traveling, since rehabilitation patients can have problems with their mobility. Also, in the moment that the physiotherapist adds a new exercise there is the option to record a personalized video which the patient can check afterwards in the moment of the exercise performance, reminding the patient how to do it properly. Furthermore, the remote monitoring has been designed using widely accepted guidelines for exercise prescription [16].

3.4   Preliminary Findings

After a previous stages of an evaluation and testing process in a real healthcare environment like a rehabilitation service of a public hospital, physiotherapy experts stated

that preliminary findings indicate that the platform provides the appropriate level of remote monitoring needed for the improvement of the current rehabilitation procedures.
They pointed out as the major contributions of our work the following key points: i)
data structure representing the concepts of the rehabilitation programmes domain; ii)
the possibility of increasing treatment adherence in rehabilitation treatments and iii) the
prospects of reducing waiting lists in rehabilitation centers as well as saving costs in
rehabilitation treatments.

Physiotherapist involved in the project consider that eFisioTrack can improve adherence since the amount of detailed monitored data obtained from patients performance
allow them to be more precise setting the rehabilitation plans. On the other side, the
system has many aspects to increase patients motivation to complete rehabilitation programmes, usually tedious for them, in a better mood.

4 Conclusions

At the time of writing, eFisioTrack has been tested in our laboratory and deployed in a
hospital. Although the telerehabilitation platform presented in this paper is not the first
of its kind, it offers new ways to improve both, physiotherapist and patient experience.
Rehabilitation experts are able to perform daily monitoring routines in places other than
the medical center, and obtain immediate statistics about all open treatments and how
well are their patients following their guidelines. In the patients case, the system offer
them new, attractive and adapted to their needs, ways to perform rehabilitation exercise,
so this could improve their adherence to expert guidelines. Also with eFisioTrack we
aim to strengthen communication between physiotherapist and patient which over time
will benefit the results of the treatment, giving to the patient the feeling of a more
centered-on-him healthcare process.

The developed platform fulfills all requirements that we defined in previous work
such as: remote monitoring management, ubiquitous access to perform rehabilitation
exercises, motion capture device integration with the application and 24/7 connectivity.
We can conclude that the design proposal is appropriate and is technically feasible and
as a future work, other devices are being analyzed for the purpose of collecting training
data in even more ubiquitous places.

Acknowledgments. This work has been funded by grants from the Spanish Ministry
of Science and Innovation (TIN2009-10855) and part financed by FEDER.

References

1. Sabaté, E.: Adherence to long-term therapies: evidence for action. No. ISBN 92 4 154599 2,
   World Health Organization (2003)
2. Pisters, M., Veenhof, C., Van Meeteren, N., Ostelo, R., De Bakker, D., Schellevis, F., Dekker,
   J.: Long-term effectiveness of exercise therapy in patients with osteoarthritis of the hip or
   knee: A systematic review. Arthritis Care & Research 57(7), 1245–1253 (2007)
3. Belza, B., Topolski, T., Kinne, S., Patrick, D., Ramsey, S.: Does adherence make a difference?: Results from a community-based aquatic exercise program. Nursing Research 51(5),
   285 (2002)

4. van Gool, C., Penninx, B., Kempen, G., Rejeski, W., Miller, G., van Eijk, J., Pahor, M., Messier, S.: Effects of exercise adherence on physical function among overweight older adults with knee osteoarthritis. Arthritis Care & Research 53(1), 24–32 (2005)
5. Tsekleves, E., Skordoulis, D., Paraskevopoulos, I., Kilbride, C.: Wii Your Health: A Low-Cost Wireless System for Home Rehabilitation after Stroke using Wii Remotes with its Expansions and Blender. In: Proceedings of The 8th IASTED International Conference on Biomedical Engineering (Biomed 2011), Innsbruck, Austria, February 16-18 (2011), doi: 10.2316/P.2011.723-058
6. Tao, Y., Hu, H.: A Novel Sensing and Data Fusion System for 3-D Arm Motion Tracking in Telerehabilitation. IEEE Transactions on Instrumentation and Measurement 57, 1029–1040 (2008)
7. Schepers, H.M., Roetenberg, D., Veltink, P.H.: Ambulatory human motion tracking by fusion of inertial and magnetic sensing with adaptive actuation. Medical & Biological Engineering & Computing 48, 27–37 (2010)
8. Zhang, S., Hu, H., Zhou, H.: An interactive Internet-based system for tracking upper limb motion in home-based rehabilitation. Medical & Biological Engineering & Computing 46, 241–249 (2008)
9. Brennan, D., Barker, L.: Human factors in the development and implementation of telerehabilitation systems. Journal of Telemedicine and Telecare 14(2), 55–58 (2008)
10. Brennan, D., Lum, P., Uswatte, G., Taub, E., Gilmore, B., Barman, J.: A telerehabilitation platform for home-based automated therapy of arm function. In: 2011 Annual International Conference of the IEEE Engineering in Medicine and Biology Society, EMBC 2011, September 3, pp. 1819–1822 (2011)
11. Liu, Y., Zhang, L., Song, Q., Shuang, F., Ge, Y.: Design and Investigation on Control System of a Rehabilitation Robot Based on Walking Gait. In: Wu, Y. (ed.) Advances in Computer, Communication, Control and Automation. LNEE, vol. 121, pp. 289–296. Springer, Heidelberg (2011)
12. Shi, X., Wang, H., Yuan, L., Xu, Z., Zhen, H., Hou, Z.: Design and analysis of a lower limb rehabilitation robot. Advanced Materials Research 490, 2236–2240 (2012)
13. Crosbie, J., Lennon, S., McGoldrick, M., McNeill, M., McDonough, S.: Virtual reality in the rehabilitation of the arm after hemiplegic stroke: a randomized controlled pilot study. Clinical Rehabilitation (2012)
14. Spencer, S.: Movement Training and Post-Stroke Rehabilitation Using a Six Degree of Freedom Upper-Extremity Robotic Orthosis and Virtual Environment. PhD thesis, University of California, Irvine (2012)
15. Wiimotelib programming library, http://www.brianpeek.com/blog/pages/wiimotelib.aspx (last checked: May 1, 2012)
16. Gordon, N.: ACSM's guidelines for exercise testing and prescription, vol. 54. Lippincott Williams & Wilkins (2009)

Technological Solution for Improving Time Management Skills Using an Android Application for Children with ADD

Alexander Alonso Molinero, Fernando Jorge Hernández,
Amaia Méndez Zorrilla, and Begoña García Zapirain

DeustoTech-Life Unit, DeustoTech Institute of Technology
Bilbao, Spain
alex.alonso@opendeusto.es,
{fernandojorge,amaia.mendez,mbgarciazapi}@deusto.es
http://www.deustotech.deusto.es

Abstract. A large body of evidence supports that people with attention deficit disorder (ADD) have difficulties organizing and remembering daily activities because they are easily distracted. Specifically, the group of school children with ADD has problems when it comes to time management and planning tasks for each subject. The main objective of this approach is to provide a support tool to solve or minimize the difficulties associated with "time management skills", to reinforce social skills and foster their motivation to perform any task. Therefore, this project presents a technological solution that allows developing that skill by an application made for Smartphones, which provides a fully customizable agenda adaptable to the needs of children with ADD and accessible by their tutors and family. This project fulfills a technical and a social purpose because it is demonstrated the acceptance of this collective to ICT using daily elements of their personal and school live.

Keywords: Smartphone, ADD, Time Management, Agenda.

1 Introduction

The attention deficit disorder with or without hyperactivity (ADD or ADHD) is a developmental disorder that appears in childhood. It is characterized by an increase of physical activity, impulsivity and attention problems. According to WHO (World Health Organization) the alterations caused by the symptoms of ADD [1] can occur in two or more environments (at home and at school), can occur before seven years old and clinically can significantly impair social, academic, or occupational activity (symptoms which significantly interfere in the person).

The prevalence of disorder is between 3 and 7% in school-aged children [2,3], while this data on adolescence and adulthood are unclear.

Academic failure is significantly high, considering that 40% of students with ADD have a low performance in school. Therefore, it requires a specific school intervention to help the child to improve academically.

J. Bravo, R. Hervás, and M. Rodríguez (Eds.): IWAAL 2012, LNCS 7657, pp. 431–434, 2012.

Basic Calendar is an Android OS-based application that allows users to navigate through a calendar to view any tasks to be done or done already, being able to alert, with a message to the server, if the task was successful or not made. Tasks are stored on a server can be modified or inserted by the tutor or the coordinator.

The objectives of Basic Calendar are manage of the tasks of the children with ADD, facilitate the management of time of the children with ADD, be helpful for both children and their parents, so that the child could find simple and enjoyable the management of his tasks, design a completely customizable application and integrate the application in the everyday life of the child.

This article describes the proposed system design in Section 2, summarizes the obtained results in Section 3, and finally, presents concluding remarks.

2   Proposed System Design

Basic Calendar has two well differentiated parts; one is the application itself that includes the Alarm Management Service, and the other one is the tasks server.

2.1   Mobile Application

Within three main categories of this application are; to provide a user friendly interface and a calendar with the possibility to scroll nimbly across the months, the ability to obtain the user's tasks from a server for both the current day, and for the next 7 days and to select any day in the calendar and to allow to confirm a task in the terminal and, consequently, transmit the confirmation to the server. Figure 1 describes the operation of the application and the service.

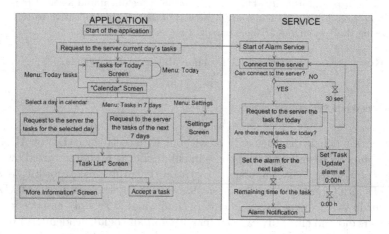

Fig. 1. High level Diagram of the application

Application realizes calendar management, shows user's alerts and connects with server to consult new tasks. Secondly, as shown on Figure 1, mobile application has a hierarchical model of a GUI.

Service manages alarms without user interaction, it synchronizes with server when device is turned on and it makes daily tasks.

2.2   Server

In the second part, it is the server which can receive a lot of requests of many devices and returns the tasks to them.

When the device sends requests, sends its own IMEI (International Mobile Equipment Identity). When the server receives the requests, checks if the IMEI is authorized in the database and if not, the connection is automatically denied.

3   Results

The system has been implemented successfully, the results obtained are divided into evaluation results gained from the pilots, and technical results.

In social results, system is fully developed and now we are testing it is performance. Pilots of this system have been tested with a group of 10 students with ADD. After each pilot, teachers and students receive a survey to fill. Questions should be valued from 1 to 10.

Results of surveys are a real feedback of application and are interesting to analyse the application operation and to check if application is useful to students to remember tasks. Table 1 shows teachers' survey results.

Table 1. Teachers satisfactory survey

Questions	% of acceptance
Insertion of new tasks are made easily	85%
Calendar management is easy	87%
Text fields are descriptive enough	92%
Images provide a better understanding of tasks	95%
Students complete all scheduled tasks	85%
Students are more organized	90%
Students usually get distracted with the mobile phone	87%

Results provide a good feedback about the ease to use of application or about the use of custom images, although surveys show some inconveniences such as distraction with mobile phone.

In technical results, the application used to support the time management skills, acts as an external management tool that aims to achieve a behaviour management of children with ADD. Therefore it is likely to be obtained positive feedbacks from the children, so that they will be more organized and effective in developing any school activity. This application has a significative impact in terms of time management skills.

In the screen of the Figure 2 the user can scroll through the months of the year and select a day to see the tasks that contains. In the screen of the Figure 3 the user can view the remaining task for the current day.

Fig. 2. Calendar screen with menu options

Fig. 3. Tasks for Today screen

Fig. 4. Real example of application

4   Conclusions

The proposed support tool helps to solve the following problem types; emotional, school performance, acceptance in school or in other activities, relationships with peers and family relations. It also helps children who suffer ADD not to be so prone to have accidents which are due mainly to the impulsivity and inattention.

This application differs from the rest because it presents a simple, reduced and intuitive interface and because can be managed remotely by parents and tutors which can insert completely customized tasks, so that the child can quickly understand the assignment.

In the future, this application may be developed for other mobile operating systems, such as Windows Phone, iPhone OS and RIM OS. And may be expanded to other collectives, such as the elderly or sufferers of Alzheimer's.

Acknowledgments. This work was partially supported by the Basque Country Department of Education. The support of AHIDA association must also be thanked.

References

1. Biederman, J.: Attention-deficit/hyperactivity disorder: a life-span perspective. The Journal of Clinical Psychiatry 59(suppl. 7), 4–16 (1998)
2. National Institute of Mental Health: Attention Deficit Hyperactivity Disorder(ADHD) (2007), http://www.nimh.nih.gov/health/publications
3. Nair, J., Ehimare, U., Beitman, B.D., Nair, S.S., Lavin, A.: Clinical review: evidence-based diagnosis and treatment of ADHD in children. Missouri Medicine 103(6), 617–621 (2006)
4. DuPaul, G.J., Stoner, G.: ADHD in the schools, assessment and intervention strategies. The Guilford Press (2003)

Author Index